NELSON CANADA *Political Science*

Braving *the* New World

Readings in Contemporary Politics

Thomas M.J. Bateman
University of Alberta

Manuel Mertin
Mount Royal College

David M. Thomas
Mount Royal College

Nelson Canada

I(T)P An International Thomson Publishing Company

Toronto • Albany • Bonn • Boston • Cincinnati • Detroit • London • Madrid • Melbourne
Mexico City • New York • Pacific Grove • Paris • San Francisco • Singapore • Tokyo • Washington

Published in 1995 by
Nelson Canada,
A division of Thomson Canada Limited
1120 Birchmount Road
Scarborough, Ontario M1K 5G4

Canadian Cataloguing in Publication Data
Main entry under title:
Braving the new world: readings in contemporary politics
Includes bibliographical references and index.
ISBN 0-17-604850-2
1. Political science.   2. World politics -
1945-   I. Bateman, Thomas Michael Joseph,
1962-   II. Mertin, Manuel. III. Thomas,
David, 1943-
JA83.B73   1995   320.9'045   C95-932159-4

Team Leader and Publisher	Michael Young
Acquisitions Editor	Andrew Livingston
Project Coordinator	Joanne Scattolon
Production Editor	Jill Young
Production Coordinator	Brad Horning
Art Director	Liz Harasymczuk
Cover/Interior Design	Liz Harasymczuk
Composition	Anita Sidey

Printed and bound in Canada
1 2 3 4   TG   98 97 96 95

Contents

ADK 0855
816 229

Unit One
The Vortex

Unit Two
Ideas & Ideologies

Unit Three
Citizenship and Democracy

Unit Four
Institutions

Unit Five
Regimes and Change

Unit Six
The Nature of Politics

Preface

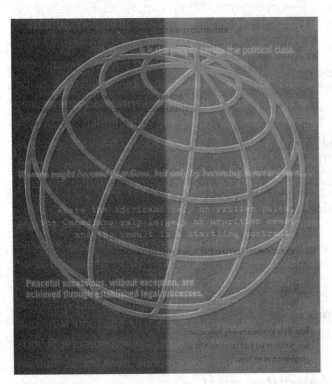

*T*his book is intended for use in introductory political science courses at the college and university level. As a new student, you may intend to major in political science, but may also be taking an introductory political science course as an interesting elective or because your academic program requires it. You will have been exposed to a great deal of electronic media coverage of world events, but may be intimidated by abstract treatments of political themes. To our "typical readers," an introductory course in political science, with its schematic texts, complex readings, and references to arcane historical events, will often appear difficult.

Such misgivings are an unfortunate reaction to a course in a discipline with the advantages political science has over other academic pursuits. Not the least of these advantages is an abundance of current, relevant, and interesting examples and case studies to animate the concepts and generalizations at the core of the discipline. On the other hand, political events constantly challenge, and sometimes render outdated, received understandings of politics and political life and defy our most careful predictions and generalizations. The study of politics and government is, therefore, a double-edged pedagogical sword: the existence of interesting, illuminating, and current case studies is countered by unpredictable and often intractable political, economic, and social change.

Textbooks used in introductory political science courses must necessarily be rigorous in their coverage of the conceptual basis of the study of politics, and they tend to present this conceptual basis as fixed. What is gained in rigour and comprehensiveness, however, is sometimes sacrificed in terms of an understanding of the dynamism of political life, especially in the current period.

We assembled this collection of readings to complement standard textbooks in the discipline, in a sense to bring the conceptual approach to politics alive and to examine the concepts "in action." We believe this collection will illuminate fundamental concerns in the discipline as well as stimulate the readers' interest in the world around them. It is one thing to be able to define concepts such as sovereignty and liberalism. It is another to understand how these ideas are used, abused, applied, interpreted, stretched, and attacked in historical situations. Political literacy requires one to think critically about issues and concepts, not simply to memorize details and definitions. The readings in this collection challenge people to think critically about the world around them and about a number of the basic concerns preoccupying political scientists.

Aside from the essays written especially for this book, we have selected others from notable books, journals, and current affairs magazines. Some of the contributors are professional writers; most are academics. The articles themselves range from the polemical to the analytical, from the partisan defence to the critical analysis, and from the short and direct to the lengthy and complex. Some are not easy. But then, some subjects simply cannot, or should not, be treated superficially. We trust that a thorough reading of the essays in this collection will both broaden and deepen knowledge of political issues; we also hope that readers will become familiar with some of the sources where intelligent discussions of politics are to be found.

We have inserted a number of pedagogical aids to set articles in context. Each article in the collection is preceded by an **editors' note** that sets the stage for—but does not summarize—the article to follow. These introductions set out the problems or issues and important ideas addressed in the article. Following each article is a **list of key words and concepts** that the reader should understand after having read the article. As well, a series of **questions** tests the reader's basic understanding of the authors' arguments and challenges the reader to think *about* the argument and how it might apply to new problems and situations. Throughout each article **key quotes** are inset to emphasize important assertions. At the end of each section, are more questions challenging readers to compare and contrast the themes and arguments made in the articles they have just read.

The essays in this book are arranged in an order that we think presents and then examines the vortex of political change defining our times. However, instructors may have their own preferences about the order in which themes and issues should be examined by students. Further, students may wish to pursue a theme or topic through a series of articles in the book. The **topic guide** at the beginning of the book is designed to facilitate this. Key themes and concepts are listed, followed by indicators of the articles in which they are considered. For example, federalism is a key theme in this book and is treated in different ways in different articles. A reader conducting research on federalism may not glean a systematic discussion of federalism from its mention in the articles by Bateman, Young, Smith, Gibbins and Youngman, Verney, or Johnstone—such a discussion will be found in lectures and textbooks—but he or she will form a solid understanding of the contexts in which federalism arises in contemporary political debates.

We owe a debt of thanks to Nelson Canada's Joanne Scattolon, Andrew Livingston, and Jill Young for their stewardship of this project, and to the reviewers of the manuscript, John Hiemstra, The King's University College; Richard Nutbrown, University of Waterloo; Henry Srebrnik, University of Prince Edward Island; and Chaldeans Mensah, Grant MacEwan Community College, who made many helpful suggestions. Colleagues have also given timely and insightful advice. Our greatest thanks is, of course, due our spouses, Jill, Jindra, and Maureen, for whose understanding and patience, as we consistently underestimated the work we had to do, we are deeply grateful.

◆ ◆ ◆

Contributors

▶ **G. Grant Amyot** is assistant professor of political science at Queen's University. He specializes in the politics of advanced industrial states. Among his publications is *The Italian Communist Party: The Crisis of the Popular Front Strategy*.

▶ **Anthony Arblaster** is reader in politics at the University of Sheffield, England. He has written *Democracy* (1987), and more recently contributed an essay in Iain Hampsher-Monk, ed., *Defending Politics: Bernard Crick and Pluralism* (1993).

▶ **Benjamin R. Barber** is Whitman professor of political science at Rutgers University and the author of many books including *Strong Democracy* (1984), *The Conquest of Politics* (1988), and *An Aristocracy of Everyone* (1992).

▶ **Thomas M.J. Bateman** taught political science at Mount Royal College in Calgary and is now completing his Ph.D. at the University of Alberta. He is the author of several articles on parliamentary and electoral reform.

▶ **Nancy Bermeo** teaches political science at Princeton University. She is the author of *Liberalization and Democratization* (1992).

▶ **Jeffrey H. Boutwell** is associate executive officer at the American Academy of Arts and Sciences. He has written widely on international security issues, including *The German Nuclear Dilemma* (1990), and co-edited *Lethal Commerce: The Global Trade in Small Arms and Light Weapons* (1995).

▶ **Robert D. Cairns** is a member of the Department of Economics and the Centre for the Study of Regulated Industries at McGill University, and received his Ph.D. in economics from the Massachusetts Institute of Technology.

▶ **James W. Carey** was the dean of the College of Communications at the University of Illinois. (1979–92). He has been the editor of several communications journals and the author of numerous monographs and articles.

▶ **Stephen Carter** is professor of law at Yale University and author of *Reflections of an Affirmative Action Baby* (1992).

▶ **Lorraine Code** is professor of philosophy at York University. She is the author of *What Can She Know? Feminist Theory and the Construction of Knowledge* (1991), and co-editor of *Changing Patterns: Women In Canada*, 2nd ed. (1993).

▶ **Bernard Crick** is emeritus professor of politics at Birkbeck College, London, and an Honourary Fellow of the University of Edinburgh. He is the author of numerous essays, and his books include *In Defence of Politics*, 4th ed. (1992), and *George Orwell: A Life* (1980).

▶ **David Frum** is a columnist with *Forbes* magazine and formerly an editor with the *Wall Street Journal*. He has recently written *Dead Right* (1994).

▶ **John Kenneth Galbraith** is Paul M. Warburg professor of economics emeritus at Harvard. He is the author of dozens of books, almost all of which are still in print, spanning a publishing career of over 40 years. He also held several senior governmental positions over the years.

▶ **Roger Gibbins** is professor and head, Department of Political Science, University of Calgary. He is the author of over 50 articles and books. His latest book, written with Sonia Arrison, is *Western Canadian Nationalism* (1995).

▶ **Mary Ann Glendon** is professor of law at Harvard University. She has a particular interest in comparative family law. Among her published works is *Abortion and Divorce in Western Law* (1987).

▶ **Frederick Johnstone** is professor of sociology at Memorial University in St. John's, Newfoundland. His interests include human rights and federalism. His *Race, Class and Gold: A Study of Class Relations and Racial Discrimination in South Africa* (1987) remains a widely cited book on South African studies. His most recent article is entitled "The New World Disorder: Fear, Freud and Federalism," in *Telos* (Summer 1994).

▶ **Charles S. Maier** is Krupp Foundation professor of European studies at Harvard. His books include *In Search of Stability* (1987), *The Unmasterable Past* (1988), *Changing Boundaries of the Political* (1987), and *The Politics of Inflation and Economic Stagnation* (1991).

▶ **Manuel Mertin** teaches political science at Mount Royal College in Calgary and is currently completing a Ph.D. thesis on comparative regional economic development in federal systems.

▶ **George W. Rathjens** is a professor in the Department of Political Science at the Massachusetts Institute of Technology (1968–). He is a former chief scientific adviser (Advanced Research) to the Department of Defence, and a former director of the Weapons Systems Evaluation Division.

▶ **Donald J. Savoie** holds the Clément-Cormier chair in economic development, Université Moncton and is a research fellow at the Canadian Centre for Management Development. He has written and edited several books and articles on Regional Economic Development and Public Administration. His latest book is *Thatcher, Reagan, Mulroney: In Search of a New Bureaucracy* (1994).

▶ **Anthony D. Smith** teaches sociology at the London School of Economics. His books include *National Identity* (1991), *Theories of Nationalism* (1983), and *The Ethnic Origins of Nations* (1986).

▶ **Jennifer Smith** teaches political science at Dalhousie University. Recent publications include articles on representative and constitutional reform, on democratic rights and electoral reform, and on the influence of American federalism on Canadian Confederation.

▶ **David M. Thomas** is the dean of the Faculty of Community Studies at Mount Royal College, Calgary. He is the general editor of *Canada and the United States: Differences that Count* (1993).

▶ **Goh Chok Tong** is the prime minister of Singapore (1990–). He was Singapore's minister of defence from 1982–91. Educated at the University of Singapore and at Williams College, he received an M.A. (Development Economics) from Williams.

▶ **Douglas V. Verney** is emeritus professor of political science at York University. He is the author of numerous articles, and his books include *Three Civilizations, Two Cultures, One State: Canada's Political Traditions* (1986).

▶ **Michael Walzer** is permanent member of the faculty of social sciences at Princeton's Institute for Advanced Study. Among his published works are *Spheres of Justice: A Defense of Pluralism and Equality* (1983), and *Thick and Thin: Moral Argument at Home and Abroad* (1994).

▶ **Meredith Woo-Cumings** is an associate professor of political science at Northwestern University. She is the author, under the name Jung-en Woo, of *Race to the Swift: State and Finance in Korean Industrialization* (1991). She is also the editor of *The Developmental State in Comparative Perspective* (forthcoming).

▶ **Robert A. Young** teaches political science at the University of Western Ontario. Recent works include *The Breakup of Czechoslovakia* (1994), and *The Secession of Quebec and the Future of Canada* (1995).

▶ **Lolleen Youngman** is a Ph.D. student at the University of Calgary. Her area of interest is gender and political representation.

Topic Guide

*T*he authors listed on the right deal with the boldfaced topics. The article number of the appropriate reading is given in parentheses after the author's name.

authoritarianism ▶ Barber (2), Maier (3), Bermeo (20)

autocracy ▶ Maier (3), Bermeo (20), Woo-Cumings (21), Tong (22), Crick (25)

bureaucracy ▶ Frum (5), Cairns (6), Woo-Cumings (21), Savoie (23)

capitalism ▶ Homer-Dixon (1), Barber (2), Arblaster (4), Frum (5), Cairns (6), Code (8), Walzer (11), Galbraith (13), Johnstone (14), Bermeo (20), Woo-Cumings (21)

citizenship/civil society ▶ Barber (2), Maier (3), Smith, A. (9), Walzer (11), Glendon (12), Gibbins (17), Johnstone (14), Verney (15), Carey (19), Bermeo (20), Crick (25)

confederalism ▶ Barber (2), Maier (3), Smith, A. (9), Young (24)

conservatism ▶ Maier (3), Frum (5), Cairns (6), Carter (10), Tong (22)

constitutions ▶ Arblaster (4), Glendon (12), Johnstone (14), Verney (15), Smith, J. (16), Gibbins (17), Young (24)

democracy —majoritarian/ direct ▶ Maier (3), Bateman (7), Amyot (18), Carey (19), Crick (25)

democracy —parliamentary/ representative ▶ Bateman (7), Verney (15), Smith, J. (16), Gibbins (17), Crick (25) Barber (2), Maier (3), Arblaster (4), Cairns (6), Bateman (7), Carter (10), Walzer (11), Glendon (12), Galbraith (13), Smith, J. (16), Gibbins (17), Amyot (18), Bermeo (20), Crick (25)

elections ▶ Bateman (7), Gibbins (17), Amyot (18)

environment ▶ Homer-Dixon (1), Barber (2), Cairns (6)

equality ▶ Homer-Dixon (1), Arblaster (4), Frum (5), Cairns (6), Code (8), Glendon (12), Galbraith (13), Gibbins (17)

ethnicity ▶ Homer-Dixon (1), Barber (2), Maier (3), Smith, A. (9), Gibbins (17), Johnstone (14), Young (24)

federalism ▶ Bateman (7), Smith, A. (9), Johnstone (14), Verney (15), Smith, J. (16), Gibbins (17), Young (24)

feminism ▶ Code (8), Glendon (12), Gibbins (17), Tong (22)

globalization ▶ Homer-Dixon (1), Barber (2), Bateman (7), Smith, A. (9), Johnstone (14), Bermeo (20), Woo-Cumings (21), Savoie (23)

Introduction

*I*n 1990 American President George Bush wanted his listeners to embrace what he called the "New World Order," which he intended as a sunny, hopeful phrase to describe the post-Cold War era in world politics. Clearly his vision was triumphalist and simplistic. Today there is as much evidence of disorder as there is of order. Consider events in Bosnia, Georgia, the Persian Gulf, Algeria, Egypt, Pakistan, Rwanda, Burundi, and Chechnya. The threat of global nuclear annihilation may have diminished only to be replaced by the equally terrifying threat of chemical/biological terrorism, and the reality of numerous "hot" wars—civil more than interstate—taking place all over the globe. Furthermore, there is considerable debate over what is really new in all of this and what is simply the return of the old. What, for example, is the meaning of nationalist uprisings in the former Soviet Union? Are they the expression of old identities long suppressed under the weight of Communist ideology? Or do these nationalist resurgences bear little resemblance to identities and loyalties that have gone before? We live in a changing world that is to be braved as much as it is to be embraced—braved because the pace of change is bewildering and unexpected things are happening, some of them truly horrific.

Bewildering change veritably characterizes the late 20th century. Who would have imagined that the United Nations, created in 1948 with 35 member states, would swell to a membership of almost 200 in less than 50 years, as established states and colonies subdivide like amoeba? The entrance to the UN building in New York is now a forest of poles flying the flags of represented countries. As if to mock the flourishing of sovereign self-assertion, whole classes of people—homeless, impoverished refugees on the one hand, and rootless, cosmopolitan entrepreneurs on the other—traverse the globe, indifferent to the political borders defining those same states. Countries of the European Union dismantle barriers to trade and human mobility in a hiccupping movement toward post-national cooperation, while other groups engage in brutal, almost medieval, hand-to-hand combat in defence of ancestral homelands, rights, and traditions proclaimed from a megaphone.

Against the images of Tiananmen Square one must consider instances of political and democratic reform. Democracy proceeds apace in South Africa, and the "hard" authoritarian regimes in Latin America are more scarce than in the 1970s and 1980s. There are signs that the "soft" authoritarianism characteristic of the East Asian countries is slowly giving way to more pluralistic politics and competitive party systems. In 1992 citizens in Canada voted in the first-ever national constitutional referendum and defeated a package of changes supported by much of the political and economic elite in the country, an outcome touted by many as the victory of the people over vested interests.

Hopes of a smooth transition to democracy and prosperity in Eastern Europe and the former Soviet Union have, however, been dashed. After the collapse of Communism, a deep disorder permeates many of these countries. Some observers doubt the very existence of a stable constitutional order in Russia. Initially smug about their "victory" over Communism, the countries of the Atlantic Alliance now grapple with public debt, welfare state dysfunction, and the seeming inability of governments to control change within the borders of states. Citizens of the so-called advanced democracies hold their political representatives in utter contempt and in some countries, for example, the United States—the birthplace of modern democracy—citizens stay away from the polls in droves.

Many recent political events challenge conventional understandings of basic political theories and generalizations. It was long thought, for example, that the development of industrial society proceeded in step with increasing prosperity, scientific knowledge and understanding, democratization, and social peace. This is the idea of modernization. Technology, industry, prosperity, rationality, and happiness seemed to flourish together.

Events have not borne out this happy scenario. First, scientific promise and impartiality, as readings in this volume indicate, are called into question. Rational bureaucratic organization seems neither rational nor organized. Democratic self-government is contradicted by the triviality of the voting exercise and the influence of organized interests. Prosperity eludes many sectors of the populations of advanced industrial democracies and most of the so-called third world. The prosperity that *is* *achieved* is bought at the price of environmental degradation. Humanity is no closer to the happiness promised by the Enlightenment. Observers refer to this sober realization of the limits of science, industry, and reason as *post-modernity*. The post-modern mood pervades much of the reflection on political events of the last decade. Some insist that the idea of modernization is being vindicated by the crisis of authoritarian regimes around the world and by the progressive melding of a democratic "world culture" with particular cultures.[1] Most contemporary intellectuals are not so sanguine.

Is the problem due to Enlightenment ideas themselves or to the way these ideas are interpreted and applied in specific cultural contexts? Leaders of the booming East Asian countries such as Singapore, Japan, South Korea, and Taiwan attribute their countries' economic success, not to Western values of individualism but to Confucian standards of order, discipline, deference, and respect for elders—all qualities academics, until recently, thought would keep the Confucian countries in the economic dark ages. In a speech reprinted in this collection, Singapore's prime minister recently argued that America's decline is traceable to its permissive social order. The East Asian experience has caused some to suggest that Western culture itself is the explanation for Western economic and political dysfunction. Hence, Samuel Huntington's controversial thesis (1993) that the coming years will be characterized by a clash of civilizations defined by culture and religion, and not ideology.[2]

The study of politics has not been left untouched by the vortex of political, social, and economic change. Political scientists were caught largely unawares by the rapidity and depth of Communism's collapse in Eastern Europe and the Soviet Union. The pace of negotiations to dismantle apartheid in South Africa, as well as the relative tranquility of the transition to nonracial democracy, were a surprise to many. In Canada political observers knew that the ruling federal Progressive

Conservative party would take a beating at the polls in 1993, but virtually no one predicted that the party of Sir John A. Macdonald would be reduced to two MPs.

Political change has challenged many core concepts in the study of politics and government. Take, for example, the idea of sovereignty. It often refers to the legitimate source of political power in a political community. The term has always been ambiguous because sovereignty has often been understood to be vested in one place but exercised in another. In constitutional monarchies, to take one example close to home, all authority is vested in the Crown but is exercised on its behalf by, among others, members of Parliament who are elected by voters. Sovereignty is further divided among branches of government, each with the ability to check the other's excesses. This historical ambiguity is now heightened by the fact that the people are no longer, if they ever were, a homogeneous mass. Different categories of citizens exercise different degrees of sovereign power. In Canada, constitutional provisions mete out special status to aboriginal peoples, women, multicultural groups, persons defined by region of residence, and a host of other groups. Such special status is not new in this country: special constitutional status for particular groups goes back to the *Constitution Act, 1867,* itself. What is new is the degree to which the myth of undivided sovereignty is contradicted by contemporary political events. Where exactly does sovereignty lie? Where should it lie? Does the possession of sovereign power depend on its effective exercise? Who or what exactly is running the political show in contemporary states?

The nation-state, another concept challenged by political change, is usually defined as a political entity characterized by clear, demarcated territory, a named population, and the existence of sovereign power over that people and territory. What is becoming obvious in the contemporary world is the degree to which the nation-state fails to meet these minimal conditions. Now, sovereign power seems to exist in supra-national entities like the United Nations, the European Union, the European Court of Human Rights, international economic and financial institutions, and transnational corporations, as well as substate groups defined by region, ethnicity, language, and even gender.

Is the traditional role of the nation-state, which was thought to be the primary unit of political power in global politics, threatened in a complex, interdependent world where the state is increasingly unable to order life within its borders, and when so much is beyond its control. Transnational corporations have larger annual budgets than do many countries. Environmental groups in different countries have more in common with one another than they do with other groups and organizations in their respective home jurisdictions. As one political sociologist wrote in the mid-1980s, the nation-state suffers from a problem of scale: it increasingly appears too small for the big things in life and too big for the little things in life.[3]

It is also unclear, to cite another important concept in political science, whether citizenship means today what it used to mean for democratic regimes. Can the political community command unqualified allegiance and sacrifice from its members in these volatile times? On what basis, then, can people be understood to be members of a political community? What exactly can and should be expected from the late 20th century citizen? Political concepts are being stretched, mutated, and in some cases, rendered nearly obsolete. The student of politics must be attentive to these developments and to the pervasive dynamic of political change itself.

Unit One of this book is appropriately entitled "The Vortex." This unit sets the global scene for the essays included in this reader. We wish to evoke the image of a funnel cloud tracking unpredictably across an expanse, stirring up, and in some cases, destroying what lies in its path, oblivious to borders and other defences. This is rather like some of the changes sweeping across the world and transcending political borders: globalizing forces of telecommunications, trade, and human migration; environmental destruction; and nationalist consciousness. In meteorological terms, a vortex is produced—albeit without a regularity that can be forecasted—by the confluence of two pressure systems creating a steep pressure gradient. The two major political "pressure systems" in the contemporary world are cultural and economic/technological forces. Neither set of forces seems to predominate. Both are equally powerful. Accordingly, the readings in this unit emphasize both economic and cultural factors and how they interact to produce rapid, unpredictable change.

Unit Two delves into the realm of political ideas and ideologies, challenging the reader to examine old forces and new contenders. Political ideas and ideologies both seek to explain and produce the sort of changes described in the previous unit. And they are influenced by those very same changes. The vortex has not left political ideas untouched. No longer can the politically literate political science student be satisfied with a survey of the "ideological spectrum" where ideologies are discretely placed along a continuum. He or she must understand populism, nationalism, the power of religion in politics, and the fundamental critique of politics and knowledge posed by feminist ideas.

Ideas and ideologies are related to politics because they have ethical implications for political actors and citizens. How indeed should people act in the political realm? This question is the subject of Unit Three, entitled "Citizenship and Democracy." Here, articles examine several themes at the heart of current discussion of democratic citizenship: the dependence of democratic life upon civil order among citizens; the idea of rights and whether the discourse of rights is constructive or destructive in democratic societies; the relationship between economy and polity in liberal democracies; and finally, the nature of diversity—territorial and otherwise—in democratic societies.

Unit Four is concerned with the institutional character of politics. Ideas and ideologies are not ethereal preoccupations of the philosopher: they are powerful forces that change minds, move people, and become embedded in the institutional context of public life. Institutions also influence what we think about politics, a fact that should be obvious to Canadians given our preoccupation with reform of many of our central political institutions in recent decades. The articles in this unit examine the politics of representation, the role of political executives, parliamentarism and federalism, political parties, and last but not least, the role of the media and journalism in democratic life.

Unit Five, "Regimes and Change," examines the transition from one regime to another, a poignant topic at a time when halting and painful steps toward democratization are being taken in many parts of the world. This unit also examines new forms of authoritarianism in East Asia; the relationship between political culture and political and economic development; the effect of globalization on domestic government; and the peaceful breakup of countries, a topic of some relevance to Canadians.

It is one of the oddities of political science that the notion at the core of the discipline defies easy definition. What are politics exactly? What does it mean to settle a conflict politically? What counts as a political victory? And further, why are conflicts dealt with politically and not in some other way? Are there not better ways to handle problems and frictions? Bernard Crick, probably one of the most thoughtful post-World War II writers on the idea of politics, addresses these issues in light of the turbulent events and new forces discussed in other essays in this book. Crick's essay in the final unit serves as a call to maturity and realism in our understanding of this essential aspect of human existence.

As can be expected in any collection of this sort, many would dispute the representativeness of essays selected under various subject headings. Is David Frum's understanding of neoconservatism representative of the neoconservative political stance? Are the East Asian regimes representative of authoritarian regimes around the world? No, on both counts. Our concern is not to include the most representative essay—if such indeed exists—but rather to raise important questions about aspects of the contemporary world and have readers think critically about arguments and where they lead.

We hope that this book will help readers become better students of politics, better critical thinkers, and better citizens.

---

1. Lucian W. Pye, "Political Science and the Crisis of Authoritarianism," *American Political Science Review* 84, No. 1 (March 1990), 3–19. Also, Francis Fukuyama, *The End of History and the Last Man* (New York: Avon, 1992).
2. Samuel P. Huntington, "The Clash of Civilizations?" *Foreign Affairs* 72, No. 3 (Summer 1993), 22–49.
3. Daniel Bell, "The World and the United States in 2013," *Daedalus* 116, No. 3 (Summer 1987), 1–32.

Unit One

The Vortex

• • •

The image of an advancing tornado is undoubtedly familiar to us. We have all seen photographs of that black, evil-looking column of rotating power that descends from the clouds. It strikes unpredictably and erratically, leaving in its wake devastation, dazed survivors, and the reminder that we have absolutely no control over the forces set in motion.

It seems to us that this image of a rampaging vortex is particularly appropriate both as the title for this first set of articles, and as a possible metaphor for what is happening in our changed and changing world. Our political skies have indeed darkened; towering thunderclouds gather. Deep low pressure areas form between unstable fronts. We do not know where and when the vortices will form and touch down—but strike some will—not only in the areas where their occurrence is normal, but now also appearing in regions hitherto relatively immune. Luck, timely warnings, and adequate preparations will reduce the casualties, but we will still be left in awe, dread, and shock at the forces unleashed.

We should not push such metaphors too far. Although each article in this unit deals with important components of our political storm systems, the authors neither paint a picture of unrelieved gloom, nor do they suggest that we are powerless to act and must simply await our fate. Sometimes, seemingly unavoidable crises can be averted or placed in abeyance—such may be the outcome of the situation in Quebec.

Homer-Dixon, Boutwell, and Rathjens discuss the very foundations of our increasingly fragile global ecosystem. They are no cornucopians: they do not believe that our science and technology will continue to fill the horn of plenty. Where will the environmental funnel cloud touch down next: vanishing salmon stocks; turbot wars; struggles over Middle East water? There are also the vortices generated by the forces of "Jihad and McWorld." In a world of resurgent fanaticism, terrorist attacks can strike anywhere. In 1993 New York's tallest building was almost destroyed, chemical or biological terrorism is now easy, and instructions on how to build the kind of bomb that destroyed an entire building in Oklahoma City are available on the internet.

Democracy as we know it, dependent upon a solid, stable, middle class, is also under enormous stress. A new economy may be emerging in which there is a professional/technical elite in what Jocelyn Létourneau has called the aeroplan class, a much larger group of marginalized "migrant" workers, and a shrinking state and public sector bureaucracy.[1]

These three articles under the general heading of "The Vortex" are, therefore, intended to make our readers sit up with a shock of recognition, and with a new awareness of the problems. What if Homer-Dixon

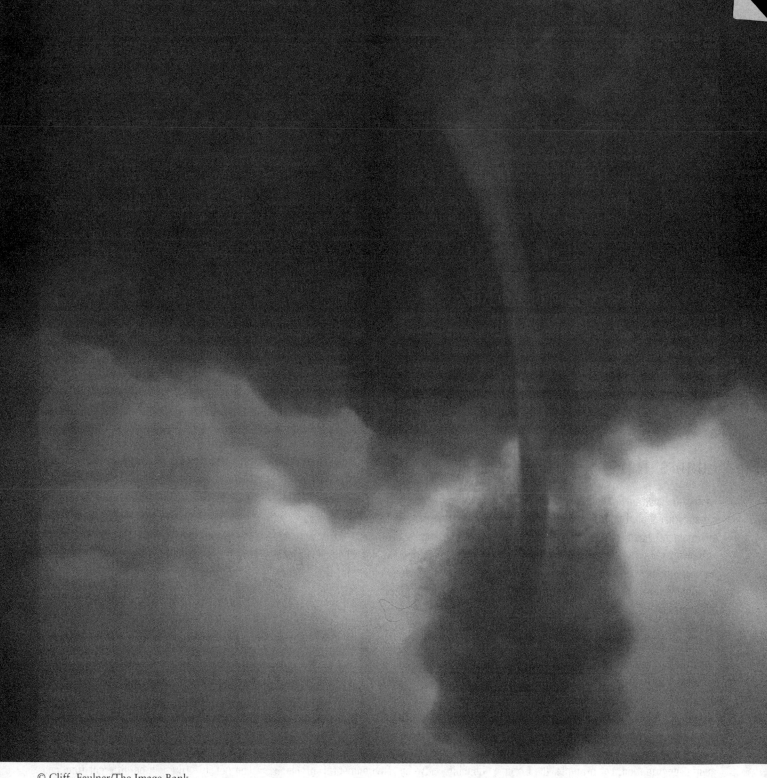

and his co-authors are right? What if McWorld's imperatives are not particularly democratic? Are we going through a serious moral crisis that precedes the growth of new values? How can we best prepare our- selves for dramatic changes in our economic, social, political, spiritual, and environmental climates? Where will the vortex strike next, and with what results?

1. For an incisive discussion of the Canadian situation, see Richard LaRue and Jocelyn Létourneau, "De l'unité et de l'identité au Canada. Essai sur l'éclatement d'un état," *International Journal of Canadian Studies* 7-8, 1993, 81–94.

1

Environmental Change and Violent Conflict

Thomas Homer-Dixon, Jeffrey H. Boutwell, and George W. Rathjens

Editors' Note

In the absence of impending nuclear holocaust, other global concerns relating to the environment have moved into the mainstream of political debate. News programs and newspaper articles routinely recount environmental destruction of various kinds: oil spills, air and water pollution, health effects of pesticides and fertilizers, top soil erosion, uncontrolled logging, and the depletion of the atmosphere's ozone layer.

Two interesting patterns stand out. First, it is easier to learn about and mobilize resources to respond to sudden environmental disasters than to longer-term environmental degradation. For example, the Exxon Valdez oil spill in Alaska drew international attention and caused the deployment of massive cleanup resources (which some think did more harm than good). Yet several

times the volume of that oil spill is either burned or dripped from the crankcases of cars and trucks in Canada every year and scarcely anything is done about it. Second, environmental destruction is often understood in apolitical terms. The depletion of the ozone layer is bad, we often hear, because it can be a health hazard to humans generally, with no other specific political or security ramifications.

University of Toronto political scientist Thomas Homer-Dixon wants to broaden our understanding of enviromental destruction and has written extensively on the close relationship between environmental problems and political conflict. In this brief but cogent article written with Jeffrey H. Boutwell and George W. Rathjens, Homer-Dixon offers an explanation for violent political conflict

grounded in environmental scarcity. Politics are often understood to be conflicts about the distribution of resources, whether these resources are land, money, oil, honour, or legal recognition. Environmental destruction, on the other hand, is often understood to present dangers of a nonpolitical nature—threats to health, for example. This article suggests, however, that there are clear connections between environmental destruction and social and political conflict. A way to reduce political conflict, they suggest, is to address growing environmental scarcity.

As you read this article, notice how political conflict in future will be different from conflict in the past. Also note how environmental issues are linked with "traditional" conflicts of an economic, ethnic, and nationalistic nature.

◆ ◆ ◆

Within the next 50 years, the human population is likely to exceed nine billion, and global economic output may quintuple. Largely as a result of these two trends, scarcities of renewable resources may increase sharply. The total area of highly productive agricultural land will drop, as will the extent of forests and the number of species they sustain. Future generations will also experience the ongoing depletion and degradation of aquifers, rivers and other bodies of water, the decline of fisheries, further stratospheric ozone loss and, perhaps, significant climatic change.

...scarcities of renewable resources are already contributing to violent conflicts in many parts of the developing world.

As such environmental problems become more severe, they may precipitate civil or international strife. Some concerned scientists have warned of this prospect for several decades, but the debate has been constrained by lack of carefully compiled evidence. To address this shortfall of data, we assembled a team of 30 researchers to examine a set of specific cases. In studies commissioned by the University of Toronto and the American Academy of Arts and Sciences, these experts reported their initial findings.

The evidence that they gathered points to a disturbing conclusion: scarcities of renewable resources are already contributing to violent conflicts in many parts of the developing world. These conflicts may foreshadow a surge of similar violence in coming decades, particularly in poor countries where shortages of water, forests and, especially, fertile land, coupled with rapidly expanding populations, already cause great hardship.

Before we discuss the findings, it is important to note that the environment is but one variable in a series of political, economic and social factors that can bring about turmoil. Indeed, some skeptics claim that scarcities of renewable resources are merely a minor variable that sometimes links existing political and economic factors to subsequent social conflict.

The evidence we have assembled supports a different view. Such scarcity can be an important force behind changes in the politics and economics governing resource use. It can cause powerful actors to strengthen, in their favor, an inequitable distribution of resources. In addition, ecosystem vulnerability often contributes significantly to shortages of renewable resources. This vulnerability is, in part, a physical given: the depth of upland soils in the tropics, for example, is not a function of human social institutions or behavior. And finally, in many parts of the world, environmental degradation seems to have passed a threshold of irreversibility. In these situations, even if enlightened social change removes the original political, economic and cultural causes of the degradation, it may continue to contribute to social disruption. In other words, once irreversible, environmental degradation becomes an independent variable.

Skeptics often use a different argument. They state that conflict arising from resource scarcity is not particularly interesting, because it has been common throughout human history. We maintain, though, that renewable resource scarcities of the next 50 years will probably occur with a speed, complexity and magnitude unprecedented in history. Entire countries can now be deforested in a few decades, most of a region's topsoil can disappear in a generation, and acute ozone depletion may take place in as few as 20 years.

Unlike nonrenewable resources—including fossil fuels and iron ore—renewable resources are linked in highly complex, interdependent systems with many nonlinear and feedback relations. The overextraction of one resource can lead to multiple, unanticipated environmental problems and sudden scarcities when the system passes critical thresholds.

Our research suggests that the social and political turbulence set in motion by changing environmental conditions will not follow the commonly perceived pattern of scarcity conflicts. There are many examples in the past of one group or nation trying to seize the resources of another. For instance, during World War II, Japan sought to secure oil, minerals and other resources in China and Southeast Asia.

Currently, however, many threatened renewable resources are held in common—including the atmosphere and the oceans—which makes them unlikely to be the object of straightforward clashes. In addition, we

---

THREE VIEWS OF THE ROLE THAT SCARCITY OF RENEWABLE RESOURCES PLAYS IN VIOLENT CONFLICT

Political and Economic Factors → **Social Conflict**

Political and Economic Factors → **Scarcity of Renewable Resources** → **Social Conflict**

Political and Economic Factors ⇄ **Scarcity of Renewable Resources** → **Social Conflict**

Ecosystem Vulnerability → **Scarcity of Renewable Resources**

Political and Economic Factors → **Social Conflict**

Political and Economic Factors → **Irreversible Scarcity of Renewable Resources** → **Social Conflict**

have come to understand that scarcities of renewable resources often produce insidious and cumulative social effects, such as population displacement and economic disruption. These events can, in turn, lead to clashes between ethnic groups as well as to civil strife and insurgency. Although such conflicts may not be as conspicuous or dramatic as wars over scarce resources, they may have serious repercussions for the security interests of the developed and the developing worlds.

Human actions bring about scarcities of renewable resources in three principal ways. First, people can reduce the quantity or degrade the quality of these resources faster than they are renewed. This phenomenon is often referred to as the consumption of the resource's "capital": the capital generates "income" that can be tapped for human consumption. A sustainable economy can therefore be defined as one that leaves the capital intact and undamaged so that future generations can enjoy undiminished income. Thus, if topsoil creation in a region of farmland is 0.25 millimeter per year, then average soil loss should not exceed that amount.

The second source of scarcity is population growth. Over time, for instance, a given flow of water might have to be divided among a greater number of people. The final cause is change in the distribution of a resource within a society. Such a shift can concentrate supply in the hands of a few, subjecting the rest to extreme scarcity.

These three origins of scarcity can operate singly or in combination. In some cases, population growth by itself will set in motion social stress. Bangladesh, for example, does not suffer from debilitating soil degradation or from the erosion of agricultural land: the annual flooding of the Ganges and Brahmaputra rivers deposits a layer of silt that helps to maintain the fertility of the country's vast floodplains.

But the United Nations predicts that Bangladesh's current population of 120 million will reach 235 million by the year 2025. At about 0.08 hectare per capita, cropland is already desperately scarce. Population density is 785 people per square kilometer (in comparison, population density in the adjacent Indian state of Assam is

SOME SOURCES AND CONSEQUENCES OF RENEWABLE RESOURCE SCARCITY

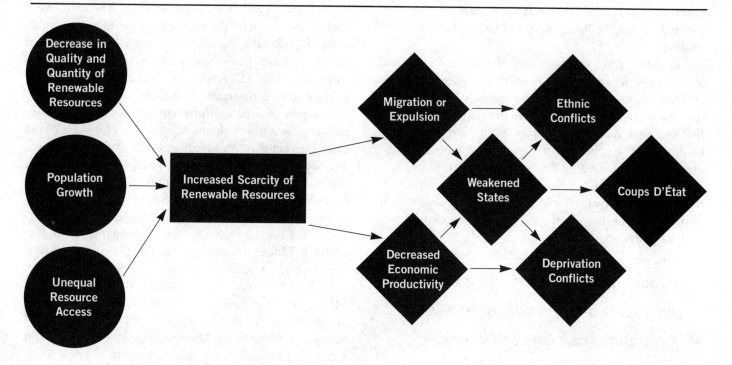

284 people per square kilometer). Because all the country's good agricultural land has been exploited, population growth will cut in half the amount of cropland available per capita by 2025. Flooding and inadequate national and community institutions for water control exacerbate the lack of land and the brutal poverty and turmoil it engenders.

Over the past 40 years, millions of people have migrated from Bangladesh to neighboring areas of India, where the standard of living is often better. Detailed data on the movements are few: the Bangladeshi government is reluctant to admit there is significant migration because the issue has become a major source of friction with India. Nevertheless, one of our researchers, Sanjoy Hazarika, an investigative journalist and reporter at the *New York Times* in New Delhi, pieced together demographic information and experts' estimates. He concludes that Bangladeshi migrants and their descendants have expanded the population of neighboring areas of India by 15 million. (Only one to two million of those people can be attributed to migrations during the 1971 war between India and Pakistan that resulted in the creation of Bangladesh.)

This enormous flux has produced pervasive social changes in the receiving Indian states. Conflict has been triggered by altered land distribution as well as by shifts in the balance of political and economic power between religious and ethnic groups. For instance, members of the Lalung tribe in Assam have long resented Bengali Muslim migrants: they accuse them of stealing the area's richest farmland. In early 1983, during a bitterly contested election for federal offices in the state, violence finally erupted. In the village of Nellie, Lalung tribespeople massacred nearly 1,700 Bengalis in one five-hour rampage.

In the state of Tripura the original Buddhist and Christian inhabitants now make up less than 30 percent of the population. The remaining percentage consists of Hindu migrants from either East Pakistan or Bangladesh. This shift in the ethnic balance precipitated a violent insurgency between 1980 and 1988 that was called off only after the government agreed to return land to dispossessed Tripuris and to stop the influx of Bangladeshis. As the migration has continued, however, this agreement is in jeopardy.

Population movements in this part of South Asia are, of course, hardly new. During the colonial period, the British imported Hindus from Calcutta to administer Assam, and Bengali was made the official language. As a result, the Assamese are particularly sensitive to the loss of political and cultural control in the state. And Indian politicians have often encouraged immigration in order to garner votes. Yet today changes in population density in Bangladesh are clearly contributing to the exodus. Although the contextual factors of religion and politics are important, they do not obscure the fact that a dearth of land in Bangladesh has been a force behind conflict.

In other parts of the world the three sources of scarcity interact to produce discord. Population growth and reductions in the quality and quantity of renewable resources can lead to large-scale development projects that can alter access to resources. Such a shift may lead to decreased supplies for poorer groups whose claims are violently opposed by powerful elites. A dispute that began in 1989 between Mauritanians and Senegalese in the Senegal River valley, which demarcates the common border between these countries, provides an example of such causality.

Population growth and reductions in the quality and quantity of renewable resources can lead to large-scale development projects that can alter access to resources.

Senegal has fairly abundant agricultural land, but much of it suffers from severe wind erosion, loss of nutrients, salinization because of overirrigation and soil compaction caused by the intensification of agriculture. The country has an overall population density of 380 people per square kilometer and a population growth rate of 2.7 percent; in 25 years the population may double. In contrast, except for the Senegal River valley along its southern border and a few oases, Mauritania is for the most part arid desert and semiarid grassland. Its population density is very low, about 20 people per square kilometer, and the growth rate is 2.8 percent a year. The U.N. Food and Agriculture Organization has included both Mauritania and Senegal in its list of countries whose croplands cannot support current or projected populations without a large increase in agricultural inputs, such as fertilizer and irrigation.

Normally, the broad floodplains fringing the Senegal River support productive farming, herding and fishing based on the river's annual floods. During the 1970s, however, the prospect of chronic food shortages and a serious drought encouraged the region's governments to seek international financing for the Manantali Dam on the Bafing River tributary in Mali and for the Diama salt-intrusion barrage near the mouth of the Senegal River between Senegal and Mauritania. The dams were designed to regulate the river's flow for hydropower, to expand irrigated agriculture and to raise water levels in the dry season, permitting year-round barge transport from the Atlantic Ocean to land-locked Mali, which lies to the east of Senegal and Mauritania.

But the plan had unfortunate and unforeseen consequences. As anthropologist Michael M. Horowitz of the State University of New York at Binghamton has shown, anticipation of the new dams raised land values along the river in areas where high-intensity agriculture was to become feasible. The elite in Mauritania, which consists primarily of white Moors, then rewrote legislation governing land ownership, effectively abrogating the rights of black Africans to continue farming, herding and fishing along the Mauritanian riverbank.

There has been a long history of racism by white Moors in Mauritania toward their non-Arab, black compatriots. In the spring of 1989 the killing of Senegalese farmers by Mauritanians in the river basin triggered explosions of ethnic violence in the two countries. In Senegal almost all of the 17,000 shops owned by Moors were destroyed, and their owners deported to Mauritania. In both countries several hundred people were killed, and the two nations nearly came to war. The Mauritanian regime used this occasion to activate the new land legislation, declaring the black Mauritanians who lived alongside the river to be "Senegalese," thereby stripping them of their citizenship; their property was seized. Some 70,000 of the black Mauritanians were forcibly expelled to Senegal, from where some launched raids to retrieve expropriated cattle. Diplomatic relations between the two countries have now been restored, but neither has agreed to allow the expelled population to return or to compensate them for their losses.

We see a somewhat different causal process in many parts of the world: unequal access to resources combines with population growth to produce environmental damage. This phenomenon can contribute to economic deprivation that spurs insurgency and rebellion. In the Philippines, Spanish and American colonial policies left behind a grossly inequitable distribution of land. Since the 1960s, the introduction of green revolution technologies has permitted a dramatic increase in lowland production of grain for domestic consumption and of cash crops that has helped pay the country's massive external debt.

This modernization has raised demand for agricultural labor. Unfortunately, though, the gain has been overwhelmed by a population growth rate of 2.5 to 3.0 percent. Combined with the maldistribution of good cropland and an economic crisis in the first half of the 1980s, this growth produced a surge in agricultural unemployment.

With insufficient rural or urban industrialization to absorb excess labor, there has been unrelenting downward pressure on wages. Economically desperate, millions of poor agricultural laborers and landless peasants have migrated to shantytowns in already overburdened cities, such as Manila; millions of others have moved to the least productive—and often most ecologically vulnerable—territories, such as steep hillsides.

In these uplands, settlers use fire to clear forested or previously logged land. They bring with them little ability to protect the fragile ecosystem. Their small-scale logging, charcoal production and slash-and-burn farming often cause erosion, landslides and changes in hydrologic patterns. This behavior has initiated a cycle of falling food production, the clearing of new plots and further land degradation. Even marginally fertile land is becoming hard to find in many places, and economic conditions are critical for peasants.

The country has suffered from serious internal strife for many decades. But two researchers, Celso R. Roque, the former undersecretary of the environment of the Philippines, and his colleague Maria I. Garcia, conclude that resource scarcity appears to be an increasingly powerful force behind the current communist-led insurgency. The upland struggle—including guerilla attacks and assaults on military stations—is motivated by the economic deprivation of the landless agricultural laborers and poor farmers displaced into the hills, areas that are largely beyond the control of the central government. During the 1970s and 1980s, the New People's Army and the National Democratic Front found upland peasants receptive to revolutionary ideology, especially where coercive landlords and local governments left

AN EXAMPLE FROM THE PHILIPPINES

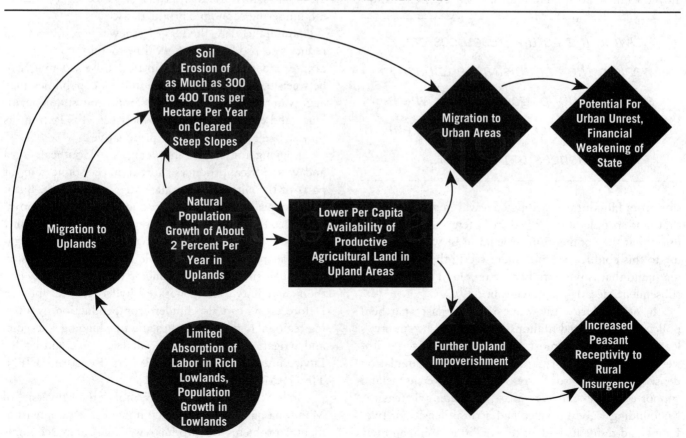

them little choice but to rebel or starve. The revolutionaries have built on indigenous beliefs and social structures to help the peasants focus their discontent.

Causal processes similar to those in the Philippines can be seen in many other regions around the planet, including the Himalayas, the Sahel, Indonesia, Brazil and Costa Rica. Population growth and unequal access to good land force huge numbers of people into cities or onto marginal lands. In the latter case, they cause environmental damage and become chronically poor. Eventually these people may be the source of persistent upheaval, or they may migrate yet again, stimulating ethnic conflicts or urban unrest elsewhere.

The short but devastating "Soccer War" in 1969 between El Salvador and Honduras involved just such a combination of factors. As William H. Durham of Stanford University has shown, changes in agriculture and land distribution beginning in the mid-19th century concentrated poor farmers in El Salvador's uplands. Although these peasants developed some understanding of land conservation, their growing numbers on very steep hillsides caused deforestation and erosion. A natural population growth rate of 3.5 percent further reduced land availability, and as a result many people moved to neighboring Honduras. Their eventual expul-

---

Dwindling natural resources can weaken the administrative capacity and authority of government, which may create opportunities for violent challenges to the state...

---

sion from Honduras precipitated a war in which several thousand people were killed in a few days. Durham notes that the competition for land in El Salvador leading to this conflict was not addressed in the war's aftermath and that is powerfully contributed to the country's subsequent, decade-long civil war.

In South Africa the white regime's past apartheid policies concentrated millions of blacks in the country's least productive and most ecologically sensitive territories. High natural birth rates exacerbated population densities. In 1980 rural areas of the Ciskei homeland supported 82 persons per square kilometer, whereas the surrounding Cape Province had a rural density of two. Homeland residents had, and have, little capital and few skills to manage resources. They remain the victims of corrupt and abusive local governments.

Sustainable development in such a situation is impossible. Wide areas have been completely stripped of trees for fuelwood, grazed down to bare dirt and eroded of topsoil. A 1980 report concluded the nearly 50 percent of Ciskei's land was moderately or severely eroded; close to 40 percent of its pasture was overgrazed. This loss of resources, combined with the lack of alternative employment and the social trauma caused by apartheid, has created a subsistence crisis in the homelands. Thousands of people have migrated to South African cities. The result is the rapid growth of squatter settlements and illegal townships that are rife with discord and that threaten the country's move toward democratic stability.

Dwindling natural resources can weaken the administrative capacity and authority of government, which may create opportunities for violent challenges to the state by political and military opponents. By contributing to rural poverty and rural-urban migration, scarcity of renewable resources expands the number of people needing assistance from the government. In response to growing city populations, states often introduce subsidies that distort prices and cause misallocations of capital, hindering economic productivity.

Simultaneously, the loss of renewable resources can reduce the production of wealth, thereby constraining tax revenues. For some countries, this widening gap between demands on the state and its capabilities may aggravate popular grievances, erode the state's legitimacy and escalate competition between elite factions as they struggle to protect their prerogatives.

Logging for export markets, as in Southeast Asia and West Africa, produces short-term economic gain for parts of the elite and may alleviate external debt. But it also jeopardizes long-term productivity. Forest removal decreases the land's ability to retain water during rainy periods. Flash floods then damage roads, bridges, irrigation systems and other valuable infrastructure. Erosion of hillsides silts up rivers, reducing their navigability and their capacity to generate hydroelectric power. Deforestation can also hinder crop production by altering regional hydrologic cycles and by plugging reservoirs and irrigation channels with silt [see "Accounting for Environmental Assets," by Robert Repetto; SCIENTIFIC AMERICAN, June 1992].

In looking at China, Václav Smil of the University of Manitoba has estimated the combined effect of environmental problems on productivity. The main economic burdens he identifies are reduced crop yields caused by water, soil and air pollution; higher human morbidity resulting from air pollution; farmland loss because of construction and erosion; nutrient loss and flooding caused by erosion and deforestation; and timber loss arising from poor harvesting practices. Smil calculates the current annual cost to be at least 15 percent of China's gross domestic product; he is convinced the toll will rise steeply in the coming decades. Smil also estimates that tens of millions of Chinese will try to leave the country's impoverished interior and northern

---

The entire Middle East faces increasingly grave and tangled problems of water scarcity, and many experts believe these will affect the region's stability.

---

regions—where water and fuelwood are desperately scarce and the land often badly damaged—for the booming coastal cities. He anticipates bitter disputes among these regions over water sharing and migration. Taken together, these economic and political stresses may greatly weaken the Chinese state.

Water shortages in the Middle East will become worse in the future and may also contribute to political discord. Although figures vary, Miriam R. Lowi of Princeton University estimates that the average amount of renewable fresh water available annually to Israel is about 1,950 million cubic meters (mcm). Sixty percent comes from groundwater, the rest from river flow, floodwater and wastewater recycling. Current Israeli demand—including that of settlements in the occupied territories and the Golan Heights—is about 2,200 mcm. The annual deficit of about 200 mcm is met by over-pumping aquifers.

As a result, the water table in some parts of Israel and the West Bank has been dropping significantly. This depletion can cause the salinization of wells and the infiltration of seawater from the Mediterranean. At the same time, Israel's population is expected to increase from the present 4.6 million to 6.5 million people in the year 2020, an estimate that does not include immigration from the former Soviet Union. Based on this pro-

jected expansion, the country's water demand could exceed 2,600 mcm by 2020.

Two of the three main aquifers on which Israel depends lie for the most parts under the West Bank, although their waters drain into Israel. Thus, nearly 40 percent of the ground water Israel uses originates in occupied territory. To protect this important source, the Israeli government has strictly limited water use on the West Bank. Of the 650 mcm of all forms of water annually available there, Arabs are allowed to use only 125 mcm. Israel restricts the number of wells Arabs can drill in the territory, the amount of water Arabs are allowed to pump and the times at which they can draw irrigation water.

The differential in water access on the West Bank is marked: on a per capita basis, Jewish settlers consume about four times as much water as Arabs. Arabs are not permitted to drill new wells for agricultural purposes, although Mekorot (the Israeli water company) has drilled more than 30 for settlers. Arab agriculture in the region has suffered because some Arab wells have become saline as a result of deeper Israeli wells drilled nearby. The Israeli water policy, combined with the confiscation of agricultural land for settlers as well as other Israeli restrictions on Palestinian agriculture, has encouraged many West Bank Arabs to abandon farming. Those who have done so have become either unemployed or day laborers within Israel.

The entire Middle East faces increasingly grave and tangled problems of water scarcity, and many experts believe these will affect the region's stability. Concerns over water access contributed to tensions preceding the 1967 Arab-Israeli War; the war gave Israel control over most of the Jordan Basin's water resources. The current Middle East peace talks include multi-lateral meetings on water rights, motivated by concerns about impending scarcities.

Although "water wars" are possible in the future, they seem unlikely given the preponderance of Israeli military power. More probably, in the context of historical ethnic and political disputes, water shortages will aggravate tensions and unrest within societies in the Jordan River basin. In recent U.S. congressional testimony, Thomas Naff of the University of Pennsylvania noted that "rather than warfare among riparians in the immediate future…what is more likely to ensue from water-related crises in this decade is internal civil disorder, changes in regimes, political radicalization and instability."

Scarcities of renewable resources clearly can contribute to conflict, and the frequency of such unrest will probably grow in the future. Yet some analysts maintain that scarcities are not important in and of themselves. What is important, they contend, is whether people are harmed by them. Human suffering might be avoided if political and economic systems provide the incentives and wherewithal that enable people to alleviate the harmful effects of environmental problems.

Our research has not produced firm evidence for or against this argument. We need to know more about the variables that affect the supply of human ingenuity in response to environmental changes. Technical ingenuity is needed for the development of, for example, new agricultural and forestry technologies that compensate for environmental deterioration. Social ingenuity is needed for the creation of institutions that buffer people from the effects of degradation and provide the right incentives for technological innovation.

The role of social ingenuity as a precursor to technical ingenuity is often overlooked. An intricate and stable system of markets, legal regimes, financial agencies and educational and research institutions is a prerequisite for the development and distribution of many technologies—including new grains adapted to dry climates and eroded soils, alternative cooking technologies that compensate for the loss of firewood and water-conservation technologies. Not only are poor countries ill endowed with these social resources, but their ability to create and maintain them will be weakened by the very environmental woes such nations hope to address.

The evidence we have presented here suggests there are significant causal links between scarcities of renewable resources and violence. To prevent such turmoil, nations should put greater emphasis on reducing such scarcities. This means that rich and poor countries alike must cooperate to restrain population growth, to implement a more equitable distribution of wealth within and among their societies, and to provide for sustainable development.

Terms & Concepts

ecological vulnerability
ecosystem
environmental refugees
independent and dependent
  variables

modernization
renewable and nonrenewable
  resources
resource capital
scarcity

short- and long-term productivity
social ingenuity
sustainable development
technical ingenuity

Questions

1. What are the several ways in which environmental scarcity can be related to political and social conflict?

2. How do you think depletion of resources in "common" areas like the oceans and the atmosphere can be stopped?

3. Can you think of Canadian examples of the causal relationships discussed by the authors?

4. What is the significance of environmental destruction? Are environmental concerns problems to be solved by clever people, or are they indications that modern industrial, scientific civilization has met its match?

5. Are the authors too pessimistic? Have we not faced crises before and overcome them? Is the present crisis any different?

6. Some argue that excessive world population growth is the root of environmental problems. Do you agree?

Jihad Vs. McWorld

Benjamin Barber

Editors' Note

Since World War II, up until the end of the 1980s, two military superpowers dominated the world scene. In addition, multinational (or perhaps more descriptively "transnational") corporations became major international actors, some having larger annual sales than the entire gross domestic product of many state economies. Now there is only one superpower left, and it exercises enormous influence not only because of its military strength but also because of the cultural and economic leverage it possesses.

State-to-state diplomacy now takes place within a changed context, in which the old rules of the game no longer apply, and in which a key development is the "globalization" of national economies and a con-comitant decline of state power, even as states still struggle to emerge and be recognized.

In this widely read article, Benjamin Barber sets out the two principal forces of the post-Cold War world: universalizing, globalizing forces of technology, information, and trade; and parochial, tribalizing forces of nationalism, ethnicity, and religious identity. The two sets of forces combine to bring us together and drive us apart simultaneously. Barber addresses a couple of themes worth noting at the outset. The first is the degree to which globalizing forces bear an American cultural imprint. Is technology noncultural or does it inevitably carry with it American cultural antecedents? The second theme is the anti-democratic or antipolitical character of both forces.

This is a powerful and provocative piece: it challenges the reader to think in global terms. The reader's main task is to first ask, as always, do I understand the relationships that Barber presents: the four imperatives of *McWorld*, the elements that make up the centrifugal forces of *Jihad*, and the antipolitical nature of both? Second, Barber uses a vocabulary that will be familiar to political scientists, but not necessarily to the general reader. He uses terms such as comity and community, sectarianism, ethnocentrism and, confederalism, which will have to be discussed and thought about, not merely glossed over.

◆ ◆ ◆

Just beyond the horizon of current events lie two possible political futures—both bleak, neither democratic. The first is a retribalization of large swaths of humankind by war and bloodshed: a threat-ened Lebanonization of national states in which culture is pitted against culture, people against people, tribe against tribe—a Jihad in the name of a hundred narrowly conceived faiths against every kind of interdepen-

Published originally in the March 1992 issue of *The Atlantic Monthly* (pp. 53–63).

dence, every kind of artificial social cooperation and civic mutuality. The second is being borne in on us by the onrush of economic and ecological forces that demand integration and uniformity and that mesmerize the world with fast music, fast computers, and fast food—with MTV, Macintosh, and McDonald's, pressing nations into one commercially homogeneous global network: one McWorld tied together by technology, ecology, communications, and commerce. The planet is falling precipitantly apart and coming reluctantly together at the very same moment.

These two tendencies are sometimes visible in the same countries at the same instant: thus Yugoslavia, clamoring just recently to join the New Europe, is exploding into fragments; India is trying to live up to its reputation as the world's largest integral democracy while powerful new fundamentalist parties like the Hindu nationalist Bharatiya Janata Party, along with nationalist assassins, are imperiling its hard-won unity. States are breaking up or joining up: the Soviet Union has disappeared almost overnight, its parts forming new unions with one another or with likeminded nationalities in neighboring states. The old interwar national state based on territory and political sovereignty looks to be a mere transitional development.

The tendencies of what I am here calling the forces of Jihad and the forces of McWorld operate with equal strength in opposite directions, the one driven by parochial hatreds, the other by universalizing markets, the one re-creating ancient subnational and ethnic borders from within, the other making national borders porous from without. They have one thing in common: neither offers much hope to citizens looking for practical ways to govern themselves democratically. If the global future is to pit Jihad's centrifugal whirlwind against McWorld's centripetal black hole, the outcome is unlikely to be democratic—or so I will argue.

MCWORLD, OR THE
GLOBALIZATION OF POLITICS

◆ ◆ ◆

Four imperatives make up the dynamic of McWorld: a market imperative, a resource imperative, an information-technology imperative, and an ecological imperative. By shrinking the world and diminishing the salience of national borders, these imperatives have in combination achieved a considerable victory over factiousness and particularism, and not least of all over their most virulent traditional form—nationalism. It is the realists who are now Europeans, the utopians who dream nostalgically of a resurgent England or Germany, perhaps even a resurgent Wales or Saxony. Yesterday's wishful cry for one world has yielded to the reality of McWorld.

The market imperative. Marxist and Leninist theories of imperialism assumed that the quest for everexpanding markets would in time compel nation-based capitalist economies to push against national boundaries in search of an international economic imperium. Whatever else has happened to the scientistic predictions of Marxism, in this domain they have proved farsighted. All national economies are now vulnerable to the inroads of larger, transnational markets within which trade is free, currencies are convertible, access to banking is open, and contracts are enforceable under law. In Europe, Asia, Africa, the South Pacific, and the Americas such markets are eroding national sovereignty and giving rise to entities—international banks, trade associations, transnational lobbies like OPEC and Greenpeace, world news services like CNN and the BBC, and multinational corporations that increasingly lack a meaningful national identity—that neither reflect nor respect nationhood as an organizing or regulative principle.

The market imperative has also reinforced the quest for international peace and stability, requisites of an efficient international economy. Markets are enemies of parochialism, isolation, fractiousness, war. Market psychology attenuates the psychology of ideological and religious cleavages and assumes a concord among producers and consumers—categories that ill fit narrowly conceived national or religious cultures. Shopping has little tolerance for blue laws, whether dictated by pubclosing British paternalism, Sabbath-observing Jewish Orthodox fundamentalism, or no-Sunday-liquor-sales Massachusetts puritanism. In the context of common markets, international law ceases to be a vision of justice and becomes a workaday framework for getting things done—enforcing contracts, ensuring that governments abide by deals, regulating trade and currency relations, and so forth.

Common markets demand a common language, as well as a common currency, and they produce common behaviors of the kind bred by cosmopolitan city life everywhere. Commercial pilots, computer programmers, international bankers, media specialists, oil riggers, entertainment celebrities, ecology experts, demographers, accountants, professors, athletes—these compose a new breed of men and women for whom religion, culture, and nationality can seem only marginal elements in a working identity. Although sociologists of everyday life will no doubt continue to distinguish a Japanese from an American mode, shopping has a common signature throughout the world. Cynics might even say that some of the recent revolutions in Eastern Europe have had as their true goal not liberty and the right to vote but well-paying jobs and the right to shop (although the vote is proving easier to acquire than consumer goods). The market imperative is, then, plenty powerful; but, notwithstanding some of the claims made for "democratic capitalism," it is not identical with the democratic imperative.

The resource imperative. Democrats once dreamed of societies whose political autonomy rested firmly on economic independence. The Athenians idealized what they called autarky, and tried for a while to create a way of life simple and austere enough to make the polis genuinely self-sufficient. To be free meant to be independent of any other community or polis. Not even the Athenians were able to achieve autarky, however: human nature, it turns out, is dependency. By the time of Pericles, Athenian politics was inextricably bound up with a flowering empire held together by naval power and commerce—an empire that, even as it appeared to enhance Athenian might, ate away at Athenian independence and autarky. Master and slave, it turned out, were bound together by mutual insufficiency.

The dream of autarky briefly engrossed nineteenth-century America as well, for the underpopulated, endlessly bountiful land, the cornucopia of natural resources, and the natural barriers of a continent walled in by two great seas led many to believe that America could be a world unto itself. Given this past, it has been harder for Americans than for most to accept the inevitability of interdependence. But the rapid depletion of resources even in a country like ours, where they once seemed inexhaustible, and the maldistribution of arable soil and mineral resources on the planet, leave even the wealthiest societies ever more resource-dependent and many other nations in permanently desperate straits.

Every nation, it turns out, needs something another nation has; some nations have almost nothing they need.

The information-technology imperative. Enlightenment science and the technologies derived from it are inherently universalizing. They entail a quest for descriptive principles of general application, a search for universal solutions to particular problems, and an unswerving embrace of objectivity and impartiality.

Scientific progress embodies and depends on open communication, a common discourse rooted in rationality, collaboration, and an easy and regular flow and exchange of information. Such ideals can be hypocritical covers for power-mongering by elites, and they may be shown to be wanting in many other ways, but they are entailed by the very idea of science and they make science and globalization practical allies.

Business, banking, and commerce all depend on information flow and are facilitated by new communication technologies. The hardware of these technologies tends to be systemic and integrated—computer, television, cable, satellite, laser, fiber-optic, and microchip technologies combining to create a vast interactive communications and information network that can potentially give every person on earth access to every other person, and make every datum, every byte, available to every set of eyes. If the automobile was, as George Ball once said (when he gave his blessing to a Fiat factory in the Soviet Union during the Cold War), "an ideology on four wheels," then electronic telecommunication and information systems are an ideology at 186,000 miles per second—which makes for a very small planet in a very big hurry. Individual cultures speak particular languages; commerce and science increasingly speak English; the whole world speaks logarithms and binary mathematics.

Moreover, the pursuit of science and technology asks for, even compels, open societies. Satellite footprints do not respect national borders; telephone wires penetrate the most closed societies. With photocopying and then fax machines having infiltrated Soviet universities and *samizdat* literary circles in the eighties, and computer modems having multiplied like rabbits in communism's bureaucratic warrens thereafter, *glasnost* could not be far behind. In their social requisites, secrecy and science are enemies.

The new technology's software is perhaps even more globalizing than its hardware. The information arm of international commerce's sprawling body reaches out and touches distinct nations and parochial cultures, and gives them a common face chiseled in Hollywood, on Madison Avenue, and in Silicon Valley. Throughout the 1980s one of the most-watched television programs in South Africa was *The Cosby Show*. The demise of apartheid was already in production. Exhibitors at the 1991 Cannes film festival expressed growing anxiety over the "homogenization" and "Americanization" of the global film industry where for the third year running, American films dominated the awards ceremonies.

America has dominated the world's popular culture for much longer, and more decisively. In November of 1991 Switzerland's once insular culture boasted best-seller lists featuring *Terminator 2* as the No. 1 movie, *Scarlett* as the No. 1 book, and Prince's *Diamonds and Pearls* as the No. 1 record album. No wonder the Japanese are buying Hollywood film studios even faster than Americans are buying Japanese television sets. This kind of software supremacy may in the long term be far more important than hardware superiority, because culture has become more potent than armaments. What is the power of the Pentagon compared with Disneyland's?

...culture has become more potent than armaments.

Can the Sixth Fleet keep up with CNN? McDonald's in Moscow and Coke in China will do more to create a global culture than military colonization ever could. It is less the goods than the brand names that do the work, for they convey life-style images that alter perception and challenge behavior. They make up the seductive software of McWorld's common (at times much too common) soul.

Yet in all this high-tech commercial world there is nothing that looks particularly democratic. It lends itself to surveillance as well as liberty, to new forms of manipulation and covert control as well as new kinds of participation, to skewed, unjust market outcomes as well as greater productivity. The consumer society and the open society are not quite synonymous. Capitalism and democracy have a relationship, but it is something less than a marriage. An efficient free market after all requires that consumers be free to vote their dollars on competing goods, not that citizens be free to vote their values and beliefs on competing political candidates and programs. The free market flourished in junta-run Chile, in military-governed Taiwan and Korea, and, earlier, in a variety of autocratic European empires as well as their colonial possessions.

The ecological imperative. The impact of globalization on ecology is a cliché even to world leaders who ignore it. We know well enough that the German forests can be destroyed by Swiss and Italians driving gas-guzzlers fueled by leaded gas. We also know that the planet can be asphyxiated by greenhouse gases because Brazilian farmers want to be part of the twentieth century and are burning down tropical rain forests to clear a little land to plough, and because Indonesians make a living out of converting their lush jungle into toothpicks for fastidious Japanese diners, upsetting the delicate oxygen balance and in effect puncturing our global lungs. Yet this ecological consciousness has meant not only greater awareness but also greater inequality, as modernized nations try to slam the door behind them, saying to developing nations, "The world cannot afford *your* modernization; ours has wrung it dry!"

Each of the four imperatives just cited is transnational, transideological, and transcultural. Each applies impartially to Catholics, Jews, Muslims, Hindus, and Buddhists; to democrats and totalitarians; to capitalists and socialists. The Enlightenment dream of a universal rational society has to a remarkable degree been realized—but in a form that is commercialized, homogenized, depoliticized, bureaucratized, and, of course, radically incomplete, for the movement toward McWorld is in competition with forces of global breakdown, national dissolution, and centrifugal corruption. These forces, working in the opposite direction, are the essence of what I call Jihad.

JIHAD, OR THE LEBANONIZATION OF THE WORLD
◆ ◆ ◆

OPEC, the World Bank, the United Nations, the International Red Cross, the multinational corporation...there are scores of institutions that reflect globalization. But they often appear as ineffective reactors to the world's real actors: national states and, to an ever greater degree, subnational factions in permanent rebellion against uniformity and integration—even the kind represented by universal law and justice. The headlines feature these players regularly: they are cultures, not countries; parts, not wholes; sects, not religions; rebellious factions and dissenting minorities at war not just with globalism but with the traditional nation-state. Kurds, Basques, Puerto Ricans, Ossetians, East Timoreans, Quebecois, the Catholics of Northern Ireland, Abkhasians, Kurile Islander Japanese, the Zulus of Inkatha, Catalonians, Tamils, and, of course, Palestinians—people without countries, inhabiting nations not their own, seeking smaller worlds within borders that will seal them off from modernity.

A powerful irony is at work here. Nationalism was once a force of integration and unification, a movement aimed at bringing together disparate clans, tribes, and cultural fragments under new, assimilationist flags. But as Ortega y Gasset noted more than sixty years ago, having won its victories, nationalism changed its strategy. In the 1920s, and again today, it is more often a reactionary and divisive force, pulverizing the very nations it once helped cement together. The force that creates nations is "inclusive," Ortega wrote in *The Revolt of the Masses*. "In periods of consolidation, nationalism has a positive value, and is a lofty standard. But in Europe everything is more than consolidated, and nationalism is nothing but a mania...."

This mania has left the post-Cold War world smoldering with hot wars; the international scene is little more unified than it was at the end of the Great War, in Ortega's own time. There were more than thirty wars in progress last year, most of them ethnic, racial, tribal, or religious in character, and the list of unsafe regions doesn't seem to be getting any shorter. Some new world order!

The aim of many of these small-scale wars is to redraw boundaries, to implode states and resecure parochial identities: to escape McWorld's dully insistent imperitives. The mood is that of Jihad: war not as an instrument of policy but as an emblem of identity, an expression of community, an end in itself. Even where there is a shooting war, there is fractiousness, secession, and a quest for ever smaller communities. Add to the list of dangerous countries those at risk: In Switzerland and Spain, Jurassian and Basque separatists still argue the virtues of ancient identities, sometimes in the language of bombs. Hyperdisintegration in the former Soviet Union may well continue unabated—not just a Ukraine independent from the Soviet Union but a Bessarab Ukraine independent from the Ukrainian republic; just Russia severed from the defunct union but Tatarsa severed from Russia. Yugoslavia makes even the disured, ex-Soviet, nonsocialist republics that were once the Soviet Union look integrated, its sectarian fatherland springing up within factional motherlands like weeds within weeds within weeds. Kurdish independence would threaten the territorial integrity of four Mid-Eastern nations. Well before the current cataclysm Soviet Georgia made a claim for autonomy from the Soviet Union, only to be faced with its Ossetians (164,000 in a republic of 5.5 million) demanding their own self-determination within Georgia. The Abkhasian minority of Georgia has followed suit. Even the good will established by Canada's once promising Meech Lake protocols is in danger, with Francophone Quebec again threatening dissolution of the federation. In South Africa the emergence from apartheid was hardly achieved when friction between Inkatha's Zulus and the African National Congress's tribally identified members threat-

ened to replace Europeans' racism with an indigenous tribal war. After thirty years of attempted integration using the colonial language (English) as a unifier, Nigeria is now playing with the idea of linguistic multiculturalism—which could mean the cultural breakup of the nation into hundreds of tribal fragments. Even Saddam Hussein has benefited from the threat of internal Jihad, having used renewed tribal and religious warfare to turn last season's mortal enemies into reluctant allies of an Iraqi nationhood that he nearly destroyed.

The passing of communism has torn away the thin veneer of internationalism (workers of the world unite!) to reveal ethnic prejudices that are not only ugly and

---

This is religious as the Crusaders knew it: a battle to the death for souls that if not saved will be forever lost.

---

deep-seated but increasingly murderous. Europe's old scourge, anti-Semitism, is back with a vengeance, but it is only one of many antagonisms. It appears all too easy to throw the historical gears into reverse and pass from a Communist dictatorship back into a tribal state.

Among the tribes, religion is also a battlefield. ("Jihad" is a rich word whose generic meaning is "struggle"—usually the struggle of the soul to avert evil. Strictly applied to religious war, it is used only in reference to battles where the faith is under assault, or battles against a government that denies the practice of Islam. My use here is rhetorical, but does follow both journalistic practice and history.) Remember the Thirty Years War? Whatever forms of Enlightenment universalism might once have come to grace such historically related forms of monotheism as Judaism, Christianity, and Islam, in many of their modern incarnations they are parochial rather than cosmopolitan, angry rather than loving, proselytizing rather than ecumenical, zealous rather than rationalist, sectarian rather then deistic, ethnocentric rather than universalizing. As a result, like the new forms of hypernationalism, the new expressions of religious fundamentalism are fractious and pulverizing, never integrating. This is religious as the Crusaders knew it: a battle to the death for souls that if not saved will be forever lost.

The atmospherics of Jihad have resulted in a breakdown of civility in the name of identity, of comity in the name of community. International relations have sometimes taken on the aspects of gang war—cultural turf battles featuring tribal factions that were supposed to be sublimated as integral parts of large national, economic, postcolonial, and constitutional entities.

THE DARKENING FUTURE OF DEMOCRACY

◆ ◆ ◆

These rather melodramatic tableaux vivants do not tell the whole story, however. For all their defects, Jihad and McWorld have their attractions. Yet, to repeat and insist, the attractions are unrelated to democracy. Neither McWorld nor Jihad is remotely democratic in impulse. Neither needs democracy; neither promotes democracy.

McWorld does manage to look pretty seductive in a world obsessed with Jihad. It delivers peace, prosperity, and relative unity—if at the cost of independence, community, and identity (which is generally based on difference). The primary political values required by the global market are order and tranquillity, and freedom—as in the phrases "free trade," "free press," and "free love." Human rights are needed to a degree, but not citizenship or participation—and no more social justice and equality than are necessary to promote efficient economic production and consumption. Multinational corporations sometimes seem to prefer doing business with local oligarchs, inasmuch as they can take confidence from dealing with the boss on all crucial matters. Despots who slaughter their own populations are no problem, as long as they leave markets in place and refrain from making war on their neighbors (Saddam Hussein's fatal mistake). In trading partners, predictability is of more value than justice.

The Eastern European revolutions that seemed to arise out of concern for global democratic values quickly deteriorated into a stampede in the general direction of free markets and their ubiquitous, television-promoted shopping malls. East Germany's Neues Forum, that courageous gathering of intellectuals, students, and workers which overturned the Stalinist regime in Berlin in 1989, lasted only six months in Germany's mini-version of McWorld. Then it gave way to money and markets and monopolies from the West. By the time of the first all-German elections, it could scarcely manage to secure three percent of the vote. Elsewhere there is growing evidence that *glasnost* will go and *perestroika*—defined as privatization and an opening of markets to Western bidders—will stay. So understandably anxious

are the new rulers of Eastern Europe and whatever entities are forged from the residues of the Soviet Union to gain access to credit and markets and technology—McWorld's flourishing new currencies—that they have shown themselves willing to trade away democratic prospects in pursuit of them: not just old totalitarian ideologies and command-economy production models but some possible indigenous experiments with a third way between capitalism and socialism, such as economic cooperatives and employee stock-ownership plans, both of which have their ardent supporters in the East.

Jihad delivers a different set of virtues: a vibrant local identity, a sense of community, solidarity among kinsmen, neighbors, and countrymen, narrowly conceived. But it also guarantees parochialism and is grounded in exclusion. Solidarity is secured through war against outsiders. And solidarity often means obedience to a hierarchy in governance, fanaticism in beliefs, and the obliteration of individual selves in the name of the group. Deference to leaders and intolerance toward outsiders (and toward "enemies within") are hallmarks of tribalism—hardly the attitudes required for the cultivation of new democratic women and men capable of governing themselves. Where new democratic experiments have been conducted in retribalizing societies, in both Europe and the Third World, the result has often been anarchy, repression, persecution, and the coming of new, noncommunist forms of very old kinds of despotism. During the past year, Havel's velvet revolution in Czechoslovakia was imperiled by partisans of "Czechland" and of Slovakia as independent entities. India seemed little less rent by Sikh, Hindu, Muslim, and Tamil infighting than it was immediately after the British pulled out, more than forty years ago.

To the extent that either McWorld or Jihad has a *natural* politics, it has turned out to be more of an antipolitics. For McWorld, it is the antipolitics of globalism: bureaucratic, technocratic, and meritocratic, focused (as Marx predicted it would be) on the administration of things—with people, however, among the chief things to be administered. In its politico-economic imperatives McWorld has been guided by laissez-faire market principles that privilege efficiency, productivity, and beneficence at the expense of civic liberty and self-government.

For Jihad, the antipolitics of tribalization has been explicitly antidemocratic: one-party dictatorship, government by military junta, theocratic fundamentalism—often associated with a version of the *Führerprinzip* that empowers an individual to rule on behalf of a people. Even the government of India, struggling for decades to model democracy for a people who will soon number a billion, longs for great leaders; and for every Mahatma Gandhi, Indira Gandhi, or Rajiv Gandhi taken from them by zealous assassins, the Indians appear to seek a replacement who will deliver them from the lengthy travail of their freedom.

THE CONFEDERAL OPTION

◆ ◆ ◆

How can democracy be secured and spread in a world whose primary tendencies are at best indifferent to it (McWorld) and at worst deeply antithetical to it (Jihad)? My guess is that globalization will eventually vanquish retribalization. The ethos of material "civilization" has not yet encountered an obstacle it has been unable to thrust aside. Ortega may have grasped in the 1920s a clue to our own future in the coming millennium.

> Everyone sees the need of a new principle of life. But as always happens in similar crises—some people attempt to save the situation by an artificial intensification of the very principle which has led to decay. This is the meaning of the "nationalist" outburst of recent years...things have always gone that way. The last flare, the longest; the last sigh, the deepest. On the very eve of their disappearance there is an intensification of frontiers—military and economic.

Jihad may be a last deep sigh before the eternal yawn of McWorld. On the other hand, Ortega was not exactly prescient; his prophecy of peace and internalism came just before blitzkrieg, world war, and the Holocaust tore the old order to bits. Yet democracy is how we remonstrate with reality, the rebuke our aspirations offer to history. And if retribalization is inhospitable to democracy, there is nonetheless a form of democratic government that can accommodate parochialism and communitarianism, one that can even save them from their defects and make them more tolerant and participatory: decentralized participatory democracy. And if McWorld is indifferent to democracy, there is nonetheless a form of democratic government that suits global markets passably well—representative government in its federal or, better still, confederal variation.

With its concern for accountability, the protection of minorities, and the universal rule of law, a confederalized representative system would serve the political needs of McWorld as well as oligarchic bureaucratism or meritocratic elitism is currently doing. As we are already beginning to see, many nations may survive in the long term only as confederations that afford local regions smaller than "nations" extensive jurisdiction. Recommended reading for democrats of the twenty-first century is not the U.S. Constitution or the French Declaration of Rights of Man and Citizen but the Articles of Confederation, that suddenly pertinent document that stitched together the thirteen American colonies into what then seemed a too loose confederation of independent states but now appears a new form of political realism, as veterans of Yeltsins's new Russia and the new Europe created at Maastricht will attest.

By the same token, the participatory and direct form of democracy that engages citizens in civic activity and civic judgment and goes well beyond just voting and accountability—the system I have called "strong democracy"—suits the political needs of decentralized communities as well as theocratic and nationalist party dictatorships have done. Local neighborhoods need not be democratic, but they can be. Real democracy has flourished in diminutive settings: the spirit of liberty, Tocqueville said, is local. Participatory democracy, if not naturally apposite to tribalism, has an undeniable attractiveness under conditions of parochialism.

Democracy in any of these variations will, however, continue to be obstructed by the undemocratic and antidemocratic trends toward uniformitarian globalism and intolerant retribalization which I have portrayed here. For democracy to persist in our brave new McWorld, we will have to commit acts of conscious political will—a possibility, but hardly a probability, under these conditions. Political will requires much more than the quick fix of the transfer of institutions. Like technology transfer, institution transfer rests on foolish assumptions about a uniform world of the kind that once fired the imagination of colonial administrators. Spread English justice to the colonies by exporting wigs. Let an East Indian trading company act as the vanguard to Britain's free parliamentary institutions. Today's well-intentioned quick-fixers in the National Endowment for Democracy and the Kennedy School of Government, in the unions and foundations and universities zealously nurturing contacts in Eastern Europe and the Third World, are hoping to democratize by long distance. Post Bulgaria a parliament by first-class mail. Fed Ex the Bill of Rights to Sri Lanka. Cable Cambodia some common law.

Yet Eastern Europe has already demonstrated that importing free political parties, parliaments, and presses cannot establish a democratic civil society; imposing a free market may even have the opposite effect. Democracy grows from the bottom up and cannot be imposed from the top down. Civil society has to be built from the inside out. The institutional superstructure comes last. Poland may become democratic, but then again it may heed the Pope, and prefer to found its politics on its Catholicism, with uncertain consequences for democracy. Bulgaria may become democratic, but it may prefer tribal war. The former Soviet Union may become a democratic confederation, or it may just grow into an anarchic and weak conglomeration of markets for other nations' goods and services.

Democrats need to seek out indigenous democratic impulses. There is always a desire for self-government, always some expression of participation, accountability, consent, and representation, even in traditional hierarchical societies. These need to be identified, tapped, modified, and incorporated into new democratic practices with an indigenous flavor. The tortoises among the democratizers may ultimately outlive or outpace the hares, for they will have the time and patience to explore conditions along the way, and to adapt their gait to changing circumstances. Tragically, democracy in a hurry often looks something like France in 1794 or China in 1989.

It certainly seems possible that the most attractive democratic ideal in the face of the brutal realities of Jihad and the dull realities of McWorld will be a confederal union of semi-autonomous communities smaller than nation-states, tied together into regional economic associations and markets larger than nation-states—participatory and self-determining in local matters at the bottom, representative and accountable at the top. The nation-state would play a diminished role, and sovereignty would lose some of its political potency. The Green movement adage "Think globally, act locally" would actually come to describe the conduct of politics.

This vision reflects only an ideal, however—one that is not terribly likely to be realized. Freedom, Jean-Jacques Rousseau once wrote, is a food easy to eat but hard to digest. Still, democracy has always played itself out against the odds. And democracy remains both a form of coherence as binding as McWorld and a secular faith potentially as inspiriting as Jihad.

Terms & Concepts

Americanization
antipolitics
authoritarianism
capitalism
civil society
confederation
cultural homogenization
democracy
ecological imperative

Führerprinzip
globalization
hyperdisintegration
hypernationalism
information-technology imperative
Jihad
market imperative
McWorld
nationalism

parochialism
religion
resource imperative
sovereignty
transnational organizations
tribalism
universalization

Questions

1. Barber sees both *Jihad* and *McWorld* as challenges to democracy. How do they both threaten democracy and how do the threats differ?

2. What is Barber's democratic antidote, and how much faith does he have in it?

3. Can the forces of *Jihad* and *McWorld* be found in Canada? Give examples.

4. Is *McWorld* truly a universal, globalizing set of forces, or is it American international pre-eminence?

5. Is Barber too hard on the world of *Jihad* —a world trying to escape the clutches of domination, exploitation, and *McWorld*?

Democracy and Its Discontents

Charles S. Maier

Editors' Note

"Democracy and Its Discontents" tackles a question that runs through, or appears in some form, in a large number of the articles in this reader. Have democracies become unruly and more difficult to govern? Reading the first two essays in this volume, (*Homer-Dixon* and *Barber*), one might think so. Charles Maier, however, points out that *real* political crises "threaten civil war or dictatorship." We do not have to fully agree with him (the Great Depression of the 1930s was without doubt a real crisis) to concede the point that what we are experiencing in Europe and North America is not societal breakdown.

The kind of crisis to which Maier refers is described as a form of "civil discontent," and above all, as a moral crisis. Such moral crises are not new, and the current one has characteristics in common with its predecessors, including: a broad distrust of politics, leaders, and political institutions; impatience with corruption; a sense of historical disorientation; and major ("seismic") shifts in intellectual orientation and in public perception and confidence. Two of his most interesting points are how our views of history—and the kind of history we read—change, and how we have now moved from "ethnocultural generalizations to biological

ones." The recent searing controversy over race, genes, and IQ that is raging in the United States is clear evidence in support of this latter point.

Maier also notes the upsurge in populism, discussed at length elsewhere in this book, and we must not forget the role played by the media. Maier ends with a plea similar to the one made by Anthony Smith in his discussion of European nationalism (Unit Two, Article 9)—a plea for multiple loyalties, tolerance, historical awareness, and an appreciation of the moral choices we face.

◆ ◆ ◆

MORAL CRISES IN HISTORICAL PERSPECTIVE

◆ ◆ ◆

How should one make sense of the malaise that currently sours public opinion in the countries of Europe, in Japan and North America? It reveals itself most saliently in tremendous electoral volatility as political parties are deserted for new formations and leaders. Consider the disintegration of Japan's Liberal Democrats; the obliteration of Canada's Progressive Conservatives; the populist appeal of Ross Perot; the attrition of the mainstream German parties for Greens on the left and xenophobes on the right; the willingness of voters in Poland and former East Bloc countries to vote for recycled communists; the Zhirinovsky phenomenon in Russia. Most recently Italian voters turned sharply toward the unconventional electoral formations of the Italian "Freedom Alliance": the refurbished neo-fascists, the plebiscitary fan clubs of television magnate Silvio Berlusconi, and the pugnacious regionalists of the Northern Leagues.

Elections provide only the most spectacular index of public impatience. Political leaders have found it difficult to follow through on laboriously negotiated national pledges such as Meech Lake, Maastricht or the North American Free Trade Agreement. Great breakthroughs become mired in complexity: How many out-

---

Do these manifestations mean that democracies, as some might propose, have become ungovernable?

---

side Brussels still retain the 1992 vision of the European Community as a transforming venture? And social cohesion apparently frays at a level even more basic than politics. Citizens become uneasy at the noticeable presence of the foreign-born, worry about the burdens on welfare and the pool of jobs, and view imported mores, languages and religious manifestations as a threat to national identity. Casual resort to deadly force seems to have become more acceptable, whether among American gangs or German skinheads. Commentators point out, and everyday life seems to confirm, a general erosion of civility, which has taken on "an ideological edge."[1] Only a few years after Eastern Europeans sought to recover the autonomy of civil society, the quality of civil society, Western and Eastern, seems significantly degraded. No wonder that the common exhilaration that attended the collapse of communism has largely dissipated. How difficult it is today to recover the spirit of the crowds in Leipzig or Wenceslaus Square.

Do these manifestations mean that democracies, as some might propose, have become ungovernable? Are they more unruly? Certainly they are not in comparison to 15 or 20 years ago. There are probably fewer public demonstrations, fewer bombings, fewer assassinations, fewer strikes, more moderate wage claims than during the 1970s. (To be sure, the record may yet deteriorate further.) In the 1970s, too, critics discerned a crisis of

governability. What they usually referred to, however, were excessive demands on the state and economy, as postwar growth deteriorated into stagflation. The crisis then was purportedly the result of "overloaded democracy," shortsighted mass pursuit of present entitlements at the expense of saving for the future. Whether or not this analysis is accepted for the 1970s, today's discontents are different. Citizens do not so much confront their states with demands as they back away in disillusion. If there is a crisis, it is of a different sort.

WHAT KIND OF CRISIS?

◆ ◆ ◆

The crisis of the 1970s tended to focus on issues of economic distribution. In the market arena wage earners and employers seemed locked in a struggle, over income shares, that inhibited productive saving and investment. In the political arena delegates for the same classes as well as pensioners, the military and other interests all struggled for government subsidies and benefits—a continuing tug-of-war then diagnosed by some as the "fiscal crisis of the state."[2] In the 1970s the vicious circle of declining productivity and employment, higher welfare needs and state expenditures as a share of stagnating income, persisting inflation, increased political contentiousness; wage militancy, lower investment and so on seemed impossible to break. State deficits persist in the 1990s, but in most Western societies a cap seems to have been placed on public claims on national income. Unemployment remains preoccupying in Spain, France, American cities and elsewhere. Nonetheless, the discontents of the 1990s do not manifest themselves preeminently as an economic crisis. An economic crisis is one in which poor economic performance—high unemployment, a decline in growth or an actual fall in output, sometimes a great inflation—imposes massive public hardship and dominates political debate. The market societies, at least to date, have learned to be less perturbed.

Neither does the disaffection of the 1990s constitute a political crisis—again with the proviso, at least not yet. Real political crises threaten civil war or dictatorship. They emerge when contending parties cannot resolve deep ideological differences and thus paralyze institutions. The French and Spanish Republics from 1934 through 1936, the Weimar Republic in 1923 and again after 1930, the United States in the late 1850s and perhaps in the late 1960s underwent political crises. The communist regimes experienced their own political crises at the end of the 1980s, and the lands of the former Soviet Union may have not yet emerged. (Whether ethnic conflicts over territory or political rights, as in Canada, the former Czechoslovakia, and of course the former Yugoslavia, count as political crises depends upon their mode of resolution, whether consensually or by force.) Whereas political crises often emerge out of intense party loyalties, the public mood under study here involves a profound distrust of traditional parties. Granted, the rejection of traditional party organizations can evolve into the emergence of fierce new loyalties. But the crisis today retains its pre-political properties. It is less conflictual, more rooted in a civil society (actually in structures that are less developed than civil society) that has become distrustful of the state.

If it constitutes neither an economic nor a political crisis, how should contemporary public dissatisfaction be summarized? It is best described by the term "civic discontent" or even "moral crisis." Moral crises can help generate political crises, and they reveal characteristic economic symptoms even if they do not originate in economic causes. The economic manifestations involve distribution more than production: moral crises are nurtured by growing inequality of incomes, feverish and often conspicuous consumption and the frenzied pursuit of windfall gains in real estate and speculative finance. Ivan Boesky and Michael Milken, for example, testify to moral crises, not economic ones.

"Crisis" is a strong and often overused term. Still, it is justified, for it signifies a precarious systemic state in which an organism or a society hovers between decomposition and a rallying of collective energy. Undergoing a crisis does not preclude a recovery of vitality, but it does suggest that the society and states that emerge after an extended period of turbulence shall have been transformed, not merely restored. One can understand more of what is currently at stake by contrasting two preeminent nineteenth-century analysts of crisis. Karl Marx, of course, believed economic crises to be deepening ineluctably before his eyes. They unfolded as the consequence of class conflict, restlessly stripping away all illusions about the power of capital, transforming political and property regimes in their wake. His conservative contemporary Jacob Burckhardt, however, remained preoccupied by a cultural degeneration (akin to what I mean by "moral crisis") that he ascribed to the advent of mass politics, the resort to militarism and the feverish pursuit of wealth. As Burckhardt wrote with foreboding in the 1870s, "The first great phenomenon to follow the [Franco-Prussian] war of 1870–1871 was a further extraordinary intensification of money-making....Art

and science have greatest difficulty in preventing themselves from sinking into a mere branch of money-making and from being carried away on the stream of general unrest...."[3]

One need not share Burckhardt's fear of democracy to grasp his premonitions of moral crisis after 1870: the force of mass upheaval, the spectacular international realignment, the rash of new fortunes, a renewed threat of anti-Semitism. Others would share these misgivings. A few years later the once-ardent national poet, Giosuè Carducci, wrote scathingly about united Italy and the ugliness of its capital, now the site of clientelistic politics and real estate speculation. Italy was not the only country to be afflicted by a sense of historical decay and moral degeneration. In the Third French Republic one scandal after another agitated (or titillated) the public: the son-in-law of President Jules Grévy, it was disclosed, peddled the Legion of Honor out of the Elysée; the would-be developers of the Panama Canal thoughtfully placed a sizable number of parliamentary deputies on their payroll. In the United States rife corruption tarnished the administration of Ulysses Grant, the administration of New York City and the presidential candidacy of James G. Blaine. Germany underwent a plutocratic orgy during its brief *Gründerzeit*. All the nation-states constructed or reconstructed between 1860 and 1870 on the basis of popular nationalism seemed to be mired in networks of venality.

Political mobilization of the male population led apparently neither to a lofty democracy nor an austere liberalism, but to regimes based on manipulated public opinion. The instruments might be shameless patronage or rigged elections—entrenched by interparty agreement in Restoration Spain after 1874 or achieved by voting restrictions in Hungary and the American South. Given the discrepancy between the high ideals of liberalism and its shabby realities, it was no surprise that the generation of intellectuals after 1870 developed a new conservative sociology of politics. Its positivist theorists spared no effort to discredit democratic pretensions. William Graham Sumner borrowed from Darwin to criticize social reform. In Italy Gaetano Mosca updated Machiavelli's political analysis, while Pasquale Turiello yearned for a regenerative war. In France Hippolyte Taine repudiated the French Revolution, and Fustel de Coulanges praised the collectivist vigor and ancestral cults of the ancient city. A generation later Georges Sorel and Vilfredo Pareto heaped disdain on soft-minded bourgeois humanitarians. Other critics of liberalism proposed schemes for technocratic governance by experts. They sought scientific social intervention, championed imperialism and worried about eugenic decay. They despised left-wing reformers as self-interested demagogues and yearned for authority. They envisaged military competition as calisthenic and invigorating, the "sole hygiene of the world." So much hope had attended the creation of the new nation-states; how corrupt and shabby they seemed to be turning out!

CRITERIA OF MORAL CRISES

◆ ◆ ◆

After having lived through its own Gilded Age in the 1980s, the United States should find the civic climate of the 1870s and 1880s familiar. Moral crises of democracy have since recurred periodically, in some cases localized, at other times across national boundaries. Dating them with precision remains difficult. Although they peak during the course of a decade or even more briefly, with their antecedents and ideological sequels they can take a quarter-century to play out completely. Not all characteristics need emerge simultaneously, and contemporaries often decry prejudice, corruption or other civic defects without discerning a systemic crisis. But symptoms were pervasive and deep enough to justify a diagnosis of moral crisis in Europe and the Western hemisphere during the 1870s and 1880s, in Central Europe in the 1920s and in Western Europe in the late 1930s, and during the past decade the West has at least created the preconditions for a new era of civic discontents.

Moral crises, to consider the first dimension, are marked by a feeling of historical aftermath and disorientation.

Admittedly the typology remains imprecise. Critics will discern symptoms of decline in every passage of history, and jeremiads alone cannot substantiate the existence of a moral crisis. Insofar as they find a wide audience, they get taken as evidence for the conditions they denounce. The diagnosis of moral crisis is thus highly self-reflective. As such it is prone to exaggeration and must be invoked with caution. Still, one can go beyond cultural commentary to discern a profound shift of public attitude along three dimensions: a sudden sense

of historical dislocation, a disaffection with the political leadership of all parties and a recurring skepticism about doctrines of social progress. Each of these developments tends to entail the others such that they hang together as a whole.

Moral crises, to consider the first dimension, are marked by a feeling of historical aftermath and disorientation. Intellectuals share a widespread perception that a great historical moment has been succeeded by a shabby area of routine transactions—poet W.H. Auden's "low dishonest decade." There is a gnawing conviction that great causes have either been achieved ("the end of history") or betrayed; in any case they are over.[4] Public activity seems to amount to the streetsweeping required after a great confetti-strewn triumphal parade.

The sensation of letdown usually follows some supreme national experience. Italian and German unification, the American Civil War and other struggles of the era from the late 1850s to 1870 defined or renegotiated the nation-states of the West (and Japan). "We shall not succeed in banishing the curse that besets us, that of being born too late for a great political era, unless we understand how to become the forerunners of a greater one," wrote Max Weber in his inaugural lecture of 1895.[5] So, too, the First World War, with its grandiose claims of transforming states and international relations, could not but leave a later spiritual vacuum. Participants often felt ignored and devalued. Latecomers shared a sense of missing out, the need to generate a new crusade or sometimes just to discredit the old one. In the aftermath of 1989's collapse of communism, a similar feeling of anticlimax has succeeded initial euphoria.

In periods of moral crisis international politics no longer offers familiar principles and alignments. Not only have the great simplifying struggles passed, but the new issues are less clear-cut and harder to order using grand principles. Restructured nation-states change their relative power, and major countries have to negotiate predictable new coalitions, usually only after painful faltering and expedients. The new complexity encourages irresolution, which in turn bequeaths a sense of collective failure, as the years of appeasement sadly demonstrated. Whether the arguments for restraint and accommodation in the 1930s were well-founded or shortsighted, they left a corrosive feeling of inadequacy. Similarly, no matter how imposing the practical difficulties of intervention, most Western onlookers have felt soiled by their passivity during the ferocious assault on the Bosnian Muslims. High hopes for Europe seem hollow before this lack of capacity or volition. So they did after Ethiopia, the Spanish Republic, Austria and

Czechoslovakia were wiped out in the late 1930s. Once undertaken, the struggle against Nazism helped to expiate and overcome the moral crisis of the late 1930s. What equivalent recuperation will be possible now is not at all clear.

Moral crises reveal, as their second dimension, a broad distrust of political representatives regardless of ideology. The moment of opportunity for the nonpolitical politician arises. In this respect the moral crisis might seem to constitute a reaction by civil society against its political class. However, the roots of distrust spring from more primitive resentments than civil society. They are tribal, not associational, and thus not to be identified with the process that East Europeans carried through in the late 1980s. The East European project involved reclaiming political activity through the empowerment of voluntary associations. The moral crisis involves a rejection of the nomenklatura or political class on behalf of territorial loyalties and idealized local ties.

One major expression of this distrust of elites emerges as a new impatience with long-tolerated patterns of corruption. Bribery and kickbacks, which had long been shrugged off or ignored as a transaction cost of public business, now become perceived as an intolerable symptom of decay. The press focuses on corruption, and trials and interrogations confirm the general distrust of political and financial leaders. *Mani pulite* ("clean hands"), the massive anticorruption drive in Italy, prodded a long-overdue scrutiny of the representational system. The Recruit scandal in Japan has shaken decades of unquestioned Liberal Democratic clan rule. Such upheavals can be constructive if they lead to durable reforms; often, they yield just a few spectacular trials and a brief housecleaning; in today's circumstances they can amplify the revulsion against the political class as a whole.

Periods of moral crisis are marked most profoundly by seismic shifts in intellectual orientation and social thought. In this climate conservative critiques of mass politics tend to seem more persuasive, while ideologies of the left lose their credibility. Collectivist ideas and movements fragmented in the 1870s and 1880s. In our current era, Marxism flagged as a plausible ideology at least a decade before the communist systems collapsed. Intellectuals more generally abandon their commitment to ideas of progress and projects for equality. Again, complexity overwhelms. Reformers tire of difficult causes or become overwhelmed by contemplating the evils that have accompanied them. They see the French Revolution exclusively in terms of the Reign of Terror, socialism exclusively as the Gulag—the perception

always insisted on by conservative critics, but now wearily acquiesced in by leading journals of opinion and intellectuals who had long sought to uphold distinctions.

Relatedly, there is a new stance toward historical knowledge as a form of public self-awareness. Historical writing is prized more for its narrative and evocative capacity and less for its explanatory possibilities. Practitioners renounce earlier (or later) social-scientific ambitions; they focus on the discipline's elegiac mission. History today thus becomes the basis for a memory industry which seeks to recreate mood and feeling. Readers ask less analysis and more evocation. Landscape and place seem more compelling; the past, more viscous.

Responding to similar impulses, political and social analysts tend to abandon their earlier confidence in reform for an emphasis on social intractability. Social stratification earlier attributed to unequal opportunity seems far more difficult to overcome and is ascribed to more persistent categories. Classes harden into apparent castes; racial and ethnocultural distinctions are interpreted as the fundamental social reality, to be celebrated by some, taken as a challenge for policy by fewer, acquiesced in by more. The issue in each of these generalizations is not the truth or error of the analysis, but the recourse to it and the consequences that are drawn. Social stratification, criminality and violence seem so overwhelming that they require deep structural explanation. But in contrast to earlier periods of reform, fewer political leaders believe in institutional reform. More

---

Periods of moral crisis are marked most profoundly by seismic shifts in intellectual orientation and social thought.

---

police and harsher sentences in the United States, limitation of asylum and residence rights in Germany and France, exemption of wealthier regions from the burdens of the poorer in Italy, all emerge as the counsels of realism.

Finally, ethnocultural generalizations yield to biological ones: distinctions are increasingly defined as genetic, and sciences emphasize the biological bases of behavior, including deviance. Professional anthropology, which started in the 1860s with an emphasis on the unity of mankind, evolved by the 1870s and 1880s into a study of the distinctions between higher and lower races. Today's laboratory researchers announce that they have discovered the putative gene for alcoholism or homosexuality winding its insidious way through strands of DNA. Liberals are relieved that the burden of individual guilt can thus be mitigated, but sometimes fail to think through the ethical or policy implications of the alleged finding. Sociobiology is extended as a key to explain all human behaviour. The issue here is not whether these contributions are sound or not; very few can resolve that question. But the interest in the experiments and the supposed results reflects a renewed skepticism about the possibilities for purposeful social reform, change that significantly enhances equality of outcomes. Today's conventional wisdom is deeply conservative.

Some commentators here and abroad celebrate social pluralism as multiculturalism (German Greens are into *multikulti*) and urge going with the fragmented flow. Others lament the loss of a common civic allegiance and hope to reverse the current. Both stances recognize a sense of decomposition and the loss of a hitherto functioning civic myth. If societal divisions are presumed to be grounded in nature or in ancestral culture, neither side should be surprised that the only settlement of conflicting claims must ultimately be by force or territorial partition. Territory becomes the one adjustable variable, since society cannot overcome its biological or cultural diversity. And whereas territorial adjustment used to involve the conquest of irredenta from their foreign masters, now it involves civil war or negotiated secession. Sometimes the relatively disadvantaged want to renegotiate or dismantle the federal pact, as in the former Soviet Union, sometimes the relatively advantaged (the Lombard League), sometimes both (Alberta and Quebec, Slovakia and the Czech lands).

All these symptoms, it will be noted, involve changes in collective attitudes and psychology. The shifts in public mood may correspond to the discovery of real constraints. An intoxicating historical victory—1865, 1871, 1918, 1989—may indeed bequeath an aftermath of quotidian politics and new resentments. Corruption and criminality may indeed have become more brazen; it may have attracted or recruited ethnic outsiders. Nonetheless, the perceptions and reactions constitute the crisis, not the phenomena in their own right. Societies make their peace with objective pathologies for many years and decades. The mafia extracts tribute, politicians get kickbacks, inequality remains. (Revolutionary crises, after all, occur not necessarily as inequality peaks, but when it becomes perceived as unacceptable.) A moral crisis indicates that patience has run out.

This observation leads to the final characteristic of a moral crisis: open-endedness. Moral crises, with their sense of collective disillusion, can generate heightened xenophobia, a surly distrust of institutions, a cynicism about politics, a resentment of elites. Societies can slip deeper into despair over ethnic or ideological pluralism. Surprisingly, however, a moral crisis can also provoke societies to recover the public commitments they earlier abandoned. Moral crises are grave, but not necessarily lethal, and if some have undermined liberal democracy, others have prompted, albeit belatedly, a renewed sense of civic mission. Under committed leaders, societies can seek to remoralize politics, to overcome legacies of corruption or entrenched patterns of racism or withdrawals into isolationism. The politics of resentment and of renewed moralization are both possible responses to moral crises of democracy, and sometimes they can follow each other.

PRINCIPLES IN CONTENTION

◆ ◆ ◆

Elements of moral crisis, if not the entire syndrome, recur periodically, from the disillusionment after Versailles to the resentments of the McCarthy era. Ultimately, however, the great international struggles of 1914 to 1989—the First World War, the struggle against Hitler and imperial Japan, the Cold War—subsumed or redirected the recurring impulses of moral crises and political disorientation. The long war (a harsher view of what John Gaddis has termed "The Long Peace") imposed urgent political and military tasks on Western publics, justified activist state policies and imposed common ideological agendas.[6] The moral crises of democracy, in contrast, comprise a flight from politics, or what the Germans call *Politikverdrossenheit*: a weariness with its debates, disbelief about its claims, skepticism about its results, cynicism about its practitioners. It should not be surprising that the temptation to escape the political should revive as the discipline of the Cold War fades.

Disillusion with politics by the 1990s has undermined successive sets of expectations. Contemporary disaffection no longer focuses on the state's claim to regulate economic activity, which was preeminently contested in the 1970s and 1980s. Marxists, social democrats and reformers of every stripe then underwent a chastening process of reeducation and emerged purged of their earlier confidence in the state. Confident young economists and editors assured them that the market could best allocate most collective as well as private goods: access to land, to resources, to the radio and television spectrum, to education. For now a minimal consensus has been reached on the primacy of markets with a continuing regulatory role for government. Skepticism about politics in the 1990s reverts instead to questioning the most basic task of government, that of assuring peace over a given territory on anything other than the most ethnically exclusive basis. Every country, in this vision of despair, tends toward a *Volksgemeinschaft* or toward hopeless civil strife. Samuel Huntington recently claimed in this journal that the West confronts a new conflict among civilizations, not easily overcome.

Must this somber a prognosis be accepted? What outcome should one expect from contemporary civic discontents? Moral crises do not necessarily doom liberal regimes, but they provide a powerful opportunity for political outsiders to capitalize on the perceived defects and corruption of "the system." Outside political entrepreneurs can combine several appeals: they claim to represent success in the managerial or commercial world where competence is really tested, they can mock the parasites "inside the beltway" or ensconced in legislature and bureaucracies who have made a living out of public office, and they plausibly claim to transcend old partisan or class divisions in the name of an underlying national interest. This familiar rhetoric mingles accents of renewal and derision.

Electorates today remain poised between contending visions of political community. If the traditional parties that speak for reenergizing the public sphere can produce plausible and attractive leaders, they can channel public dissatisfaction into an era of renewed reform. This was the American outcome in the 1930s and the early 1960s, and I, for one, hope that the United States shall later be able to claim it was the result of the 1990s. Throughout this century, indeed through the nineteenth as well, reform coalitions periodically mobilized to open the political system, enlarge the boundaries of effective citizen participation, spread the benefits of economic progress. In each Western country, success required augmenting the normal constituencies of the left with the concerned electorate of the center. These coalitions worked for distributive change, for the reallocation of privileges and wealth and the expansion of public goods. But even these intervals of reform have been cut short either by war or by their own inner tensions. For the reformist coalitions tend finally, as they did by the 1970s, to result in a rash of social movements and contradictory economic outcomes that lose the reformers their centrist supporters. In the aftermath of these difficulties, former reformist and radical intellectuals repent

of their earlier enthusiasm. They are literally de-moralized but now to the benefit, not of traditional conservatives as a decade ago, but increasingly of apparently diverse movements and political entrepreneurs: in the ex-Eastern Bloc countries, former communist apparatchiks reborn as national populists; in the West, vociferous regionalists and highly successful business and media leaders.

TERRITORIAL POPULISM

◆ ◆ ◆

Does common politics unite such diverse challengers? Their common theme is that the average voter has lost control of the political and economic forces that control his life; parties in power have become absorbed only in perpetuating their tenure; outside peoples and abstruse concepts have achieved too great an influence. Identity—defined as the expectation of predictable relationships within a given spatial domain, familiar faces in familiar places—must be defended. The remedy is to realign a meaningful territory and political voice. If this is populism (the term is imprecise, but alternatives are difficult) it is territorial populism: the politics of turn in the broadest sense.

But every moral crisis generates territorial populism...

Territorial populists rally supporters in reaction to the fragmentation of social cohesion for which reformist policies are blamed. They claim to simultaneously fight for jobs at home, scrape away encrusted bureaucracies and overcome social fragmentation. Whether through xenophobic appeals, regionalism or a rejection of supranational economic commitments, they reaffirm the validity of a bounded political domain. They contest the perceived diffusion of decision-making to supranational authorities or offshore enterprises. They promise to restore a sense of identity and to repatriate decisions to a cohesive community on a familiar home territory. *"Ein Volk, ein Reich, ein Führer"* was once the most ruthless of such rallying cries; it expressed the most rigorously simplistic answer to the moral crisis of the post-World War I era. But every moral crisis generates territorial populism as a political nostrum. And sooner or later it tends to single out as deviant and subversive those groups on the ethnic territory that stand for complexity and alternative principles of solidarity: immigrant communities and vulnerable minorities, Jews, homosexuals and the old imagined conspiracies of Masons and intellectuals that seemed so insidious in Franco's Spain and Vichy France. One can hear the echoes of this sad discourse even in present-day Italy.

In theory, territorial populism can remain tolerant and reformist, but it skids easily to what is thought of as the right. Familiar right-wing motifs tend to reemerge: an appeal to ethnic exclusiveness, the desire to reinvigorate the national unit, the contempt for the existing parliamentary class. American sociologists in the 1950s referred to a "new" right, but it is no longer new. Some of the contemporary territorial populisms, though not all, are reliably neo-fascist; they rehabilitate the records of the interwar fascist leaders; their participants threaten violence as a political recourse; they allow themselves the unbridled contemptuous language that was part of the fascist or Nazi repertory. These harsh tonalities of politics emerged in the first era of moral crisis during the 1870s and 1880s; they marked the language of Action Française, Austrian political anti-Semitism, Italian fascism and German national socialism; the contempt is heard among some of the ideologues of the Northern Leagues and National Alliance, and of course from Mr. Zhirinovsky. On the other hand are many leaders who eschew this violence, who modulate their appeals or who adopt the cracker-barrel wisdom of the down-home businessman or the flashy success of the modern media czar. They avoid authoritarian rhetoric, but appeal to a plebiscitary support for national salvation.

Fascism, recall, emerged as a specific historical movement in an adversarial relationship with an energized socialism and communist left, the foe whose success in 1917–18 helped trigger fascism's own historical appearance, but with which fascism shared repressive attributes. The new territory champions arise in a moment of leftist exhaustion; they reject the complex multiethnic societies fascism also attacked, but they currently face no major ideological adversary. Just as the postwar years in Eastern Europe sometimes witnessed the phenomenon of anti-Semitism without Jews (or with very few), the current nationalism is a right without a left. Nonetheless, the fact that five years after the fall of the Berlin Wall one sees the spread of political formations so reminiscent of interwar nationalist authoritarianism remains one of the stunning surprises of post-communist history. And that some of the formations that openly admire the interwar dictators should be participating in governments in countries where these predecessors once ruled is doubly astonishing. A new right? Yes, but at the same time it is a retro-right.

Not every moral crisis deepens sufficiently for territorial populism to prevail. However, periods of moral crisis tend always to provoke such a coalition as an inherent component of their historical dynamic. The political effort to impose an imagined territorial cohesion is in fact a key indicator of such crises. This does not mean that the territorial populists will win in the long run; they may indeed represent hopeless responses to a resolute choice of complexity and cosmopolitanism. Pat Buchanan and David Duke enjoyed only evanescent celebrity status. So far support for the German right remains below 10 percent, as its successive avatars have since 1950. The Front National has given French citizens and observers a few frissons but has not gained significant parliamentary strength. In the United States, Franklin Roosevelt trounced the uneasy coalition of nativist populism in 1936, and President Clinton will presumably repeat this achievement in 1996. But no matter what the outcome, the contest cannot be fun. It touches ugly chords of prejudice, it raises nationalistic instincts that the West has not had to contend with for many decades, and it introduces an element of incalculability into each country's public life and into the relations of nations with each other. During moral crises and their aftermath, the advocates of cosmopolitanism and compromise, pluralism and rationality are never in full control. Nonetheless, tenuous leadership is no mean achievement. It would be far more perilous to try to outbid territorial populists, for such a policy will always skid out of control.

DEMOCRACY BEYOND BORDERS

◆ ◆ ◆

To overcome a moral crisis is to rehabilitate principles of civic allegiance that look beyond the control of territory. If the United States is to serve as an anchoring force in global civil society, it must provide a plausible alternative vision to territorial populism abroad as well as at home. That means reaffirming commitments to civic inclusiveness, not just ethnicity; avoiding retreats into protectionism; encouraging common international projects and loyalties beyond ethnic or even cultural kinship. American policy should redefine the Wilsonian agenda that justified early U.S. ventures into great-power politics and whose concept of self-determination still remains so appealing, such that self-determination is separated from its original territorial focus. Such an approach cuts against the grain of contemporary micronationalism, but by the mid-1990s proposals for ethnic aggregation or the encouragement of multiple loyalties are more urgent than disaggregation.

It is time for confederalism, cantonization and overlapping citizenship claims to receive more creative attention. Of course, the idea of encouraging confederal frameworks will appear utopian when warring ethnic groups are determined to seek exclusive territorial states. Nonetheless, frameworks for ethnic reaggregation—if only in regional economic institutions at first—will seem appropriate once again, and pressures toward reconstruction of units that are now merely battlegrounds will become pressing agenda items. As confederal structures reemerge, they might well include participants that are not drawn directly from the contested territory. The Council on Security and Cooperation in Europe and the European Union have roles to play beyond their original purview in helping to organize such structures in Europe, and their delegates should play a role as continuing board members, as should U.S. nominees. The appropriate levels of aggregation and boundaries will be contested in every case. To grant every people its own sovereignty is not feasible, but they can have their representation, their cultural institutions, a share of the public purse and a delegation in international overarching structures such as enlarged European Union, CSCE or analogous institutions that might be constructed elsewhere. Indeed, the formation and strengthening—the widening and deepening—of such institutional networks might eventually help democracies combat the anomie that has permitted indifference, tribalism and fragmentation to advance. This recovery will not be quick or easy; moral crises of democracy tend to be protracted and contagious. They will only be reversed by a commitment beyond borders and across frontiers.

Notes

1. William Grimes, "Have a #%!&$@$! Day," *The New York Times*, October 17, 1993, section 9, page 1.
2. James O'Connor, *The Fiscal Crisis of the State*, New York: St. Martin's Press, 1973.
3. Jacob Burckhardt, *Force and Freedom: An Interpretation of History*, ed. James Hastings Nichols, New York: Meridian Books, 1955, a translation of *Weltgeschichtliche Betrachtungen*, pp. 297–300, and pp. 256–300 more generally.
4. Francis Fukuyama, *The End of History and the Last Man*, New York: Free Press, 1992.
5. Max Weber, *Gesammelte Politische Schriften*, 3rd ed., Johannes Winckelmann, ed., Tübingen: Mohr Siebeck, 1972, p. 24.
6. Compare G. John Ikenberry, "The Long War," Council on Foreign Relations discussion paper, and John Lewis Gaddis, *The Long Peace; Inquiries into the History of the Cold War*, New York: Oxford University Press, 1987.

Terms &
Concepts

class and caste
confederalism
cosmopolitanism
demagogues
democratic pretensions
elegiac mission
ethnic aggregation
ethnocultural generalizations
evocation vs. analysis
historical dislocation

irridenta
jeremiads
malaise
memory industry
nationalist authoritarianism
neo-fascists
objective pathologies
patronage
plebiscitary fan clubs
politikverdrossenheit

retro-right
social intractability
social pluralism
sociobiology
supranationalism
technocratic governance
territorial populists
volksgemeinschaft
xenophobes

Questions

1. Why does Maier think that the "moral malaise" is so important? What are its three dimensions, and aren't economic problems even more serious?

2. Does the author's argument apply to Canada, or is it written in such a way that it focuses on the problems facing the United States and Europe, and has only limited applicability to us?

3. How does he define "crisis"? Do we not always tend to think we are in one, and what does he say this one has in common with its predecessors?

4. Why is there an attempt to "escape from politics"? How is this linked to the rise of conservatism and the eclipse of the left-wing agenda?

5. What does Maier have to say about "seismic shifts" in intellectual orientation? Does he exaggerate these shifts?

6. Does it appear that President Clinton will in fact triumph, as Roosevelt did, over the "uneasy coalition of nativist populism" that opposes him—or has Maier underestimated the forces in play?

Unit
One   Discussion Questions

1. The editors have used the vortex metaphor to discuss what is happening. Can you think of other metaphors to describe the paradoxical nature of the changes that are taking place?

2. To what extent do the analyses in this section imply that we face really new challenges, or have we coped with similar problems before?

3. Do you think that we can ignore the effects of the changes discussed in this section: are we going to be able to isolate ourselves morally, physically, spiritually and materially from changes of this magnitude?

Annotated
Bibliography

Daedalus, Spring 1995, Vol. 124, No. 2. This issue is entitled "What Future for the State," and it contains a number of excellent essays.

Elkins, David J. *Beyond Sovereignty: Territory and Political Economy in the Twenty-First Century.* Toronto: University of Toronto Press, 1995. A provocative look at the future of the nation-state and other conventional forms of political organization.

Heilbroner, Robert. *Visions of the Future: The Distant Past, Yesterday, Today, Tomorrow.* Oxford/New York: Oxford University Press/New York Public Library, 1994. Heilbroner's latest collection of essays reflects a considerable amount of pessimism about our ability to save our environment and continue our systems of "ceaseless accumulation."

Hobsbawm, Eric. *The Age of Extremes A History of the World, 1914–1991.* New York: Pantheon Books, 1994. Hobsbawm is an eminent British historian. This ambitious, sweeping, work focuses on the economic and social forces that have shaped the 20th century, particularly capitalism and socialism. He does not find much to look forward to!

Homer-Dixon, Thomas F. "Environmental Scarcities and Violent Conflict." *International Security* 19:1 (Summer 1994), 3–40. A more detailed discussion of environmental issues, and the future, than the article in this volume.

Huntington, Samuel. "The Clash of Civilizations." *Foreign Affairs* (Summer 1993), 22–49. An important and controversial contribution to the debate about the post-Cold War nature of international relations, stressing the persistence of cultural boundaries, and their reassertion.

Kaplan, Robert. "The Coming Anarchy." *Atlantic Monthly* (January 1994). A highly readable discussion of change as seen "on the ground," especially in Africa. Relies heavily on Homer-Dixon's work, and adds to it.

Kennedy, Paul. *Preparing for the Twenty-First Century.* New York: Harper Collins, 1993. Superpower decline and enormous economic change—and what is to be done. Kennedy is Dilworth professor of history and director of International Security Studies at Yale.

Luttwak, Edward N. "Where are the Great Powers?" *Foreign Affairs* 73:4, 23–28. Even the United States is now hamstrung; Americans will have to learn to "ignore avoidable tragedies" and blind themselves to injustice.

Magnusson, Warren. "De-Centring the State." In *Canadian Politics*, 2nd ed., edited by James P. Bickerton and Alain-G. Gagnon. Peterborough: Broadview, 1994. Environmentalism, new politics, and sovereignty at the end of the 20th century.

O'Brien, Conor Cruise. *On the Eve of the Millennium.* Concord: Anansi, 1994. A reflection on the status and future of Enlightenment values at the end of the second millennium.

Unit Two

Ideas and Ideologies

◆ ◆ ◆

The title of this section is purposefully general. Do all of the following seven readings contain ideas? Definitely. Do they all contain ideologies? That depends on how ideology is defined. If one defines it as a "project of creating social perfection by managing society," as Kenneth Minogue does, then ideologies have disappeared, at least temporarily, with the collapse of communism.[1] If one defines ideology as a system of ideas that interprets the world, then one has to judge whether the "isms" discussed here are capable of fulfilling this function and whether, in fact, they do so for significantly large numbers of people.

The placement of this unit in this book also betrays our views of ideologies. For us, they are deeply affected by the "vortex," but are, in themselves, also capable of changing its direction. This is, of course, a debate along the lines of chickens and eggs and which came first; it is about dependent and intervening variables, and the interplay between ideas, "mentalities," institutions, culture and economics. Scholars approach these questions in very different ways. Neo and post-Marxists will still see strong economic causation, even determinism, at work. Francis Fukuyama has declared that the battle of ideologies is over;[2] liberal–democracy has triumphed over its totalitarian opponent, communism. Samuel Huntington argues

that the clash of ideologies is increasingly a clash between "civilizations," each with ancient roots.[3] Ideologies, as we have traditionally viewed them, are eurocentric. They are difficult to transplant. For example, liberal individualism does not sit easily with Confucian hierarchy, as the reading by Go Chok Tong illustrates (Unit Five, Article 22).

Western ideologies are also under attack from within. Liberalism, or at least reform liberalism and democratic socialism, are under assault on a number of fronts. Neoliberals and neoconservatives think that the whole idea of the welfare state must be readdressed. Populists object to liberals' unwillingness to act in support of majoritarian demands. Liberalism's emphasis on individualism and individual rights does not sit well with communitarians or with certain religious fundamentalisms.

Students should therefore be cautious when dealing with ideologies. Beware of labels, for they are in transition and are value laden. (What are the differences, if any, between a neoliberal, a neoconservative, and a new conservative?) Note that the list of ideologies is growing. To the hitherto standard labels, such as fascism or socialism, we now have to add both revivals of older beliefs, such as nationalism and ethnocentrism, and powerful new forces, such as feminism (in all its different forms) and environmentalism.

Photo courtesy of Canapress.

As you read this unit, we ask that you consider what these differences in political belief systems mean. Are they merely academic generalizations and abstractions, and of little individual consequence? Or are they a vital aspect of our collective life, capable of moving political mountains?

1. Kenneth Minogue, "Ideology after the Collapse of Communism," *Political Studies* 41, 4 (1993), 19.
2. Francis Fukuyama, "The End of History," *The National Interest* 16 (Summer 1989).
3. Samuel Huntington, "The Clash of Civilizations?" *Foreign Affairs* 72, 3 (Summer 1993), 22–49.

4

Liberal Values

Anthony Arblaster

Editors' Note

The most pervasive political ideology in the Western world is liberalism. It infuses most of our ideas about the nature and status of the individual person, the principles of equality and liberty, and the role of the state. So pervasive is liberalism that we often do not recognize the ideological character of our liberal attitudes and assumptions. Liberal ideas, writes British political scientist Anthony Arblaster, make up "a large part of the intellectual air we breathe" and comprise the commonplaces of our day. As a result, liberalism as a distinct political ideology is often hard to identify. Opposing political doctrines have incorporated many liberal words and principles. At the same time, liberalism has become something of a term of derision. Especially in the United States but also in Canada, it is identified with big, expensive government and permissiveness in matters of public morality.

This article provides an extended discussion of the values at the heart of liberalism. You will almost certainly recognize many of your own beliefs in this account. Who would dis-

agree with the liberty of a person to choose his or her own way of life as long as it does not harm others? Who can dispute the principle of being left alone, free from arbitrary interference by others? But things are not as simple as they appear. Many of the common arguments for individual freedom and untrammelled debate and toleration, are either simplistic or are contradicted by historical evidence. It is not true for example, that a liberal society is necessary for the fostering of the arts and sciences: many of the West's most celebrated achievements in these areas were made under illiberal social and political conditions.

Further, freedom is widely considered not simply a condition of being left alone but rather the possession of a requisite degree of power or ability to realize one's goals. This often requires the aid and support of others, including coercive political institutions, which liberals are otherwise wont to regard as oppressive. The solid core of liberalism may not be as resilient as it appears.

Liberalism is ambivalent about the relationship between polity and economy. Some liberals think that the natural economic complement of a liberal polity is free-market capitalism while others, like John Maynard Keynes, argue that capitalism needs to be domesticated in order to preserve both liberal polity and capitalist economy. Others maintain that capitalism is simply incompatible with liberal values of equality and equal opportunity.

As you read this excerpt from Arblaster's 1984 book, *The Rise and Decline of Liberalism in the West*, make note of the liberal values Arblaster presents and the criticisms he makes of them. Description and criticism are intertwined. Also, disabuse yourself from any direct association between liberalism and the Liberal Party of Canada or the Democratic Party in the United States. Liberalism is a deeper, more complex set of ideas than any political party can embody at any one time.

◆ ◆ ◆

CONSTITUTIONALISM AND THE RULE OF LAW

◆ ◆ ◆

For as in absolute governments the King is law, so in free countries the law *ought* to be King; and there *ought* to be no other.

THOMAS PAINE, COMMON SENSE[1]

Freedom, privacy and tolerance are ideals, at first no more than dreams, which in order to be realized (made real) must be embodied in rules, customs and institutions. We have already seen that traditionally liberals have regarded the state as the principal threat to the individual and her freedom. How is this danger to be met?

The first step is to assert, as a matter of fundamental principle, that the power and authority of the state or government is not absolute, but limited. There are two main ways by which this principle is established. The first is by making consent the basis of legitimate government. It can be argued, of course, that any government needs a measure of consent from the governed in order to function effectively at all. But the liberal position is not this pragmatic one: it is argued as a matter of principle that since government is for the benefit of society, so it ought to be based on the consent or support of society. Government must be thought of, not as autonomous, but as answerable and accountable for its actions. Consent is normally sought, and accountability enforced, through the device of elections. But whose consent does it need? To whom is it answerable? The commonest rhetorical answer was 'the nation', or 'the people'. But this *was* rhetorical since it was often not clear who exactly was included in these rather vague entities. 'The people' seldom meant all of the people. It seldom meant even all of the male people. The political nation to which the government was answerable was not until quite recently identified with the whole population. Consent was required only from a minority of the propertied classes. Nevertheless, in spite of its limited application, the principle of accountability was in itself a check on government, especially when it was contrasted with the absolute and unlimited authority which some theorists, such as Bodin and Hobbes, had thought the state ought to have, and which some rulers were bold enough to claim and occasionally powerful enough to use.

But there were other methods which, from this point of view, were not less important. The essence of them was the placing of the state or government within a restricting framework of constitutional provisions and fundamental law. The state and its institutions must operate within limits which are either laid down in an explicit, written constitution, or take the form of a rather more vaguely conceived body of 'fundamental' laws and customs. The revolutionary states of the late eighteenth century celebrated their newness with written constitutions; but it was also held that England had been a constitutional, and therefore, free state since 1688, although it had no comparable single document to cite.

Among the constitutional provisions of the new United States of America, one of the most important in limiting the power of government was held to be the device of the separation of powers. This represented a challenge not only to absolutism, but also to the theory of sovereignty, which had been used to give intellectual support to absolutism and to the more general principle of the supremacy of the state. Hobbes had argued that the only adequate bulwark against division, civil conflict and chaos within a society was the establishment of a single and indivisible ultimate authority—a sovereign. Sovereignty was indivisible by definition; for if authority was divided, a further authority would be needed to arbitrate between the parties in case of dispute, and that further authority would therefore be the effective sovereign. Hobbes's argument is irrefutable—so long as one thinks in terms of sovereignty. But first in practice, and later in theory, liberals have moved away from the idea of sovereignty. They have preferred to run the risks of conflict inherent in arrangements whereby state authority is divided. For, unlike Hobbes, their fear of a final and undivided power-cum-authority is greater than their fear of the possible consequences of splitting it up. Hence institutional safeguards against despotism are provided by the separation of powers—the allocation of different portions of the authority of the state to separate institutions, each of which will act as a rival to, and a check on, the others.

The power of the state was to be further circumscribed by the placing of the state within the limits of established law. Government is to be carried on according to 'the rule of law'. This notion, however, is by no means a clear one. Human laws do not, after all emanate directly from God or nature, even if they are thought to be based on divine or natural law. They have to be formulated by someone, even if it is not the king or sovereign. The transference of the law-making function from a king to a parliament or other assembly does not in

From *The Rise and Decline of Western Liberalism*, 1984, pp. 71–91 (Oxford: Basil Blackwell).

itself provide any guarantee against unjust or tyrannical laws. However, it was argued that an elected and accountable assembly would find it more difficult to enact laws which were clearly partial or oppressive. And there were other restrictions on their law-making powers. Laws could only be made within the framework of the constitution. Or, if no explicit constitution existed, appeal was made to something like 'the spirit of the laws', to the traditional sense of what was legitimate and what rights it was accepted that people possessed, even if these were not inscribed in any particular document. Finally the implementation and interpretation of the laws were to be placed in the hands of institutions which would be independent of the government of the day. In these various ways it was hoped that the 'rule of law' could be separated from, and raised above the mere will of the body that did actually make the laws.

But the rule of law meant still more than this. It meant an end to the arbitrariness which was so marked a feature of absolutist rule. It represented an attempt to replace the rule of whim by the rule of rules: *'Freedom of Men under Government* is, to have a standing Rule to live by, common to every one of that society and made by the Legislative Power erected on it.'[2] Part of the meaning of the rule of laws was simply a minimum of consistency and impartiality. If something was permitted, then it was permitted to all. If something was an offence, then it was an offence no matter who committed it. The law was supposed to be impartial as between classes, between rich and poor, between the titled aristo-

---

...there is an ambiguity in the liberal attitude towards both state power and the law.

---

crat and the starving beggar who hardly had a name. Of course, in a society of economic inequality this impartiality is not without its ironies, as Anatole France observed: 'The law, in its majestic equality, forbids the rich as well as the poor to sleep under bridges, to beg in the streets, and to steal bread.' Still, it was held to be an essential part of a rational society, and one which offered some security to the individual, that he or she should know where they were in relation to the laws. They should know what they could do with impunity, and what not. They should be able to know what measure of punishment awaited them if they committed an

offence of a certain kind. The notion that law was nothing but the will of the sovereign, whoever or whatever that might be, was, in the liberal view, a recipe for uncertainty, insecurity, favouritism and arbitrariness. No man could be safe in possession of either his rights or his property so long as such a principle held sway. Even if he himself took no part in the making of laws, directly or indirectly, it was essential that those laws should have a certain reliability and permanence, and that they should be impartial as between individuals and classes.

Through such principles and devices as these it was hoped that the power of the state could be limited and the rights of the individual made reasonably secure. But there is an ambiguity in the liberal attitude towards both state power and the law. On the one hand there is the liberal view that the state is the chief threat to the individual and his freedom. This is supported by the picture of society as essentially a self-regulating mechanism, so that state or government 'interference' is often regarded as not merely unnecessary but positively disruptive: 'The more perfect civilisation is, the less occasion has it for government, because the more does it regulate its own affairs, and govern itself...how often is the natural propensity of society disturbed or destroyed by the operations of government.'[3] Paine looked forward to a steady reduction in the power and activity of the state as society improved.

This tendency in liberalism is reinforced by the stress which many liberals have placed on the supposed antithesis between laws and freedom. Thus Berlin, in reference to both Hobbes and Bentham, says that "Law is always a "fetter", even if it protects you from being bound in chains that are heavier than those of the law."[4] All this points in the direction of an anarchist opposition to state, government and laws. Yet the purpose of the liberal apparatus of constitutionalism and the separation of powers is not to dissolve the power of the state but only to curb it. And although law may always be a fetter, liberals readily accept that such fetters are necessary, and have made 'the rule of law' one of their most conscious slogans.

Imprisonment is the most blatant and basic way in which someone's liberty can be taken away. And from the moment of the fall of the Bastille the prison became a specially potent symbol or epitome of the kind of tyranny against which liberals were fighting.[5] Yet liberals have for the most part accepted prisons and imprisonment as necessary social institutions for the indefinite future. It seems that it is not imprisonment as such to which they object, but its arbitrary use. This is, however, no safeguard against a tyranny which operates through laws, as many contemporary authoritarian regimes in fact do. Such cases ought to make liberals more cautious than they usually are about using 'the rule of law' as a norm and a slogan. Structures of law such as those which enforce racial separation and inequality demonstrate the need for a concept of justice by which laws themselves can be judged.

So there are ambiguities in the liberal commitment to law. They claim to be suspicious of the state and its power, yet accept it as an indefinitely necessary evil. In so doing, they accept, too, that there are necessarily limits to the freedom which the individual can expect to enjoy within the context of an 'orderly' society. The commitment to freedom is not quite as absolute as it is sometimes made to appear.

LIBERALISM AND DEMOCRACY

◆ ◆ ◆

Liberty is more essential then democracy

TITLE OF AN ARTICLE BY SALVADOR DE MADRIAGA, *INDIAN AND FOREIGN REVIEW*, 1 JANUARY 1968

'Liberal democracy' is such a common phrase that it is natural to imagine that the coinage denotes a perfectly harmonious marriage between the two constituent principles. In fact the alliance, like many real-life marriages, has been an affair of compromises and concessions from the start, and of the partners it was liberalism which was

---

Liberals were afraid...[of]...a new tyranny still more powerful than the old ones.

---

always the more reluctant. Liberals wished to replace absolutism by limited government; and limited government was taken to mean government by consent. But whose consent? Once the notion of consent becomes current it is difficult to establish convincing arguments for limiting its application, especially since the arguments in its favour were characteristically couched in a universalist style which tended to contradict any principle of selection or exclusion. The idea of consent tends towards democracy.

Bourgeois liberals were thus increasingly hoist by their own petard. They valued the principle of consent in so far as it applied to themselves, but became fearful

when it was taken over by radical spokesmen for the lower classes. Understandably so, since as C.B. Macpherson has reminded us, democracy was not until very recently something of which everyone was expected to approve. On the contrary:

> Democracy used to be a bad word. Everybody who was anybody knew that democracy in its original sense of rule by the people or government in accordance with the will of the bulk of the people, would be a bad thing—fatal to individual freedom and to all the graces of civilized living.[6]

Democracy meant essentially the rule of 'the mob'. Liberals were afraid that the overthrow of the old monarchical or aristocratic autocracies would lead to their replacement, not by the minimal state which most of them wanted, but by a new tyranny still more powerful than the old ones. Its power would derive precisely from its superior claims to legitimacy. Against a government which could claim to be enacting the will of the people, what safeguards could stand firm? Dissident minorities would appear merely as disgruntled and self-interested factions unwilling to accept the elementary democratic principle of majority rule. Dissident individuals would be in an even weaker position. In this way liberals saw the principle of consent, intended by them as a curb on government and as a basis for protecting individual rights, leading to a popular or democratic dictatorship which could offer a more serious threat to liberty than any known before.

Fears of this kind were expressed by some of the American Founding Fathers. 'Give all power to the many, they will oppress the few. Give all power to the few, they will oppress the many', said Hamilton. And Jefferson protested: 'One hundred and seventy three despots would surely be as oppressive as one...an *elective despotism* was not the government we fought for.'[7] Many of them despised 'the people', and were openly hostile to the idea of democracy.[8] From these attitudes sprang the carefully devised constitutional arrangements intended to curb the power of the state by dividing it. These anxieties and hostilities remain as a recurring theme in liberal writings of the nineteenth century, even among those who, like Mill, were in principle in favour of the widest popular participation in politics. Lord Acton explicitly distinguished between the liberal and the democrat:

> As to Democracy, it is true that masses of new electors are utterly ignorant, that they are easily deceived by appeals to prejudice and passion, and are consequently unstable, and that the difficulty of

explaining economic questions to them, and of linking their interests with those of the State, may become a danger to the public credit, if not to the security of private property. A true Liberal, as distinguished from a Democrat, keeps this peril always before him.[9]

It was not only property which the ignorant masses were held to threaten. Others believed that culture and civilization were also in danger. Matthew Arnold's book of 1869 might have been called 'Culture *versus* Anarchy', since it saw culture, which depends on order and authority, as menaced by working-class demonstrations in favour of parliamentary reform—'demonstrations perfectly unnecessary in the present course of our affairs'.[10]

But above all, democracy was seen as a potential threat to individual freedom. Whether one thought in terms of majority rule, or the sovereignty of the people, the danger was there. The point is essentially a logical one. Freedom is a matter of the absence of constraints and restrictions which prevent the individual from doing what he wants. Democracy is a matter of how governments are chosen and to whom they are answerable. There is no necessary connection between the two issues: 'the opposite of liberalism is totalitarianism, while the opposite of democracy is authoritarianism. In consequence, it is at least possible in principle that a democratic government may be totalitarian, and that an authoritarian government may act on liberal principles.'[11] The fact that a government is elected will not in itself prevent it from restricting people's freedom. Quite the contrary, in fact. An 'elective despotism' would be less easily challenged than one the basis of which was patently arbitrary.

The anxiety is exacerbated if democracy is identified not simply with majority rule, but with the more exalted doctrine of popular sovereignty. Liberals are unhappy with the idea of sovereignty in any circumstances. But the concept of popular sovereignty is doubly objectionable because it implies the existence of a recognizable entity which can be called 'the people'. This offends against the liberal doctrine that society is made up of discrete individuals, or at the most, groups, all with their particular and distinct wills and interests. Notions such as 'the general interest' and 'the general will' not only obscure this: they also provide governments with plausible excuses for overriding the concrete interests of particular individuals and groups. According to Bernard Crick it is the essence of what he terms 'politics' to recognize and accept the essential diversity of the various groups and interests which make up society. Therefore 'politics' has to be defended against democracy, for 'The democratic doctrine of the sovereignty of the people threatens…the essential perception that all known advanced societies are inherently pluralistic and diverse, which is the seed and the root of politics.'[12]

It might be thought that one way of counteracting such a danger would be to encourage greater popular participation. The involvement of the widest range of groups and individuals might well ensure that particular interests were taken into account, and that decisions were not taken without due contest and debate. But, as we have seen, participation is regarded by many liberals as a *threat* to privacy and freedom. Others go further and see it as a step towards totalitarianism. Thus Rousseau, one of the leading theorists of democracy, has become a favourite target of contemporary liberal polemics. According to J.L. Talmon, who represents himself as a defender of liberal democracy, Rousseau 'demonstrates clearly the close relation between popular sovereignty taken to the extreme, and totalitarianism' precisely because of his insistence on 'the active and ceaseless participation of the people and of every citizen in the affairs of the State'. Talmon concludes 'Liberty is safer in countries where there are numerous levels of non-political private and collective activity, although not so much direct popular democracy, than in countries where politics take everything in their stride, and the people sit in permanent assembly.'[13] Talmon is a conservative rather than a strictly liberal writer, but this is one of many points where liberal and conservative thinking now overlap. Crick makes the same point when he asserts that the doctrine of popular sovereignty 'if taken too seriously, is an actual step towards totalitarianism. For, quite simply, it allows no refuge and no contradiction, no private apathy even.'[14] Mill made a similar, though perhaps more sophisticated case, when he argued that democracy implies not only a certain style of government but also a certain type of society, in which 'public opinion' will enjoy an unprecedented ascendency. This powerful force, with its intolerance of deviance and non-conformity, will constitute a most serious threat to liberty and diversity. There is one major puzzle about liberalism's portrayal of all these various democratic monsters—the tyranny of the majority, popular participation, and public opinion. All of them assume that the pressure of the mass, the majority, or the public, will be a monolithic force in pushing in a single direction. But if, as liberals ceaselessly reiterate, society is composed of individuals and/or diverse groups and interests, if 'a people doesn't exist except as an abstract conception' (to repeat Dwight Macdonald's words), how is it that diverse individuals nevertheless act in this ominous unified manner when they come together? There is a sharp contradiction here between the liberals' pluralistic and individualistic analysis of society, and the liberal fear of democracy with its accompanying mythology of mobs and monolithic masses.

At worst liberals see democracy, 'taken to the extreme', as a threat to liberty, property and culture. At best it can be a means to liberty, provided the principles of democracy are revised and qualified in a way which

---

Liberal democracy is limited democracy.

---

provides safeguards against the danger of popular tyranny. It becomes so by being converted into 'liberal democracy', a formulation in which, as Guido de Ruggiero very candidly put it, 'the adjective Liberal has the force of a qualification.'[15] Democracy has increasingly been seen not as an end in itself, but as a means to preserving liberty, individuality and diversity: 'The distinctive features of democratic government, at least as we understand it in the western world, are intended to secure a maximum of liberty for citizens.'[16] The appearance of this bland statement in a representative 'introduction' to political philosophy indicates that this is now the consensus view. Democracy, in its existing limited representative forms, is believed to serve that purpose well. But proposals for extending democracy, or enlarging popular participation are another matter. Liberal democracy is limited democracy. Unlimited democracy is potentially, if not actually, totalitarian, and threatens the liberal values and institutions of personal freedom, private property and the market economy.

These are the fears which have inspired the description of the British political system as one of 'elective dictatorship', and led to revived demands for either a written constitution or a bill of rights in Britain. Attractive as a bill of rights may sound, the clear intention of its contemporary protagonists is to create a constitutional barrier to some of the more radical policies which might be enacted by a left-wing government with strong popular support, and in particular to prevent enactment of policies which might involve attacks on private property, and private economic power, such as the ownership of newspapers and television companies. These fears are not very different from those aroused by popular political movements and extensions of the franchise in the nineteenth century.

REASON, SCIENCE AND PROGRESS
◆ ◆ ◆

Reason, which has always been, and still is, a highly prestigious term, is also one of the most complex and elusive in the vocabulary of ideas. We have already noted that it has at least two general meanings, both of which figure prominently in liberal thinking. The narrower and more precise of these identifies reason with the ability to think logically, to make calculations and deductions. The broader conception is not necessarily antithetical to this, but is larger and more positive in its claims. The first conception, strictly interpreted, has no application to ends, only to means. It has nothing to say about ends, except as to whether they are 'realistic'—that is, attainable given the world as it is.

The other conception is not so confined. It has something to say about ends as well as means. Only certain purposes of the individual and of society deserve to be called rational. Tolerance, for example, is a rational policy, because it respects the limits of human knowledge, and makes no claim to certainty or rightness in areas, such as morals and religion, where such assurance cannot rationally be justified. Cruelty and the infliction of suffering, are likewise irrational, since it is evident that in all normal circumstances people try to avoid suffering and unhappiness. Reason is thus not morally neutral. Reason is not compatible with intolerance or dogmatism, or with cruelty and callousness.[17] It was therefore in the name of reason as well as humanity—for the two go together—that the liberals of the Enlightenment campaigned against the power of the Catholic Church and against the judicial use of torture. In this sense of the word reason is 'a normative and not a neutral scientific term', to quote Stuart Hampshire.[18]

Both of these conceptions of reason have played a part in liberalism. Hence some of the conflicts and ambiguities within liberalism itself. The larger concept of reason has made many liberals active enemies of religion, or at least of religion in its more dogmatic and superstitious forms. This is the way in which the historian J.B. Bury used the term reason in his *A History of Freedom of Thought* (1913), when he entitled his chapter on Greece and Rome 'Reason free' that on the Middle Ages 'Reason in prison'. Such hostility to Catholicism now seems rather old-fashioned in Anglo-Saxon countries, though not necessarily in countries such as Italy, Ireland and Portugal where the Roman Catholic Church still retains considerable political and ideological power. Many liberals would still want to insist on a connection between reason and tolerance, and tolerance is still at odds with religious bigotry.

Similarly, reason is often contrasted with tradition, custom and prejudice. The fully rational man will take nothing on trust, nothing on authority. He will think things through for himself, and make up his own mind. A characteristic example is provided by John Maynard Keynes, who wrote retrospectively (and not uncritically) of himself and his Cambridge contemporaries of the early 1900s: 'We repudiated entirely customary morals, conventions, and traditional wisdom....We recognized no moral obligation on us, no inner sanction, to conform or to obey. Before heaven we claimed to be our own judge in our own case.'[19] Such attitudes are incompatible with the hold which habit and prejudice often exert over people's minds and lives. In this respect liberals are at odds with conservatives of the traditional Burkean variety. Nothing in Burke is more significant of his challenge to the Enlightenment than his open defence of prejudice:

> instead of casting away all our old prejudices, we cherish them to a very considerable degree, and, to take more shame to ourselves, we cherish them because they are prejudices....Prejudice renders a man's virtue his habit; and not a series of unconnected acts. Through just prejudice, his duty becomes a part of his nature.[20]

From Burke to W.B. Yeats and Michael Oakeshott, conservatives have consistently expressed their mistrust of reason (or rationalism), and their faith in the virtues of tradition and custom. But the whole tendency of the liberal Enlightenment was in direct conflict with these celebration of prejudice, custom and habits of thought unthinkingly inherited from the past.

This contraposition of reason to authority and tradition set liberals at odds with conservatives and with the power of established religion. But the definition of reason as calculation created a different kind of problem for liberalism. It raised the question of what value liberalism attaches to feeling; whether liberalism has a theory of imagination and art to rival the place occupied in its philosophy by reason and science. The younger Mill's account of his upbringing is well known: how the process of intellectual 'cramming' led to a complete personal breakdown at the age of twenty, which in turn sent him in quest of 'that culture of the feelings' which had been so totally neglected by Bentham and his father. This experience led Mill to adopt a more critical attitude towards Benthamism, and take an interest in the Anglicized version of German idealism represented by Coleridge and to some extent the young Thomas Carlyle. But it is doubtful whether Mill succeeded in assigning to art and imagination a much larger role than that of providing refreshment to the rational man when he is tired by his intellectual and reforming exertions.

Creative writers of liberal conviction were, naturally enough, particularly disturbed by the priority which calculation so evidently enjoyed over feeling in *laissez-faire* liberalism. This led Shelley, in *A Defence of Poetry*, to attack the prevalent narrow notion of utility, according to which 'the exercise of the imagination is most delightful, but...that of reason is more useful.' He argued—and he must have been one of the first to argue—that the accumulation of knowledge and the 'unmitigated exercise of the calculating faculty' had outstripped men's capacity to know how to use this great power to control and exploit nature:

> There is now no want of knowledge respecting what is wisest, and best in morals, government, and political economy, or at least what is wiser and better than what men now practise and endure. But...We want the creative faculty to imagine that which we know; we want the generous impulse to act that which we imagine...our calculations have outrun conception; we have eaten more than we can digest.[21]

Shelley, despite his 'Romantic' label, was in no sense an anti-rationalist. On the contrary, he was, through Paine and Godwin, a direct heir of Enlightenment radicalism. But as an artist he was perplexed to know what role there was for him, and for the poet, in the developing industrial capitalist society. And as a radical democrat he saw that the political economy of liberalism was not producing the universal benefits which its proponents had predicted.

But it would be unfair to liberalism not to recognize that anxieties about the relations between rationality and feeling have been a recurring theme within the liberal tradition. In the twentieth century it has been a preoccupation of E.M. Forster and Lionel Trilling, among others, and even Keynes felt the force of D.H. Lawrence's vehement criticisms of the rationalism of the Cambridge–Bloomsbury circles to which he (Keynes) belonged: 'The attribution of rationality to human nature, instead of enriching it, now seems to me to have impoverished it. It ignored certain powerful and valuable springs of feeling. Some of the spontaneous, irrational outbursts of human nature can have a sort of value from which our schematism was cut off.'[22] A sort of value, certainly, but what sort? The claim that is made for imagination by writers from Blake, Wordsworth and Coleridge, through Keats and Shelley to Yeats, is that imagination as well as, if not more than, reason gives men access to truth. Hence Keat's 'Beauty is Truth', and Blake's many exclamations against eighteenth-century rationalism and empiricism: 'All that is Valuable in Knowledge is Superior to Demonstrative Science, such as is Weighed or Measured.'; 'God forbid that Truth should be Confined to Mathematical Demonstration!'[23] Historically and theoretically liberalism has had difficulty in responding sympathetically to such claims and criticisms because of its close association with empiricist and, to a lesser extent, rationalist theories of truth and knowledge. This is one source of that alienation of modern literature from the liberal ideology about which Trilling in particular has written at some length.[24]

But while liberalism has never developed a satisfying theory of art and imagination, it *has* laid claim to a special relationship with science, as we saw earlier. Liberalism is claimed to be the application of the scientific approach to politics and social life. And conversely, or reciprocally, science is held to represent the outstanding expression of the liberals' commitment to reason and empiricism. The interest shown by the radical liberals like Paine, Jefferson and Joseph Priestley in inventions and technological developments, at the time of the British industrial revolution, is neither surprising nor coincidental. Material and technological progress was as integral a part of the world-wide advance of reason and enlightenment as was the sweeping away of feudal privileges, superstition and bigotry.

To begin with at least, the liberal conception of progress was of this uncomplicated kind, and apart from

---

Liberalism has not been immune from the general loss of self-confidence which the capitalist world has experienced in this century.

---

isolated figures like Shelley, most doubts about the economic and social effects of industrialization were expressed by radicals and conservatives who stood well outside the liberal mainstream. But misgivings about the supposed benefits of uncontrolled technological change, and about the unlimited exploitation of the planet and its limited resources, are now widespread. And apart from that, the political experience of the twentieth century has made any simple belief in continuous linear progress very hard to sustain. Liberalism has not been immune from the general loss of self-confidence which the capitalist world has experienced in this century. Keynes faithfully recorded the change of mood in the essay already quoted. He described his own generation as having been 'among the last of the Utopians, or meliorists as they are sometimes called, who believe in a continuing moral progress'. By the 1930s he had come to see this belief as mistaken. It ignored the 'insane and irrational springs of wickedness in most men', and it underestimated the extent to which 'civilisation was a thin and precarious crust erected by the personality and the will of a very few, and only maintained by rules and conventions skilfully put across and guilefully preserved.'[25] In the 1940s Cyril Connolly described himself as being one of thousands of 'Liberals without a belief in progress, Democrats who despise their fellow men'.[26] Yet it is significant that those who in recent years have attacked what they call the 'technocratic' character of our society, such as Theodore Roszak, have been denounced by orthodox liberals as 'Luddites' and champions of unreason or irrationalism. Clearly the traditional syndrome which links reason with science, technology and progress is still powerful.

Reason is still regularly invoked as a talisman by liberals, though clearly not always with the same meaning. Reason, for example, is often associated with persuasion and contrasted with force. It is claimed that the quintessential liberal method of going about things is to seek to persuade others, not by what are derogatorily termed 'emotional' appeals, but by rational arguments. Thus Paul Johnson, in a popular history of England, referred to 'the great tripod of the liberal ethic' as being 'the rejection of violence, the reaching of public decisions through free argument and voluntary compromise, and the slow evolution of moral principles tested by experience and stamped with the consensus.'[27] It is one thing to identify these as ideals, or aims, towards which liberals always strive. It is quite another to claim, as Johnson does, that these ideals have actually prevailed in English history, or more generally in the practice of liberalism. Leaving that aside for the moment, it is important to see what the liberals' professed faith in rational persuasion assumes. It assumes that rationality is, in principle, the universal possession of human beings. It also assumes that it is better to persuade than to compel, better that people should do something voluntarily than compulsorily. But what liberalism also assumes is that appeals to rationality can and do work. Or in other words, that rationality not merely can, but does, play a larger part in determining people's decisions and attitudes than their prejudices, feelings and material interest—using 'material' in a broad sense to include people's class-based concern with status, reputation and

---

Liberals constantly hope, or even believe, that people can be persuaded to sacrifice 'selfish' personal, group or class interests...

---

security as well as more narrowly economic considerations. Liberals constantly hope, or even believe, that people can be persuaded to sacrifice 'selfish' personal, group or class interests for the sake of some seemingly nobler goal, or even in the name of enlightened self-interest. They are equally constantly surprised and disappointed when this does not happen. This sets them apart from conservatives, who take a less optimistic or rationalistic view of human nature, and Marxists, who do not expect ideals or rational arguments to outweigh the commitment of a class and its members to their own interest as they perceive them.

But what happens when appeal to reason and attempts at persuasion fail? What then? Very often we are not told. Thus Talmon declares that as far as 'the final aims of liberal democracy' are concerned, 'the use of force is considered as an evil'—by contrast, of course, with 'totalitarian democracy', which resorts readily to the use of coercion.[28] What Talmon does not say is whether the use of force is also considered to be a *necessary* evil. For to suggest that liberalism as a political practice involves, or has involved, the renunciation of force as non-rational, is quite false. It can and has been argued that the liberal belief in reason and liberal respect for the rights and freedom of the individual point logically in the direction of anarchism and pacifism. And liberalism does come close to anarchism at times—in the case of Paine, for example. But liberalism is not anarchism. As we have seen, it may not like prisons, but it has not pulled them down. And although some liberals have been pacifists, they have been a minority. The dominant tradition of liberalism has never renounced either coercion or killing. Whether we think of liberals like Paine and Jefferson, Byron and Garibaldi, fighting in wars of national independence or liberation, or of rebels like the Russian Decembrists, or of the liberal imperialists, or of liberal opponents of fascism and South African racism, or of liberal supporters of the Vietnam War, the

conclusion must be the same: most liberals have always been prepared to use force and fight wars when it seems to them that persuasion and argument were no longer effective. Even if the dubious liberal hypothesis of an antithesis between reason and force or violence is accepted, there is still a glaring contrast between the self-image and the reality of liberalism in this respect. Whatever qualms of conscience they may have, liberals generally do not renounce force in politics, and to that extent their own claims to be committed exclusively to the use of reason and persuasion are bogus.[29] I cannot see what other conclusion is possible.

LIBERALISM AND CAPITALISM

◆ ◆ ◆

There are thus significant discrepancies between the reality of liberalism and its public self-image. Liberals have always been happy to advertise their commitments to freedom, tolerance, reason and the rule of law. Contemporary liberals are willing to endorse 'liberal democracy', though previously not all liberals were prepared to be counted as democrats. I have tried to suggest that these commitments are seldom as unambiguous and as straightforward as they are sometimes made out to be. But the overall picture is further complicated by those commitments which used on occasions to be openly avowed, but have more recently become, for most liberals, sources of embarrassment and unease. So, without ever being generally or openly abandoned, they are relegated to a limbo where they lurk half-concealed like rocks which the liberal steersman wishes to avoid, but which for that very reason cannot be wholly ignored. These half-hidden commitments are mostly to do with the relationship of liberalism to capitalism. In particular they involve the issues of private property, inequality and class.

Liberalism grew up together with Western capitalism, and even today liberal-democratic political systems only flourish in advanced capitalist countries. Attempts to establish such systems in ex-colonial countries of the Third World have collapsed, and even those countries which once looked like exceptions to this general rule, such as Uruguay, Chile and India, have had their electoral systems and civil liberties destroyed or threatened. This can hardly be coincidental. And there are at least two schools of thought which, from opposite angles, would argue strongly that it is not.

On the one hand Marxists argue that capitalism, contains, rather than supports, liberal democracy. The state and the political system are autonomous and sovereign agencies through which the popular will can, if it so wishes, change or abolish capitalism. They are subordinate to the nature and purposes of the capitalist economy. Where there are signs that democracy may lead to a political assault on capitalism, democracy is either distorted—as in Italy, in order to exclude the Communist Party from office—or destroyed—as in Chile in 1973—to prevent this. Tolerance is only extended to those who do not seriously threaten democracy, which accepts and administers capitalism rather than seeking to abolish it. There are, in other words, quite narrow limits to the freedom and democracy which capitalism can and will allow.

From the opposite political position, there are those economists and politicians, like F.A. Hayek, Milton Friedman, Keith Joseph and Margaret Thatcher, who argue that there can be no liberal democracy, no individual freedom, without capitalism. Socialism and fascism are the alternatives—state-dominated economies which are authoritarian, if not totalitarian, in their power over society as a whole. Not only should our concept of freedom include economic freedom—the freedom to compete in the making of profits—but other kinds of freedom are dependent upon the existence of economic freedom. The existence of economic power in private hands is a safeguard of individual liberties because it limits the power of the state. The position of Hayek, Friedman and their followers is fundamentally that of liberals from Adam Smith to Herbert Spencer. But mainstream liberalism has changed since then, and their position on the British political spectrum now appears as an ultra-conservative one; though it doubtless seems less eccentric in countries such as the USA, Australia and Japan, where the entire spectrum of politics lies further to the right.

It is nearly 60 years since Keynes, the leading liberal economist of the twentieth century, and a supporter of the British Liberal Party, published his historic essay, 'The End of Laissez-Faire'. In it Keynes explicitly rejected many of the central tenets of the old creed:

> The world is *not* so governed from above that private and social interest always coincide. It is *not* so managed here below that in practice they coincide. It is *not* a correct deduction from the principles of economics that enlightened self-interest always operates in the public interest. Nor is it true that self-interest generally *is* enlightened....[30]

Rejecting the doctrine of a natural harmony of interests, as well as the slightly more sophisticated argument that the intervention of the state will in the end only make

things worse, Keynes went on to suggest what the form and direction of state action should be. He did not attack what he called 'doctrinaire State Socialism' primarily on moral grounds, but for pragmatic reasons: it offered policies which were no longer relevant, remedies for ills which were being abolished in any case by the steady movement of capitalist enterprises away from a competitive obsession with profits towards rationalized monopoly or near monopolies: 'They are, as times goes on, socialising themselves....The battle of Socialism against unlimited private profit is being won in detail hour by hour.' Nevertheless Keynes argues in favour of giving the state a more positive role in managing the economy: 'The important thing for government is not to do things which individuals are doing already, and to do them a little better or a little worse; but to do those things which at present are not done at all.' Keynes was not a socialist economist, and unlike some of his social democratic followers, he was not so confused as to suppose that what he was recommending was a gradualist shift from capitalism to socialism. On the contrary, his explicit intention was to secure adjustments in capitalism which would enable it to survive in a more rational and humane, and therefore more stable, form:

> These reflections have been directed towards possible improvements in the technique of modern capitalism by the agency of collective action. There is nothing in them which is seriously incompatible with what seems to me to be the essential characteristic of capitalism, namely the dependence upon an intense appeal to the money-making and money-loving instincts of individuals as the main motive force of the economic machine.[31]

Keynes did not despise the pursuit of wealth. He played the stock-market himself with considerable success. He regarded the pursuit of wealth as a comparatively harmless employment of energies which might otherwise be deflected into more dangerous channels. But his more serious defence of capitalism was the traditional one. What he called 'individualism', by which he meant scope 'for the exercise of private initiative and responsibility' in the economic field, was in his view 'the best safeguard of personal liberty' and 'of the variety of life'.[32]

So Keynes, although he shocked many liberals—and social democrats—by the novelty of his proposals, was perfectly candid about his own commitment to capitalism, based as it was upon quintessentially liberal arguments. 'The difficulty is that the capitalist leaders in the City and in Parliament are incapable of distinguishing novel measures for safeguarding capitalism from what they call Bolshevism.'[33] Later liberals have usually been less blunt in their defence of capitalism, and their unease is reflected in the various less provocative euphemisms that are commonly used—'free enterprise', 'the mixed economy', and so forth. Nevertheless, allowing for some differences of opinion over the extent of desirable state intervention or management, support for capitalism remains the basic liberal position. Hostility to what, like Keynes, they typically refer to as *state* socialism, remains constant.

If pressed, most contemporary liberals, including many social democrats, would probably offer a defence of capitalism along the same lines as Keynes. They might well reject the neo-conservative campaign to rehabilitate *laissez-faire*, but they would agree with Keynes that capitalism does allow and encourage individual enterprise and initiative as socialism supposedly does not. It is not possible (they would argue), and it is not realistic to seek to separate individual economic enterprise from all the other expressions of personal energy and ability. If there is to be scope for individuals to express themselves, this must include the opportunity to 'get on' economically. It is not realistic to think that people will exert themselves if they are to get no material reward from it. There are, of course, other incentives besides purely economic ones, but economic incentives cannot be disregarded. Even the Communists have discovered this, they point out gleefully. Opportunities for the individual must include economic opportunities.

It must follow from this that liberals regard a measure of inequality as not only unavoidable but positively desirable. Keynes was, as usual, quite explicit about this.[34] But it has become ever more difficult for liberals to admit this, since economic inequality is now so widely associated with social injustice. Yet if economic incentives are to operate effectively, and if economic opportunities are to mean anything, individuals must be able to make money and to keep it once they have made it. Of course liberals can hardly afford to renounce altogether the slogan of 'equality'. Like freedom and democracy it is now too prestigious a term to be completely abandoned to one's political opponents. The equality which liberals claim to believe in is equality of opportunity. People should be given an equal 'start' in life, but if energy, ability and merit are to achieve their 'due' reward, they will end up unequally. The principle that such virtues should be rewarded precludes the possibility of a high degree of overall economic and social equality. Liberals subscribe to the classic bourgeois idea of the career open to talent. Merit, not birth or title or privilege, should be rewarded. Hereditary inequality is

unacceptable. Inequality which reflects merit or desert is not.

But at this point we encounter yet another contradiction within liberalism. The principle of equality of opportunity, of providing to every one an equal 'start' in

---

...liberals assign a higher priority to the freedom to acquire money and use it as you please than they do to equality of opportunity...

---

life, implies that it should not be possible to transmit wealth, privilege and advantage from one generation to the next. But endowing one's children or heirs with money, a privileged education and other advantages beyond the common lot is precisely what many parents want most of all to do with the money they have acquired. To prevent them from doing this for the sake of equality of opportunity would require 100 percent death duties and other drastic measures to prevent the passing on of wealth and advantage. This would not only act as a powerful disincentive to individual economic enterprise. It would also be an attack on the rights of property. So if liberals took the principle of equality of opportunity really seriously, they would be obliged to qualify their commitment to two central institutions of capitalism: individual economic incentives, and private property. By and large liberals have not been prepared to do this, any more than they have been prepared to prevent the rich from buying a superior education for their children, with all the social and career advantages that normally accompany it. Clearly in practice liberals assign a higher priority to the freedom to acquire money and use it as you please than they do to equality of opportunity, or to the principle that rewards should accrue to merit alone.

Perhaps this is not surprising. We have already noted that the liberal principle of respect for the individual and his/her rights does not extend to the renunciation of all coercion or killing. The theoretical individualism of the liberals is constantly modified by their acceptance of the legitimacy of more mundane or 'realistic' demands of politics and economics. So it is not out of character that liberalism should be reluctant to interfere with the rights of property and inheritance, even though a consistent regard for the equal rights of all individuals requires such interference. We have already noticed how deeply and how early ideas of possession entered into liberal thought. We are said to *possess* rights, and to *possess* our bodies and their labour, in the same way as we (may) possess material property. But these more metaphysical forms of ownership should not divert our attention from the great importance which liberalism attaches to property in the most elementary material sense of the word.

The self-interest which liberalism generally attributes to the individual is assumed to take, in part, the form of the desire for material possessions. This is neither sordid nor irrational since, as Keynes pointed out, it is through material possessions and money that men and women can enlarge their own lives and a variety of life-styles become possible. But liberals also connect freedom with private property in terms of the independence which property confers on its owners. This is an abiding theme of liberal argument, and it has a variety of implications, not all of them equally attractive. For example, it was contended by Whigs and liberals that the poor and propertyless were, by virtue of their poverty, at the mercy of both the rich and governments. They were susceptible to bribery. They were dependent rather than independent. There was truth in this; and one conclusion might have been that it was desirable to make the poor less poor, and spread property rather more evenly through the nation as a whole. But eighteenth-century Whigs drew a different conclusion. They held that it proved the rightness of restricting the franchise and political participation generally to men who already possessed enough property to make them immune to bribery at its usual level.

To argue that the secure possession of enough to provide a modestly comfortable standard of life forms a basis for personal independence is reasonable. But the logic of this argument points in the direction of what might be called a Rousseauist type of society: a society composed of self-employed artisans owning their own homes and means of production; by implication a society necessarily without extremes of wealth and poverty. That is the level and type of property ownership which confers independence. But property ownership on a larger scale—the ownership of houses in which other people live, and of offices and factories in which other people work—self-evidently places those who are tenants or employees in a position of dependence. Yet liberalism, in its defence of private property as a bulwark of individual freedom, has not discriminated between the small-scale ownership which promotes independence, and the large-scale ownership which generates dependence and exploitation. They have not much concerned themselves with the power of property, nor

sought actively to redistribute it on a more equal basis. Nor has there been an effective liberal attack on the inheritance of property. In other words, neither the professed liberal commitment to equality of opportunity and rewards for talent and merit, nor the association of private property with personal independence, has been allowed to interfere with the rights of property as such. When it comes to the choice of priorities, respect for private property, however acquired and on however large a scale, has taken precedence over concern with equality of opportunity and personal independence.

This indicates one of the many limitations which the actual commitments of liberalism place upon its theoretical individualism. The concept of 'the individual' is in essence universal and egalitarian. As individuals we are all equal, of equal worth and with equal rights. The egalitarian character of individualism could quite reasonably be held to require in practice a high degree of economic and social equality. The very least that it requires is equality of opportunity. Yet in practice even this lies beyond liberalism because it requires extensive interference with the rights of property and the accumulation and transmission of wealth. Again, if private property provides a firm foundation for individual freedom, then every individual should share in it; yet liberals have never been happy about expropriation or the compulsory redistribution of property, or indeed about any form of what is tendentiously called 'levelling down'. Property and capitalism do not often figure prominently in the definition of liberalism, or lists of liberal values, which liberals themselves put on display. But I think we are justified in concluding that both play a far more important part in determining the concrete historical character of liberalism than has often been recognized.

This in turn raises the still more awkward question of class. How a class is defined, and on what basis a particular social group maintains its position and privileges, are difficult and much debated questions which cannot be entered into here. It will, however, be generally accepted that the ability to transmit wealth and advantage from one generation to the next is at least one of the means by which a perhaps temporary elite converts itself into an entrenched class. Thus, in so far as liberals are unwilling seriously to obstruct the process of passing on wealth and property from one generation to the next, they are in effect acquiescing in the maintenance of class and class privileges.

But it would not for this reason be true to say that the liberals are consciously and openly committed to the maintenance of a class society. If anything, the opposite is closer to the truth. Historically liberalism has involved a frontal assault on feudal privileges. And conceptually liberal individualism is by nature universalist: it does not think of people as members of classes or other social or national groups, but as individuals, fundamentally alike and equal members of the human species. Phrases like 'regardless of colour, class or creed' are part of the stock-in-trade of liberal political rhetoric. No liberal has ever offered the kind of overt defence of a stable class struc-

---

...the commitment to the individual...is constantly diluted by the liberal commitment to...liberal 'realism.'

---

ture which can be found in conservative writers like Burke, T.S. Eliot, and Yeats. Yet liberals are not levellers in the ordinary sense of the word. They do not share the substantive notions of equality to be found in Rousseau or socialist writers. But they do believe in equality before the law, in equal civil and political rights, and in equality of opportunity.

Once again we encounter a contradiction between the proclaimed principles of liberalism and its actual commitments. And since this contradiction exists *within* liberalism, what it has produced among liberals is a constant evasiveness and uneasiness about the whole question of class. They cannot defend class, but they are unwilling to attack it. So they prefer to pretend that it doesn't exist, or that it is withering away, or that it doesn't really matter anyway. The liberal attitude to class is a classic case of bad faith. There are many good reasons, both historical and conceptual, for regarding liberalism itself, and its priorities, as an essentially middle-class or bourgeois political creed. And many liberals would themselves concede this, without necessarily allowing that this in itself limits the relevance or importance of the liberal values. Yet beyond this they shy away from looking any more closely at the realities of class or its impact on their own complex of beliefs and attitudes.

Thus although in principle the commitment to the individual and his or her rights stands at the centre of liberal theory, in reality this commitment is constantly diluted by the liberal commitment to other apparently less central principles, or simply by liberal 'realism'. Contemporary liberals attack 'utopians' for their apparent willingness to sacrifice the real, living individuals of today to some distant future goal or harmony or happi-

ness. In practice, however, liberals accept the right of at least liberal-democratic states to conscript young men and send them off to die in wars fought for goals which are often equally uncertain and 'Utopian'. Liberal writers present imprisonment as the absolute antithesis of personal freedom; yet they accept the use of imprisonment by the liberal state for a vast range of offences, not all of which by any stretch of argument could be regarded as infringements of, or threats to, the liberties of others. They are fond of quoting Kant's dictum about treating each individual as an end rather than a means to some further end. Yet they normally accept the legitimacy of using punishments and penalties as deterrents. The concept of 'the individual' is asexual: it makes no distinction between men and women. Yet it is extraordinary how few of the liberal champions of the rights of man have also been champions of the equal rights of woman. John Stuart Mill stands out as an honourably consistent exception to the general rule. Of course this unthinking exclusion of half the human race is not peculiar to liberalism. Socialism, which is supposed to extend radical thought and practice beyond the confines of liberalism, has also been blighted by it. And it is not a question of 'blaming' liberals for this failure, as if they could realistically have expected to think otherwise. Nevertheless, we must note this as one further way in which liberals have failed to be consistent in their individualism. To be sure, such consistency would have required a degree of penetrating radicalism which is rare at any time and in any creed. But this is only another way of saying that the practice of liberalism has turned out to be a great deal less radical and subversive of established forms of inequality and oppression that one might expect if one looked only at liberal theory, and accepted it at its own valuation.

[In the first part of this book] I have tried to outline what I take to be the essentials of the liberal world-view, the liberal theory of politics, society and individual and social values. All this assumes that there is some constant hard-core of liberalism, and that the word is not simply over-stretched to cover a variety of disparate and unconnected phenomena. Nevertheless, such an approach runs the danger of presenting too unified and too fixed a picture of something which has taken different shapes at different times, and which also has a history and a development which need to be charted. For liberalism is not reducible to a set of general and abstract propositions. It is a historical movement of ideas and a political and social practice. We misread its character and underestimate its chameleon talents if we abstract too much from its actual history.

Notes

1. Thomas Paine: *Common Sense,* ed. Isaac Kramnick (1776, Penguin edn., 1976) p. 98.
2. Locke: *Two Treatises of Government*, Second Treatise, ch. 4, 22.
3. Paine: *Rights of Man*, Part II, ch. 1 (Penguin edn., p. 187).
4. Berlin: *Four Essays*, footnote, p. 123.
5. See Lionel Trilling: *The Opposing Self* (Secker & Warburg, 1955) pp. 52–3.
6. C.B. Macpherson: *The Real World of Democracy* (Oxford University Press, 1966) p. 1.
7. Thomas Jefferson: *Notes on the State of Virginia*, in *The Portable Thomas Jefferson*, ed. Merrill D. Peterson (Penguin, 1977) p. 164.
8. See Richard Hofstadter: *The American Political Tradition* (Jonathan Cape, 1962, 1967 edn.) p. 4.
9. Letter to Mary Gladstone, 24 April 1881, quoted in Bullock and Shock (eds.), *The Liberal Tradition*, p. 124.
10. Matthew Arnold: *Culture and Anarchy*. This observation and his invocations of order and authority occur in the final paragraph of ch. 2.
11. F.A. Hayek: *Studies in Philosophy, Politics and Economics* (Routledge & Kegan Paul, 1967) p. 161.
12. Crick: *In Defence of Politics*, p. 62.
13. J.L. Talmon: *The Origins of Totalitarian Democracy* (1952, Sphere Books edn 1970) pp. 46–7.
14. Crick: *In Defence of Politics*, p. 60.
15. Guido de Ruggiero: *The History of European Liberalism* (Beacon Press, 1959) p. 379.
16. D.D. Raphael: *Problems of Political Philosophy* (Pall Mall, 1970) p. 142.
17. I have here repeated in a condensed form some points made at greater length in my article 'Socialism and the idea of science' in Bkikhu Parekh (ed.) *The Concept of Socialism* (Croom Helm, 1975).
18. Stuart Hampshire, "Russell, radicalism and reason' *New York Review of Books*, 8 Oct. 1970, an exceptionally interesting review of the third volume of Bertrand Russell's *Autobiography*.
19. J.M. Keynes: 'My Early Beliefs', in *Essays in Biography*, Collected Writings, Vol. X, (Macmillan, 1972) p. 446.
20. Edmund Burke: *Reflections on the Revolution in France,* ed. Conor Cruise O'Brien (Penguin, 1968) p. 183.
21. Percy Bysshe Shelley: *A Defence of Poetry*, in *Complete Works of Percy Bysshe Shelley* Roger Ingpen and Walter E. Peck (eds.) (Ernest Benn, 1965) Vol VII, p. 134.
22. Keynes: 'My Early Beliefs', *Essays in Biography*, pp. 448–9.
23. William Blake: Annotations to Reynolds's 'Discourses', in *Complete Writings*, Geoffrey Keynes (ed.), (Oxford University Press, 1966) pp. 474–5.
24. See Lionel Trilling: *The Liberal Imagination* (Secker & Warburg, 1951), especially the Preface and 'The Function of the Little Magazine'.
25. Keynes: *Essays in Biography*, p. 447.
26. 'Palinurus' (Cyril Connolly): *The Unquiet Grave* (Hamish Hamilton, 1951 edn.) p. 7.

27. Paul Johnson: *The Offshore Islanders*, (Weidenfeld & Nicolson, 1972) pp. 421–2.
28. Talmon: *The Origins of Totalitarian Democracy*, pp. 2, 3.
29. For a fuller critique, see Roy Edgley: 'Reason and Violence', *Radical Philosophy*, 4, Spring 1973. Reprinted in Stephan Korner (ed.) *Practical Reason* (Yale University Press, 1974).
30. J.M. Keynes: *Essays in Persuasion*, Collection Writings, Vol. IX (Macmillan, 1972) pp. 287–8.
31. Ibid., pp. 290–3.
32. J.M. Keynes: *The General Theory of Employment Interest and Money* (Macmillan, 1936) pp. 374, 380.
33. J.M. Keynes: *Essays in Persuasion*, p. 299.
34. J.M. Keynes: *The General Theory*, p. 374.

Terms & Concepts

absolutism	individualism	progress
consent	John Maynard Keynes	rationalism
death duties	"liberal realism"	Romanticism
economic freedom	liberalism's "actual commitments"	rule of law
enlightened self-interest	merit	self-regulating society
Enlightenment	mixed economy	state socialism
equality of opportunity	pacifism	tyranny of the majority

Questions

1. What is the liberal attitude toward equality and democracy?

2. Liberalism is often a defence of the private realm against state intervention. Has this defence treated men and women equally? Is there a gender bias built into liberal values?

3. Arblaster argues that liberalism has a half-hidden commitment to capitalism. Is capitalism the friend or the enemy of liberal values?

4. Is liberalism neutral with respect to different cultures and ways of life, or does it favour some ways of life over others?

5. Is Arblaster too dismissive of the attempts liberal societies have made to equalize opportunities for their citizens? Does he place too much stock in death duties as a means of realizing liberal ideals?

6. Liberalism's commitment to fairness and individualism imply a meritocratic social, political, and economic order. To what extent do you think Canadian society meets the meritocratic ideal?

It's Big Government, Stupid

David Frum

Editors' Note

Conservatism can be understood as both an ideology and a disposition. It can be a systematic set of propositions to explain and change the world, or it can be an attitude one may have toward the wisdom of tradition, change in general, or perhaps certain types of social and political change.

In the last 15 years conservatism has become identified with a sustained critique of public policies designed to protect people from the consequences of the contingencies of life such as unemployment, sickness, and old age. Conservatism is now generally identified with the attack on the state as a giant unlimited liability insurance company.

Historically, conservatives were different from liberals in the sense that they recognized the duty of the privileged groups to provide for the needs of the less fortunate. In the post-World War II era, some conserva-

tives saw the welfare state as a corruption of this historical principle because welfare benefits were made a matter of recipients' right rather than providers' moral obligation. So conservatism became the label for a political program to scale back the welfare state and allow for the re-emergence of more traditional means of social support. Furthermore, the scaling back of the welfare state would help end "welfare dependency" and spur people first to self-reliance and then to self-respect, diminishing the need to rely on charity, whatever its source. The ideology of "neoconservatism" was born. Its proponents now dominate the American Congress.

This article by journalist David Frum is a trenchant critique not only of the welfare state, but, curiously, of conservatives themselves, especially American conservative political leaders. As you read this article,

note how he weaves economic arguments into a political case for the conservative position. Note how Frum's neoconservatism differs from that of some who want the state to cultivate a certain form of moral character through the legislation of codes of public morality; and that of others, like Patrick Buchanan, who identify the conservative political stance with the promotion of American nationalism.

Though Frum is a Canadian by birth, his brand of conservatism is particularly American. Conservatives outside of the United States would bristle at his polemic against the state and the idea of collective responsibility. Indeed, many conservatives would regard the unfettered operation of market forces as the solvent of those traditional attachments and loyalties that conservatives seek to preserve. To them, Frum's cure would be worse than the disease.

◆ ◆ ◆

Journalists who covered Patrick J. Buchanan's abortive 1992 presidential campaign heard some remarkably stinging invective from him about the crushing burden of Big Government. When pressed for details, however, Buchanan could bring himself to name only three specific civilian budget cuts. He would repeal half the 1990 congressional pay raise, eliminate the National Endowment for the Arts, and end all foreign-aid programs—for a grand-total savings of some $13.2 billion. Yet in the 1992 fiscal year, the United States government spent nearly $1.5 trillion, an amount equal to the entire gross domestic product of united Germany. From that vast ocean of money, fed by roaring rivers of unnecessary and destructive spending, greasy with floating blobs of waste, the man who regards himself as the most fearless conservative in America would blot up rather less than 1 percent.

However marginal some of Buchanan's views may be, his timidity in the face of Big Government is all too typical of American conservatives, including even Ronald Reagan. Reagan owed his 1980 presidential victory to what seemed at the time an inspired political stroke. There would be no more threats to throw widows out into the snow, no more Taft- and Goldwater-style calls for self-reliance, cheese-paring, and pay-as-you-go, no more flinty frugality. Rather than fight and lose the battle over the welfare state for the hundredth time, Reagan would change the subject from spending to taxes. Later, after the tax cuts had worked their supply-side magic in the form of increased revenue, there would be plenty of time to start chopping away at the excesses of Big Government.

And indeed, federal revenues did shoot upward in the booming 80's—even revenues from the personal income-tax cut, just as the supply-siders had predicted. Unfortunately, federal spending swelled even faster. Conservatives would later pin the blame for this spending binge on a hostile Democratic Congress. But a quick flip through the pages of the budget documents of the decade shows that spending grew fastest for Republican constituencies: pensioners, farmers, and veterans. In the end, Reagan's two administrations piled up more debt, in inflation-adjusted dollars, than Franklin D. Roosevelt and Harry Truman had incurred to win World War II. Then, in the following four years, George Bush accumulated three times more debt (again adjusting for inflation) than Woodrow Wilson had taken on to fight World War I.

Conceivably, the failure of the Reagan gambit might have persuaded conservatives—in government and out—to redouble their zeal for scaling back the functions of the state. But that is not what happened. Most people on the Right accepted the view that anything Reagan had left undone simply could not be done.

Thus, in the spring of 1992, *Policy Review* sent a questionnaire to twenty moderate-to-conservative Senators. What would you do, the magazine asked, to cut $25 billion from the budget? The real news was not that only five bothered to answer, or that only one of the five, the Colorado Republican Hank Brown, had any useful suggestions to offer. The real news was that *Policy Review*, the organ of the Heritage Foundation, the intellectual armory of Reaganism, thought that $25 billion—or less than 2 percent of federal expenditure—was as ambitious a spending-cut target as it could realistically set.

Whatever they might say in their after-dinner speeches or in their op-ed pieces, conservatives had effectively thrown in the towel on government spending. As Heritage despairingly wondered, in the briefing book it compiled for the new Bush administration in 1989: "If Ronald Reagan and his 'Reaganauts' could only *slow down* the growth of government spending, not reverse it or eliminate wasteful programs, what hope is there for any other conservative President…?" Understandably, post-Reagan conservatives have been greatly tempted to stop thinking about shrinking government, and to look for a new and less frustrating message.

The message they have found is summed up in the phrase "the culture." As the always quotable Buchanan wrote in defense of his controversial speech to the 1992 Republican convention in Houston: "We cannot raise the white flag in the culture war, for that is a war about who we are. Nor can conservatives become conscientious objectors—because culture shapes politics, culture is the Ho Chi Minh trail to power. Surrender this province, and we lose America."

Precisely what is meant by "the culture" has always been more than a little unclear. Some conservatives, like Hilton Kramer and Samuel Lipman of the *New*

Criterion, use the term to encompass arts and letters, the sciences, and intellectual life generally, all of which, they fear, are being politicized and degraded. Other conservatives, like Midge Decter and William J. Bennett, appear principally to be talking about morality—and in particular, the attitude of the mass media, the entertainment industry, and the nation's religious, political, and intellectual leaders toward morality. Still other conservatives

---

The problem is that a politics of opposition to cultural decay in any or all of these senses cannot work as a substitute for a politics of opposition to Big Government.

---

use the term to mean the civilization created on this continent by European immigrants—a civilization they see as threatened by the assaults of multiculturalism.

The problem is that a politics of opposition to cultural decay in any or all of these senses cannot work as a substitute for a politics of opposition to Big Government. For perhaps the most important force driving the social trends that offend conservatives, from family breakup to unassimilated immigration, is the welfare function of modern government. The nearly $1 trillion the federal government spends each year on social services and income maintenance—and the additional hundreds of billions spent by the states—is a colossal lure tempting citizens to reckless behavior. Remove those heaps of money, and the penalties would again deter almost everyone from personal misconduct, as they did before the welfare state was set up in 1933, and as they even continued to a lesser extent to do before its huge expansion in 1965.

The great, overwhelming fact of a capitalist economy is risk. Everyone is at constant risk of losing his job, or having his business destroyed by a competitor, or seeing his investment portfolio crash. Risk makes people circumspect. It disciplines them and teaches them self-control. Government subsidy, by contrast, does for many who are not rich what her millions did for the late socialite Barbara Hutton—it enables them to engage in destructive behaviour without immediately suffering the consequences.

Twenty years ago, an economist named Sam Peltzman noticed that drivers who wore seat belts, while suffering far fewer accidents than drivers who did not,

inflicted far more. The welfare state functions as a political safety belt, reducing the riskiness of all of our lives; and, just as with real safety belts, there are what Peltzman called "feedback effects" from our newfound sense of personal security. Some of these effects are undoubtedly good. Unemployment insurance, by easing fears of job loss, does seem to relax workers' anxieties about technological change. Other effects are not so good.

Consider the example of what ranks in conservative thinking as perhaps the most corrupted institution in American society: the university. Suppose that there were no student loans, and very little general state aid to higher education; imagine that every student (save those who could win a scholarship from the university itself) were paying the full cost of his own tuition and that the university had no sources of income other than tuition, alumni and corporate gifts, endowment income, and grants from government exclusively for specific research projects. In such a world, the universities would not look at all like the schools that now enrage conservative critics of American higher education.

Forced to spend their own money, the less motivated students, or those seeking only (as one conservative academic once put it) to prove the negative point that they were not so idle and incompetent as to fail to get a B.A., would drop away. The students who remained, paying $1,000 or more per course, would become discriminating consumers. Some demand for film studies, black studies, gay studies, and courses on the novels of Louis L'Amour would linger on—but in a cash-on-the-barrelhead university, the demand for them would be much less.

So, pretty quickly, would the supply. How and why the likes of Jacques Derrida, Michel Foucault, and Frantz Fanon have come to loom so large in American higher education is a big and vexing question. But at least part of the answer is that American universities teach what they do for the same reason Polish factories under Communism used to turn out pairs of boots with two left feet: the factories made what pleased them; and because the consumers were paying with soft currency, they took whatever it pleased the factories to make. With consumers—i.e., students—paying real money—i.e., their own—the universities would no longer be able to get away as easily with teaching useless or politicized junk.

Nobody can promise that the end of state aid to universities would chasten them immediately. Organizations like the Ford and Rockefeller Foundations could still channel billions to the universities' most destructive personalities and functions. It would take a generation, possibly more, for the prankster and sophists in the academy to retire. But surely if large-scale state aid to higher education had never been tried, the universities would be more wholesome places from the conservative point of view today, and if massive aid ended tomorrow, they would tend over time to become more wholesome.

Furthermore, with greater sacrifices demanded of the families of those seeking higher education, the proportion of Americans going on to college would shrink. That in turn would mean that state governments could no longer count on the colleges to remedy the deficiencies of the high schools. America turns out students the way General Motors once turned out cars: slovenly workers on the line count on a highly paid team of fixers at the end of the line to redo and repair their bungled labors. If there were fewer fixers, the schools would have to be run like a Toyota line instead: the job would have to be done right the first time.

Similar "feedback effects" drive the crisis of family breakdown. Welfare can never be reformed in a way that simultaneously encourages people to work and provides them with a decent livelihood if they do not. I am not suggesting—not very confidently anyway—that abolishing welfare would undo the harm the program has done. It is quite possible that this trap cannot be escaped through the same route by which it was entered. But if welfare had never been expanded in the middle 1960's, if a sixteen-year-old who got pregnant in 1994 had the same unpleasant options her counterpart did in 1964— beg her furious parents for help, drop out of school and take a job, or somehow persuade the father to marry her and take a job himself—is it not probable that she would be as unlikely to give birth out of wedlock as her 1964 predecessor was?

Of course the world—or "the culture"—in which the teenager of 1994 lives is not so hostile to illegitimacy as the world in which her grandmother lived. But if the culture that abhorred illegitimacy has vanished, perhaps it has done so because it is hard for most people to believe for very long in the wrongness of something that the government rewards. The English jurist James Fitzjames Stephen observed 130 years ago that while it is true that most people refrain from stealing because they believe stealing to be wrong, and not because they fear hanging, it is also true that the reason most people believe stealing to be wrong is that thieves are hanged.

It really should not surprise anyone that the welfare state has weakened family structures. That was what the welfare state's social programs were meant to do. The family used to be connected by its members' mutual responsibility for child-rearing, unemployment, sickness, old age, disability, and burial. But while strict mutual responsibility did a fair job of deterring illegitimacy and abandonment, it never succeeded very well in coping with illegitimacy and abandonment once they occurred. The welfare state was designed to replace and improve upon those old family functions. It thus reduced the economic importance of the family—which, predictably, weakened the family's stability.

To be sure, there is little clamor for going back to the old ways. Social Security is more reliable, more generous, more efficient, and less intrusive than one's children; and from the child's point of view, even a 15.3-percent payroll tax is a lot less trouble than having to look after a bedridden old mother in the spare room. Certainly, it is more agreeable to slice "duty" out of the lexicon, to visit one's aged parents knowing that it is someone else's job to provide for them, or to drop one's children off at a day-care center instead of begging a favor from one's sister or mother.

Hence, it is not very realistic of conservatives to expect that the pre-welfare-state family can survive in a welfare-state world. Hence, too, the conservative search for (in Bennett's words) "economic and social policies that support the two-parent family" is bound to be disappointed. "Supporting the family" in Washington parlance is code for subsidies and welfare programs like family leave and day care. But these are the very forces in modern life that strike at the family's core economic logic, the sexual division of labor, leaving only affection to hold families together—and affection is not always a trustworthy glue.

Through yet another "feedback effect," the welfare state is also heavily responsible for the balkanization of American society that so worries conservatives. Henry George compared the act of raising a single tariff to hurling a single banana into a cage of monkeys: all the unlucky monkeys shriek and rage until bananas are thrown at them, too. So long as society keeps hurling economic and psychic rewards at everyone who claims victimhood, it is futile for conservatives to demand that America's warring ethnic, religious, racial, and even sexual minority groups stop their complaining and concentrate instead on what unites them as Americans. If billions of dollars can be extracted by any group that can represent itself as piteous enough, political entrepreneurs will play on their followers' grievances, mobilizing their resentments, intensifying their group identify, and whipping up suspicion of outsiders.

Conservatives who wish to direct their full attention to "the culture" say that they are attempting to preserve bourgeois values. But they are unlikely to succeed in a world arranged in such a way as to render those virtues at best unnecessary and at worst active nuisances.

What are the bourgeois virtues anyway? The paramount ones are thrift, diligence, prudence, sobriety, fidelity, and orderliness. Compared to the military, saintly, and romantic virtues—zeal, courage, passion, love of beauty, pride, and indifference to worldly goods—it is not a very poetic list. But the prosaic bourgeois virtues are the virtues that settled America (combined, of course, with a canny eye for the quick buck), and they developed into a national norm because they were essential to survival in a country that was, until the 1930's, simultaneously rich in opportunities and full of terrible dangers from which there was scant protection except for one's own resources and the help of friends and family.

The opportunities remain, but the dangers have dwindled. Why be thrifty any longer when your old age and health care are provided for, no matter how profligate you may be in your youth? Why be prudent when the state ensures your bank deposits, replaces your flooded-out house, buys all the wheat you can grow? Why be diligent when half your earnings are taken from you and given to the idle? Why be sober when the government runs clinics to cure you of your drug habit as soon as it no longer amuses you? Why be faithful when there are no consequences to leaving your family in search of newer and more exciting pleasures?

True, some virtues linger on after they have outlived their usefulness. True, too, the bourgeois virtues retain much of their usefulness when combined with talent. If diligence can earn you $150,000 a year as an engineer, you will be diligent, even if President Clinton helps himself to half the proceeds. If your mental life is interesting to you even when you are cold sober, those taxpayer-funded clinics will not beckon. But for the less capable and the less resourceful, who always outnumber the more, things look rather different.

If the old American culture and the old American character were rational responses to the riskiness of life, one cannot radically reduce that riskiness and expect the old culture and the old character to persist. The children of a self-made man are different from their father: more optimistic, often more generous, more sensitive, and more tolerant, but less careful, less provident, less hard-working, less self-controlled. In the same way, the citizens of a socially insured America naturally act and think differently from the citizens of a self-reliant America.

Conservatives, who prefer the older character, are fooling themselves in thinking that it can be rebuilt without returning to the older way of life that brought such a character into being. But they are also fooling themselves in thinking that Reagan defined the limits of any

---

In the same way, the citizens of a socially insured America naturally act and think differently from the citizens of a self-reliant America.

---

conceivable shrinkage of the redistributive and regulating functions of the American government.

The welfare state that conservatives are frightened to fight is a desperately unstable institution. Its costs rise without respite because it tempts people into ever-greater helplessness and dependence on it. The faster its costs rise, the more the economy that supports the welfare state stagnates, in large part because of the disincentives created by the high taxes it requires, but also because its temptations sap the brutal acquisitive drive that propels economies forward.

Thus, as the government sectors of the world's two dozen welfare states have swelled, their budget deficits have soared, their growth rates have slowed, their unemployment rates have risen, and their poor have behaved in increasingly pathological ways Comparatively speaking, the trend by which spending outruns resources has not yet gone very far in the United States—only 14 percent of federal revenues are now spent to pay interest on the federal debt, while neighboring Canada pays 35 percent—but the proportion is climbing.

As it does, terrible resentment will be ignited. If taxpayers now think that they send money to Washington and get little in return, wait until one dollar in six or one dollar in five vanishes right off the top to the federal government's creditors. Pressed by taxes, angered by the declining quality of public services, feeling cheated by government and not knowing why, the voters sink deeper and deeper into the mistrustful mood that characterized the electorate in 1992, when almost one voter in five cast a ballot for the most sinister demagogue to seek the presidency since Huey Long was cut down in 1935.

Some conservatives take comfort in the welfare state's travails, assuming that the edifice will collapse by itself. Irving Kristol says that we are living through the "end-game" of the welfare state. The editors of the *Wall Street Journal* cite polls in which a clear majority of Americans claim that they would prefer to receive fewer services from the government and pay less in taxes than receive more and pay more. Republican Congressman Newt Gingrich's theory is that within the next half-dozen years, the number of people who understand that they are never going to get their money's worth out of Social Security will for the first time outnumber those for whom the system is a net benefit: the baby boomers will realize that Social Security is a bad deal and will rebel against it. But the ricketiness of the welfare state does not embolden Gingrich to vote against it. Precisely the opposite: it excuses him from doing much of anything while waiting for the inevitable end.

Nothing, however, is inevitable and very few things are even predictable. And even if the welfare state does collapse, it is not preordained that a more enterprising, self-reliant, and virtuous society will emerge from the rubble. For as the United States keeps its commitments to the old with ever-heavier impositions on the young; as it tends the sick with invisible taxes on the healthy; as it hastens the promotion in the labor force of blacks and Hispanics with laws that penalize whites and Asians; as it supports the poor in ways that abuse the neighborhoods and schools that formerly belonged to the middle class—as it does all this, a lot of free-floating intergroup animosity will be released into the atmosphere. Animosity is always someone's opportunity. In 1992 Patrick Buchanan hoped it would be his; he happened to be wrong, but next time he, or someone like him, may come a little closer to being right.

Anticipating this dangerous outcome, conservatives should be acting now to avoid it, by doing what the conservatives of the 1950's did—discarding all consideration of what the public at the moment wants to hear, and trying to prepare its mind to respond intelligently to the crisis ahead.

Such a course of action may demand perhaps too much of Republican politicians, but conservative intellectuals are another matter. They should be at work on something a little more ambitious than the Republican party's next campaign manifesto. They should be showing the public the necessary connection between the social pathologies it loathes and fears and the social programs it still rather likes—and not just the programs for the poor that have created the underclass, but also the broader policies and laws that have corroded the economic functions of the family, set ethnic groups at one another's throats in pursuit of set-asides and special favors, outlawed the expression of moral outrage at irregular conduct, and diminished the necessity of thrift.

Conservatism was never supposed to be a sunny political ideology or an easy sell. It was always a doctrine for the tough-minded. But the Reagan interlude turned conservative heads. It mislead conservatives into thinking that most Americans were with them—not just casually or accidentally, but fundamentally, even when conservative ideology might deny them some benefit out of the Treasury or morally condemn something it would give them pleasure to do. And as conservatives have discarded the uncomfortable fact that the people are not really with them—not at the moment, at least—they have tried to adapt to the popular will, sacrificing in the process their old hostility to Big Government.

Twelve years of twisting and struggling to escape this trap have just entangled conservatives ever more deeply in it. Is there a way out? Only one: conservative intellectuals will have to care less about the immediate electoral prospects of the Republican party and more about telling unpalatable truths—in the hope of making those truths prevail to the point of becoming the conventional political wisdom of the future.

Terms & Concepts

Big Government	family's core economic logic	nationalism
bourgeois virtues	"feedback effects"	Reaganism
dependency	more wholesome places	risk
"end-game" of the welfare state	multiculturalism	"the culture"

Questions

1. What is "family breakdown"? What is its source in Frum's view?

2. What are the sources of the bourgeois virtues?

3. Frum argues that conservatism is a "doctrine for the tough-minded." Why? Does the evidence from trends in Canadian public policy support his contention?

4. Why, according to Frum, are people so stupid?

5. What would Frum's stripped-down state do?

6

On a Necessary Tension of a Democratic Society

Robert D. Cairns

Editors' Note

Economist Robert D. Cairns tries to find and defend a middle ground in the ongoing debate about the role of the state in a capitalist democracy. Taking a moderate post-Cold War social democratic perspective; he argues that capitalism and state need each other if democracy is to exist. The market and the state have different functions, play by different rules, and aim for different outcomes but are bound together in a symbiotic relationship. Public choice theorists believe that most of the state's functions can be stripped away and either disappear altogether or become subject to market forces. Cairns considers these theorists just as naive and misguided as those radical socialists who want to eliminate the market altogether.

Cairns defends the role of the state as the defender of social or collective interests. He also clearly recognizes the danger that democracy can easily degenerate into either plutocracy or mob rule, and argues for balanced participation.

Social democracy is a double-balancing act: the individual interests represented in the market need to be balanced by the social interests represented by the state. To enable the state to play this role, the individual interests of entrepreneurs must be aggregated and balanced by the collective interests of those they employ. This balancing act is also reflected in some of the hybrid public-private activities of the modern liberal demo-

cratic state: Crown corporations competing in the marketplace; private utility monopolies regulated by the state; and public health care delivered by medical professions organized into professional corporations.

Social Democratic parties everywhere are trying to redefine their ideological position in view, first, of the collapse of communist extreme to which they presented the moderate alternative and, second, of the undermining of the Keynesian welfare state, which they supported. Cairns advances this task of redefinition considerably.

◆ ◆ ◆

Neo-conservative "public choice" theory holds that political action, or government intervention, is a coercive interference with voluntary transactions in the market. The public demand on the state for redistributional policies is also viewed as a retarding force on social well-being. A conflict between market and state is the underlying premise. Ideally, the neo-conservative "minimal state" would limit itself to contract enforcement and national defence.

On the contrary, historically the state and market have developed in parallel. This essay emphasizes that the market is itself a political instrument, with attendant advantages and disadvantages. An active state is warranted not only for reasons of distributive justice, but for the efficient operation of a complex industrial economy. Evidence suggests that some—certainly not all—state intervention and regulations lead to efficiency as well as distributional gains in an industrial society. Furthermore, the role of the state is founded on shared collective values, including compassion and moral sense, the expression of which is precluded in the individualistic market.

To view the market as a political institution, rather than an abstract, external "invisible hand" in social relations, has implications beyond the day-to-day formulation of economic policy; it helps give substance to the concept of democracy and individual participation in industrial society.

Markets are important and valuable institutions within Canadian society. Many times, when I hear an attack on markets in general, I sense that the underlying purpose of the critics is to afford their particular group a market advantage by political means. By the same token, when I hear extravagant praise of the virtues of the market, what I am really hearing is a demand that some interest groups relinquish their political means of advancement. Neither of these positions promotes the admittedly vague goals that policy ought to promote, namely the benefit of society as a whole and the dignity of the individual.

I have come to the following proposition: from an analytic and historic standpoint, if a line is to be drawn, it is more reasonably drawn *around* the market and the state, not *between* them. This has important implications for the way that social democrats ought to approach the setting of policy.

MARKETS AND POLITICS
◆ ◆ ◆

When economists speak of a market, what they refer to is a more-or-less idealized mechanism by which interactions between or among *individuals* are facilitated. The interactions are held to be for mutual benefit; otherwise, if an individual did not benefit, he or she would refuse to take part. The fact that a market exchange takes place is *prima facie* evidence of mutual benefit. Economists allow that the relative bargaining strengths and wealth of the individuals, i.e., their "endowments," may be unequal and hence one individual may be more able to hold out for a better deal than another; but however unequal are endowments, markets are of mutual benefit to all involved. Most economists accept uncritically the existence of unequal endowments—and, thereby, inequality of opportunity. This is a weak spot in the argument, only partially answered by appeals to realism or "positivism," or by arguments about the extent of social mobility.

The state, on the other hand, is the predominant *collective* mechanism. Through it individuals can be induced or coerced (sometimes economists do not distinguish) to do things they otherwise would not do. Ideally, the state promotes some measure of collective benefit, but historical experience unfortunately illustrates an inherent tendency for the state to deviate from any reasonable interpretation of collective benefit.

It is a truism that the role of government has grown rapidly in this century in all Western industrialized countries. This growth troubles certain economists. When introducing a symposium on the subject, Myrhman (1985, p. 276) observed that conservatives would limit government to the "minimal state consist[ing] of defence, police and the legal system, all the necessary institutions to define, protect and enforce property rights and to solve conflicts between subjects." For such economists growth of the state beyond these limits is a coercive infringement of individual prerogatives—and hence of the market. A conflict between market and state is the underlying premise.

In the last generation economists have invaded the domain of political scientists, applying such theories of individual "rent-seeking" to political outcomes. For such "public choice" economists the political process is very different from the democratic ideal. Based on the

From *Social Democracy Without Illusions* by Richards, John, Robert D. Cairns and Larry Pratt, eds. (Toronto: McClelland & Stewart, 1991) (pp. 29–45). Used by permission of the Canadian Publishers, McClelland & Stewart, Toronto.

analogy of individuals seeking to maximize their well-being by exchange in ordinary markets, they view politics as another form of market in which self-seeking interest groups attempt to promote their own advantage, irrespective of the effect produced on the rest of society. Implicit in much of this analysis is the idea that the economic marketplace, working ideally, can provide an efficient distribution of income, promote participation by all citizens, and promote the "collective benefit." Interventions by government are viewed typically as the result of undesirable rent-seeking by interest groups.

To be fair to this approach, it is undeniably true that special interest groups promote government policies in their members' interest while wrapping them in the rhetoric of the public good. Consider milk marketing boards, which control supply by requiring dairy farmers to produce no more than their individual quotas. At the time of the system's introduction, the quota system reduced supply, raised milk prices, and clearly benefited existing farmers. But the next generation of dairy farmers has had to buy quotas from existing farmers before producing milk. Farmers have bid milk quota prices up to substantial levels, and the net income remaining to them after paying the interest cost on the quota may be close to what it would have been in an unregulated market. It is a wasteful system that does not benefit farmers beyond the first generation and worsens income distribution by increasing the price of an essential food. Social democrats who criticize proposals for imposing sales taxes on food would do well to recognize the tax implicit in the operation of agricultural marketing boards, a tax that does not augment government revenues.

> *...if interest groups pressuring for government intervention are rent-seeking, it also must be true that those who advocate a greater role for the market are so motivated.*

Other examples of rent-seeking abound, and are convincing evidence that government policies can work against the broad public interest. On the other hand, the critique cannot be true in general. Our social safety nets arose as a result of government policies. Moreover, if interest groups pressuring for government intervention are rent-seeking, it also must be true that those who advocate a greater role for the market are so motivated. There is no reason to suppose that the Business Council on National Issues or other supporters of the Canada-U.S. trade agreement have acquired an enlightened concern for the well-being of all Canadians, any more than has the textile workers' union, which advocates protection against foreign competition.

Our view of government, then, must be realistic. It must admit the role of a multitude of special interest groups working against the public interest and seeking special advantage. Social democrats ought to be honest enough—and if they hope to have credibility among the majority of voters, will have to be honest enough—to concede that some of their own policies, promoting the interest of their supporters, are not in the interest of the general public. Yet our view must also retain idealism, insisting that society, through institutions that promote both collective and individual interaction, has the potential to improve its future. Neither capitalism nor socialism can be looked upon as the ideal culmination.

Social democrats must admit the need for balance between social and personal, between collective and individual aspirations. Put differently, there must be an ongoing tension between the political and market domains.

Even though there is *tension*, it is not historically accurate to view the market and the political system as having developed in *conflict*. Rather, they developed hand-in-hand. We measure the beginnings of civilization from the point at which codified laws governing social relations began to be promulgated. It is part of the tradition of the English-speaking world that legislative and public concepts of democracy grew in parallel with the growth of commerce. Closer to the present, North (1985, pp. 388ff) outlines reasons for government growth in the United States in the nineteenth century, reasons likely applicable to other countries. Change in technology led to change in economic organization, increased trade, and increased division of labour in production. All this increased the number of special interest groups that turned to government to fulfil various needs, including enforcement of the complex contracts that emerged from the new technology. North (1985, p. 390) gives the particular example of farmer's political agitation in the midwestern states: "The best predictor of farm political activity, i.e. the variability of income, is a direct function of growing dependence on the world market." In summary, the growth of interest group politics paralleled, and was a result of, the extension of markets.

North implies that extension of the market (as measured in increased division of labour and extension of trade) is inextricable from extension of politics. To North a central factor in the pace of change, and presumably the extent of change, is the institutional environment. Institutions, then, matter. Like a gas in a bottle, one might say, the market takes the shape of its institutional container. The market is really a political institution. It is *defined by*, not simply *limited by*, the regulations that govern economic transactions.

Nor are the institutions of society purely technologically determined. Armstrong and Nelles (1986) give the example of telecommunications, a timely one for the contemporary debates on deregulation. Canadian jurisdictions were the first to regulate telecommunications, before the turn of the twentieth century; the Americans followed shortly thereafter. Armstrong and Nelles's thesis is that the monopoly accorded to Bell Canada was "made" by the political and market processes, not "born" by the technology. If the technology is such that unit costs fall as firm size increases, then unit cost is lowest when one producer supplies the entire market and optimal policy may be that government permits a "natural monopoly" and regulates its price. While some aspects of telecommunications technology are natural monopolies, other aspects are not. For example, there never was any reason to accord a monopoly through regulation of entry in the production of telephones themselves. Recent changes in "terminal equipment" technology make this point obvious now. For generations an aspect of regulation served no ostensible public policy purpose; on the other hand, the protected market gave Northern Telecom an opportunity to develop into a technological leader in terminal equipment. Changing telecommunication technology has changed the social costs of continuing the protected market and has led to a rethinking of the appropriate form of regulation. But if the debate is properly understood, new technology has not justified an abstract intellectual attack on the desirability, in appropriate circumstances, of regulation as an instrument to realize policy goals.

A simultaneous concern for the social good and for the dignity of the individual requires a tension between collective and individual interests, between politics and markets, and not the suppression of one to the advantage of the other. The existence of exchange and a market implies more than one person, which in turn implies a social and moral context; we cannot imagine a market without political interaction. Nineteenth-century classical economists recognized the political nature of markets and accepted the functioning of greed only to the extent that individualistic competition constrained or eliminated its evil effects. They were explicit that only when a competition harnessed human greed to advance collective goals could it be given free rein.

The market is not the natural touchstone by which social progress may be judged. On the contrary, regulation and the market are natural complements. The market depends on political regulation for its definition and adequate functioning and is thus a political institution. As such it is to be judged on the basis of its performance relative to other possible political institutions. Having established this much, we should consider the benefits of markets.

To an economist the greatest benefit of a market is efficiency. Given an initial distribution of wealth as morally acceptable, competitive markets produce optimal quantities of all goods and services, optimal in the sense that no slack exists and one individual or group can be made better off only at the expense of some others. If scarcity of goods and services is an important constraint, then this property of markets is important. Presumably, as social wealth increases—as scarcity diminishes—the appeal of efficiency diminishes somewhat.

A second benefit, related to the idea of efficiency but not identical to it, is that competitive markets have a ring of natural justice to them. An alternative way of stating the efficiency property is that the competitive price of any good exactly equals the cost (more precisely the marginal cost) of its production. One must pay into the system (in the price paid for a good or service) exactly the sacrifice imposed on society (the marginal cost) to produce what one takes out of the system. This argument gains moral appeal as individuals are moved from the margin of subsistence, so that material demands are less pressing. The moral claim of markets to justness is not absolute, but it is sufficiently compelling to have attracted those socialists, such as Oskar Lange, who a half-century ago interested themselves in optimal pricing for a socialist economy.

A third benefit of markets is their contribution to individual dignity; markets accord independence. With a well-functioning market a productive individual can be assured of the ability to exchange his or her labour, or the fruits thereof, for the material needs he or she cannot produce. The satisfaction of one's own material needs and those of one's dependants, which are among the most coercive aspects of life, does not depend on conformity to a particular bureaucratic imperative. The anonymity of market exchange encourages employers to hire the most productive, consumers to seek the least expensive, regardless of the personal characteristics of the other party to the exchange. Hence markets can provide incentives to break down discrimination and established sources of power. Yet it must also be recognized that exploitation and discrimination of individuals by those with power is often exercised in markets.

All of these benefits require the existence of competition among individual consumers and firms. Whether industrial society conforms more or less to competitive theory is a continuing debate. Some insist that it does. Winn (1985), for example, finds evidence of considerable economic mobility among minority groups in Canada. On the other hand, the modern corporation has a hierarchical neo-feudalistic organization and executives espouse an ethos of "knowing your place"; it is clearly not atomistically competitive. Consider Newman's (1975, p. 144) statement of the "theology of free enterprise":

> Adherents of the creed genuinely believe that virtue can be certified by worldly accomplishment, that success is tangible evidence of holy favour. Power is no judge of values, but it acts instinctively to create order, because no order can exist without power and no power exists without order. That's why businessmen place so much emphasis on institutions and hierarchies in which people know and keep their place. It is this deeply felt faith in institutions that is at the heart of the capitalist ethic.

It is schizophrenic to hold that egoist behaviour in the economic realm is invariably salutary while egoism in a political setting is invariably contrary to social welfare or individual freedom.

The economic view of markets is that competition by atomistic individuals leads to social benefit, through a continual shaking up of entrenched interest. But the "creed" emphasizes hierarchy, order, and power. Newman (1975, p. 185) characterizes "the corporate order [as] a system of private governments lacking the restraints of public accountability." In another passage a bank director notes that "no individual in Canada, to my mind, can do much without the support of the chartered banks" (Newman, 1975, p. 110). The idea of corporation as quasi-government returns us to the idea that markets develop in step with government.

What political structures will evolve, including what market structures? That is the question central to the protection of the social good and individual dignity, not whether the market of economic models will dominate, or whether the economy will be "market-oriented." None of this denies that in many circumstances the advancement of social good and individual dignity will be aided by a greater reliance on individual market transactions.

GAINS TO COLLECTIVE ACTION

◆ ◆ ◆

I have argued that market and non-market forces can be harnessed into a creative tension, that they are not in a simple position of conflict. They place constraints on one another and define each other's range of operation. It is schizophrenic to hold that egoistic behaviour in the economic realm is invariably salutary while egoism in a political setting is invariably contrary to social welfare or individual freedom. Especially in a complicated society that respects the rule of law, the economic measure of social welfare in terms of aggregate willingness-to-pay for commodities traded by all consumers cannot provide a means to evaluate the appropriate role of governments or of markets.

Buchanan (1987, pp. 245–46), one of the founders of the public choice school of economics, notes that "the differences in the predicted results stemming from market and political interaction stem from differences in the structures of these two institutional settings rather than from any switch in the motives of persons as they move between institutional roles." Clearly the *motives* of individuals do not change; they are, after all, the same persons in both settings. But one may argue that their *choices* are expanded or restricted by the political structure within which they operate. In competitive markets it is possible to pursue nothing but one's selfish advantage. By "political interaction," to use Buchanan's expression, it is possible to change laws and institutions that can help raise society from a non-optimizing ("Cournot-Nash" in the jargon) equilibrium to a superior solution for all concerned. Improved legal sanctions, for example, may prevent or limit the emergence of non-co-operative behaviour, in the same way as the economic theory of oligopoly stresses that political sanction on behalf of a cartel's decisions aids cartel cohesion.

A mundane example is city traffic laws. Political decisions about driving on one side of the road, speed limits, traffic lights, parking, etc. increase the efficiency of the "market" of urban transportation relative to the alternative of unregulated "free competition." Admittedly, flexible, creative, non-traditional approaches might be even more useful. To continue with the traffic example, society would likely be better off without urban automobile traffic.

This implies that the legitimate role of the state is much greater than protection of the status quo through defence, police, and contract enforcement. The state is justified not solely or even mainly by efficiency. Man is the only moral, as well as the only rational, animal. Man is not only egotistical but compassionate. A minimal extension of the role of the state beyond protection of the status quo is to protect those to whom the notion of optimality of freely negotiated contracts cannot conceivably apply because they cannot participate in a market. The government must protect children, the aged, the handicapped, and others who might die or live in misery if left to their own devices in an anarchistic market. Compassion for such individuals is where the modern welfare state begins; the capacity for collective compassion is a fundamental measure of a civilized society. Children, for example, are citizens, not "consumption goods." They enter in their own right into the "social welfare function," not just as arguments in the "utility functions" of some adults. One would not take a doll away from someone who regularly beat it; one would a child.

Once the need for collective compassion is admitted, debate over the welfare state becomes a matter of degree. It cannot be reduced to the outcome of interest group calculations—even if welfare lobbies, nurses' unions, and doctors' associations do vie for political influence at the margin. A society must collectively decide—whether explicitly or implicitly—what to do about the economic well-being of single-parent families, of those who might be ruined financially by medical expenses, of those who market productivity collapses because technological change renders their skills obsolete, of those who suffer psychological and social debilitation from unemployment, or—to cite a controversial group—of the employable who refuse to work.

Choices must be made. A totally collectivist society in which welfare state transfer payments approached 100 per cent of gross national product (GNP) would be socially stagnant, not progressive. (A professor of mine, Robert Bishop, once observed that brotherly love is a scarce resource, which must be economized in policy-making.) This is the thrust of McCallum and Blais's (1987) work. In comparison of national rates of growth of GNP among industrialized countries, they find a negative effect when transfer payments become very high. However, they find a range of attractive choice: at intermediate levels (of transfer payments relative to GNP) an increased share of transfer payments increases rates of economic growth. McCallum and Blais (1987, pp. 14ff) offer two reasons for the positive contribution, to a point.[1] First, the welfare state may help foster co-operation among groups by creating a climate of social consensus. Second, the guarantee of at least partial compensation may overcome the drag on economic growth exercised by politically organized groups that lose from technological and social change. While adoption of any such change may have positive net social benefits, it will almost certainly create identifiable groups of losers as well as winners. In a pluralist democracy, it is to be expected that the losers mobilize to block changes from which they stand to lose.

...the greatest risks in our economy are borne, not by shareholders... but by workers.

There is further rationalization of these results, one that is in keeping with the historical fact that increased growth and expansion of the market have gone hand-in-hand with the development of the state. This argument has to do with the high level of risk in any market economy—the inherent uncertainty surrounding the rewards to be realized in the future from investment today. Contrary to the emphasis on much economic work, the greatest risks in our economy are borne, not by shareholders, who are in the final analysis basically "rentiers," people who receive income from property, but by *workers*. Workers' potential losses from unfavourable market events—plant closure, economic depression, rising interest rates, etc.—involve their basic livelihood, not just an accountant's assessment of their financial net worth. Unemployment to a family living primarily on the wages of its working members means not only an immediate decline in living standards, but increased family problems, psychological stresses, and lost prestige for its members in the community. The welfare state—especially unemployment insurance, has also other programs such as universal health care insurance—has shifted some of the economic risk facing the individual workers to the entire community. To this extent the welfare state, far from being an inefficient redistribution of income from the productive to the "lazy," actually contributes to economic efficiency.

The rhetoric of the right is to shift risk back to the individual worker: redundant workers should be fired: unemployment insurance and welfare benefits should be reduced. This is all in the name of individual responsibility and market competitiveness. But human skills are an investment; they are even called "human capital" in economists' jargon. The returns to these skills can be eliminated by events beyond the control or predictive capacity of the individual. Increasing the strength of the safety net lowers the risk of investing in "human capital" and increases the willingness of people to do so.

During the period of high unemployment in the 1980s—when the private and social opportunity costs of training were low—there developed an acute shortage of skilled workers in many sectors across the country, including my own city of Montreal. This means that either the expected return (difference between skilled and unskilled wage level) is too low or the risk in acquiring skills is too high. Human skills are fast becoming the driving element of the economy. The risk of acquiring these skills should be lowered, and the welfare state is an important means of doing so.

One further observation is that, while workers assume a good deal of market risk, they have very little role in economic decision-making. As "human capital" becomes ever more important, one can expect workers to seek an increasingly active role in economic decision-making (cf. Richards, Mauser, and Holmes, 1988). If this is achieved, and some measure of it seems inescapable, then managers—within both corporations and government—must yield a measure of their traditional managerial autonomy. Such a change would affect the nature of political institutions and, hence, the market. The desirability of such change, from the perspective of democratizing society, will be discussed below. A strong labour movement tends to strengthen a country's social programs. An increased role for labour in economic decision-making may also be desirable for reasons of efficiency. Another of McCallum and Blais's (1987) findings was that increasing unionization tends to reduce rates of economic growth, but centralizing wage bargaining damps this effect and can overcome it. In countries with centralized bargaining, policy is more apt to be formulated with meaningful input from organized labour, which in turn assumes some responsibility for policy decisions.

Here in Canada collective bargaining obviously needs an overhaul. As measured by percentage of working time lost to strikes and lockouts, Canada's strike rate has worsened relative to major OECD countries in the last two decades. We have exceeded Britain's rate and rank second only to Italy. Strikes are valuable and legitimate as organized labour's ultimate weapon, but they cannot serve as the basis for industrial relations. Strike action in industries serving the public harm, not employers and employees who would then have an incentive to bargain seriously, but third parties. Even in the private sector, where collective bargaining is an important institution, labour can only fight for a bigger share of an existing pie.

With property safety nets growth may be aided by an increase in social consensus and also by institutional reforms that serve to internalize the effects of interest group actions (McCallum and Blais, 1987, p. 15). In particular, if labour has a greater role in decisions, it will internalize more the effects of its actions—both within firms and in politics. Increased labour power will have the further beneficial effect of increasing the share of employment in secure, well-paying jobs. Such institutional changes in organized labour's role may release unions from their excessive focus on decentralized collective bargaining and encourage them to be a critical force for collective advance.

Policies that increase growth of national income tend to be accepted in a secular society (Waterman, 1983, p. 380). If they also serve to redistribute income more equally, they acquire a moral force as well. How, then, do we explain the vigour of the contemporary attack on the welfare state? In the 1960s and 1970s there was admittedly naiveté on the left about the capacity of collective processes to solve all social problems. The welfare state is one of the great accomplishments of post-war industrial society, but it cannot solve all problems, such as environmental degradation, or even eliminate all poverty. From exaggerated expectations in the welfare state many have succumbed to exaggerated scepticism. Government is an easy target for frustrated hopes, and some have now developed excessive faith in the market as an institution to solve all problems.

A PERSPECTIVE ON ECONOMIC ANALYSIS

As we social democrats confront changed circumstances, we must become psychologically more accepting of the constructive role of markets in our society and not seek solely to accentuate their destructive potential. I am not suggesting we forsake scepticism of markets or abandon our commitment to collective solutions to social problems. Civilization advances by refining its institutions, including the market. Refinement of the market may be accomplished through better combinations of both regulation *and* deregulation. As circumstances change, the appropriate scope of market transactions also changes.

If economists had truly digested the interest group theory of politics, they would be equally sceptical of proponents of the trade agreement with the United States.

Many theories of mainstream economists, though sometimes presented in an ideologically biased way, are really fairly neutral. For example, social democrats have to date rejected the theory of political "markets," according to which political outcomes depend on competition among special interest groups for favourable government policy. At best, social democrats interpret the model to mean no more than a vulgarization of the traditional socialist thesis that under capitalism property-owning interest groups (or classes) exercise overwhelming political power, that political conflict can largely be reduced to conflicts between those who do and do not own property, and that appropriate strategy is to support the current claims of the latter. While I have insisted that selfish pursuit of self-interest by special interest groups does not explain all political action, it can hardly be disputed that such self-interested activity occurs—or that special interest groups allied to social democratic parties are themselves actively engaged in such behaviour.

The criticism I make of my profession is not of the theory of political markets, but of its selective application. To the extent economists saw the 1988 trade debate in interest group terms, for example, they criticized the opponents as a collection of special interest groups seeking to preserve tariffs and other market impediments that redistribute income from the Canadian consumer to themselves. If economists had truly digested the interest group theory of politics, they would be equally sceptical of proponents of the trade agreement with the United States. The managed trade arising from the "free trade" agreement simultaneously requires continual interpretation by binational regulatory agencies and limits the scope for Parliament to govern. Such a change is in the interest of major business lobbies desirous of lessening popular constraints on their actions.

I use this example to urge upon social democrats a tolerance of mainstream economics; its new developments are not ideological sophistry. This does not mean we accept the uses made of the market by particular powerful interests. But it does mean we accept the market as a legitimate constraint on the scope of politics and the size of the public sector relative to GNP.

SOME VIEWS ON POLICY

◆ ◆ ◆

If we accept the market as a legitimate, potentially useful political institution in our society, that has implications. For example, just as uncritical advocacy of market (including contracting) solutions to all social issues will be rejected, so too, will uncritical reliance on political (collective) solutions. Acceptance of an inevitable individual-collective tension implies abandonment of ideological positions; we must justify any particular public policy through careful thought and argument.

What does this mean in practical terms? There can be no progress if defence of the welfare state is the only *raison d'être* of a social democratic party. It becomes quite literally a conservative force in a period of great technological and social change. It does our society little service for social democrats to stand in the way of all technological change. To the extent we succeed in blocking change, the change will simply occur in other countries, leaving Canadians with obsolete high-cost production processes and lower living standards that can only be preserved by recourse to ever-increasing protection. Social democrats have the obligation to propose policy to manage change.

A first principle for any social democratic government is that the costs of innovation not be borne by particular groups of workers whose skills are rendered obsolete by technological change and who are thrown out of work. It must be widely accepted that such costs are to be borne by society as a whole, in other words, by those who gain the benefits through better goods and services at lower prices or through new jobs elsewhere in the economy. Were this principle fully accepted—and among most economists it is a subject for the appendix to the treatise on gains from free trade—unions would not automatically resist technological change as equivalent to job loss. It is a principle that enhances both the efficiency of the economy and the dignity of workers.

Such a principle may ultimately be endorsed even by the present governing party. The sharp and broadly based dislocations that the Canada-U.S. trade agreement will bring, to some sectors at least, may force even the Conservatives to come to grips with this problem. Social democrats must go further than this first principle. A second principle is a greater degree of worker involvement in the decision-making of their own firms. We cannot foresee the future, but this surely is the most obvious way in which individuals can attain a greater degree of control over their lives. It promotes democracy in the broadest sense of popular participation in the making of decision. Richards *et al.* (1988) found that the majority of workers wanted greater control over their own working environments, especially over decisions affecting them directly, such as scheduling of work and holidays. These findings, as the authors point out, are not definitive, but they are in agreement with any social democrat's institution. The idea of worker input will advance slowly—in the thinking of social democrats as well as that of conservatives—and at this personal level the process may make its most significant start.

In the promotion of democracy at the workplace, a social democratic government could aim for 25–30 per cent worker representation on "mundane" decision-making bodies; the percentage and scope of workers-influenced decisions could then possibly increase over time. Nonetheless, a quarter is a sufficiently significant minority position for collective worker actions to place limits on the vagaries of marketplace forces; it would be consonant with promoting the dignity of the individual and the benefit of society as a whole. Presumably worker representatives on such bodies would remain part of the work force; worker participation in management should not become a paternalistic method of individual career advancement.

While collective bargaining is a valuable institution that has in the past advanced democracy at work, further advances require that unions go beyond it. Union leaders must show an enlightened concern for broad social issues, which, I suspect, occupy them less now than in the beginnings of industrial unionism. For union leaders to interest themselves in broad issues of policy requires no great theoretical leaps; it would be a worthwhile, achievable goal.

Technological change is one field needing practical social democratic policy; another is government regulation of business. What should be our responses to the deregulation debate? Consider four industries: telecommunications, airlines, electrical utilities, and trucking.

It is simply not acceptable that deregulation and recourse to market forces raise the price of basic telephone service to the point of a significant reduction in the percentage of telephone subscribers in any community. Telephone service has strong implications for social cohesiveness and individual ability to interact with others in the society. By the same token, uncritical defence of regulatory imposition of "flat rates" for local service is not defensible. Such a policy amounts to subsidy by those who need a telephone of those who, for example, use local telecommunication facilities for data transmission or telephone solicitation. Social goals may be best protected in this case by approximate social costs.

Airline fare deregulation also has been very controversial on the left. There are now many people with very price-sensitive demand for airline services, whereas there were not in the early days of air travel when financial viability of commercial airlines was uncertain in the face of thin demand. As the industry matured, over-regulation led to higher-than-necessary average fares, and underutilization of capacity. There is little public policy justification to support regulation that limits the travel options of a price-sensitive public in order to provide empty seats on which businessmen may spread their newspapers. None of this eliminates the justification for regulation of safety standards.

Uniform pricing of electricity at all hours of the day leads to substantial inefficiencies. Particularly in hydro-electrical systems, the fixed capital costs (dams, generators, distribution grids) far exceed the operating costs that vary with electrical consumption. The cost of providing for growing peak demand includes both the capacity and operating costs; the cost of off-peak demand is operating costs only. Uniform pricing encourages wasteful peak demand, discourages use at off-peak hours, and requires investment by provincial utilities in capital-intensive capacity that need not be installed. Canadian electrical utilities are typically Crown corporations and hence public investment is being diverted from more socially constructive uses such as health and education toward hydroelectric dams. Yet, proposals for regulatory reform to adopt marginal cost time-of-day pricing are met with distrust on the part of social democrats.

On the other hand, some industries could be rendered more efficient by more regulation. Abouchar (1987) argues that heavy trucks cause far more damage to highways than their fuel and other taxes cover, not to mention their contribution to such externalities as congestion, air pollution, and traffic accidents. In this case, increased regulation and taxation could induce some transport to be diverted from truck to train and could contribute to an improved transportation system. The issues are complex: other regulations, such as those preventing back-hauling by trucks, clearly do not contribute to an efficient system.

In summary, as technological and social conditions change, so too, must regulation. This conclusion follows from the public policy purpose of regulation—which is to protect the social good and individual dignity. A refusal to allow for reform, like a refusal to allow for regulation, must eventually be inimical to these goals.

A third institution needing attention by social democrats is the Crown corporation. I do not automatically advocate the establishment of new Crown corporations, or the maintenance of existing Crown corporations, or the privatization of them, except on reasoned public policy grounds. There are many reasons for establishing Crown corporations, but they do not imply the abandonment of markets. In Canada we have a tradition of Crown corporations competing in markets with private enterprises. Each form of organization has advantages and disadvantages, and competition between forms has had generally beneficial results. There is no reason not to extend this competition further. Competing Crown corporations could be set up in the same industry but report to different ministers or even to different levels of government. The discipline of market forces could be an important means to make these corporations more accountable to government.

Beyond this, I think it is worth re-emphasizing that institutions should be developed so that labour has a role in decision-making. Decisions cannot be left to management and shareholders whose risk is frequently minimal. We cannot tolerate markets in which workers can be made "redundant" by technological change and simply jettisoned—as Canada Post has repeatedly tried to do. This means more than social safety nets, even

though these must remain strong and safe from political attack. On the other hand, work incentives also need to be retained. And there must be a greater acceptance of change—with democratic participation in business decisions.

All this requires flexibility. And flexibility means a scepticism toward bureaucratic modes of thought. Regulation and publicly owned firms have many virtues, but they should be recognized as being most useful in periods of stability. In periods of rapid technological and social change, looser forms of social control must be accepted. This looser control, however, should include internal workers participation in management decisions. Indeed, if such participation can be achieved, then such currently popular regulations (in social democratic circles) as laws restricting plant closures may be counter-productive. If labour participates effectively in major corporate decisions regarding the opening of new plants and the closing of old ones, then such decisions will only be made where workers losing jobs are adequately compensated. The economy will be able to divest redundant inefficient industries with less (and internalized) dislocation. Supporting redundant industry ceases to be a drain on funds destined to finance social safety nets and ceases to impair the growth of other industry. For example, Canada Post, an arm of government, and its unions have an opportunity to formulate new approaches to worker displacement arising from technological change. It is a failure of the government *and* of the institution of collective bargaining that Crown corporations are not generating experiments in dealing with this problem.

Canadian society needs flexibility, economic agility, security of "human capital," and imaginative government. Although the market provides a constraint to our advancing collective ties, we need to find ways to help markets work better. Maturity of social democratic thought requires that we learn to live with the tension between market and state, not seek to eliminate it.

Notes

1. The estimated optimum ratio of transfer payments to GNP is about one-sixth. This result is of some curiosity value, because it is close to the current median of the seventeen countries examined. But one hesitates to quote the particular value with too great faith: confidence limits are fairly wide.

References

Aboucher, A. (1987). Presentation to Canadian Economic Theory Conference, Montreal (June).

Armstrong, C., and V. Nelles (1986). *Monopoly's Moment*. Philadelphia: Temple University Press.

Buchanan, J. (1987). "The Constitution of Economic Policy," *American Economic Review*, LXXVII, 3 (June), pp. 243–250.

McCallum, J., and A. Blais (1987). "Government, Special Interest Groups and Economic Growth," *Public Choice*, 54, pp. 3–18.

Myrhman, J. (1985). "Introduction: Reflections on the Growth of Government," *Journal of Public Economics*, 28, pp. 275–85.

Newman, P.C. (1975). *The Canadian Establishment*, Vol. I. Toronto: McClelland and Stewart.

North, D.C. (1985). "The Growth of Government in the United States: An Economic Historian's Perspective," *Journal of Public Economics*, 28, pp. 383–99.

Richards, J.G., G. Mauser, and R. Holmes (1988). "What do Workers Want? Attitudes Toward Collective Bargaining and Participation in Management," *Relations Industrielles*, XLIV, 1, pp. 133–52.

Waterman, A.C. (1983). "The Catholic Bishops and Canadian Public Policy," *Canadian Public Policy*, IX, 3 (September), pp. 374–82.

Winn, C. (1985). "Affirmative Action and Visible Minorities: Eight Premises in Quest of Evidence," *Canadian Public Policy*, XI, 4 (December), pp. 684–700.

Terms & Concepts

accountability
capitalism
collective compassion
collective interests
Crown corporations
deregulation
efficiency

equity
interest groups
labour relations
managed trade
markets
"minimal state"
neoconservatism

political market
public choice theory
regulation
social consensus
social democracy
welfare state
workplace democracy

Questions

1. It is generally assumed that investors bear the greatest risks in a capitalist economy? Cairns disagrees and would argue that you as students, for example, bear greater risks. Do you agree?

2. Cairns accuses the state, which he calls "the collective mechanism," of sometimes undermining the collective interest. How, according to him, does this happen?

3. What, if any, is the difference between the collective interest defended by Cairns and the popular interest defended by the populist (see Unit Two, Article 7)?

4. What, if any, effect does a free trade agreement like the Canada-U.S. (FTA) have on the state's ability to be the collective mechanism?

5. Cairns claims that the market is ultimately a political institution defined by political regulation. What necessary (and unnecessary) government regulation goes into your grocery shopping?

7

Mad as Hell: Reflections on Canadian Populism

Thomas M.J. Bateman, Manuel Mertin, and David M. Thomas

Editors' Note

A spectre is haunting European and North America politicians — the spectre of populism. In virtually every western democracy grassroots populist movements have sprung up in reaction to the difficulties faced by post-modern democracies. A spate of books and articles (some of which are listed in the bibliography at the end of this unit), have recently appeared on the topic. The Reform Party, Canada's most prominent contemporary populist party, was catapulted from one seat in the federal election of 1988 to within two seats of official opposition status in the 1993 election. In the United States, Ross Perot came from nowhere to garner 19% of the popular vote in the 1992 election. Populists are challenging governments not just on specific policy issues but also on some of our most widely and deeply held political values: the very character of representative democracy is at issue.

In an essay written specifically for this volume, Bateman, Mertin, and Thomas peel back the various layers of Reform-style populism only to discover that, beneath the glossy veneer of a more direct democracy, the creed is rife with ideological faultlines. Representative democracy has two prominent rationales: to overcome the difficulties in governing a mass society in a large country, and to protect the polity from degenerating into a tyranny of the majority. The reader finds out that populists only emphasize the first of these rationales. Besides being an analysis of populist institutional and policy prescriptions, the paper also investigates the type of conditions that generally give rise to populism and discovers that the present atmosphere of uncertainty and unease is an ideal breeding ground.

It is doubtful, though, at least from the authors' perspective, that populism will re-invigorate the democratic state after the sapping experiences of globalization, interdependence, supranational control, and internal disaggregation. One reason lies in the nature of movement parties themselves. Since they respond to popular issues, populist parties find it difficult to be ideologically coherent, a point recently made by former Reform policy adviser and political scientist Tom Flanagan.[1] Their agenda is thus likely to

---

1. Tom Flanagan, *Waiting for the Wave* (Toronto: Stoddart, 1995).

be highjacked by any major parties whose ideological position happens to mirror public opinion on the issues of the year, or by parties pragmatic enough to graft popular positions onto such issues to their existing programs.

Finally, these parties do not fit well into the parliamentary mould. The "us the people" versus "them the political establishment" attitude of populists becomes problematic when they enter parliaments or legislatures in significant numbers, or when they win an election. Populist legislators tend to become part of the political establishment and the system, if not their ambition, makes the maintenance of close links to "the people" difficult. If they do stay true to their populist roots, they will be ineffective in a system playing by different rules. In either scenario, disappointment among the followers seems inevitable. After a dizzying ride, even the best wave deposits the surfer near the shore.

◆ ◆ ◆

Canadians are angry. They see taxes going up, services going down, and public debt still increasing. They distrust politics and politicians, and deeply resent overt patronage at a time when all are told of the need to make sacrifices. Concerns over immigration, nothing new in themselves, are linked to questions about job loss, welfare fraud, crime, and the erosion of Canadian social values: many people want a melting pot, not a mosaic. Special interest groups are seen as manipulating the political and legal system and as thwarting the "common sense of the common people." Elites are no longer deferred to and there is a growing demand for accountability. The welfare state itself is regarded as a liability and not as a benefactor. And, increasingly, nationalist sentiment outside Quebec takes the form of resistance to Quebec's demands and defense of provincial equality and the constitutional status quo.

Many of these concerns are not new, but some are, and the resulting *mix* of sentiments and policy proposals has become a powerful factor in Canadian political life at a time when other forces are also pressing in upon a beleaguered federal state. Populism is back!

Canada has been closer to the European welfare-state model than to the American version. Health care policies are a clear example of this. It should not, therefore, be a surprise to find that reactions of European citizens to globalization and the overloaded state are similar to the reactions of many Canadians even though local and regional political cultures differ greatly.[1] One such reaction is often given the name "populism," and populist parties and leaders have emerged in virtually every western democracy: Perot in the United States, Le Pen in France, Bossi and Berlusconi in Italy, and Manning in Canada. Merely listing these names immediately illustrates a serious problem: the term "populism" is used by academics to describe a phenomenon that seems to exhibit certain similarities of outlook and behaviour, but it is not the term necessarily used by those individuals described in this manner to refer to themselves. (And although members of the Reform Party, including the leader, often do call themselves populists, they would not agree that a Preston Manning has anything in common with a "fascist bully-boy" like Le Pen.)[2] The term might, therefore, be seen as pejorative, and at the very least, it remains rather general for it "can refer to a particular political style, a particular method of political organization, an organization of particular social groups, a particular political program, or some combination of these elements."[3] Contemporary populism has been defined by Peter McCormick

as being as much a mood as a systematic philosophy. It is built on a number of factors: a common-sense celebration of the average citizen, a preference for direct democracy devices, (recall, referendum, initiative) to allow direct ongoing influence by the electors, an identification with small-scale business capitalism (family farms and small business), a tendency to blame outside forces (sometimes sinister in nature) for economic and social problems and to see solutions in simple or even simplistic terms (such as recurrent conspiracy theories), a strong feeling of community and traditional values that borders on xenophobia, a project of reform rather than revolution to solve economic and social ills, and a distrust of parties leading to a preference for non-partisanship that usually co-exists with strong support for a dominant leader.[4]

But even if a precise definition is elusive, it is still our contention that populist parties are worthy of close

Article prepared for this publication (1995).

study *especially at a time of rapid change*, that populism as a cluster of related ideas about politics *has mutated* and is now a full-fledged attack on the welfare state and the ways in which it is run, and that populist assumptions are *deeply paradoxical*, particularly in that populism contains a strong "anti political" element even as it advocates political action and reform. At the moment populist parties are clearly right wing in orientation, but it must be noted that the populism of the past took both left as well as right-wing forms. There were always those who believed in the need for collective action, for cooperative effort, and for strong measures to reduce social inequality. Western Canadian populism was never simply an agrarian revolt and always had a strong urban base.[5] Thus, even though present-day populism in Canada and Europe stresses the need to downsize the state, to recreate opportunities for small-business capitalism, to use technology to revitalize and reform democracy, to allow people to suffer the full consequences of their own actions, and to return power to the people by taking it away from elites and special interest groups, this does not preclude the possibility that there could arise a radical populism of the left, unlikely though this may now seem.[6] Bankers, militarists, and business tycoons are not yet back on the populist hit list, but as globalization and government restraint proceed apace, they could displace immigrants, bureaucrats, unions, special interest groups, and mainstream politicians as the new enemy.

To understand populism's appeal we will discuss its links to political culture and the economic environment, to democratic theory, to policy proposals, and to institutional reform. This is followed by a summary of some of the more important contradictions raised by a populist outlook, for it is such anomalies that reveal the difficulties as well as the promise of populist claims. Canadian examples are emphasized as these will be more familiar to readers, but the context for this discussion is one that is truly international.

POPULISM AND ITS ENVIRONMENT

◆ ◆ ◆

Populism in the past has been a response to economic uncertainty and crisis. American and western Canadian populism during the early 1920s was rooted in, although not limited to, an agricultural sector reeling from a post-war recession. Likewise, both left and right-wing populism in western Canada during the 1930s occurred during a Great Depression aggravated by pests and drought. During both these periods many suffered a calamitous erosion in their economic condition. All suffered from a loss of control over their lives, and judging by other occurrences of populism, its appearance may also be a response to anticipated or actual change for the

---

Populism has also found roots in western Canada...even during economic boom times.

---

worse in noneconomic terms. For example, racist populists during the late 19th century in the southern United States feared the changes that the emancipation of blacks was going to bring about for whites. Similarly, racist populists in France, Germany, and even Canada fear the impact of increasing non-European immigration on what they see as a heretofore racially homogenous population. Populism has also found roots in western Canada in the context of regional isolation and alienation, even during economic boom times. Of course racist backlashes to immigration and regional isolation cannot be entirely divorced from economic uncertainty, but it would be an oversimplification to submerge them in the economic theme. The most revealing common denominator is a reaction to actual or anticipated deterioration in the quality of life of a significant portion of the population, accompanied by a profound distrust of the elites deemed responsible. Feelings of uncertainty, powerlessness, and loss of control are crucial by-products. In such conditions populism is one possible political response, the rise of a charismatic leader another and, of course, both may coincide.

What sort of changes or anticipated changes are then at the root of populism in industrialized countries such as Canada? Since World War II, Canadians had been living in a period of unprecedented prosperity. Growth was taken for granted, and with it a real and continuous increase in the standard of living. Government intervention in the economy kept recessions and unemployment at minimal levels. The expanding economy and tax base ensured the affordability of extensive social programs.

The first serious signs that all was not well appeared during the 1970s. Two oil crises within six years had a profound impact in all countries. In the western world they produced simultaneous stagnation and inflation (stagflation) that the conventional economic levers at the disposal of governments could not control. Other, more gradual developments compounded the loss of state control: international trade increased and barriers to it were gradually dismantled; national economies became more specialized and interdependent; international trade aided by instant communication moved larger proportions of financial transactions from the national to the international level; interest and exchange rates became determined by international money markets; the shift into a post-industrial, service-based economy created structural unemployment that taxed the welfare state even during economic upturns, never mind during recessions when cyclical unemployment was added. Huge, chronic, government deficits were the result in many countries, especially Canada, despite increased taxes. All these factors spell instability, uncertainty, and loss of control for citizens and governments.

In Canada, non-European immigration is changing the cultural composition of society more than ever. Constitutional reform has allowed a variety of groups to push for particular constitutional rights or protection, which, if one views rights as a zero-sum game, may diminish the rights of the majority. Special interest groups are accused of imposing a "tyranny of minorities over democratic majorities."[7] In addition, some of the old regional grievances in western Canada have not been satisfactorily addressed. There remains a popular feeling that the West is not effectively enough represented in the federal government, thus, it either suffers economically or cannot fully realize its economic potential. Meanwhile Quebec, in particular, is seen as being coddled, overrepresented, and as using the threat of separation to extort economic gains from Ottawa. These feelings, while not new, are most likely to resurface when economic times are difficult and citizens are trying to find explanations for the decline.

The resurgence of populism should not, therefore, come as a surprise, and given the circumstances, neither should its particular agenda. What does need explanation, however, is the composition of the populist following. There can be little doubt that the Reform Party is the largest populist organization in Canada, both in the way in which it sees itself[8] and, as we shall see later, in terms of its policies. A recent survey of Reform Party activists conducted at the 1992 party convention showed that 38% of the delegates were 60 years of age or older. Less than 5% were under 30.[9] For comparison, among NDP delegates less than 19% were 60 years or older, and among Progressive Conservative delegates more than 40% were under 30.[10] Analysis of the 1993 federal election confirms the strong support for Reform among older voters. But this is not the only notable feature about the Reform following. Richard Sigurdson

observes that the Reform Party encompasses two theoretical strains, which he calls "postmodern antimodernism" and "postmodern hypermodernism." The former seeks to provide a sense of security, including security of identity, and opposes the new values and lifestyles of contemporary society. Thus besides worrying about economic insecurity, the antimodernists worry about immigration, multiculturalism, and alternative lifestyles. Manning's attacks on "humanism" or "secular fundamentalism" and his own emphasis on Christianity may also appeal.[11] Although Sigurdson does not make this linkage, it would make sense for this antimodernism to appeal particularly to the older followers.

Hypermodernism, on the other hand, actually embraces many of the recent cultural and economic changes. The shift to service industries together with modern communications technology is seen to increase the feasibility of self-reliance and increased, more direct political participation.[12] This strain is aimed at a segment of this new service class, "its knowledge-based, technologically oriented, entrepreneurial element."[13] Indeed, delegate characteristics seem to show that the Reform Party has been successful with this segment. While the largest single professional category among delegates were retirees (25%), business owners, self-employed professionals, and professional employees collectively constituted 47% of delegates.[14]

Of course, many of the Reform Party policy prescriptions to cure Canada's perceived ailments would be held in common by both hypermodern and antimodern groups. It is the ability of the Reform Party to hold together these retired and modern professional segments that makes this particular populist organization powerful, buttressed by members' belief that they are a far more democratic, grass-roots, organization than their political rivals. Democracy, however, is a slippery concept, and populists have a particular understanding of it.

POPULISM AND DEMOCRACY

◆ ◆ ◆

Democracy can be understood, first, as a set of political norms and ideals and, second, as a set of institutional arrangements that give some concrete form and expression to those norms. The norms are engrained in modern political consciousness: fundamental human equality, individual freedom as an essential human need and attribute, political self-government as a bulwark against arbitrary power and exploitation, and the consequent reconciliation of the individual person and the community through shared responsibility for one's life and that of the community. The institutional consequences involve mechanisms facilitating citizen consent to government, checks on the exercise of political power and, usually, some means of maintaining or attaining a modicum of economic equality on the basis of which personal and political self- government can be exercised.

Populists speak the language of democracy. They draw on the powerful moral content of the democratic ideal and use it as an indictment of current democratic practice. For populism, the core of democracy is the sovereignty of the people, concretely reflected in the will of the majority. The majority is the vessel of common sense, simple virtues, and true national character. The true compass of democratic politics, says Reform Party leader Preston Manning, is "the common sense of the common people." We need only the mechanisms to discern it.

Populists consider the problem of democracy to be that its ideals have been honoured more in the breach rather than in the observance. Consequently, the populist democratic mission is to revitalize democracy—to close the gap between theory and practice—by advocating a host of institutional reforms that would *restore* power to the people. The rhetoric of restoration is key because it allows populists to project themselves at once as both conservative and reformist.

What is the nature of the democratic malaise that populism seeks to remedy? Criticisms are directed, first, at the parliamentary system. In Canada, populists argue that parliamentary democracy dangerously concentrates power in the executive branch of government and, particularly, in the hands of the prime minister. Government is a series of "four-year dictatorships"; between elections, the government is unreachable, unresponsive, and uncaring. The election of constituency-based representatives to Parliament is of no help. Party discipline is so strictly enforced by party whips that MPs, once elected, vote as they are told by party elites regardless of the wishes of the constituents. Instead of representing the people to the government, Canadian MPs represent Ottawa and the party to the people.

Second, criticisms are directed at the "political class" in general. This seemingly amorphous group constitutes a quasi-conspiratorial cadre composed of politicians, political party functionaries, bureaucrats, "special interest group" leaders, media elites, academics, and other hangers-on who pretend to be in mutual contention but who are really birds of a feather. They all feed, say the populists, on government largesse and either hold the people in contempt or are indifferent to

their concerns. In Canada the political class is regionally concentrated in the populous provinces of Ontario and Quebec—or, according to Alberta MP David Kilgour, in the Toronto-Ottawa-Montreal corridor—and so populists rail against the political class not only for its elitism but also for its regional insensitivity.

Third, populists imbibe the general dissatisfaction with the welfare state, alleging that its very size and complexity gives the lie to democratic accountability. Welfare programs, say the populists, are the product of special interest group lobbying; they create dependency among client groups; accordingly, they fail to achieve their stated objectives. They are far too expensive for taxpayers to support, but because of bureaucratic inertia they are difficult to reform or remove once implemented.

Hence, democratic revival includes the simultaneous reform of the democratic political process and welfarist public policies. Indeed, populists are confident that once the will of the people is expressed, the bloated welfare

---

It is the people versus the political class...

---

state will be its target. This is an important rhetorical point. Populism provides a strategy by which criticisms of the so-called social safety net can be cast in terms of the reform of the democratic political system. Neoconservative economic and social policies thus blend nicely with the populist critique of democratic institutional arrangements. Hence, populism is now attractive to groups and interests that one would not normally consider populist and that were once the enemies rather than allies of earlier populist movements.[15]

These three criticisms can be summarized in the following way: democracy is the will of the people governing the affairs of the country; democracy has been hijacked by a collection of elites who have more in common with each other than with the people in whose name they purport to act; and finally, democracy suffers from the "tyranny of minorities."[16] It is the people versus the political class, "us" versus "them." Power must be restored to the people.

This populist critique is a sanguine departure from a more circumspect tradition of democratic thought that sees dangers as well as virtues in democratic government. The founders of the American republic argued that the governed had to be controlled as carefully as the government. Simply put, tyranny is the principal problem of government and while democracy is a remedy for the tyranny of the one or the few, it is also the recipe for the "tyranny of the majority." In *The Federalist Papers*, James Madison argued that every political community is vulnerable to "faction," defined as "a number of citizens, whether amounting to a majority or minority of the whole, who are united and actuated by some common impulse of passion or of interest, adverse to the rights of other citizens, or to the permanent and aggregate interests of the community."[17]

Madison's factions are what we would now call special interest groups and he distrusted them as much as do contemporary populists. But the key for him is that the majority can behave as a faction as easily as any minority. "Pure democracy" is simply the vehicle for tyranny of the majority. Later writers expressed concern about the moral authority majority opinion was to develop. According to Alexis de Tocqueville, the French aristocrat who wrote a magisterial study of American democracy in the 1830s, the majority "possesses a power that is physical and moral at the same time, which acts upon the will as much as upon the actions and represses not only all contest but all controversy."[18]

Liberal democrats sought to limit (without destroying) democratic power through a series of institutional contrivances. One was the idea of representation, whereby the people would elect officials to rule them on their own behalf. The hope was that representatives would be public-spirited agents who would "refine and enlarge the public views" and protect the people from their worst tendencies.[19] Representation was elitist by design. British philosopher and parliamentarian Edmund Burke proposed a theory of representation as trusteeship that, he hoped, would achieve the same end.

Another contrivance was federalism, the creation of two levels of government operating over the same electorate, each level possessing constitutionally specified powers and able to resist the incursions of the other. Further, checks and balances were created *within* the structure of government to enable public officials to resist the ambitions of their colleagues. These measures were counter-majoritarian to be sure, but nonetheless democratic at the same time.

Tocqueville noticed the despotic tendencies in democratic government. The despot, he argued, thrives on the indifference of his subjects. If people care neither about their government nor about their fellows, they don't have the power nor inclination to unseat the despot. In democracy, conditions of equality also produce indifference: "Equality places men side by side, unconnected by any common tie...."[20] The isolated individual is weak,

puny, and impotent. This democratic antipolitics must be countered, Tocqueville warned. People need to be drawn outside of themselves to see the condition of their fellows, to unite with them in common purposes.

The contrivance to produce such fellow feeling is civil and political association, the voluntary union of like-minded people in the pursuit of a common purpose, often referred to as "civil society." This association enlarges the heart and gradually brings the democratic citizen into the public square, where he or she must be if democratic life is to survive. In other words, democratic life is not just a matter of individuals aggregated into decision-making units of majorities and minorities; it is a complex web of relationships and intermediate institutions between the otherwise isolated individual and the machinery of government. Among such intermediate institutions one can count the family, religious organizations, organized volunteer associations, and trade and professional groups. They are a buffer between the individual and the concentrated power of the state. They are also a means of linking the citizen to the political community.

The long tradition of counter-majoritarianism in democratic thought is thus frontally assaulted by populists. Populists wonder why the majority is something to be feared. Indeed, strident populists allege that "in a democracy, the people are never wrong."[21] Crucial assumptions are made by populists about "the people": that it is a homogeneous, singular entity, that its voice is audible, and that its will is pure. These are precisely the assumptions about which political thinkers for the past several centuries have been circumspect.

POPULISM AND PUBLIC POLICY
◆ ◆ ◆

Older Canadian populist movements characterized the anti-democratic special interests as distant political elites in conspiracy with the captains of big business and finance—the "Fifty Big Shots" was Alberta Premier William Aberhart's famous phrase. Hence, populism had a radical, left-wing flavour and usually implied some role for government in countering the destructive influence of big business. Contemporary populism targets government and the political class but is largely silent about business. The only concern is that business becomes a special interest when it lines up for handouts in the form of subsidies and tax concessions from government. Otherwise the market is the central organizing principle of populist public policy reform. Free the market, the prescription goes, and wealth, growth, employment, and prosperity will follow. This is the core of the populist Reform Party's "hyper-modernist neo-conservative economic agenda."[22]

Populist anti-elitism is expressed in distrust for government solutions to social problems. In fact, government is really the cause of many problems rather than simply an inadequate cure for them. The welfare state experiment, say contemporary populists, is a failure and the social safety net must drastically be cut back so that people will rely on their own, their families', and their communities' resources rather than government. This will simultaneously simplify the work of government and revivify nongovernment social institutions.

Not only does the welfare state produce unintended consequences, it is also too expensive. Politicians and bureaucrats have vested interests in "bribing the people with their own money" at election time by promising expensive social programs. These become burdens on present and future generations, forcing governments to tax wantonly and borrow money to finance the people's heightened expectations. Government borrowing becomes "taxation without representation": future generations will be saddled with the cost of today's profligacy. And government spending is always less efficient than market allocations of resources. Populists thus place government debt reduction high on the list of policy priorities. Related to these prescriptions are proposals for the elimination of all manner of subsidies and grants for regional development, the arts, and funding of special interest groups — political incest in its purest form.

Slightly more controversial among populists is support for free trade, interprovincially and internationally. The Reform Party of Canada supports both in principle but its members appear to be more ambivalent.[23] The reasons for this ambivalence are unclear but perhaps have something to do with threats to political sovereignty, worries about international finance, and the loss of traditional jobs attendant upon globalizing trade and production. Hence, free trade may be a point of friction in the odd coalition of post-modern antimodernists and post-modern hyper-modernists in the Reform Party camp.

The populist affirmation of the colour-blind equality of individual Canadians flows from populist anti-elitism. In Canada, populists resoundingly oppose any policy appearing to cater to Quebec, the largest "special interest group" in the country. Thus official bilingualism founded on the personality principle[24] is an anathema to populists, as is the constitutional idea of recognition of

Quebec as a distinct society within Canada. Other preferential policies like multiculturalism and affirmative action are also targets for populist ire.

Because of populism's kinship with nativism and even xenophobia, immigration has become a sensitive issue in North America and Europe.[25] The 1990 platform of the Reform Party of Canada opposed any immigration policy "designed to radically or suddenly alter the ethnic makeup of Canada."[26] Critics detected a thinly veiled racism. The policy was subsequently modified to concentrate on the economic and social consequences of too high a number of immigrants entering Canada each year.

A final policy area in which populism has claimed the moral high ground is criminal justice policy. Populists trace crime to the breakdown of social institutions like the family and to a permissiveness in the treatment of offenders. Populists assert a simple theory of moral agency and rational calculation: criminals deserve to be punished and stiff punishment will deter prospective offenders. The democratic deceit is that polls report that the people consistently support capital punishment but the political class systematically ignores them. Let the people speak, say the populists.

Populist positions on public policy are not straightforward or settled. Sometimes populists assert the relentless logic of individualism and the market in their policy proposals, and sometimes they assert the value of communities and the moral order against it. Sometimes they are willing to defer to the judgment of the people, as in capital punishment, but sometimes are more ambivalent, as on the question of access to abortion and euthanasia. Sometimes populist policies bear the taint of racism and bigotry, but sometimes they trumpet the principle of colour-blind individual equality before the law. This is the dialectic of symbol and substance at the heart of the populist mind and indeed of all political debate.

POPULISM AND INSTITUTIONAL REFORM

◆ ◆ ◆

Populists are known for more than their assertion of the common sense of the average person or wisdom of democratic majorities. They have also been at the forefront of calls for the reform of political institutions, especially in North America. Indeed, in the early parts of this century, populists attempted some of the most radical reforms of democracy yet seen — from the attempt by the United Farmers of Alberta in the 1920s to eliminate political parties to the institution of a nonpartisan unelected committee of "experts" charged with implementing the electoral will of Alberta voters in the 1930s.

The reformist populist impulse continues, now augmented by an anger at the political system borne of a decline in political deference and the frustration of unmet high expectation.[27] Many populist reform ideas are now shared by a great many others who would not describe themselves as populists. What distinguishes this populist institutional reform agenda is the particular aggregation of reform items as well as the rhetorical spin offered as justification for them.

Chief among targets for populist reform is the parliamentary system of government. Here populists combine with others in the call for relaxation of party discipline so that MPs can be freed from the dictates of their parties and vote the wills of their constituents. In case the newly freed MPs fail to act as delegates of the constituents, their electors should have recourse to a recall mechanism whereby elected representatives can be fired mid-term by their constituents.[28] Lest elected officials feel too comfortable once in office, populists call for the slashing of salaries, perquisites and benefits, as well as for the limitation of electoral terms. In addition, discretionary powers of the head of government, such as the timing of election calls, legislative sittings, and budget pronouncements, as well as the making of executive appointments, should be removed. While MPs are to be *freed* from party discipline, they are to be more closely *tied* to the will of constituents.

Implicit in the calls for parliamentary reform is a critique of party politics. Populist sentiment ranges from utter disdain for parties to a concern to democratize them. Certainly the parliamentary wings of parties are to be clipped. Aside from the above limitations on the party leadership, populists call for greater caucus control of the executive branch. Since leadership is often considered the quintessence of elitism, reformers target party leadership selection processes for change. Traditionally, parties held leadership conventions to which each constituency association would send delegates usually selected on the basis of the candidate of their choice. As much as a third of convention delegates were party functionaries of one kind or another who were not selected by party members. Such processes are now routinely criticized as elitist.

Here populism has happily converged both with developments in communications technology and crises in mainstream party memberships to prompt the direct election of party leaders. Direct election processes have been used sporadically in the last 12 years in Canada but they are increasingly becoming the norm. Even the federal Liberal Party will hold its next leadership selection by direct membership ballot. The "televoting" process is now in use by different parties in many provinces; in 1994 it was used for the election of the Alberta Liberal leader (and a technological debacle resulted). Of the 1992 Nova Scotia Liberal Party leadership selection, one observer reported: "It afforded all members of the party the possibility of participating in the choice of leader without leaving their living rooms."[29]

In addition to leadership selection, populists seek to harness technology for MP/MLA constituency consultations. "Electronic town hall meetings" are an attempt to recreate the intimate, deliberative atmosphere of a local meeting while surmounting the limitations of geography and the segmented, hurried lives of modern citizens. In the spring of 1994 the Reform Party experimented with such an event on the subject of euthanasia in Preston Manning's Calgary South West riding. This is a format that has since been repeated. Typically, a television audience containing articulate activists representing both sides of the issue banters with a panel of "experts" while poll results are reported from television viewers. These responses to questions are compared with studio audience results and, in the case of the euthanasia electronic town hall, with the results of a scientific survey, conducted earlier, of a sample of a larger population on the same questions. If the purpose of an electronic town hall is to educate the participants in the discussion and facilitate the exercise of democratic deliberation, one has to wonder about some of the features of these events. Reporting the results of a survey held *before* the meeting, for example, serves neither function. If the event is staged by one party, and its MPs speak to the issues, it is difficult to differentiate grassroots democracy from a party forum. Since the event needs to be staged for television broadcast, it has to be managed to a much greater degree than a real town hall meeting. Certainly, the participation of those watching at home is limited and passive. Spontaneity is undermined by staging and electronic circuit capacities. All this invites manipulation by the partisan organizers, who decide which issues they want to raise in these meetings and then do so without neutral mediators. Finally, the role of MPs becomes dubious. Are they to be bound by the decisions made by the participants, which would relegate them to a delegate role completely inconsistent with our form of parliamentary government, or are these town halls a nonbinding consultative process inconsistent with principles of grassroots democracy? While real town hall meetings may work for small communities (but even in ancient Athens they often became the forum of dema-gogues and made some tyrannical decisions), the elec-tronic variant differs in enough ways from the genuine town hall version to make its democratic value highly suspect.

Canadian populism is primarily a western regional phenomenon and so has blended with a long tradition of regional discontent.[30] The we/they populist orientation is well suited to the discourse of western alienation. Accordingly, Canadian populism is intertwined with the eternal Canadian debate about federalism. But the issues are complex, and the inner tensions and contradictions of populism are clearly apparent here. On the one hand, populism's emphasis on "the people" has universalist, centralist, pan-Canadian institutional implications: if there is but one people, there is no need for the protec-tion of distinct sociological particularities, be they terri-torially concentrated or not. Institutionally, this suggests a centralized federalism.[31] Here populism meshes with the principle of "national culture," and identity and often takes on the ideological trappings of liberal indi-vidualism. Hence, much of Preston Manning's rhetoric echoes many (but not all) of Pierre Trudeau's views of the Canadian polity. The "governing principle" of a new Canadian constitution would be, according to Manning, "the equality of all Canadians."[32]

On the other hand, populism has a communitarian thrust that prizes the local — the particular — and defends it against intrusions from without, especially when the community is western Canada and the "with-out" is the more populous, insensitive, self-centred cen-tral Canada. Western populists have taken a number of approaches to federalism. Some have sought decentral-ization of federal powers to enhance the autonomy of provincial communities and bring government "closer to the people." Some have crossed over into Western sepa-ratism. Others have argued for strengthening the voice of the regions in central government institutions, thereby easing the centralist/decentralist tension. The Triple E Senate reform proposal embodies this latter position.

A poignant illustration of the relationship between populism and federalism is offered by recent controver-sies involving Sikhs in public service in Canada. One controversy involves a decision by the RCMP to allow practising Sikhs to wear turbans as part of their police uniforms. A group of RCMP veterans (and a great many other Canadians) considered this an attack on one of Canada's greatest national symbols, a dangerous conces-sion to the politics of difference and interest group whin-ing, and a further step in the decline of Canadian national culture.[33] The second controversy involves the

resounding defeat of a motion before the national deci-sion making body of the Royal Canadian Legion to require Legion branches to allow the wearing of reli-gious headgear (including turbans) in Legion facilities across the country. One of the most reasoned arguments in favour of the Legion policy was that decisions on such matters were best left to local branches to decide for themselves: a distant national head office should not have the authority to impose a national standard on local branches, especially if it violates an *existing* national standard.

The federalist contradiction here should be obvious: the substantive issue is much the same in each case yet one response sets a national standard while the other response asserts local autonomy. Both views represent populist perspectives on federalism. The contradiction is

---

"The people" is the pea in the populist shell game...

---

due in part to political opportunism. Bigots will dress their prejudices in the finest garb possible to carry the day. But the contradiction is also due to an inherent ten-sion between the local and the universal. This tension is concealed by repeated populist references to "the peo-ple." The heart of the matter is that the identity and location of "the people" change with context, issue, and political goal. "The people" is the pea in the populist shell game, changing location and form according to the demands of political opportunity. If "the people" is defined as those who belong to the Legion, then a uni-form national policy is favoured; if "the people" is that group affiliated with a local branch, then authority should rest there. The same ambiguity applies to pop-ulist perspectives on federal political institutions and their reform.

The final area of populist institutional reform agita-tion is also the area for which it is best known: direct democracy. There can surely be no simpler expression of giving power to the people, we are told, than letting them have direct influence on matters of public policy through referenda, citizen initiatives, and constituent assemblies. Without going into details, the referendum is the posing of a substantive policy or constitutional ques-tion to eligible voters for their response. The response is yes or no. The wording of questions, the timing of refer-enda, the degree to which referendum results are binding upon governments, the rules under which campaigns for each side are run, and the frequency with which referenda should be used are all matters on which there is much debate and disagreement. But the principle is simple enough.

Citizen initiatives take the principle of referenda a step further. With this mechanism, citizens can circulate a petition to require the government to place a public policy issue before voters in a referendum. Public policy development can be taken from the hands of the politicians and issues which elites would rather avoid, such as capital punishment, can be put on the public agenda.

Given Canada's continuing constitutional traumas, it is not surprising that the politics of constitutional change would be affected by populist agitation. Indeed, the failure of the Meech Lake Accord can in large part be attributed to English Canada's revulsion at the closed, elitist, paternalistic manner in which the accord was negotiated and pitched to Canadians. Similar criticisms were levelled at the Charlottetown Accord even though it was put to a referendum vote in 1992 and was preceded by "the most intensive, extensive, exhaustive and exhausting round of public consultations and intergovernmental negotiations on the constitution that has occurred in any country during this century."[34] Constitutional populism will ensure that referenda on proposed constitutional amendments will form an indelible part of Canada's constitutional future.

However, referenda are ratification mechanisms, leaving the development of public policies or major constitutional amendments to the political class. How can the people wrest control over this phase of the political process? The answer typically has been the constituent assembly, an extraordinary convention of rank-and-file Canadians who consider the constitution and formulate a set of amendments for the public to ratify in a referendum. Such a process could take constitutional change almost completely out of the hands of the political class, a prospect that sends shivers up the spines of liberal democrats across the land.[35]

CONCLUSION

◆ ◆ ◆

What are we to make of all of this? It is obvious that populism—and the rise of any populist party—must be placed within the context of those larger forces that shape our societies. We must take globalization into account where, for the new elites of old states, borders cease to matter (and for whom a new mark of status is the accumulation of aero-miles). We have to look at the

overall and dramatic decline of established parties, and at the possibility of democracy without the type of parties we have known since World War Two. We must also, and perhaps most significant of all, connect the emergence of populism to changes in collective attitudes and to the existence of a deep moral malaise within democracies. Electorates, as Maier notes, "remain poised between contending visions of political community."[36]

It is, therefore, a mistake to see populism as simply a product of economic and technological change, or as due only to the bungling and short-sightedness of those who have held power, or merely as a reaction to new social forces. It is all of these and more: it is a new right and a "retro-right," it is hyper-modern and deeply traditional. The startling tensions within populism, and in particular within the Reform Party as a current example, have already been touched upon implicitly if not always explicitly in this article. What remains to be done is to sum up such paradoxes. They conveniently cluster around three headings.

First, the populist view of democracy itself is particularly vulnerable to the clash of opposing principles and can produce effects that are, if anything, the opposite of what was intended. Populist MPs are supposed to represent the people who elected them, to ascertain their wishes, to stay in touch and to do what people want. This requires that a consensus or majority view be found. But which consensus are we talking about?

It might be a claimed consensus amongst constituents as a whole, Reform party members in a constituency, the Reform Party itself, a province, a class of citizens (the middle class for example), or even the country. In other words, the very idea of consensus lends itself to manipulation, and what is taken to constitute such a consensus will depend upon the questions posed and the answers that are deemed to count. What is taken to constitute the majority's will depends entirely upon who is being counted, and for what purposes the counting is being done. The more general the question, the more likely there will be agreement: "Are you in favour of the death penalty?" Answer—yes. "Shall all murderers be executed?" Answer—we're not sure. So, which questions a responsible MP asks and which group of citizens represents the will of the people will alter the results in a dramatic way, and this allows representatives to pick and choose how and when they are to be seen as subservient to the public's wishes.

The whole idea of subservience seems to be at odds with the populist notion that we do not need individuals who hide behind a manipulated consensus, ("I have no choice; I must follow"), but a completely new breed of politicians. These knights of a political round table will supposedly abstain from the perks of office and the abuse of patronage should power be obtained, avoid the temptations of Ottawa life (even though the latter idea may seem an oxymoron), and remain above the juvenile antics practised in the House of Commons. They are also supposed to be relatively immune to the drives of the marketplace with its emphasis on getting ahead, succeeding financially, and realizing one's individual dreams. The older Calvinist virtues of thrift, foresight, and prudence are supposed to supplant the current North American ethos of easy money and aggressive self-interest. This is a tall order. These ideas are in some ways simply incompatible; what is being asked is that principled and self-disciplined politicians, worthy of our trust, must also do our bidding.

The need to be seen as the servant of an aroused populace leads naturally to the temptation to exaggerate the public's visceral reactions to such things as crime,

---

...in most populist parties it is the voice of the leader that counts.

---

immigration, and new social movements. Yet to play up fears and to pose such emotive issues in the starkest possible terms is merely to play a very old—and very cynical—political game. Populist discourse can easily degenerate into the very rhetoric that the new political party wishes to avoid; it becomes a manipulative game played to keep people in power, or to get them there. This was why the Reform Party's use of the slogan "the Mulroney deal" as a synonym for the Charlottetown Accord created such protest. It harked back to such old-style politics.

A final democratic irony to contemplate is that in most populist parties it is the voice of the leader that counts. Without Preston Manning the Reform Party would not exist. The leader incarnates what people want, but what they want is often far from clear. They want a party that is an anti–party, but they want a party that wins, and scores off its opponents. The party and its leader are therefore often forced into normal party-like behaviour. People distrust political leaders, but follow one powerful enough to appeal directly to the populace over the heads of the party's senior members. Democracies must always be very wary of such appeals. For every Franklin Roosevelt or Charles de Gaulle there is a Napoleon Bonaparte or a Benito Mussolini.

Technology, seen as a possible democratic solution, is just as much the problem and will remain so. If one believes in the "will of the people," technology might now appear to give us a chance to let this will be heard via polls, instant voting and electronic town hall meetings. But who sets the rules and decides on and asks the questions? Who get to be party members, and who do not? Can anyone join? Who pays the considerable bills? How do we get reasoned debate and ongoing deliberative opinion formation if we rely on a snapshot approach and just sit at home pushing buttons? Why are we prepared to believe media talk show hosts and not our elected political representatives? Our technology is as much a cause of our problems as a cure: it is homogenizing, globalizing, and Americanizing at the same time that it helps to destabilize and fragment our communities as we retreat into a private world of entertainment. Populists, to their credit, are at least thinking about democracy, but their attempts to see that there is less "politics" and more democracy could easily leave us with far too little politics, and far too much reliance on supposed expressions of an ascertained popular will derived from some sort of instant opinion poll and unmediated by group activity. Populism often assumes that a national consensus exists along with a national culture and national values, all of which must be protected. However, populists are also localists, who wish to defend provincial or regional rights, who think in terms of decentralization, and who resent central domination even if backed by a majority. So which majorities are to count?

Second, populism, certainly in Canada, represents a very unusual collection of political ideas that sit uneasily together. Populists are the defenders of federalism as expressed through the argument for provincial rights and for a senate within which each territorial unit is equal. (Defence of territory seems to be the only thing that can or should override a national majority.) This is a Madisonian-type argument for checks and balances, and controls on the majority, to prevent it acting as a faction. There is a strong and very traditional distrust of Ottawa and Eastern control. A reformed senate is seen as a real check upon simple weight of numbers. Yet numbers are supposed to be what matters, especially on such things as moral questions. Why, therefore, should a territorially based senate be able to decide upon questions such as abortion or capital punishment and possibly override a clear national majority? Why are provincial governments, often elected with far less than 50% of the vote, seen as more legitimate than national interest groups with widespread support? To this fixation with territory and boundaries there is no easy answer.

Within the Reform outlook there is often a strong sense of Canadian nationalism; national cohesion and territorial integrity are important. There is a strong sense of "love it as it is or don't come here." Such pan-Canadian feelings do not, however, come to terms with Quebec's aspirations, and do not accord different federal strokes to different federal folks. The creation of national bilingualism in federal institutions is deeply resented. Therefore a Pierre Trudeau is applauded for standing up to Quebec and for Canada, but hated for his language policies (which the government of Quebec did not ask for) and for his Eastern elitism.

Even Trudeau's famous Charter of Rights is seen in very different ways depending upon which interests it is being used to defend. Unelected judges could easily become the target of populist wrath, particularly as the Charter has begun to be used to defend special groups as well as individuals. Yet Manning sees the Charter as a necessary democratic backstop, and as a guarantee that a majority cannot abuse its powers. This is a particular Canadian irony given the nature of the Charter, and it also qualifies as another paradox that has a bearing on our notions of democracy as well as on policy: what courts do is cause a different kind of political debate to take place—one driven particularly by the law professors, feminist scholars, advocacy groups and that most unrepresentative of all occupations—judges.

If we turn to economic policy, similar deep contradictions are to be found. How can there be a strong Canada if the powers of the central government are so reduced that national policy making becomes almost impossible? One strong element of populism now stresses the need for a free-trading, competitive, global marketplace. In this marketplace power is in the hands of banks, investment houses, pension fund managers, and nongovernmental institutions; the people have little or no say in such a largely invisible world except as consumers of products. The marketplace is the natural order and the cult of efficiency rules. Such sentiments sit very uneasily with ideas of strong community, shared values and the need for political power to be placed in the hands of the voters. This is also an American economic world, and it raises the spectre of Canada's deepest historic fear—absorption by the United States. Solutions made in the U.S. are advocated, and could have precisely the opposite effects to those which is intended, for we could end up with U.S. problems if we implement such answers. It is not difficult to imagine, for example, that under the impact of cost-cutting we could create a much more American style health care system, one that would be a good deal more expensive. However, these expenses will be borne by the consumers, not the government itself. This represents political sleight-of-hand, not genuine cost-cutting.

If parts of the state apparatus, at any level, are cut adrift and privatized, or placed under independent regulatory bodies, it could be even harder for citizens to obtain satisfaction. People may be in for a shock when they find out that the functions once at least nominally under political control are now in other hands, and politicians will increasingly be able to deflect and duck responsibility by saying that X or Y is no longer part of their mandate. Perhaps a massive reduction in government will encourage more self-reliance, but in the policy arena the greatest paradox is the amount of trust now placed in the marketplace as a neutral regulator and as a way of returning power to the people: "Such an argument, and the political agenda stemming from it, would leave earlier populist democrats turning in their graves."[37] Will the policies designed to bring politicians to heel, such as recall, do anything at all about the very real imbalances in political power that exist, and enable life's foot-soldiers to wield any more influence over how our society is run? One does not have to be a socialist to suspect that, in policy terms, populists at present are very selective in their targets, naive in their views on the marketplace and paradoxical about which interests count and what causes our problems in the first place.

When the deeper questions of policy are raised it brings to the forefront the third area of paradox, and this is the odd coalition of social and political interests that make up the basis of support for Reform's brand of populism. Rooted in western Canada, particularly Alberta, it is strongly regional. But far more people voted Reform in Ontario than in either Alberta or British Columbia, and Ontario is the historic enemy. Reformers tend to favour free trade,[38] but Ontarians in general harbour deep reservations about its effects. Quebec favours both free trade and decentralization: this fits the new populist agenda but Quebec's other demands are unacceptable because they make Quebec "distinct," which is deemed unfair. If the Reform Party's populist agenda fractures it is, therefore, likely to be along regional lines and/or, as a result of differing views on a range of questions such as abortion, euthanasia, gender, the role of courts, and the Charter.

Any discussion of regionalism and nationalism would be incomplete without a reference to political myths. Such myths are a narrative of events in a dramatic form, believed to be true not because the historical evidence is compelling but because they make sense of our present experience and "tell the story of how it came about."[39] Such myths promise not the abolition of politics but the "restoration of an authentic political society."[40] The problem is, authentic political societies require one thing above all—territory. In Canada's case the demands for a "new Canada" might be taken to mean the need for territorial cohesion and the imposition of "order" upon a multi–ethnic, multinational, geographically fragmented, heterogeneous state. Or, paradoxically, our myths can reinforce localism, can help convince us that the state is too remote or uncontrollable, run by others and not by us, so that "we" would be better off with a territorial home of our own. Territorial populism is Janus-faced and its supporting myths, in Canada at least, are contradictory and regionalized. "The West Wants In" has now disappeared from the Reform Party's letterhead, but has the West really made its mind up?

All of this does not mean that we should be unduly pessimistic about the paradoxical nature of much of what populism promises. That fact that Canada's version of populism is such a mixture of elements prevents it from being monolithic and will probably force Reform to act somewhat like a brokerage party. There can be no wish, as there is among some European populists, to establish an authoritarian form of rule. The debate that the new populist agenda has triggered could help to revitalize our moral sensibilities; to make us more aware of the need for a tolerant and highly pluralistic federation; to kindle a desire to balance global market forces with stronger political directives; to even reinforce Canadian nationalism as we see where we are headed. The Reform Party's promise of a new Canada does not mean that the one we will get, with or without Reform's agenda being implemented, is the one populists seem to have in mind. History plays strange tricks, especially upon politicians.

Notes

1. Hans-George Betz, "The New Politics of Resentment: Radical-Right-Wing Populist Parties in Europe," *Comparative Politics* 25 (1993), 413–27.

2. See Stanley Hoffman "France: Keeping the Demons at Bay," *The New York Review of Books*, March 3, 1993; also Jane Kramer, "Letter From Europe," *The New Yorker*, May 30, 1988.

3. Alvin Finkel, *The Social Credit Phenomenon in Alberta* (Toronto: University of Toronto Press, 1989), 202.

4. Peter McCormick, "The Will of the People: Democratic Practice in Canada and the United States," *Canada and the United States: Differences that Count*, edited by David Thomas (Peterborough: Broadview Press, 1993), 189.

5. Finkel, *The Social Credit Phenomenon in Alberta*, 210.

6. John Richards, "Populism: A Qualified Defense," *Studies in Political Economy* 5 (1981), 5–27.

7. David Laycock, "Reforming Canadian Democracy? Institutions and Ideology in the Reform Party Project," *Canadian Journal of Political Science* 27 (1994), 213–248.

8. Preston Manning, *The New Canada* (Toronto: Macmillan Canada, 1992), 6–7.

9. Keith Archer and Faron Ellis, "Opinion Structure of Party Activists: The Reform Party," *Canadian Journal of Political Science* 27 (1994), 277–308, 286.

10. Ibid.

11. Richard Sigurdson, "Preston Manning and the Politics of Postmodernism in Canada," *Canadian Journal of Political Science* 27 (1994), 269–70.

12. Ibid., 270–73.

13. Ibid., 271.

14. Archer and Ellis, "Opinion Structure of Party Activists," 286.

15. The National Citizens Coalition, a right-wing business lobby, has advocated populist democratic reforms because these techniques in its opinion

will allow the hitherto silent Canadian majority to veto tax increases and other forms of government largesse. See National Citizens Coalition, "Direct Democracy: Trusting and Empowering the People: A Submission to the [B.C.] Select Standing Committee on Parliamentary Reform," December 18, 1992.

16. Manning, *The New Canada*, 320.
17. James Madison, "Federalist #10" in James Madison, Alexander Hamilton, and John Jay, *The Federalist Papers*, edited by Clinton Rossiter (New York: Mentor, 1961), 77–84.
18. Alexis de Tocqueville, *Democracy in America*, vol. 1, trans. Henry Reeve (New York: Vintage 1945), 273.
19. Madison, "Federalist Paper #10."
20. Tocqueville, *Democracy in America*, vol. 2, 112.
21. Andre Carrell, Administrator, City of Rossland, British Columbia, "Direct Democracy," a speech to the Annual General Meeting of the Canada West Foundation, May 28, 1994.
22. Sigurdson, "Preston Manning and the Politics of Postmodernism in Canada," 276.
23. Archer and Ellis, "Opinion Structure of Party Activists," 296.
24. For the distinction between the territorial and personalty principles in official language policy see: Kenneth McRoberts, "Making Canada Bilingual: Illusions and Delusions of Federal Language Policy" in *Federalism and Political Community: Essays in Honour of Donald Smiley*, edited by David Shugarman and Reg Whitaker (Peterborough: Broadview, 1989), 141–72.
25. Betz, "The New Politics of Resentment."
26. Reform Party of Canada, *Principles and Policies* (1990).
27. For empirical support and analysis, see The Royal Commission on Electoral Reform and Party Financing, *Reforming Electoral Democracy*, vol. 1 (Ottawa: Supply and Services, 1991), 223–28; also Peter Dobell and Byron Berry, "Anger at the System," *Parliamentary Government*, January 1992, 3–17, and Stephane Dion, "Rising Cynicism: Who is to Blame?" *Canadian Parliamentary Review* (Winter 1993–94), 33–35.
28. See Peter McCormick, "The Will of the People: Democratic Practice in Canada and the United States" in *Canada and the United States*, edited by David M. Thomas, 182–186.
29. Leonard Preyra, "The 1992 Nova Scotia Liberal Leadership Convention," *Canadian Parliamentary Review* (Winter 1993–94): 2; see also "Reforming the Leadership Convention Process," *Canadian Parliamentary Review* (Autumn 1993), 5–11.
30. It is important to bear in mind, however, that the Reform Party did surprisingly well in Ontario in the 1993 federal election, electing one MP and garnering 20% of the provincial vote. The Reform Party must deal with a tension between its Western regionalist populism and its pan-English Canada populist appeal.
31. Canadian populism of the right-wing variety supports the free market against government intrusion. Logically, this moves populism in the direction of the enforcement of national (or even global) economic, industrial, and educational policy standards to counter provincial protectionism. Hence, on the economic front, populism is also centralist.
32. Manning, *The New Canada*, 306.

33. Few realize that the current RCMP head gear arrived via the Boer War and was adopted through the agency of Baden Powell by the Boy Scouts. Hollywood cemented the public's view that this was "the" uniform to wear.

34. Ronald L. Watts, "Overview" in *Canada: The State of the Federation*, edited by Ronald L. Watts and Douglas M. Brown, *1993* (Kingston: Institute for Intergovernmental Relations, 1993), 5.

35. See, for example, Janet Ajzenstat, "Constitution Making and the Myth of the People" in *Constitutional Predicament: Canada After the Referendum of 1992*, edited by Curtis Cook (Montreal and Kingston: McGill-Queen's University Press, 1994), 112–26.

36. Charles S. Maier, "Democracy and Its Discontents," *Foreign Affairs* 73 (1994), 60; reprinted in this volume (Unit One, Article 3).

37. Laycock, "Reforming Canadian Democracy," 244.

38. Archer and Ellis, "Opinion Structure of Party Activists," 298.

39. Henry Tudor, *Political Myth* (London: Pall-Mall Press, 1972), 124.

40. Ibid. 103.

Terms & Concepts

citizen initiatives
direct democracy
electronic town hall meeting
federalism
globalization
immigration
interest groups
majoritarianism
minority rights

nationalism
neoconservatism
parliamentary democracy
political myths
political parties
popular will
populism
post-industrialism
postmodern antimodernism

postmodern hypermodernism
postmodernism
referenda
regionalism
representation
representative democracy
territorial populism
welfare state

Questions

1. What differentiates current Canadian populism from
   a. its Canadian predecessors?
   b. the manifestations of populism in other contemporary democracies?

2. A question that arises in the discussion of direct democracy is whether the will of the people is always right. Is there such a thing as the "popular will"? Is it, by definition, always correct? Does this matter? After all, representatives make mistakes too.

3. Populism has had an association with the left as well as the right. Are there current trends that might result in a rebirth of left-wing populism?

4. The Reform Party elected a significant number of MPs in the 1993 election. Has this created problems for a party that is populist in nature?

Feminist Theory

Lorraine Code

Editors' Note

This opening chapter from *Changing Patterns: Women in Canada,* 2nd ed. (Toronto: McClelland & Stewart, 1993) differs from others in this unit in that it neither deals with feminism as an issue nor offers a critique. Rather, it elaborates first-year textbook treatments in which feminism is discussed often in a more cursory or fragmentary manner. In this reading Lorraine Code, a professor of philosophy at York University and widely published author on feminist theory, first presents a historical perspective of various theories that influenced the relationship between the sexes and then explains how these were challenged. This is followed by an explanation of, and differentiation among, the many strains of contemporary feminism, which are then grouped into two broad categories: feminisms of equality and feminisms of difference.

Feminists contend that contemporary gender inequality is rooted in patriarchy, which has been entrenched for millennia. It has shaped human values, beliefs, culture, religion, institutions and, in the last couple of centuries, even science, to reinforce and perpetuate male domination. The earliest philosophers ranked men above women—and note that this was grounded in "nature." Organized religion has also, for the most part, relegated women to inferior status. Indeed, when we study history—major civilizations explored by studying the actions of their almost invariably male rulers, with the help of records kept by male scribes according to what they saw as important, and then interpreted by mostly male historians[1]—we can easily be forgiven for believing that the preeminence of men must be part of the natural order of things. Feminists reject this view and provide evidence to the contrary.[2]

The problem in understanding the feminist critique(s) is, therefore, one common to all ideologies; separating premises based upon assumptions (women are more nurturing than men) from those based on facts (women bear children) and then evaluating the conventions derived from both. This task is made very difficult by the pervasiveness of the conventions. They are around us everywhere, from the wedding veil to the *chador.* Professor Code argues that our societies have been constructed on many dubious gender-based assumptions. Her article establishes a solid foundation for understanding and putting into context this prominent challenge to most conventional belief systems.

◆ ◆ ◆

1. Germaine Greer makes a compelling case of the historical suppression of female artists in *The Obstacle Race: The Fortunes of Women Painters and Their Work,* (New York: Farrar Strauss Giroux, 1979).
2. For example, see Riane Eisler, *The Chalice and The Blade: Our History, Our Future,* (San Francisco: Harper & Row, 1988).

Contemporary feminism, which came into being with the student and civil-rights movements of radical protest in the 1960s, is an active, evolving, politically engaged movement. As such, it has been instrumental in effecting fundamental social changes. Feminism is also a theoretical project whose purposes are to understand the power structures, social practices, and institutions that disadvantage and marginalize women, and to devise innovative strategies of social transformation that will promote women's emancipation. British feminist Juliet Mitchell observes that feminism is "an ideological offspring of certain economic and social conditions. Its radicalism reflects the fact that it comes to prominence at points of critical change and envisages it with an imagination that goes beyond it."[1] Mitchell's observation points to the close connections between feminist practice, which works to transform material and social conditions, and feminist theory, which develops out of that practice and informs it. Theory is constantly modified by what proves effective in practice, and practice is shaped by theory; so any apparent separation between theory and practice in this chapter will be made only for purposes of analysis. This account of changing feminist theories is intended to describe the theoretical context in which the emancipatory practices that are detailed in subsequent chapters have evolved in Canadian society.

Feminist theorists work to develop critical analyses of how, in patriarchal societies, women and men tend, generally, to live different lives and have different experiences. These experiences can be differentiated along sex-gender lines even as they differ also according to class, race, age, ethnicity, religion, and numerous other attributes and variables. Patriarchal societies are those in which men have more power than women and readier access than women to what is valued in the society or in any social sub-group. In consequence of this power and privilege differential, men in such societies or groups occupy positions that permit then to shape and control many, if not most, aspects of women's lives. Most known societies are patriarchal to a greater or lesser degree, although they exhibit specific variations in how power is distributed and manifested. Feminist theorists seek to understand this uneven distribution of power and privilege: to examine how it came into being, how the oppression of women by men is related to other forms of social oppression, such as racism, classism, homophobia; and to develop strategies to eradicate it. The point of studying the situations and ideologies that oppress women is to work towards producing social change.

Feminists differ in how they identify the primary feature(s) of women's oppression, in the theoretical questions they place high on their agendas, and in the strategies they develop for challenge and change. Yet, although these issues are approached from different angles and with carrying estimations of their significance, there are several common feminist themes. In particular, feminists want to understand how the organization of production, reproduction, sexuality, and socialization, in their shifting manifestations, has determined women's circumstances throughout history and across cultural, class, and racial boundaries.[2]

Production, in this context, includes all of the processes that go into producing and distributing food, clothing, shelter, and the other material necessities of human lives. It is primarily, but not solely, an economic category, for it also includes political and cultural activity. Reproduction refers not just to conceiving and bearing children, and giving birth, but also to raising children, ministering to the physical and emotional needs of husbands, lovers, and children, and caring for the elderly and the sick. The boundaries between reproduction and socialization, and between reproduction and sexuality, are not rigid ones, for women are socialized to use their reproductive capacities in certain approved ways. They are expected to socialize their children to perpetuate acceptable sexual reproductive behaviour. In patriarchal societies, women's sexuality is subject to strict censure and control by social pressures that define and enforce permissible modes of female sexual expression. Hence, for feminists, both sexuality and socialization are political matters, although different ideological strands within feminism accord these various structures and activities differing importance. Likewise, the structures and practices identified as oppressive to women have changed throughout history and been variously shaped by class, race, culture, and other social positions.

The starting point of feminist theory, then, is in women's lives: in the varied experiences of women; and in the concrete situations where they live and are differently marginalized and disadvantaged. Theoretical

From *Changing Patterns: Women in Canada* by Burt/Code/Dorney (pp.19–57). Used by permission of the Canadian Publishers, McClelland & Stewart, Toronto.

analysis is integral to feminism, because women's experiences do not speak for themselves. For this reason, consciousness-raising was crucially important in the early years of the current women's movement. Women needed to learn from each other how to see and name their experiences of oppression and how to recognize the commonalities of their circumstances. Theory—and consciousness-raising—are still fundamental to the movement in its self-critical project; revising its initial assumptions of female sameness (sisterhood), deriving ever more subtle analyses of the effects of patriarchy, defining and redefining the problems that have to be faced, and evaluating new strategies for change.

Marilyn Frye develops a useful image to show why it is so difficult to see the minuscule oppressive structures of everyday life in an allegedly democratic, free society.[3] Frye notes that if one examines one wire of a birdcage, one can neither see the other wires nor understand why the cage is so confining. One might wonder why the bird would not just fly around that wire and go free. The same thing would happen if one were to inspect each wire separately—it would not be apparent why any single wire would constrain the bird. It is only by stepping back to examine the entire structure—the interconnected and mutually enforcing system of barriers—that one can see why the bird is trapped. Similarly, it is necessary to stand back from particular oppressive social practices to see their mutual reinforcement; to see, as a feminist, how patriarchy is constructed out of practices that, considered singly, may not seem to be particularly significant or oppressive. Yet together these practices form an intractable structure.

Over the last two and a half decades, there has been a major shift within feminism from an earlier focus on women as a caste, class, or homogeneous group to a concentration upon differences among women. It can no longer be assumed that there is a single, essential 'women's experience' out of which universal analytic categories can be developed. Differences of race, class, and sexual practices are just a few of the differences that have become primary focal points of theoretical discussion. Contemporary feminist theorists face the tasks of accounting for differences among women's experiences and, simultaneously, of discerning common threads and themes that make these experiences specific to women. The task, now, is to develop theoretical tools that will make it possible to examine the samenesses and differences in women's lives without losing sight of the boundaries of commonality or of specificity. These are delicate tasks, for experience is always structured and mediated by a complex of material, social, cultural, historical, and unconscious forces. There is no 'pure, untainted' experience; and the forces that shape it are often complex and difficult to understand. Furthermore, it is always just as important to account for the absence of women from social practices and institutions as it is to produce analyses of visible oppression. Thus feminists have to learn to see how standard theoretical analyses of social practices often justify, or mask, women's absence. Finally, in performing these tasks a theorist faces a curious paradox: consciousness of the effects of sex-gender seems to be *necessary* to the very existence of feminism, even though feminists are committed to eradicating the oppressive consequences of sex-gender expectations.[4] And all of these tasks must be performed without losing sight of the fact that sex-gender-specific exclusions and oppressions work differently across the social order. The goal of these projects is not only to produce knowledge about women—to make women visible—but also to develop informed, critical analyses of the structures of power and privilege that keep women in their socially assigned places and are stubbornly resistant to change.[5]

Women in the industrialized Western world grow to womanhood in circumstances where it is assumed that (to quote Adrienne Rich):

> women are a subgroup, that "man's world" is the real world, that patriarchy is equivalent to culture and culture to patriarchy...that generalizations about "man", "humankind", "children", "blacks", "parents", "the working class" hold true for women, mothers, daughters, sisters, wet-nurses, infant girls, and can include them with no more than a glancing reference here and there, usually to some specialized function like breast-feeding.[6]

Patriarchial assumptions about the appropriate places for women to occupy in 'man's world' are so seamlessly woven into the ideologies and policies of most Western cultures that they seem to dictate the 'natural' way for things to be.[7] Because of the persistence of these beliefs, it is especially important for feminist theory to maintain its continuity with the consciousness-raising practices of the late 1960s and early 1970s. Women need to go on learning how to see their personal and seemingly idiosyncratic experiences as the effects of systemically oppressive beliefs and practices.

No feminist theorist could take on all aspects of patriarchy at once. Yet Frye's birdcage image stands as a reminder that concentrating on any one aspect may cause one to lose sight of the interwoven patterns of oppression that patriarchy perpetuates. Feminists have to develop a "doubled vision"[8] so they can at once challenge specific patriarchal practices and step back to see how those practices reinforce and are reinforced by the whole social structure. They have to see what else needs to be tackled for any practice really to be changed. and to estimate how changing one practice might affect the whole.

BIOLOGICAL DETERMINISM: *ANCIENT VIEWS*

◆ ◆ ◆

Many of the ideas and practices that have worked to maintain women's disadvantaged social positions have their roots in the history of Western thought. The belief that a woman's nature and all of her possibilities are determined by her biology—specifically her reproductive biology—is one of the most ancient and persistent of these ideas. It has long been used to justify a range of social practices designed to keep woman 'in her place.' Assumptions about 'women's nature' have described what that nature allegedly is, but have also prescribed what a woman should be.

Biological determinism has its best-known ancient formulation in the philosophy of Aristotle (384–322 B.C.). Despite vast increases in the sophistication of biological knowledge, which make the 'facts' on which Aristotle based his normative claims look quite naive, views remarkably similar to his have persisted even throughout the twentieth century. In their political, revisionary projects feminists repeatedly find themselves required to counter modern versions of Aristotelian beliefs to the effect that women are not capable (physically, intellectually, or emotionally) of holding certain kinds of jobs, or that placing children in day care is a violation of a mother's *natural* role.

Woman's place in the Aristotelian scheme of things is defined purely by her essential function, which is seen as a biological, reproductive one. Her rational capacities are declared to be underdeveloped and inferior in comparison with those of men. Hence men are to rule over women, in whom the irrational element of the 'soul' tends naturally to overrule the rational element. Aristotle writes:

> The male is by nature superior, and the female inferior; and the one rules, and the other is ruled; this principle, of necessity, extends to all mankind. Where there is such a difference as that between soul and body, or between men and animals...the lower sort are by nature slaves, and it is better for

them as for all inferiors that they soul be under the rule of a master.[9]

In Aristotle's view, neither women, children, nor slaves can be citizens. Because only citizens can participate in the political life of the Greek city state, women are barred from such participation, as are children and slaves. Furthermore, because virtue, through which the best human qualities are realized, is achievable only through participation in political activity, virtue, too, in its highest forms, is inaccessible to women (and to slaves and children).

Aristotle maintains that even in respect to their own essential function—the reproduction of the species—women play an inferior part. The male parent's contribution to the offspring is the soul: that which makes it essentially human. The female parent contributes only crude physical matter in the form of menstrual blood (catamenia). According to Aristotle, hers is a passive contribution, by contrast with semen, which he regards as an active substance, "for the catamenia have in their nature an affinity to the primitive matter."[10] This unformed matter, then, awaits insemination by the male parent to endow it with human form and human capacity. Women's contribution to reproduction is merely to provide the material that is to be acted upon and to offer a place of incubation to the future infant. Hence, both with respect to rationality, which distinguishes human beings from other Aristotelian 'natural kinds,' and with respect to reproductive function, women are inferior to men. Their inferior position is biologically determined, according to the natural order of things, and no further explanation for their civic status is required.

Aristotle's philosophy underpins most Western theories about human nature from classical times up to the twentieth century. As Beverley Baines shows in her chapter in this book, Aristotelian conceptions of the biologically determined inequality of women and men can even be discerned in the assumptions that underlie much of nineteenth- and twentieth-century legal practice.[11] Yet it was by no means inevitable that Aristotle should develop the functionalist, biological-determinist ideas that he did. From the earliest days of developing theories of human nature there were well-known alternative possibilities, which might have opened up quite different ways of thinking about women and about the relations between women and men. In fact, Aristotle seems to have articulated his position partly in reaction to a startling and innovative proposal about the social relations between the sexes that was developed by his own teacher, Plato (427–347 B.C.).

In the *Republic*, Plato has *his* teacher, Socrates, describe an ideal society in which every citizen will perform the function best suited to his or her 'natural' capacities. Future merchants, craftspeople, and tradespeople will receive training appropriate to the acquisition of the skill they need for their occupations; and those who are to form the military forces will receive an education designed to make them suitably courageous, yet neither rash nor cowardly. The ruling, guardian class will be responsible for maintaining harmony within the state and governing it wisely. Its members will receive a rigorous training in music and the arts, gymnastics and athletics, mathematics, and all of the highest arts of reason.

Remarkably for his time and even for ours, Socrates intends that the guardian class should be composed of both women and men, who will receive exactly the same education. He maintains that there is *nothing* in female nature to prevent women's participation, arguing, "There is no pursuit of the administrators of a state that belongs to a woman because she is a woman or to a man because he is a man. But the natural capacities are dis-

---

Women might become guardians, but only by becoming honorary men...

---

tributed alike among both creatures, and women naturally have a share in all pursuits and men in all—yet for all the woman is weaker than the man."[12] Hence, "Women of this kind ... must be selected to cohabit with men of this kind and to serve with them as guardians since they are capable of it and akin by nature."[13] Socrates explicitly states, then, that there are no specifically female traits, either biological or psychological, that would naturally exclude women from these pursuits. So that child-rearing will not interfere with the education and other activities of women of the guardian class, Socrates establishes a set of social arrangements in which there will be no conventional family structures. Children, who will be born as a result of brief periods of co-habitation in designated marriage festivals, "will be taken over by the officials appointed for this, men or women or both" and raised communally.[14]

It would be a mistake to claim, on the basis of this radical proposal, that Plato was a feminist. He puts forward a proposal quite different from Aristotle's of how women might live in a 'man's world,' but there is little doubt that it is a man's world, and it is unlikely that the

kind of equality he advocates would be acceptable to twentieth-century feminists. The guardians' educational system is modelled upon an extension of educational practices designed for the *male* citizens of the Greek polis. The proposal is that women should participate equally in men's activities and pursuits, devised and elaborated so as to bring out the best in masculine nature. Women might become guardians, but only by becoming honorary men: by having men make room for them within male-defined structures. Present-day variations on this theme, where women are admitted to business and other high-status occupations on the (often implicit) condition that their 'femininity' not be permitted to count, are only too familiar.

In any case, it is Aristotle's conceptions of women's nature that provide the basis for virtually all of Western theory up to the eighteenth century, and they offer the principal rationale for maintaining patriarchal social arrangements. Even late Platonists, who were influenced by other aspects of Plato's philosophy, did not take up his novel ideas about women or about equality between the sexes. In fact, it was not until the development of liberalism in the eighteenth century that the first serious challenges to biological determinism were articulated.

THE LIBERAL CHALLENGE

◆ ◆ ◆

Liberal political theory, especially as it developed in Britain and France in the eighteenth and nineteenth centuries, prepared the way for a fundamental challenge to biological determinism. The early liberal feminists' contention that women's inferior social status was a consequence of their lack of education and opportunity, and not of their nature, opened the way for a re-examination of traditional assumptions about 'women's nature.' Moreover, the social and economic upheavals that accompanied the Industrial Revolution undermined the idea that women's natural, biologically determined place is in the home. As women began to work in factories there was a growing differentiation between the activities that they performed at home and at work. In the face of such practical evidence, it could no longer so easily be maintained that women were fitted only to perform a biologically determined role. These challenges and alternatives are significant feminist milestones, for they undercut the sense of inevitability that feminists often feel in the face of deterministic arguments. If women's circumstances can be explained by their limited access to education, opportunity, and other social resources, rather than by their 'nature,' it is possible that if the 'goods' of the society are more equally available, then women's emancipation will follow. (More recently, feminists have begun to show that biology, too, is shaped by environmental and other circumstances.)

The eighteenth century witnessed the widespread development of liberal, egalitarian political ideals, which challenged fundamental social and political beliefs and inspired the American and French revolutions. Most significantly, liberal thinking gradually came to displace the belief that political authority was based in inherited title, and that rulers, by natural right, stood in benevolent patriarchal relation to their subjects. Thomas Hobbes (1588–1679) and John Locke (1632–1704) argued that society should work as though it had been established by a freely entered contract among free and equal individuals. The role of government was to ensure the personal safety and protect the property rights of citizens who had demonstrated their capacity to know their own interests by opting into the contract. In an age when people had unquestioningly believed that members of lower social orders should simply submit to the greater wisdom of their natural superiors and rulers, these were novel ideas.

The argument that all members of society are free and equally participating individuals led feminists to contend that equality should be enjoyed by women, too. They could see no reason for it to remain a masculine privilege. Feminists had to demonstrate the limited scope of the new-found ideals of equality, for it certainly was not true that all of the early liberals were feminists or that they were united in rejecting biological determinism. Most early male liberal theorists unthinkingly assumed that the liberal 'individual' about whom their theories spoke would undoubtedly be male; and many of them clearly believed that women were inferior beings.

It was to take issue with such assumptions about female inferiority that Mary Wollstonecraft (1759–1797) wrote her famous treatise, *The Vindication of the Rights of Woman*, completed in 1792. Wollstonecraft maintains that if women were to have the same education and opportunities as men, they would be men's equals in every respect. Only because of their inferior education, she argues, do women appear to be merely emotional creatures, lacking in rationality; they are not so by nature. It is women's rights to education and equal treatment that Wollstonecraft is concerned about vindicating.

Wollstonecraft wrote her *Vindication* largely to refute the position developed by Jean-Jacques Rousseau (1712–1778) in *Emile*, his treatise on education.

Rousseau is, in a sense, the liberal individual *par excellence*. He comes across in his political writings as a man deeply committed to values of freedom, individualism, independence, and equality. Rousseau envisages a transformation of civil society into a moral society in which all men are citizens and equals, while women are virtuous wives and mothers. In *Emile* he advocates an education of young men that would develop their reason to its fullest potential and train them to tame nature and understand its secrets. Women, in Rousseau's view, are much closer to nature than men because they have a different intellectual character—they are less able to engage in abstract thought, to reason well, and to form universal judgements. But they are well endowed with taste, practical sense, and feeling. Hence, he believes, they should be educated to *complement* men, adorn their lives, raise their children, and obey them. Like nature, women must be tamed, kept in check. In particular, their sexual passions must be controlled so that men can be free from enslavement to female sensuality.

Like Aristotle, then, Rousseau is a firm believer in biological determinism. Several issues that have become contentious for twentieth-century feminists are foreshadowed in his work. Most present-day feminists reject the complementarity thesis that is implicit in Rousseau's work, according to which women and men are declared

---

When women are trained to prefer and are expected to occupy themselves with trivial tasks, they cannot help but appear feeble-minded...

---

to be different but equal and complementary; and many feminist stake issue with the idea that women should be the guardians of morals, particularly of sexual morals. In helping men to control their reputedly more robust natural sexuality, women are required to suppress or deny their own sexual desires. These expectations generate a paradoxical and oppressive view of women as both chaste and wanton, defined wholly in relation to men, and required to subordinate their self-expression to men's ideas of what they should be.

Wollstonecraft takes Rousseau to task on many of these issues. Her arguments in favour of equal education for women occupy the greater part of her treatise: she attributes all aspects of women's disadvantaged situation to their circumscribed intellectual opportunities in a patriarchal society. When women are trained to prefer and are expected to occupy themselves with trivial tasks, they cannot help but appear feeble-minded and deficient in rational capacity, she argues.

According to Wollstonecraft, women and men are created alike both in sexual feeling and rational capacity. Rather than accepting the claim that it is women's responsibility to curb excessive masculine sexual interest and indulgence, she argues that female chastity is impossible without equivalent male chastity, both practised according to a single rather than a double sexual standard. Wollstonecraft plainly regards sexual constraint as preferable to free sexual expression. She believes that reason, equally developed in both sexes, should rule over passion, which is equally strong in both sexes. The passion in which marriage begins should evolve into a rational, passionless friendship where sexuality is carefully controlled. It is her belief that such a relationship between equals can serve as a model for the structure of civil society.

Yet Wollstonecraft does not reject complementarity outright, for she believes in the maintenance of a family structure in which women would be responsible for child care. Employment outside the domestic sphere is not one of the primary rights she claims for women. If women are to perform well in the important task of mothering, she maintains, they must be educated just as men are educated. Otherwise they will be unable to give their children a rational upbringing. Her larger point is that only when women are educated so that they too can be ruled by reason will they be able to share in the opportunities of the new egalitarian society. She evidently expects that most women will enjoy these opportunities at home. Yet Wollstonecraft sees such a clear continuity between domestic and civil life that there is no stark public/private dichotomy in her work. She believes that domestic life is part of civic life and that the same capacities and virtues are appropriate to each.

In later developments of liberal theory, women's potential for intellectual achievement and their right to the franchise came to be recognized as interconnected issues. Because the franchise could be claimed only by educated property owners, women had remained effectively disqualified as potential voters. John Stuart Mill (1806–1873) was mindful of these obstacles when he wrote *The Subjection of Women*, so his arguments in favour of education and equal rights for women are, in this respect at least, directed towards a goal somewhat different from Wollstonecraft's. Nonetheless, like Wollstonecraft, Mill believes that educated women will be more likely to choose a domestic life than a career.

The major change he envisages, apart from their qualifying for the franchise, is that women will be better able to share in their husband's intellectual pursuits and to raise their children intelligently.

Equality is the dominant theme of Mill's essay: the need for "a principle of perfect equality, admitting no power or privilege on one side, nor disability on the other" to govern the relations between the sexes.[15] Like Wollstonecraft, he believes that women and men are equally rational, intelligent beings, and that the contention that women are not rational simply ignores their lack of opportunity to develop their reason. Mill is convinced that society as a whole will benefit if women are granted all of the educational opportunities available to men.

Harriet Taylor Mill (1807–1858) proposes much more radical social changes when she argues that there should be no laws concerning marriage and that a woman should retain guardianship of, and take financial responsibility for, her own children.[16] Hers was a radical challenge to patriarchy at a time when wives and children were regarded by law as the property of the father. Taylor's proposals were intended to ensure that the issue of providing for children would be irrelevant in divorce proceedings and would not be used to tie a woman into a unworkable marriage for fear of losing custody of her children. She contends that a woman should consider carefully how many children to have, rather than having a great many in order to strengthen her tie to the man who feeds her. As well, Taylor believes that if women are not to barter their persons for bread, they must not only be educated but also be permitted to enter any occupational field they wish. Clearly, Taylor would have applauded many of the successes of present-day feminists in restructuring women's participation in the work force and in bringing about reform in family law. Higher education for women, which is taken for granted as an opportunity today, was an unknown possibility when she was writing.

This early liberal emphasis upon equality of opportunity has carried over, if in a different guise, into contemporary feminist thought. And liberal rejection of deterministic explanations for women's situation has become a constant feminist theme. But original formulations of liberal theory require modification for contemporary feminist purposes. Liberal theorists write of 'men' and 'women' as homogenous groups: they rarely address questions about how their theories could bear upon the circumstances and interests of women or men who are less well situated, socially and economically, than the theorists themselves. In short, they believe that their experiences are representative of human experience as such. Furthermore, most early liberal theorists take for granted that women's concerns will, as a matter of course, be covered by analyses of men's situations and interests. Contemporary feminists have rightly insisted that analyses of men's social circumstances usually gloss over or obscure women's experiences, and that these experiences require separate analysis

THE MARXIST CHALLENGE

◆ ◆ ◆

Liberal ideology is just one of several sources of present-day feminism. An equally important ideological landmark for understanding the origins of feminist theory is the development of Marxist thought in the nineteenth century. Early Marxism was primarily an analysis of the

---

...Marxist socialism opens possibilities for analyzing the connections between class oppression and women's oppression.

---

modes of production and the social relations that accompanied the Industrial Revolution and the rise of capitalism. Although Marxist and socialist thinkers do not concentrate upon developing explicit refutations of biological determinism, their work assumes that biology cannot provide the sole explanation for social inequality and the oppression of one group of people by another. Economic factors are at least as important, if not more so. Furthermore, liberalism, despite its apparent class-lessness, is very much a bourgeois or middle-class ideology. Marxism, by contrast, is class conscious above all. In its later feminist formulations, Marxist socialism opens possibilities for analyzing the connections between class oppression and women's oppression.

According to Karl Marx (1818–1883), culture and society are rooted in material, economic conditions, and human beings are essentially social creatures, shaped by material and social circumstances. These claims contrast sharply with the liberal idea of the abstract, self-realizing individual, freely opting for membership in society. Whereas in liberal thought it is necessary to understand the individual in order to understand society, in Marxist thought the reverse is true: it is necessary to understand society in order to understand the individual. Because

Marx regards human nature as essentially historical, he maintains that it cannot be investigated in abstraction from specific historical circumstances. More specifically, human nature cannot be understood in abstraction from the organization of material productivity in the society.

Under capitalism, which is the focus of Marx's critical analysis, the two main classes are the working class (the proletariat) and the ruling class (the bourgeoisie), which owns the means of production. Members of the same class participate in similar kinds of productive activity and live in similar social and material circumstances. These circumstances shape the physical development and the personalities, attitudes, and consciousness of members of each class. The greater health and life expectancy of the ruling class, contrasted with that of the proletariat, is one example of how these processes work. Not only does the ruling class dominate the mode of production, it also determines the development and circulation of knowledge and values. Hence it generates perceptions of human nature and social reality that are distorted by its own perspective so as to make the status quo seem like the 'natural' way for things to be. It is clear, however, that capitalist social arrangements are designed to serve the interests of the ruling class. So members of the proletariat who accept the received view as 'natural' are living in a state of 'false consciousness,' which makes it difficult for them to see the world from the perspective of their own class interests.

Marx's theory of alienated labour is particularly significant for feminists. Marx argues that the root cause of such alienation is to be found in the structure of industrial production, where workers have no say in the conditions of their work or in the design of its products and are cut off from its final use. As Marx puts it: "The *alienation* of the worker in his product means not only that his labour becomes an object, assumes an *external* existence, but that it exists independently, *outside himself*, and alien to him."[17] In consequence of being constantly engaged in alienated labour, Marx believes, members of the working class are deprived of any sense of participation in the processes in which they spend most of their waking hours. They experience their work as meaningless and unfulfilling and their place in the social order as insignificant.

One of the roots of alienation is in the division of labour into isolated, minutely specialized tasks. Marx would replace this divisive situation with collective ownership of the means of production and a reorganization of the labour process that would reintegrate mental and manual labour. Alienated labour would be supplanted by the conscious, purposeful activity that Marx calls "praxis." This term refers to co-operative social activity that does involve some division of labour, but only through drawing upon the knowledge, experience, and skills of workers themselves. By contrast with alienated labour, praxis would develop in awareness of collective human needs and of the place of each person's endeavours in the scheme designed to satisfy those needs.

Marx's distrust of biological explanations is apparent in his contention that the division of labour in capitalist society is rooted in the division of labour and of power within the family. The claim is that those familial divisions are based purely on physiological factors: on differences of sex and age. Yet Marx maintains that the enslavement of a wife and children within the family is the first form of private property; and for him, private property is one of the fundamental social evils. It is an evil that cannot be rationalized by spurious appeals to biology. It is an evil that is perpetuated by capitalist social arrangements.

A more sustained analysis of women's oppression under capitalism is developed by Marx's associate,

---

...women are oppressed under capitalism because of a sexual division of labour that serves the interests of men directly.

Friedrich Engels (1820–1895), in *The Origin of the Family, Private Property and the State*, published in 1884. In the nuclear family of capitalist society, Engels sees a microcosmic mirroring of the larger, macroscopic social structure, with the husband occupying the role of the bourgeoisie and the wife the role of the proletariat. Engels attributes the privatization and denigration of household labour to the development of the nuclear family, where "the wife became the head servant, excluded from all participation in social production."[18] The solution he envisages would be for women to refuse to remain confined within the sphere of private domestic labour by entering the public world of productive work. To make this transformation possible, domestic labour and child care would have to become public, collective responsibilities.

In short, in the Marxist view, women are oppressed under capitalism because of a sexual division of labour that serves the interests of men directly. That same division of labour serves the interests of capitalism indirectly, through serving the interests of men. Women are responsible, without pay, for child-raising, cooking, attending to all of the mundane family needs, and looking after the sick and the aged, leaving men free to devote themselves fully to productivity in the public world of waged labour. Under such an arrangement, capitalist society need not pay for the reproduction of the labour power upon which it depends.

In the early years of socialist fervour there were differences of opinion among socialist women about whether 'the woman question' would be dealt with by the revolutionary changes that socialist thinkers and activists were proposing. The contrasting views of some of the leading socialist women illustrate this point. Radical German socialist Rosa Luxemburg, for example, believed that her sex was irrelevant to the issues for which she was campaigning. She saw women's oppression as one of the many miseries of capitalist society that would no longer exist after the socialist revolution. By contrast, Luxemburg's friend Clara Zetkin believed that women's issues had to be dealt with separately, in recognition of women's dual oppression by both capitalism and patriarchy. Zetkin helped to found the International Socialist Women's Congress, and it is she who, in 1910, declared March 8th as International Women's Day. That day, which is still celebrated annually in Canada and throughout the world, was set aside to commemorate a 1909 strike by female garment workers in New York, who were protesting overcrowded, poorly ventilated, dangerous working conditions and very low pay. From related motives, Russian feminist Alexandra Kollontai campaigned for a special bureau in the Russian Social Democratic Labour party to devise ways of addressing women's concerns and argued that a commitment to promoting the liberation of women should be included in the stated aims of the party. She had noted that the Social Democratic Labour Party in pre-1914 Russia showed little interest in the circumstances of working-class women.[19] Although Kollontai's initial efforts met with little success, she later managed—at least temporarily—to place women's issues on the agenda of the Bolshevik revolution. Kollontai and Zetkin both realized that patriarchy exerts a kind of oppression all of its own. It is true that its manifestations have much in common with other forms of oppression; but feminists who have focused on the forms of oppression that patriarchy creates have ensured that the distinctive features of the oppression of women receive separate analysis.

Today socialist feminists continue to debate the issue of whether Engel's scheme to deal with the 'woman question' is the best solution. It still has not been determined whether women's participation in the work force, together with the collectivization of domestic tasks and child-rearing, could work to end women's oppression.[20] What is clear, however, is that no explanation in biological terms alone can account for the ways in which women are disadvantaged and marginalized in most known societies. Material and economic factors are instrumental in perpetuating the oppression of women by men. Feminists have worked, with notable success, to transform these circumstances: campaigning for affirmative action programs, insisting on equal pay for work of equal value, and demanding safe, affordable child care arrangements.

THE FREUDIAN CHALLENGE

◆ ◆ ◆

A third and equally important source of inspiration for modern feminism has come out of the analyses of sexuality and psychosexual development initiated by Havelock Ellis (1859–1939) and Sigmund Freud (1856–1939) in the late nineteenth and early twentieth centuries. It is interesting that this line of inquiry should have come to be so significant in feminist thought, because Freud himself stated unequivocally that "anatomy is destiny": as clear a statement of biological determinism as anyone could make.[21] Indeed, Freud and the early Freudians had no doubt that psychosexual development was biologically determined. Hence feminists in the early years of the current movement were highly critical of Freud, characterizing psychoanalysis as a form of brainwashing designed to keep women quiet, passive, and in their place—especially sexually. The well-adjusted woman, in Freudian terms, was one who had learned to accept her patriarchally defined role of passive dependence in a heterosexual marriage, schooling herself to please her husband. Sexual maturity was her goal. Evidence of its achievement was the ability to achieve vaginal orgasm, to recognize male supremacy in all things, and to be content with her place in life. Kate Millett argues in *Sexual Politics* that the primary effect of Freudian discussions of female sexuality was to convince "the dispossessed that the circumstances of their deprivation are organic, therefore unalterable."[22] In short, Freudian doctrine, literally read, stands as a strong rationalization of women's subservient position in sexual relations, with its claim that their situation is biologically determined, natural. Joanna Boehnert suggests in her chapter on the psychology of women that the

intellectual and scientific respect Freud's theories commanded made it seem unnecessary to criticize any of the social and institutional restrictions on women's lives. Freudian explanations of psychosexual development seemed to be adequate and definitive.

In the light of these events, it may appear preposterous to claim Freud as one of the inspirations of contemporary feminism. Freudian theory seems to reinstate a form of determinism that can only lead women to blame themselves if they are unable to accept their natural place in the world. But psychoanalytic theory, especially since the late 1970s, has been an immensely fertile area of feminist discussion. The very need to criticize Freud's views because of their discrepancy with women's experiences opens a vitally important debate about aspects of women's lives that most political theorists ignore. In its emphasis upon sexuality, desire, primary process, and creativity, psychoanalytic theory addresses private, disorderly, and non-rational aspects of personal experience. It emphasizes the central significance of sexuality in human lives and creates space for an affirmation of female sexuality, defined and practised in women's own terms. It gives impetus to analyses of the social implications of sexuality and desire, of the relations between repression and social organization, and of the interplay between individual psychic formation and the production and maintenance of the social order.

Through analyses of the effects of parenting and socialization in producing sexual identity, feminists have developed critical readings of classical psychoanalytic texts and have explored the implications of drawing a distinction between sex and gender.[23] Second-wave feminists tended, initially, to work with a clear distinction, using the term 'sex' to refer to the biological differences in genitalia and reproductive function between male and female human beings; and 'gender' to refer to the social and psychological creation of masculine and feminine people, socialized to fulfill a complex set of requirements and expectations about what it is to be a woman—or a man. More recently feminists have hesitated to maintain so clear a distinction. Recent work on sex and sexuality has made clear that sex cannot be accepted as a simple physiological given, then to be embellished by gender. Sex, too, is to a significant degree a social construct.[24] Some feminists have argued that the sex/gender distinction merely repeats the old body/mind, nature/culture distinction, which tended to denigrate bodily, physical powers and pleasures that many feminists now want to affirm and celebrate. And 'gender' seems to divide too neatly into two, thus obscuring different manifestations of gender in different cultures, subcultures, and sexual orientations.[25] Yet despite these new debates, there is still evidence that a sex/gender-order (which varies across historical, cultural, and racial lines) dictates how people should live their sexual being. Hence questions about the psychosexual construction of masculinity and femininity are central to current feminist discussion.

"one is not born, but rather becomes a woman"

One of Freud's most articulate early feminist critics is Simone de Beauvoir (1908–1986), in her pathbreaking study, *The Second Sex*. This work stands as a milestone in the development of contemporary feminism: even those who criticize it do so within a frame of reference that de Beauvoir has created. Her observation that "one is not born, but rather becomes a woman"[26] connects directly with later feminist analyses of patriarchally constituted psychological and sexual being. At least as influential is de Beauvoir's characterization of women as "the second sex," thus designated by virtue of their creation as Other, with reference to a masculine more. De Beauvoir writes:

> Just as for the ancients there was an absolute vertical with reference to which the oblique was defined, so there is an absolute human type, the masculine.... Thus humanity is male and man denies woman not in herself but as relative to him; she is not regarded as an autonomous being....She is defined and differentiated with reference to man and not he with reference to her; she is the incidental, the inessential as opposed to the essential. He is the Subject, he is the Absolute—she is the Other.[27]

Many of the best-known present-day feminist writings amount, in effect, to a set of variations on this theme.

De Beauvoir believes that the relegation of woman to 'otherness' derives from received conceptions of female biology, and women's psychological inability to transcend it. Women are commonly portrayed as immersed in the material realm, dragged down by their physical being, slaves to the reproduction of the species. Influenced by Jean-Paul Sartre's claim that conscious beings are distinguished from material beings in their capacity to define themselves, to *transcend* their material being, de Beauvoir maintains that this capacity belongs to men but not to women. In this failure to transcend, primarily, women are Other. Because de Beauvoir

seems to accept this pessimistic picture of female biology, and of women's psychological inability to come to terms with it, many feminists have taken exception to her description of what it is to belong to the second sex. They argue that her ideas are fundamentally misogynist and that her evident horror at the 'messier' aspects of female anatomy and biological functioning places her in the camp of male detractors of femininity.

The Second Sex presents a detailed descriptive analysis of the social and psychological processes through which a female baby becomes a feminine woman. It offers a marvellous account of the construction of femininity on the basis of biological determinism. De Beauvoir's analysis covers such previously unmentionable aspects of female existence as puberty, menstruation, sexual intercourse, and childbearing. The simple fact that so much could be written about the physical, phenomenological details of what it means to live as a woman in a male-defined world astonished de Beauvoir's early readers. Their astonishment alone attests to the path-breaking character of her work.

It is worth noting that when she wrote *The Second Sex*, de Beauvoir did not consider herself to be a feminist. Like many of the socialist feminists, she believed that revolutionary socialism would bring an end to the oppression of women along with all other social injustices and that the class struggle had priority over the feminist struggle. Although she remained a socialist throughout her life, de Beauvoir later came to believe that socialist and feminist issues required separate treatment. She commented, "Feminists are women—or even men, too—who are fighting to change women's condition in association with the class struggle, but independently of it as well." She declared herself a feminist after all, "Because I realised that we must fight for the situation of women, here and now, before our dreams of socialism come true."[28] De Beauvoir remained politically involved throughout her life. She became a member of the group "Choisir" in 1971 to protest against the illegality of abortion in France. In 1977 she became editor of a new radical-feminist journal, *Questions féministes*, devoted to theoretical texts that dealt with women's oppression. In this capacity she was closely allied with the new French feminists, even though she wrote none of the texts now considered pivotal to their thinking.

Feminist theory could not have advanced as it has since the 1960s had the ground not been prepared by all of these intellectual and social developments. Even feminists who have taken issue with aspects of these lines of thought have found in them a necessary critical focus. In proceeding, now, to discuss some of the forms that feminist theory has taken in the last decades of the twentieth century, my intention is not to suggest that all was quiet in the feminist world between the early growth of liberalism and socialism and the feminist resurgence in the 1960s. Feminist activism in campaigning for the suffrage alone would attest to the falsity of such a suggestion. And the concerted activities of cultural feminists and social-reform feminists at the end of the nineteenth and the beginning of the twentieth centuries were remarkable in their social impact. Jane Errington details the activities of Canadian suffragists and Canadian social feminists in her chapter in this book. Naomi Black shows, too, how wrong it would be to claim that there were no feminist issues before the emergence of the contemporary women's movement. But the purpose of this chapter is to give an idea of some principal strands of present-day feminist theory. Certain historical movements in which these strands originated have been described in order to locate current feminism within a broader intellectual history. The next task is to examine contemporary feminism in some of its many guises.

CONTEMPORARY THEORY: *LIBERAL FEMINISM*

◆ ◆ ◆

Contemporary feminist theory draws upon the entire spectrum of ideas, causes, and political agendas discussed so far—adding to, elaborating upon, and engaging critically with them. Some twentieth-century feminists have concentrated on adapting classical political theories to feminist ends. Thus, against the background of classical liberal theory, contemporary liberal feminists argue for women's rights to enjoy the freedom and equality of opportunity claimed by the autonomous liberal individual. Betty Friedan, who is probably the best-known spokeswoman of post-1960 liberal feminism, observes in *The Feminist Mystique*: "My definition of feminism is simply that women are people in the fullest sense of the work, who must be free to move in society with all the privileges and opportunities and responsibilities that are their human and American right."[29] Feminism, as Friedan understands it, is less a theory of women's oppression by patriarchy than it is a theory of human rights.

According to liberal feminists, sex discrimination is unjust primarily because it deprives women of equal rights to pursue their own self-interest. Justice and fairness require equal opportunities for each individual,

regardless of sex. Liberal feminists deplore the informal discrimination, with its roots in biological determinism, that is generated by the assumption that women are not suited to certain kinds of work, or that they are especially suited to other—peculiarly 'feminine'—kinds. Liberals also oppose the formal discrimination that pro-

---

Women's lack of equality in public life is exacerbated by oppressive sexual standards...

---

duces an asymmetry in the legal rights of women and men in capitalist societies. Liberal feminists maintain that women's inferior social status is not freely chosen; rather, bias and discrimination block their access to equal participation with men in occupations that confer a high social status. Women's relegation to low-paid clerical and service work, for example, and their (often sole) responsibility for child care and housework diminish their freedom and autonomy in other areas of their lives. Their poverty relative to men often makes it impossible for them to exercise their legal rights or to enjoy their social rights. Women's lack of equality in public life is exacerbated by oppressive sexual standards according to which they are viewed primarily as sex objects. Hence they are limited in their freedom to dress and act as they would like, for fear of inviting unwanted sexual attention; and in their freedom to move about in public spaces, for fear of sexual assault.

Liberal feminists aim to free women from their dependent status in patriarchal society, and their efforts have met with notable success. [In her chapter in this book] Sandra Burt gives an account of some of the successes that Canadian liberal feminists have realized. Yet liberal feminists retain some ideological commitment to the belief that political decisions are the decisions made within the formal political process—that the term 'politics' should be restricted to what takes place in the public sphere. For this reason they have been less assiduous than socialist and radical feminists in their analyses of the daily politics of the 'private,' domestic sphere, and hence in their analyses of sexual power and privilege. Liberal feminists argue persuasively that women must be included equally within existing public decision-making structures. Yet they often assume that the structures themselves need no modifications beyond those that would automatically come about if women were included on an equal basis with men.

Friedan claims to have located the root of all sexist evils in the "feminine mystique," which defines woman in terms of her femininity and judges her solely according to her performance as a wife and mother. Women, in her view, must claim an identity of their own in order to shake off the effects of this mystique. Although large numbers of middle-class white American women recognized themselves in Friedan's analysis and tried to change their lives accordingly, the problem as she presents it is clearly specific to these reasonably affluent women living in the stability of a continuing marriage. Now it is true that all women are constrained by the ideology of femininity. Yet the self-realization Friedan urges is by no means equally available to all women in all economic and social circumstances. Like most liberal feminists, Friedan advocates individual solutions, taking scant account of the extent to which patriarchal capitalism sustains women's oppression. By contrast, socialist feminists, across a wide spectrum of positions, argue that oppression cannot be treated as an individual problem. It can be understood only by seeing women against the background of the social and economic circumstances that shape their lives and can be eradicated only through collective action. Whether abstract equality, or equality with men, could achieve all that is necessary for women's emancipation remains a question with no easy answer. Perfect equality could well create a set of problems all of its own, derived from a requirement to live as equals, but on men's terms. Hence, although equality would undoubtedly be preferable to subservience and oppression, many feminists argue that it would only be for want of a better solution that a feminist would be a liberal.[30]

Liberal theory can, at best, define an area of public life in which women would have unlimited formal opportunities. It offers no indication of how access to that area would, in practice, be achieved. Feminists who are critical of liberal solutions point out that autonomous, freely participating citizens need wives at home to mind the children and attend to domestic matters. Because liberal theory works with a model of society in which feminist change would merely require men to move over to make room for women, it does not challenge the extent to which those structures are defined and constructed to promote masculine well-being, understood according to a narrowly stereotyped conception of masculinity. Liberal feminism leaves masculine values intact and does not address the systemic injustices fostered by the patriarchal relations that sustain women's sexual and economic dependence.

CONTEMPORARY THEORY:
MARXIST AND SOCIALIST FEMINISM

◆ ◆ ◆

Marxist and socialist feminists are critical of liberal theory because they believe that there is no point in arguing for political liberalism unless one has a theory to show how people can achieve the economic means, and the power, to enjoy it.[31] They argue that equality of legal rights will have minimal impact upon actual social inequalities unless there are far more fundamental economic and social changes. Drawing, then, upon a Marxist analysis of class oppression, socialist feminists maintain that the capitalist economic system oppresses women as a group, just as it oppresses the working class as a whole. Yet within capitalist patriarchal society, women are subjected to additional forms of oppression that relate specifically to their sex. First, within the labour force women's work is alienated labour in the same ways that men's work is: women own neither the means of production nor the products of their labour. Second, women in the labour force commonly find themselves in positions where they are subordinate to men whose superiority is by no means obvious: hence they are doubly alienated from realizing their potential. Third, women who work at home, as housewives, are in an even more powerless position: their lives are devoted to serving others, their labour is accorded no material value, and they have limited access to the activities of the 'public' world.

Under capitalism women are the primary producers of goods and services for use within the family, yet because their labour has no monetary exchange value, it is considered worthless. But feminists differ on the question of whether domestic labour is alienated labour in the same sense that capitalist productive labour is. Some feminists maintain that the menial, non-creative, and isolating nature of household tasks marks them as alienated labour.[32] Others claim the household as the only unalienated work space in capitalist society. There, women know that what they do is useful, for they see the importance of their labour in caring for those they love and sustaining family values.[33] In the home women have more control over the pace and use of their work than office or industrial workers do. Yet these positive features have to be weighed against the fact that women's labour is undervalued. Hence some socialist feminists have argued that there should be wages for housework; and most of them maintain that women's invisible domestic labour needs to be revalued to acknowledge its vital role in reproducing the labour power upon which economic productivity depends.

These analyses have demonstrated the extent of capitalism's dependence upon women's unpaid, invisible labour. But it needs to be remembered that capitalist societies are not alone in oppressing women. Notable among socialist feminists who remind us that women's oppression cannot be fully explained by the sexual division of labour under capitalism are Michele Barrett and Gayle Rubin. Barrett observes that the sexual division of labour was not a capitalist creation: capitalism may have refined and elaborated it, but the ideology of a gendered division of labour was there to be elaborated.[34] And Rubin outlines a spectrum of patriarchal practices that oppress, subdue, and denigrate women, yet are quite independent of capitalist economics. She observes: "No analysis of the reproduction of labour under capitalism can explain foot-binding, chastity belts, or any of the incredible array of Byzantine, fetishized indignities, let alone the more ordinary ones that have been inflicted upon women in various times and places."[35] Yet Barrett also notes significant structural differences between pre-capitalist and capitalist modes of production, which are apparent in social arrangements that have direct consequences for women's lives. Capitalist society is marked, in particular, by an emphasis upon competitive mass production and by that specialized, and alienating, divi-

---

Even in the early 1990s women commonly earn sixty-seven cents for each dollar that men earn.

---

sion of labour into minute, isolated units that is a focus of Marx's critique.

These features of capitalism recall Engel's contention that the disempowering effects of the sexual division of labour would be nullified if women could enter the paid labour force as full participants. Socialist feminists have pointed out that entry into the work force does not automatically count as a liberating experience for women. Rather, many women simply find themselves doing double duty: they work for wages in the labour market and continue to do just as much unpaid domestic labour at home. Without radical social restructuring that would make good child care readily available and effect a redistribution of other household tasks, Engels's solution cannot be the ideal one.

Its problems are exacerbated by the fact that, more often than not, women in the work force earn considerably less than men do. Even in the early 1990s women commonly earn sixty-seven cents for each dollar that men earn. Some socialist feminists see this wage differential as the primary cause of women's ongoing powerlessness and oppression, even as they gain increased access to waged work. The wage differential used to be rationalized by claims that the father's income is the 'family income,' which is equitably shared within the family. This argument has been used by employers, who contend that women work only to *supplement* the family income. Yet the ideology of liberal capitalist society allows no 'interference' in 'private' family matters to ensure that the man's income really is distributed as it is thought to be: too often the ideology works to conceal the genuine poverty of women and children. Moreover, the 'family wage' argument could only apply to women who have heterosexual, patriarchal living arrangements. Single mothers and lesbian couples have no such family wage at their disposal. Feminist efforts to transform these unjust practices are achieving some success, at least in current efforts to legislate wage equity.

Women have tended to enter the labour force in temporary, unskilled jobs that offer them no security. Some socialist theorists have characterized these women as a 'reserve army of labour,' which capitalism can draw upon at times of need and dismiss into unemployment when economic circumstances dictate.[36] Such women do not achieve economic independence from men, and those who have no man tend to become dependent on social welfare. When one adds the fact that, in capitalist society, women who are 'liberated' from domesticity into the labour market are often engaged, like men, in alienated labour, it is easy to see that Engels did not have the perfect solution to women's oppression.

Moreover, just as assumptions about the family wage often mask women's inferior economic status, so too assumptions about the class to which 'the family' belongs often conceal a woman's inferior, or equivocal, class membership. A Marxist division along class lines does not offer an obvious way of designating a women's social class. She can sometimes be identified according to the class of her husband or of the man on whom she is dependent, but for a divorced, single, or independently employed woman, or for women in permanent lesbian relationships, class identification has to work quite differently.

Socialist feminists have addressed these issues by advocating alternatives both to capitalist modes of production and to the patriarchal organization of families and other social institutions. Socialists see the nuclear family as a cornerstone of women's oppression. It keeps women socially powerless, enforces compulsory heterosexuality,[37] and reproduces masculine and feminine stereotypes in the next generation. Capitalist society seems to require stereotypical feminine women to nurture men to manhood and to help them fulfill the demands of adult masculinity. As Heidi Hartmann observes, "Sexist ideology serves the dual purpose of glorifying male characteristics/capitalist values, and denigrating female characteristics/social need."[38] In sustaining a high level of demand for consumer goods and inculcating in children the competitive, free-market ideology of capitalism, the nuclear family is effective in perpetuating women's subordinate and marginal positions.

CONTEMPORARY THEORY: *RADICAL FEMINISM*

◆ ◆ ◆

Radical feminists would be in general agreement with socialist-feminist analyses of women's social and economic circumstances and with many of their strategies for change. But radical and socialist feminists differ on a fundamental question of emphasis. Whereas material, economic, and social factors are primary for socialist

---

...radical feminists contend that the oppression of women by men is the root cause of all oppressions...

---

feminists, radical feminists contend that the oppression of women by men is the root cause of all oppressions (radical = at the root).

Radical feminism was born out of women's disillusionment with New Left politics in North America, Britain, and France in the late 1960s. Women in the United States who were fighting for equality and justice in the civil-rights movement and against the war in Vietnam found themselves treated as subordinate members of these organizations and exploited as sex objects and servants (making the coffee, doing the secretarial chores) for their male co-workers. Such experiences prompted Robin Morgan to write, "Sexism is the root oppression, the one which, until and unless we *up*root it, will continue to put forth the branches of racism, class

hatred, ageism, competition, ecological disaster, and economic exploitation."[39] Sexism, as manifested in patriarchal families, gender stereotyping, pornography, wife and child abuse, and rape, became the focus of radical-feminist analysis.

The radical-feminist dictum 'the personal is political' declares that patriarchal society structures personal experiences and social relations in ways that disadvantage women. For example, the liberal slogan that the government has no place in the bedrooms of the nation, which Canadians (echoing Pierre Trudeau) proudly intoned in the late 1960s, improves upon the belief that society can legislate permissible sexual behaviour between adults. But it screens from public scrutiny such common and damaging practices as rape and sexual abuse within marriage and families. In fact, many of the everyday practices that perpetuate women's oppression occur within the home, a place that is protected by an ideology of sanctity and privacy that maintains the invisibility of women's domestic and childrearing labour.[40] Before radical feminists placed it on the public agenda, domestic violence passed as a private matter in which the law ought not to meddle. Radical and socialist feminists emphasize the systematic difference in power between women and men, which manifests itself in men's socially and legally sanctioned control over women's sexual, procreative, and emotional lives. The ideology that supports this control produces the consequence that when things go wrong in the domestic sphere, the woman is held accountable for not being appropriately obedient and submissive. Such power relations need to be undermined if women's emancipation is to be possible.

Many radical feminists maintain that any male-female relation will necessarily be oppressive to the woman; hence they conclude that female separatism is the only option. Notable among them is Mary Daly, who claims: "For men...life has meant feeding on the bodies and minds of women, sapping energy at the expense of female deaths....It is men who have sapped the lifeforce of women."[41] Daly maintains that women under patriarchy live in a condition of "robotitude," a term that refers to "the state of servitude of women in a phallocratic world."[42] This condition is induced by a system of myths devised by men and internalized by women to the point where they live unthinkingly by them. Radical feminism, for Daly, is a voyage of "woman becoming,"[43] fuelled by "gynergy" (women's energy),[44] and moving toward a full affirmation of woman-centred valued. It is a voyage toward developing a separate and self-affirming women's culture.

CONTEMPORARY THEORY:
SEXUALITY AND REPRODUCTION

◆ ◆ ◆

Socialist and radical feminism developed out of quite distinct concerns, but they have been mutually influential, with many common themes and agendas uniting their interests. One important issue of concern has been women's sexual and reproductive freedom. Feminists have been active, vocal, and often successful—although their successes are still fragile—in claiming women's right to abortion on demand, insisting upon reliable birth control, affirming women's sexual freedom in relationships—either lesbian or heterosexual—that refuse patriarchal norms and challenge male control over childbirth and child-raising.

In *The Dialectic of Sex*, one of the first radical-feminist texts, Shulamith Firestone names biological reproduction as the primary source of women's oppression.[45] She believes that women can escape from the traps of biology only through reproductive technology and communal living arrangements that supplant the nuclear family. So long as women bear children, their biology will be their destiny. In the years since Firestone made these claims, however, the revolutionary promise that she saw in reproductive technology has been seriously contested. Rona Achilles shows in her chapter here how these technologies threaten women's reproductive autonomy. Firestone urges women to reject the ideology of romantic love that encourages them to live as sex/love objects for men, deluded in the belief that romantic (heterosexual) love is the route to happiness.

Adrienne Rich focuses somewhat differently on women's reproductive lives, contending that their experiences of motherhood have been co-opted by "motherhood as institution." A complex power structure produced by the interlocking forces of law, medicine, culture, and professional expertise works to create an "invisible institution" of male control over women's bodies and minds.[46] Rich celebrates women's strengths in keeping much of the experience of motherhood for themselves despite the power of institutional control. She is impressed with some women's abilities to preserve, "even within the destructiveness of the institution: the tenderness, the passion, the trust in our instincts, the evidence of a courage we did not know we owned."[47] Women's capacity to resist patriarchal power draws upon these strengths.

In like vein, Mary O'Brien argues that men have endeavoured to negate their alienation from the reproductive process by appropriating children as their own (giving them a name and a place in the social structure). Thus they claim "ownership of the women's reproductive labour power in a sense recognizably similar to... the sense in which capitalists appropriate the surplus labour power of wage labourers."[48] Yet, she observes, "Embedded in the child is the alienated reproductive labour of the mother"[49]—alienated because patriarchal societies do not permit her to call the child her own. O'Brien maintains that this appropriation needs to be understood in dialectical relation to woman's reproductive consciousness. A woman knows that the child is hers, and it grows with her love, yet she must nurture it to be a labourer or a producer of children in its turn. Out of the strength of female reproductive consciousness, O'Brien also sees a possibility for developing a unified social consciousness that could transform the social structures that perpetuate the alienation of both reproductive and productive labour.

The belief that male-female relationships are inevitably oppressive to women has led many feminists to advocate alternatives either of the separatist kind that Mary Daly advocates or of some other variety. Some feminists recommend celibacy as the only solution, for they believe that sexual relations, whether lesbian or heterosexual, always generate dominance and oppression. Separatist lesbian feminists contend that sexual expression between women is the only acceptable sexuality for women who are seeking freedom from the exploitative requirements of patriarchy. Separatists contend that male domination is sustained by heterosexuality, which ties women to men socially, economically, and emotionally. The only way to break free, they maintain, is through female separatism. Lesbianism has an impressively subversive political potential in a society where women are defined, primarily, as sex objects for men. Adrienne Rich characterizes compulsory heterosexuality as a *"political institution"* created "to enforce women's total emotional, erotic loyalty to men." She says that heterosexuality wrenches "women's emotional and erotic energies away from themselves and all other women and from woman-identified values."[50] Rich believes that the pain a growing girl experiences in transferring her affections from a woman—her mother—to a man shows that this is an unnatural choice into which women are coerced by the patriarchal order. She urges scholars to explore the continuum of lesbian experience past and present, so that women will realize that heterosexuality is not the only option.[51] Separatist feminists believe that lesbianism offers a place for a radical restructuring of sexuality in a woman-culture founded on non-hierarchical, mutually affirming female values.

CONTEMPORARY THEORY: *FRENCH FEMINISM*

◆ ◆ ◆

Contemporary French feminism stands as a distinct and original contribution to feminist theory. French feminists are ideologically closer to socialist and radical feminists than they are to liberal feminists. They share with English-speaking radical and socialist feminists an activist origin in the student revolt in Paris in 1968. Yet French feminism has its roots in French and German philosophical traditions that are markedly different from the traditions that have shaped feminist theory in the English-speaking world. French feminists are not so much political theorists as intellectuals in a society where an intellectual can play a vociferous political role, attacking the arrogant assumptions of entrenched institutions. Perhaps in consequence their theoretical work focuses on literary and psychoanalytic theory, creativity, and sexuality. The reinterpretation of Freud by French psychoanalyst Jacques Lacan has become one of the focal points of feminist writing in France.

For Lacan, the Freudian story of human psychosexual development is a story of the 'fall' from one-ness with the mother into consciousness. That fall is, at the same time, a fall into language, which Lacan refers to as the symbolic realm. Language is the bearer of the patriarchal social order. It exists prior to the moment when a child learns it, yet it is the primary mode of expression available to any maturing child. It is through language that a preconscious child becomes a conscious human subject. Central to Lacan's discussion is the belief that entry into the symbolic order brings with it an awareness of separation-alienation from mother, self, and world. Men endeavour to overcome that separation through a (phallic) mastery, partially manifested in the patriarchal power of language. It is through language that a child learns of the greater value accorded to maleness in a world where femaleness signifies otherness.

It is small wonder, then, that language both as a subject-matter of linguistics and as the substance of literary texts has become a primary concern in French feminist writings. Julia Kristeva, for example, asserts that the conception of language itself, as it is studied by linguists, is riddled with political implications. She explores the arbitrariness of meaning, the artificiality of separating 'speaking subjects' from their context, and the power inherent in the application of linguistic labels.[52] Her aim is to understand the overweening power of masculine rationality, which privileges "reason, order, unity and lucidity," doing so "by silencing and excluding the irrationality, chaos and fragmentation that has come to represent femininity."[53] Above all (and following Lacan), Kristeva sees in language a means of designating sexual difference: a fundamental difference that manifests itself "in the relationship to power, language, and meaning,"[54] which is radically different for women and for men. With other French feminists, Kristeva is critical of feminists efforts to minimize the significance of biological, sexual difference. Women, she believes, should affirm and rejoice in their difference. In it they have a means of subverting the patriarchal order. They should use it to advantage, even if it results in their relegation to a marginal status, beyond the written text and the limits of public discourse.

Femininity, sexuality, and discourse are central topics of analysis in the works of two other French feminists: Hélène Cixous and Luce Irigaray. Characterizing traditional discourse as essentially phallocentric, Cixous speaks "about women's writing: about *what it will do*."[55] She believes that conceptions of 'masculine' and 'feminine' imprison thinkers within oppressive binary oppositions. Yet she, too, maintains that the solution is not to *deny* sexual difference, as advocates of androgyny have done, but to emphasize, write, and celebrate the feminine. Such writing, as she conceives of it, does not "annul differences but stirs them up, pursues them, increases their number."[56] Hence no one 'pair' of differences, such as the traditional male/female dichotomy, is privileged, yet difference is always a central topic of discussion.

French feminists read texts, then, to see what is left out: they read the gaps and exclusions in a text as manifestations of power in discourse. Rather than concentrating their critical attention on modes of material production, they examine cultural production to discern what its artefacts say—and resist saying—about their creators. French feminists draw upon the potential of the comic, the ironic, the mimetic, to reveal the arbitrariness of patriarchal assumptions by 'making them strange.' Irigaray advocates a subversive feminine discourse that 'writes from the margins' to displace (phallocentric) male discourse.[57] In miming the masculine, this writing points to the ephemerality of masculine power with its exclusive claim to occupy the dominant speaking positions. It celebrates the power of female sexuality, pleasure, and desire. There is no question, here, that women should try to be just like men: rather, the point is that their strength is in their difference. French feminists displace the univocal voice of the masculine tradition with a plurivocality that constantly affirms difference. Since women's most visible difference is bodily, it is the female body that is to be foregrounded, as a source of disruptive female desire and creativity.

In their writings on sexuality, feminine creativity, and power structures that are constructed around sex and class privilege, contemporary French feminists examine many of the same physical and psychological implications of being a woman in a man's world that de Beauvoir analyses in *The Second Sex*. Yet contemporary French feminists differ markedly from de Beauvoir in their celebration of bodily femininity and in the challenges they pose to the theories and cultural artefacts that systematically devalue it. They expose standard analyses of the 'human condition' as androcentric and heterosexist; maintaining that even the word 'human' refers only to *men's* theories and inventions. It is but one small example of the entrenched phallocentricity of language and discourse, which needs to be unmasked, ridiculed, and subverted. Elaine Marks and Isabelle de Coutivron remark that French feminists, fittingly, have "stolen the intellectual tools of patriarchy and, in many cases, [have] turned them against their inventors."[58]

CONTEMPORARY FEMINISM: *DIVERSITY AND COMMONALITY*

◆ ◆ ◆

Distinction among the separate strands that have, historically, gone into the making of feminist theory tend to obscure the commonalities that initially united feminists of seemingly disparate ideological persuasions. Feminists of the early years of the 'second wave' rallied around a common cause in their opposition to patriarchy. They focused on their new-found similarities and celebrated the sisterhood of all women. In the 1980s difference became the most pressing item on the feminist agenda. Groups of women who could not see themselves as the 'women' that feminism claimed to be speaking for criti-

...early second-wave feminism was primarily the creation of white, middle-class, affluent, educated, and usually heterosexual women.

cized the early second-wave theorists for assuming a falsely universal category of 'woman.' The fact is that, for all its ideological differences, early second-wave feminism was primarily the creation of white, middle-class, affluent, educated, and usually heterosexual women. Its

generalizations about the experience of women took for granted a homogeneous female position in society that could not capture such specificities as race, class, culture, age, or sexual preference, in whose terms women's experiences were as different from one another as they were similar in virtue of their 'femaleness.' Feminists of the 1990s are attempting to work through issues of commonality and difference, to determine the extent to which it is legitimate to claim a common feminist cause in the face of the exclusions and marginalizations within feminism that assumptions of sisterhood tended to produce.[59]

Black feminists have been especially articulate in pointing out how consistently feminist discourse, articulated out of white middle-class experience, has arrogated to itself the right to speak for all women, black or white, rich or poor, heterosexual or lesbian. Women of colour have been particularly critical of an analogy that was drawn by white feminists in the 1970s, between the social positions of women and blacks. This so-called equation attests to an implicit racism both in the language and in the presuppositions of early second-wave theory.[60] In producing this analogy, white feminists simply ignored the enormous power differential, in predominantly white societies, between black and white women. They failed to take into account the effects of institutionalized racism in maintaining black women in poverty relative to white women, and in situations of more acute marginalization and differently restricted options. Moreover, in claiming the feminist cause as the primary political cause, white feminists could not see the urgency, for black women and other racially marginalized women, of making alliances with the oppressed men of their own racial or ethnic groups, in their struggles against forms of oppression whose effects often were more acute than patriarchal oppression. 'The patriarchy,' too, has usually been white and middle-class; relations between women and men in other classes and races cannot adequately be analysed on the same patriarchal model.

Issues of universality and diversity have generated a paradox at the centre of feminist theory in the 1990s. Feminism seems, still, to require the consciousness-raising that enables women to claim some measure of unity 'as women,' even while they concentrate on understanding differences. There is something persuasive, still, about Nancy Cott's observation: "The value accorded to 'sexual difference' in feminist theory has increased at the same time that the universality of the claim for sisterhood has been debunked. Ethnic, racial, and sexual diversity among women is stressed more than ever before in feminist theory, but so is the emphasis on how women (as a whole) differ from men (as a whole)."[61] But these urgent issues that centre around differences within feminism have the effect of problematizing the very idea that it is possible to refer to 'women as a whole' in any but an unjustly reductive way. Hence the historical goal of achieving equality for women has to be refined and redefined if it is to retain any legitimacy as a feminist project.

EQUALITY AND DIFFERENCE

◆ ◆ ◆

The question of equality forms a thread that runs through most of the early feminist texts and is highly contested in the pluralistic feminisms of the 1990s. Few feminists would deny that there is still some force in the (primarily liberal) claim that social justice demands equality before the law, with respect to opportunities for education and employment, to property ownership and remuneration for work, and to all matters of human rights. Plato's proposal in the *Republic* draws feminist attention because of the equality of educational opportunity he proposes for women and men. The early liberal preoccupation with issues of equality was one of the principal inspirations of contemporary feminist thought; and feminists still claim, and dispute, the value of working toward equality. Yet arguments to the effect that achieving equality *between the sexes* is the primary feminist goal are highly problematic. Both feminists and anti-feminists (albeit for different purposes) read such claims to mean that women want to be just like men. Yet it would be a rare feminist, today, who would name equality with men as the aim of her efforts to promote women's causes. Plato's scheme in the *Republic*, with its reliance on a masculine model, indicates why this idea is problematic.

The liberal vision of equality is similarly contentious. It provides ready support for a claim that women and men are equal, but different, and hence should occupy different but complementary places in society. Hence it translates too easily into a belief that women—even enlightened and educated ones—are best suited to be wives and mothers. Mill's belief that an equally educated woman will be prepared—and pleased—to share in her husband's pursuits shows that the equality he envisages is to be understood strictly on male terms, and that it derives primarily from the experiences of an affluent and propertied class of men. None of the arguments in favour of equality between the sexes

has been able to show how the unalike can be treated equally; for 'equality' tends to mean sameness of goals, rights, and opportunities.

To state the goal of feminism as one of achieving equality with men amounts to approving of how men are and claiming that women want to be like that too. But the question "equality with *which* men?" could never be answered, "Oh, of course, with all." Women would never have claimed equality with men who are

---

Modern (liberal) feminists who campaign for equality with men forget that men themselves are not equal under capitalism.

---

oppressed because of race, class, religion, ethnicity, or any other attribute. They do not want equality with coal miners, or with industrial workers sterilized by the chemicals they work with, or with men infected with cancer from pollutants in asbestos mines.[62] Modern (liberal) feminists who campaign for equality with men forget that men themselves are not equal under capitalism. Setting out to achieve equality with men requires opting into a utopian myth according to which all men can in fact (not just in theory) achieve success in proportion to their natural initiative, intelligence, and energy. It takes no account of the structural social impediments that locate men quite differently in relation to the powers and privileges that affluent societies appear to hold out to everyone.

Now, in a formal, abstract sense, women probably do want the freedom to achieve such status as *their* initiative, intelligence, and energy allow. But in patriarchal, capitalist societies, equality is more abstract than it is real. Women are not likely to achieve any real emancipation from the oppressions that have shaped their lives, as long as the structures of such societies remain intact, simply stretching a little to make space for women. If neither the rhetoric nor the practice of equality can accommodate differences between women, between men, and between women and men, then its value is questionable. As long as putative labour-market equality can (even implicitly) require women to conceal evidence of pregnancy, to work until labour begins, or to refrain from having children, then women's relevant differences from the (masculine) labour-market norm are not being taken into account.[63]

Questions of difference have never been adequately addressed in liberal capitalist societies, whose moral theories and common wisdom agree in declaring that it is both immoral and unjust to treat individuals differently. In the rhetoric of democratic societies it is simply taken for granted that all should be treated alike and equally. And traditional moral theories emphasize the importance of impartiality and equality in moral decisions, arguing that these values will be preserved only if moral decisions are based on reason alone, with no appeal to emotions. If the differences that are now central to feminist analysis are to be taken adequately into account in moral and political decision-making, then different ways of thinking about difference have to be developed.

A productive and controversial debate about sexual differences in moral consciousness was stimulated by Carol Gilligan's 1982 book *In a Different Voice*.[64] Analyzing the responses of a group of male and female subjects to Lawrence Kohlberg's tests for measuring moral development, Gilligan concluded that there are two moral systems. One system, which she perceived in the responses of her male subjects, approaches morality as a complex of rights and principles that provide a basis for making moral decisions. This approach to moral problems contrasts with a kind of response more common in her female subjects, according to which human lives are a network of social relationships and judgements of 'right' and 'wrong' depend upon the kinds of response, and care, that a specific situation demands. Traditionally, moral philosophers have believed that rights and principles are the proper issues for moral debate, for they can yield universally valid solutions. Questions about feelings and caring have been relegated to a realm of sentiment that is so idiosyncratic and particular that it does not lend itself to moral analysis.

There is a persistent belief in the history of Western thought that it is *reason*, rationality, that distinguishes human beings from other living creatures. According to this belief, the best realization of human possibilities will be achieved through the cultivation of reason. Now the emphasis upon rights and principles in moral theory derives from this veneration of reason. The argument goes that it is only through the use of reason that moral principles and rights can be discerned. Hence in the historical examples discussed earlier in this chapter, the education of the 'reason' is a constant theme. It was in consequence of their allegedly inferior rational capacities that women were deemed inferior to men. Wollstonecraft's claims for equal female access to the domain of reason can be understood in light of this belief. In the theories that inform the moral ideology of

late twentieth-century capitalist societies, as Gilligan shows, the belief persists that rationally discerned, universal, impartial moral principles constitute the proper 'stuff' of moral judgements. The capacity to act upon such principles is heralded as the mark of achieved moral maturity; and it is commonly believed that women are deficient in this capacity.

There is a still more subtle problem about reason for feminists. Genevieve Lloyd shows that reason itself, both as a distinguishing human characteristic and as a character ideal, is defined, throughout history, by exclusion of the traits that are traditionally associated with women and femaleness.[65] Lloyd demonstrates the near-impossibility simply of revaluing and celebrating these undervalued traits to claim for them a value equal to that accorded to 'masculine' traits. Much more radical deconstructions and reconstructions are required. In Gilligan's work, then, although she claims that both moral 'voices' are available alike to women and men, it is still not clear how such a sex-undifferentiated interplay could work, in practice. The 'different' voice that Gilligan hears has been associated with lesser female preoccupations, throughout a long and oppressive history. Her work appears to suggest that both voices should be permitted to speak freely and both sets of concerns accorded equal worth. But much more needs to be done in identifying the specificity of these voices—not just to women and men, but to a small and fairly homogeneous group of subjects—before the transformative potential of her work can be assessed. Meanwhile, Gilligan's research is remarkable for the sheer volume of productive, innovative debates it has generated around issues of rights and care.

Feminists are faced with the necessity of transforming a social system that has been constructed and informed by the assumption that what a select and privileged group of men do is the normal *human* thing to do, as Simone de Beauvoir's analysis of female Otherness makes clear. In the history of western thought, 'humanness' has been androcentrically defined; when women— or members of other races and cultures—think, speak, or act differently, their behaviour is judged deviant because of its divergence from that norm. Attributions of difference tend to lose sight of the fact that difference is a symmetrical relation. If women are different from men, or blacks from whites, or lesbian women from heterosexual women, then men, and whites, heterosexuals are, by the same token, different from women, blacks, lesbians. If members of any one of these groups speak in a 'different' voice, then they all do. The different voice in which the morality (and rationality) of the white male tradition has long been speaking—and drowning out all other voices by calling them 'different'—is itself but one voice among many. It may have legitimate things to say: it has gone to some lengths to ensure that its pronouncements count as the only respectable ones. But the other voices that are insisting on their share of the speaking places in the 1990s are emphasizing the partiality, the narrow specificity, of that masculine voice.

North American culture has been built on a ideology of sameness and conformity, which has produced the effect that when differences are noted, they tend to be noted judgementally, as deviant from a norm. An observed difference, in this conformist context, often provides a pretext for condemnation. Indeed, the history of woman's place in patriarchal society is a history of judgements to the effect that woman is different from man, and *hence* inferior (Other), The consequences have been apparent in the exploitative and oppressive practices that feminists have been working to displace.

In the process, many early feminist theorists concentrated upon de-emphasizing and/or defusing difference, arguing in favour of 'genderblind' laws, policies, and practices. They believed that this would be the best route to equality. These feminists claimed that taken-for-granted polarities are less stark than they seem to be; and they argue in terms of difference-in-sameness, sameness-in-difference, with a goal of understanding and tolerance. Such a program has never seemed to offer enough to the feminists who have maintained that women's differences from one another, and from men, have to be affirmed and celebrated. That program is unacceptable to feminists who believe that social structures and institutions have to be reformed so that they can deal adequately with all of the myriad differences between and among people.

Gilligan's work was inspired by a difference she perceived between her experiences as a woman and the theory she was teaching. She comments: "I was teaching the theory of adolescent development based on a view that maturity was being autonomous and independent. But I had never experienced that. It was clearly based on the male development cycle."[66] Gilligan did not just notice a difference and conclude that it must be sex-based: she cites evidence to support her conclusions. But what she does with the discrepancy between her *experience* and the accepted *theory* is particularly feminist. It tends still to be assumed, in 'malestream'[67] thought, that if experiences fly in the face of established theory, then so much the worse for the experiences. Theories are granted an intellectual authority that overrides experiences, so that if certain experiences do not 'fit' the theory, then the assumption is that there is something wrong with the experiences, not with the theory. Women, and other marginalized people, are familiar with the coercive power of theory and expertise in scientific, technological societies. But, like Gilligan, growing numbers of feminists are asking the revolutionary, subversive question: "What is wrong with this theory that it cannot explain my experience and the experiences of other women?" These are the questions feminists are asking as they work both in theory and in practice to undermine the silencing effects of theoretical, patriarchal power structures.

Notes

1. Juliet Mitchell, "Reflections on Twenty Years of Feminism," in Juliet Mitchell and Ann Oakley, eds., *What is Feminism?* (New York: Pantheon Books, 1986), 48.

2. These are the four constant structures of women's oppression designated by Juliet Mitchell in the title essay of her *Women: The Longest Revolution*, first published in 1968 (London: Virago Press, 1984).

3. Marilyn Frye, *The Politics of Reality: Essays in Feminist Theory* (Trumansburg, N.Y.: The Crossing Press, 1983), 4–5.

4. Nancy Cott draws attention to this paradox in her "Feminist Theory and Feminist Movements: The Past Before Us," in Mitchell and Oakley, *What is Feminism?* 49.

5. For feminist analyses of power, *see*: Anne Ferguson, "Motherhood and Sexuality: Some Feminist Questions," and Jana Sawicki, "Foucault and Feminism: Towards a Politics of Difference," both in *Hypatia: A Journal of Feminist Philosophy I*, no. 2(1986); Kathy Ferguson, *The Feminist*

Case Against Bureaucracy (Philadelphia: Temple University Press, 1984); and Sandra Lee Bartky, *Femininity and Domination* (New York: Routledge, 1990).

6. From Adrienne Rich's remarks at the Columbia University Seminar on Women and Society, 1976. Quoted by Hester Eisenstein in her *Contemporary Feminist Thought* (London: Allen & Unwin, 1984), 74.

7. Joan Kelly observes: "It has been a strength of patriarchy in all its historical forms to assimilate itself so perfectly to socioeconomic, political and cultural structures as to be virtually invisible." In Joan Kelly, *Women, History, and Theory* (Chicago: University of Chicago Press, 1984), 61.

8. *See*: Joan Kelly, "The Doubled Vision of Feminist Theory," in Kelly, *Women, History, and Theory*.

9. Aristotle, *Politics*, trans. Benjamin Jowett, in Richard McKeon, ed., *The Basic Works of Aristotle* (New York: Random House, 1941), 1254b.

10. Aristotle, *De Generatione Animalium*, trans. Arthur Platt, in McKeon, *Basic Works of Aristotle*.

11. *See*: Judith Hicks Stiehm, "The Unit of Political Analysis: Our Aristotlelian Hangover," in Sandra Harding and Merrill Hintikka, eds., *Discovering Reality* (Dordrecht: Reidel, 1983), 31–43.

12. Plato, *Republic*, trans. Paul Shorey, in Edith Hamilton and Huntington Cairns, eds., *The Collected Dialogues of Plato* (Princeton, N.J.: Princeton University Press, Bollingen Series, 1961), 455d–e.

13. Ibid., 456b.

14. Ibid., 460b.

15. J.S. Mill, "The Subjection of Women," in John Stuart Mill and Harriet Taylor Mill, *Essays on Sex Equality*, ed. Alice Rossi (Chicago: University of Chicago Press, 1970), 125.

16. *See*: John Stuart Mill and Harriet Taylor Mill, "Early Essays on Marriage and Divorce" (1832), in *Essays on Sex Equality*.

17. Karl Marx, *The Economic and Philosophical Manuscripts of 1844* (New York: International Publishers, 1964), 96.

18. Friedrich Engels, *The Origin of the Family, Private Property and the State* (New York: International Publishers, 1972), 65.

19. For an extended account of the contribution of women to the early socialist movement, *see*: M.J. Boxer and J.H. Quataert, eds., *Socialist Women: European Socialist Feminism in the Nineteenth and Early Twentieth Centuries* (New York: Elsevier, 1978).

20. These issues are debated in the essays collected in Lydia Sargent, ed., *Women and Revolution: A Discussion of the Unhappy Marriage of Marxism and Feminism* (Boston: South End Press, 1981).

21. Sigmund Freud, *Sexuality and the Psychology of Love*, ed. Phillip Reiff (New York: Collier Books, 1963), 181.

22. Kate Millett, *Sexual Politics* (New York: Avon Books, 1971), 187.

23. Noteworthy among texts that approach this task are: Juliet Mitchell, *Psychoanalysis and Feminism* (New York: Pantheon Books, 1974); Dorothy Smith and David Smith, *Women Look at Psychiatry* (Vancouver: Press Gang Publishers, 1975); Nancy Chodorow, *The Reproduction of Mothering: Psychoanalysis and the Sociology of Gender* (Berkeley: University of California Press, 1978); P. Susan Penfold and Gillian Walker, *Women and the Psychiatric Paradox* (Montreal: Eden Press, 1983); and Hannah Lerman, *A Mote in Freud's Eye: From Psychoanalysis to the Psychology of Women* (New York: Springer, 1986).

24. See, for example, Thomas Laqueur, *Making Sex: Body and Gender from the Greeks to Freud* (Cambridge, Mass.: Harvard University Press, 1990); and Suzanne J. Kessler, "The Medical Construction of Gender: Case Management of Intersexed Infants," *Signs: Journal of Women in Culture and Society* 16, no. 1 (Autumn 1990).

25. See in this connection Judith Butler, *Gender Trouble: Feminism and the Subversion of Identity* (New York: Routledge, 1990); and Denise Riley, *'Am I That Name?' Feminism and the Category of 'Women' in History* (Minneapolis: University of Minnesota Press, 1988).

26. Simone de Beauvoir, *The Second Sex,* trans. H.M. Parshley (New York: Knopf, 1953), 301.

27. Ibid., xviii–xix.

28. Simone de Beauvoir, *Simone de Beauvoir Today: Conversations with Alice Schwartzer, 1972–1982* (London: Chatto & Windus, 1984), 32.

29. Betty Friedan, *The Feminine Mystique* (New York: Dell, 1963), 317.

30. See, for example, Marion Tapper, "Can a Feminist Be a Liberal?" *Australasian Journal of Philosophy,* supplement to Vol. 64 (June 1986). These last points are paraphrased from Tapper's paper, 47. See also Lorraine Code, "Simple Equality is Not Enough," in the same volume.

31. Some theorists distinguish between Marxist and socialist feminism, arguing that Marxist concerns are more purely economic whereas socialist feminists are concerned to effect more wide-ranging social reforms. But Josephine Donovan, for example, claims, "Contemporary 'Marxist feminism' is more appropriately called 'social feminism' to point up that it no longer represents an undiluted Marxism but a Marxism modified...by radical feminism." In Josephine Donovan, *Feminist Theory* (New York: Frederick Ungar, 1985), 66. The term 'socialist feminism' will be used in the rest of this chapter.

32. *See*: Shiela Rowbotham, *Woman's Consciousness, Man's World* (Harmondsworth: Penguin Books, 1973); and Zillah Eisenstein, "Developing a Theory of Capitalist Patriarchy and Socialist Feminism," in Z. Eisenstein, ed., *Capitalist Patriarchy and the Case for Socialist Feminism* (New York: Monthly Review Press, 1979).

33. *See*: Susan Sontag, "The Third World of Women," *Partisan Review* 60 (1973).

34. *Cf:* Michele Barrett, *Women's Oppression Today: Problems in Marxist Feminist Analysis* (London: Verso, 1980).

35. Gayle Rubin, "The Traffic in Women: Notes on the 'Political Economy' of Sex," in R. Reiter, ed., *Towards an Anthropology of Women* (New York: Monthly Review Press, 1975), 163.

36. This thesis is advanced, for example, by Iris Young in "Beyond the Unhappy Marriage: A Critique of the Dual Systems Theory," in Sargent, *Women and Revolution.*

37. *See*: Adrienne Rich, "Compulsory Heterosexuality and Lesbian Existence," in A. Snitow, C. Stansell, and S. Thompson, eds., *Desire: The Politics of Sexuality* (London: Virago Press, 1983), for a superb and extensive radical-feminist analysis of the political implications of compulsory heterosexuality.

38. Heidi Hartmann, "The Unhappy Marriage of Marxism and Feminism," in Sargent, *Women and Revolution,* 28.

39. Robin Morgan, *Going Too Far: The Personal Chronical of a Feminist* (New York: Random House, 1977), 9.

40. There have been significant changes in the workings of this ideology in Canada in the 1980s, largely in response to feminist political pressure. (See Sandra Burt's chapter in this book.) But feminists in Britain continue to express concern at the reluctance of the law to intervene in domestic disputes. *See:* Katherine O'Donovan, *Sexual Divisions in Law* (London: Weidenfeld & Nicholson, 1985).

41. Mary Daly, *Gyn/Ecology: The Metaethics of Radical Feminism* (Boston: Beacon Press, 1978), 173.

42. Ibid., 53.

43. Ibid., 1.

44. Ibid., 34.

45. Shulamith Firestone, *The Dialectic of Sex: The Case for Feminist Revolution* (New York: Bantam Books, 1970).

46. Adrienne Rich, *Of Woman Born: Motherhood as Experience and Institution* (New York: Bantam Books, 1981), 58.

47. Ibid., 285.

48. Mary O'Brien, *The Politics of Reproduction* (London: Routledge & Kegan Paul, 1981), 58.

49. Ibid.

50. Rich, "Compulsory Heterosexuality," 217.

51. Ibid., 227ff.

52. Perhaps the most accessible of Kristeva's many works to those unfamiliar with the French tradition is *About Chinese Women* (London: Boyars, 1977).

53. Toril Moi, *Sexual/Textual Politics* (New York: Methuen, 1985), 160.

54. Julia Kristeva, "Women's Time," *Signs: A Journal of Women in Culture and Society* 7, no. 1 (1981), 21.

55. Hélène Cixous, "The Laugh of the Medusa," in Elaine Marks and Isabelle de Courtivron, eds., *New French Feminisms* (New York: Schocken Books, 1981), 245.

56. Ibid., 254.

57. Irigaray's two most frequently cited works, *Speculum de l'autre femme* and *Ce sexe qui n'en est pas un,* have been translated into English and published by Cornell University Press.

58. Marks and Courtivron, *New French Feminisms,* 35. The tools referred to are those developed by such French theorists as Jacques Derrida and Michel Foucault, but the reference could apply to the entire French intellectual tradition, with its emphasis on reason and the suppression of the body. See also Toril Moi, ed., *French Feminist Thought* (Oxford: Basil Blackwell, 1988).

59. For a good analysis of some of these issues, see Elizabeth V. Spelman, *Inessential Women: Problems of Exclusion in Feminist Thought* (Boston: Beacon Press, 1988).

60. *See:* Bell Hooks, *Ain't I a Woman? Black Women and Feminism* (Boston: South End Press, 1981), 102; Bell Hooks, *Feminist Theory from Margin to Center* (Boston: South End Press, 1984); and Patricia Hill Collins, *Black Feminist Thought: Knowledge, Consciousness, and the Politics of Empowerment* (London: Unwin Hyman, 1990).

61. Cott, "Feminist Theory," 59.

62. These are Zillah Eisenstein's examples in *The Radical Future of Liberal Feminism* (New York: Longman, 1981), 231.

63. Explicit requirements of this sort are less commonly evident than they were prior to contemporary feminist challenges. In 1960, for example, a

woman scientist in the United States was told in the early days of her employment, "If you become pregnant, you'll get fired." She reports, "So I got pregnant, and they never knew it. I just wore a lab coat one size larger....I came back two days after the baby was born, and I never told a soul there that I had a child." Vivian Gornick, *Women in Science* (New York: Simon and Schuster, 1983), 102. Such overt prohibitions are not so common in the 1990s, but workplace discrimination of a subtler sort is documented almost every day.

64. Carol Gilligan, *In a Different Voice: Psychological Theory and Women's Development* (Cambridge, Mass.: Harvard University Press, 1982).

65. *See*: Genevieve Lloyd, *The Man of Reason* (Minneapolis: University of Minnesota Press, 1984). Recent feminist work in the philosophy of science endeavours to explain the invisibility of women and 'the feminine' in scientific practice, with its ideals of rational objectivity. *See*: Ursula Franklin, "Will Women Change Technology or Will Technology Change Women?" CRIAW *Papers* (1985); and Sandra Harding, *The Science Question in Feminism* (Ithaca, N.Y.: Cornell University Press, 1986).

66. *The Guardian* (U.K.), April 1982.

67. This is Mary O'Brien's term, introduced in *The Politics of Reproduction*, and now a widely accepted term in feminist discourse.

Terms & Concepts

absolute human type	French feminism	oppression
alienation	Freud	patriarchy
Aristotle	gender equality	Plato
biological determinism	Industrial Revolution	radical feminism
capitalism	language	reproductive freedom
complementarity thesis	liberal feminism	Rousseau
difference in feminism analysis	liberalism	social feminism
domestic labour	Marxism	socialism
equality in feminism analysis	Mill, J.S.	socialization
exploitation	"natural" capacities	

Questions

1. The metaphor of a bird in a cage is frequently used by feminist writers. Explain the metaphor.

2. What was most influential in Marx's explanation for female exploitation?

3. Is there a common core of beliefs among the various strains of feminism?

4. Have the battles of feminism been largely won? What is there left to be done?

5. What, if any, are the differences between a women's group and a feminist group?

National Identity and the Idea of European Unity

Anthony Smith

Editors' Note

Western European countries are unique in that their state and cultural boundaries coincide substantially. This compartmentalization was achieved at horrendous costs through centuries of ongoing warfare culminating in two world wars. The French historian Ernest Renan was absolutely correct when he wrote that "unity is ever achieved by brutality."[1] Still, despite the bloodletting, even individual *European* states are not made up of one nation, and some ethnic groups claim distinctness from nations in which others would like to include them. But the experience with nationalist wars did lead to a constructive outcome: the European Economic Community (now the European Union) had as one of its avowed purposes the integration of economies not only for greater prosperity but also to make war among members impossible. On both counts it has succeeded admirably, but what happens to national identity when many traditional state functions are shifted to a supranational organization like the European Union, which then plays increasingly meaningful roles in the lives of its citizens? This is the topic of Anthony Smith's article.

Smith, a professor of sociology at the London School of Economics, examines the complex phenomena that make up identities, including an insightful treatment of two very different traditions of nationality, and the potential basis for a European identity. What will it take to make Europeans feel strongly European? Brussels administered educational programs, the European song contest, a European flag, or the ECU (European Currency Unit)? Or will it take an uglier stimulus—for example, xenophobia?

The article easily transcends the fairly narrow themes in its title and becomes an authoritative treatment of national identity in the 1990s. Note that Smith distinguishes among the levels and dimensions of national identity, and shows how the common understanding of this concept is being challenged by universalizing trends such as the emerging new federal structures in Europe. Finally, the relevance of the topic should not escape Canadians familiar with measures taken to bring about a sense of Canadian unity, an ongoing process more than 125 years after unification.

1. Ernest Renan, "What is a Nation," in Mark O. Dickerson, Thomas Flanagan, and Neil Nevitte, eds. *Introductory Readings in Government and Politics*, (Toronto: Nelson Canada, 1995), 21.

There is nothing new about the idea of European unity. It can be traced back to Sully, Podiebrad, perhaps even Charlemagne and the Holy Roman Empire. Nor is there anything new about national identity. Even if not as old as nationalists would have us believe, national consciousness can be traced back to the later Middle Ages, to the wars of the Scots, English and French in the fourteenth century, to Joan of Arc, to Spanish unification under the Catholic monarchs, and certainly to the Elizabethans and the age of Shakespeare: though not until the next century, in the Puritan Netherlands and England, can one discern the first flowerings of popular (albeit religious) *nationalism*, and not until the American and French Revolutions does nationalism appear as a fully fledged secular ideology.[1]

So why should there be such interest now in the European idea and its relationship to national identities? Is it simply the fact that European unification, in whatever form, is for the first time a distinct possibility—that we can 'make Europe' where previous generations could only dream about it? Or is it rather that the sheer pace of social and political change has forced us to reassess rooted structures like the nation-state, and hallowed values like national identity?[2]

Clearly, modern technologies and communications have led many people to question the old certainties. They grope in some confusion towards a new type of social order, yet are afraid to let go of the old. They wonder whether the new structures and identities that may be forged will answer to their needs and interests as well as the habitual and familiar ones. What exactly will a vast, over-arching 'Europe' mean for individuals and families? Will the seat of authority become still more impersonal and remote? Will it be less sensitive to local problems and needs? What does growing European unification mean for the values, heritages and cultures of Europe's many ethnic communities, regions and nations?

There is a more fundamental reason for the current interest in the cultural impact of European unification. It lies in the problem of 'identity' itself, one that has played a major part in European debates over the past 30–40 years. At issue has been the possibility and the legitimacy of a 'European identity', as opposed to the existing national identities. For nationalists, the nation is the sole criterion of legitimate government and of political community. Does this exclude the possibility of a European identity and political community? Or can, and must, a unified Europe be designated a 'super-nation'? Alternatively, should we regard a United States of Europe as a new type of 'supranational' identity and community? What exactly does that mean? These issues are central to the continuing debates between pro-and anti-Europeans, between federalists, Gaullists and today's Bruges Group.

I hope to show that some of these debates are exaggerated in their assumptions and scope. It is true that at the practical level of policy the claims of these competing identities—the European and the national—may come into conflict. This appears to have been the case recently, when the states of Europe, responsive to national public opinion, were in disarray over foreign policy over the Gulf War and then over Yugoslav conflicts. A common European cultural identity, if such there be, does not yet have its counterpart on the political level; to date, each state of the European Community has placed its perceived national interests and self-images above a concerted European policy based on a single presumed European interest and self-image.

At the conceptual level, however, the contradiction between a European identity and existing national identities may be more apparent than real. It rather depends on the version of nationalist doctrine held. If we hold to a Romantic doctrine and view the nation as a seamless, organic cultural unit, then the contradiction becomes acute. If, on the other hand, we accept a more voluntaristic and pluralistic conception and regard the nation as a rational association of common laws and culture within a defined territory, then the contradiction is minimized. For in this version—which is the one generally accepted in Western countries—individuals may choose to which nation they wish to belong, and there is, as we shall see, room for competing focuses of identity. So the conflict between the claims of the nation and those of a looser European identity becomes more situational and pragmatic, even if in a political crisis it could never be eliminated. I shall return to this key question below.

FIRST CONSIDERATIONS: METHOD
◆ ◆ ◆

Though there have been many studies of the economic organizations and political institutions of the European Community, relatively little attention has been devoted to the cultural and psychological issues associated with European unification—to questions of meaning, value and symbolism. What research there has been in this

This article first appeared in *International Affairs*, London, 68.1, 1992 (pp. 55–76) and is reproduced with permission.

area has suffered from a lack of theoretical sophistication and tends to be somewhat impressionistic and superficial. This is especially true of attitude studies, in which generalizations over time are derived from surveys of particular groups or strata at particular moments. In few areas is the attitude questionnaire of such doubtful utility as in the domain of cultural values and meanings.[3]

Clearly, what is needed in this field is a series of case-studies over time of *changes* in collective perceptions and values, as recorded in literature and the arts, in political traditions and symbolism, in national mythologies and historical memories, and as relayed in educational texts and the mass media. Such studies rarely focus on the European dimension as such. Rather, they address changes in the content of *national* symbolism and mythology, ethno-history and collective values and traditions, which may or may not include an opening towards a wider, European dimension, but whose central focus is continuing process of reconstructing or re-imagining the nation.[4]

Such studies form a useful point of departure for investigations into the complex relationships between national identities and the processes of European unification in the sphere of culture and values. Here I shall concentrate specifically on the cultural domain and its links with politics, leaving on one side the processes of economic and political integration that form the main concern of European studies. I shall focus on five interrelated areas.

◆ The impact and uses of the pre-modern 'past' or 'pasts' of ethnic communities and nations in the continent of Europe, and the ways in which pre-modern structures and images continue to condition modern processes and outlooks.

◆ The origins and nature of collective, cultural identities, and more specifically of *national* identities, and their consequences for social and political action.

◆ The growth of globalizing tendencies in communications, education, the media and the arts, which transcend national and even continental boundaries, bringing a truly cosmopolitan character to society that surpasses internationalism.

◆ Allied to these tendencies, fundamental geopolitical and ecological changes in the world at large-often of an unpredictable nature, like the dangers of a shrinking Soviet Union or a Middle Eastern vortex, or of pollution and epidemic disease—which affect changing values.

◆ The processes of regional or continental unification, of which Europeanization is only the most explicit

and advanced example. Here the question is not just the history of an idea or process, but the changing contents and boundaries of 'Europe' in the context of a rapidly evolving world.

MULTIPLE IDENTITIES

◆ ◆ ◆

A comparative method using case-studies of national identity and culture needs some kind of theoretical framework; and given the nature of our problem, a logical starting-point is the concept of collective cultural identity. This would refer not to some fixed pattern or uniformity of elements over time, but rather to a sense of shared *continuity* on the part of successive generations of a given unit of population, and to shared *memories* of earlier periods, events and personages in the history of the unit. From these two components we can derive a third: the collective belief in a common *destiny* of that unit and its culture. From a subjective standpoint, there can be no collective cultural identity without shared memories or a sense of continuity on the part of those who feel they belong to that collectivity. So the subjective perception and understanding of the communal past by each generation of a given cultural unit of population—the 'ethno-history' of the collectivity, as opposed to a historian's judgement of that past—is a defining element in the concept of cultural identity, and hence of more specific national and European identities.[5]

From this starting-point we might go on to characterize the cultural history of humanity as a successive differentiation (but also enlargement) of processes of identification. In the simplest and earliest societies, the number and scale of such identities were relatively limited; but as populations organized themselves into more complex agrarian societies in a variety of political formations, the number and scale of such identifications multiplied. Where once gender, age, clan and tribe had provided the chief units of identity, now there were also village communities, regions, city-states, religious communities and even empires. With the growing stratification of such societies, classes and status groups (castes, estates, ethnic communities) also took on vital roles as focuses of identification in many societies.

In the modern era of industrial capitalism and bureaucracy, the number and in particular the scale of possible cultural identities have increased yet again. Gender and age retain their vitality; class and religious loyalties continue to exercise their influence; but today, professional, civic and ethnic allegiances have proliferated, involving ever larger populations across the globe. Above all, *national* identification has become the cultural and political norm, transcending other loyalties in scope and power.

Yet however dominant the nation and its national identification, human beings retain a multiplicity of allegiances in the contemporary world. They have *multiple* identities. These identifications may reinforce national identities or cross-cut them. The gendered perceptions of the male population may reinforce their sense of national identity, whereas those of the female part of the

---

...national identification has become the cultural and political norm, transcending other loyalties in scope and power.[6]

---

same collectivity may detract from it. The class allegiances of upper and middle classes may subjectively fuse with their sense of national identification, whereas the class solidarities of workers may conflict with their national loyalties. Similarly, some collective religious sentiments can reinforce a sense of national identity, as we witness today in Ireland, Poland and Israel; whereas some other kinds of religious loyalty transcend and thereby diminish purely national identities, as in the case of Roman Catholicism and Islam.[6]

Under normal circumstances, most human beings can live happily with multiple identifications and enjoy moving between them as the situation requires. Sometimes, however, one or other of these identities will come under pressure from external circumstances, or come into conflict with one of the individual's or family's other identities. Conflicts between loyalty to a national state and solidarity with an ethnic community, within or outside the boundaries of that state, may lead to accusations of 'dual loyalties', and families may find themselves torn between the claims of competing communities and identities. There is in fact always the potential for such identity conflicts. That they occur less often than one might expect is the result of a certain fluidity in all processes of individual identification.

At this point it becomes important to observe the distinction between individual and collective identification. For the individual, or at any rate for most individuals, identity is usually 'situational', if not always

optional. That is to say, individuals identify themselves and are identified by others in different ways according to the situations in which they find themselves; as when one goes abroad, one tends to classify oneself (and be classified by others) differently from one's categorization at home.[7]

Collective identities, however, tend to be pervasive and persistent. They are less subject to rapid changes and tend to be more intense and durable, even when quite large numbers of individuals no longer feel their power. This is especially true of religious and ethnic identities, which even in pre-modern eras often became politicized. It is particularly true of national identities today, when the power of mass political fervour reinforces the technological instruments of mass political organization, so that national identities can outlast the defection or apathy of quite large numbers of individual members. So we need to bear this distinction between the collective and the individual levels of identity in mind and to exercise caution in making inferences about collective sentiments and communal identifications on the basis of individual attitudes and behaviour.[8]

NATIONAL IDENTITY: SOME BASES AND LEGACIES

◆ ◆ ◆

This preliminary survey of the types and levels of *cultural* identity provides a general framework for analyzing specifically *national* identities. Here it may be useful to take together the first two areas of analysis—the impact of the pre-modern past and the nature and consequences of national identity—since in Europe at any rate it is mainly through such identities that these 'pasts' have been retained and mediated.

The concept of national identity is both complex and highly abstract. Indeed the multiplicity of cultural identities, both now and in the past, is mirrored in the multiple dimensions of out conceptions of nationhood. To grasp this, we need only enumerate of few of these dimensions. They include:

◆ the territorial boundedness of separate cultural populations in their own 'homelands';
◆ the shared nature of myths of origin and historical memories of the community;
◆ the common bond of a mass, standardized culture;
◆ a common territorial division of labour, with mobility for all members and ownership of resources by all members in the homeland;

◆ the possession by all members of a unified system of common legal rights and duties under common laws and institutions.

These are some of the main assumptions and beliefs common to all nationalists everywhere. Drawing on these, we may define a nation as a named human population sharing a historical territory, common memories and myths of origin, a mass, standardized public culture, a common economy and territorial mobility, and common legal rights and duties for all members of the collectivity.[9]

This definition is just one of many that have been proffered for the concept of the 'nation'. But, like most others, it reveals the highly complex and abstract nature of the concept, one which draws on dimensions of other types of cultural identity, and so permits it to become attached to many other kinds of collective identification—of class, gender, and religion. National identifications are fundamentally multidimensional. But though they are composed of analytically separable components—ethnic, legal, territorial, economic and political—they are united by nationalist ideology into a potent vision of human identity and community.

The ideology of nationalism which emerged in Western Europe and America in the late eighteenth century was premised on the belief in a world of exclusive nations. The basic goals of nationalists everywhere were identical: they sought to unify the nation, to endow it with a distinctive individuality, and to make it free and autonomous. For nationalists, the nation was the supreme object of loyalty and the sole criterion of government. There was no legitimate exercise of political power which did not emanate expressly from the nation, for this was the only source of political power and individual freedom.[10]

Yet there were also important differences between nationalists in their conceptions of the nation. In fact we can usefully distinguish two main models of the nation, which emerged out of different historical contexts and which retain a certain importance even in our era. The first, or 'Western', model of the nation arose out of the Western absolutist states whose rulers inadvertently helped to create the conditions for a peculiarly territorial concept of the nation. The second, or 'Eastern', model emerged out of the situation of incorporated ethnic communities or *ethnies* (from the French), whose intelligentsias sought to liberate them from the shackles of various empires.

The Western model of the nation tended to emphasize the centrality of a national territory or homeland, a common system of laws and institutions, the legal equal-

ity of citizens in a political community, and the importance of a mass, civic culture binding the citizens together. The Eastern model, by contrast, was more preoccupied with ethnic descent and cultural ties. Apart from genealogy, it emphasized the popular or folk element, the role of vernacular mobilization, and the activation of the people through a revival of their native folk culture—their languages, customs, religions and rituals, rediscovered by urban intellectuals such as philologists, historians, folklorists, ethnographers and lexicographers.[11]

The contrast between these two concepts of the nation should not be overdrawn, as we find elements of both at various times in several nationalisms in both Eastern and Western Europe. And it is perhaps more important for out purposes to underline the distinction between the concepts of the nation and of the state. The latter is a legal and institutional concept. It refers to autonomous public institutions which are differentiated from other, social institutions by their exercise of a monopoly of coercion and extraction within a given territory.[12] The idea of the nation, by contrast, is fundamentally cultural and social. It refers to a cultural and political bond which unites in a community of prestige all those who share the same myths, memories, symbols and traditions. Despite the obvious overlap between the concepts of state and nation in terms of common territory and citizenship, the idea of the nation defines and legitimates politics in cultural terms, because the nation is a political community only in so far as it embodies a common culture and a common social will. This is why today no state possesses legitimacy which does not also claim to represent the will of the 'nation', even where there is as yet patently no nation for it to represent. Though the vast majority of contemporary states are 'plural' in character—that is, they have more than one ethnic community within their borders and so cannot claim to be true 'nation-states' in the strict sense—they aspire to become at least 'national states' with a common public culture open to all citizens. Their claim to legitimacy, in other words, is based on the aspiration of a heterogeneous population to unity in terms of public culture and political community, as well as popular sovereignty.[13]

This reiterated reference to a community of common public culture reveals the continuing influence of ethnicity and its common myths, symbols and memories in the life of modern European nations. On the one hand, these nations seek to transcend their ethnic origins, which are usually the myths and memories of the dominant ethnic community (the English, the northern

French, the Castilians); on the other hand, in a world of growing interdependence, they very often feel the need to revert to them to sustain community as well as to justify their differences. The link with the distinctive premodern past serves to dignify the nation as well as to explain its mores and character. More important, it serves to 'remake the collective personality' of the nation in each generation. Through rituals and ceremonies, political myths and symbols, the arts and history textbooks—through these the links with a community of origin, continually reshaped as popular 'ethno-history' are reforged and disseminated.

In this respect, national identifications possess distinct advantages over the idea of a unified European identity. They are vivid, accessible, well established, long popularized, and still widely believed, in broad outline at least. In each of these respects, 'Europe' is deficient both as idea and as process. Above all, it lacks a premodern past—a 'prehistory' which can provide it with emotional sustenance and historical depth. In these terms it singularly fails to combine, in the words of Daniel Bell *a propos* ethnicity, 'affect with interest', resembling rather Shelly's bright reason, 'like the sun from a wintry sky.'[14]

Recently it has been suggested that nationalism's halcyon days are drawing to a close, and that the current spate of fissiparous ethnic nationalism runs counter to the 'major trends' of world history, which are towards ever-larger economic and political units. In other words, that substance is belied by appearance—that today's ethnic nationalisms are divisive and have lost the breadth and power of the former mass democratic and civic nationalisms of Western Europe.[15]

Others take the view that the current renewal of ethnic nationalism represents the shape of the future 'postindustrial' society, one whose economy is based increasingly on the service sector and on the social and cultural needs of consumers. They argue that in such societies the means of communication and information become much more important than mass production of commodities; that the mass media, telecommunications and computerized information spawn smaller but dense networks for those who share the same ethno-linguistic networks of language, symbols and culture. This, they argue, is the reason why we are witnessing the proliferation of ethnic nationalisms; they are intrinsic to a postindustrial 'service society.'[16]

There are in fact a number of reasons why we are witnessing an ethnic revival today, and why it is challenging the accepted frameworks of the national state. For one thing, the state itself has become immensely

more powerful, both as an international actor and *vis-à-vis* society within its boundaries. Its powers, scope and capacity for intervention in every sphere of social life—and will to do so—have increased profoundly since 1945 (helped, no doubt, by the powers conferred on it by the

---

Third, the impact of public, mass education systems...also creates divisions along pre-existing ethnic lines.

---

exigencies of two world wars). Second, the spread of literacy and the mass media to the remotest hinterlands of European and other states has raised the level of consciousness and expectations of minority peoples, who witness national protests and movements in neighbouring territories almost as soon as they occur. Third, the impact of public, mass education systems, while on the face of it uniting a given national population into a single civic culture, also creates divisions along pre-existing ethnic lines. By forcing all its different peoples to employ a single civic language and by preaching allegiance to national symbols and historical myths, the state's elites may actually stir up resentment and bitterness at the neglect of minority cultures and the suppression of minority peoples' histories. The latter have not been entirely forgotten among the relevant peoples themselves; they remain embedded in separate folklore, customs, myths and symbols. State intervention, literacy and civic culture, and mass education and the mass media tend to rekindle these memories and regenerate these ancient cultures in new forms.

So recent political developments in Western as well as Eastern Europe, not to mention the Third World, offer few grounds for hope of an early end to the proliferation of ethnic nationalisms, even if their intensity periodically diminishes. What we are currently witnessing is no more than the latest of the periodic waves of ethnic nationalism that have swept different parts of the world since the early nineteenth century, and such demotic ethnic nationalisms have always accompanied the more territorial state-based nationalisms of ethnic majorities since the first stirrings of Serb, Greek and Irish nationalisms. There is therefore little warrant for regarding recent ethnic nationalism as inimical or irrelevant to the 'major trends' of economic development or world history, as long as most of the world's trade, production and consumption is still organized in terms of relations between sovereign (if increasingly interdependent) national states.[17]

If we disregard the evolutionary undertones of these recent interpretations of nationalism, we are left with the problem of determining the relative strength and influence of European nations, their cultures and their myths from their ethnic pasts at the turn of the second millennium. Anthropologists have begun to explore some of the cultural aspects of the ethnic identity of such European nations as the Basque, the Breton and the Greek, but much research still needs to be conducted into the continuing impact of ethno-histories, of ethnic myths and symbols, and of the different value systems embodied in various popular traditions, ceremonies and rituals. There is also much work to be done on the recent revival of cultural heritages and political traditions in the wake of new concepts of multiculturalism, which have gained ground following demographic shifts and population migrations.

Given the multiplicity of language groups and ethnic heritages in Europe, it is reasonable to expect the persistence of strong ethnic sentiments in many parts of the continent, as well as the continuity or periodic revival of national identities, fuelled by the quest for ethnic traditions and cultural heritages of distinctive myths, memories and symbols.

A GLOBALIZING CULTURE?

◆ ◆ ◆

Against these predictions must be set the 'major trends' of world history that so many have discerned and welcomed. These include:

◆ the rapid growth of vast transnational companies, with budgets, technologies, communications networks and skill levels far outstripping those of all but the largest and most powerful of contemporary national states;

◆ the rise and fall of large power blocs based on one or other military 'superpower', and forming a military-political network of client-states in an increasingly interdependent international system of states; and

◆ the vast increase in the scale, efficiency, density and power of the means of communications, from transport to the mass media, from telecommunications to computerized information and transmission.

What this means, in the most general terms, is an accelerating process of globalization: of trends and processes that transcend the boundaries of national states and ethnic communities, and that serve to bind together into common economic, political and cultural patterns the various populations into which the globe is at present divided.[18]

That such trends and processes can be observed is not in question. It is not difficult to point to processes that transcend national boundaries, and appear to unite different populations in those respects. This is as true of patterns of world trade, nuclear proliferation and diplomatic language as it is of styles in modern art, fashion and television serials. The question is whether there is anything new in such boundary-transcending activities and processes, and whether they serve to unite distinctive populations in more than superficial respects. Do they, in other words, portend that global cosmopoli-

---

Can there be a truly cosmopolitan culture, one that is genuinely "post-national" in form and content?

---

tanism of which Marx and Engels, as well as so many liberals, dreamed?

We should perhaps recall in this context the many imperial cultures that sought to integrate, even homogenize, ethnically different populations, from the Hellenizing policies of Alexander and his successors right up to the Russification policies of the later Romanovs. Here, too, the conscious intention to overleap local boundaries was evident, as was also the case with the 'world religions' of Buddhism, Islam and Christianity. It is true that today the English language and American cultural styles can reach an even wider audience and penetrate much more of the globe. But do they, can they, have as profound an effect? Can there be a truly cosmopolitan culture, one that is genuinely, 'post-national' in form and content? The answer to such a question may have a profound bearing on the possibility of a European cultural identity.

It is undeniable that we are witnessing an immense and rapid growth of communications and information technology, spanning the globe; and with it a slower but definite, albeit uneven, increase in literacy and mass education in many countries. There is also considerable convergence in parts of each state's education system: an emphasis on technology, a concern with mathematics and science, an interest in at least one other *lingua franca,* and so on. In other parts of each education system, however, there is a conscious retention of national difference: in literature, in history, in the arts. In so far as the state can control and use the instruments of mass education effectively, this policy of national self-maintenance is not to be underestimated.[19]

This is not to deny the possibility that governments may actively intervene to try to change popular perceptions of their identity. One could cite here not only the recent efforts of the British government to change the content of the history curriculum to accord with its perceived 'national interests,' but also the efforts of France and Germany to change earlier perceptions of each other, through the use of symbols, through massive youth exchange programmes, and by subsidizing academic studies of common history, all of which have after 25 years had a significant effect. (Whether the efforts of the Council of Europe to encourage changes in national histories, on both the academic and the official levels, have been effective is open to doubt.)

At the same time, there are clear limits to what governments can achieve. Thus the recent uneasy position of the German government during the Gulf War shows up clearly the constraints on governments which are at all responsive to public opinion. The same is true for other governments in such recent foreign policy crises as Yugoslavia or the Lebanese hostage situation.

There is another side to the question of cultural globalization—what will a truly cosmopolitan culture involve? Will it resemble the imperial prototype, on this occasion various versions of Americanization? Or will it be something genuinely new? The evidence to date suggests neither alternative. What a 'post-modernist' global culture is more likely to resemble is the eclectic patchwork we are witnessing in America and Western Europe today—a mixture of ethnic elements, streamlined and united by a veneer of modernism on a base of scientific and quantitative discourse and computerized technology.[20]

This is not to deny the global diffusion of some aspects of modern Euro-American culture, especially popular music, films, videos, dress and some foods. The worldwide spread of consumer commodities, of art styles in furnishing, of architecture and the visual arts, not to mention the mass media and tourism, is evidence of a global nexus of markets for similar products and the ability of consumer industries to mould shared tastes, in some degree at least. But even here, ethnic and class factors intrude. The appreciation and assimilation of Western styles and cultural products is generally adaptive; the audiences in Third World countries tend to interpret these products and experiences in ways that are specific to the perceptions and understanding of their own peoples.[21]

Side by side with this adaptive Westernization, there is also a more or less conscious rediscovery of and return to indigenous styles and values. This process was stimulated by political nationalism or by a vaguer consciousness of and pride in the past of particular peoples and cultural areas, and has been continuing since the early nineteenth century—first in Central and Eastern Europe, then in the Middle East and India, then in the Americas, and finally in Africa and Eastern Asia. In each case, myths and memories of an ancient ethnic past (not necessarily strictly that of the revivalists themselves) have been reappropriated, often through a process of vernacular mobilization in which the peasant masses are treated as a repository of truth, wisdom and culture.

The revival of ethnic myths, memories and traditions, both within and outside a globalizing but eclectic culture, reminds us of the fundamentally memoryless nature of any cosmopolitan culture created today. Such a culture must be consciously, even artificially, constructed out of the elements of existing national cultures. But existing cultures are time-bound, particular and expressive. They are tied to specific peoples, places and periods. They are bound up with definite historical identities. These features are essentially antithetical to the very nature of a truly cosmopolitan culture. Herein lies the paradox of any project for a global culture; it must work with materials destined for the very projects which it seeks to supersede—the national identities which are ultimately to be eradicated.

THE EUROPEAN 'FAMILY OF CULTURES'

◆ ◆ ◆

This, then, is where the European project must be located; between national revival and global cultural aspirations. Thus expressed, it makes the old debate between pan-Europeans and anti-Europeans seem faintly antiquated.

That debate centred on the possibility and desirability of creating a unified Europe 'from above', through economic and political institutions, perhaps on the model of German unification in the nineteenth century. Pan-Europeans conceded that there would be local delays and problems, but believed that European unity was imperative to prevent a recurrence of any European 'civil war', to create a third power between East and West and to secure a prosperous future for Europe's peoples. They also argued that the route of 'state-making' from above through bureaucratic incorporation and the building of institutions was the only way forward. Just as in the past dynastic states had moulded the first nations in the West, so today the framework of a United States of Europe and swift political union, based firmly in the Western heartlands, would forge a European consciousness in place of the obsolete national identities.

Anti-Europeans countered by pointing to the 'unevenness' of Europe's peoples and states, to the difficulties of deciding the boundaries of 'Europe', to the continuing strength of several European national states and to the linguistic and ethnic pluralism of Europe's mixed areas. But at the root of their opposition to pan-Europeanism, whether unitary or federal in character, was their belief in the overriding importance of existing national identities and the ethnic histories and cultures they enshrined. Behind the economic facade and the agonizing over subsidies and monetary union, the embattled camps of Brussels and Bruges agreed on the mutual incompatibility of 'Europe' and 'national' identity.[22]

But is there any warrant for this dichotomic view of cultural identities and for the battle cries on either side. We have already seen that, sociologically, human beings have multiple identities, that they can move between them according to context and situation, and that such

---

...what does it mean to feel and be European?

---

identities may be concentric rather than conflictual. None of this is to deny the cultural reality and vivid meanings of these identities, which, transmitted through successive generations, are not exhausted by the often fickle volitions and changing perceptions of individuals. At the same time, there is plenty of historical evidence for the coexistence of concentric circles of allegiance.[23] In the ancient world it was possible to be Athenian, Ionian and Greek all at the same time; in the medieval world, to be Bernese, Swiss and Protestant; in the modern Third World to be Ibo, Nigerian and African simultaneously. Similarly, one could feel simultaneously Catalan, Spanish and European; even—dare one say it?—Scottish-or-English, British and European.

But if the possibility of being intensely French or British *and* intensely European exists, what does it mean to feel and be European? Is 'Europe' merely the sum total of its various national identities and communities? If so, is there not something quite arbitrary about aggregating such identities simply because certain otherwise unrelated communities happen to reside in a geographi-

cal area which is conventionally designated as the continent of Europe?—Which raises further questions about the eastern and southern boundaries of Europe, as well as about important internal geographical and historical divisions within that continent.

On the other hand, if 'Europe' and 'European' signify something more than the sum total of the populations and cultures that happen to inhabit a conventionally demarcated geographical space, what exactly are those characteristics and qualities that distinguish Europe from anything or anyone else? Can we find in the history and cultures of this continent some thing or things that are replicated elsewhere, and that shaped what might be called specifically 'European experiences'?

There are a number of areas in which one might seek for specifically European characteristics, qualities and experiences. The first is linguistic. Though not all the languages of Europe belong to the Indo-European family, the vast majority do, and though there are important linguistic fault-lines between Latin, Germanic and Slav sub-families, there has been sufficient movement across these lines to speak of at least a tenuous interrelationship which is modern as well as prehistoric. At the same time, the disastrous political consequences of drawing ethnic inferences from purely linguistic relationships suggests serious limitations in this area for any support for the European idea in ethno-linguistic terms.[24]

A second area of enquiry is that of cultural geography and territorial symbolism. The recent idea of a European 'home' from the Urals to the Atlantic is supported by the lack of any serious geographical barriers (apart from the Alps and Pyrenees, and perhaps the Carpathians and the Rhine—and the Channel?), and by the protected geopolitical space between the Atlantic and the Mediterranean into which successive 'barbarian' ethnic communities poured and in which they found permanent shelter and adjacent homes. But what may be true in the north and west has no counterpart in the south and east. The Mediterranean forms a unifying internal (Roman?) lake—*mare nostrum*—rather than an impermeable boundary, while to the east the rolling plains, as the terrified populations found in the face of Hun and Mongol onslaughts and as the shifting boundaries of Poland-Lithuania and Russia-Ukraine bear witness, afford neither defence not borderland. Besides, where is the geographical centre of the European homeland? In Burgundy or along the Rhine? In Berlin or Prague, or Budapest? In the Benelux countries, or in Provence or norther Italy? All these are historical claims, not geographical 'facts.'[25]

Third, there is the old issue of religious cleavages. Might this not provide a test of European inclusion and exclusion? There is a clear sense, going back at least to the Crusades and probably even to Charles Martel, in which Europeans see themselves as not-Muslims or as not-Jews. The history of resistance to Arab and Turkish Muslim encroachment provides potent memories, though there is the great exception of Spain and its Moorish and Jewish conduits for the enormous legacy of Arab Islam to Christian European culture.

What of the inter-Christian divides? The most potent is still that between 'Western' Christendom (Catholic and Protestant) and Eastern Orthodoxy. Hungarians, for example, emphasize their Western connections through their historic 'choice for the West' over 1,000 years ago, in contrast to the Russians, for example, who chose Greek Byzantine Orthodoxy. But this brings problems of its own, not least for the position of Greece and potentially Serbia in the European Community. If religion is a real criterion of identity, should not Poland, rather than Greece, be a member of the new Europe? And what of that other great division, between the Protestant and Catholic states of Europe? Politically, Catholic-Protestant divisions may have declined, but how far, again, does this extend to the vast majority of Europeans in small towns and villages? This is another aspect of the wider question of the gulf between urban elites and rural masses in Europe over perceptions of and attitudes to Europe and European unification.

Fourth, there is the more inchoate sense of the 'outsider', which has recently found expression in various European countries, directed at immigrants and guestworkers. Might not the older nationalistic exclusive attitudes to foreigners now become 'Euro-nationalist' exclusion of blacks, Asians and other non-Europeans? There is some evidence for this. But it is difficult to disentangle it from the older attitudes. If it is the case, it supports the idea that there is a continuum between collective cultural identities, as I have argued. This may well be reinforced after 1992, when common passports and European frontiers will help to 'create' an element of perceived common identity for those who travel beyond the European frontiers—and for those who seek to enter (or return to) them. The effect of such frontiers on creating an *out-group*, so vital to the formation of identity, depends of course on the degree of unity of perceptions and sentiments among the Europeans themselves, and on the degree of common political action, especially in the field of defence and foreign policy, which a more united Europe can evolve. The evidence in these fields to date has not been encouraging.

We are thrown back on history, and specifically on political and legal traditions and cultural heritages and symbolisms. Here, if anywhere, we may hope to find experiences and collective memories that differentiate the communities of Europe from other communities, and which, in some degree at least, provide common reference points for the peoples of Europe.

This is an area which, of its nature, is not amenable to rigorous positivistic criteria. We are dealing with shared memories, traditions, myths, symbols and values, which may possess subtly different meanings and significance for different communities in the area conventionally designated as Europe. The Roman heritage, for example, penetrated certain areas more than others, and some not at all. Christianity embraced most of the continent eventually, but it did so unevenly and split early into separate cultural and ethnic traditions. The various attempts to recreate the Roman Empire foundered, but they left their imprint on some areas of Europe more than others. Even such 'event-processes' as the Crusades, the Renaissance, the Reformation and the Enlightenment affected some areas, peoples and states more than others, and a few hardly at all.

So what is common to all Europeans? What can they be said to share and in what respects can they be said to differ from non-Europeans? To these kind of questions there can never be satisfactory answers. Europeans differ among themselves as much as from non-Europeans in respect of language (Basques, Finns, Hungarians), territory (Russians, Greeks, Armenians), law (Roman, Germanic), religion (Catholic, Orthodox, Protestant) and economic and political system (democracy, communism, unitary state, generalism, etc.)—*as well as* in terms of ethnicity and culture.

On the other hand, there *are* shared traditions, legal and political, and shared heritages, religious and cultural. Not all Europeans share in all of them; some share in particular traditions and heritages only minimally. But at one time or another all Europe's communities have participated in at least *some* of these traditions and heritages, in some degree.

What are these partially shared traditions and heritages? They include traditions like Roman law, political democracy, parliamentary institutions, and Judeo-Christian ethics, and cultural heritages like Renaissance humanism, rationalism and empiricism, and romanticism and classicism. Together they constitute not a 'unity in diversity'—the official European cultural formula—but a 'family of cultures' made up of a syndrome of partially shared historical traditions and cultural heritages.

The idea of a 'family of cultures' resembles Wittgenstein's concepts of 'family resemblances' and of the 'language game', which features several elements, not all of which figure in each particular example of the game. What we have instead is a 'family' of elements which overlap and figure in a number of (but not all) examples. So, for example, the Italian Renaissance and its humanism found its way into many, but not all, parts of Europe, as did the spirit and methods of the French Enlightenment. 'Europe' here represents a field favourable to diffusion and cross-fertilization of cultural traditions, but one of uneven receptivity. Specific European states or communities may reveal only certain of the above traditions or heritages, or only to a limited extent. But the sum total of all Europe's states and communities has historically revealed a gamut of overlapping and boundary-transcending political traditions and cultural heritages, which together make up what we may call the European experience and the European family of cultures.

There has always been such cultural cross-fertilization in various parts of Europe. What now needs to be established is how far those shared traditions and heritages have become part of each of Europe's national

---

When the British working classes took package holidays to Spanish beaches, were they even exposed to Spanish, let alone European, culture?

---

identities, how far each national tradition has embraced and assimilated these 'trans-European' cultural heritages; how far Romanticism, Roman law or parliamentary democracy has taken on a peculiar national form, or conversely the extent to which French, or German, classicism and humanism partake of some shared trans-European tradition.

It is important here to distinguish between families of culture and political or economic unions. The latter are usually deliberate creations; they are consciously willed unities, rationally constructed sets of institutions, the kind of frameworks that some European states are trying to hasten and others to delay. Families of culture, like a *lingua franca*, tend to come into being over long time-spans and are the product of particular historical circumstances, often unanticipated and unintentional. Such cultural realities are no less potent for being so

often inchoate and uninstitutionalized. Thus the sentiments and identities that underpin the Islamic *umma* or community of Muslims are no less significant than any official Islamic social and political institutions.[26]

But this very lack of institutionalization poses severe difficulties for the researcher. One of them is the problem of interpreting recent trends and developments as in some sense, European manifestations. Can the growth of mass tourism, for example, be interpreted as a contribution to a more European identity? The fact that many more Europeans can and do travel abroad is open to several interpretations. When the British working classes took package holidays to Spanish beaches, were they even exposed to Spanish, let alone European, culture? Has the long-standing German love affair with Italy made any difference to the intensity of German nationalism, in this or the last century? Or shall we rather agree with Karl Kautsky that the railways are the greatest breeder of national hatreds (and by implication the most potent force for anti-Europeanism).[27]

Or take the astonishing growth of large-scale 'European' music festivals and travelling art exhibitions. Do these great events testify to a new 'European spirit'? Can they not equally be seen as expressions of local pride, be it in Edinburgh or Spoleto, Moscow or Leeds, in the Royal Academy or the Louvre or the Prado? By their nature such artistic events are all-inclusive; great artistic events are as likely to be shown in America or Japan and include contributions from all parts of the world. Europe may well have become a 'great museum' for the heritage industry, but only its greater openness and capitalist spirit have given it the edge over other tourist centres and 'great museums' in the Middle East or Asia.[28]

Given these problems, where may we look for signs of a possible European identification—and among whom? It is one thing for elites in Brussels, Strasbourg and some European capitals to identify with and work for a united Europe, quite another to attribute such sentiments and beliefs to the great mass of the middle and working classes, let alone the surviving peasantries of Southern and Eastern Europe. Whence will *they* derive a sense of European identity?

One answer often given suggests the mass, standardized, public education system. The problem here is that there is no pan-European system, only *national* systems; and what they teach, or omit to teach, is determined by *national*, not European, priorities. In other words, education systems are run by and for national states. Until there is a single, centralized, unitary European state, we cannot expect too much from the national education systems of each European state. This can be confirmed by a glance at schoolroom texts in history, civics and literature. Even when they include positive reference to contemporary Europe, the bulk of such texts are national in content and intent. The recent study of French school history textbooks by Suzanne Citron is a striking case in point.[29]

What about the mass media? Are they equally tied to purely national criteria of choice and content? Here there is clearly more variety as between different European national states. Yet even here, national priorities are very much in evidence: news stories tend to be relayed or at least interpreted from a national standpoint, drama, comedy shows, children's tales, even the weather reports accord the national state and its literature and outlook first place. Given the linguistic and historical barriers and the national frameworks of most mass media institutions, this is only to be expected.

Some changes are occurring in these areas, and given the political will of the elites, more rapid changes may soon take place. But the question still remains; how will the new 'European message' be received? Will it be reinterpreted by audiences and pupils in ethnic and national terms, as with so many cultural products? For until the great majority of Europeans, the great mass of the middle and lower classes, are ready to imbibe these European messages in a similar manner and to feel inspired by them to common action and community, the edifice of 'Europe' at the political level will remain shaky. This is all too clear today in respect of foreign policy and defence. where we are witnessing the need for European governments to respond to their national public opinion and the failure of Europeans to agree on a common policy. Once again, the usual divisions of public opinion between European states have been exposed, and with them the tortuous and divided actions of Europe's governments. Once again, too, the division between Britain and the Continent has become plain, and with it the crucial relationship of all European states to American political leadership. The 'European failure' only underlines the distance between the European ideal and its rootedness in the popular consciousness of Europe's national populations—and hence the distance between European unification at the political and cultural levels and the realities of divergent national identities, perceptions and interests within Europe.

Clearly these are areas for detailed and intensive research, which would focus not on ephemeral attitudes but on what is taught and portrayed and how it is received by the majority of Europe's populations. In more concrete terms, this means examining the ways in which news and documentaries are purveyed; how far a European dimension is added to, and received in, matters of art, music and literature; how far education systems are harmonized and teachers and taught acculturated to the different values, goals and forms of education and training, and how far history textbooks are rewritten to accommodate a European standpoint.[30]

If this were not problematic enough, there is the deeper question of popular myths and symbols, and historical memories and traditions. Here we are placed firmly back in the pre-modern past of each national state. There is no European analogue to Bastille or Armistice Day, no European ceremony for the fallen in battle, no European shrine of kings or saints. When it comes to the ritual and ceremony of collective identification, there is no European equivalent of national or religious community. Any research into the question of forging, or even discovering, a possible European identity cannot afford to overlook these central issues.[31]

We encounter similar problems when it comes to the question of a genuinely European political mythology. The founding fathers of the European movements, such as Coudenhove-Kalergi, recognized the problem. They tended to look back to the imperial myths of the Carolingian and Ottonian Holy Roman Empire and to the medieval urban civilization centred on the Rhine as their models of a 'golden age' of European Christendom. But as a modern political *mythomoteur*, these models

---

It is possible for the new Europe to arise without 'myth' and 'memory'?

---

are deeply flawed. Secularism has made deep inroads into the political consciousness of most classes in several European states, too deep for any genuine religious revival to be less than divisive. Besides, the imperial format of such myths is profoundly inimical to the spirit of democracy which the West espouses and Eastern Europe so ardently seeks. There is also the persistent unease over locating one's guiding myth in a particular part of Europe at the expense of the rest. Once again, these models assert the primacy of 'the West' as the home of innovation and progress, traceable to that early spirit of capitalism in the free cities of late medieval Europe.[32]

It is clear that such historical *mythomoteurs* are inappropriate for the modern European project. But where else can one look for the necessary political mythology? It is possible for the new Europe to arise without 'myth' and 'memory'? Have we not seen that these are indispensable elements in the construction of any durable and resonant collective cultural identity?

Here lies the new Europe's true dilemma: a choice between unacceptable historical myths and memories on the one hand, and on the other a patchwork, memory-less scientific 'culture' held together solely by the political will and economic interest that are so often subject to change. In between, there lies the hope of discovering that 'family of cultures' briefly outlined above, through which over several generations some loose, over-arching political identity and community might gradually be forged.

EUROPE IN A WIDER WORLD

◆ ◆ ◆

At present the tide is running for the idea of European unification as it has never done before. This is probably the result of dramatic geopolitical and geocultural changes, which remind us that the future of 'Europe', as indeed of every national state today, will be largely determined by wider regional, or global, currents and trends. The most immediate of these, of course, has been the dramatic shift in world power resulting from the adoption of perestroika in the Soviet Union and the liberation of the states of Eastern Europe and the republics of the former Soviet Union to determine their own political future. But this same current may serve simultaneously as a model and a warning; what may flow so suddenly and vigorously in one direction may equally swiftly change course, for reasons that have nothing to do with intra-European developments, and in so doing reverse the climate that seemed so conducive to the project of European unification.

There are many other currents and trends affecting the chances of fulfilling a European project. We may cite several:

◆ dramatic regional developments, like the vortex of conflict in the Middle East, into which European states may be drawn, severally or together;

◆ the dangers of ethnic conflict, separatism and large-scale wars in other parts of the world such as the Indian subcontinent or Africa, which may again involve one or more European states and so divide the interests of those states and even threaten, by example, their stability and cohesion;

◆ the impact of waves of migrants and guest-workers on the economies and societies of European states, which may differentially affect their attitudes and priorities;

◆ larger problems of environmental pollution and ecological disaster, as well as epidemic disease, which may require both individual action by each European states and wider, perhaps global, responses which may pre-empt the integration of Europe; and

◆ problems of large-scale crime and terrorism, which may again call for immediate action by individual states, or by bodies larger and more powerful than any European organization.

The point of this list, which could be extended, is simply to underline the dramatic pace and scope of change within which the project of European unification must locate itself. Unification is in fact one of several possible responses to wider changes; but these trends do not all work in the same direction, and they may be reversed. Hence the importance of basing any European project on firm and deep cultural and social foundations that are to some extent independent of economic and political fluctuations, even of the much vaunted trends of mass democracy and popular capitalism.

There is another and equally important issue raised by the project of European unification and its relationship with nations and nationalism. Identities are forged out of shared experiences, memories and myths, in relation to those of other collective identities. They are in fact often forged through opposition to the identities of significant others, as the history of paired conflict so often demonstrates. Who or what then, are Europe's significant others? Until now, the obvious answers were the protagonists of the ideological Cold War. In this context Europe was often seen as a third force *between* the respective superpower blocs, though there was always something unreal about such a posture. Now, however, the problem of relationship to other identities has become more perplexing. To whom shall Europe be likened, against whom shall it measure itself? Today's geopolitical uncertainty makes a direct comparison and relationship with the United States ambiguous; Europe is increasingly wholeheartedly a part of the 'capitalist' and 'democratic' camp of which the United States is likely to remain the military leader. Shall Europe look to Japan as its *alter ego*? But Japan is an ethnically almost homogeneous society, it poses no military or political threat, and its economic rivalry is still mainly directed at the United States.

There is another, a less pleasing, possibility: the relationship of a unifying Europe to a disaggregated Third World. There is the prospect of an increasingly affluent, stable, conservative but democratic European federation, facing and protecting itself from, the demands and needs of groupings of states in Africa, Asia and Latin America. To some extent this prospect is still mitigated by the remaining ex-colonial ties between certain European and certain African or Asian states. But were the European project to achieve its political goals, it would also entail, not just economic exclusion, but also cultural differentiation and with it the possibility of cultural and racial exclusion. The forging of a deep continental cultural identity to support political unification may well require an ideology of European cultural exclusiveness.

These dangers are well known in respect of the maintenance of national identities by individual European states. In many respects, it is European institutions that are leading the struggle against racial discrimination, ethnic antagonism and anti-semitism, though with mixed success. The deeper question remains. Is not the logic of cultural exclusion built into the process of pan-European identity formation? Will not a unified Europe magnify the virtues and the defects of each of Europe's national identities, precisely because it has been built in their images? And might a European 'super-nation' resemble in its external as well as its internal policies and relations, this national model?[33]

This is a fear that has been often expressed. It is one that still haunts the European political arena, as each of Europe's national states seeks to influence the future shape of a European union along the lines of its own self-image. In its relations with minorities inside Europe, as well as with states and peoples outside the continent, these images have not been appealing ones. Here too lies an agenda for policy-oriented research, one beset by sensitive issues and thorny problems.

Facing and understanding these problems is a precondition for forging a pan-European identity that will eschew these undesirable and self-defeating images and features. Shaping a cultural identity that will be both distinctive and inclusive, differentiating yet assimilative, may yet constitute the supreme challenge for a Europe that seeks to create itself out of its ancient family of ethnic cultures.

Notes

1. On the forerunners of the idea of European unity, see Denis de Rougemont, *The meaning of Europe* (London: Sidgwick & Jackson, 1965).

2. This article was prepared for a seminar series on 'Europe in the 1990s: forces for change', held at the RIIA in 1991 and funded by the Economic and Social Research Council.

3. Studies of European economic and political integration go back to Karl Deutsch *et al.*, *Political community and the North Atlantic area* (Princeton, NJ: Princeton University Press, 1957) and Ernest B. Haas, *Beyond the nation state* (Stanford University Press, 1964). Cf. William Wallace, *The transformation of Western Europe* (London: Pinter/RIIA, 1990), ch. 4.

4. See, for example, the essays in Eric Hobsbawm and Terence Ranger, eds., *The invention of tradition* (Cambridge: Cambridge University Press, 1983), and also in Elisabeth Tonkin, Maryon McDonald, and Malcolm Chapman, eds., *History and ethnicity* (London: Routledge, 1989).

5. For studies of ethnic identity, see George de Vos and Lola Romanucci-Rossi, eds., *Ethnic identity: cultural continuities and change* (Chicago, ILL.: University of Chicago Press, 1975), and A.L. Epstein, *Ethnos and identity* (London: Tavistock, 1978).

6. On the relationships between religion and nationalism, see Donald E. Smith, eds., *Religion and political modernisation* (New Haven, Conn.: Yale University Press, 1974), and Pedro Ramet, ed., *Religion and nationalism in Soviet and East European politics* (Durham, NC: Duke University Press, 1989). For some case-studies of the relationships

between gender and nationality, see Floya Anthias and Nira Yuval-Davis, eds., *Woman-nation-state* (London: Macmillan, 1989).

7. For the concept of 'situational ethnicity' see J.Y. Okamura, 'Situational ethnicity', *Ethnic and Racial Studies* 4: 4 (1981), pp. 452–65.

8. On the 'individualistic fallacy' see E.K. Scheuch. 'Cross-national comparisons with aggregate data', in Richard L. Merritt and Stein Rokkan, eds., *Comparing nations: the use of quantitative data in cross-national research* (New Haven, Conn.: Yale University Press, 1956).

9. This definition summarizes long and complex discussions of the many definitions of 'nation'. See, *inter alia*, Karl Deutsch, *Nationalism and social communication* (2nd edn. New York: MIT Press, 1966), ch. 1; and Walker Connor, 'A nation is a nation, is a state, is an ethnic group, is...', *Ethnic and Racial Studies* 1: 4 (1978), pp. 377–400.

10. For fuller discussions of nationalist ideologies, see Elie Kedourie, *Nationalism* (London: Hutchison, 1960); Elie Kedourie, ed., *Nationalism in Asia and Africa* (London: Weidenfeld & Nicolson, 1971): and A.D. Smith, *Theories of nationalism* (2nd edn., London: Duckworth, 1983). On the multi-dimensionality of national identity, see A.D. Smith, *National identity* (London: Penguin, 1991), ch. 1.

11. On the distinction between these types of nationalism, see Hans Kohn, *The idea of nationalism* (2nd edn., New York: Macmillan, 1967), and A.D. Smith, *The ethnic origins of nations* (Oxford: Blackwell, 1986), ch. 6.

12. I have adapted the definitions given in the introductions to Charles Tilly, ed., *The formation of national states in Western Europe* (Princeton, NJ: Princeton University Press, 1975), and Leonard Tivey, ed., *The nation-state* (Oxford: Martin Robertson, 1980).

13. See Walker Connor's seminal article, 'Nation-building or nation-destroying?', *World Politics* 24 (1972), pp. 319-55; and Ernest Gellner, *Nations and Nationalism* (Oxford: Blackwell, 1983).

14. See Daniel Bell, 'Ethnicity and social change', in Nathan Glazer and Daniel P. Moynihan, eds., *Ethnicity: theory and experience* (Cambridge, Mass.: Harvard University Press, 1975).

15. This argument is presented in the last chapter of Eric Hobsbawm, *Nations and nationalism since 1780* (Cambridge: Cambridge University Press, 1990).

16. This argument is presented with force and clarity by Anthony Richmond in 'Ethnic nationalism and post-industrialism', *Ethnic and Racial Studies* 7: 1 (1984), pp. 4-18; it is also implicit in Benedict Anderson, *Imagined communities: reflections on the origin and spread of nationalism* (London: Verso, 1983).

17. The ethnic revival in the West in the 1970s suggests the difficulty of 'reading' any 'major trends' of world history. Regions and ethnic communities are being revitalized *alongside* a strengthened national state and an overarching European Community. On ethnic nationalisms in the West see Milton Esman; ed., *Ethnic conflict in the Western world* (Ithaca, NY: Cornell University Press, 1977), and A.D. Smith, *The ethnic revival in the modern world* (Cambridge: Cambridge University Press, 1981).

18. For a discussion of globalization, see Mike Featherstone, ed., *Global culture: nationalism, globalisation and modernity* (London: Sage, 1990).

19. For a searching analysis of the role of mass, public education systems in shaping national identities, see Gellner, *Nations and nationalism*.

20. The argument is presented fully in A.D. Smith, 'Towards a global culture?', *Theory, Culture and Society* 7 (1990), pp. 171-91.

21. This point is documented in Philip Schlesinger, 'On national identity: some conceptions and misconceptions criticised', *Social Science Information* 26: 2 (1987), pp. 219-64.

22. For the early debates between pan-Europeans, see Miriam Camps, *What kind of Europe? The Community since de Gaulle's veto* (London: Oxford University Press, 1965), and Wallace, *The transformation of Western Europe*, ch. 4.

23. On the idea of concentric circles of allegiance see James Coleman, *Nigeria: background to nationalism* (Berkeley, CA: University of California Press, 1958), appendix.

24. On Europe's linguistic divisions, see Andrew Orridge, 'Separatist and autonomist nationalisms; the structure of regional loyalties in the modern state', see C. Williams, ed., *National separatism* (Cardiff: University of Wales Press 1982), and John Armstrong, *Nations before nationalism* (Chapel Hill, NC: University of North Carolina Press , 1982), ch. 8.

25. On Europe's protected geopolitical position, see introduction, Tilly, ed., *The formation of national states*; for Europe's problematic eastern boundaries, see Raymond Pearson, *National minorities in Eastern Europe, 1848–1945* (London: Macmillan, 1983), and Roger Portal, *The Slavs* (London: Weidenfeld & Nicolson, 1969).

26. On the Islamic *umma* and the Muslim states, see Erwin Rosenthal, *Islam in the modern national state* (Cambridge: Cambridge University Press, 1965). Pan-Europeans have sometimes tried to construct culture areas through the deliberate manufacture of myths, symbols and traditions: see Lord Gladwyn, *The European idea* (London: New English Library, 1967).

27. On Karl Kautsky's argument, see Horace Davis, *Nationalism and socialism: Marxist and labor theories of nationalism* (London, New York: Monthly Review Press, 1967). There is evidence that mass tourism among the younger generations of Western Europe, which grew up in an era of peace has confirmed their lack of national antagonisms.

28. European elites, going back to feudal nobility and clergy, have always been more cosmopolitan and open to outside influences than the middle and lower classes: see Armstrong, *Nations before nationalism*, ch. 3, and Smith, *The ethnic origins of nations,* ch. 4.

29. Suzanne Citron, *Le mythe national* (Paris: Presses Ouvriers, 1988), analyses the strongly nationalistic content and framework of French school history textbooks based on Lavisse, which came into use during the late nineteenth century under the Third Republic. The continuing debate in Britain over the place of British, even English, history, as opposed to European and world history illustrates the same issues; see Raphael Samuel, ed., *Patriotism: the making and unmaking of British national identity* (London: Routledge, 1989), vol. 1, and Juliet Gardiner, ed., *The history debate* (London: Collins & Brown, 1990).

30. Even this does not take us to the heart of the problem. We need also to explore people's attachments to national landscapes, or myths thereof; to certain events and heroes from the national past; to certain kinds of social

institutions and mores, food, family life and village community: and how far all these are felt to override, conflict with or deny a more overarching European identity that is inevitably more abstract, intellectual and political.

31. The centrality of such rites and ceremonies for creating and maintaining collective cultural identities is only now receiving the attention it deserves. See e.g., John Breuilly, *Nationalism and the state* (Manchester: Manchester University Press, 1982), ch. 16; Hobsbawm and Ranger, eds., *The invention of tradition*.

32. The primacy of Western Europe as a 'core' to the northern, southern and especially eastern 'peripheries' (which in medieval times were sparsely inhabited) was seized on by the myth-makers of the European idea: see Gladwyn, *The European idea*, and de Rougemont, *The meaning of Europe*.

33. A fear summed up in Johan Galtung, *The European Community: a superpower in the making* (London: Allen & Unwin, 1973), but with recent events taking on a new meaning: namely, the fear that Germany's economic domination might influence the political shape of a future Europe, and the chances of greater cultural and racial exclusiveness, at the expense mainly of Third World migrants but stirring all too vivid memories of the Nazi past. Fears, like memories, are no less real for being intangible and difficult to research.

Terms & Concepts

collective identities	globalization	pan-European identity
cultural identity	legitimacy	political culture
ethnic nationalism	multiple identities	religion
ethnicity	mythology	sovereignty
European Union	national identity	state-based nationalism
family of cultures	nationalism	supranationality

Questions

1. One might expect that education, the "broadening of minds," would counteract the parochial (narrowing) aspects of nationalism. Yet, Smith maintains that education has been a factor in fragmenting states along ethnic lines. What role has education played in forming your national identity?

2. If one holds multiple national identities, does it matter for political cohesion in which order of priority one holds them? For example, does

it matter whether one feels French first and European second, or European first and French second?

3. Can we expect that a European identity be produced by supranational European institutions?

4. Can the Romantic doctrine and the voluntaristic and pluralistic doctrine of nationalism be found in Canada or is only one present? Which one?

5. What could foster a cohesive sense of European nationalism?

Conservatives' Faith, Liberals' Disdain

Stephen Carter

Editors' Note

Religious belief creates difficult problems for the study and practice of politics. The dominant view among social scientists is that religions are traditional, prescientific, even superstitious belief systems whose force in people's lives fades with the spread of scientific knowledge and industrial social organization. Such a result is particularly welcome for many thinkers because they see religion as inherently intolerant, dogmatic, and resistant to the necessary compromises that make political life possible—in other words, a prime source of social and political instability. Indeed, liberal democratic political thought arose in part as a reaction to competing religious claims to public power. The liberal solution to the dilemma is to establish a division between public and private affairs and relegate religious matters to the private realm.

The nature of religious belief, however, is more complex than this. First what is the relationship between religion and modernization, and is it natural to assume that as one increases in importance the other will decline? Or is religious belief innate, or at least a means of resisting the disruptions of capitalist tehnological society? "No sooner does a country like Iran undergo enormous modernization than a fundamentalist dictatorship takes over."[1] Second, instability and violence have not waned with the spread of the scientific civilization. Evidence suggests that violence has never been more intense than in the 20th century: perhaps religion was not the main culprit after all. The enemies of politics are far more numerous.

Third, many scholars argue that religious belief has a *positive* influence on political life. Basic ethical principles of human dignity and consideration for others are found in the tenets of major religions. Further, these principles affect, however imperfectly, the attitudes of believers and those around them in their roles as citizens and members of civil society.

So there is a deep ambivalence attached to the place of religion in the modern world. The United States illustrates the ambivalence poignantly: its constitution prohibits the establishment of any religion in law and public policy; yet its coinage bears the inscription, "In God We Trust" and nary a presidential address finishes without an appeal for God's blessings upon the American people. The following article by Yale law professor Stephen Carter addresses the ambivalence with which Americans treat religious belief. In particular, he is interested in the use of religious ideas and forms of speech in political debate and comes to some surprising conclusions. As you read the article, think about the status of religion in our society, and the nature of political argument.

---

1. Robert Wuthnow, "Understanding Religion and Politics," *Daedalus* 120, No. 3 (Summer 1991), 5.

It is, in some ways, a strange and boisterously wonderful time to be an American. As the twentieth century marches toward its close, for the first time in its history America has begun to take halting steps toward an aggressive pride in its diversity, toward respecting and understanding its pluralism rather than dumping everyone into a simmering melting pot intended to boil us all down to a common essence. It is both tragic and paradoxical that now, just as the nation is beginning to invite people into the public square for the different points of view that they have to offer, people whose contribution to the nation's diversity comes from their religious traditions are not valued unless their voices are somehow esoteric. One thinks, for example, of the Colorado school district that ordered, with federal court approval, the Bible and books on Christianity be removed from a classroom, while books on Native American religious

---

What is going on here in America, where religion was once thought to be so important that the Constitution was amended to protect its free exercise?

---

traditions—and, for that matter, on the occult—were allowed to remain.[1] And then there is the prominent feminist who grumbled in the summer of 1991 that there are too many Catholics on the Supreme Court—discussing Roman Catholics the way that Pat Buchanan discusses homosexuals.[2] And consider the fact that for all the calls for diversity in the hiring of university faculty, one rarely hears such arguments in favor of the devoutly religious—a group, according to survey data, that is grossly underrepresented on campus.[3]

What is going on here in America, where religion was once thought to be so important that the Constitution was amended to protect its free exercise? This is an America that once gloried in the smart show of religion in the public square, most notably and most recently in the sixties, when the civil rights and antiwar movements were awash in openly and unapologetically religious rhetoric which politicians fell all over themselves to endorse, to emulate, and to amplify.

What has happened can be captured in one word: abortion. In 1973, the Supreme Court decided in *Roe v. Wade* that the right to privacy (which, despite some sniping, was firmly established in past decisions) was broad enough to encompass a pregnant woman's decision on whether to carry the pregnancy to term.[4] For many religious conservatives, *Roe* was like a cold shower. All at once, the nascent pro-life movement (which actually began a few years before *Roe,* as a response to efforts to liberalize abortion laws) exploded into the national prominence. The very same Christian fundamentalists who had preached for decades that their followers should ignore the secular world, perhaps not even vote,[5] looked around and decided that the secular world was on the verge of destroying the right religious cocoons in which they had bound their communities. The Roman Catholic Church saw a nation that had suddenly committed itself to the destruction of lives that the church had, for centuries, called sacred. And so the public rhetoric of religion, which from the time of the abolitionist movement through the era of the "social gospel" and well into the 1960s and early 1970s had largely been the property of liberalism, was all at once—and quite thunderously, too—the special province of people fighting for a cause that the left considered an affront. Since the 1970s, liberals have been shedding religious rhetoric like a useless second skin, while conservatives have been turning it to one issue after another, so that by the time of the 1992 Republican Convention, one had the eerie sense that the right was asserting ownership in God—but that the left had yielded its rights.

Nowadays, public religious appeals are generally associated with conservative causes, which might explain why liberals often seem overenthusiastic in the rush to register their distaste for religion. The sociologist James Davison Hunter, in his fine book *Culture Wars,* quotes a 1981 address in which the President of Yale University told incoming freshmen that politically active Christian evangelicals were "peddlers of coercion."[6] Garry Wills records the objections of some authors to the appointment of a Jesuit as the head of the New York Public Library.[7] And in a widely reported instance that I would like to think apocryphal, a woman who addressed a feminist conference in California and described herself as a Jewish atheist received a ringing ovation, as though by purging herself of religiosity she

---

had somehow accomplished a great good.* Political candidates who make a show of their religiosity—or who show the danger signs of taking their religious commitments seriously—are treated with suspicion by mass media not quite sure how to present this unfortunate malady to the public. (How often one hears on the news a political report beginning, "Her opponent, a born-again Christian...".)

Curiously, the mass media seem willing to overlook this difficulty—religiosity—in candidates they like, even as the media emphasize the same factor in those they dislike. Garry Wills has noted the peculiar media attitude toward the two ordained ministers in the 1988 presidential primary campaigns, Pat Robertson and Jesse Jackson:

> While asking what Jackson "really wants," they kept looking for what he was "really" saying under the ornamental flourishes of Scripture language. If reporters had not shown a determination to keep Robertson boxed into his religious past, and an obliviousness to Jackson's religious rhetoric, the similarities of the two preachers would have been more frequently noticed.[8]

Similarly, in the 1992 campaign, the media often treated President Bush's speeches to religious organizations as pandering—but when Bill Clinton spoke, for example, to a black Baptist group, he was given credit for shrewdness. (Notice how both descriptions bespeak an assumption of insincerity.) Nor is this effect limited to political candidates. One can scarcely read about any statement by the Reverend Jerry Falwell without being reminded in so many words of his religious involvement. On the other hand, when pundits discuss the work of the Reverend Martin Luther King, Jr., the only member of the clergy whose life we celebrate with a national holiday, the fact of his religious calling is usually treated as a relatively unimportant aspect of his career, if, indeed, it is mentioned at all.

The liberal reluctance to acknowledge the religious content of the civil rights movement is a close cousin to another societal blind spot: the refusal to admit the centrality of religion to most of the black community itself. As a group, black Americans are significantly more devout than white Americans. By some measures, a recent study concluded, black Americans are "the most

religious people in the world." For examples, black Americans are "more likely than any other Americans to have high levels of confidence in the church or organized religion" and "much more likely than other Americans to be church members and to attend church weekly."[9]

One reason for the liberal unease with the black community's religiosity may be that the black Protestant churches—as well as the growing Islamic movement—are characterized by a deep theological and social conservatism. For example, black Americans are much more likely than other Americans to treat the Bible as literal truth,[10] a key element of fundamentalism, are heavily represented in the nation's more conservative Protestant denominations,[11] and are among the most likely to support a return to traditional roles for women, a useful measure of social conservatism.[12] Indeed, black Americans as a group seem to follow the general rule that the degree of measurable religiosity is a good predictor of the degree of social conservatism.

To be sure, there are deeply religious people on the left and there are hypocrites and atheists on the right. But the seeming instinctive mistrust of God-talk by contemporary liberals, and its ready embrace by conservatives, has badly damaged the public image of American religion—and provides strong, sad evidence of the way in which the abortion issue has so distorted our political dialogue that the public square, which once welcomed explicit religious witness, now views with suspicion people who talk about God in public.

The way in which the problem of public religious dialogue is inseparable from the problem of abortion was well illustrated in the spring of 1990, when New York City's controversial Roman Catholic archbishop, John Cardinal O'Connor, wrote an article in a church publication warning that Catholic politicians who supported abortion rights were "at risk of excommunication." (He did not, as was widely reported, actually threaten to excommunicate anyone, although several other Catholic bishops have made explicit threats, and at least one has carried it out.) Perhaps to tweak the nose of New York Governor Mario Cuomo, a pro-choice Catholic who has sparred with the cardinal before, O'Connor cited the martyred saint Thomas More, one of the locquacious Cuomo's favorite philosophers: "While he remained committed to his king, his first obligation was to Almighty God. Catholics in public

---

*This story is usefully compared with a very different and much happier tale about feminist writer Gloria Steinem who was asked how Judaism had led her to feminism and responded, "It was the other way around." See Allen R. Myerson, "Editions of the Passover Tale: This Year in Profusion," *New York Times,* April 4, 1993, Section 4, p. 2.

office must also have this commitment to serve the state; but service to God must always come first."[13]

Excommunication is, formally, a recognition that a Catholic has separated from the church. It does not mean that one is no longer a Christian, for it does not undo the rite of baptism. Nor does it, as some in the media reported, represent a sentence of damnation, which the Catholic church holds to be the privilege of God alone; but it does separate the excommunicant from the sacraments, including communion and last rites. Over the centuries, the possibility of excommunication has been one of the most dreadful for many Catholics to contemplate; it was the threat of excommunication, so the folklore has it, that led Emperor Henry IV to stand in the snow at Canossa, begging forgiveness from Pope Gregory VII for daring to thwart papal edicts.

But this is pluralistic America in the twentieth century, not theocratic Europe in the eleventh, and the words of a prince of the church no longer cause the nation's leaders to fall on their knees in the snow. Instead, they call press conferences. Pro-choice forces understandably jumped all over O'Connor's statement, calling on the cardinal, almost in so many words, to mind his own business. *Vanity Fair* informed its readers that O'Connor was "a fanatic, in the sense that any religious zealot unquestioningly committed to a rigid set of beliefs is a fanatic."[14] Other critics were more respectful. An editorial in the *New York Times* began by disavowing any intention of judging "the moral discipline that John Cardinal O'Connor imposed on Roman Catholics...including those holding public office," and ended by accusing him of imposing "a religious test" on Catholic office-seekers and forcing Catholic politicians

---

What precisely does it mean to be an American and religious?

"to choose between looking like heretics and looking like stooges."[15] Catholic politicians quickly chose up sides. New York's Governor Mario Cuomo, whose position is that he publicly supports abortion rights although personally opposed to abortion, called the cardinal's statement "mean-spirited." Former vice presidential candidate Geraldine Ferraro, also a Roman Catholic, warned that the voters might "get angry at the church's attempt to tell legislators how to vote." Not all prominent Catholics objected. Hugh Carey, Mario Cuomo's predecessor as governor, said he was distressed that his

fellow Democrats were "gloating and gleeful that their party will kill more fetuses than the other party."[16]

But not even all Catholics who agreed with the merits of the cardinal's position thought his intervention wise. Joseph Cardinal Bernardin, archbishop of Chicago, the nation's largest Catholic archdiocese, argued that the church would accomplish more through teaching and persuasion than through threats. Father Richard P. O'Brien, the head of the theology department at Notre Dame, worried that if other prelates took O'Connor's approach, "practicing Catholics could not run for office," because non-Catholics would doubt their independence.[17] This, of course, is the very fear that John F. Kennedy tried to put to rest in his 1960 presidential campaign, with his emphatic declaration that "I do not speak for my church on public matters—and the church does not speak for me."[18]

Among non-Catholics, too, the debate raged, and two New Yorkers perhaps captured it best. Asked about O'Connor's remarks, former New York mayor Ed Koch, his long-time friend, shrugged: "That's his job."[19] Burt Neuborne, a law professor at New York University, put the other side of the matter succinctly: "When you accept public office, you're not a Catholic, you're not a Jew. You're an American.[20]

Which is, in a nutshell, the problem. What precisely does it mean to be an American and religious? What is the proper scope of the influence of the religious self on the public self? How hard are politicians, and others in the public square, required to work to make this separation—and is the separation possible or even desirable? Governor Cuomo, in a very thoughtful address at Notre Dame in 1984, argued that the separation can and must be made in order for devoutly religious individuals to function as elected officials in a secular polity.[21]

Again, if one but turns the clock back to the 1950s, the battle lines over these tough questions were drawn rather differently. In February of 1956, in the midst of one of the most turbulent periods of the civil rights movement, Joseph Rummel, the Roman Catholic Archbishop of New Orleans, issued a pastoral letter condemning racial segregation as a sin. The letter, which rested on traditional church teachings, came at a delicate but auspicious moment. The Montgomery bus boycott was but two months old. The Southern states were crafting legal strategies to resist Supreme Court edicts to integrate their schools. In the middle of the month, Rummel's letter was read in all 120 Roman Catholic churches in the archdiocese, the South's largest. Next, in an editorial in a church publication, Rummel forbade Roman Catholic legislators to support a pending bill that would have required segregation in all of Louisiana's private schools, warning that to do so would be to risk "automatic excommunication."[22] White supremacist Catholic legislators were quick to blast what they evidently considered a violation of the separation of church and state. Racial segregation, they argued, was not "a matter of revealed religion" and therefore was "outside the church province."[23] Sneered one, "The editorial makes no difference."[24] Thus, the rhetoric of the 1950s was just like the rhetoric of the 1990s, except that in 1956, the liberals cheered and the conservatives got mad.

Then, in the early 1960s, several prominent segregationists *were* excommunicated for refusing to follow the church's teaching that racism was wrong. Again, there was no liberal outcry that the Catholic bishops who commanded their flocks to take a public political position against segregation or risk separation from the sacraments were wrongly interjecting their religious views into politics; no popular magazines call the bishops "religious zealot[s] unquestioningly committed to a rigid set of beliefs." Nobody, except a handful of conservatives, seemed to think the excommunications mocked Kennedy's promise that his church did not speak for him, nor he for it. Indeed, given the strong support of many Southern Protestants for segregation, this controversy places the demands that John Kennedy disavowed any intention to be bound by the teachings of his church in a somewhat different light. (After all, Kennedy's famous disavowal came in a quickly crafted speech delivered in Houston before a group of conservative white Protestant ministers.)[25]

What is one to make of all this? For one thing, there is much depressing evidence that the religious voice is required to stay out of the public square only when it is pressed in a conservative cause. A few years ago, when Roman Catholic bishops in the United States overwhelmingly endorsed a nuclear freeze, only a few nervous conservatives objected. (In an interesting twist, Defense Secretary Caspar Weinberger, who opposed the bishops on the merits of their view, defended their right as religious leaders to get involved in secular political issues.) In many parts of the world (but not all) the Roman Catholic Church has acted as an independent moral force, calling for change in brutal dictatorships and, at times, leading the charge. For liberals suddenly to decide that they dislike the image of the Catholic Church as a moral force in human affairs when they dislike the content of the moral message is to emulate those hypocritical conservatives who gleefully (and

properly) seize on the reports of Amnesty International as evidence of horror made real in Iraq or Cuba or North Korea, but who (wrongly) consider it politically motivated interference in our domestic affairs when Amnesty turns its critical eye on conditions in American prisons.

Catholicism, like any religion worth its salt, is a mass of complexities. There have been Catholic horrors over the centuries, wars, inquisitions, corruptions, and vast moral silences. There have also been plenty of secular Catholic heroes, the most prominent recent example being Nobel Laureate Mother Teresa, who has achieved folk-hero status for her work among the destitute and dying of India. Indeed, for many liberals, it might be said that Mother Teresa embodies all that is best in public avowals of religious purpose, just as Ronald Reagan, while president, very likely embodied all that is worst. Which is why an interesting coda to this chapter involves a meeting between the two of them. A few months after

---

Now imagine, for a moment, a Reagan so moved by the words that he suddenly decided to turn his presidency into a political effort to do the will of God, as interpreted by Mother Teresa.

---

he was shot by John Hinckley, Reagan had a visit from Mother Teresa, who told him: "You have suffered the passion of the cross and have received grace. There is a purpose to this. Because of your suffering and pain you will now understand the suffering and pain of the world. This has happened to you at this time because your country and the world need you."[26]

Strong words, these, from a Nobel Laureate whom many consider holy and some regard as a saint. Now imagine, for a moment, a Reagan so moved by the words that he suddenly decided to turn his presidency into a political effort to do the will of God, as interpreted by Mother Teresa. Thus he might have declared, for example, a holy war on poverty and disease. Probably he would have been lauded: he would have been no irrational zealous religionist, improperly mixing church and state, but a man devoted to a good and moral cause. Of course, Mother Teresa opposes poverty and abortion with equal vehemence. Suppose the inspired Reagan had chosen abortion instead of poverty as the object of his religious ire. Would he then have been condemned as a religious zealot by our secular culture? One shudders to think that the answer might turn on which part of Mother Teresa's work he chose to pursue.

Notes

1. See *Roberts v. Madigan*, 921 F. 2d 1047 (10th Cir. 1990).
2. The comment about the Supreme Court was made by Florence Kennedy, a member of the board of directors of the National Organization for Women, in connection with the nomination of Clarence Thomas to the Supreme Court, and was promptly repudiated by Patricia Ireland, the group's president. The comment typified an unsubtle anti-Catholic theme in much of the academic, intellectual, and mass media response to the Thomas nomination. I am constrained to add, lest the reader mistake my point, that I was not a supporter of Thomas's and that I believed Anita Hill's charges of sexual harassment.
3. See, for example, the discussion of the religious views of scientists and social scientists in Robert Wuthnow, *The Struggle for America's Soul: Evangelicals, Liberals, and Secularism* (Grand Rapids, MI: William B. Eerdmans, 1989) pp. 143–57.
4. *Roe v. Wade* 410 U.S. 113 (1973).
5. See E.J. Dionne, Jr., *Why Americans Hate Politics* (New York: Simon & Schuster, 1991), pp. 209–210.
6. James Davison Hunter, *Culture Wars: The Struggle to Define America* (New York: Basic Books, 1991), p. 144.
7. Garry Wills, *Under God: Religion and American Politics* (New York: Simon & Schuster, 1990), pp. 90–91.
8. Garry Wills, *Under God*, p. 63.
9. George Gallup, Jr., and Jim Castelli, *The People's Religion: American Faith in the 90's* (New York: Macmillan Publishing Co., 1989), pp. 122–23.
10. Ibid., p. 123.
11. Wade Clark Roof and William McKinney, *American Mainline Religion: Its Changing Shape and Future* (New Brunswick: Rutgers University Press, 1987) p. 123.
12. Gallup and Castelli, *The People's Religion*, p. 196.
13. Quoted in Ari L. Goldman, "O'Connor Warns Politicians Risk Excommunication Over Abortion," *New York Times*, June 15, 1990, p. A1.
14. Leslie Bennetts, "The Holy Terror of Cardinal O'Connor," quoted in Richard John Neuhaus, "The Immutable Rebels," *First Things*, Dec. 1990, p. 62.
15. Editorial, "The Cardinal Gets Tougher," *New York Times*, June 17, 1990, section 4, p. 20.
16. Cuomo, Ferraro, and Carey quoted in Frank Lynn, "The Stakes Are Raised for Catholic Politicians," *New York Times*, June 17, 1990, section 4, p. 5.

17. Quoted in Ronald Brownstein, "Catholicism a Political Issue Again," *Los Angeles Times,* June 22, 1990, p. A1.

18. "Remarks of Senator John F. Kennedy on Church and State," reprinted as Appendix C to Theodore H. White, *The Making of the President 1960* (New York: Atheneum, 1988), p. 393.

19. Quoted in Kenneth L. Woodward, "An Archbishop Rattles a Saber," *Newsweek*, June 25, 1990, p. 64.

20. Quoted in Howard Kurtz, "O'Connor's Warning on Abortion Causes Political Uproar," *Washington Post,* June 16, 1990, p. A13.

21. Mario Cuomo, "Religious Belief and Public Morality: A Catholic Governor's Perspective," *Notre Dame Journal of Law, Ethics, and Public Policy* 1 (1984): 13.

22. "Catholics Warned on School Measure," *The Times-Picayune* (New Orleans), Feb. 25, 1956, p. 1.

23. Bernard Taper, "A Reporter at Large: A Meeting in Atlanta," *The New Yorker,* Mar. 17, 1956, p. 78.

24. Quoted in "The Nation: Segregation Fronts," *New York Times*, Feb. 26, 1956, p. 2E.

25. For an account of the hasty decision to give the speech and the hasty effort to draft it, see White, *The Making of the President* 1960, pp. 259–62.

26. Quoted in Laurence I. Barrett, *Gambling with History: Ronald Reagan in the White House* (Garden City, N.Y.: Doubleday, 1983), p. 124.

Terms & Concepts

abolitionist movement
Amnesty International
Christian fundamentalists
contemporary liberals
desegregation
excommunication

God-talk
Martin Luther King, Jr.
Mother Teresa
public religious dialogue
Roe v. Wade
Ronald Reagan

secular political issues
separation of church and state
social gospel
theocratic Europe

Questions

1. What is the role of religion in liberal democratic societies? Do liberals have a double standard regarding religion, and if so, what are the criteria for approving of "good" religious beliefs and disapproving of others?

2. Several observers argue that religious belief and motivation has increased in the non-Western world in the last decade. Is this so? If so, what might be the reasons for this development?

3. Is religion really ideology? Or can we call socialism or nationalism religions?

4. What Canadian examples can you find to illustrate Carter's argument?

5. What does this article suggest about the nature of political debate? Is it carried on according to strict rules of logic? Cite examples from the article to explain your position.

Unit Two

Discussion Questions

1. Do any of the belief systems discussed seem to explain our world better than the others? Do they really matter anyway, as we go about our daily lives?

2. Do ideas, in particular ideologies, drive events and actions, or are they simply a reflection and interpretation of what has already occurred?

3. Are the old, resurgent, forces of nationalism, religion, and territorialism going to eclipse the more recent, secular ideologies—even (constitutional) liberalism?

4. Does feminism seem to have any "natural allies" in terms of the other ideologies?

Annotated Bibliography

Arblaster, Anthony. *The Rise and Decline of Western Liberalism*. Oxford: Basil Blackwell, 1984. This is an acclaimed critical analysis of liberalism, from which the excerpt in this unit has been taken. We strongly suggest that you read the whole of Chapter 4 on "Liberal Values."

Ball, Terrence and Richard Dagger. *Political Ideologies and the Democratic Ideal*. New York: Harper Collins, 1991. This reader provides a historical foundation for traditional ideologies as well as their current derivatives; includes analysis of various "liberation ideologies."

Betz, Hans-Georg. "The New Politics of Resentment: Radical Rightwing Populist Parties in Western Europe." *Comparative Politics* 25:4 (July 1993). A thought-provoking analysis of the current rise of populism in France, Italy, and Germany.

Brooks, Geraldine. *Nine Parts of Desire: The Hidden World of Islamic Women*. New York: Doubleday, 1995. A fascinating exploration of the private and public role of women in Islamic countries.

Dworkin, Ronald. *A Matter of Principle*. Cambridge. Cambridge, Mass.: Harvard University Press, 1985. An examination of the balance struck between liberty and equality in liberalism.

Eisler, Riane. *The Chalice and the Blade: Our History, Our Future*. San Francisco: Harper and Row, 1988. A thought-provoking sociocultural investigation of gender relations—past, present, and future.

Flanagan, Tom. *Waiting for the Wave: the Reform Party and Preston Manning*. Toronto: Stoddart, 1995. An insider's account of the tension between pragmatism and ideology in a populist party.

Folkertsma, Marvin J., Jr. *Ideology and Leadership*. New Jersey: Prentice Hall, 1988. The author focuses on what political ideas and beliefs inspired leaders such as Roosevelt, Martin Luther King, Stalin, Mao, Hitler, and Khomeini.

Frum, David. *Dead Right*. New York: New Republic Books/Basic Books, 1994. A sweeping, polemical attack on the state by a leading neoconservative.

Fukuyama, Francis. *The End of History and the Last Man*. New York: Free Press, 1992. A seminal work on the "triumph" of liberal democracy.

Gilligan, Carol. *In a Different Voice*. Cambridge, Mass.: Harvard University Press, 1982. A very important and frequently cited contribution to the debate surrounding gender difference.

Hubbard, Ruth. *The Politics of Women's Biology*. New Brunswick: Rutgers, 1990. Hubbard, who decided to write about science after becoming a respected biologist, shows the subjectivity of science; science is patriarchial and has been part of the power structure that has kept women subjugated.

Ignatieff, Michael. *Blood and Belonging: Journeys into the New Nationalism*. Toronto: Viking, 1993. A study of nationalism in several contemporary locations; also made into a TV documentary.

Kamenka, Eugene. Nationalism: Ambiguous Legacies and Contingent Futures." *Political Studies*, special issue, 1993. In a useful and special issue of this journal, Kamenka offers a sobering analysis of the past and future of nationalism.

Limbaugh, Rush. *The Way Things Ought To Be*. New York: Pocket Books, 1994. The full ferocity of the "new" conservatism in the United States is evident in this volume.

Minogue, Kenneth. "Ideology After the Collapse of Communism." *Political Studies* 41, 4 (1993). An attempt to redefine ideology and limit the use of the term.

Pateman, Carole. "Feminism and Democracy." In *Democratic Theory and Practice,* edited by Graeme Duncan. Cambridge: Cambridge University Press, 1983. By one of the foremost critics of polyarchy, which, she believes, purposefully and wrongly limits the political participation of women and of citizens of lower socio-economic status.

Radcliffe Richards, Janet. *The Sceptical feminist: a Philosophical Inquiry*. London: Penguin, 1980. The author traces the nature of gender inequality, identifies its causes, and critically assesses the arguments justifying it.

Richards, John, Robert D. Cairns, and Larry Pratt, eds. *Social Democracy Without Illusions*. Toronto: McClelland and Stewart, 1991. A collection of useful essays on some of the key questions facing Canadian social democrats.

Rorty, Richard. "The Intellectuals at the End of Socialism." *Yale Review* 80: 1 & 2, (April 1992). A leading scholar discusses the role of left-wing intellectuals as the left collapses.

Rosenblum, Nancy, ed. *Liberalism and the Moral Life*. Cambridge: Harvard University Press, 1989. A collection of essays laying out the key debates in which liberalism is currently embroiled.

Sandel, Michael, ed. *Liberalism and its Critics*. New York: New York University Press, 1984. A collection of articles on the assault on American liberalism.

Sigurdson, Richard. "Preston Manning and the Politics of Postmodernism in Canada." *Canadian Journal of Political Science* 27:2 (June 1994). Hypermodernism meets the retro-right, and globalization encounters parochialism.

Smith, Anthony. *National Identity*. London: Penguin, 1991. A concise and balanced review of ethnic and other forms of nationalism.

Walker, Connor. "Beyond Reason: The Nature of the Ethnonational Bond." *Ethnic and Racial Studies* (July 1993). An interesting discussion of a vital topic.

Unit Three

Citizenship and Democracy

• • •

Citizens in liberal democracies express very little confidence in their governments' problem-solving abilities, harbour feelings of cynicism and resentment against elected politicians, and tend to blame government for whatever ails them. How could such a gulf emerge between the citizen and the state in a regime in which the people are held to rule themselves through their representatives? This paradox requires explanation.

Articles in the previous units of this book suggest some answers. Representation, for example, is not so simple and straightforward an idea as is often thought. There are a variety of ways in which a representative may relate to his or her constituents, each one with specific implications for institutions like parties, electoral systems, and parliamentary government. Another explanation is that the prevailing liberal political ideology exalts the autonomous individual who considers his or her own interest in isolation from that of others. This process has been aggravated by economic changes threatening the middle class, leading citizens increasingly to see each other as competitors for pieces of a shrinking economic pie. Rapid technological and political change, to cite another explanation, has left states scrambling to catch up, offering old and ineffective solutions to new problems.

Another way to look at the problem is to think about the meaning of citizenship. Canada is among a small number of countries for which citizenship is a matter of official government promotion. In the eyes of many, Canada does not demand a great deal of its new citizens. In other countries, immigration is either denied or discouraged. For example, German citizenship is all but refused to persons who are unable to demonstrate German ethnic lineage. Many countries require their citizens to serve in the military for a period of their lives. What can be expected of citizens? Is citizenship a set of entitlements, a set of obligations, or a blend of the two? If the latter, exactly what entitlements and obligations are at issue in democratic citizenship?

These issues lead to a more fundamental question: Does democratic government require a certain minimal moral character among citizens, or is it enough to obey the law? If the former, then the contemporary democratic malaise may be explained in terms of a decline in citizens' moral character. For some, democratic government rests on moral as well as material foundations and if the regime does not foster the health of civil society, self-government itself is threatened. In other words, a society of liberty and equality requires a minimal moral sense of fellow-feeling and communal obligation in order to survive. For others, however, to require citizens to conform to a moral standard of character is to defeat the very purpose of democratic government, which is to allow and encourage diversity in this and other areas of life. For others still, to agree with the prin-

Photo courtesy of Canapress.

ciple that moral character is necessary is to agree on relatively little; the debate then shifts to the content of that moral character, an extremely controversial matter indeed.

The articles in this section examine these issues in various ways. Michael Walzer's contribution probes the concept of civil society and its status in different political ideologies. Mary Ann Glendon addresses herself to one of the most popular—and misunderstood—ideas in North American liberal democracy: the notion that each citizen possesses rights that all others have a duty to respect. John Kenneth Galbraith stresses the

material, economic foundations of liberal society in his article, while Frederick Johnstone discusses the complicated politics of identity and considers some institutional implications.

Citizenship and democracy are of interest not merely to academics and political science students. Almost everyone is a citizen of some country. And everyone having citizenship in a democratic society must consider what he or she may expect from the political community, and what he or she is prepared to contribute to it. These readings will challenge you to reflect on these questions.

The Idea of Civil Society

Michael Walzer

Editors' Note

In 1987, then playwright and dissident Vaclav Havel observed that after decades of exposure to "the radiation of totalitarianism," people in his native Czechoslovakia were almost drained of the sense of ease, cheerfulness, and spontaneity he noticed in foreigners. Look, he wrote, at how people behave toward one another in stores and offices and on the streetcars:

> ...they tend to be surly, selfish, impolite and disobliging; for the counter staff, customers are often an imposition: they serve while talking among themselves. When asked a question, they reply with distaste (if they know an answer at all). Drivers yell at each other, people in lineups elbow ahead and snap at each other. Bureaucrats don't care how many people

are waiting to see them, or how long they wait. They often make appointments and fail to keep them. They get no pleasure from helping people and have no regrets when they can't.[1]

Such is the consequence of the imposition of a singular ideological vision unconnected to the realities of human life, Havel argued. Civil society is crushed by an omnipresent state fearful of any human relationship carried on outside its control.

The following article by Princeton University political theorist Michael Walzer argues for the existence and revitalization of civil society. Readers should not think, however, that the health of civil society is something only

people in former Communist countries have to worry about. He suggests that life "on the ground" in North America and Europe increasingly lacks tolerance and fellow-feeling, and that the rich complexity of associational life is threatened.

As you read this article watch out for three elements: 1) Walzer's critique of ideologies, 2) the subtle but important relationship between state and civil society, and 3) a hint of agreement between neoconservatives and people on the ideological left. Consider also the possibility that associational life may not be in decline, only in transition. Perhaps the PTA no longer commands parents' time and attention, but the daycare parental advisory board does.

◆ ◆ ◆

---

1. Vaclav Havel, "Stories and Totalitarianism," in Paul Wilson, ed., *Open Letters: Selected Prose, 1965–1990* (London: Faber and Faber, 1991), 348.

My aim in this essay is to defend a complex, imprecise, and, at crucial point, uncertain account of society and politics. I have no hope of theoretical simplicity, not at this historical moment when so many stable oppositions of political and intellectual life have collapsed; but I also have no desire for simplicity, since a world that theory could fully grasp and neatly explain would not, I suspect, be a pleasant place. In the nature of things, then, my argument won't be elegant, and though I believe that arguments should march, and sentences following one another like soldiers on parade, the route of my march today will be twisting and roundabout. I shall begin with the idea of civil society, recently revived by Central and East European intellectuals, and go on to talk about the state, the economy and the nation, and then about civil society and the state again. These are the crucial social formations that we inhabit, but we don't at this moment live comfortably in any of them. Nor is it possible to imagine, in accordance with one or another of the great simplifying theories, a way to choose among them—as if we were destined to find, one day, the best social formation. I mean to argue against choosing, but I shall also claim that it is from within civil society that this argument is best understood.

The words "civil society" name the space of uncoerced human association and also the set of relational networks—formed for the sake of family, faith, interest, and ideology—that fill this space. Central and East European dissidence flourished within a highly restricted version of civil society, and the first task of the new democracies created by the dissidents, so we are told, is to rebuild the networks; unions, churches, political parties and movements, cooperatives, neighbourhoods, schools of thought, societies for promoting or preventing this and that. In the West, by contrast, we have lived in civil society for many years without knowing it. Or, better, since the Scottish Enlightenment, or since Hegel, the words have been known to the knowers of such things but they have rarely served to focus anyone else's attention. Now writers in Hungary, Czechoslovakia, and Poland invite us to think about how this social formation is secured and invigorated.

We have reasons of our own for accepting the invitation. Increasingly, associational life in the "advanced" capitalist and social democratic countries seems at risk. Publicists and preachers warn us of a steady attenuation of everyday cooperation and civic friendship. And this time it's possible that they are not, as they usually are, foolishly alarmist. Our cities really are noisier and nastier than they once were. Familial solidarity, mutual assistance, political likemindedness—all these are less certain and less substantial than they once were. Other people, strangers on the street, seem less trustworthy than they once did. The Hobbesian account of society is more persuasive than it once was.

Perhaps this worrisome picture follows—in part, no more, but what else can a political theorist say?—from the fact that we have not thought enough about solidarity and trust or planned for their future. We have been thinking too much about social formations different from, in competition with, civil society. And so we have neglected the networks through which civility is produced and reproduced. Imagine that the following questions were posed one or two centuries ago to political theorists and moral philosophers: what is the preferred setting, the most supportive environment, for the good life? What sorts of institutions should we work for? Nineteenth- and twentieth-century social thought provides four different, by now familiar, answers to these questions. Think of them as four rival ideologies, each with its own claim to completeness and correctness. Each is importantly wrong. Each neglects the necessary pluralism of any civil society. Each is predicated on an assumption I mean to attack: that such questions must receive a singular answer.

DEFINITIONS FROM THE LEFT
◆ ◆ ◆

I shall begin, since this is for me the best-known ground, with two leftist answers. The first of the two holds that the preferred setting for the good life is the political community, the democratic state, within which we can be citizens: freely engaged, fully committed, decision-making members, And a citizen, on this view, is much the best thing to be. To live well is to be politically active, working with our fellow citizens, collectively determining our common destiny—not for the sake of this or that determination but for the work itself, in which our highest capacities as rational and moral agents find expression. We know ourselves best as persons who propose, debate, and decide.

This article first appeared in *Dissent,* Spring 1991 (pp. 293–304) and is reproduced with permission.

This argument goes back to the Greeks, but we are most likely to recognize its neoclassical versions. It is Rousseau's argument or the standard leftist interpretation of Rousseau's argument. His understanding of citizenship as moral agency is one of the key sources of democratic idealism. We can see it at work in a liberal such as John Stuart Mill, in whose writings it produced an unexpected defense of syndicalism (what is today called "workers' control") and, more generally, of social democracy. It appeared among nineteenth- and twentieth-century democratic radicals, often with a hard populist edge. It played a part in the reiterated demand for social inclusion by women, workers, blacks, and new immigrants, all of whom based their claims on their capacity as agents. And this same neoclassical idea of citizenship resurfaced in the 1960s in New Left theories of participation, where it was, however, like latter-day revivals of many ideas, highly theoretical and without much local resonance.

Today, perhaps, in response to the political disasters of the late sixties, "communitarians" in the United States struggle to give Rousseauian idealism a historical reference, looking back to the early American republic and calling for a renewal of civic virtue. They prescribe citizenship as an antidote to the fragmentation of contemporary society—for these theorists, like Rousseau, are disinclined to value the fragments. In their hands, republicanism is still a simplifying creed. If politics is our highest calling, then we are called away from every other activity (or, every other activity is redefined in political terms): our energies are directed toward policy formation and decision making in the democratic state.

I don't doubt that the active and engaged citizen is an attractive figure—even if some of the activists that we actually meet carrying placards and shouting slogans aren't all that attractive. The most penetrating criticism of this first answer to the question about the good life is not that the life isn't good but that it isn't the "real life" of very many people in the modern world. This is so in two senses. First, though the power of the democratic state has grown enormously, partly (and rightly) in response to the demands of engaged citizens, it can't be said that the state is fully in the hands of its citizens. And the larger it gets, the more it takes over those smaller associations still subject to hands-on control. The rule of the demos is in significant ways illusory; the participation of ordinary men and women in the activities of the state (unless they are state employees) is largely vicarious; even party militants are more likely to argue and complain than actually to decide.

Second, despite the singlemindedness of republican ideology, politics rarely engages the full attention of the citizens who are supposed to be its chief protagonists. They have too many other things to worry about. Above all, they have to earn a living. They are more deeply engaged in the economy than in the political community. Republican theorists (like Hannah Arendt) recognize this engagement only as a threat to civic virtue. Economic activity belongs to the realm of necessity, they argue, politics to the realm of freedom. Ideally, citizens should not have to work; they should be served by machines, if not by slaves, so that they can flock to the assemblies and argue with their fellows about affairs of state. In practice, however, work, though it begins in necessity, takes on a value of its own—expressed in com-

---

...in the Marxist here and now, political conflict is taken to be the superstructural enactment of economic conflict, and democracy is valued mainly because it enables socialist movements and parties to organize for victory.

---

mitment to a career, pride in a job well done, a sense of camaraderie in the workplace. All of these are competitive with the values of citizenship.

The second leftist position on the preferred setting for the good life involves a turning away from republican politics and a focus instead on economic activity. We can think of this as the socialist answer to the questions I began with; it can be found in Marx and also, though the arguments are somewhat different, among the utopians he hoped to supersede. For Marx, the preferred setting is the cooperative economy, where we can all be producers-artists (Marx was a romantic), inventors, and artisans. (Assembly-line workers don't quite seem to fit.) This again is much the best thing to be. The picture Marx paints is of creative men and women making useful and beautiful objects, not for the sake of this or that object but for the sake of creativity itself, the highest expression of our "species-being" as *homo faber*, man-the-maker.

The state, in this view, ought to be managed in such a way as to set productivity free. It doesn't matter who the managers are so long as they are committed to this goal and rational in its pursuit. Their work is technically important but not substantively interesting. Once productivity is free, politics simply ceases to engage anyone's attention. Before that time, in the Marxist here and now, political conflict is taken to be the superstructural enactment of economic conflict, and democracy is valued mainly because it enables socialist movements and parties to organize for victory. The value is instrumental and historically specific. A democratic state is the preferred setting not for the good life but for the class struggle; the purpose of the struggle is to win, and victory brings an end to democratic instrumentality. There is no intrinsic value in democracy, no reason to think that politics has, for creatures like us, a permanent attractiveness. When we are all engaged in productive activity, social division and the conflicts it engenders will disappear, and the state, in the once-famous phrase, will "wither away."

In fact, if this vision were ever realized, it is politics that would wither away. Some kind of administrative agency would still be necessary for economic coordination, and it is only a Marxist conceit to refuse to call this agency a state. "Society regulates the general production," Marx wrote in *The German Ideology*, "and thus makes it possible for me to do one thing today and another tomorrow...just as I have a mind." Because this regulation is nonpolitical, the individual producers are free from the burdens of citizenship. They attend instead to the things they make and to the cooperative relationships they establish. Exactly how one can work with other people and still do whatever one pleases is unclear to me and probably to most other readers of Marx. The texts suggest an extraordinary faith in the virtuosity of the regulators. No one, I think quite shares this faith today, but something like it helps to explain the tendency of some leftist to see even the liberal and democratic state as an obstacle that has to be, in the worst of recent jargons, "smashed."

The seriousness of Marxist antipolitics is nicely illustrated by Marx's own dislike of syndicalism. What the syndicalists proposed was a neat amalgam of the first and second answers to the question about the good life: for them, the preferred setting was the worker controlled factory, where men and women were simultaneously citizens and producers, making decisions and making things. Marx seems to have regarded the combination as impossible; factories could not be both democratic and productive. This is the point of Engels's little essay on authority, which I take to express Marx's view also. More generally, self-government on the job called into question the legitimacy of "social regulation" or state planning, which alone, Marx thought, could enable individual workers to devote themselves, without distraction, to their work.

But this vision of the cooperative economy is set against an unbelievable background—a nonpolitical state, regulation without conflict, "the administration of things." In every actual experience of socialist politics, the state has moved rapidly into the foreground, and most socialists, in the west at least, have been driven to make their own amalgam of the first and second answers. They call themselves *democratic* socialists, focusing on the state as well as (in fact, much more than) on the economy and doubling the preferred settings for the good life. Because I believe that two are better than one, I take this to be progress. But before I try to suggest what further progress might look like, I need to describe two more ideological answers to the question about the good life, one of them capitalist, the other nationalist. For there is no reason to think that only leftists love singularity.

A CAPITALIST DEFINITION
◆ ◆ ◆

The third answer holds that the preferred setting for the good life is the marketplace, where individual men and women, consumers rather than producers, choose among a maximum number of options. The autonomous individual confronting his, and now her, possibilities—this is much the best thing to be. To live well is not to make political divisions or beautiful objects; it is to make personal choices. Not any particular choices, for no choice is substantively the best: it is the activity of choosing that makes for autonomy. And the market within which choices are made, like the socialist economy, largely dispenses with politics; it requires at most a minimal state—not "social regulation," only the police.

Production, too, is free even if it isn't, as in the Marxist vision, freely creative. More important than the producers, however, are the entrepreneurs—heroes of autonomy, consumers of opportunity—who compete to supply whatever all the other consumers want or might be persuaded to want. Entrepreneurial activity tracks consumer preference. Though not without its own excitements, it is mostly instrumental: the aim of all entrepreneurs (and all producers) is to increase their market power, maximize their options. Competing with one another, they maximize everyone else's options too, filling the marketplace with desirable objects. The market is preferred (over the political community and the cooperative economy) because of its fullness. Freedom, in the capitalist view, is a function of plenitude. We can only choose when we have many choices.

It is also true, unhappily, that we can only make effective (rather than merely speculative or wistful) choices when we have resources to dispose of. But people come to the marketplace with radically unequal resources—some with virtually nothing at all. Not everyone can compete successfully in commodity production, and therefore not everyone has access to commodities. Autonomy turns out to be a high-risk value, which many men and women can only realize with help from their friends. The market, however, is not a good setting for mutual assistance, for I cannot help someone else without reducing (for the short term, at least) my own options. And I have no reason, as an autonomous individual, to accept any reductions of any sort for someone else's sake. My argument here is not that autonomy collapses into egotism, only that autonomy in the marketplace provides no support for social solidarity. Despite the successes of capitalist production, the good life of consumer choice is not universally available. Large numbers of people drop out of the market economy or live precariously on its margins.

Partly for this reason, capitalism, like socialism, is highly dependent on state action—not only to prevent theft and enforce contracts but also to regulate the economy and guarantee the minimal welfare of its participants. But these participants, insofar as they are market activists, are not active in the state: capitalism in its ideal form, like socialism again, does not make for citizenship. Or, its protagonists conceive of citizenship in economic terms, so that citizens are transformed into autonomous consumers, looking for the party or program that most persuasively promises to strengthen their market positions. They need the state but have no moral relation to it, and they control its officials only as consumers control the producers of commodities, by buying or not buying what they make.

Because the market has no political boundaries, capitalist entrepreneurs also evade official control. They need the state but have no loyalty to it; the profit motive brings them into conflict with democratic regulation. So arms merchants sell the latest military technology to foreign powers, and manufacturers move their factories overseas to escape safety codes or minimum-wage laws. Multinational corporations stand outside (and to some extent against) every political community. They are known only by their brand names, which, unlike family names and country names, evoke preferences but not affections or solidarities.

A NATIONALIST RESPONSE

◆ ◆ ◆

The fourth answer to the question about the good life can be read as a response to market amorality and disloyalty, though it has, historically, other sources as well. According to the fourth answer, the preferred setting is the nation, within which we are loyal members, bound to one another by ties of blood and history. And a member, secure in membership, literally part of an organic whole—this is much the best thing to be. To live well is to participate with other men and women in remembering, cultivating, and passing on a national heritage. This is so, on the nationalist view, without reference to the specific content of the heritage, so long as it is one's own, a matter of birth, not choice. Every nationalist will, of course, find value in his or her own heritage, but the highest value is not in the finding but in the willing: the firm identification of the individual with a people and a history.

Nationalism has often been a leftist ideology, historically linked to democracy and even to socialism. But it is most characteristically an ideology of the right, for its understanding of membership is ascriptive; it requires no political choices and no activity beyond ritual affirmation. When nations find themselves ruled by foreigners, however, ritual affirmation isn't enough. Then nationalism requires a more heroic loyalty: self-sacrifice in the struggle for national liberation. The capacity of the nation to elicit such sacrifices from its members is proof of the importance of this fourth answer. Individual members seek the good life by seeking autonomy not for themselves but for their people. Ideally, this attitude ought to survive the liberation struggle and provide a foundation for social solidarity and mutual assistance. Perhaps, to some extent, it does: certainly the welfare state has had its greatest successes in ethnically homogeneous countries. It is also true, however, that once liberation has been secured, nationalist men and women are commonly content with a vicarious rather than a practical participation in the community. There is nothing wrong with vicarious participation, on the nationalist view, since the good life is more a matter of identity than activity—faith, not works, so to speak, though both of these are understood in secular terms.

In the modern world, nations commonly seek statehood, for their autonomy will always be at risk if they lack sovereign power. But they don't seek states of any particular kind. No more do they seek economic arrangement of any particular kind. Unlike religious believers who are their close kin and (often) bitter rivals, nationalists are not bound by a body of authoritative law or a set of sacred text. Beyond liberation, they have no program, only a vague commitment to continue a history, sustain a "way of life." Their own lives, are emotionally intense, but in relation to society and economy this is dangerously free-floating intensity. In times of trouble, it can readily be turned against other nations, particularly against the internal other minorities, aliens, strangers. Democratic citizenship, worker solidarity, free enterprise, and consumer autonomy—all these are less exclusive than nationalism but not always resistant to its power. The ease with which citizens, workers, and consumers become fervent nationalists is a sign of the inadequacy of the first three answers to the question about the good life. The nature of nationalist fervour signals the inadequacy of the fourth.

CAN WE FIND A SYNTHESIS?

◆ ◆ ◆

All these answers are wrongheaded because of their singularity. They miss the complexity of human society, the inevitable conflicts of commitment and loyalty. Hence I am uneasy with the idea that there might be a fifth and finally correct answer to the question about the good life. Still, there is a fifth answer, the newest one (it draws

---

Ideally, civil society is a setting of settings: all are included, none is preferred.

---

upon less central themes of nineteenth- and twentieth-century social thought), which holds that the good life can only be lived in civil society, the realm of fragmentation and struggle but also of concrete and authentic solidarities, where we fulfil E.M. Forester's injunction, "only connect," and become sociable or communal men and women. And this is, of course, much the best thing to be. The picture here is of people freely associating and communicating with one another, forming and reforming groups of all sorts, not for the sake of any particular formation—family, tribe, nation, religion, commune, brotherhood and sisterhood, interest group or ideological movement—but for the sake of sociability itself. For we are by nature social, before we are political or economic beings.

I would rather say that the civil society argument is a corrective to the four ideological accounts of the good life—part denial, part incorporation—rather than a fifth to stand alongside them. It challenges their singularity but it has no singularity of its own. The phrase "social being" describes men and women who are citizens, producers, consumers, members of the nation, and much else besides—and none of these by nature or because it is the best thing to be. The associational life of civil society is the actual ground where all versions of the good are worked out and tested...and proved to be partial, incomplete, ultimately unsatisfying. It can't be the case that living on this ground is good in itself; there isn't any other place to live. What is true is that the quality of our political and economic activity and of our national culture is intimately connected to the strength and vitality of our associations.

Ideally, civil society is a setting of settings: all are included, none is preferred. The argument is a liberal version of the four answers, accepting them all, insisting that each leave room for the others, therefore not finally accepting any of them. Liberalism appears here as an anti-ideology, and this is an attractive position in the contemporary world. I shall stress this attractiveness as I try to explain how civil society might actually incorporate and deny the four answers. Later on, however, I shall have to argue that this position too, so genial and benign, has its problems.

Let's begin with the political community and the cooperative economy, taken together. These two leftist versions of the good life systematically undervalued all associations except the demos and the working class. Their protagonists could imagine conflicts between political communities and between classes but not within either; they aimed at the abolition or transcendence of particularism and all its divisions. Theorists of civil society, by contrast, have a more realistic view of communities and economies. They are more accommodating to conflict—that is, to political opposition and economic competition. Associational freedom serves for them to legitimate a set of market relations, though not necessarily the capitalist set. The market, when it is entangled in the network of associations, when the forms of ownership are pluralized, is without doubt the economic formation most consistent with the civil society argument. This same argument also serves to legitimate a kind of state that is liberal and pluralist more than republican (not so radically dependent upon the virtue of its citizens). Indeed, a state of this sort, as we shall see, is necessary if associations are to flourish.

Once incorporated into civil society, neither citizenship nor production can ever again be all-absorbing. They will have votaries, but these people will not be models for the rest of us—or, they will be partial models only, for some people at some time of their lives, not for other people, not at other times. This pluralist perspective follows in part, perhaps, from the lost romance of work, form our experience with the new productive technologies and the growth of the service economy. Service is more easily reconciled with a vision of human beings as social animals than with *homo faber*. What can a hospital attendant or a school teacher or a marriage counsellor or a social worker or a television repair-person or a government official be said to *make*? The contemporary economy does not offer many people a chance for creativity in the Marxist sense. Nor does Marx (or any socialist thinker of the central tradition) have much to say about those men and women whose economic activity consists entirely in helping other people. The helpmate, like the housewife, was never assimilated to the class of workers.

In similar fashion, politics in the contemporary democratic state does not offer many people a chance for Rousseauian self-determination. Citizenship, taken by itself, is today mostly a passive role: citizens are spectators who vote. Between elections they are served, well or badly, by the civil service. They are not at all like those heroes of republican mythology, the citizens of ancient Athens meeting in assembly and (foolishly, as it turned out) deciding to invade Sicily. But in the associational networks of civil society—in unions, parties, movements, interest groups, and so on—these same people make many smaller decisions and shape to some degree the more distant determinations of state and economy. And in a more densely organized, more egalitarian civil society, they might do both these things to greater effect.

These socially engaged men and women—part-time union officers, movement activists, party regulars, consumer advocates, welfare volunteers, church members, family heads—stand outside the republic of citizens as it is commonly conceived. They are only intermittently virtuous; they are too caught up in particularity. They look, most of them, for many partial fulfillments, no longer for the one clinching fulfillment. On the ground of actuality (unless the state usurps the ground), citizenship shades off into a great diversity of (sometimes divisive) decision-making roles; and, similarly, production shades

off into a multitude of (sometimes competitive) socially useful activities. It is, then, a mistake to set politics and work in opposition to one another. There is no ideal fulfillment and no essential human capacity. We require many settings so that we can live different kinds of good lives.

All this is not to say, however, that we need to accept the capitalist version of competition and division. Theorists who regard the market as the preferred setting for the good life aim to make it the actual setting for as many aspects of life as possible. Their singlemindedness takes the form of market imperialism; confronting the democratic state, they are advocates of privatization and laissez-faire. Their ideal is a society in which all goods and services are provided by entrepreneurs to consumers. That some entrepreneurs would fail and many consumers find themselves helpless in the marketplace— this is the price of individual autonomy. It is , obviously, a price we already pay: in all capitalist societies, the market makes for inequality. The more successful its imperialism, the greater the inequality. But were the market to be set firmly within civil society, politically constrained, open to communal as well as private initiatives, limits might be fixed on its unequal outcomes. The exact nature of the limits would depend on the strength and density of the associational networks (including, now, the political community).

The problem with inequality is not merely that some individuals are more capable, others less capable, of making their consumer preferences effective. It's not that some individuals live in fancier apartments than others, or drive better-made cars, or take vacations in more exotic places. These are conceivably the just rewards of market success. The problem is that inequality commonly translates into domination and radical deprivation. But the verb "translates" here describes a socially mediated process, which is fostered or inhibited by the structure of its mediations. Dominated and deprived individuals are likely to be disorganized as well as impoverished, whereas poor people with strong families, churches, unions, political parties, and ethnic alliances are not likely to be dominated or deprived for long. Nor need these people stand alone even in the marketplace. The capitalist answer assumes that the good life of entrepreneurial initiative and consumer choice is a life led most importantly by individuals. But civil society encompasses or can encompass a variety of market agents: family businesses, publicly owned or municipal companies, worker communes, consumers cooperatives, nonprofit organizations of many different sorts. All these function in the market even though they have their origins outside. And just as the experience of democracy is expanded and enhanced by groups that are in but not of the state, so consumer choice is expanded and enhanced by groups that are in but not of the market.

It is only necessary to add that among the groups in but not of the state are market organizations, and among the groups in but not of the market are state organizations. All social forms are relativized by the civil society argument—and on the actual ground too. This also means that all social forms are contestable; moreover, contests can't be won by invoking one or another account of the preferred setting—as if it were enough to say that market organizations, insofar as they are efficient, don't have to be democratic or that state firms, insofar as they are democratically controlled, don't have to operate within the constraints of the market. The exact character of our associational life is something that has to be argued about, and it is in the course of these arguments that we also decide about the forms of democracy, the nature of work, the extent and effects of market inequalities, and much else.

Civil society simply is that place where the stakes are lower, where, in principle at least, coercion is used only to keep the peace...

The quality of nationalism is also determined within civil society, where national groups coexist and overlap with families and religious communities (two social formations largely neglected in modernist answers to the question about the good life) and where nationalism is expressed in schools and movements, organizations for mutual aid, cultural and historical societies. It is because groups like these are entangled with other groups, similar in kind but different in aim, that civil society holds out the hope of a domesticated nationalism. In states dominated by a single nation, the multiplicity of the groups pluralizes nationalist politics and culture; in states with more than one nation, the density of the networks prevents radical polarization.

Civil society as we know it has its origin in the struggle for religious freedom. Though often violent, the struggle held open the possibility of peace. "The establishment of this one thing," John Locke wrote about toleration, "would take away all ground of complaints and

tumults upon account of conscience." One can easily imagine groundless complaints and tumults, but Locke believed (and he was largely right) that tolerance would dull the edge of religious conflict. People would be less ready to take risks once the stakes were lowered. Civil society simply is that place where the stakes are lower, where, in principle at least, coercion is used only to keep the peace and all associations are equal under the law. In the market, this formal equality often has no substance, but in the world of faith and identity, it is real enough. Though nations don't compete for members in the same way as religions (sometimes) do, the argument for granting them the associational freedom of civil society is similar. When they are free to celebrate their histories, remember their dead, and shape (in part) the education of their children, they are more likely to be harmless than when they are unfree. Locke may have put the claim too strongly when he wrote, "There is only one thing which gathers people into seditious commotions, and that is oppression," but he was close enough to the truth to warrant the experiment of radical tolerance.

But if oppression is the cause of seditious commotion, what is the cause of oppression? I don't doubt that there is a materialist story to tell here, but I want to stress the central role played by ideological singlemindedness: the intolerant universalism of (most) religions, the exclusivity of (most) nations. The actual experience of civil society, when it can be had, seems to work against these two. Indeed, it works so well, some observers think, that neither religious faith nor national identity is likely to survive for long in the network of free associations. But we really don't know to what extent faith and identity depend upon coercion or whether they can reproduce themselves under conditions of freedom. I suspect that they both respond to such deep human needs that they will outlast their current organizational forms. It seems, in any case, worthwhile to wait and see.

STILL A NEED FOR STATE POWER

◆ ◆ ◆

But there is no escape from power and coercion, no possibility of choosing, like the old anarchists, civil society alone. A few years ago, in a book called *Anti-Politics*, the Hungarian dissident George Konrad described a way of living alongside the totalitarian state but, so to speak, with one's back turned toward it. He urged his fellow dissidents to reject the very idea of seizing or sharing power and to devote their energies to religious, cultural, economic, and professional associations. Civil society appears in his book as an alternative to the state, which he assumes to be unchangeable and irredeemably hostile. His argument seemed right to me when I first read his book. Looking back, after the collapse of the Communist regimes in Hungary and elsewhere, I can easily see how much it was a product of its time—and how short that time was! No state can survive for long if it is wholly alienated from civil society. It cannot outlast its own coercive machinery; it is lost, literally, without its firepower. The production and reproduction of loyalty, civility, political competence, and trust in authority are never the work of the state alone, and the effort to go it alone—one meaning of totalitarianism—is doomed to failure.

The failure, however, has carried with it terrible costs, and so one can understand the appeal of contemporary antipolitics. Even as Central and East European dissidents take power, they remain, and should remain, cautious and apprehensive about its uses. The totalitarian project has left behind an abiding sense of bureaucratic brutality. Here was the ultimate form of political singlemindedness, and though the "democratic" (and, for that matter, the "communist") ideology that they appropriated was false, the intrusions even of a more genuine democracy are rendered suspect by the memory. Post-totalitarian politicians and writers have, in addition, learned the older antipolitics of free enterprise—so that the laissez-faire market is defended in the East today as one of the necessary institutions of civil society, or, more strongly, as the dominant social formation. This second view takes on plausibility from the extraordinary havoc wrought by totalitarian economic "planning." But it rests, exactly like political singlemindedness, on a failure to recognize the pluralism of associational life. The first view leads, often, to a more interesting and more genuinely liberal mistake: it suggests that pluralism is self-sufficient and self-sustaining.

This, is, indeed, the experience of the dissidents: the state could not destroy their unions, churches, free universities, illegal markets, *samizdat* publications. Nonetheless, I want to warn against the antipolitical tendencies that commonly accompany the celebration of civil society. The network of associations incorporates, but it cannot dispense with, the agencies of state power; neither can socialist cooperation or capitalist competition dispense with the state. That's why so many dissidents are ministers now. It is indeed true that the new social movements in the East and the West—concerned with ecology, feminism, the right of immigrants and national minorities, work place and product safety, and

so on—do not aim, as the democratic and labor movements once aimed, at taking power. This represents an important change, in sensibility as much as in ideology, reflecting a new valuation of parts over wholes and a new willingness to settle for something less than total victory. But there can be no victory at all that doesn't involve some control over, or use of, the state apparatus. The collapse of totalitarianism is empowering for the members of civil society precisely because it renders the state accessible.

Here, then is the paradox of the civil society argument. Citizenship is one of many roles the members play, but the state itself is unlike all the other associations. It both frames civil society and occupies space within it. It fixes the boundary conditions and the basic rules of all associational activity (including political activity). It compels association members to think about a common good, beyond their own conceptions of the good life. Even the failed totalitarianism of, say, the Polish communist state had this much impact upon the Solidarity union. It determined that Solidarity was a Polish union, focussed on economic arrangements and labor policy within the borders of Poland. A democratic state, which is continuous with the associations, has at the same time a greater say about their quality and vitality. It serves, or it doesn't serve, the needs of the associational networks as these are worked out by men and women who are simultaneously members and citizens. I shall give only a few obvious examples, drawn from American experience.

Families with working parents need state help in the form of publicly funded day care and effective public schools. National minorities need help in organizing and sustaining their own educational programs. Worker-owned companies and consumer cooperatives need state loans or loan guarantees; so do (even more often) capitalist entrepreneurs and firms. Philanthropy and mutual aid, churches and private universities, depend upon tax exemptions. Labor unions need legal recognition and guarantees against "unfair labor practices." Professional associations need state support for their licensing procedures. And across the entire range of association, individual men and women need to be protected against the power of officials, employers, experts, party bosses, factory foremen, directors, priests, parents, patrons: and small and weak groups need to be protected against large and powerful ones. For civil society, left to itself, generates radically unequal power relationships, which only state power can challenge.

Civil society also challenges state power, most importantly when associations have resources or supporters abroad: world religions, pan-national movements, the new environmental groups, multinational corporations. We are likely to feel differently about these challenges, especially after we recognize the real but relative importance of the state. Multinational corporations, for example, need to be constrained, much like states with imperial ambitions; and the net constraint probably lies in collective security, that is, in alliances with other states that give economic regulation some international effect. The same mechanism may turn out

---

The civility that makes democratic

politics possible can only be learned

in the associational networks...

---

to be useful to the new environmental groups. In the first case, the state pressures the corporation; in the second it responds, to environmentalist pressure. The two cases suggest, again, that civil society requires political agency. And the state is an indispensable agent—even if the associational networks also, always, resist the organizing impulses of state bureaucrats.

Only a democratic state can create a democratic civil society; only a democratic civil society can sustain a democratic state. The civility that makes democratic politics possible can only be learned in the associational networks; the roughly equal and widely dispersed capabilities that sustain the networks have to be fostered by the democratic state. Confronted with an overbearing state, citizens, who are also members, will struggle to make room for autonomous associations and market relationships (and also for local governments and decentralized bureaucracies). But the state can never be what it appears to be in liberal theory, a mere framework for civil society. It is also the instrument of the struggle, used to give a particular shape to the common life. Hence citizenship has a certain practical pre-eminence among all our actual and possible memberships. That's not to say that we must be citizens all the time, finding in politics, as Rousseau urged, the greater part of our happiness. Most of us will be happier elsewhere, involved only sometimes in affairs of state. But we must have a state open to our sometime involvement.

Nor need we be involved all the time in our associations. A democratic civil society is one controlled by its members, not through a single process of self-determination but through a large number of different and uncoordinated processes. These needn't all be democra-

tic, for we are likely to be members of many associations, and we will want some of them to be managed in our interests, but also in our absence. Civil society is sufficiently democratic when in some, at least, of its parts we are able to recognize ourselves as authoritative and responsible participants. States are tested by their capacity to sustain this kind of participation—which is very different from the heroic intensity of Rousseauian citizenship. And civil society is tested by its capacity to produce citizens whose interests, at least sometimes, reach farther than themselves and their comrades, who look after the political community that fosters and protects the associational networks.

IN FAVOR OF INCLUSIVENESS
◆ ◆ ◆

I mean to defend a perspective that might be called, awkwardly, "critical associationalism." I want to join, but I am somewhat uneasy with, the civil society argument. It can't be said that nothing is lost when we give up the singlemindedness of democratic citizenship or socialist cooperation or individual autonomy or national identity. There was a kind of heroism in those projects—a concentration of energy, a clear sense of direction, an unblinking recognition of friends and enemies. To make one of these one's own was a serious commitment. The defense of civil society doesn't seem quite comparable. Associational engagement is conceivably as important a project as any of the others, but its greatest virtue lies in its inclusiveness, and inclusiveness does not make for heroism. "Join the associations of your choice" is not a slogan to rally political militants. And yet that is what civil society requires; men and women actively engaged—in state, economy, and nation, and also in churches, neighbourhoods, and families, and in many other settings too. To reach this goal is not as easy as it sounds; many people, perhaps most people, live very loosely within the networks; a growing number of people seem to be radically disengaged—passive clients of the state, market dropouts, resentful and posturing nationalists. And the civil society project doesn't confront an energizing hostility, as all the others do; its protagonists are more likely to meet sullen indifference, fear, despair, apathy, and withdrawal.

In Central and Eastern Europe, civil society is still a battle cry, for it requires a dismantling of the totalitarian state and it brings with it the exhilarating experience of associational independence. Among ourselves what is required is nothing so grand; nor does it lend itself to a singular description (but this is what lies ahead in the East too). The civil society project can only be described in terms of all the other projects, against their singularity. Hence my account in these pages, which suggest the need (1) to decentralize the state so that there are more opportunities for citizens to take responsibility for (some of) its activities; (2) to socialize the economy so that there is a greater diversity of market agents, communal as well as private; and (3) to pluralize and domesticate nationalism, on the religious model, so that there are different ways to realize and sustain historical identities.

None of this can be accomplished without using political power to redistribute resources and to underwrite and subsidize the most desirable associational activities. But political power alone cannot accomplish any of it. The kinds of "action" discussed by theorists of the state need to be supplemented (not, however, replaced) by something radically different: more like union organizing than political mobilization, more like teaching in a school than arguing in the assembly, more like volunteering in a hospital than joining a political party, more like working in an ethnic alliance or a feminist support group than canvassing in an election, more like shaping a co-op budget than deciding on national fiscal policy. But can any of these local and small-scale activities ever carry with them the honor of citizenship? Sometimes, certainly, they are narrowly conceived, partial and particularist; they need political correction. The greater problem, however, is that they seem so ordinary. Living in civil society, one might think, is like speaking in prose.

But just as speaking in prose implies an understanding of syntax, so these forms of action (when they are pluralized) imply an understanding of civility. And that is not an understanding about which we can be entirely confident these days. There is something to be said for the neoconservative argument that in the modern world we need to recapture the density of associational life and relearn the activities and understandings that go with it. And if this is the case, then a more strenuous argument is called for from the left: we have to reconstruct that same density under new conditions of freedom and equality. It would appear to be an elementary require-

ment of social democracy that there exist a *society* of lively, engaged, and effective men and women—where the honor of "action" belongs to the many and not to the few.

Against a background of growing disorganization—violence, homelessness, divorce, abandonment, alienation, and addiction—a society of this sort looks more like a necessary achievement than a comfortable reality. In truth, however, it was never a comfortable reality, except for the few. Most men and women have been trapped in one or another subordinate relationship, where the "civility" they learned was deferential rather than independent and active. That is why democratic citizenship, socialist production, free enterprise, and nationalism were all of them liberating projects. But none of them has yet produced a general, coherent, or sustainable liberation. And their more single-minded adherents, who have exaggerated the effectiveness of the state of the market of the nation and neglected the networks, have probably contributed to the disorder of contemporary life. The projects have to be relativized and brought together, and the place to do that is in civil society, the setting of settings, where each can find the partial fulfillment that is all it deserves.

Civil society itself is sustained by groups much smaller than the demos or the working class or the mass of consumers or the nation. All these are necessarily fragmented and localized as they are incorporated. They become part of the world of family, friends, comrades, and colleagues, where people are connected to one another and made responsible for one another. Connected and responsible: without that, "free and equal" is less attractive than we once thought it would be. I have no magic formula for making connections or strengthening the sense of responsibility. These aren't aims that can be underwritten with historical guarantees or achieved through a single unified struggle. Civil society is a project of projects; it requires many organizing strategies and new forms of state action. It requires a new sensitivity for what is local, specific, contingent—and, above all, a new recognition (to paraphrase a famous sentence) that the good life is in the details.

Terms & Concepts

antipolitics of free enterprise
associational networks
autonomous individual
citizenship
civic virtue
civil society
communitarians
consumerism

cooperative economy
"critical associationalism"
democratic socialists
egalitarian civil society
homo faber
ideological singlemindedness
Marx
Marxist antipolitics

multinational corporations
nationalism
pluralism of associational life
politics and antipolitics
republicanism
sociability
the good life

Questions

1. What does Walzer mean when he argues that civil society is a "setting of settings" that "incorporates and denies" each of the four standard ideological accounts of the good life?

2. Vaclav Havel (1992) wrote that "if everyone doesn't take an interest in politics, it will become the domain of those least suited to it." Compare this statement with Walzer's acceptance of Western citizens' limited political participation. Does Walzer place too little stress on the demands of citizenship?

3. Walzer makes a distinction between the kind of choice offered by capitalism and that offered by the pluralism of civil society. What does he mean?

4. How would you propose to revitalize civil society in the formerly Communist countries? Should full-bore marketization be part of the plan?

5. What evidence is there for the existence of civil society in Canada? Is it thriving or atrophying?

Rights Talk

Mary Ann Glendon

Editors' Note

Can you imagine the abortion debate couched in terms *other* than the competing and mutually exclusive rights of women and the unborn? Can you imagine freedom being understood in terms *other* than the right to do whatever you want? It is hardly possible to imagine contemporary North American political debate carried on without reference to the idea of rights. "The naked self," argues political scientist Benjamin Barber, "comes to the bargaining table weak and puny; the language of rights clothes it."[1]

The rights discourse is well developed in the United States, but Canadians are becoming increasingly familiar with it due to their proximity to the United States and to the incorporation of the Canadian Charter of Rights and Freedoms into the Canadian constitution in 1982. The rights discourse is of

recent vintage, becoming prominent only since the end of World War II. Historically, rights were understood as immunities defining the limits of government's legislative authority. Carefully designed political institutions were thought to be as important for the protection of people's liberties as any declaration of rights. A transformation began with the view that rights are entitlements that people can claim and that others have an obligation to honour.

In this excerpt from her book, *Rights Talk: The Impoverishment of Political Discourse*, Harvard law professor Mary Ann Glendon explores the "romance of rights" in the American public imagination. She is especially interested in the "absolutist" character of the American rights dialect, namely the notion that rights are absolute claims on

which there can be no compromise. She is no enemy of rights but she has deep concerns about how they are used to shape public discussion in the American setting. She asks her readers to think critically about American-style "rights talk" and to give it no more or less importance than it deserves.

As you read this selection, note the importance Glendon places on the importance of words as communicators of meaning. Note also the relationship she attempts to draw between rights talk and threats to civil society. There is an antipolitical thrust in rights talk that careful readers will notice in Glendon's argument. In this respect her essay should be read in conjunction with the readings by Bernard Crick (Unit Six, Article 25) and Michael Walzer (Unit Three, Article 11).

◆ ◆ ◆

---

1. Benjamin Barber, "The Reconstruction of Rights," *The American Prospect* (Spring 1991), 36.

And where freedom is, the individual is clearly able to order for himself his own life as he pleases?

Clearly.

Then in this kind of state there will be the greatest variety of human natures?

There will.

This, then, seems likely to be the fairest of states, being like an embroidered robe which is spangled with every sort of flower.

—PLATO, THE REPUBLIC [1]

Our own ways of thinking and speaking seem so natural to us that very often it is only an empathetic outsider who can enter into our view of the world, and spot a peculiarity in it. Thus it took an aristocratic Frenchman, resolved to make the best of living in a democratic age, to notice that the everyday speech of the Americans he encountered on his travels here in 1831 and 1832 was shot through with legalisms. Tocqueville's ten-month journey took him all over what was then the United States, from Massachusetts to Georgia, from New Orleans to the territory that is now Wisconsin. Wherever he went, he found that lawyers' habits of mind, as well as their modes of discourse, "infiltrate through society right down to the lowest ranks." [2] Foreign observers today are still struck by the degree to which law and lawyers have influenced American ways of life. [3]

Tocqueville attributed the legal cast of common parlance to the fact that in America, unlike in Continental Europe, most public men were lawyers. [4] Though skeptical about the power of the law as such to exert much direct influence on human behavior, he regarded this American penchant as a social phenomenon of the utmost importance. For he believed that legal ideas could, under certain circumstances, help to shape the interior world of beliefs, attitudes, dreams, and yearnings that are the hidden springs of individual and social action. To be sure, he was in general accord with his great predecessor Rousseau that "the real constitution of the State" is composed "of morality, of custom, above all of public opinion." [5] Rousseau had likened a nation's laws to the arc of an arch, with "manners and morals, slower to arise, form[ing] in the end its immovable keystone." [6] But neither Rousseau nor Tocqueville was inclined to underrate the arc's supporting role. As he listened to the speech of Americans in all walks of life, Tocqueville became convinced that law and lawyers had left an unusually strong imprint on the "manners and morals" of the new nation, and therefore on its unwritten constitution. Not only was legal language "pretty well adopted into common speech," but a legalistic spirit seemed to pervade "the whole of society, penetrating each component class and constantly working in secret upon its unconscious patient, till in the end it has molded it to its desire." [7]

Tocqueville's observations are even more pertinent to contemporary American culture than they were to the small democratic republic of our forebears. Americans today, for better or worse, live in what is undoubtedly one of the most law-ridden societies that has ever existed on the face of the earth. The reach of government and law have extended to a degree that Tocqueville and his contemporaries would have found hard to imagine. The proportion of legally trained individuals among our government officials, and in the population at large, moreover, is higher than ever. A great communications and entertainment industry now reports on and dramatizes their doings. We are surrounded by images of law and lawyers.

In addition, middle-class Americans are apt to have many more firsthand contacts with the legal system than did their ancestors. In an earlier day, anyone who was not wealthy, and was able to abstain from violence, had a good chance of living his or her whole life without seeing the inside of a law office or a courtroom. By the middle of the twentieth century, however, Americans commonly had brief dealings with lawyers as they purchased or sold homes, made wills, or settled estates. At the same time, eligibility expanded for jury service, an experience which rarely fails to leave a deep impression even on those who initially view it as a nuisance. When divorce became a mass phenomenon, multitudes of men and women had their own "day in court" of sorts, either as parties or witnesses. In the phrase of legal historian Lawrence Friedman life in modern America has become "a vast, diffuse school of law." [8]

This "legalization" of popular culture is both cause and consequence of our increasing tendency to look to law as an expression and carrier of the few values that are widely shared in our society: liberty, equality, and the ideal of justice under law. With increasing heterogeneity, it has become quite difficult to convincingly articulate common values by reference to a shared history, religion, or cultural tradition. The language we have developed for public use in our large, multicultural society is thus even more legalistic than the one Tocqueville heard, and it draws to a lesser degree on other cultural resources.

Legality, to a great extent, has become a touchstone for legitimacy.

Few American statesmen today are—as Abraham Lincoln was—equally at home with the Bible and Blackstone. Political figures now resort primarily to legal ideas and traditions when they seek to persuade, inspire, explain, or justify in public settings. Legality, to a great extent, has become a touchstone for legitimacy. As a result, certain areas of law, especially constitutional, criminal, and family law, have become the terrain on which Americans are struggling to define what kind of people they are, and what kind of society they wish to bring into being. Legal discourse has not only become the single most important tributary to political discourse, but it has crept into the language that Americans employ around the kitchen table, in the neighborhood, and in their diverse communities of memory and mutual aid.

The law talk that percolates through American society today, however, is far removed from nineteenth-century versions. For one thing, it has been through the fiery furnace of critical theory, from Oliver Wendell Holmes Jr.'s insistence on strict analytical separation between law and morality, to the "realist" fact-skeptics and rule-skeptics of the 1930s, to their latter-day epigones of the right and left. Secondly, though the legal profession still contains many more planners and preventers than litigators, it is the assertiveness of the latter rather than the reverse of the former that migrates most readily through the media into the broader culture. Finally, law-talk in Tocqueville's day was not nearly so saturated with rights talk as it has been since the end of World War II. In short, legal speech today is a good deal more morally neutral, adversarial, and rights-oriented than it was in 1831.

There is no more telling indicator of the extent to which legal notions have penetrated both popular and political discourse than our increasing tendency to speak of what is most important to us in terms of rights, and to frame nearly every social controversy as a clash of rights. Yet, for most of our history, political discourse was not so liberally salted with rights talk as it is today, nor was rights discourse so legalistic. The high season of rights came upon the land only rather recently, propelled by, and itself promoting, a gradual evolution in the role of the courts.

The marked increase in the assertion of rights-based claims, beginning with the civil rights movement of the 1950s and 1960s, and the parallel increase in recognition of those claims in the courts, are sometimes described as a rights revolution. If there is any justification for using the overworked word "revolution" in connection with these developments, it is not that they have eliminated the ills at which they were aimed. Indeed, the progress that has been made, substantial as it is, serves also to heighten our awareness of how deep, stubborn, and complex are the nation's problems of social justice. What do seem revolutionary about the rights-related developments of the past three decades are the transformations they have produced in the roles of courts and judges, and in the way we now think and speak about major public issues.

At least until the 1950s, the principal focus of constitutional law was not on personal liberty as such, but on the division of authority between the states and the federal government, and the allocation of powers among the branches of the central government. In keeping with Hamilton's observation in *Federalist* No. 84 that "the Constitution is itself, in every rational sense, and to every useful purpose, A BILL OF RIGHTS," the theory was that individual freedom was protected mainly through these structural features of our political regime. The Supreme Court saw far fewer cases involving free speech, association, religion, and the rights of criminal defendants than it does now, not only because such issues were less frequently litigated, but because, until relatively recent times, many important provisions of the Bill of Rights were thought to apply only to the federal government. Gradually, however, the Supreme Court developed its "incorporation" doctrine, through which more and more of the rights guaranteed by the first eight amendments to the Federal Constitution were declared to have been made binding on the states (incorporated) by the Fourteenth Amendment. This process accelerated in the 1960s when the Warren Court vigorously began to exercise the power of judicial review as a means of protecting individual rights from interference by state as well as federal governments.[9] Today the bulk of the Court's constitutional work involves claims that individual rights have been violated.[10] In the 1980s, even though a majority of justices on the United States Supreme Court began to adopt a slightly more deferential attitude toward the elected branches of government, the rights revolution continued, as many state supreme courts began interpreting state constitutions to confer more rights on individuals.[11]

The trendsetters of the legal academic world were quick to recognize the burgeoning of individual rights as the central legal drama of the times. The top legal minds of the New Deal era had been virtuosos of legislation and administrative law, specialists in taxation, antitrust, and labor; architects and engineers of the regulatory state and the new federalism. With the civil rights generation, however, legal attention shifted to the courts. The study and teaching of constitutional law gained in excitement and prestige. Older constitutional law professors who had given pride of place to federal-state relations and the commerce clause were succeeded by men and a few women who focussed on advancing equality and personal liberty by means of rights. To a great extent, the intellectual framework and the professional ethos of the entire current population of American lawyers have been infused with the romance of rights. In legal education, an intense preoccupation with the Bill of Rights and the courts tends to obscure the important roles that federalism, legislation, and the separation of powers still can and must play in safeguarding rights and freedom. The rights revolution has contributed in its own way to the atrophy of vital local governments and political parties, and to the disdain for politics that is now so prevalent in the American scene.

Unlike the New Dealers (who resembled the Founders in their attention to the overall design of government and to the functions and relations among its specialized organs), many bright, ambitious public lawyers of the 1960s had a narrower and less organic view of law, government, and society. They saw the judiciary as the first line of defense against all injustice, and came to regard the test case as preferable to ordinary politics. To no small degree, this shift of the energy and interests of public-law lawyers from legislation and regulation to adjudication reflected growing sensitivity to the obvious and persistent racism of many local laws, institutions, and practices. Encounters with corrupt and prejudiced officials has soured many activists and intellectuals of the civil rights era on legislatures and local governments, while their faith in the judiciary was strengthened by a series of bold Supreme Court rulings that seemed to wipe out ancient wrongs with a stroke of the pen. Landmark cases in the criminal-law area, and above all, the Court's celebrated 1954 desegregation decision in *Brown v. Board of Education*,[12] shone like beacons, lighting the way toward an America whose ideals of equal justice and opportunity for all would at last be realized. Many hopeful men and women came to believe that the high road to a better society would be paved with court decisions—federal court decisions. At the elbow, so to speak, of wise Supreme Court justices, would be renowned social scientists, lawyers armed with theories generated in the best law schools, and teams of young law clerks, fresh from the classroom and bearing the very latest word on constitutional law. The civil rights movement thus did not exploit as fully as it might have the opportunities opened up by its voter registration drives and by the historic one-person, one-vote decisions of the Supreme Court.[13]

Our justifiable pride and excitement at the great boost given to racial justice by the moral authority and the unanimous Supreme Court decision in *Brown* seems, in retrospect, to have led us to expect too much from the Court where a wide variety of other social ills were concerned. Correspondingly, it seems to have induced us to undervalue the kind of progress represented by an equally momentous social achievement: the Civil Rights Act of 1964. The time-honored understanding that difficult and controversial issues should be decided by the people through their elected representatives, except where constitutional text and tradition clearly indicated otherwise, began to fray at the edges. A text, it became fashionable to say in the 1970s, has no determinate meaning, and tradition is as likely to be oppressive as nourishing. To many activists, it seemed more efficient, as well as more rewarding, to devote one's time and efforts to litigation that could yield total victory, than to put in long hours at political organizing, where the most one can hope to gain is, typically, a compromise. As the party system gradually fell prey to large, highly organized, and well-financed interest groups, regular politics came to seem futile as well as boring, socially unproductive as well as personally unfulfilling.

Gradually, the courts removed a variety of issues from legislative and local control and accorded broad new scope to many constitutional rights related to personal liberty. Most dramatic of all, perhaps, from the average citizens point of view, was the active role that lower federal court judges assumed in many parts of the country, using their remedial powers to observe the everyday operations of prisons, hospitals, and school systems. Court majorities with an expansive view of the judicial role, and their academic admirers, propelled each other, like railwaymen on a handcar, along the line that led to the land of rights. The example of the civil rights movement inspired many other victims of injustice to get on board. In the 1970s, the concerns of women crystallized around the idea of equal rights. Soon, persons and organizations devoted to social and related causes—such as preventing the abuse and neglect of children, improving the treatment of the mentally and physically disabled, eliminating discrimination based on life-style, protecting consumers from sharp practices, preventing cruelty to animals, and safeguarding the environment—began to articulate their concerns in terms of rights.

As we have reconceptualized increasing numbers and types of issues in terms of entitlements, a new form of rights talk has gradually come into being. This change in our habits of thought and speech is a social phenomenon of equal importance to the legal developments whose course it has paralleled. The significance of this aspect of the rights revolution comes into even sharper focus when one takes a comparative perspective.

In the years since the end of World War II, rights discourse has spread throughout the world. At the transnational level, human rights were enshrined in a variety of covenants and declarations, notably the United Nations' Universal Declaration of Human Rights of 1948.[14] At the same time, enumerated rights, backed up by some form of judicial review, were added to several national constitutions. (Great Britain, with neither judicial review nor a single-document constitution, became something of an anomaly in this respect.) Nor was the rush to rights confined to "liberal" or "democratic" societies. American rights talk is now but one dialect in a universal language of rights. The American version of rights talk, however, displays several unusual features. Intriguing differences have emerged between the formulations of rights in American contexts and the ways in which rights are proclaimed and discussed in many other liberal democracies.

We do not, of course, normally think of our own way of speaking as a dialect. But American rights talk does possess certain distinctive characteristics that appear both in our official declarations and in our ordinary speech. As an initial example of the latter, consider the lively discussions that took place in the wake of the Supreme Court's first controversial flag-burning decision in June 1989.[15] On the day after the Court ruled that burning the American flag was a form of expression protected by the First Amendment to the Constitution, the *Today* show invited a spokesman for the American Legion to explain his organization's discontent with that decision. Jane Pauley asked her guest what the flag meant to the nation's veterans. He gave a standard reply: "The flag is the symbol of our country, the land of the free and the home of the brave." Jane was not satisfied.

"What exactly does it symbolize?" she wanted to know. The legionnaire seemed exasperated in the way people sometimes get when they feel there are certain things that should not have to be explained. The answer he came up with was, "It stands for the fact that this is a country where we have the right to do what we want." Of course he could not really have meant to espouse a principle that would have sanctioned the very act he despised. Given time for thought, he almost certainly would not have expressed himself in that way. His spontaneous response, however, illustrates our tendency, when we grope in public settings for the words to express strong feelings about political issues, to resort to the language of rights.

Later that same day, a man interviewed on National Public Radio offered a defense of flag-burning. He said, "The way I see it, I buy a flag. It's my property. So I have a right to do anything I want with it." Let us put aside the fact the flag involved in the case happened to be a stolen one. What is striking about this man's rights talk is that, like the outburst of the legionnaire, it was couched in absolute terms. In neither case was the choice of words idiosyncratic. How often, in daily speech, do all of us make and hear claims that whatever right is under discussion at the moment trumps every other consideration?

When roused to speak out about issues of great importance, we often find ourselves repeating the experience of the righteously indignant legionnaire. We are apt to begin, as he did, by speaking from the heart, choosing some formula that carries a rich train of associations for us personally and for like-minded people. When our spontaneous efforts are challenged, or meet with real or feigned incomprehension on the part of a listener, we often find that words temporarily fail us. Like the legionnaire when ordered to "unpack" the symbol by a television interviewer, we may be temporarily tongue-tied. On such occasions, we often begin to speak about rights, and to do so in a distinctive manner that I have called the American rights dialect. This dialect, whose features are illustrated in more detail in the chapters that follow, is pervasive. When People for the American Way asked a thousand young Americans what makes America special, most of them quite properly mentioned our famous rights and freedoms.[16] One after another, however, the young men and women expressed themselves in the same language that came so easily to the legionnaire. One said that America's uniqueness lay in "individualism, and the fact that it is democracy and you can do whatever you want." Another said: "Our freedom to do as we please, when we please," Another: "That we really don't have any limits." And so on.[17]

Yet a moment's reflection tells us that these extravagant beliefs and claims cannot possibly be true. We have criminal laws that put rather decisive limits on our ability to do anything we want. Thus the Supreme Court in the flag case was careful to point out that the First Amendment does not protect verbal incitement to imme-

---

...in its simple American form, the language of rights is the language of no compromise.

---

diate breach of the public peace. As for property, our ownership rights are limited by the rights of our neighbors, by zoning laws, by environmental protection measures, and by countless other administrative rules and regulations. The property-rights enthusiast on public radio probably does not even have the right to burn dead leaves in his own back yard. To speak in this careless fashion is not without consequences; in fact, it sets us up to fail twice over—first, by cheapening or betraying our own meaning (The flag "stands for the fact that this is a country where we have the right to do what we want"), and second, by foreclosing further communication with those whose points of view differ from our own. For, in its simple American form, the language of rights is the language of no compromise. The winner takes all and the loser has to get out of town. The conversation is over.

Plato in *The Republic* made the idea of a state where everyone is free to say and do what he wants sound highly attractive—a "city full of freedom and frankness," with an amazing profusion of lifestyles.[18] But as Socrates disingenuously extols the delights of absolute freedom, his interlocutor, Adeimantus, grows uneasy. In such a city, one would not have to participate in government, or even to be subject to government—unless one wished. One would not need to go to war when others did, or even to keep the peace—unless one was so disposed. The "humanity" of such cities, Socrates continues, is "quite charming"—just look at all the persons sentenced to death or exile who are permitted to walk about the streets. And see how indulgent the citizens are toward the character defects of public men—so long as such men profess to be friends of the people.

Plato's image of the city where license reigns supreme makes a strong initial appeal to that part of us that delights in freedom and variety. "Just as women and children think an assortment of colors to be of all things

most charming, so there are many men to whom this state, which is spangled with the manners and characters of mankind, will appear to be the fairest of states." Socrates observes. But as its implications unfold, we and Adeimantus begin to suspect that this sort of freedom may lead straight to the eclipse of anything we would recognize as meaningful liberty.

Some listeners to American rights talk might reach the conclusion that Americans have nothing in common with those ancient Greeks who claimed that moderation, balance, and limits were what distinguished their civilization from the peoples they called barbarians. Others, noting that the Greeks are reputed to have honored their own ideals quite frequently in the breach, might say that we are simply less hypocritical. Much that passes for normative in the media, the universities, and the entertainment industry suggests that modern Americans have rejected many traditional social constraints in principle and thrown them off in fact. But the total picture is a good deal more complex. Most American parents, to cite an obvious instance, remain deeply concerned with setting limits and helping their children achieve self-control. To some extent, families are aided in these efforts by the various communities in which they participate. It seems likely, too, that most Americans agree in principle that our regime is an experiment in *"ordered* liberty" (in Justice Cardozo's locution)[19]—though they may not agree on the relative scope to be given to the two components of that ambiguous concept. Why then does our public rhetoric so regularly gloss over the essential interplay between rights and responsibilities, independence and self-discipline, freedom and order?

The distinctive traits of our American rights dialect can be discerned at both of the great "moments" in the history of human rights. The first of these moments was marked by the late eighteenth-century American and French revolutionary declarations, and the second by the wave of constitution-making and the international human rights movement that emerged in the wake of World War II. The language that evolved to promote and implement the rights proclaimed at those crucial junctures partakes everywhere of certain common characteristics, but everywhere has its own local accent. The common features are well-known. From the treatises of seventeenth-and eighteenth-century philosophers, the ideas of natural right and equality gave shape, momentum, and definite direction to scattered and diffuse social forces. They spoke to as yet unnamed longings; they awakened sleeping hopes, fired imaginations and changed the world.[20] The eighteenth-century "rights of man," like modern "human rights," all mark a stand against the abuse and arbitrary exercise of power. They are landmarks in the recognition of the dignity of the individual human person and of our potential to be free and self-determining. These common characteristics, together with the contemporary thrust toward the internationalization and "universalization" of human rights, give to rights discourse everywhere a superficial appearance of unity. The path of the United States diverged somewhat from those of most other Atlantic-European nations, however, at each of these great watersheds in the history of rights.[21] The parting of the ways was already evident in 1789 when the French *Declaration of the Rights of Man and the Citizen*, in contrast to the *Declaration of Independence*, emphasized that individuals have duties as well as rights.[22]

In the years since the end of World War II, "rights" have entered importantly into the cultural schemes of meaning of peoples everywhere. But rights were imagined differently from one place to another. And even slight divergences in such matters are of potentially great interest, for the world of meanings is where we human beings spend most of our lives, "suspended in webs of significance" that we ourselves have spun.[23] The way we name things and discuss them shapes our feelings, judgements, choices, and actions, including political actions. History has repeatedly driven home the lesson that it is

---

American rights talk is set apart by the way that rights, in our standard formulations, tend to be represented as absolute, individual, and independent of any necessary relation to responsibilities.

---

unwise to dismiss political language as "mere rhetoric." When Vaclav Havel in 1989 gained a platform from which to address the world, he chose to deliver one of his first major speeches on "the mysterious power of words in human history."[24] The Czech president's message was a somber one, for his purpose was to remind us that while exhilarating words like "human rights" recently have electrified society "with their freedom and truthfulness," one need not look far back into the past to find words and phrases whose effects were as deadly as they were hypnotic. Most sobering of all, said Havel, the very same words that can at some times be "rays of light," may turn under other circumstances into "lethal arrows."

It thus seems worthwhile—as well as interesting—to try to identify those characteristics that make our version of rights talk a special dialect; to explore the difference in shades of meaning between our own and other forms of rights discourse; and to probe the discrepancies as well as the similarities between our public rights talk and the ways we speak at home, at work, in the neighborhood, and in the church or mosque or temple. The contrast with other countries is not a dramatic one, but rather a matter of degree and emphasis. American rights talk is set apart by the way that rights, in our standard formulations, tend to be represented as absolute, individual, and independent of any necessary relation to responsibilities. The simplicity and assertiveness of our version of the discourse of rights are more noticeable when viewed in the light of the continuing dialogue about freedom and responsibility that is taking place in several other liberal democracies.

All over the world, political discourse is increasingly imbued with the language of rights, universal, inalienable, inviolable. Yet, subtle variations in the way rights ideas are presented can have broad and far-reaching implications that penetrate nearly every corner of the societies involved. Take, for example, the way a country depicts itself to new citizens in naturalization proceedings. When my adopted Korean daughter, Sarah, became an American citizen, our country's official national symbolism was on prominent display at her naturalization ceremony. That day, Sarah and several hundred other immigrants heard a solemn recital in Boston's famed Faneuil Hall of all the rights and freedoms that would henceforth be theirs. As a souvenir of the occasion, she was given a red-white-and-blue pamphlet in which the Commissioner of Immigration and Naturalization explained "The Meaning of American Citizenship':

> This citizenship, which has been solemnly conferred on you, is a thing of the spirit—not of the flesh. When you took the oath of allegiance to the Constitution of the United States, you claimed for yourself the God-given unalienable rights which that sacred document sets forth as the natural right of all men.[25]

Rights dominate the notion of citizenship from the top to the bottom of the American system, from the literature distributed at federal buildings throughout the country to the pronouncements of the United States Supreme Court (which once referred to citizenship as "the right to have rights").[26]

Our close neighbor, Canada, presents quite a different face to its new citizens. To be sure, Canadian citizenship literature, and Citizenship Court judges, prominently mention rights, but they lay still greater stress on the importance of participation in the political life of a multicultural society.[27] The great writer on cities, Jane Jacobs, delights in telling how, when she became a citizen of Canada, she was instructed by the judge that the most important thing about being a Canadian is learning to get along well with one's neighbors. Just talk? Perhaps. But it is the kind of talk we do not easily forget. Words spoken in a formal setting, on a day marking an important change of status, carry a special charge. Like the words of the marriage ritual, they etch themselves on our memories.

Formal proclamations of fundamental rights, too, have a different flavor from country to country. Without falling into the error of equating official statements of aspirations with representations of reality, one learns what the drafters of such documents deemed important, and what ideals have become part of the state-sponsored folklore. Try, for example, to find in the familiar language of our Declaration of Independence or Bill of Rights anything comparable to the statements in the Universal Declaration of Human Rights that "Everyone has duties to the community," and that everyone's rights and freedoms are subject to limitations "for the purposes of securing due recognition and respect for the rights and freedoms of others and of meeting the just requirements of morality, public order and the general welfare in a democratic society."[28]

These differing official pronouncements do not spring from nowhere. The language of the United Nations Declaration is a melding of the Anglo-American rights tradition with the more nuanced dialect of rights and responsibility associated with the Romano-Germanic legal traditions. These traditions in turn are informed by a somewhat different amalgam of Enlightenment political philosophy from that which inspired the American founders. It made a considerable difference, for example, that natural rights theories were elaborated for us principally by Hobbes and Locke, without the glosses added within the continental tradition by Rousseau and Kant.

To be sure, ideas that are absent from the text of our foundational documents can be, and often are, supplied by interpretation in court decisions. Thus, American lawyers know that, from the very beginning, the United States Supreme Court has acknowledged implicit limits on our constitutional rights and has imposed obligations on citizens to respect each other's rights. Jurists are also well aware that ordinary private law—contracts, torts, domestic relations—is replete with reciprocal duties. Nevertheless, it is the language emblazoned on our monumental public documents, far more than the numerous limitations buried in the text of individual court decisions, that lodges in the collective memory, permeates popular discourse, and enters into American habits of mind.

The most distinctive features of our American rights dialect are the very ones that are most conspicuously in tension with what we require in order to give a reasonably full and coherent account of what kind of society we are and what kind of policy we are trying to create: its penchant for absolute, extravagant formulations, its near-aphasia concerning responsibility, its excessive homage to individual independence and self-sufficiency, its habitual concentration on the individual and the state at the expense of the intermediate groups of civil society, and its unapologetic insularity. Not only does each of these traits make it difficult to give voice to common sense or moral intuitions, they also impede development of the sort of rational political discourse that is appropriate to the needs of a mature, complex, liberal, pluralistic republic.

Our rights talk, in its absoluteness, promotes unrealistic expectations, heightens social conflict, and inhibits dialogue that might lead toward consensus, accommodation, or at least the discovery of common ground. In its silence concerning responsibilities, it seems to condone acceptance of the benefits of living in a democratic social welfare state, without accepting the corresponding personal and civic obligations. In its relentless individualism, it fosters a climate that is inhospitable to society's losers, and that systematically disadvantages caretakers and dependents, young and old. In its neglect of civil society, it undermines the principal seedbeds of civic and personal virtue. In its insularity, it shuts out potentially important aids to the process of self-correcting learning. All of these traits promote mere assertion over reason-giving.

For a heterogeneous country committed to an ongoing experiment in ordered liberty, these are grave matters. Obstacles to expression and communication can hobble a collective enterprise which depends heavily upon continuing public liberation. Our rights talk is like a book of words and phrases without a grammar and syntax. Various rights are proclaimed or proposed. The catalog of individual liberties expands, without much consideration of the ends to which they are oriented, their relationship to one another, to corresponding responsibilities, or to the general welfare. Lacking a grammar of cooperative living, we are like a traveler who can say a few words to get a meal and a room in a foreign city, but cannot converse with its inhabitants.

Our communicative deficiency is more serious than a mere traveler's, however, for it seals us off from our fellow citizens. By indulging in excessively simple forms of rights talk in our pluralistic society, we needlessly multiply occasions for civil discord. We make it difficult for persons and groups with conflicting interests and views to build coalitions and achieve compromise, or even to acquire that minimal degree of mutual forbearance and understanding that promotes peaceful coexistence and keeps the door open to further communication. Our simplistic rights talk regularly promotes the short-run over the long-term, sporadic crisis intervention over systemic preventive measures, and particular interests over the common good. It is just not up to the job of dealing with the types of problems that presently confront liberal, pluralistic, modern societies. Even worse, it risks undermining the very conditions necessary for preservation of the principal value it thrusts to the foreground: personal freedom. By infiltrating the more carefully nuanced languages that many Americans still speak in their kitchens, neighborhoods, workplaces, religious communities, and union halls, it corrodes the fabric of beliefs, attitudes, and habits upon which life, liberty, property, and all other individual and social goods ultimately depend.

Yet this need not be so. There are several indications that our rights-dominated public language does not do justice to the capacity for reason or the richness and diversity of moral sentiments that exist in American society. If this is the case, we could begin to refine our rhetoric of rights by recognizing and drawing on our own indigenous resources. A refined rhetoric of rights would promote public conversation about the ends towards which our political life is directed. It would keep competing rights and responsibilities in view, helping to assure that none would achieve undue prominence and that none would be unduly obscured. It would not lend itself to the notion that freedom is being able to do anything you want.

The critique of the American rights dialect presented here rejects the radical attack on the very notion of rights that is sometimes heard on both ends of the political spectrum. It is not an assault on specific rights or on the idea of rights in general, but a plea for reevaluation of certain thoughtless, habitual ways of thinking and speaking about rights. Let us freely grant that legally enforceable rights can assist citizens in a large heterogeneous country to live together in a reasonably peaceful way. They have given minorities a way to articulate claims that majorities often respect, and have assisted the weakest members of society in making their voices heard. The paradigms of civil rights at home and universal human rights around the world undoubtedly have helped to bring to light, and to marshal opinion against, oppression and atrocities. We Americans justifiably take a great sense of pride in our particular tradition of political liberty. Many of us harbor, too, a patriotic conviction that, where freedom is concerned, the United States was there first with the best and the most. From there, however, it is but a step to the more dubious proposition that our current strong, simple version of rights is the fulfillment of our destiny toward freedom, or to the still more questionable notions that, if rights are good, more rights must be even better, and the more emphatically they are stated, the less likely it is that they will be watered down or taken away.

In a reflective mood, even the most ardent rights enthusiast must concede some substance to the persistent critiques from right and left[29] that trace their origins, respectively, to Edmund Burke's concern about the social costs of rights,[30] and Karl Marx's dismissal of rights as mostly smoke and mirrors.[31] The prevailing consensus about the goodness of rights, widespread though it may be, is thin and brittle. In truth, there is very little agreement regarding *which* needs, goods, interests, or values should be characterized as "rights," or concerning what should be done when, as is usually the case, various rights are in tension or collision with one another. Occasions for conflict among rights multiply as catalogs of rights grow longer. If some rights are more important than others, and if a rather small group of rights is of especially high importance, then an ever-expanding list of rights may well trivialize this essential core without materially advancing the proliferating causes that have been reconceptualized as involving rights. Can it really be the case, as an article in *The New Republic* suggests in 1990, that "so long as I eat tuna fish and support the use of primates in AIDS research," my endorsement of the idea of human rights is rendered problematic?[32] At some point one must ask whether an undifferentiated language of rights is really the best way to address the astonishing variety of injustices and forms of suffering that exist in the world.

On the bicentennial of our Bills of Rights, Americans are struggling to order their lives together in a multicultural society whose population has grown from fewer than four million in 1791 to over 250 million men, women, and children. No longer "kindly separated' (as Jefferson put it) "by nature and a wide ocean" from much of the world,[33] we are now acutely conscious that we spin through time and space on a fragile planet where friend and foe alike are locked in ever-tighter webs of interdependence. Creative, timely, and effective responses to the social and environmental challenges presently facing us will not easily emerge from habits of thought and discourse that are as individualistic, rights-centered, and insular as those now current in the United States. Until recently, we have stood in this respect at the opposite pole from the Soviet Union and the countries that were within its political sphere of influence. In those nations, political discourse was long characterized by excessively strong and simple duty talk. Civic responsibilities and the general welfare were officially exalted at the expense of rights, the individual, and particular communities. Now, however, in one of the most remarkable political upheavals in history, public discourse in those countries has begun to correct for exaggerated and impoverished notions of duty and community. The discourse of rights and the idea of civil society have become important elements of experiments in democratic socialism and social democracy. The doors and windows of the East are opening to winds bearing seeds of change from all directions.

No one knows how these processes will play out in the new Europe. One thing is certain, however. As Paul wrote to the Corinthians, the world as we know it is continually passing away. The question for Americans therefore is not whether our own rights tradition will change, but what it will become. Like Moses, who never entered the promised land, but glimpsed it from afar, our Founding Fathers had a vision of an America where all citizens were endowed with certain inalienable rights, but they lived in a country where this vision was only partially realized. In recent years, we have made great progress in making the promise of rights a reality, but in doing so we have neglected another part of our inheritance—the vision of a republic where citizens actively take responsibility for maintaining a vital political life. The rights tradition we have constructed on the foundation laid by those who have gone before us has served that nation well in many ways. From what springs of meaning can it be nourished and renewed?

Notes

1. Plato, "The Republic," in *The Dialogues of Plato*, Benjamin Jowett trans. (Chicago: Encyclopedia Britannica, 1952), Book VIII, 409.

2. Alexis de Tocqueville, *Democracy in America*, trans. George Lawrence, ed. J.P. Mayer (Garden City, New York: Doubleday Anchor, 1969), I, 270.

3. E.g., Franz Wieacker, "Foundations of European Legal Culture," 37 *American Journal of Comparative Law* 1, 6 (1990).

4. Some historians have remarked on the legalistic character of American society even in the early colonial days when lawyers were scarce and citizens were supposed to be visible saints. See Daniel R. Coquilette, "Introduction: The 'Countenance of Authoritie'," in *Law in Colonial Massachusetts* (Boston: Colonial Society of Massachusetts, 1984), xxi.

5. Jean-Jacques Rousseau, "The Social Contract," in *The Social Contract and Discourses*, trans. G.D.H. Cole (London: Dent Dutton 1973), 206. Cf. Tocqueville, *Democracy in America*, I, 305, 307.

6. Rousseau, *The Social Contract*, 207.

7. Tocqueville, *Democracy in America*, I, 270.

8. Lawrence M. Friedman, "Law, Lawyers, and Popular Culture," 98 *Yale Law Journal* 1579, 1598 (1989).

9. Gerald Gunther, *Individual Rights in Constitutional Law,* 4th ed. (Mineola, N.Y.: Foundation Press, 1986), 95; Laurence H. Tribe, *American Constitutional Law,* 2d ed. (Mineola, N.Y.: Foundation Press, 1988), 772–73, 776.

10. Lawrence Baum, *The Supreme Court,* 2d ed. (Washington: Congressional Quarterly, 1985), 160, 162, 166.

11. State court activism in this area was urged (and perhaps stimulated) by Justice William Brennan in "State Constitutions and the Protection of Individual Rights," 90 *Harvard Law Review* 489 (1977).

12. *Brown v. Board of Education of Topeka,* 347 U.S. 483 (1954).

13. *Reynolds v. Sims,* 377 U.S. 533 (1964), foreshadowed in *Baker v. Carr,* 369 U.S. 186 (1962).

14. The United Nations Universal Declaration of Human Rights was adopted by the General Assembly on December 10, 1948. U.N.-sponsored international covenants on Economic, Social and Cultural Rights and on Civil and Political Rights were ready for signature in December 1966 and came into force a decade later. Most of the major powers, but not, so far, the United States, have ratified these covenants. The United States did, however, sign the Declaration and the Helsinki Final Act of 1975 which calls for a nonbinding commitment to stated international norms of human rights. We have also ratified a small number of human rights treaties addressed to particular topics: slavery, forced labor, political rights of women, the status of refugees, genocide, and torture.

15. *Texas v. Johnson,* 109 S. Ct. 2533 (1989), reaffirmed in *United States v. Eichman,* 110 S. Ct. 2404 (1990).

16. People for the American Way, *Democracy's Next Generation* (Washington: People for the American Way, 1989), 14.

17. Ibid., 67–69.

18. Plato, *The Republic,* 409.

19. *Palko v. Connecticut,* 302 U.S. 319, 325 (1937).

20. There is a vast literature on the history and theory of rights and natural right. Works that I have found of particular interest are: Ronald Dworkin, *Taking Rights Seriously* (Cambridge: Cambridge University Press, 1977); Richard E. Flathman, The Practice of Rights (Cambridge: Cambridge University Press, 1976); John Finnis, *Natural Law and Natural Rights* (Oxford: Clarendon Press, 1986); Charles Fried, *Right and Wrong* (Cambridge: Harvard University Press, 1978); Morton Horwitz, "Rights," 23 *Harvard Civil Rights—Civil Liberties Review* 393 (1988); Michael J. Sandel, *Liberalism and the Limits of Justice* (Cambridge: Cambridge University Press, 1982); Leo Strauss, *Natural Right and History* (Chicago: University of Chicago Press, 1953); Michel Villey, *Le Droit et les Droits de l'Homme* (Paris: Presses Universitaires de France, 1983).

21. See, generally, Louis Henkin, *The Age of Rights* (New York: Columbia University Press, 1990); Morton Keller, "Powers and Rights: Two Centuries of American Constitutionalism," 74 *Journal of American History* 675 (1987).

22. "Declaration of the Rights of Man and of the Citizen" in *Constitutions et documents politiques,* 10th ed., ed. Maurice Duverger (Paris: Presses Universitaires de France, 1986), 17.

23. Clifford Geertz. The *Interpretation of Cultures* (New York: Basic Books, 1973). See also James Boyd White, *When Words Lose Their Meaning* (Chicago: University of Chicago Press, 1984).

24. Vaclav Havel, "Words on Words," *The New York Review of Books,* January 18, 1990. (Speech on receiving the Peace Prize of the German Booksellers Association.)

25. U.S. Department of Justice, Immigration and Naturalization Service, *A Welcome to U.S.A. Citizenship* (Washington: U.S. Government Printing Office, 1977), 3.

26. *Trop v. Dulles*, 356 U.S. 86, 102 (1958) (Warren, C.J.).

27. Participation in community and political life is the single most strongly emphasized theme in the official booklet distributed to prospective Canadian citizens. Department of the Secretary of State of Canada, *The Canadian Citizen* (Ottawa: Department of the Secretary of State, 1985).

28. United Nations Universal Declaration of Human Rights, Article 29.

29. See, especially, Martin P. Golding, "The Primacy of Welfare Rights," 1 *Social Philosophy and Policy* 119 (1984); Richard E. Morgan, *Disabling America: The "Rights Industry" in Our Time* (New York: Basic Books, 1984); Michael Sandel, *Liberalism and the Limits of Justice* (Cambridge: Cambridge University Press, 1982); Richard Stith, "Living without Rights—In Manners, Religion and Law," in *Law and the Ordering of Our Life Together,* ed. Richard J. Neuhaus (Grand Rapids: Eerdmans, 1989), 54; Michel Villey, *Le Droit et les Droits de l'Homme* (Paris: Presses Universitaires de France, 1983); Tom Campbell, *The Left and Rights* (London: Routledge & Kegan Paul, 1983).

30. Edmund Burke, *Reflections on the Revolution in France,* ed. J.G.A. Pocock (Indianapolis: Hackett Publishing, 1987). Burke contrasted the abstract rights of liberty and equality with "the *real* rights of men" (his emphasis) which he described as a patrimony from our forefathers, the product of practical reason and the experience of men in civil society, rather than sterile theorizing about "natural" or "universal" man. Among these "real" rights (the rights of Englishmen) Burke listed several, beginning with the right to live under law:

> They have a right to the fruits of their industry and to the means of making their industry fruitful. They have a right to the acquisitions of their parents, to the nourishment and improvement of their offspring, to instruction in life, and to consolation in death. Whatever each man can separately do, without trespassing upon others, he has a right to do for himself; and he has a right to a fair portion of all which society, with all its combinations of skill and force, can do in his favour. In this partnership all men have equal rights, but not to equal things. (p. 51).

31. Marx was as scornful as Burke of the "so-called *rights of man*," and even more emphatic in condemning their failure to take into account human sociality. In his view, the "liberty" of the French declaration was merely the liberty "of man regarded as an isolated nomad, withdrawn into himself." It was "founded...upon the separation of man from man"; indeed, it was the very "right of such separation." As for equality, it did not go beyond the idea of man as "an individual separated from the community." It was but the right to be equally treated "as a self-sufficient

nomad." Karl Marx, "On the Jewish Question," in *The Marx-Engels Reader*, ed. Robert C. Tucker (New York: Norton, 1972), 24, 40, 41.

32. Robert Wright, "Are Animals People Too?" *New Republic*, 12 March 1990, 20, 27.

33. Thomas Jefferson, "Inaugural Address," in *The Life and Selected Writings of Thomas Jefferson* (New York: Modern Library, 1944), 323.

Terms & Concepts

Bill of Rights
Brown v. Board of Education
civil rights movement
civil society
"communicative deficiency"
constitutionalism
Founding Fathers
human rights

individualism
legalism
legalization of popular culture
legitimacy
litigation
New Deal
ordered liberty
political discourse

reciprocal duties
rights talk
Rousseau
the American rights dialect
Tocqueville
UN Universal Declaration of
    Human Rights
Vaclav Havel

Questions

1. What are the features of the American rights dialect?

2. Think of three public policy issues where rights come into conflict. Is rights talk helpful in sorting out competing interests?

3. Glendon believes words are important and, further, that laws have an effect on people's thinking and acting regardless of the enforcement of those laws. If so, would a law prohibiting euthanasia or assisted suicide be of any worth even if it were never enforced?

4. The Canadian Charter of Rights and Freedoms opens with the following provision: "The Canadian Charter of Rights and Freedoms guarantees the rights and freedoms set out in it subject only to such reasonable limits as can be demonstrably justified in a free and democratic society." Does this provision address Glendon's concerns about rights talk?

5. What does the fixation with rights imply for the power and status of the judiciary? Is a very powerful judiciary undemocratic?

The Culture of Contentment

John Kenneth Galbraith

Editors' Note

In this excerpt from his 1992 book *The Culture of Contentment*,[1] John Kenneth Galbraith, prolific author and former economic adviser to U.S. presidents, makes a compelling case that class conflict, the existence of which is generally denied in American social science literature, is becoming acute in the United States. Coming just a few months before the Watts riots in Los Angeles, this observation appeared to be prescient enough to catch considerable attention.

The idea of class struggle is, of course, most closely associated with Karl Marx, who saw it as the motive force of all history. Class struggle, when combined with the boom-bust cycles of capitalism, would drive the working class inexorably towards revolution. That this did not happen was due in part to the achievement of universal suffrage and to

the emergence of liberal and socialist political parties. It was also due to the conclusion arrived at by many economists that the government itself had to play a major economic role.

Probably the best known advocate of reform liberalism and state intervention was John Maynard Keynes, later Lord Keynes. He firmly believed that his prescriptions for state intervention in the economy would help moderate the cycles of capitalism. Capitalism with a human face could deliver prosperity and security for all. Faced with the Great Depression, Franklin Delano Roosevelt, called a crypto-communist by many at the time, brought in the New Deal, thereby helping to save capitalism.

Why, then, violent class conflict in a late 20th century democratic welfare state?

According to Galbraith, the American version of the welfare state has been a victim of its own incomplete success. It has helped make the majority content with their affluence, but has kept a significant and growing minority poor and hopeless. The latest figures available for the United States show that the top 20% of U.S. households own nearly 80% of the nation's wealth.[2] Democracy has become a tyranny of the contented, and the results are foreboding.

John Kenneth Galbraith continues to be a very forceful, though, as of late, lonely voice for reform liberalism. He dismisses his numerous critics with the remark that conventional wisdom (now neoconservatism) is usually outdated by the time it has become convention. You will enjoy Galbraith's dry, irreverent wit. Here is an economist who writes for everyone, not just for colleagues.

◆ ◆ ◆

1. John Kenneth Galbraith, *The Culture of Contentment* (New York: Houghton Mifflin, 1992). This excerpt was first printed in *New Statesman & Society* (May 8, 1992).
2. *The Globe and Mail*, April 17, 1995. Data come from the U.S. Federal Reserve and are for 1989.

On no matter is American social thought in its accepted and popular manifestation more insistent than on social class or, more specifically, the absence thereof in the United States. We have a classless society; to this we point with considerable pride. The social mythology of the Republic is built on the concept of classlessness—the belief, as President George Bush once put it, that class is "for European democracies or something else—it isn't for the United States of America. We are not going to be divided by class."

Yet presidential oratory, however well-intended and even eloquent, does not serve entirely to suppress the truth. Determinedly and irrevocably into the American language has come the modern reference to "the underclass". There are individuals and families who, it is conceded, do not share the comfortable well-being of the prototypical American. These people, this class, are concentrated in the centres of the great cities or, less visibly, on deprived farms, as rural migrant labour, or in erstwhile mining communities. Or they are the more diffused poor of the Old South and of the region of the Rio Grande in Texas. The greater part of the underclass consists of members of minority groups, blacks or people of Hispanic origin. While the most common reference is to the underclass of the great cities, this is at least partly because its presence there is the most inescapably apparent.

So much is accepted. What is not accepted, and indeed is little mentioned, is that the underclass is integrally a part of a larger economic process and, more importantly, that it serves the living standard and the comfort of the more favoured community. Economic progress would be far more uncertain and certainly far less rapid without it. The economically fortunate, not excluding those who speak with greatest regret of the existence of this class, are heavily dependent on its presence.

The underclass is deeply functional; all industrial countries have one in greater or lesser measure and in one form or another. As some of its members escape from deprivation and its associated compulsions, a resupply becomes essential. But on few matters, it must be added, is even the most sophisticated economic and social comment more reticent. The picture of an economic and political system in which social exclusion, however unfortunate, is somehow a remediable affliction is all but required. Here, in highly compelling fashion, the social convenience of the contented replaces the clearly visible reality.

Appreciation of this reality begins with the popular, indeed obligatory, definition of work. Work, in the conventional view, is pleasant and rewarding; it is something in which all favoured by occupation rejoice to a varying degree. A normal person is proud of his or her work.

In practical fact, much work is repetitive, tedious, painfully fatiguing, mentally boring or socially demeaning. This is true of diverse consumer and household services and the harvesting of farm crops, and is equally true in those industries that deploy workers on assembly lines, where labour cost is a major factor in the price of what is finally produced. Only, or in any case primarily, when this nexus between labour cost and price is broken or partly dissociated, invariably at higher income levels, does work become pleasant and, in fact, enjoyed. It is a basic but rarely articulated feature of the modern economic system that the highest pay is given for the work that is most prestigious and most agreeable. This is at the opposite extreme from those occupations that are inherently invidious, those that place the individual directly under the command of another, as in the case of the doorman or the household servant, and those involving a vast range of tasks—street cleaning, garbage collection, janitorial services, elevator operation—that have an obtrusive connotation of social inferiority.

There is no greater modern illusion, even fraud, than the use of the single term *work* to cover what for some is, as noted, dreary, painful, socially demeaning and what for others is enjoyable, socially reputable and economically rewarding. Those who spend pleasant, well-compensated days say with emphasis that they have been "hard at work", thereby suppressing the notion that they are a favoured class. They are, of course, allowed to say that they enjoy their work, but it is presumed that such enjoyment is shared by any *good* worker. In a brief moment of truth, we speak, when sentencing criminals, of years at "hard labour". Otherwise we place a common gloss over what is agreeable and what, to a greater or lesser extent, is endured or suffered.

From the foregoing comes one of the basic facts of modern economic society: the poor in our economy are needed to do the work that the more fortunate do not do and would find manifestly distasteful, even distressing.

And a continuing supply and resupply of such workers is always needed. That is because later generations do not wish to follow their parents into physically demanding, socially unacceptable or otherwise disagreeable occupations; they escape or seek to escape the heavy lifting to a more comfortable and rewarding life. This we fully understand and greatly approve; it is what education is generally meant to accomplish. But from this comes the need for the resupply or, less agreeably, for keeping some part of the underclass in continued and deferential subjection.

To see these matters in the clearest light, one must first look at their resolution in western Europe.

In the past 40 years in Germany, France and Switzerland, and in lesser measure in Australia and Scandinavia, the provision of outside workers for the tasks for which indigenous labourers are no longer available has been both accepted and highly organised. The factories of the erstwhile German Federal Republic are manned, and a broad range of other work is performed, by Turks and Yugoslavs. Those in France are similarly supplied by what amounts to a new invasion of the Moors—the vast influx from the former North African colonies. Switzerland has long relied on Italian and Spanish workers. The industrial north of Italy, in turn, has depended heavily on a reserve army of the unemployed from the south—the more backward Mezzogiorno—and now increasingly from North Africa. The British economy has been sustained in no small part by migrants from the former dominions—India, Pakistan, Bangladesh and the West Indies.

The employment of these workers goes beyond manufacturing establishments and factory assembly lines to a wide range of jobs. Restaurants, household and other personal services and less elegant public employments are all their conceded domain. In the large and generally excellent Swiss hospitals, decline and death would, it is said, be probable, if not inevitable, in the absence of the menial foreign staff. Swiss highways would not be repaired without them, or snow or city garbage removed. This is work that the older Swiss workforce does not do. Nor, to repeat, do native workers man the assembly lines or undertake the non prestigious tasks in Germany, France or elsewhere in western Europe in any nearly sufficient way.

There are marked further advantages in this arrangement—in the availability of this admitted underclass. If it becomes unneeded, it can be sent home or, as more often, denied entry. This has been accomplished in Switzerland with such precision in the past that involuntary unemployment has been often in the low hundreds.

Most important of all, these workers, coming as they do from countries and occupations (mostly poor and tedious peasant agriculture) with much lower incomes, are impressed by their new comparative well-being. They are not, accordingly, as assertive as to wage and other claims as would be local workers, and their assertiveness is further tempered by the fact that they are not, with some progressive exceptions, voting and participating citizens. Many, once a certain financial competence is acquired, plan to return home. And some may have entered the country illegally, which usefully enforces their silence.

Not much has been made of this migration, some ethnic tension apart, and even less of the fact that in the years since the second world war it has been essential for western European economic life. That is because the offspring of the traditional older working class have gone on to the more pleasant and remunerative employments, the employments that are also called work. Still less has been made of a functionally similar underclass in the United States. Here too it has one of the uncelebrated but indispensable roles in modern capitalism. Both its character and also its uses are, however, rather more ambiguous and diverse than those of the foreign workers in Europe, those who are often called guest workers to emphasise their seemingly temporary role.

In the latter years of the last century and until the first world war, American mass-employment industry and the less agreeable urban occupations drew their workforce extensively from eastern Europe as well as from the labour surplus of American farms. As this supply diminished, poor whites from the Appalachian plateau and, in greatly increasing numbers, blacks from the south moved to take their place. The assembly plants and body shops of Detroit were once staffed by workers from the adjacent farms and small towns of Michigan and Ontario, as well as by immigrants from Poland and elsewhere in Europe. As that generation went on to personally more attractive or socially more distinguished occupations, the assembly lines there reached out to more distant refugees from poor farming and mining areas and to the erstwhile sharecroppers and other deprived rural workers of the Deep South. With the latter recruitment, Detroit became a city of largely black population; the automobile industry would not have survived had it had to rely on the sons and daughters of its original workers. Nor would many other public and private services have been available in tolerable form.

In more recent times, migration from Mexico, Latin America and the West Indies has become a general source of such labour. For many years now, legal provision has been made for the importation of workers for the harvesting of fruit and vegetables, there being very specific acknowledgement that this is something native-born Americans cannot be persuaded in the necessary numbers to do. There is here, somewhat exceptionally, a clear legal perception of the role of the underclass.

In the US immigration legislation of 1990, there was at last some official recognition of the more general and continuing need for immigrant labour. Although much of the discussion of this measure turned on the opening of the door to needed skilled workers (and compassionately to relatives of earlier migrants), the larger purpose was not in doubt. There would be a new and necessary recruitment of men and women to do the tasks of the underclass. Avoided only was mention of such seemingly brutal truth. It is not thought appropriate to say that the modern economy requires such an underclass, and certainly not that it must reach out to other countries to sustain and refresh it.

It is important to note and emphasise that the contribution of the underclass is not confined to disagreeable industrial and agricultural employment. In the modern urban community, as noted, there is a vast range of tedious or socially demeaning jobs that require unskilled, willing and adequately inexpensive labour. To this need the underclass responds, and it makes urban life at the comfortable levels of well-being not only pleasant but possible. There is, however, the darker side.

In the inner cities of the United States, as less dramatically in Europe—Brixton and Hackney in London, areas in France where North African migrants are heavily concentrated—there is a continuing threat of underclass social disorder, crime and conflict. Drug dealing, indiscriminate violence, other crime and family disorientation and disintegration are now all aspects of everyday existence.

In substantial part, this is because a less vigorously expanding economy and the movement of industry to economically more favoured locations have denied to the underclass those relatively stable and orderly industrial employments once available in the large cities. But also, and more importantly, the normal upward movement that was for long the solvent for discontent has been arrested. The underclass has become a semi-permanent rather than a generational phenomenon. There has been surprisingly little comment as to why minority communities in New York, Chicago, Los Angeles and elsewhere, once poor but benign and culturally engaging, are now centres of terror and despair. The reason is that what was a favouring upward step in economic life has now become a hopeless enthralment.

Yet, considering the sordid life to which the modern underclass is committed, and especially when their life is compared with that of the contented majority, it is an occasion for wonder that the discontent and its more violent and aggressive manifestations are not greater than they are. One reason, evident in Europe and also important in the United States, is that for some of the underclass life in the cities, although insecure, ill-rewarded and otherwise primitive, still remains, if tenuously, better than that from which they escaped. The great black migration to the north after the second world war was from a rural existence, classically that of the sharecropper, with rudimentary shelter and clothing; no health care; hard farm labour; exploitative living costs; little in the way of schooling; no voting rights; forthright, accepted and enforced racial discrimination; and, with all, extreme invisibility. Urban life, however unsatisfactory, was an improvement. So also for those moving in the recent past from Latin America. For many the comparison is not with those who are more fortunate but with their own past position. This latter comparison and its continuing memory in the culture unquestionably has had the same tranquillising effect on the American underclass as it has on that in Europe. It is one unnoted reason, along with ineligibility because of recent arrival or illegal presence, that underclass voter turnout in elections is relatively low.

While the urban areas inhabited by the underclass have seen outbreaks of violence, notably the widespread riots in the second half of the 1960s in the US, with the recent echo in Los Angeles [last week], the more surprising thing, nonetheless, is their relative tranquillity. This, however, it will be evident from the foregoing, is something on which no one should count in the future. It has existed in the past because, as noted, the underclass has been in the process of transition—that from a lesser life, and with the prospect of generational escape. As this process comes to an end—as membership in the underclass becomes stable and enduring—greater resentment and social unrest should be expected. A blockage in the movement upward and out of the underclass will not be accepted. However, although it will not be accepted, it will not in the ordinary course of events be anticipated.

It is not in the nature of the politics of contentment to expect or plan countering action for misfortune, even disaster, that, however predictable and predicted, is in the yet undisclosed future. Such planning, involving as it always does public action—provision of good educational opportunity, good public housing and health care, competent attention to drug addiction, family counselling, adequate welfare payments—is systemically resisted by the contented electoral majority. In what is the accepted and, indeed, only acceptable view, the underclass is deemed the source of its own succour and well-being; in the extreme view, it requires the spur of its own poverty, and it will be damaged by any social assistance and support.

The reaction of the community of contentment to the miseries and violence of the urban slums, and the probable reaction if the violence becomes more extreme, is readily predictable. Aiding prediction, as ever, is the fact that the future, in some measure, is already here.

The first development, one we can already see, is resort by the contented in the larger cities to a laager mentality—the hiring of personal, neighbourhood or apartment security guards or the escape to presumptively safe suburbs. In Manila in the Philippines, affluent urban enclaves—the golden ghettos—are distributed over that poverty-ridden metropolis, each with its own impenetrable fence and stern security force. In less formal fashion, something of the same can now be seen in the modern American city, and this development could be, and one can doubtless say will be, greatly extended. In contrast with steps to tackle and ameliorate the economic and social forces shaping the despair and violence of the slums, such a protective remedy has an appealing element of immediacy and practicality: seemingly far better and surer the effect of outlays for security guards than the more distant hope from some rehabilitative expenditure in the inner city.

The second reaction is the likelihood, indeed near certainty, of what will happen if urban discontent, crime and violence increase: this will be attributed not to the social situation but to the inferior, even criminal, disposition of the people involved. Such is already the case. A major answer to crime, disaffection and disorder in the central cities is now a call for heavier law enforcement, including a more extensive use of the death penalty and more facilities for detention. No other current situation produces such inflammatory rhetoric. This mood, in the event of still worse violence, could, in turn, lead readily to armed repression, first by the local police, then by military force. The obvious fact that people of comfortable circumstance live peacefully together and those afflicted by poverty do not goes largely unnoticed. Or, if noticed, it is not discussed amid the clamour for a clamp-down on what seems an intrinsically ill-behaved and violent citizenry. Were one permitted one confident prediction, it would be of the likelihood of an increasingly oppressive authority in areas of urban desolation.

Articles of this genre are expected to have a happy ending. With awareness of what is wrong, the corrective forces of democracy are set in motion. And perhaps they would be now were they in a full democracy—one that embraced the interests and votes of all the citizens. Those now outside the contented majority would rally, or, more precisely, could be rallied, to their own interest and therewith to the larger and safer public interest. Alas, however, we speak here of a democracy of those with the least sense of urgency to correct what is wrong, the best insulation through short-run comfort from what could go wrong—a democracy run by and for the contented majority, in which those who do not share in its benefits do not participate.

There is special occasion here for sadness—for a sad ending—for what is needed to save and protect, to ensure against suffering and further unpleasant consequence, is not in any way obscure. Nor would the resulting action be disagreeable. There would be a challenge to the present mood of contentment with its angry resentment of any intrusion, but, in the longer run, the general feeling of security in well-being would be deepened.

The central requirement cannot be escaped: almost every action that would remedy and reassure involves the relationship between the citizen and the state. In the communist world in the long years before collapse all concessions to the market were resisted as concessions to capitalism; they were inconsistent with the accepted principles of socialism. It was, however, almost certainly by such concessions, especially in the diverse world of consumer goods and services and agriculture—economic activity beyond the reach and competence of the command system—that communism cum socialism might have been saved. In a perverse way, the same is now true of modern capitalism. Although intervention by the state on a wide and varied front once saved capitalism, there is now a resistance to the state action that is necessary to ensure an economically successful and socially tranquil future. The dialectic of the modern capitalist, or more precisely the modern mixed, economy, all but exclusively involves the role of government. In the dialectic this is extensively ideological; in everyday manifestation it is highly pragmatic. And, to repeat, no subtlety conceals the needed attitude and action.

But on nothing has the culture of contentment been so successful as in shaping the accepted attitude toward the state. In some areas—the armed services, the procurement of highly technical weaponry—the state's performance is, to be sure, approved. In the conduct of foreign policy, real and rhetorical, the provision of social security and the rescue of failing financial institutions, its adequacy is assumed. Where, however, regulation to forestall the socially damaging or self-destructive tendencies of the system or to rescue the poor is involved, state action is held to be deeply inadequate and seriously counterproductive.

The required change in policy begins with the overall or macroeconomic performance of the economy. In a time of economic recession such as that of the early 1990s, there is a strong case not only for low interest rates but also for increased public expenditure, especially on roads, bridges, airports and other civic needs, and on unemployment compensation and welfare payments, all to employ of protect the unemployed and those otherwise adversely affected.

But there is here a conflict with the tenets of the age of contentment: it is not the comfortable who would thus be aided. And lurking also is the eventual tax effect. During the 1980s, the burgeoning years of contentment, there was a large continuing deficit in the US federal budget. Though a topic for voluble discourse, it was less of a threat to the contented than the taxes that would have reduced it. In the ensuing recession, a deliberate addition to the deficit, primarily for those outside the community of contentment, which might renew the call for higher levies on those inside, became unthinkable.

The controlling role of taxation continues. The only effective design for diminishing the income inequality inherent in capitalism is the progressive income tax. Nothing in the age of contentment has contributed so strongly to income inequality as the reduction of taxes on the rich; nothing, as has been said, would so contribute to social tranquillity as some screams of anguish from the very affluent. That taxes should now be used to reduce inequality is, however, clearly outside the realm of comfortable thought. Here the collision between wise social action and the culture of contentment is most apparent.

The present and devastated position of the socially assisted underclass has been identified as the most serious social problem of the time, as it is also the greatest threat to long-run peace and civility.

Life in the great cities in general could be improved, and only will be improved, by public action—by better schools with better-paid teachers, by strong, well-financed welfare services, by counselling on drug addiction, by employment training, by public investment in the housing that in no industrial country is provided for the poor by private enterprise, by adequately supported recreational facilities, libraries and police. The question once again, much accommodating rhetoric to the contrary, is not what can be done but what will be paid.

Terms & Concepts

capitalism
classless society
democracy
income disparity
inequality

laager mentality
labour cost
macroeconomic performance
migration of labour
mixed economy

politics of contentment
the underclass
welfare state

Questions

1. Given that there always has been an economic underclass in the United States, why is it being driven to revolt now?

2. How has the underclass been managed more successfully in western Europe?

3. Is there any evidence that class conflict is increasing in Canada? Are we following the U.S. trend? What evidence can you cite?

4. Representative democracy is supposed to prevent a tyranny of the majority (see Unit Two, Article 7 on populism). What went wrong?

5. The welfare state will never make everyone comfortable. The more it succeeds, the greater the comfortable majority and the less powerful the poor minority. Is Galbraith simply being too idealistic?

Quebeckers, Mohawks and Zulus: Liberal Federalism and Fair Trade

Frederick Johnstone

Editors' Note

Discussions of federalism are usually technical, detailed, boring accounts of divisions of powers, degrees of decentralization, fiscal arrangements, taxing authority, and the intricacies of amending formulas—in other words, good prescriptions for bouts of insomnia. Not so with this article. Frederick Johnstone takes his readers on a roller coaster ride through the turmoil of the late 1980s and early 1990s, careening through the pantheon of Greek gods, the homelands of apartheid, and the 1990 confrontation at Oka, Quebec. It is a biting, witty polemic on the one hand, and a penetrating look at the issues at the heart of federal political arrangements on the other.

As Benjamin Barber points out in "Jihad vs McWorld" (Unit One, Article 2), the nation-state is being assailed by forces from above and below. While international organizations and transnational corporations effectively transfer sovereign powers upward, subnational groups defined by territory, ethnicity, national identity, or other characteristics claim greater autonomy relative to the political community, in part in reaction to the homogenizing forces of globalization. Johnstone extends the argument to federal societies. Federalism, he argues, is a good mechanism to balance individual human rights with group rights, the placeless logic of the global economy

with the logic of place of local communities, or, in general, the abstract and universal with the concrete and particular. Federalism allows and requires people to live astride this dualism.

Parts of this article are quite difficult, but fear not. Johnstone's argument rings through, despite his use of ideas and references culled from remote times and places. For example, from the world of art Johnstone opposes two sculptures. The first is Nefertiti, the ancient Egyptian queen depicted in a bust with slender neck and delicate features, effortlessly supporting an elaborate headress. Venus von Willendorf, on the other hand, is a very old statuette (now displayed in Austria) depicting a squat, plump, fleshy, and presumably fecund women. The "chthonian ooze" is a reference to a Greek word indicating what is on or beneath the surface of the earth—as opposed to what is in the heavenly realms. The Greek god Apollo is the sun-god, the god of music and poetry, the thoughtful, serene, cool, distant, ethereal god. Dionysius, on the contrary, is the god of wine; he represents the sensual, earthly, passionate, volatile dimension of life as it is lived "on the ground" in time and space. Federalism, according to Johnstone, incorporates the Apollonian and Dionysian dimensions of life into a workable and satisfactory political arrangement.

◆ ◆ ◆

SOCIAL NATURE:
PLACELESS LOGIC AND THE LOGIC OF PLACE*
◆ ◆ ◆

All over the world, from Europe to Canada, from South Africa to Tibet, the complacent post-war consensus of liberal-Marxist cosmopolitanism is facing heretical challenges to Enlightenment assumptions of abstract universalism. Old realities of group and place are just not going away. In Europe, Maastricht mega-statism is on the rocks, while in North America, NAFTA news about joining Mexico is about as popular as joining East Germany. Canada is trying to accommodate Mohawks and Quebeckers, and is handing over one fifth of its land mass to the Inuit in a new place called Nunavut. In South Africa the ANC is trying *not* to accommodate Zulus, and China is trying to keep the lid on Tibet. Meanwhile, the globalization steamroller of free trade is squashing things flat, from French cheese to Canadian jobs, and people who resist this Sell-Your-Mother-For-The-Cheapest-Price philosophy are labelled "foolish old peasants," for wanting to protect their local worlds.

But resist they do. The brash agenda of political and economic universalism comes up against a stubborn obstacle: the foolish people. An old tension is still in play; between localism and globalism, individual and group, particular and universal, placeless logic and the logic of place. The old peasants are back in the picture, and the real fools turn out to be those who thought they could ever be rid of them.

While Danes demur, the experts pontificate. "No change to the script!" They still claim to know what is best and to be able to tell everyone what to do. The irony is not lost on old peasants in the Canton of Uri. Imagine trying to tell them where to go. They have just observed the 700th anniversary of Swiss democracy and they remain to be convinced about the wisdom of handing things over to the Brussels bureaucrats or turning the Alps into ten-lane free-trade highways for ten-ton trucks.[1]

Camille Paglia rethinks "the West" as a dialectical drama of chthonian and anti-chthonian forces in which the "hard Apollonian line of Western separatism" transcends but never fully escapes the all-encompassing ooze of mother-earthly Dionysian flux.[2] After decades of "social constructionism," nature is back in the picture.[3] Paglia's bold critique of the Great Escape has political implications. The Willendorf-Nefertiti tension, between chthonian connectedness and Apollonian separatism, is not just about art. It is the aesthetic expression of a basic political tension between self and tribe, humans and nature, person and place, logic and landscape, denatured mind and nature-place-group.

This tension is still in play. The jet-thrust of Nefertiti head-power, of Apollonian flight, tries to escape the earthy pull of gravity, the chthonian pull of nature-place-group. Modernism de-natures mind. The precious ballet of post-modernism daintily sidesteps the ooze. But it is rudely shocked by Serbian guns, disintegrating states, civil wars. The stage fills with Zulu spears, Mohawk Warriors, medieval flags.

In the middle of it all, as usual, the decent folk from Canada are keeping the peace, sitting in airports waiting for mortar shells to land on their heads in half-baked UN peace-keeping missions, while the UN walks backwards into a new kind of role: peace-maker-among-thugs. The Khmer Rouge thugs, the Mogadishu thugs, the ethnic cleansing thugs, all make a mockery of the old niceties of peace-keeping.[4] Eyeless in Bosnia. What to do? The Canadian general, back from Sarajevo, tells it like it is, on US prime-time. His words are echoed later

Reprinted by permission of *Telos* (Fall 1992), pp. 71–91.
*This is a continuation of an earlier article. See my "Quebec, Apartheid Lithuania and Tibet: The Politics of Group Rights," in *Telos* 85 (Fall 1990); pp. 56–62.

by the UN chief-of-mission to Somalia, who resigns in protest. "If you are going in, go in strength, secure a beachhead, negotiate from strength. Forget all that soft-headed do-goodism or you'll get your head blown off."[5]

Crisis explodes old UN assumptions, about peace-keeping-with-permission, non-interventionism, existing states. While the UN dithers, the National Geographic changes its world map six times in six months. Meanwhile, back in Mogadishu, the teenage toughs in homemade tanks wait to see if the do-gooders are finally getting their act together. And sitting in the airport, writ-

---

People turn out to have landscapes. The voice of the Innu is heard in the land.

---

ing home to small Ontario towns, the peacemakers agree: geography lessons were never quite like this at school. Indeed. People come and go, talking of...capitalism and socialism...?...No Armenians and Kurds! And CNN is there. "This is a place called Slovenia. You may not have heard of it before. But now you have." Landscapes turn out to be social. The Lake of Two Mountains erupts in sound. "We are the Mohawks of Oka, and this is what it means to us to be of this place. (So don't go on building this golf course on the graves of our ancestors, or we'll blow you up?") People turn out to have landscapes. The voice of the Innu is heard in the land. "This is this place and we are us and this is what it means to us to be here." Nature is back in the picture. In a new place called Nunavut something old becomes clear: social nature, as a given, grounded, pre-Enlightenment fact.

More names to learn, like Boipatong and Inkatha, as the decent chaps move on, to Station Zulu. The vast anti-apartheid military-industrial complex creaks and groans into the harsh new-world-order glare of a post-apartheid stage on which the wrong things keep happening. Black civil war? Script writers are confused. The bit players seem to be taking over the show. And the global audience is not sure what to do. The old morality play is over, but the Greek Chorus is still standing around.

After years of heavy-duty anti-apartheid DraiNo, things should be running fairly clear. But dazed plumbers throw up their hands. "Don't ask me about the Zulus." What was supposed to be happening is not happening and what was not is. Is there a blockage in

the pipe? Decades of double-think on Africa has not helped. The demonization of apartheid meant the usual round of taboos and victimology. The writing was on the wall, the message was clear. Forget tribalism in Africa, black-on-black violence, black human rights abuse, political persecution, aid scams, female circumcision etc.—talking about that is cultural imperialism. Criticize white dictatorship, but lay off everything else. Whites sticking it to blacks is an outrage but blacks sticking it to blacks is okay. Whites denying blacks votes is an outrage, but blacks mutilating black girls is okay.

Everyone could point the finger. Places like Malawi could point the finger. Everyone could sign solemn resolutions against apartheid. A strange assortment of black dictators, one-party-states, emperors-for-life, colonel-torturers and clitoris-cutters could make speeches about human rights. The Organization of African Unity turned into a bizarre kind of Black-Dictators-Against-Apartheid Club and double-think on Africa became double-think about the ANC. This does not mean the anti-apartheid crowd simply became cheer-leaders for the ANC. But with the ANC acting as a government-in-exile, led by a martyr/saint, there was not much questioning of the party line, on national liberation, socialist change, a unitary state, the end of tribalism—or about black violence as just an apartheid issue, a Zulu problem, a white plot.[6]

The party line on group rights is understandable. Ethnicity was indeed badly compromised and manipulated by apartheid. Is not ANC universalism the progressive antidote to a poisonous past? In some ways yes. But as UN soldiers from Ontario head for Station Zulu, questions mount. What exactly is going on? Who should be helped now: just the ANC alliance, or other groups as well? And what about the party line on issues such as a unitary state? What can be said about federalism and ethnicity? Can one say one thing to Mohawks and another to Zulus? Or is that a double standard on human rights? Can Canadians hand over a fifth of Canada to the Inuit in a new place called Nunavut but not question the party line on the Zulus?

The global anti-apartheid bandwagon thus comes to an awkward stop. There is a more critical stance, about the past, about the future, about "the good guys." This is evident for example in the recent controversy about the ANC camps. What is significant here is not so much the confirmation of earlier allegations of ANC abuses but the questioning of the party line (and of the absence of that by anti-apartheid media in the past).[7] And it is evident in a more reflexive appraisal of the Western anti-apartheid movement, such as the Adam-Moodley report, which in its general themes transcends its

Canadian focus. Predicated on a "tough and hard-nosed realism," which seeks to "substitute sober analysis and strategic pragmatism for moral outrage," while eschewing "the abdicating relativism of postmodernists" and warning that "the task of outside intervention is not to select winners or losers, but to facilitate democratization" in a process including "all legitimate political actors." It criticizes the politically correct fixation on the ANC, the national group-therapy functions of anti-apartheid in the West, and the image-enhancing DayGlow effect of global devil-bashing (i.e., Canada may not have made much difference to apartheid, but anti-apartheid certainly made a difference to Canada).[8]

From Sarajevo airport to Station Zulu, old certainties about modern progress are fading fast, as ethnic and

---

The challenge is to stake out a compromise position which transcends but retains universalism...

---

regional forces remake the world, redefine the UN, and renew debate about the social order. From the Lake of Two Mountains to the Canton of Uri, old peasants question the party line, and modern experts are confused. Nature may be back in the picture again, but is this not dangerous stuff? Does not nature-place-group sound like "nature-blood-tribe" or "fatherland-fascism"? This is a dangerous trail. It comes uncomfortably close to racism. Balkan rage, ethnic cleansing, genocide. On the other hand, the universalistic road has problems of its own. The hegemonic steamroller of homogenizing universalism has been clanking along, squashing things flat. The driver may not care, but the flattened people do. Populist resistance indicates underlying problems too long ignored by modernizing elites. The challenge is to stake out a compromise position which transcends but retains universalism, rather than simply inverting it into its opposite: xenophobic chauvinism and autarchic protectionism. Politically, it means liberal federalism and, economically, fair-trade.

FEDERAL COMPROMISE: LIBERAL FEDERALISM OR FEDERAL POPULISM?

◆ ◆ ◆

Federalism is the classic political compromise between individual and group. It makes concessions to groups.

But this can be dangerous to individuals. So it has to be "liberal" federalism, if individual rights are to be secure. Groups and regions can be recognized in ways that a unitary state does not, but there must be paramount concern for individual rights—this is the hallmark of Western democracy. The idea of human rights is perhaps the greatest accomplishment of Western civilization and it would be foolish to take it for granted. Was that not, after all, the main legacy of Auschwitz: to establish once and for all, through the UN, the idea of universal human rights?

This needs to be remembered in the current debate about federalism. This is a problem, for example, with Paul Piccone's "federal populism": an almost total silence on human rights.[9] Piccone has taken the discussion a long way, and recognizes the fascism problem. But his devastating critique of universalism is in danger of going too far in the opposite direction. Unlike liberal federalism, his federal populism provides no constitutional or institutional mechanisms to counter this problem. He unduly conflates the critique of liberalism with that of the unitary state, so that a progressive defense of populism ends up being based on a questionable (and typically left-anarchist) underestimation of the achievements of the liberal state. This is not logically necessary or politically wise. In fact it misunderstands the nature of the federal compromise. Liberal federalism does not entail the repudiation of universalism per se: if it did, it would not be a compromise but a reversal into tribalism. What is at issue is not universalism but how things are balanced. Liberal federalism balances the universal and the particular, individual and group, liberalism and populism. Does federal populism? Where is the liberal side of the equation in federal populism?

With the present resurgence of ethnic cleansing, neo-Nazi violence and Moslem-Hindu bloodbaths, this is no idle issue.[10] The left-anarchist quest for utopian community is well and good, but there is also a need for a few guarantees that anarchism is inherently unable to provide.[11] If within the populist framework all one is left with is "the vindication of people's really existing culture,"[12] weird things may be done in the name of particular cultures and there will be no principles in terms of which to criticize them, no mechanisms in terms of which to resist them. One cannot criticize postmodernism for being relativizing and trivializing, and then dismiss human rights on the ground that they are universalizing and "totalizing." Surely human rights merit more than a few dismissive comments about the "terminal" problems of liberalism. Is it possible to have a theory of social justice that is in no way universalistic? Is it not dangerous to jettison the universals and go with group justice? If one has second thoughts when being cooked by the cannibals, perhaps it is a bit too late. The Lombard League may not be cannibals, or fascists. But say they were? Should one's right to life and liberty be paramount over the right to cultural autonomy? If so, in terms of what principle? What will happen if Quebeckers do set up an independent state? Either it will be a tribal state, in which case there is the problem of fascism, or it will be a smaller version of the liberal state.

Balance, not universalism, is the key issue. Federalism straddles two worlds, but one foot must be securely out of the chthonian ooze. Paglia's critique of the "hard Apollonian line of Western separatism" understands the pathos of its futile attempt to escape from the nature loop. But this is no namby-pamby deconstructionist denial of the meaning of the text, the text of the West, the progressive thrust. The West escapes out of the ooze. Not everyone does. But it still has a foot in it. It tries to forget or to romanticize, what it cannot fully evade. In the end, it is a story of both: of Apollonian sky-time and Dyonysian earth-space.

Aesthetics deals with synthesis (e.g., Egyptian earth-sky) but does not have to deal with compromise. Politics does. But in dealing with the human condition, aesthetic synthesis is a metaphor about political compromise. Liberal federalism is a compromise. It permits group power but not a tribal state. It affirms nature-place-group, but not the scalping of neighbours who belong to the wrong groups. Respecting the old peasants does not mean giving them a blank check. Liberal federalism provides a safety net. It guarantees individual rights against the group. The self is secure and separate from nature-place-group. This safety net is not just about rights, but about dignity. While federalism recognizes the dignity of group, universalism liberates dignity from group, the ascriptive tyranny of birth and nature-place-group. The emancipatory thrust of the Great Escape is not just for freedom but for dignity. Origin and kinship become irrelevant to human dignity in the great Alexandrian library of global citizens, in the great Judaeo-Christian-Enlightenment-Liberal-Marxist project of Western universalism.

Aesthetics and politics thus speak about the same things in different ways. Aesthetics is about nature without knowing it is about politics, and federalism is about politics without knowing it is about nature. Paglia's comments on the Mona Lisa have implications for the Canton of Uri. Humanism implodes on the inner contradictions of its own naturalism; so does de-natured universalism on the gravitational pull of nature-place-group. Humanism is not expunged. But nature is back in

the picture: human nature, social nature; the *sexual personae* of Michelangelo, the *social personae* of Mohawks.[13]

Leonardo struggles with nature, modernity tries to escape. Adam Smith, Karl Marx and Talcott Parsons proclaim the gospel of achieved status, of meritocratic universalism, of total disconnectedness. Free trade revives the placeless logic of the never-sleeping market place, from Hong Kong to Wall Street. But this denies, evades, suppresses the ties of place. Why deny the unde-

---

Human rights are a Western idea.

---

niable? Why not work with it instead? Federalism is bold. It works with dangerous forces, of nature-place-group, but with the gloves on. After all, there are ethnic scalpers around. Poisonous snakes from the chthonian ooze should not be handled with bare hands. The human rights of a liberal state are essential to counter group problems of fascism and fundamentalism.

If human rights mean limits to cultural relativism, so be it. That is indeed the meaning of the Western text. Human rights *are* a Western idea. So is not having your clitoris cut off. Who needs to apologize for that? Is anyone going to apologize to the 80 million African women who have had their clitorises cut off? There has to be an Archimedean point in human rights (as Amnesty International assumes there is, to the discomfort of various regimes). How else can one question things such as ethnic cleansing, Islamic sexism, Arab slavery, let alone outright genocide? That does entail taking provocative positions now, just as it has in the past. It means that the Islamic state is just as much a systemic human rights problem as the Leninist state and the apartheid state. Islamic fundamentalists may not live to hear that, but then neither did the Leninists, who dismissed human rights as "bourgeois nonsense." The real nonsense is the appeasement of fascist fundamentalism, the 30-year UN gag order on female circumcision, the grotesque rationalizations of things such as the anti-Rushdie *fatwa* (assassination order). Accusations of cultural imperialism just rationalize a double standard about human rights (that human rights are Universal when it comes to South African blacks but Imperialism when it comes to Islamic women). For liberal federalism, respect for local culture is not a blank check for cultural relativism. Universal human rights are inherently incompatible with clitoris cutting, sexual slavery and the shooting of writers who dare to be free.

Liberal federalism is thus a balancing act. It means accommodating groups but avoiding fascism by entrenching individual rights. This is what is obtained in successful cases such as Canada and Switzerland. This is also the issue in Canada's constitutional struggle today: how to find a new balance, which better accommodates groups and regions without jeopardizing individual rights. Canadian federalism is a successful compromise, born out of historical accommodations between different groups which did not wish to suppress diversity in the name of modernity. French, English, natives and others have gone on being French, English, natives and others, within a pluralistic federal state which permits them to do so. But this is a liberal state, with an overarching structure of individual rights and federal powers. Two recent attempts at "renewed federalism" (the Meech Lake Accord of 1987, the Charlottetown Accord of 1992) provoked a marathon debate. The failure of Meech led to the new and improved Charlottetown package, which was also rejected, in a national referendum in October 1992. But this means less than it seems, since the status quo is already a fairly successful balancing act, and further reforms (e.g., Nunavut) can and will be made in more incremental and less sweeping ways.

What does the simultaneous collapse of Charlottetown and the creation of Nunavut mean? It illustrates the Canadian balance. It means that "actually existing Canadian federalism is a pragmatic compromise between Trudeau's universalistic federalism and Joe Clark's more decentrist, group-oriented idea of Canada as a "community of communities." And the debate gave new voice to both sides. Anyone who thinks that cultural particularity somehow died with the rise of modernity should take note of how all these negotiations brought them back in the picture to better accommodate distinct groups such as Quebeckers and natives (who want more groups rights), and marginal regions (East and West) which want more clout in a Triple E Senate (elected, equal, effective). And if the accords failed it was partly because for some they did not go far enough on group rights. For example, Meech was killed by the single word of a single man: native leader Elijah Harper, whose "No" in the Manitoba Legislature prevented unanimous consent to a deal which excluded natives. Charlottetown was more inclusive, but dealt with so many contentious issues as to make unanimous consent even more difficult. Similarly, for some who said no, it was departing too far from individual rights. Most Canadians, it turns out, are unwilling to go much further down the road of special status for distinct groups. They are unwilling to let one province, Quebec, have much

more in the way of special power, though they are willing to give natives some form of self-government resembling provincial power. They like the pluralistic federal system, but wish to preserve the over-arching framework of liberal democracy: the paramountcy of individual rights (of equal citizens with equal rights), the equality of provinces (of equal provinces with equal powers), and a strong federal government (pursuing national goals and standards such as medicare).

This came most dramatically to the fore in the abrasive interventions of Trudeau and Mordechai Richler. Trudeau has always attacked Quebec nationalists and opposed special status for Quebec, in the name of a pluralistic federalism allowing individuals to be French rather than imposing Frenchness on individuals. His devastating attacks on both Meech and Charlottetown as sell-out deals which betrayed Canada to appease greedy provinces did not mince words.[14] If Trudeau's individualistic federalism (not to be confused with unitary statism) is galling to Quebeckers, so is Richler's brash use of his platform as world-famous-author to lambast Quebec nationalism as a narrow, exclusionary, chauvinistic, tribalistic project with anti-semitic and neo-fascist overtones.[15] Nothing annoys French intellectuals more than when Richler says that "when I hear French crowds marching through the streets shouting 'Le Quebec pour les Quebecois,' I do not think they are referring to people whose last name is Ginsberg." Some wanted to ban his book (which, of course, made it a best-seller). But that is what tribalism means. That is the down side of nature-place-group. Some people feel left out, unwanted, a bit worried about their scalps perhaps. This is Richler's ways of saying that tribal logic is dangerous. Most Canadians agree. They support the *status quo*, in its indirect solution to the problem of group rights.

This is a distinctive feature of liberal federalism. The indirect solution means vesting power in regions and individuals rather than groups. The latter wield power without group rights as such being entrenched in the Constitution. This is true both of Canadian and Swiss federalism. Quebeckers do not have special rights because they are French, but have group power because they reside in a province in which the majority of individuals are French, in a federal system in which provincial governments have distinct powers. Inuit in the new "ethnic homeland" of Nunavut will not have special rights because they are Inuit but because they are the majority of individuals in that territory. Swiss federalism involves a similar territorialization of rights. Swiss Germans do not have special rights as such, but the majority of people in the Canton of Uri have a lot of power to decide what happens in the Canton of Uri. The old peasants never did actually entrench group rights. Group power works through territorial rather than group rights. Cantons have powers rather than groups having rights.[16]

What *are* entrenched are individual rights. The bottom line is that Canada and Switzerland are first and foremost liberal democracies in which individual rights are supreme, although significantly tempered by nature-place-group. This is what makes liberal federalism different from apartheid. The Inuit "ethnic homeland" of Nunavut will not be an ethnic state of "bantustan," with the kind of separate citizenship of apartheid homelands (which served to de-legitimize black claims to a common South African citizenship with universal rights). Leaving Canada is an option, but being in it means being part of an overarching structure of liberal democracy. Cultural pluralism does not mean rights relativism. The Inuit will still be subject to Canadian law. And since being in Canada also means being part of what the UN ranks as one of the best countries in the world, Quebeckers, Mohawks, Inuit, Cree, Newfoundlanders and other distinct groups are unlikely to secede. Interestingly enough, they do have that right. Unlike Kurds and Scots (and Californians), they belong to a place in which secession is actually possible. Quebeckers even had a referendum on this in 1980 (which the separatists lost).

Of course, federal paramountcy is anathema to Quebec separatists. Their problem, however, is that most Quebeckers are not too interested in seceding from Canada unconditionally. Moreover, the rest of Canada will not consider the separatist idea of "sovereignty-association," in which Quebec would be both in and out of Canada at the same time. Separatists invented this idea to fudge the issue for the 1980 vote, when they realized they could not gain sufficient support for outright independence. They still advocate it today for the same reason, though such a move now would be ignored as meaningless by the rest of Canada (and could land Quebec in a Slovakian mess).[17] As long as Quebec is in, it will have to put up with the over-arching claims of a liberal state. This is not too difficult, however, because Canadian federalism allows Quebec a great deal of autonomy (and generous transfers). Furthermore, the Notwithstanding Clause of the 1982 Constitution permits provincial governments to override certain Charter rights under certain conditions. This was a compromise Trudeau had to make with the provinces in order to gain their consent to the 1982 reform package, and his new individual-leaning Charter of Rights. This is how the Quebec government currently enforces its controversial Inside/Outside sign law, banning English outdoor signs, without breaking the law of the land.

Paramountcy is also a tricky issue for natives since, unlike Quebec, various Treaty Indians claim to have already been "nations" and to still be so today. Some native leaders actually reject the idea of native self-government as a threat to unceded sovereignty, and opposed the "progressive" 1992 Accord on these grounds.[18] This is the basic problem for hard-line liberals like Trudeau. What can they say to the Mohawks, to the Cree? Get Lost? Even for Canadian natives the issue is not cut-and-dried. Thus, in the current debate about native self-government, native women have been embarrassing the mostly male native leaders by insisting on Charter paramountcy (of the Charter of Rights) in any new scheme, because of the appalling rate of sexist violence against women in the native's "really existing culture." For them, universal and enforceable rights are hardly "oppressive." Balance, not universalism, is the issue, and that is what Canadian federalism is about.

FREE TRADE CRISIS: POPULIST RESISTANCE AND FEDERALIST ECONOMICS

◆ ◆ ◆

Politically, the crisis of universalism points towards federalism, which has to be *liberal* if it is to be clearly and categorically free from the fascism/apartheid side of cultural particularism. But what about the crisis of economic universalism? This also requires a balancing act: a federalist critique of free trade that goes beyond knee-jerk protectionism, that rejects the arrogant assumptions of market absolutism without denying the benefits of the market place and liberal trade.

Those assumptions are being questioned by the old peasants, who know what a "level playing field with Mexico" really means. When they hear about "short term pain for long term gain," they know who is likely to feel the pain and who will benefit from the gain. They know what this Buy-And-Sell-Anything-For-The-Cheapest-Price game means. It means selling your birthright for a mess of potage. Sure, people may get Mexican sneakers at K-Mart for ten dollars, but in exchange for no longer being able to produce anything themselves. And without a productive job or a protective government they will be left at the mercy of global capital: dependent, weak, expendable, cheap. Again, the Canadian case is instructive here. As free trade looms larger on the world agenda, the Canadian case is of interest on at least four levels: its price tag, the macho elitism it is packaged in, the populist resistance it generates, and the alternative economics it implies.

Before buying into NAFTA it might be worthwhile consulting Mel Hurtig's report on the Canada-US Free Trade Agreement (FTA). Not many economic reports spend 30 weeks on the best-seller list. But this is a dramatic story, about what happens when one gives up the proverbial bird in hand for two in the bush. The fact is that Canada has always been a successful and liberal trading nation. But the FTA was a new kind of *hara-kiri* economics, in which one cuts one's throat to become "more competitive." It was a sell-out deal which made blanket concessions in exchange for no real benefits. In the first three years of the FTA (1989–92), Canada lost about 600,000 jobs and 1000 factories, its merchandise trade surplus with the US declined by over $6 billion, and its global balance of trade in goods and services went from a surplus of about $13 billion to a deficit of about $10 billion.[19] Most of the lost jobs have been prime manufacturing jobs. Since 1990 Canada has lost manufacturing jobs at triple the US rate, and the unemployment insurance bill has risen by $7 billion.[20] Ontario (Canada's manufacturing heartland) has been devastated. Toronto's unemployment rate is now higher than the national average, and one in ten people are on welfare. This would have been unthinkable five years earlier.

Numbers aside, of equal interest is the political debate between the advocates of macho elitist free-trade and left-populist fair-trade. Canadians, who have always been successful traders, were told that their world class economy was a basket case and that they were foolish old peasants who should make more concessions to American capital, if they were to "stand up like real men in a tough world." But it is not easy to fool the old peasants. As the dismal results roll in, they have few illusions about what the neoconservative agenda really means, as they witness what Hurtig refers to as the "de-industrialization of Canada" into a "warehouse economy." Mulroney became the most unpopular leader in modern Canadian history[21] and the new plan to extend FTA into NAFTA with Mexico, where manufacturing wages are 800 percent lower than Canada, is going over like a lead zeppelin.[22]

As Thatcher belatedly came to realize, after trying to catch up with the Japanese by doing things the Japanese would never have dreamt of doing, *hara kiri* economics leaves one bleeding. The brash model of entrepreneurial individualism leads to a loss of economic and cultural sovereignty which even conservatives find hard to swal-

low. The truth is that neoconservatives are not really neoconservatives: they are neo-liberals. Conservatives and anarchists both have some respect for the old peasants. It is liberals and Marxists who do not. British conservatives think in thousand-year Agincourt terms. Brussels bureaucrats are just little blips on the millennial radar screen, and there are some itchy fingers on the trigger. Likewise in North America, populist leaders such as Preston Manning (of the insurgent Reform Party in Western Canada) and Ross Perot (in his attack on NAFTA) tap into social discontent "down on the farm" about lost worlds, banks foreclosing, companies exiting, and foreigners profiting: about rootless money, placeless logic, homeless values.

Global GATTists have more than populist protest to worry about. Free trade also provokes ecological resistance, as can be seen from the big tuna fish fight. The powerful American eco-lobby already has GATT on the defensive on things such as the dolphin-destructive Mexican tuna trade, and the Euro-eco-lobby is not far behind on things such as Malaysian tropical lumber.[23] This is just a sign of things to come, especially with Gore in the White House. Those who think free tradism is a blank check for eco-destructive economics are in for a surprise. Malaysian eco-fascists ("We'll cut down every damn tree if we want to") are in trouble. It is not just a cheap labor issue anymore. The eco-critique of free trade broadens not only the terrain of resistance but the force of critique, since ecological theory involves the same repudiation of market absolutism as does social critique: the same affirmation of context, the same rejection of disconnected universalism, of Newtonian mechanics, of the objectification of nature, space, time and place.

Free trade critique is thus fueled by a potent combination of populist and ecological resistance, in the name of an alternative, more socially and ecologically responsible economics. It is unclear just what this is, since it is still defined primarily by what it is not. But despite the heady rhetoric of "global competition," the days of market absolutism are numbered and people shocked by jobless wastelands, gutted programs and disappearing dolphins will pull out Schumacher again, the old Gandhian essays, about "two million villages" and "Buddhist economics."[24] along with ecological theory, small-scale development theory affirms the context of place, of nature-place-group, of local ways, local production, in ways that the atomic individualism of market theory does not. Along with social democratic theory, it sees a role for community and government in ways that *laissez faire* market theory does not. Along with anarchist theory, it respects the old peasants in ways that peasant-hating Marxism does not. Actually it respects the old peasants in ways that both Marxist and modernization theory (which are inverted forms of each other) do not. As development theories go, free-tradism is just warmed-over modernization theory, re-hashed Rostow, with the same old fantasy of endless growth through freer trade. Is the Hong Kong model really the solution to the world's problems? What is the fate of the Amazonian rainforest and the Newfoundland outport within this model? It is as if nothing has happened in development theory in the last 30 years.

Ironically, as the 21st century approaches, "utopian" Schumanomics turn out to have more staying power than "hard-nosed" Reaganomics and "realist"

It makes sense to protect the neighbourhood. It is not misguided to think that local and national governments are still good tools for that.

Thatcheromics, which are imploding everywhere. Clintonomics is a backlash of place, for local benefits, investment, growth. There are no easy solutions to structural decline, imploding Keynesianism and four trillion dollar debts. But that is what Robert Reich's emphasis on "grassroots economics" and "immobile assets" is about: a new resistance to placeless logic by a logic of place, to placeless economics by what Schumacher called "economics as if people mattered."

As it turns out, free trade has a negative-feedback-loop. The globalization steamroller squashes things flat, from Ontario jobs to Saskatchewan farms, from Pacific dolphins to Malayan teak. And local costs of economic universalism point, along with those of political universalism, toward some compromise between the global and the local, commodities and people, future and past, experts and peasants, depressing intellectuals and the

old salts—some compromise between placeless logic and the logic of place, between the Hong Kong stock exchange and the Canton of Uri. A federalist economics?[25] The label is not important. But the idea is. It makes sense to protect the neighbourhood. It is not misguided to think that local and national governments are still good tools for that. It may be necessary to re-think what one can afford, and what one is entitled to. But a "level playing field with Mexico"? Must one become mere cannon fodder in the global war of capital, which takes no prisoners, wants as little government control as possible, and would be only too happy to have a high-tech version of 19th century wage slaves, policed by Gatt RoboCops?

Perhaps not. Nor are Quebeckers and Mohawks willing to give up the ghost. So one can look for a compromise, that gives one a say, through one's neighborhood in the bigger game, the political game, the economic game. Federalism and fair trade are ways of doing that, imperfect yes, but popular for self-respecting people who refuse to simply lie down and accept their modern fate within a universalizing script. The old peasants are back in the picture. The script is being questioned, changed, rewritten. And not least of all by Canadians, who sometimes worry about their place in history but who, it turns out, are actually out there in the global crisis doing world-historical things such as stopping people from scalping each other in Bosnia, resisting free trade threats to their social democratic state, and dealing with old group issues through new group schemes such as Nunavut. Like Schopenhauer's porcupines, Canadians seek out the middle ground: "On on a cold winter's day a group of porcupines squeezed very close to each other, using their mutual warmth to prevent death from cold. Soon, however, they felt each others quills, which once again made them draw apart from one another. But the need for warmth brought them together again, only for the problem to repeat itself, so that they found themselves driven to and fro between the two sufferings until they finally found an intermediate distance affording them the most comfort possible."[26]

Notes

1. Old peasants of Schwvz and Uri, Declaration of 1291, and Referendum of 1992. In the Referendum of Dec. 6, 1992, 16 of 23 Swiss Cantons said "No" to closer ties with the EEC. For an account of Swiss particularism, see Willi Geutschel, "Switzerland, for Example: 700 Years and Still Going Strong," in *Telos* (Summer 1991), pp. 155–186.

2. Camille Paglia, *Sexual Personae: Art and Decadence from Nefertiti to Emily Dickinson* (New York: Vintage, 1991).

3. See, for example, Paglia's review of Germaine Greer's book on menopause, in *People* magazine (Nov. 30, 1992).

4. The 1991 Cambodian Accord sent a nice message to the Khmer Rouge killing-field gang. "Don't worry, stick around, you're okay. Perhaps you can even take over again. After all, what is a million dead Enemies of the People? A Crime against Humanity? No, that's dead Jews. So don't worry, be happy." Who designed this accord? The Idi Amin Fan Club? Unfortunately dead Enemies of the People (unlike certain other dead groups) have no one to stand up for them. What Pol Pot needs is not a Peace Accord but a Wanted Poster.

5. Canada is the world's leading peace-keeper and the only country that has participated in every UN peace-keeping mission since the first one in 1947. With less than 1% of the world's population, Canada has been doing 10% of the world's peace-keeping and is currently involved in 13 such operations. One Canadian, (Sgt. Michael Ralph, a Newfoundlander), was recently killed in Bosnia, and another has written a popular song about the United Nations Protection Force (UNProFor), called "We are the UNProFor," about how "We go to countries/That are at war/And try to make their world/A better place/We leave our families/And so much more/And go to lands of atrocities/We work and sweat and even die/God I wonder/I wonder why...."

6. For example, see Rupert Taylor, "The Myth of Ethnic Division: Township Conflict on the Reef," in *Race and Class*, Vol. 33, No. 2 (1991), which defends "the idea of a unitary South Africa" against various federalist heresies.

7. *Telos* was one of the first journals to publicly ask the question "What happened in Quatro?" See Johnstone, *op. cit.*, p. 61. In October 1992 a commission of inquiry reported that prisoners in ANC camps were tortured and killed, and it denounced ANC officials for acts of brutality.

8. Heribert Adam and Kogila Moodley, *Democratizing Southern Africa: Challenges for Canadian Policy* (Ottawa: Canadian Institute for International Peace and Security, 1992), pp. 3, 10, 19 and 60. This report is hardly politically correct—especially when it describes anti-apartheid meetings in which a "bewildered Canadian church audience" suddenly found itself "in the middle of South African struggle antics," with readings supplied by the "Socialist Challenge Section of the Fourth International in the Canadian State," music by the "Euphonious Feminist Non-Performing Quintet" and Canadian Indians telling ANC leaders about the struggle of First Nations in Canada for ethnic homelands, group rights and separate development.

9. Paul Piccone, "The Crisis of Liberalism and the Emergence of Federal Populism," in *Telos 89* (Fall 1991), pp. 7–44.

10. Because liberalism is strong on individuals but weak on groups it is both strong and weak on the 1990s immigration crisis in the West. Liberal *federalism* has a role to play here precisely because it is strong on both. Neo-nazi violence shows the need for universalism and human rights. On the other hand, it is a mistake to treat populist resistance to immigration as merely an expression of racism, remediable by means of psychological counselling for misguided zombies. That presupposes that minorities have rights but majorities do not. The fact that many Canadians are not happy about Mounties wearing turbans is not just a question of racism. If it were, then Sikhs would have no right to ask non-Sikhs to take off their shoes in their temples. One cannot simultaneously affirm and deny cultural rights in an absolute way. One cannot demand the right to transform a host culture while denouncing its impact on one's own culture as "cultural imperialism" (like Toronto's black poets demanding that white poets not be allowed to write about "black matters"). Federalism is relevant here. For example, if Quebeckers feel less threatened by immigration than some other groups, it is partly because they have special immigration powers over the selection and settlement of immigrants—something which, interesting enough, is not controversial in Canada and is not considered racists. Neither is the fact that Swiss Cantons actually have a say concerning who becomes a Swiss citizen. The federalist logic deals with issues of cultural protection in ways that abstract universalism does not. On the other hand, as a compromise, it is not merely a logic of group.

11. This is why liberalism is ultimately (and ironically) a better means of achieving some left-anarchist values than anarchism itself, which naively thinks that anti-statism paves the way for freedom.

12. Piccone, *op. cit.*

13. On Renaissance Form and Italian Art, see Paglia's *Sexual Personae, op. cit.*, Chapter 5. In its contradictory messages, Donatello's David signals both the victory and the defeat of Renaissance humanism, the inescapable problems of the Great Escape.

14. For example, Trudeau's Chinese restaurant speech at *La Maison du Egg Roll* in Montreal just before the 1992 referendum helped to swing voters against the group-rights-oriented Accord. See *Maison du Egg Roll* speech, October 1, 1992, and Pierre Trudeau, "Trudeau Speaks Out," in *Maclean's* (Sept. 28, 1992). According to Richard Johnston's polling, Trudeau's Egg Roll speech knocked 20 points off the Yes vote outside Quebec, See *Globe and Mail* (Dec. 31, 1992).

15. Mordechai Richler, *Oh Canada! Oh Quebec!* (Toronto: Penguin, 1992). This is the book version of an article originally published in the *New Yorker*.

16. On the indirect, territorial solution, see Johnstone, *op. cit.*, pp. 61–2, and Piconne, *op. cit.*, p. 37.

17. The disintegration of the 74-year-old Czechoslovak Federation on January 1, 1993 is a clear warning to Quebec of how sovereignty-association fantasies can back-fire. In June 1992, Slovak voters gave their leader, Vladimir Meciar, a mandate to strike a better deal with Prague (just as Quebeckers may give such a mandate to Jacques Parizeau, leader

of the separatist Parti Quebecois, which may well win the next provincial election in Quebec). In a typically Quebec fashion, Meciar demanded full sovereignty, including a seat at the UN, but continuing $1 billion-a-year subsidies from the Czechs. The Czech reaction to this have-your-cake-and-eat-it idea was summed up by Ivan Tomek, an analyst at the Public Opinion Research Institute in Prague. "They want to go, f—k them. I am sorry to use such language, that's the way people are talking." Meciar had to choose between sovereignty or association. Yet 1992 polls showed that only 8 to 15% of Slovaks wanted independence, and that about 66 to 75% of Czechs and Slovaks wanted to remain in a common state. See Kitty McKinsey, "Nervous Slovaks Set to Ring in Independence," in *The Montreal Gazette* (Dec. 28, 1992). Appearances notwithstanding, the disintegration of the Czechoslovakian nation-state was not popular, nor would the disintegration of the Canadian nation-state be any more popular.

18. For example, in the October 1992 Referendum, Treaty Six Chiefs took out full page newspaper ads insisting on separate rights and separate development.

19. Mel Hurtig, *The Betrayal of Canada* (Toronto: Industry Stoddart, 2nd ed., 1992), pp. 22 and 56.

20. Conference Board of Canada, *Canadian Press* (Nov. 10, 1992).

21. See for example Jeffrey Brooke, *Breaking Faith: The Mulroney Legacy of Deceit, Destruction and Disunity* (Toronto: Key Porter Books, 1992).

22. On growing populist resistance to NAFTA, see Bob Davis, "U.S. Grassroots Coalition Unites Against NAFTA," in *The Wall Street Journal* (December 26, 1992). The Citizen Trade Campaign "includes not only traditional foes of free trade such as labor unions, and those wary of the pact such as environmentalists, but also a broad assortment of consumer groups, farm groups, foundations, animal rights activists, religious organizations and even the Rev. Jesse Jackson....Teamsters sit down with Greenpeace..."

23. In August 1991, a GATT panel ruled that a U.S. law protecting dolphins violated international trade agreements because it discriminated against tuna from Mexico. (Mexican nets, which snag dolphins with tuna, are now illegal in the U.S. but considered permissible by GATT). Under new GATT rules, foreign governments would have even more grounds for challenging U.S. environmental laws as restraint-on-trade.

24. E.F. Schumacher, *Small is Beautiful: Economics as if People Mattered* (New York: Harper, 1973). Federalism could also be defined as politics as if community mattered.

25. Because of the autonomous economic powers of Canadian provinces, which are currently resisting neo-conservative attempts to introduce "free trade," Canada already has a kind of federalist economics. These powers have enabled Quebec to chart a distinct course with some guaranteed benefits. Take beer for example. The reason there is such a thing as Newfoundland beer is because of federalist economics: to sell beer in Newfoundland, Canadian breweries have to brew it there. Free trade would mean the end of Newfoundland beer and, for that matter, it would also mean problems for American beer. Like Canadian provinces, American states wield all kinds of federalist economic powers (including hundreds of wine and beer regulations in over 40 states), which are

threatened by international trade agreements like NAFTA and GATT. See Penelope Lemov, "NAFTA, US States on Collision Course," in *Congressional Quarterly* (Dec. 1992). A 1992 GATT-panel ruling on beer imports threatens to invalidate regulations in many US states. See Bob Davis, *op. cit.*

26. As cited in Jean-Loup Amselle, "Tensions Within Culture," in *Social Dynamics,* Vol. 18, No. 1 (1992), pp. 42–65.

Terms & Concepts

ANC
apartheid
Archimedean point in human
  rights
cultural relativism
ethnic cleansing
ethnic homelands

fair trade
FTA
GATT
group rights
individual rights
laissez-faire
liberal federalism

NAFTA
placeless logic versus the logic of
  place
populist resistance
Schopenhauer's porcupines
tribalism
universal human rights

Questions

1. What are the two main dynamics of the contemporary world, according to Johnstone?

2. Does the porcupine metaphor accurately describe the Canadian condition? If so, in what respects? If not, what other metaphor is more apt?

3. One could argue against Johnstone that the universal human rights he asserts against the tribalist and fascist tendencies of localism are very much a part of the globalized homogenizing trends the logic of place rebels against. In other words, McWorld and McRights are aspects of the same problem. Does this criticism have merit? What are its implications if it does?

4. Do the people have a right to an undemocratic regime if they want? If so, do they not also have a right to a tyranny of the majority if they so desire? How can their desires be determined?

5. Johnstone applauds the Canadian balance or middle ground. Have Canadians moved away from this position since the article was published in 1992.

Unit Three Discussion Questions

1. You have just been appointed Minister of Immigration and Citizenship for Canada. You have reflected on the state of citizenship and democracy and Canada. What recommendations, if any, would you make to your cabinet colleagues on changes to immigration and citizenship rules? Why?

2. Federalism in many countries is about divided loyalties. Some argue that for this reason federalism is an inherently unstable form of government. Do you agree?

3. How does political ideology affect citizenship? How would David Frum, for example, differ with John Kenneth Galbraith on the rights and duties of citizenship? Does feminism have a unique contribution to make to the debate on citizenship?

4. What is required of citizens in order for democratic self-government to function, if not flourish? Should such requirements be encouraged or enforced?

Annotated Bibliography

Abu-Laban, Yasmeen. "The Politics of Race and Ethnicity: Multiculturalism as a Contested Arena." In *Canadian Politics, 2nd ed.*, edited by Bickerton, James P., and Gagnon, Alain-G. Peterborough: Broadview, 1994, 242–63. An examination of the career of the concept of multiculturalism in Canada.

Bissoondath, Neil. *Selling Illusions: The Cult of Multiculturalism in Canada*. Markham: Penguin, 1994. A provocative critique of Canadian multiculturalism and affirmative action.

Cairns, Alan C., and Cynthia Williams, eds. *Constitutionalism, Citizenship, and Society in Canada*. Toronto: University of Toronto Press, 1985. A widely read collection of essays by leading Canadian scholars.

Carmichael, Don, Tom Pocklington, and Greg Pyrz. *Democracy and Rights in Canada*. Toronto: Harcourt Brace Jovanovich, 1991. A collection of philosophical essays on ethical problems in democratic societies, including pornography, native self-government, and free speech.

Elshtain, Jean Bethke. *Democracy on Trial*. Concord, ON: Anansi, 1993. A fervent plea for the renewal of American civil society.

Etzioni, Amitai, ed. *Rights and the Common Good*. New York: St. Martin's Press, 1995. A comprehensive collection of essays by leading communitarian scholars, including Christopher Lasch, Benjamin Barber, and Mary Ann Glendon.

Havel, Vaclav. *Summer Meditations*. Translated by Paul Wilson. Toronto: Viking, 1992. A collection of essays on the political and spiritual dimensions of life after Communism by the dissident Czech playwright who became president, first, of Czechoslovakia, and then the Czech Republic.

Holmes, Stephen. *The Anatomy of Anti-Liberalism*. Cambridge, MA: Harvard University Press, 1993. A trenchant critique of communitarians and other critics of liberalism.

Kaplan, William, ed. *Belonging: The Meaning and Future of Canadian Citizenship*. Montreal & Kingston: McGill-Queen's University Press, 1993. A wide-ranging collection of essays by Canadian academics and social commentators.

Kymlicka, Will. *Recent Work in Citizenship Theory.* Ottawa: Multiculturalism and Citizenship Canada, 1992. An excellent review of the academic literature on the nature and meaning of citizenship.

Phillips, Derek L. *Looking Backward: A Critical Appraisal of Communitarian Thought.* Princeton: Princeton University Press, 1993. A critical examination of the historical evidence about "community," and its relevance and applicability to our era.

Phillips, Susan P. "New Social Movements in Canadian Politics: On Fighting and Starting Fires." In *Canadian Politics.* 2nd ed., edited by Bickerton, James P., and Gagnon, Alain-G. Peterborough: Broadview, 1994, 188–206. An introduction to feminist, environmental, and aboriginal rights movements in Canada.

Seidle, F. Leslie, ed. *Equity & Community: The Charter, Interest Advocacy and Representation.* Montreal: Institute for Research on Public Policy, 1993. A collection of essays exploring the effect of the Canadian Charter of Rights and Freedoms on political culture and the articulation of interests in Canadian society.

Taylor, Charles. *Reconciling the Solitudes: Essays on Canadian Federalism and Nationalism.* Montreal & Kingston; McGill-Queen's University Press, 1993. A collection of essays on national identity, Quebec, and Canada by one of Canada's most internationally renowned thinkers.

Young, Iris Marion. *Justice and the Politics of Difference.* Princeton: Princeton University Press, 1990. A critical examination of the relationship between universal citizenship and group differences based on gender, ethnicity, and race.

Unit Four

Institutions

◆ ◆ ◆

Our ideologies seem to be shifting markedly. We face startlingly different, and new, economic and political problems linked to global questions, such as climate. There is a renewed demand for public input into political processes, although, paradoxically, there is also a denigration of the role of politicians and of the state itself. Political institutions, which are not merely physical structures, but are in fact complex patterns of organized interaction, governed by rules and norms, are under siege at the same time as even more is demanded of them. Some people look for change and want reform, others tune out and dream of winning a lottery. Anger and dissatisfaction with our institutions seem widespread.

The articles in this unit all address the question of institutional reform, coming at it in very different ways. There are now deep divisions in many countries over what kind of institutions, or even what kind of constitution, should be in place. What rule systems and choice systems should be used? In Canada's case we see the attempt to combine majoritarian institutions, based upon British parliamentary practice, with the more "consensual" institutional needs of a federal system and, in addition, there is the question of how Quebec is to fit into the picture. Canada also has prime ministerial government, linked to cohesive parties, in contrast to the U.S. presidential/congressional model, which is always there as a reminder of an alter-

native available to us. There is often an optimistic faith that, by tinkering with our institutions, we can radically alter the way our political system operates and, in so doing, change our political culture. There is some evidence that attitudes *do* change as the state imposes new forms of social discipline on a population, as the rules and norms are altered, and as public debate is transformed.

Whatever system is created, the few will always govern the many, even though our constitutional fictions and electoral processes proclaim that the people are sovereign. Not even the introduction of referendums or other elements of direct democracy can get around the fact that representational issues are extremely complex. The article by Gibbins and Youngman illustrates this clearly. They review some of the key choices we face with regard to the actual mechanisms of electoral representation, and the paradoxes and prospects that ideas for reform create.

Political parties, sometimes referred to as "parapolitical" institutions, may be in serious decline or may be mutating, regrouping, becoming more compact and more aggressive. This raises the question as to where "traditional" left-right ideologies will fit into this new, more high-tech and populist partisan world, where spin doctors may reign supreme. There is no doubt that the voters are volatile. In a recent British by-election, of every 100 people who had voted Conservative at the last election, only 22 did so this

Photo courtesy of Canapress.

time—the biggest swing in a constituency in Britain since the Great Depression year of 1933. In Canada there is an extraordinary turnover rate in the House of Commons, demonstrated graphically by the results of the 1993 election.

The very significant differences in power between Canadian prime minister and American president have been starkly illustrated recently by the election of a Republican Congress, led by Newt Gingrich, which created serious difficulties for the president. Contrast this with Jean Chrétien's control over the House of Commons. The point is, our two systems are *institutionally* so different because they were set up to achieve different ends in the first place. In this section, Douglas Verney investigates Canada's unique case in more detail.

For the past 30 years the prevailing view in Canada would appear to have been that the constitution was in need of major surgery. Perhaps there is, of late, a return to the politics of constitutional conservatism; yet inertia is not acceptance, satisfaction, or pride.

Canadians, of course, compare their institutions to those in the United States, and there was a time when they viewed American institutions with almost complete disdain. Such a time could come again. However, there appear to be fewer reservations at the moment, even though the details of the actual operation of the U.S. system are not well known. (How many people realize that in the U.S. Senate, senators representing a population base of only 10% of the American population can block legislation?)

The media, key mechanisms for the transmission of political ideas and information, strongly affect how you feel about all of this. As is the case with all institutions, the media too are in transition. What is happening to the media will have extremely important consequences for the ways in which democracies operate, and there has been a spate of recent works on this subject.

Thus, each of the five articles in this unit reveal institutions under stress. Our rule systems are changing as organizations strive to adapt—but many institutions are, as we know, highly resistant to change, and institutionalized behaviour and culture are deeply rooted.

Incorporating Canada's Other Political Tradition

Douglas Verney

Editors' Note

Douglas Verney is a noted Canadian political scientist who teaches at York University. One of his best known works is an exhaustive examination of Canada's constitutional and political development entitled *Three Civilizations, Two Cultures, One State: Canada's Political Traditions.*[1] In this book he discusses, at length, the changing relationships between and among Britain, Canada, the province of Quebec, and the United States. He stresses the unique quality of our constitutional arrangements—both formal and informal—and how dependent their workings have been upon an acceptance of executive power.

In this short essay he deals with certain vital aspects of Canada's constitutional evolution. It is important to bear in mind that it was published in 1989, before the failure of the Meech Lake Accord and all that has happened since. Verney, in fact, assumed the Accord would pass and that there would therefore be new and important additions to our constitutional evolution. In retrospect, we know differently.

We seem to have arrived at a point in our political development when our federal/parliamentary state is being hounded from all sides, and our institutions and traditions may themselves be the cause of many of our difficulties. The Senate seems unacceptable as it stands but we cannot agree on a substitute, or on the representational principles upon which it should be based. The workings of the parliamentary system and party discipline, combined with the distorting effects of the electoral system, produce governments that seem unaccountable except once every four to five years. Many in the West are, as ever, in an angry mood, and Quebecers, even those among them who are federalists, think that Canadians have abandoned their belief in a bicultural compact. Taxpayers are in a state of near revolt, and Ottawa and the provinces are at loggerheads over economic and social policy.

It was not always so; Verney reminds us that once Canada seemed blessed with the best elements of the British and American models of governance. It was successfully federal *and* parliamentary and managed to avoid the kinds of problems that beset Britain (especially the Irish question) and the United States (a civil war and continuing violence). So what went wrong? Verney's answer is that "the federal principle" could only co-exist with the traditions of parliamentary government under

---

1. Douglas Verney, *Three Civilizations, Two Cultures, One State: Canada's Political Traditions* (Durham: Duke University Press, 1986).

certain conditions, and these conditions have ceased to exist. It is therefore important to note what these former conditions were, why they have ceased to function, and why we have not been able to create a satisfactory substitute.

What therefore makes this piece important, apart from its historical perspective and optimistic conclusion, is that it reflects an older assumption that what matters in Canada are institutions, and the executive power vested in those who lead them. The public's reaction to their exclusion from the constitutional debate, the rise of new political and economic forces, and an emphasis on rights and various forms of equality, mean that our institutional focus may have to change.

◆ ◆ ◆

I

◆ ◆ ◆

At one time Canada had the best of both worlds. It inherited the Westminster parliamentary tradition, but without the burden of a Buckingham Palace or a House of Lords. The substance of the British political system was transferred to Canada, but not its archaic forms, except for the wording of the British North America Act.[1] Like Britain, Canada after 1867 was governed by a Cabinet responsible primarily to a House of Commons under a two-party system of alternating majorities. It was the party with the majority that ruled.

Canada also tentatively entered another political world, the world of federalism. It adopted the distribution of powers between a federal government and a number of provincial governments. At the same time, it avoided such American doctrines as republicanism, popular sovereignty, the separation of powers, checks and balances, and limited government. Of all the American principles, federalism alone was extracted, and only one part of federalism, the distribution of powers. The other part, the veto exercised within federalized institutions, could not be adopted because the veto lay with the imperial authorities. Canada enjoyed strong cabinet government both at the centre and in the provinces. What some have called "interstate federalism" and I shall call "half federalism," the distribution of powers was tempered by the conventions of a Westminster-inspired constitution, by majority rule, not a veto.

The new Dominion enjoyed more than the parliamentary tradition inherited from the United Kingdom and the federal principle inspired by the United States.

Like both these countries it developed a two-party system. Canada managed to escape the violence that had marred the United States in the early 1860s and that was to engulf the United Kingdom when the Irish, like the Southerners, determined on secession. Unlike the Irish, the people of Quebec preferred to vote for MPs who belonged to the governing party. As a result, a wonderful Canadian system of double majority rule emerged. The English-speaking Canadians enjoyed majority rule in Ottawa and most of the provinces. Members of the French-speaking Roman Catholic minority were able to exercise majority rule in their province of Quebec.[2]

The remarkable polity which Canada pioneered came to be known as "parliamentary federalism." So successful was this system of government that it was copied elsewhere. Australia adopted parliamentary federalism in 1900 and India followed suit in 1950.

II

◆ ◆ ◆

If this novel political system was so successful, why have there been increasing demands in Canada for a change?

One popular explanation is that the desire for at least a modification of the British North American Act came about because of social and economic changes in Quebec. As the province grew politically more restive in the 1960s it looked for a time as if it might become another Ireland: but fortunately Montreal did not become another Belfast. Some of the more extreme separatists appear to have compared Quebec with Algeria, where the FLN helped to drive out the French *colons*. They hoped that the FLQ would drive out *les anglais*. To

Reprinted by permission from *Federalism and Political Community: Essays in Honour of Donald Smiley*, David P. Shugarman and Reg Whitaker, eds. (pp. 187–202), published by Broadview Press, 1989.

judge by the sales of Pierre Valliéres' popular account of francophone history, many *Québecois* shared his view that they were treated as *nègres blancs*.[3] Certainly it was in Quebec that discontent with the BNA Act first manifested itself.

The view that Canada's political problems can all be traced to Quebec, while plausible, deserves closer scrutiny. There was a constitutional crisis in Canada it is true (with violence in 1970), but in 1975 there were also constitutional crises in Australia and India, the other two systems that were parliamentary and federal.[4] These other crises cannot be attributed to Quebec.

At the very least, then, we should study the nature of parliamentary federalism more carefully. Perhaps it was not what it seemed to be, or perhaps it changed over time.[5] The Westminster tradition of majority rule had been under pressure in all these countries as a result of demands for a more federal system in which provinces and states could play an important role. There were also strains resulting from the shift in power from the United Kingdom to the United States, so that it was Washington's example rather than Westminster's that appealed to the younger generation.

In short, we need to examine the structure of parliamentary federalism, not just Quebec's dissatisfaction.

III

I have argued elsewhere that the Canada of 1867 ought not to be described in terms of parliamentary federalism. At that time, Canada was governed as a colony from London through a form of what I have called "imperial federalism."[6] This imperial federalism provided three umpires, one for each of the branches of government. The three imperial empires (in principle) had power to veto. For the executive there was the Colonial Secretary and British Governor-General; for the legislature, Parliament at Westminster; and for the judiciary, the Judicial Committee of the Privy Council. As the empire retreated, the umpires gradually disappeared. The paternal Governor-General went first between 1878 and 1931, then the Privy Council in 1933 and 1949, and finally the Westminster Parliament in 1931, 1949, and 1982. Canada thus remained half-federal, with the distribution of powers, but without the veto. The vacuum left by the imperial umpires was filled by Ottawa, but only in part.

Quebec was merely the first province to notice what was happening. Long before the Parti Québécois became

a force to be reckoned with, the Liberal government of Quebec under Jean Lesage, a former cabinet minister in Ottawa, set up an office of intergovernmental affairs. It did so in 1960, immediately after assuming power. Since then other provinces, and the Federal Government, have followed suit. The study of Canada's political traditions suggested to me that there might be a contradiction between parliamentary supremacy and federalism, the two partners in parliamentary federalism. More recently, in a paper delivered at Osgoode Hall Law School in 1987 I have asked whether, in view of the growing power of the Supreme Court of Canada, any compromise is possible between parliamentary supremacy and judicial review.[7] It is not necessary to review these arguments here.

IV

Instead, we may now take the argument a stage further. The controversy over Canadian federalism has tended to centre on the distribution of powers between the Federal Government (in Section 91 of the BNA Act) and the provincial governments in Section 92. But the distribution of powers is only half of what federalism is all about. In other words, when the umpires were withdrawn Canada was not federal, nor was it quasi-federal, to use K.C. Wheare's description. It was half-federal.

The other half of the federal principle involves the transformation of such institutions of the central government as the Senate into bodies that incorporate the federal principle. In his constitutional proposals, Mr. Trudeau resisted this notion, arguing that the Westminster tradition of parliamentary government precluded having the cabinet responsible to any body other than the House of Commons. (Despite this belief he felt able to adopt as his slogan "renewed federalism".[8])

We have long recognized just how wrong were those people who in 1867 thought that the problems of Canada's new federal structure would be resolved by a Senate representing each of the main regions of the country equally. The Senate was appointed, not elected, and its role as an institution representative of the regions did not develop. Canada was to be parliamentary, but not fully federal.

And so, without a powerful Senate, and without the imperial umpires, Canada has had to wrestle with the problem of incorporating its other political tradition, federalism. Senate reform is increasingly taken seriously, even by academic political scientists. What I shall call "legislative federalism" may well become an important topic of debate in the 1990s.

V

♦ ♦ ♦

Until recently Canadian scholars have been more interested in the executive's role in making federalism work. Over the decades, Canada has gone through a number of stages in its development towards a more federal system. The first stage was the type of executive federalism that Professor MacGregor Dawson and others described: a federalized cabinet. This I shall call, somewhat clumsily, *Federal Cabinet Executive Federalism.*

The first stage of executive federalism consisted of a federal cabinet that included men [sic] drawn from all the provinces. Dawson implied that it was the Canadian equivalent of the American Senate: executive rather than legislative federalism.[9] Dawson had no doubts as to where the responsibility of the cabinet lay. It was to the House of Commons alone. "One master is enough" he noted.[10] In Dawson's view Canada's parliamentary federalism had proved sufficiently adaptable to be able so to modify the Westminster tradition of parliamentary government as to match the American Senate by means of a federalized cabinet.[11]

Such was the theory, and for many Canadians it is assumed to have been the practice. Yet in recent years the practice seems to have fallen short of the ideal.[12] How was a Liberal Prime Minister to include in his cabinet MPs from all the provinces if a province (for example Alberta in the Trudeau era) stubbornly refused to elect a single Liberal to Parliament? And how was a Conservative Prime Minister like Joe Clark in 1979 to appoint an adequate number of Quebec ministers when Quebec still voted overwhelmingly Liberal?

Moreover, are we to assume that those MPs who were available were all of ministerial calibre? Could they seriously be compared to American Senators, those quasi-ambassadors from semi-sovereign states? Even those MPs who were of ministerial timber often had difficulty in protecting the interests of their provinces in cabinet. Here secrecy and collective responsibility were the rule. There was no veto. All that such ministers could do if they wished to register a protest was to resign. But when James Richardson of Manitoba and Jean Marchand of Quebec resigned, nothing happened. The federal juggernaut rumbled on.

Of course any federal cabinet *must* include persons from across Canada. So must the Canada Council and countless other national bodies. But they are not federal in the sense that representatives of the smaller provinces can exercise anything reasonably approaching a veto. Yet strangely enough, Dawson's notion of a Canada enjoying what I have called Federal Cabinet Executive Federalism, a federalized institution that was the Canadian counterpart of the American Senate, with its filibusters and vetoes, has not been repudiated.

VI

♦ ♦ ♦

The second stage in the development of a more federal system has been the "Executive Federalism" associated with Donald Smiley. To distinguish it from the Dawson variety I shall call it *First Ministers' Executive Federalism.* From now on it is to Professor Smiley's federal-provincial type that I refer. In this form of executive federalism the possibility of a veto by one or more provincial premiers emerged.

First Ministers' Executive Federalism developed gradually out of a dawning recognition that merely to distribute power between two orders of government was not enough, especially when the imperial umpires were withdrawn. These two sets of institutions, federal and provincial, had somehow to be linked together. From its beginnings in what was called "cooperative federalism" and "federal-provincial diplomacy," executive federalism developed into the full-blown televised First Ministers' Conference we know today.

Until the constitutional debates of 1981, individual First Ministers were widely thought to exercise a veto, at least by convention.[13] However, federalism depends on a legal framework, not on conventions about which governments may differ. The limitations of the First Ministers' Conference format became obvious in 1981 when agreement on the constitution was reached during a kitchen discussion in the middle of the night while the Quebec delegation was asleep. Yet it was at this point that the First Ministers' Conference was incorporated into the Constitution Act 1982 in some perverse Canadian version of one of Parkinson's laws.[14] The First Ministers' role was extended by the Meech Lake Accord of 1987—just as it was becoming clear that it was legislative, not executive, federalism that needed to be incorporated into the Constitution. Let us consider for a moment some of the features of legislative federalism:

1. an impartial Speaker
2. parliamentary rules of procedure to ensure fair treatment of all parties
3. a legislative agenda agreed to in advance by all parties
4. a parliamentary secretariat serving all members impartially
5. public and leisurely debate of all issues in accordance with the norms of liberal democracy

Compare this set of arrangements with the somewhat ad hoc procedure governing First Ministers' Conferences:

1. The Prime Minister is in charge, as in a cabinet meeting.
2. There are no parliamentary rules of debate. Having been opposed all morning by a majority of premiers in the 1981 discussion of the principle of a Charter of Rights and Freedoms, the Prime Minister simply adjourned the meeting for lunch and afterwards proceeded to a clause by clause discussion of his proposal.
3. The agenda is circulated by the Prime Minister to the First Ministers.
4. However, the agenda for these Conferences is prepared by the Federal Government's own Federal-Provincial Secretariat.
5. There *are* public sessions, before the TV cameras, but these are largely for prepared statements. Real debate takes place behind closed doors and often over lunch and dinner.
6. At a First Ministers' Conference, Quebec's premier, representing over a quarter of the country's population, is neatly transformed into one of eleven equal First Ministers. Behind closed doors, pressure can be brought to bear on the odd man out.

Such brief encounters (one is tempted to call this institution Brief Encounter Executive Federalism, or BEEF) allow none of the leisurely, public, and thorough debate that takes place in a legislature. Meetings frequently end inconclusively and in acrimony, sometimes postponed until after an election. One may well ask whether this really is the best way to run a country and to deal with such important and controversial issues as constitutional reform.

It is true that the relationship between the Prime Minister of Canada and the premier of Quebec has been far more cordial than that of their two illustrious predecessors. Even so, the Meech Lake Accord of 1987 was reached only during all-night bargaining, after which the First Ministers urged the constitutional bodies involved, the House of Commons, Senate, and provincial legisla-

tures, not to tamper with their handiwork. So delicate was the consensus that it seemed in danger of falling apart as a result of provincial elections in which a couple of the First Ministers were replaced. Clearly, this form of ad hoc executive federalism has considerable limitations, to put it mildly.

VII

♦ ♦ ♦

If neither Federal Cabinet Executive Federalism nor First Ministers' Executive Federalism can be regarded as a permanent solution to Canada's constitutional problems, we are forced to consider the obvious alternative: legislative federalism, where all the rules of parliamentary debates are observed. While in principle legislative federalism has its attractions, it also has its defects. It is unpopular in Ontario. Here the Westminster tradition of a government responsible solely to the lower house, and majority rule governed by the old Grit principle of rep. by pop. and no nonsense about a veto, is rightly cherished.[15]

Even if we discount the views of Ontario, which would be most unwise, legislative federalism presents a number of practical problems. These will have to be attended to once debate starts in earnest over the proposed "Triple-E" Senate, one that would be Equal, Elected, and Effective.[16]

The first "E," Equality, presents a very difficult problem. How is a province like Ontario to accept equality in the Senate with all the other provinces? Having had 24 senators of its own since Confederation (out of the present 104), it is not likely to give up its share without a struggle. It is true that the present Senate is a relatively powerless body, so that the number of senators is not all that important, but its replacement is a different matter altogether.

One alternative, which proponents of equal representation in the Senate might have to consider, is to argue that the present Senate should be abolished, not reformed. In its place they could recommend a new and improved institution, one based on the existing executive federalism. At First Ministers' Conferences the Ontario premier is accustomed to being simply one of eleven equal First Ministers. He appears to accept this arrangement. In other words, the problem of equality could be resolved by recommending the creation of a new body in terms of the present arrangements for First Ministers' Executive Federalism.

The Second "E" Elected, also presents a problem. How are First Ministers who have enjoyed such a powerful role in Federal-provincial relations to be persuaded to allow themselves to be replaced or upstaged by an American-style elected Senate? Surely there is a simple answer to this question: they will not permit it.

The only way of overcoming the opposition of the First Ministers to a rival elected upper house is once again to take as the model the First Ministers' Conference, not the present Senate. In other words, the premiers themselves would have to be allowed to head provincial delegations to the new body. It could be argued that as elected MLAs their presence would in a sense fulfil the demand for an elected body.

Of course it would not be practicable for First Ministers to be in constant attendance in the new body. They might be able to be present for important occasions, for example, the final stages of a constitutional debate, but day-to-day representation would be handled by a Minister of Intergovernmental Relations and his deputies—as at the United Nations and in the European Community. In other words, it would not be feasible to attempt to impose an American-style Senate on top of the First Ministers' Conference. Rather, this conference should be transformed into a permanent legislative body

---

Many Canadians are going to resist the notion of an effective upper house.

---

with many of the characteristics of a normal parliamentary institution.

Even so, other problems remain. What would be the role of the Prime Minister? Would he be excluded from the new body? And what would be the relationship of this new institution, a House of the Provinces, with the government of the day, which traditionally has been responsible only to the House of Commons?

This leads us to the third "E" of the Triple-E Senate proposal, its Effectiveness. It is difficult to see how the new House could be effective in a system accustomed to responsible government, that is, responsibility to the lower house. Dawson expressed views held by many people today when he said "One master is enough." It is difficult to envisage Canadians taking seriously an alternative to what we may call "lower-house parliamentarism." "Lower-house parliamentarism" has long been regarded by many Canadians, including Pierre Trudeau,

as the *only* form of government consistent with a parliamentary system. This is not so. In the United Kingdom itself, a unitary state, the upper house enjoyed a veto until the Parliament Act of 1911. In other parliamentary countries, for example Sweden, it was long taken for granted that government should come to terms with *two* houses of the Riksdag, one of which represented the provinces. In 1906 an anglophile Liberal prime minister boldly suggested that Sweden should adopt the British system of lower-house parliamentarism. This attracted the wrath of Swedish conservatives as being contrary to Sweden's political traditions. The Liberal government was defeated and the proposal was dropped.

Many Canadians are going to resist the notion of an effective upper house. Not only are most people, like Mr. Trudeau, imbued with what they perceive to be the Westminster tradition, but they do not appear to see the connection between the proposal for an effective upper house and the federal principle. To them, the distribution of powers (which I have called half-federalism) is enough. Had Canadians wanted full federalism, some might say, they would have introduced it long ago. However, we may have to qualify our statement. If it turns out that Canadians in the western provinces and Quebec want full federalism, the supporters of the present system may prove to be primarily Ontarians.

There are two sets of Canadians for whom the federal principle is not paramount. One group consists of conservatives. In England the conservative tradition has been so powerful that at no time has any form of federalism for Scotland, Ireland, and Wales ever been seriously considered.[17] Similarly in English Canada, the conservative tradition has been so strong that an appointed Senate has been tolerated for over 120 years. Few political scientists have written with passion against this non-elected institution.[18] Some describe it as innocuous. They rarely indicate that it conflicts with the federal principle and sustains the "representation by population" demanded by Ontario before Confederation and supposedly modified by the creation of the Senate.

In addition to conservatives there are social democrats who have little interest in an effective upper house.[19] Many would simply like the Senate to be abolished, for experience suggests that an effective upper house tends to be an obstacle to radical reform. Consequently, if a New Democratic government ever took power in Ottawa its programme might be rejected by the upper house, as in Australia in the 1970s.

People in Ontario are likely to be particularly concerned about any new body which provides representatives from other provinces with a veto. It is the conventional wisdom in Toronto that Confederation was introduced largely to overcome the deadlock (and the veto) that characterized government in the Province of Canada in the early 1860s. For Ontarians there would have to be emphasis on ways for overcoming the veto, for example through a joint vote of the two houses (as in Sweden between 1866 and 1970), or through a conference committee (as in the United States).

Supporters of full federalism, mindful of the capacity of the United States to survive Senate vetoes, may be tempted to argue that the veto is essential for an effective upper House of the Provinces. However we must never forget that Canada is different from the United States. For example, Canada has a disciplined party system which in the House of Commons and provincial legislatures manifests itself in predictable parliamentary voting behaviour. It is possible that Canadian representatives in the new House would behave as individuals, like American senators, but equally possible that they would emulate the Australians, where bitter partisan battles occur in both houses.

On the other hand, suppose our model is not the existing upper house in the United States or Australia but our own first ministers' conference. Here the debate does not appear to be primarily partisan. Were legislative federalism in Canada to take the novel route of being the transformation of the present executive federalism into a permanent parliamentary body without the infusion of partisanship, the issue of the veto would become less intractable. The Meech Lake Accord already provides a veto for each province on a number of vital issues. It is true that observers like Eugene Forsey oppose these vetoes because they may result in stalemate.[20] On the other hand, the First Ministers who signed the Accord, the provinces that have ratified it, and a variety of observers from *The Globe and Mail* to Professor Peter Hogg think it might work.

Once again, therefore, if we think of the Triple-E proposals in terms not of a reformed Senate but of a new, improved, and transformed First Minsters Executive Federalism, it becomes less problematic.

VIII

◆ ◆ ◆

Whether legislative federalism will be incorporated into Canada's parliamentary tradition depends very much on whether the present executive federalism, in either of its forms, is seen to be inadequate and needs to be replaced.

Many Canadians, and especially Ontarians, will take a lot of convincing before they conclude that what they have been enjoying is only half-federalism, and that full federalism is preferable. They may not be upset to learn that what they have had up to now has been the distrib-

---

...many people fear that present trends are balkanizing Canada.

---

ution of powers but not the federalization of central institutions. Federal Cabinet Executive Federalism and First Ministers' Executive Federalism have yet to be perceived for what they are: stages in the development towards a more federal system, in which legislative federalism will play an important role.[21]

Indeed, many people fear that present trends are balkanizing Canada. They do not want more federalism. They still have to be persuaded that the replacement of executive federalism by legislative federalism will bring back to a single centre (Ottawa) decisions which increasingly have been made by First Ministers in eleven different capitals.

The title of this paper is "The incorporation of Canada's other political tradition." During the 1960s and 1970s, the "other" political tradition to be incorporated was of course that of French-speaking Canadians. It is arguable that this tradition has not yet been perceived (at least in English-speaking Canada outside Ottawa) as being capable of being incorporated. Be that it may, it no longer makes sense to examine francophone Canada in isolation. The criticisms of the present system, which this paper has described as half-federal, have come from other parts of Canada as well.

Those of us who live in Ontario wonder whether the new Quebec-West axis which brought us Meech Lake and Free Trade is going to affect us adversely. Economically, of course, Ontario will remain the powerhouse of Canada. Politically, however, Ontario's dominance may be in decline. Confederation in 1867 was not intended to produce "rep. by pop." or majority rule. But in effect Confederation did give Ontario considerable clout. It is not for nothing that Toronto has been the bogeyman for so many people outside Ontario. Any reform of the Canadian political system will necessarily be in the direction of greater federalism and less emphasis on the majority rule which has allowed Ontario's MPs in the House of Commons to carry the most weight. Not surprisingly, Ontarian academics from George Grant onwards (he used to live in Ontario) have long been on the defensive with regard to the Canadian political system—and to its political economy.

Ontario's academics need to be just as concerned with their province's intellectual contribution to Canada as they are with its political economy. They have seen the ferment of ideas first in Quebec and more recently in the West (where Donald Smiley's formative years were spent). History should remember the city of Toronto not only for its interesting architecture and satisfying twentieth-century lifestyle but for its contribution to the political ideas that can inspire all Canadians. After all, the great cities from Athens onwards have been not only aesthetically pleasing but important symbols of the political vitality of Western civilization.

It would be a pity if Toronto a thousand years hence were to be viewed as a latterday Leptis Magna. That great city, it will be recalled, is admired not for its contribution to the political development of Rome but for its replication of Roman architecture. What remains of Leptis Magna are the ruins of a Roman city transplanted to Africa. As far as one can tell, its primary contribution was that of an outpost of empire. Until recently Toronto too was an outpost of empire: "Loyal She Remains."[22] Nowadays Toronto is the leading metropolis of a great and independent country about to embark on a new era in both its internal constitutional arrangements and its external economy.

It is no accident that we are witnessing today in Canada a transition from a parliamentary system of government which, though it was an imperial legacy with imperial umpires, gave Canada the best of both worlds, thanks to its North American federal features. The transition now is towards a new and equally distinctive Canadian political system, as novel a form of government as were the British and American systems in their formative years. If so, Canada may be entering the best of all possible worlds, with its legislative federalism as much as inspiration to others as parliamentary federalism was in the heyday of the Dominion.

Notes

1. The Constitution Act 1982, among other things, discarded the archaic language used in the British North America Act of 1867, except in its opening paragraphs addressed "To the Queen's Most Excellent Majesty: Most Gracious Sovereign..."
2. On 17 April 1886 the Quebec Legislative Assembly recalled Canada's experience and passed a unanimous resolution favouring Home Rule for Ireland. J.L. Hammond, *Gladstone and the Irish Nation* (Hamden, Conn.: Archon Books, 1964 reprint), 476n.
3. Pierre Valliéres, *White Niggers of America* (Toronto: McClelland and Stewart, 1971). Now largely forgotten in English-speaking Canada, this little book was a best-seller in Quebec. It was one of the few modern books on Canada in the Delhi University Library in 1984—there were multiple copies.
4. In June 1975 Mrs. Gandhi declared an Emergency and jailed a number of MPs, including the Opposition leaders. In November 1975 the Governor General of Australia, Sir John Kerr, dismissed the Prime Minister, Gough Whitlam.
5. Arend Lijphart has drawn attention to the changes in the "Westminster" system, arguing that in its traditional form it now exists only in New Zealand. Arend Lijphart, *Democracies: Patterns of Majoritarian and Consensus Government in Twenty-one Countries* (New Haven: Yale University Press, 1984), 16–20.
6. Douglas V. Verney, *Three Civilizations, Two Cultures, One State: Canada's Political Traditions* (Durham, NC: Duke University Press, 1986), Chapter 5, "The 'Reconciliation' of Parliamentary Supremacy and Federalism."

7. Douglas V. Verney, "Parliamentary Supremacy versus Judicial Review: Is a compromise possible?" *Journal of Commonwealth and Comparative Politics*, 27, 2, 1989, 29–44.

8. Pierre Elliott Trudeau, *A Time for Action: Toward the Renewal of Canadian Federalism* (Ottawa: Ministry of Supply and Services, 1978).

9. "The Cabinet has in fact taken over the allotted role of the Senate as the protector of the rights of the provinces and it has done an incomparably better job." R. MacGregor Dawson, *The Government of Canada* (revised edition, Toronto: University of Toronto Press, 1957) 211–12.

10. Dawson, *Government of Canada*, 209.

11. "Professor McKay has rightly called attention to the fact that today many Canadians expect the Senate to have some of the prestige and glamour of the House of Lords on the one hand and some of the power and importance of the United States Senate on the other..." Dawson, *Government of Canada*, 331.

12. "...until the St. Laurent era, cabinets contained an apparently adequate intrastate element in their operation." Donald V. Smiley and Ronald I. Watts, *Intrastate Federalism in Canada* (Toronto: University of Toronto Press, 1985), 6.

13. In his white paper *The Amendment of the Constitution of Canada* (Ottawa: Information Canada, 1965), the Minister of Justice, Guy Favreau, delineated four general principles:

    > The fourth general principle is that Canadian Parliament will not request an amendment directly affecting federal-provincial relationships without prior consultation and agreement with the provinces. This principle did not emerge as early as the others, but since 1907, and particularly since 1930, has gained increasing recognition and acceptance. The nature and degree of provincial participation in the amending process, however, have not lent themselves to easy definition.

14. C. Northcote Parkinson noted that an institution often acquires respectability just as it becomes obsolescent. Thus the North Atlantic Treaty Alliance moved into a permanent headquarters in Paris just before the French Government withdrew from the alliance. NATO had to relocate in Brussels. See *Parkinson's Law: and other Studies in Administration* (Boston: Houghton Mifflin, 1957).

15. Before 1867 the old Province of Canada consisted of two equal sections, Canada West (later Ontario) and Canada East (Quebec). After the 1851 census indicated that Canada West had become the more populous section, the Grits (or Liberals) in Canada West argued strongly in favour of representation by population. Confederation came about after a compromise which gave English-speaking Canadians majority rule in Ontario, the Maritime Provinces and the Dominion, and francophones majority rule in Quebec. The French-speaking Canadians had expected the Senate to temper the principle of majority rule at the Federal level. This did not happen. The principle of majority rule and "rep. by pop." has continued to have many adherents in Ontario to this day.

16. The "Triple-E Senate," a proposal sponsored by the premiers of Alberta and British Columbia, was inspired by a proposal of the Canada West Foundation entitled *Regional Representation: the Canadian Partnership* (Calgary: Canada West Foundation, 1981).

17. Notably in the *Report of the Royal Commission on the Constitution* (London: HMSO, Cmnd. 5450, 1973).

18. "Senate reform...has long since ceased to be the subject of serious consideration in political science." F.A. Kunz, *The Modern Senate of Canada 1925–1963: A Re-Appraisal* (Toronto: University of Toronto Press, 1965), 367.

19. As long ago as 1935 the League for Social Reconstruction recommended the abolition of the Senate.

20. "The fact is that we now have a Constitution so rigid, so hard to amend, that it will be the devil of a job to get anything new of any consequence into it, and the devil of a job getting anything old of any consequence out of it." *The Globe and Mail* (Toronto), March 17, 1987, A7.

21. In this paper I have dealt with only one of Canada's central institutions, the Senate and its possible replacement. Other central institutions requiring investigation are the Supreme Court, a parliamentary institution which, following the Meech Lake Accord, may become fully federal, and the office of the Governor-General. This office is still thought of in parliamentary and not federal terms.

22. *Loyal She Remains* (n.a.) (Toronto: United Empire Loyalist Association, 1984). Before the second world war, public school children in Ontario studied a geography textbook which described their country's proud role in the British Empire.

> The Empire extends from the farthest north to the farthest south, from farthest east to farthest west, girdling the globe with lands over which floats the Union Jack, proud symbol of power, of justice, and of freedom...Under the Union Jack live representatives of all the races of the world, from the lowest and most degraded savage to the finest types of the highest civilization.

Ontario Public School Geography (n.a.) (Toronto: W.J. Gage Nineteenth Edition, n.d.), 249.

Terms &
Concepts

British North America Act
Canada's "other" political tradition
collective responsibility
conventions
double majority rule
Federal Cabinet Executive
    Federalism
First Ministers' Executive
    Federalism

half-federalism
imperial authorities
imperial federalism
interstate federalism
judicial review
legislative federalism
lower-house parliamentarism
Meech Lake Accord
parliamentary federalism

popular sovereignty
quasi-federalism
republicanism
separation of powers
the federal principle
Triple-E Senate
Westminster tradition

Questions

1. What are the key features of "parliamentary federalism"?

2. Why is the absence of "Imperial Umpires," and the lack of a powerful Senate so central to the problems we now face?

3. What is "executive federalism"? Why has it been so important, and why is it not likely to be a permanent solution to our problems?

4. Why do you think that Verney was such an optimist about our ability to transform our "half-federal" system into something that worked better?

5. Is Verney still trapped by institutionalist assumptions about the way the system works?

The Grass is Always Greener: Prime Ministerial vs. Presidential Government

Jennifer Smith

Editors' Note

Political executives, particularly prime ministers and presidents, fascinate us. To study a prime minister or a president is to investigate power, personality, intrigue, policy, and a political system in action. It is to examine how a political race was run, how public confidence was won or lost, what happened at moments of crisis, and how history will judge those who have ruled us. It is the stuff of popular novels, extensive academic biographies, and journalistic exposés.

In this concise article Jennifer Smith focuses upon the very different legislative-executive relationships that exist in the Canadian parliamentary system and the United States' presidential system. It is no great surprise that, in spite of public interest in the subject of leadership, so little is known of the details of office and of the systems of government.

The media deal with personalities, not the overall system.

Canadian students, when asked who is the more powerful, a prime minister or a president, will usually pick the latter. As Smith points out, this may be due to the immense military power of the United States and to the president's foreign policy role. What such a superficial comparison does not do, however, is take into consideration the enormous constraints upon a president compared with the powers of a prime minister backed by a majority government.

It can be argued that what really constrains a Canadian prime minister is the power of the provinces. An American president certainly does not have to face the equivalent of a regular First Ministers' Conference with

state governors, nor does he have to deal with the equivalent of a Quebec—not even Texas fills these shoes! But he (and one day she) does have to deal with Congress, with its powerful lower house and an even more powerful Senate.

Smith emphasizes that, in terms of efficiency, the office of prime minister is "the clear winner." Note, however, her comments when we compare what she refers to as a more "democratic" standard. Canadians may pay a price for the ability to pass legislation that the government of the day deems desirable. Americans, on the other hand, will have to wait a long time for such things as a comprehensive approach to universal health care, if indeed agreement is ever reached on this matter. So they pay a price too.

INTRODUCTION

◆ ◆ ◆

The word *execute* is derived from the Latin *exsequor,* which means "follow out." And so the political executive is understood to follow out something, namely, the will of the legislators as expressed in the laws. This is stated clearly in the American constitution, which requires that the president take care to execute the laws faithfully. But there must be more to the executive than that, otherwise the American philosopher of pragmatism, George Dewey, was rightfully dismissive of the American exemplar of a chief executive. Interviewed on the point at the turn of the century, Dewey responded with disdain: "I am convinced that the office of the president is not such a very difficult one to fill, his duties being mainly to execute the laws of Congress."[1]

The American constitution supplies some clues about the more formidable side of the executive. For instance, the president is commander-in-chief of the army and navy, and of the militia of the states. Here we have the executive in armour, the military might of the entire nation at his disposal. Thus the modern executive is not merely the servant of the legislature but a powerful initiator of action in his own right.

It is instructive that in both cases—the executive as follower and the executive as initiator—mention is made of the legislature. The story of the modern executive in constitutional governments is largely about the executive-legislative relationship, and at bottom it revolves around the question of which is dominant. Obviously the answer will vary from one system of government to the next, but there are two main models: presidential and parliamentary. And there are two neighbouring countries—the United States and Canada respectively—which are leading examples of each.

Since the two models are so different, it might seem that to compare them is like comparing apples and oranges—not very fruitful, so to speak. Yet people do compare them in order to better understand them, indeed, often to determine which is the better, and endeavour normally inspired by a "grass is greener" sentiment and a pre-established standard of judgement. One of the most sensational examples in the history of political science is an essay published in 1884 by Woodrow Wilson, long before he became president of the United States. Wilson was troubled by the "clumsy misrule" of an overbearing Congress, and sought to make Congress more amenable to direction by the president. He thought he saw an answer in the parliamentary model, which often enables a prime minister and his cabinet to control the legislature.[2]

How ought we to compare the presidential apple and the prime ministerial orange? There are a number of possibilities, ranging from an historical account of the origins of the offices to a description of the way each functions today. In a short essay like this, the more direct approach is to begin with the obvious yet fundamental questions of political science. Who qualifies? How long? How chosen? What constitutional powers and limits? To simplify, we will consider these questions under the following headings: selection; term and removal; powers.

1) SELECTION

◆ ◆ ◆

The selection of a president and the selection of a prime minister are as different as night and day. In the case of the American president, the process is nightmarishly complicated and insufferably long. In the case of the Canadian prime minister, it is uncomplicated and short—although occasionally nasty and brutish. There are other differences. The American process is older; it is watched by the world; and it is governed by written rules. The Canadian event is watched only by Canadians, and there are almost no written rules. Let us give seniority its due and begin with the Americans.

For a non-American, the rules of selection outlined in the constitution seem to belong to another era, as indeed they do, and it is hard to see how they square with what actually transpires. Yet they still provide the constitutional framework of the selection process. The framers of the American constitution were not happy with the idea of the Congress electing the president, since that would make for a weak executive dependent upon the favour of the legislative branch. But they were just as troubled by the idea of direct election by the people, since that would mean another kind of dependence—dependence on the whim of popular opinion. Moreover, they doubted that voters would know enough about the candidates to be able to exercise good judgement in choosing among them. In the end, they hit upon the expedient of the Electoral College.

Reprinted by permission from *Canada and the United States: Differences that Count,* David Thomas, ed. (pp. 148–61), published by Broadview Press, 1993.

The Electoral College is basically a method of indirect election, and it is state-based. Each state's membership is equal to its share of senators and members of the House of Representatives. Voters in the states elect their Electoral College representatives, who in turn meet to elect a president and vice-president. The framers of the constitution thought that voters would choose politically knowledgeable electors who could be counted on to make better choices than the voters themselves. It was a sensible enough scheme that went awry with the development of political parties.

The ideal of independent electors quickly turned into the reality of partisan electors as political parties soon came to dominate the presidential selection process. Once electors became partisans who could be counted on to register their respective parties' choices, their role in the process no longer mattered. What does matter is the outcome of the vote in each state, particularly since a winner-take-all system is in effect. The winning candidate in a state almost always takes all of the state's Electoral College votes.[3] Thus presidential hopefuls normally face a two-phase process. The first is to gain the nomination of a political party, which today means the Republican Party or the Democratic Party. As Ross Perot's participation in the 1992 presidential election demonstrates, it is possible to run as an independent—but also very difficult to win that way. The second phase is the presidential campaign proper.

The race to gain the party's nomination is long, expensive, and arduous. It takes over a year and is marked by a series of electoral contests, state by state. More than two-thirds of the states hold primaries, and the remainder hold caucus conventions.[4] The primaries and the caucus conventions serve two functions, one of which is to choose delegates to the national convention that each party holds in the summer months before the November election. At the national convention, delegates choose the party's presidential and vice-presidential candidates, but since most of them are committed, the outcome in recent years has been predictable. This points to the real function of the primary and caucus contests, which is to test the field of candidates.

At the beginning of the "presidential sweepstakes," the field of candidates tends to be large, since the main criteria for entry are skill at fundraising and overweening ambition, more or less in that order. Money—lots of it—is an absolute *sine qua non*, since American campaigns rely heavily on media advertising. There is matching public financing available to candidates—the government will match individuals' contributions up to a limit of $250—but if they decide to accept it, they must follow spending limitations. In 1992 the spending limit for the nomination phase was $33 million.[5]

Prospective candidates work hard to win the early contests because, as the saying goes, money follows power. The losers tend to drop out, and as the contests draw to a close, a winner emerges. Technically, the winner has accumulated a majority of committed delegates, which is why the choice of the party convention is normally a foregone conclusion. Once the parties have nominated their presidential and vice-presidential candidates at the conventions, the second phase of the campaign opens, and the contenders face one another in the general election. Public financing is available again, a flat amount with no matching requirements. In 1992 it was $55.2 million for each of the major party candidates. Other candidates for president qualify if they receive at least 5% of the vote and do not spend more than $50,000 of their own money on the campaign. However, if they turn down public financing, there is no limit on the amount of money that they can raise and spend. This was precisely the option chosen by the independent candidate, Ross Perot, who spent a staggering $60 million of his own money on his 1992 campaign.[6]

It is worth pausing to consider the implications of the primary, which is a unique American institution. Primaries vary in kind from state to state, but essentially they are open electoral contests. They test the candidates' popular appeal among registered voters of the party, not just the party notables. As a result, they encourage "outsiders," candidates whose main assets are financial and organizational, not long years of faithful party service. Moreover, because the primaries are so closely watched, they also favour candidates who play well to the world's most sophisticated media. The incumbent president, Bill Clinton, is a good example of a long-shot candidate with the right stuff. When the race began, he was a little-known governor of an obscure state, certainly not a Washington insider or a Democrat with national experience and a national profile. But he had a strong organization and demonstrated skill in communicating to voters through the media. As president, of course, he is learning on the job, which is another way of saying that the selection process is no guarantee of quality in office.

The fact that the primary system is so wide open to prospective candidates points to a significant difference between the American and Canadian systems. Whatever else it is, the Canadian route to the prime ministership is still very much a party process dominated by party notables and party activists. As in the American case, the nomination phase is capped by a party leadership convention, but en route to it there is nothing like a primary system in operation. Instead, delegate-selection meetings are held in each riding, a riding being the Canadian equivalent of a congressional district. The meetings are open to party members only, and the purpose is to select a slate of delegates to the convention. For the most part these delegates are committed to a particular candidate.

Skirmishes among the candidates and their supporters at the riding meetings are not unknown. Organizers work hard to get their supporters out, some of them newly minted partisans, and unregulated amounts of money are spent to this end. However, in the Canadian case the amounts are in the range of thousands of dollars, not millions of dollars. Setting aside transportation and organization costs, there is little to spend money on at the riding meetings, and not much time to spend it in, since this phase of the process is completed within two or three months. Moveover, in addition to riding delegates, there are a significant number of *ex officio* delegates who attend the leadership conventions of the national parties. Generally speaking, they include party officials, all former and serving elected representatives at both levels of government, and senators. The New Democratic Party sets aside a share of delegate seats for union representatives.

The divergence between the two systems widens at the convention itself, for often there is nothing predictable about the Canadian event at all, one reason being the significant number of *ex officio* delegates, many of whom are uncommitted. The decision-making rules at the convention require the lowest candidate after each ballot to drop off, and balloting continues until one of the candidates gains a majority of the votes cast. Finally, and again in contrast to the American system, at the conclusion there are two prizes—the party leadership *and* an obedient party. For the party in power—the governing party—there is an additional prize: the office of prime minister.

This last point was demonstrated by the 1993 leadership convention of the federal Progressive Conservative party. Prime Minister Brian Mulroney indicated his intention not to run again early in the year, an announcement that immediately set the stage for a convention to choose his successor. In accordance with the unwritten rules of parliamentary government, Governor General Raymon Hnatshyn, the vice-regal substitute for the Queen of Canada, appointed the new Conservative leader chosen at the party convention, Kim Campbell, to be the monarch's chief counsellor, and asked her to form a government, that is, to name a new cabinet. Canadians had an opportunity to decide the fate of the new prime minister some months later; she and her party went down to a crushing defeat, and the Liberals under Jean Chretien then formed a new majority government.

2) TERM AND REMOVAL

◆ ◆ ◆

For Americans, the constitution issues some clear guidelines on the term of office and the removal of a president. Looking to fix the president's term differently from those of members of Congress,[7] the framers decided on four years. Initially this was accompanied by unlimited re-eligibility, and then an understanding, based on the precedent set by the first president, George Washington, that an incumbent would seek to serve no more than two terms. The precedent held until Franklin Roosevelt won re-election to a third (1940) and then a fourth term (1944), arguing wartime exigencies. An unhappy Republican Congress passed a constitutional amendment imposing a two-term limitation, and the twenty-second amendment was ratified in 1951.

To impeach an official means to bring charges against him in what amounts to a political trial. The eighteenth century was the heyday of impeachment trials in England, so it is understandable that the framers would turn to the practice for a method of early removal from office. It is applicable to the president, vice-president, and civil officers of the United States, and the grounds are "Treason, Bribery, or other high Crimes and Misdemeanors." Congress does the impeaching. The House of Representatives is empowered to decide whether to proceed against an individual, and should it so decide, the trial is prosecuted before the Senate, where a conviction requires a vote of two-thirds of the members present.

The constitutional provisions on impeachment have an antique ring to them, and in the case of a president have been triggered only once, when the House of Representatives voted to impeach Andrew Johnson, who had assumed the presidency when Abraham Lincoln was assassinated. Johnson, a recalcitrant southerner from the point of view of the northern-dominated "Radical Congress," escaped impeachment in the Senate by exactly one vote. In our century, Richard Nixon skated rather close to an impeachment in the wake of the Watergate scandal, since the House Judiciary Committee began work on impeachment proceedings. However, Nixon resigned before anything could come of them.[8]

The Twenty-Fifth Amendment, ratified in 1967, establishes rules governing the succession in the event of presidential death, resignation or disability. Essentially the vice-president assumes the office, which is the major purpose of the position of vice-president. The tricky part of the amendment is the determination of presidential disability, particularly if there is disagreement among the principals themselves. The rules are cumbersome, and seem to have been neglected altogether in the confusion

---

Where the Americans rely on written rules, the Canadians rely largely on unwritten ones, and the result is a startling contrast.

---

immediately following the attempted assassination of President Reagan in 1981. Secretary of State Haig thought he was in charge and said so in a White House press conference, a claim dismissed by others in the administration. In the end, with the president recovering nicely in hospital from the gunshot wound, the rules of the Twenty-Fifth were never invoked.

Where the Americans rely on written rules, the Canadians rely largely on unwritten ones, and the result is a startling contrast. What prime ministerial term? The only applicable written rule stipulates that no House of Commons shall continue longer than five years, which fixes the outer boundary of a government's term. But a prime minister can call an election anytime within the five years. At least he can if he is in control. The other side of the equation is the House of Commons, and it is important to remember that in parliamentary systems, a prime minister and his government must have the confidence of the chamber, that is, the support of a majority of the members. If the prime minister's party forms the majority, which is often the case, there is no problem of confidence. The practice of party discipline ensures majority support. However, if his party is in a minority, he needs the support of members of other parties, which renders his position and that of his government less secure.

On the question of removal, guiding precedents are lacking and legal rules are non-existent. In Canada, no sitting prime minister has been forced openly by his party to resign. It could happen, of course, but probably only if the senior ministers resigned en masse in order to force the issue. Prime Minister Mulroney's decision not to lead his party in a third general election illustrates the usual practice followed when a prime minister becomes

an electoral liability—in the party's eyes if not his own. He decides to leave, possibly after some encouragement, and the party gets an opportunity to choose a successor who, it is hoped, will lead the troops to another election victory.

3) POWERS

On the question of powers, the contrast between the two executives deepens. In the American case, the applicable constitutional provisions are brief but certainly clear. Article II, which is devoted to the office and powers of the president, opens by vesting executive power in him. What this might mean is amplified later in the article, when the president is named Commander-in-Chief of the army and navy, and of the militia of the constituent states. He is assigned a power to make treaties, and to appoint ambassadors, senior officers of government, and Supreme Court judges, but only with the agreement of the Senate. He is empowered to receive ambassadors and officials from other countries.

In addition to these war and foreign policy powers, there are important domestic powers. The president heads the "executive Departments" (the public service) because he is empowered to appoint (with the agreement of the Senate), remove, and supervise senior officials. He appoints federal judges, again with the Senate's agreement. And in the elegant eighteenth-century prose characteristic of the constitution, he is required to "take Care that the Laws be faithfully executed." He also has a power to grant pardons to individuals convicted of offences. On the legislative front, he is assigned the duty of addressing the Congress on the state of the union and recommending to it legislative measures that he finds necessary. Finally, his signature is required for bills to become law, which means that he has a veto power. The Congress can override the veto, but only by a two-thirds vote in each chamber.

A striking feature of the president's executive power is that the Congress manages to share in it, even in the foreign affairs field. Moreover, in Article I, which deals with the legislative branch, we find that Congress is assigned the power to declare war, as well as having the all-important taxing and spending powers. The upshot is that Congress and the president need to cooperate in some fashion in order to govern.

Few presidents can be said to have dominated Congress, even when, as in the case of the current president, their party has a majority of the seats in both houses. Still, most observers agree that in this century there has been a shift from a Congress-centred government to a president-centred government.[9] One reason is that Congress delegated significant legislative powers to the executive branch during the "New Deal" era of the 1930s, when President Franklin Roosevelt introduced major programmes to counteract the effects of the Great Depression. Another is the impressive array of management resources available to the modern president: the White House Staff; the Executive Office of the President, which includes permanent agencies like the National Security Council and the Office of Management and Budget; and the departments of cabinet.

It is worth pausing here to consider the American cabinet. It includes the heads of all the major federal government departments[10] who, as mentioned above, are appointed by the president with the agreement of the Senate. Although the word denotes a collective, in fact the cabinet is not a collective body because it does not make decisions collectively. Indeed, presidents are not much inclined to hold cabinet meetings. Nor is the cabinet responsible to the Congress, although its members individually appear before congressional committees to answer questions about their respective departments, just as they answer to the president. Occasionally presidents arrive in office determined to work a "cabinet government"—President Jimmy Carter is an example—but the effort has always come to nothing. Instead, presidents seem to end up relying on the advice of a small number of individuals, perhaps cabinet secretaries of key departments like the State Department and the Treasury Department, perhaps senior White House staffers.

By contrast, in Canada the cabinet, of which the prime minister is the leading member, is very much a collective. As a result, it is not possible to talk about the "powers of the prime minister" without reviewing cabinet government. To begin, the constitution vests executive power in the Queen of Canada, who is the head of state. She is represented by the Governor General when she is not here, and she rarely is. The "real" executive is the cabinet, on whose advice the Governor General always acts.[11] The cabinet is responsible to the House of Commons for the advice that it tenders to the Governor General. It is important to notice that the advice covers purely executive matters as well as legislative matters. For example, since cabinet members are usually heads of government departments, they oversee the administration of the laws. Thus they exercise purely executive powers. But they also hold seats in the Commons, which means that they participate in the legislative branch as well. Thus they advise the Crown on proposed laws, and

shepherd them through the House of Commons. The convention of party discipline, particularly when the cabinet's party is in the majority, permits the cabinet to dominate the legislature.

How does the prime minister fit into this picture? Since the written constitution is silent on the powers of the prime minister, it is essential to recall the selection process as described above. Asked by the Governor General to form a government because she[12] is the leader of the party with the most seats in the House of Commons—not necessarily a majority—the prime minister's first notable power is in evidence in the construction of a cabinet. She not only appoints ministers—almost always from among party colleagues elected to the House of Commons—she can dismiss them at any time and without offering any reasons for doing so. She is in charge of the organization of the cabinet and the agenda of the cabinet. She controls senior civil servant appointments, and appointments to central agencies. The latter include the Prime Minister's Office, the counterpart of the White House Staff, and the Privy Council Office, which assists the cabinet. The prime minister also monopolizes the considerable patronage available to the government, unlike an American president who, as noted earlier, must share so many senior appointments with the Senate.

The timing of elections is an especially important decision that the Canadian prime minister makes, subject to the five-year limitation noted earlier in the essay. Obviously, she will try to time the election to suit her party's prospects and her own. By contrast, an American president has to fight an election at a prescribed time, and it may not suit him at all. Consider the example of President Clinton's predecessor, George Bush. Between September 1990 and March 1991, polls recorded that approval rates of President Bush reached record highs, at one point over 90% of those polled. This was the period when the United States prosecuted the Gulf War against Iraq. Any prime minister in a comparable situation would want to take advantage of it by calling an election after an appropriate interval. President Bush had not such option. He watched his popularity sink from an all-time high in March, 1992, to a low in November, 1992, precisely when he had to fight the election.[13]

CONCLUSION

◆ ◆ ◆

At first glance the American presidency seems to be an immensely powerful office, a perception linked to the country's military and economic strength and fed by the omnipresent American media. On closer examination, it is evident that there are significant constraints on a president's powers. At bottom, these constraints arise out of the fact that the president faces institutional rivals whose political careers are not dependent on his. This is a result of the design of the American system of government, which is often described as one of separate branches (executive, legislative and judicial) with shared powers.

The framers of the constitution found many ways to separate the branches, some of which we have noted, like term of office and selection. Members of the House of Representatives, senators, and the president have different terms of office, and are elected by different constituencies. For a member of the House it is a congressional district, for a senator it is a state, and for the president, the nation. Even age requirements differ. For a representative it is twenty-five, for a senator it is thirty, and for a president, thirty-five. We might expect that political parties would hook these politicians together, and to some extent they do, but not in the fashion of parliamentary parties. And separateness is the reason. American representatives, senators, and candidates for president do not stand or fall together in electoral terms. Put another way, few presidents have "coat-tails" that congressional candidates can ride to office. Yet they share powers.

The constitutional fact of shared powers means that cooperation between the branches is required in order for the government to function. Power is diffused. The president needs to exercise powers of persuasion, not just over members from the opposing party, but sometimes over members from his own. A Canadian prime minister at the head of a majority party faces nothing remotely comparable to this so long as she takes care to keep her caucus united behind her. Power is centralized, not diffused. So it is easy to see why Woodrow Wilson, looking for ways to enhance the office of president in relation to the Congress, was tempted by the parliamentary model.

How should we judge these two offices? As always, it depends on the standard of judgement. Wilson's standard was executive effectiveness, and in that race the office of prime minister is the clear winner. But if we use a democratic standard that emphasizes openness and consultation, the office of president is the clear winner.

Notes

1. John Bartlett, *Familiar Quotations*, 12th ed. (Boston: Little, Brown and Company, 1951), p. 638.

2. Woodrow Wilson, "Committee or Cabinet Government?" in Ray Stannard Baker and William E. Dodd, eds., *The Public Papers of Woodrow Wilson: College and State*, Vol. 1 (New York and London: Harper and Brothers, 1925), p. 128. See also Wilson's famous book, *Congressional Government: A Study in American Politics* (Boston and New York: Houghton Mifflin Company, 1885 and 1913).

3. It is up to the states to decide how their electors are chosen, and the general practice is a state-wide system. In other words, in each state the party chooses a slate of electors who are committed to the party's presidential and vice-presidential candidates. Occasionally states have devised systems allowing for a split vote, which Maine did in 1972 by requiring that electors be chosen by congressional district. That year the Republicans carried the districts and therefore the whole of the state's electoral votes anyway. Electors still meet in their respective state capitals about six weeks after the election to cast their votes formally. At this stage, there is always the possibility of the "faithless" elector. This occurred in the 1976 presidential election, when a Washington state elector pledged to Gerald Ford, the Republican party's candidate for president, voted instead for Ronald Reagan.

4. The caucus convention is a traditional method of choosing delegates to a party's national convention, and it is simply a meeting of party members, usually at the county level, to choose delegates to a state convention, who in turn will select delegates to the national convention. The states which use it hold open party caucuses at the local level, that is, caucuses open to registered party voters who wish to attend. The widely watched "Iowa caucuses", which come early in the schedule of primaries and caucuses, are an example of the genre. For a fuller discussion see Theodore J. Lowi and Benjamin Ginsberg, *American Government: Freedom and Power*, 2nd ed. (New York and London: W.W. Norton & Company, 1993), pp. 527–32.

5. Susan Welch, John Gruhl, Michael Steinman, John Comer, *Understanding American Government*, 2nd. ed. (Minneapolis/St. Paul: West Publishing Company, 1993), p. 247.

6. *Ibid.*, p. 247. The amount of public financing available to presidential candidates is only a portion of the amount spent during the presidential campaign. This is because there is no limit on the amount of money that individuals and organizations, particularly the PACs (political action committees), can spend independently in support of particular candidates. The 1988 presidential campaign is estimated to have cost $500 million. Estimates of the 1992 campaign are not available, although the figure is expected to be higher again. By comparison, in the 1988 general election in Canada, the political parties and eligible independent candidates received just under $20 million in public financing. Independent spending on advertising by individuals, business and labour organizations is estimated to have been $4.7 million. For figures in the Canadian case, see the Report of the Royal Commission on Electoral Reform and Party Financing, *Reforming Electoral Democracy*, Vol. 1 (Minister of Supply and Services Canada, 1991), p. 337, 371.

7. The Congress is the Senate and the House of Representatives. The phrase "member of Congress" is confusing because it might refer to a senator or a member of the House.

8. The phrase, "civil officers", includes federal judges, including judges of the Supreme Court, and cabinet officers. It excludes members of Congress and military and naval officers. Only one Supreme Court justice has been the subject of impeachment proceedings. Samuel Chase was the target of the victorious Jeffersonians in 1894, but they failed to get a conviction against him in the Senate. For a full discussion of impeachment see Raoul Berger, *Impeachment: The Constitutional Problems* (Cambridge: Harvard University Press, 1973).

9. Theodore J. Lowi and Benjamin Ginsberg, *American Government: Freedom and Power*, 2nd ed. (New York: W.W. Norton & Company, 1993), pp. 247–309.

10. There are fourteen departments, listed here in order of their establishment: State (1789); Treasury (1789); Defense (1789); Interior (1849); Agriculture (1862); Justice (1870); Commerce (1903); Labor (1913); Health and Human Services (1953); Housing and Urban Development (1965); Transportation (1966); Energy (1977); Education (1979); Veterans Affairs (1989).

11. The issue of the Governor General's "prerogative" is debated occasionally, and essentially revolves about the question of whether he has any

prerogative power left, that is, an independent sphere of power not taken over and regulated by Parliament. Most observers say no, but Canada's late, great constitutional expert, Senator Eugene Forsey, vigorously refuted the "rubber stamp theory of the Crown". See "Crown and Cabinet" in his *Freedom and Order: Collected Essays* (Toronto: McClelland and Stewart Limited, 1974), pp. 21–72.

12. Given the gender of Canada's last prime minister, Kim Campbell, the pronoun "she" is used in the remainder of the essay.

13. Lowi & Ginsberg, pp. 306–7.

Terms & Concepts

Article II	diffusion of power	impeachment
caucus conventions	Electoral College	initiator
"coat-tails"	ex-officio delegates	primaries
collective responsibility	fixed terms	unwritten rules
confidence	follower	

Questions

1. What are the key differences between the Canadian and American cabinets?

2. Is the American system more "democratic"?

3. What aspects of the executive-legislative relationship seem to make the office of prime minister more powerful than that of his or her American counterpart?

4. What reforms suggested over the past few years would move Canada far closer to the American model? Are there forces at work that seem to be pushing us toward a more American-style system?

5. How are the powers of each executive linked to the operations of the party system? Why does the current situation in both countries provide a graphic illustration of this?

The Institutional Expression of Multiple Identities: The Electoral Reform Debate

Roger Gibbins and Loleen Youngman

Editors' Note

Most Canadians take their electoral system for granted. They have an intuitive sense of how it operates but are only vaguely aware of its particular virtues and vices.

While the debate on institutional reform has become a veritable national sport in Canada in the last 15 years, the electoral system has not been one of the footballs to be kicked around. Politicians and royal commissions have preferred to tinker with the current system. Obviously, the beneficiaries of the current system—the people who are elected— have no incentive to change the rules. And populists have sought to remove political power from representatives altogether in the name of direct democracy.

As Roger Gibbins and Loleen Youngman of the University of Calgary point out, there are new forces that may cause Canadians to take a fresh look at electoral reform. Among these is the burgeoning consciousness of ethnic, racial, and gender diversity. Increasingly, groups defined by demographic or non-territorial characteristics (rather than territory or province) consider legislative assemblies illegitimate if they do not "mirror" the demographic composition of the population as a whole. This view implies that non-Aboriginals, for example, cannot represent or speak for Aboriginals. Therefore, Parliament must have Aboriginal MPs, or in the alternative, Aboriginal peoples must be represented in some other institutional context.

"Mirror representation" has obvious common sense and political appeal. There are, however, also some problems. How do we prevent an endless proliferation of demands for group representation? How do we know that a representative from a certain group will indeed know and act on the wishes of that group? Is it desirable to assume that only Aboriginals can represent Aboriginals, or women only women? Will this cause people to refuse even to try to understand others? Underlying the complex and at times tedious debate about the details of electoral reform are some fundamental questions about representation, citizenship, and the recognition of diversity in a political community.

◆ ◆ ◆

Federal states such as Canada have always provided some measure of institutional expression for the multiple identities that individuals bring to political life. More specifically, the electoral system has given voters the opportunity to highlight different aspects of their political personality by participating in local, provincial, and national elections. However, the capacity of the Canadian electoral system to permit full expression of multiple identities is constrained in three important ways. First, electoral constituencies are defined by geography; there are no constituencies that group voters by gender, ethnicity, language, or other demographic characteristics. In this respect, territorial identifications have an institutional trump over all others. Second, because only a single representative is elected in any given constituency, that representative is inherently limited in mirroring the multitude of political identities for which his or her constituents seek expression. Finally, the ballot itself precludes any complexity of expression. While voters may bring a complex host of identities and interests into the voting booth, in the final analysis all of these must be expressed through a single X, printed with a blunt pencil on a piece of paper.

These constraints would not be particularly problematic if voters were concerned only about bringing territorial identities into play in the electoral process. After all, those identities are already brought into bold relief by the territorial construction of constituencies and, thus the final act of compression through the ballot only adds further emphasis to territoriality. However, one of the more striking features of the contemporary scene is the emergence of new forms of political identities that lack territorial definition. As individuals increasingly seek institutional representation for gendered and ethnic identifications, and indeed for political identities expressed through such new social movements as environmentalism and feminism, the existing electoral system seems increasingly restrictive. Territorial constituencies, single-member representation, and a simple X no longer capture the complexity of multiple political identities in a rapidly changing world. Hence the electoral reform debate re-emerges as a matter for serious political debate.

In the following discussion we examine the history and evolution of the electoral reform debate in Canada. Here the discussion will show that even though the electoral system was designed along territorial lines, major failures in territorial representation sparked the first significant calls for electoral reform. We will then explore how the electoral reform debate expanded in recent years to include a new set of representational concerns. Most of this article will address a number of reform alternatives. We conclude with a review of the discussion on institutional expression of multiple political identities, and the role that electoral reform might play in that expression.

THE EVOLUTION OF
THE ELECTORAL REFORM DEBATE

◆ ◆

The fundamentals for the first round of the electoral reform debate were put into place by Professor Alan Cairns. Writing in 1969, Cairns argued that Canada's first-past-the-post, single-member plurality system dis-

Article prepared for this publication (1994).

torts the translation of votes into seats in a number of important ways.[1] First, it tended to over-reward the party winning the largest share of the popular vote and, thus, inflated parliamentary majorities in the House. Second, it tends to penalize minor parties with diffuse national support. Here the primary example has been the CCF/NDP and its persistent failure to win a share of seats commensurate with its share of the popular vote. Third, the system tended to over-reward parties with concentrated regional support; the primary historical example is provided by the Social Credit party whose Alberta base between 1935 and 1957 consistently generated more seats than one would expect from the party's share of the popular vote. Fourth, and most relevant to the present analysis, Cairns argued that the major parties were more broadly reflective of the national electorate with respect to their popular vote than they were with respect to the regional distribution of their seats in the House of Commons. Simply put, when the electoral system translates votes into seats it inadvertently produces regionalized parliamentary parties and, therefore, regionalized national governments. The electoral system, thus, worked to fragment rather than integrate the national party system and political community.

Cairns' critique of the electoral system gained strength over the next 15 years. In western Canada, the Liberals won a reasonable share of the popular vote but were unable to convert that vote into a proportionate number of elected MPs. Across the four general elections held from 1972 to 1980, they received 25.6 percent of the regional popular vote but came away with only 8.6 percent of the western Canadian seats in the House of Commons.[2] The Liberal nadir came in 1980 when the party won a majority government but in the process captured only two seats (2.6 percent) in western Canada with 23.4 percent of the regional vote.[3] Throughout the time when the Liberals were struggling for a reasonable seat return in the West, the Conservatives were struggling with the same lack of success in Quebec where, in the four general elections from 1972 to 1980, the party averaged only two seats (2.7 percent) while receiving on average 16.2 percent of the provincial popular vote.[4]

Neither Quebec nor the West, it should be stressed, suffered any loss of representation in the House itself, for proportional representation was guaranteed by the formula used to determine the provincial distribution of seats. The problem was that the electoral system did not ensure adequate regional representation within the winning party, *and thus within the government of the day.* Proposals for electoral reform, therefore, sought to ensure that national parties would have elected members from across the country even in those circumstances where the first-past-the-post system would not yield such results. They generally incorporated some form of proportional representation, usually tacked on to conventional single-member districts, to guarantee that a party forming the national government would never lack elected representation from across the country.[5]

In short, the electoral system was to be reformed to guarantee what the parties themselves apparently could not guarantee—broadly representative government. When, in the absence of reform, the Progressive Conservatives provided just such a government in 1984 and again in 1988, electoral reform disappeared as a matter of public interest and debate. For nine years Canadians had a national government with significant caucus and cabinet representation from every region of the country. Then, the 1993 federal election reopened the reform debate for many Canadians by illustrating once more how the electoral system can distort the translation of party shares of the popular vote into seats in the House. The most dramatic evidence was provided by the Progressive Conservatives, who captured 16.0 percent of the national popular vote but won only two seats (0.7 percent) in the House of Commons. The distortions, however, were not limited to the Tory debacle. The NDP won 6.9 percent of the national popular vote, but only nine (3.1 percent) seats. In Quebec, the sovereigntist voice of the Bloc Québécois was amplified by the electoral system when 49.2 percent of the vote garnered 72.0 percent of the provincial seats for the Bloc, enough seats for the Bloc to form Her Majesty's Loyal Opposition in the House. In the four western provinces the voice of the Reform Party was amplified in a similar fashion: 38.2 percent of the vote resulted in 60.7 percent of the regional seats. And, in Ontario, the Liberals swept all but one of the province's 99 seats with only 52.8 percent of the vote.

For other Canadians, admittedly, the 1993 results provided less compelling evidence for electoral reform. Bloc, Liberal, and Reform supporters all had reasons to be happy with the status quo, although Reform paid a price in Ontario where the 20 percent of the popular vote won by the party yielded but a single seat.[6] If the Tory debacle had marginalized particular regional or social constituencies, then perhaps a stronger case for reform could be made, but this marginalization did not occur. The only group that appeared to lack adequate representation in the new House as a direct consequence of the Tory rout were the Tories themselves; no region or recognizable social grouping had lost its parliamentary or government voice. Finally, it should be noted that the

1993 election results did not raise earlier concerns about the lack of effective regional representation within the national government, for Canadians ended up with a Liberal government enjoying reasonably strong elected representation from all regions of the country. Yet while the reform evidence provided by the 1993 election may be less than conclusive, there are other currents stirring in the political environment which, in conjunction with the 1993 results, could well propel electoral reform back onto the national agenda.

THE NEW REFORM AGENDA

◆ ◆ ◆

The new electoral reform debate that has emerged in the wake of the 1993 election is driven by concerns that are quite different from earlier issues. The essential theme of the new debate is the decline in the importance of territoriality in the Canadian political culture.

The Canadian electoral system is based on the *territorial representation* of geographically-bounded constituencies that can then be aggregated by province and region. It is now apparent, however, that increasingly mobile citizens are identifying more and more with characteristics other than their place of residence. These characteristics are often descriptive in nature and tap gender, racial, ethnic, and linguistic identifications. While in the past the representation of regions within national parties and thus within the national government was a primary source of concern for those interested in electoral reform, now the *unrepresentative nature of Parliament* has come to the fore as attention is focussed more and more on the failure of legislative bodies to accurately reflect the diversity of the population. It is often argued that elected legislatures should serve as a "portrait of the nation," reflecting not only its regional character and the relative strength of its political parties but also its social, ethnic, racial, and gender compositions. Of particular concern to date is the underrepresentation of Aboriginals, visible minorities, and especially women, who constitute over 50 percent of the population but only 18 percent of the MPs elected in 1993.

The current debate, then, is new in at least two respects: it moves away from territory as the primary focus of representation and shifts attention from the composition of the government, and the attendant composition of legislative parties, to the composition of the legislature itself. In these respects, it poses a more vigorous challenge to the institutions of Canadian federalism; the challenge is not only to accommodate more effectively the traditional territorial and linguistic cleavages within the Canadian political community but, at the same time, to accommodate a growing number of nonterritorial interests and concerns. As a consequence it brings into play more radical and comprehensive notions of electoral reform that tackle not only the for-

---

...the challenge is...to accommodate a growing number of nonterritorial interests and concerns.

---

mal electoral process but also the means by which parties nominate candidates and finance their internal operations.

To understand why more radical notions of electoral reform are coming into play, we must take a moment to explore the arguments lying behind the new debate. While there are no legal restraints barring women, Aboriginals, and visible minorities from Canadian legislatures, systemic discrimination has limited these groups' electoral and representational success.[7] Although the representativeness of the House of Commons and provincial legislatures has improved in the past decade, progress has been slow. For example, the Canadian Advisory Council on the Status of Women predicts that, if change continues at its current pace, it will take 45 years (nine elections) before men and women have equal numerical weight in the House.[8]

But why should the composition of legislative institutions "mirror" Canadian society beyond capturing the regional composition of the electorate? The strongest argument in favour of mirror representation is based on the assumption that a legislature is undemocratic unless it reflects the major divisions in society. This viewpoint was articulated by Kathy Megyery in one of the research studies for the Royal Commission on Electoral Reform and Party Financing (the Lortie Commission, tabled in 1991): "...a system that does not, over time, come closer to adequately representing its citizenship calls into question the legitimacy of its democratic institutions."[9] The argument, then, is that improving demographic representation in legislative bodies would not only counter inequalities in the broader political order but would also strengthen the democratic legitimacy of the political community.

A second argument for mirror representation states that there are specific social benefits to be derived from mirroring demographic diversity in legislatures. An individual from an underrepresented or disadvantaged group can identify with an MP on the basis of physical similarities (for example, gender or race), and for this reason perceive him or herself as being more adequately represented. Mirror representation thereby enhances a group's sense of identification with the political community, increases opportunities for participation in decision-making, and provides potential career opportunities for group members.[10] Mirror representation in this sense is closely linked to the idea of "identity politics" and its assumption that voters desire representatives who possesses characteristics similar to their own.[11]

The most controversial argument is that mirror representation will alter the functioning of politics. This argument assumes that different groups or subsets of society have "distinctive values, attitudes and concerns which may have an impact on legislative behavior and the content of public policy."[12] If, in other words, the composition of legislative assemblies is changed, the values, operating styles, and policy products of those assemblies will also change. It is assumed that institutions are shaped by the nature of their incumbents and, thus, can be transformed by changing their composition.

The call for more accurate mirror representation in legislative assemblies is a complex and contentious issue.

All of these arguments run up against the inability of the existing electoral system to provide effective accountability for new forms of group representation. The central problem is that group representation by its very nature transgresses territorial boundaries, and therefore does not fit comfortably with the present system of territorial representation and its geographically-defined constituencies. If an MP claims to speak for "women," she does so on behalf of all women and not just those in her own constituency. However, a legislator claiming to represent group interests other than those of a territorial constituency is not subject to re-election or dismissal by the group he or she claims to represent. The critically important electoral linkage between the representative and the represented is severed as a consequence.

The call for more accurate mirror representation in legislative assemblies is a complex and contentious issue. Nonetheless, it has also become the dominant issue in the contemporary debate on electoral reform. For those who feel that mirror representation in legislative bodies should be improved, the question remains how this can be achieved without doing violence to other representational values in the Canadian democratic state.

OPTIONS FOR ELECTORAL REFORM

There are at least five ways to increase diversity and thereby group representation within Parliament: 1) altering the party nomination system; 2) affirmative gerrymandering; 3) creating separate constituencies; 4) changing the electoral system to one based on some form of proportional representation; and 5) Senate reform designed to capture both social and territorial diversity. Some of these proposals reach beyond the formal electoral system to address the party nomination process while others, such as those calling for separate constituencies based on gender or race, are much more radical in character than those emerging from the earlier debate and its preoccupation with regional representation.

Reforms to the Party Nomination System

Before an individual can serve as a legislative representative, he or she must first be nominated by a political party in a constituency and then be elected to represent that constituency; it is an extremely rare event when an individual is elected as an independent candidate without the endorsement and support of a political party. Thus, it is a two-stage struggle to achieve a legislative seat.[13] In the 1993 general election, women constituted only 23 percent of all major party candidates, a proportion still well in excess of the number of Aboriginal or visible minority candidates.[14] It is not surprising, therefore, that women are numerically underrepresented in the House of Commons. It is also not surprising that the nomination process has come under increasing critical assessment by those interested in promoting the more proportionate representation of women in legislative assemblies.

The Lortie Commission on Electoral Reform and Party Financing cites two structural barriers to women's entry to politics: the cost of the nomination process and the lack of party support for women seeking nomination, a lack linked in turn to the decentralized nomination system used in Canada.[15] The cost of contesting a party nomination is a major difficulty for potential women and minority candidates. Nomination costs for competitive urban ridings can exceed $50,000,[16] and pre-writ election spending and the costs of the party nomination contest are neither regulated by federal legislation nor reimbursed from public funds. Financing nomination campaigns is particularly problematic for women, who are more likely to come from nontraditional career backgrounds, have less financial security, and have more difficulty getting bank loans to support an inherently risky political career. In addition, women have less access to business contacts, corporate donors and moneyed networks than do men.[17] In all these respects, it can be assumed that Aboriginal peoples and visible minorities encounter the same barriers.

The second problem encountered by potential women and minority candidates is the decentralized nomination system currently in place, whereby local constituency organizations select party candidates. Although the party leader typically has a veto power with respect to nominations, this power is seldom used. Nor is the party leader often active in the recruitment of constituency candidates. (An exception to this was the Liberal party's strategy of recruiting women and male "star" candidates for the 1993 campaign, a strategy that required the active intervention of leader Jean Chrétien.) The decentralized nomination system is important in the context of the present discussion because it restricts more centralized control over the nomination process. This means in turn that parties are unable to establish effective quotas for the number of female and minority candidates; they can only hope that 295 independently conducted constituency nominations yield a party slate that is broadly representative of the national electorate.

The Lortie Commission made a number of recommendations to address the representational problems posed by the nomination process. To reduce the financial burden of contesting party nominations, the Commission recommended that: 1) employers be required to grant employees leaves of absence if the latter seek nomination and, if successful, election; 2) spending limits be imposed on all candidates seeking party nomination; 3) tax receipts be granted for contributors to nomination campaigns; and 4) childcare expenses "incurred by the primary caregiver" while seeking nomination be tax deductible.[18] The Commission also recommended the establishment of formal search committees in registered political parties to promote the nomination of "broadly representative candidates."[19] To encourage the nomination of female candidates in competitive seats, the Commission proposed financial incentives: "We recommend...the reimbursement of each registered political party with at least 20 percent female MPs be increased by an amount equivalent to the percentage of its women MPs up to a maximum of 150 percent."[20] The Commission also suggested that this measure should be eliminated once the overall percentage of female MPs equals or surpasses 40 percent.

Although these recommendations have considerable potential, it should be noted that they have yet to be debated in the House of Commons. Nor do they address the problem of local party control over the nomination process. Although the central party offices may be motivated to nominate more female and minority candidates, the incentive structures must also be changed at the constituency level. This could be achieved by offering financial rewards to constituency associations that nominate women or minority candidates; such rewards could be provided by the national party organizations or by differential public reimbursements for campaign costs. Steps could also be taken to create nomination procedures that encourage greater participation by women and minorities. For example, the NDP required that each nomination for the 1993 election be contested by an equal number of men and women; the result was that 38 percent of the NDP candidates were women. However, and as the electoral fortunes of the NDP illustrate, increasing the representativeness of candidates does not alone lead to a more representative House.

Reforms to the nomination system may be the least controversial and therefore most likely means available to encourage mirror representation. They would not require changes to the formal election process itself and, thus, may avoid some of the anxieties (discussed below) associated with more radical forms of electoral reform. However, they would entail further public regulation of the internal affairs of political parties—an intrusion of the state into the private sphere that will not go unchallenged. Nor would such reforms alone *ensure* the selection of women and minority candidates or greater mirror representation within legislative assemblies. Moreover, as representation within those assemblies will continue to be based on territorial constituencies, the accountability of group representatives will remain a problem.

Affirmative Gerrymandering

Affirmative gerrymandering is the redrawing of electoral boundaries in a manner that increases the voting power of a minority group or interest. This technique is used in the United States, where electoral lines have been drawn to increase the concentration of minority groups such as blacks, Hispanics, and Asians within specific electoral districts.[21] The 1982 amendment to the Voting Rights Act prohibits the "dilution of the minority vote" by any device, including the drawing of electoral boundaries. Any minority group that constitutes at least 5 percent of the state population is allowed to seek the protection of the law to ensure that its vote is not diluted. Similar legislation could be passed by the Canadian Parliament. Appeals for affirmative gerrymandering could also be made through the courts by invoking section 3 (voting rights) and section 15 (equality rights) of the Charter. Prior legal cases invoking section 3 have established the precedent that electoral boundary commissions should respect "community of interest" when constructing boundaries. Perhaps, then, a minority group could reasonably argue that it represented a community of interest that should be reflected in the design of constituency boundaries.

However, and notwithstanding the possible legislative and constitutional opportunities for affirmative gerrymandering, this approach is unlikely to provide a solution to Canada's representation problems. First, affirmative gerrymandering would do nothing to increase the representation of women in legislative assemblies. As women and men are evenly distributed throughout the country, the redrawing of electoral boundaries, short of creating separate male and female districts, would not increase the number of elected women. Second, it is by no means clear that affirmative gerrymandering would increase other forms of social diversity within the House or provincial legislatures. Part of the problem stems from the territorial distribution of Aboriginal peoples and visible minorities. For the most part (Indian reserves and Alberta Métis settlements are a clear exception), neither has sufficient territorial concentration to make affirmative gerrymandering possible.[22] Furthermore, the lower turnout and voter eligibility of minority groups (many minorities counted in the census are not Canadian citizens) means that even a constituency with a *large minority population* may not contain enough *minority voters* to elect a minority representative.

Federalism presents a third obstacle to affirmative gerrymandering. Although a group may constitute a significant minority in the country as a whole, it may be distributed across a number of provinces in a manner that cannot be accommodated by affirmative gerrymandering. However, the constitution would have to be amended before constituencies crossing provincial boundaries could be created. If affirmative gerrymandering were to be used to ensure the representation of minority interests, other important communities of interest must be broken up. Affirmatively gerrymandered districts are usually spread out geographically and, thus, may fragment the representation of various territorial and economic interests held to be important by the electorate. Finally, it should be noted that enhancing the voting power of minorities does not in itself ensure representation, broadly defined. Voting is restricted to elections, whereas representation occurs between elections.[23] Although affirmative gerrymandering increases the probability of electing a minority representative, it cannot ensure that substantive mirror representation will take place within legislative assemblies. For all of these reasons, affirmative gerrymandering holds little potential for addressing representational problems within the Canadian federal state.

Reserved Representation

Reserved representation ensures the selection and election of minority candidates by creating separate seats for minority groups. This system is used in the New Zealand Parliament to ensure Maori representation, and has been recommended by the Lortie Commission as a means to improve Aboriginal representation in Canada.[24] Some have also argued that separate constituencies should be established for men and women to ensure equal repre-

---

...reserved representation would

ensure Aboriginal representation

within Parliament.

---

sentation of the sexes in Parliament.[25] Both ideas were floated in the 1991–92 constitutional debate when various formats for an elected Senate were under discussion.

Under the Lortie Commission plan, Aboriginal peoples would have the option of registering as either Aboriginal voters or "regular" voters. If the number of persons registering within a province as Aboriginal voters were large enough to merit the creation of an Aboriginal seat, then a reserved Aboriginal riding would be created in which only Aboriginal candidates could run and only Aboriginal voters could vote. Such a system of reserved representation would ensure Aboriginal representation within Parliament. It could also provide an important means of electoral empowerment to the large and amorphous urban Aboriginal population, a population that may lie beyond the reach of Aboriginal self-government.

Not surprisingly, the Lortie recommendations and the larger principle of reserved Aboriginal constituencies are not without their problems.[26] First, the dispersion of Aboriginal peoples across Canada, and the dispersion of *specific* Aboriginal peoples, means that many provinces would not have sufficient numbers to merit an Aboriginal seat. This problem, of course, becomes more acute if we think not of Aboriginal seats but rather of status Indian, Métis, and Inuit seats. Second, the creation of reserved seats would be based on the number of registered *voters*, whereas district sizes are now measured by the total *population* within the riding. In reserved seats, the representation of children, nonvoters, and those ineligible to vote would be neglected. A third problem with the Lortie recommendations is that they would require Aboriginal voters to publicly declare their identifications; no other group in Canada is required to do so, nor is such a requirement desirable. Such a system may also require voters to prove their Aboriginal status, which could be a very controversial requirement given the lack of constitutional guidance in matters of Aboriginal status. Finally, it is worth noting that the pressure for guaranteed or even improved Aboriginal legislative representation is not coming from Aboriginal communities, whose focus at present, and quite likely for some time to come, is on the design and implementation of Aboriginal self-government. Reser-ved representation in federal institutions is seen at best as a supplement to the far more important self-government initiative.

The most serious general problem of reserved representation is the assumption that a single identification—for example, gender or Aboriginal status—is the most important identification for the voter and that it remains so across time. Establishing gender-based constituencies, for example, would assume that gender identification takes precedence over racial, linguistic, territorial, or other political identifications. Even if this might be the case at a single point in time, one's primary identification may change over a lifetime or even between elections. Thus gender-based or racially-based constituencies lack flexibility; they lock voters into a single political identity. While it might be argued that the present system of territorial representation does the same thing, the creation of reserved constituencies based on other criteria would compound rather than resolve the existing problem.

At present, there is no evidence of significant public support for reserved representation, or at least for the application of this principle beyond Aboriginal peoples. Although reserved seats for women and visible minorities would ensure mirror representation in Parliament, it would be far too radical a departure from the existing Canadian political culture to be acceptable unless all other avenues of representational reform were to be blocked. Fortunately, more conventional avenues of reform are available.

Proportional Representation

Comparative studies on women in politics demonstrate that Canada's first-past-the-post electoral system (FPTP) is neither advantageous to women's legislative recruitment nor a reliable vehicle for ensuring mirror representation. Simply put, it is difficult to achieve mirror representation at the constituency level when there is only one elected representative who must be male *or* female, a visible minority *or* not, an Aboriginal *or* not. It is equally difficult to ensure mirror representation within legislative assemblies when their membership is completely determined by elections in single-member constituencies, a process more analogous to a crap shoot than to anything else. It is also difficult for political parties to impose gender and racial quotas within the context of single-member constituencies and the decentralized nomination process discussed above.

Given this critique, it is important to note that Canada's use of the FPTP system is becoming increasingly idiosyncratic. While Britain and the United States also use the FPTP system, the majority of western democratic states employ more complex balloting and/or districting. The single transferable vote (STV) and proportional representation (PR) list systems, which produce a more diversified and nuanced legislative "portrait of the nation," are both widely used. Their utilization of multimember constituencies loosens the above-mentioned FPTP constraints on mirror representation. The STV system does not enforce the proportional representation of political parties, as nothing in the formula requires proportionality. Rather, the system attempts to reflect the attitudes of the electorate accurately by selecting the preferred *candidates* rather than the preferred parties.[27] The system is designed to serve the electors rather than the political parties, and electors are free to cross party lines when listing their preferences. Thus, a voter may chose to vote not on the basis of party but on the basis of environmentalism, and thus would rank candidates according to their "greenness." A voter could also rank candidates by their support for or opposition to feminism, by their more general ideological orientation, or by any other criteria, including demographic characteristics. A kindred spirit to the STV system, and one that is frequently confused with it, is the alternative vote (AV) system which also uses preferential ballots. The AV system is used for elections to the Australian House of Representatives.

The PR-list systems comprise a different alternative again, one that does not allow voters to distinguish between candidates. Parties select a slate or list of candidates for multimember constituencies; the candidates are rank-ordered by the party rather than by the voters, who cast one vote for the party of their preference. Theoretically, if a party receives 30 percent of the vote, it should receive 30 percent of the seats, although the precision of proportionality varies with constituency size. Due to centralized party control over the candidate lists, the PR-list system is open to gender and racial quotas. While voters cannot rank candidates by gender or race, or by any other social or ideological characteristic, the parties can. Moreover, the parties can ensure that particular candidates are elected by placing them at the top of their list.

All of these alternatives to the electoral status quo have some appeal for Canadians interested in promoting more broadly representative legislative institutions. For example, the PR-list system would allow quotas to be set to ensure diversity in the House; parties could be required to alternate male and female candidates on their lists, with a minimum number of visible minorities or Aboriginal persons in the top third of the list. In a less intrusive reform, political parties themselves might opt for such a strategy in the expectation that it would enhance their electoral appeal. However, the adoption of the PR-list system would also weaken accountability. The chances of a candidate being elected would depend almost entirely on where he or she was placed on the party list and, thus, candidates would likely be more responsive to party rather than constituency demands. A second and related criticism is that voters would be encouraged to vote on the basis of party alone; the individual characteristics of the representatives would diminish in importance. A third criticism is that a PR-list system would allow parties to nominate "group" candidates who in fact might be antagonistic toward group goals; for example, female candidates who oppose the interests of the women's movement.

The STV options has greater potential appeal in that it would allow voters themselves to choose the identification they wished to have represented in the legislature.[28] For example, a voter in one election could base her preferences on environmental concerns and in the next on women's issues, or regional interests, or economic concerns. The resulting legislature would not necessarily mirror society, although the STV system could be coupled with quotas to avoid this problem. Since candidates are ranked by the voter and not by the party, candidates in the STV system are less likely than candidates in the PR-list system to be unresponsive to constituency needs. Also, since candidates are individually

---

The electoral alternatives are (or at least should be) of growing interest to those concerned with the lack of mirror representation in Canadian legislative assemblies.

---

assessed by the electorate, "group" candidates that are antagonistic to group goals are less likely to succeed. In the case of both the STV and the PR-list systems, their effectiveness in facilitating the election of female and visible minority candidates varies with the district magnitude; larger districts (those electing a substantial number of representatives) are more promising for mirror representation than are smaller districts. Ideally for mirror representation, the STV and PR-list systems should be based on single provincial districts.[29]

The electoral alternatives discussed above, and the STV in particular, have long been of considerable attractiveness to those acquainted with the intricacies of electoral reform, and they are (or at least should be) of growing interest to those concerned with the lack of mirror representation in Canadian legislative assemblies. At the same time, they have never found significant support among voters or the mainstream parties. The single-member, first-past-the-post electoral system currently used for the House of Commons and provincial legislatures has proven to be extremely resistant to fundamental reform, and there is little evidence that either the public or the partisan mood is about to change. Even the distortions arising from the 1993 election results have produced little more than a ripple of support for electoral reform. However, the issue may still come onto the national agenda through the backdoor of Senate reform.

Senate Reform

This is neither the time nor the place to discuss Senate reform in any detail. It is an important matter to note, however, because a reformed Senate is almost certain to be an elected Senate and, therefore, any discussion of Senate reform will necessitate a debate on electoral reform. We would argue, moreover, that an elected Senate is likely to employ one or more of the reform alternatives discussed above. This argument stems from the belief that a Senate elected along the lines of the STV would best meet the traditional demand for more effective regional representation *and* the growing demand for the more effective legislative representation of nonterritorial communities such as those based on gender and race.

As we noted at the beginning of this discussion, the contemporary scene is marked by the emergence of non-territorial political identities that are jockeying for institutional representation. It would therefore be difficult and certainly undesirable to engage in any substantive public debate on Senate reform without coming to grips with how a reformed Senate would serve nonterritorial interests and communities. The trick will be to find a way that a reformed Senate can meet both the old issues of regional representation and the new political agenda dominated by nonterritorial politics. In this context it is important to stress that the Senate is first and foremost a *federal* chamber, and that federalism has traditionally been designed to accommodate territorial communities. If a balance is to be found between the old issues and the new agenda, it will be found in adopting a method of election for the Senate that is quite different from that used at present for the House of Commons. In turn, however, electoral innovation with respect to the Senate may touch off a more wide-ranging and fundamental public debate on electoral reform to the House than we have witnessed to date.

In short, a debate on Senate reform will permit, indeed, will require a parallel debate on the role that elections should play in the democratic politics of the 21st century. We will have to address how a reformed upper house can be expected to meet a cacophony of regional and nonterritorial interests. We will be forced to address whether our political interests should be aggregated within provincial, multimember constituencies quite different from those used to elect MPs, or indeed whether the representation of nonterritorial interests requires that the nation itself be treated as one large constituency. We will be forced to consider ballot formats that are more in line with the complex political identities of contemporary citizens, identities which cannot be adequately expressed by a single X scrawled once every four or five years on the federal ballot. It will be a debate that will tax our political imaginations, but also one that could also lead to a vigorous articulation of a new sense of political community.

CONCLUSIONS

Although the 1993 election provided striking illustrations of how the Canadian single-member, first-past-the-post plurality system can significantly distort the translation of votes into seats, it is unlikely that the results themselves will overcome the inertia of the status quo. Despite repeated evidence of failure with respect to regional representation, despite the disproportionate amplification of discordant voices that resulted from the 1993 election results, and despite growing agitation about the representational quality of legislative institutions, the electoral system has proven to be even more resistant than the constitution to reform. Certainly there is no partisan imperative for reform. The Liberal, Bloc, and Reform parties all profited from the system, at least to a degree, in the 1993 election, and the two parties who were the clear losers, the Progressive Conservatives and the NDP, were also marginalized as partisan actors on the national stage; their complaints will not find a significant audience. This does not mean, however, that the electoral system is immune to change. A renewal of the Senate reform debate, an intensification of concern over the representation of women, ethnic minorities, or Aboriginal peoples in the House of Commons, populist pressure to institute recall mechanisms, or exposure to electoral reform initiatives in other countries could ignite by themselves or in combination a renewed electoral reform debate in Canada.

Should electoral reform once again climb up the national agenda, the debate will be very different than it was in the late 1970s and early 1980s, because the underpinnings of the debate have been transformed in a variety of important ways. Questions of regional representation are likely to recede in the face of a growing and much more complex debate surrounding gender, ethnic, and Aboriginal representation. This new focus in turn is likely to lead to more radical reform proposals than we have encountered to date, proposals that will embrace multimember and proportional representation systems with greater enthusiasm than we have witnessed in the past, and that may challenge the territorial definition of political constituencies. Populist measures designed to constrain representative government will further cross-cut and confuse the earlier emphasis on territorial representation. Although western Canadians were the major players in the electoral reform debates of the recent past, other players are likely to come to the fore when the debate reopens.

In this new and potentially very contentious debate, it is by no means clear that western Canadians will have a regionally distinct perspective. To the extent that they do, it will be one anchored in a regional commitment to an elected Senate. In fact, the most probable scenario for successful electoral reform is one that brings together Senate reformers and feminists. While this coalition may strike some as unlikely, it could well emerge through a shared commitment to reform based on the STV model. By themselves, neither Senate reformers nor feminists are likely to generate enough public enthusiasm for electoral reform to occur, but together they might just pull it off.

Notes

1. Alan C. Cairns, "The Electoral System and the Party System in Canada, 1921–1965," *Canadian Journal of Political Science,* Vol. 1 (1968), 55–80.

2. It is important not to attribute all of the Liberals' woes in western Canada to the perverse effects of the electoral system. For a discussion of how the Liberals were also the architects of their own misfortune, see David E. Smith, *The Regional Decline of a National Party: Liberals on the Prairies* (Toronto: University of Toronto Press, 1981).

3. The imposition of the National Energy Program shortly after the 1980 election was not seen as a coincidence in the West.

4. For a discussion of the adverse impact of the electoral system on both Conservative fortunes in Quebec and internal politics within the party, see George C. Perlin, *The Tory Syndrome: Leadership Politics in the Progressive Conservative Party* (Montreal: McGill-Queen's University Press, 1980).

5. For example, see W.A.W. Neilson and J.C. Macpherson (eds.), *The Legislative Process in Canada: The Need for Reform* (Montreal: Institute for Research on Public Policy, 1978); William P. Irvine, *Does Canada Need a New Electoral System?* (Kingston: Institute of Intergovernmental Relations, 1979); David Elton and Roger Gibbins, *Electoral Reform... The Need is Pressing, The Time is Now* (Calgary: The Canada West Foundation, 1981).

6. Nationally, the Liberals won 60 percent of the seats with 41.2 percent of the popular vote, the Bloc won 18.3 percent of the seats with 13.5 percent of the vote, and Reform won 17.6 percent of the seats with 18.7 percent of the vote.

7. Royal Commission on Electoral Reform and Party Financing, *Reforming Electoral Democracy,* Vol. 1 (Canada: Minister of Supply and Services, 1991), 97.

8. Marina Jimenez, "Slow going on the long road to Ottawa," *Saskatoon Star Phoenix,* August 14, 1993, D3.

9. Kathy Megyery (ed.), *Women in Canadian Politics—Towards Equity in Representation* (Toronto: Dundurn Press, 1991), xvii.

10. Jerry Perkins and Diane L. Fowlkes, "Opinion Representation versus Social Representation or, Why Women Can't Run as Women and Win," *American Political Science Review* 74 (1980), 92.

11. Hanna Pitkin, *The Concept of Representation* (Berkeley: University of California Press, 1967), 78.

12. Pippa Norris and Jodi Lovenduski, "Women Candidates for Parliament: Transforming the Agenda?" *British Journal of Political Science* 19 (1989), 107.

13. Lynda Erickson, "Women and Candidacies for the House of Commons," in Megyery, *Women in Canadian Politics*, edited by Kathy Megyery (1991), 110.

14. While the number of women candidates can be easily determined, the number of candidates who are visible minorities is less easily determined. Thus the assumption about the low number of visible minority and Aboriginal candidates for the major parties must at this point be treated as precisely that—an assumption.

15. *Royal Commission on Electoral Reform and Party Financing*, 107. We assume that these barriers also work in a similar fashion for Aboriginal peoples and visible minorities.

16. Janine Brodie, "Women and the Electoral Process in Canada," in *Women in Canadian Politics*, edited by Kathy Megyery, 40.

17. Ibid., 46.

18. *Royal Commission on Electoral Reform and Party Financing*, 93, 117–19.

19. Ibid., 121.

20. Ibid., 273.

21. Affirmative gerrymandering has also been proposed as a means to increase the voting power and elected representation of gays and lesbians in the United States. To be effective, however, this would require some geographic concentration of the gay and lesbian population, something that does not seem to be characteristic of the Canadian scene.

22. Affirmative gerrymandering may be easier with respect to provincial constituencies than with respect to federal constituencies, given that the former are smaller in terms of both population and geographic scope.

23. Jennifer Smith, "Commentary," in *Drawing Boundaries: Legislatures, Courts and Electoral Values*, edited by John C. Courtney, Peter MacKinnon and David E. Smith (Saskatoon: Fifth House Publishers, 1992), 41.

24. See Robert A. Milen (ed.), *Aboriginal Peoples and Electoral Reform in Canada* (Toronto: Dundurn Press, 1991).

25. See Christine Boyle, "Home Rule for Women: Power-Sharing Between Men and Women," *Dalhousie Law Journal*, (1983), 790–809.

26. For a more expanded discussion, see Roger Gibbins, "Electoral Reform and Canada's Aboriginal Population: An Assessment of Aboriginal Electoral Districts," *Aboriginal Peoples and Electoral Reform*, edited by Robert A. Milen (1991), 153–84.

27. W.J.M. Mackenzie, *Free Elections* (London: George Allen & Unwin Ltd., 1958), 69.

28. The AV option also allows the voter some choice among political identities, but the fact that only one candidate is to be elected in any given constituency reduces the range of choice and the complexity of voter strategies.

29. A criticism of provincial districts is that in larger provinces such as Ontario and Quebec, small ideological parties and/or candidates would be elected. If this is indeed a problem, minimum quotas can be set to prevent "fringe" groups from entering the legislatures. For example, the German system has a 5 percent threshold for legislative representation in the lower house.

Terms &
Concepts

affirmative gerrymandering
Alternative Vote
Canadian Advisory Council on the
   Status of Women
constituency
electoral reform
federal chamber
first-past-the-post electoral system
group representation

Her Majesty's Loyal Opposition
incumbents
Lortie Commission
mirror representation
multiple political identities
party nomination
PR-list
proportional representation
regionalized national governments

regionalized political parties
reserved representation
Senate reform
single and multimember
   constituency
single transferable vote
territorial representation
Triple-E Senate

Questions

1. What do Gibbins and Youngman mean by the phrase "multiple political identities"?

2. Describe some common reform proposals to enhance the representativeness of legislative assemblies. What problems are associated with each?

3. What role should political parties have in determining the slate of candidates they support in elections? Should constituency associations or party leadership be able to select candidates? Should voters in an election be given the opportunity to select the party and candidate(s) of their choice separately or should both preferences be combined into one vote?

4. To what extent can and should the members of a legislative assembly "mirror" the sociodemographic features of the electorate? What criteria should be used to select the groups for mirror representation?

5. Gibbins and Youngman suggest that Canadian Senate reformers in future may contemplate an alliance with feminists to achieve their goals. What would be the nature of this alliance and how likely is it to form?

Democracy Without Parties: A New Politics?

G. Grant Amyot

Editors' Note

Political parties are odd institutions. They are considered in law to be private associations, yet they have great importance for the functioning and, indeed, constitutional nature, of democratic government. (Parliamentary government is unintelligible unless one understands the centrality of parties.) Parties create their own rules of membership and operation, yet their representatives seek to attain political office and impress a partisan stamp upon government. To try to capture this dual nature of parties, political scientists often call them "parapolitical" organizations. Parties are odd also in the sense that they project themselves as democratic, member-driven organizations— many incorporate the word "democracy" or "democratic" into their names—even as they daily confirm what one observer called the "iron law of oligarchy."[1]

Some experts believe parties to be in decline in Western democracies, overtaken by polling, populist leaders, professional policy advisers, and interest groups. But the decline thesis has its critics who suggest that parties are in transition, not in decline, and that parties are tremendously flexible organizations able to incorporate new techniques and practices into their operations. Further, they argue that people make their voting choices on the basis of party and that their partisan choices are fairly stable from election to election. It is worthwhile, however, to examine whether the emergence of new parties centred on leaders—like Silvio Berlusconi's *Forza Italia*, and Ross Perot's "United We Stand America"—represents a new phenomenon. Also, does the Canadian trend toward televoting mechanisms to select party leaders represent a boon or a danger to parties? And will the prominence of professional pollsters and advertising consultants, working within and outside of political parties, render parties, as organizations with a base in the citizenry, a thing of the past?

Amyot's essay, then, should lead you to consider whether parties are in decline or only in transition. Consider whether his conclusion follows from the body of his essay. Does he give reasons why parties will prevail over the forces working against them?

---

1. Robert Michels, *Political Parties: A Sociological Study of the Oligarchical Tendencies of Modern Democracy* [1911] (New York: Collier, 1962).

Are political parties necessary? While they are still a fact of life in Western democracies, there are clear signs of their decline, which have led many to question their role and effectiveness. Party loyalties among voters are weakening, as more and more voters take up an independent stance among parties. Policies seem to emanate from the bureaucracy and increasingly lack real alternatives. Major interests have their own pressure groups to represent their points of view. Most recently, the party organizations have lost even a large part of their prominence in fighting elections to staffs of pollsters, fundraisers, and strategists. These professionals serve the leaders, who have upstaged their parties in the media and seem to dominate them as never before.

Furthermore, many citizens are not just disaffected from the existing parties, but criticize parties as such. Suggestions for more free votes in the House of Commons, greater accountability of individual MPs to their constituents, or the use of referenda on major issues all recall turn-of-the-century populist attacks on party government as corrupt and unresponsive to the will of the people. Have parties in fact outlived their usefulness? Are they destined to be replaced by a new politics, a nonparty form of democracy characterized by independent voters, charismatic leaders, and opinion polling?

PARTIES IN DEMOCRATIC THEORY

◆ ◆ ◆

The preceding notion is not as outlandish as it may seem; in spite of the major role that parties have played in democratic politics, they do not have a firm footing in the liberal-democratic tradition of political thought that has underpinned it. For classical liberal thinkers, party in the modern sense was unnecessary and indeed harmful. Politics was about the rational pursuit of the public interest, and liberals believed that all citizens, if they used their faculty of reason, would arrive at roughly similar conceptions of that interest. Correct reasoning would tend to create unity in the polity, rather than division. Not all classical liberals, of course, went as far as Rousseau in his antipathy to factions that would distract the citizenry from the search for the general will, but his thought illustrates this facet of their views in an extreme form. Generally speaking, reason would dictate a frame-

work of human laws, reflecting natural law, that would preserve the rights of the citizens vis-à-vis the state, and legislators were meant to work together to formulate this framework.

At any rate, politics for classical liberals was not primarily about the struggle of conflicting interests, for the public interest was beyond particular concerns. Therefore legislators were to be chosen for their highly developed powers of reason and their disinterestedness, rather than as delegates or representatives of their constituents. As Burke said in his often-quoted speech to the electors of Bristol: "Parliament is a deliberative assembly of one nation, with one interest, that of the whole; where, not local purposes, not local prejudices ought to guide, but the general good, resulting from the general reason of the whole" (1826, 335; Beer, 1969, 20–22).

While Burke defended the embryonic parties of his day—the Whig "connexions"—his conception of politics does not allow for strong party discipline. In his view, each individual member of Parliament (and each citizen) had to be free to follow his own reason in the pursuit of the public interest, although the ideal situation would be one of unanimity around a conception of that interest. Burke's famous definition of party— "a body of men united for promoting by their joint endeavours the national interest upon some particular principle in which they are all agreed" (1826, 335)—suggests something quite different from the disciplined parties of today, which are held together by more substantial and complex links than principle alone. When only principle binds a group of citizens together, there is always the potential for differing individual interpretations of that principle; indeed, individual freedom is necessary to the search for the true common good.

One of the greatest principles which early liberals thought a fit and noble basis for the organization of party was the struggle against "tyranny." In Burke's case, this meant the attempts of the ministers of George III to rule in disregard of constitutional traditions: "When bad men combine, the good must associate" (Burke, 1826, 336ff.). Later, Utilitarians such as Bentham viewed democracy itself principally as a means of controlling the government, which otherwise might use its powers to oppress the people. While the common good remained the goal, they recognized that both reason and desire inhabit human nature, particularly when men and women are placed in positions of power. These

G. Grant Amyot, "Democracy Without Parties: A New Politics?" In Alain-G. Gagnon and A. Brian Tanguay, eds., *Canadian Parties in Transition,* 2nd ed. Scarborough: Nelson Canada, 1994. Reprinted by permission.

conceptions are difficult to apply to the present-day situation, however, when all parties accept the democratic basis of the constitution and when, in an era of positive government, opposition parties have a role that goes far beyond checking governmental "tyranny."

Other liberal-democratic thinkers, such as John Stuart Mill, shared these views but at the same time laid a greater emphasis on citizen participation as a goal in itself. However, Mill's favoured locales for this participation were the workplace and local government, which could, in many cases, allow for direct democracy. It is only in the work of 20th-century scholars such as C.B. Macpherson that parties are seen as the principal vehicles for citizen participation.[1]

In the 20th century, the politics of interest achieved primacy over the politics of principle, in theory as well as in practice. Pluralist writers, such as Arthur Bentley, began to argue that politics was the struggle of a multiplicity of different interest groups, each striving to attain its goals in bargaining with the others. The pure pluralist scheme replaces parties almost completely with interest groups, and in the weak party discipline of the United

---

For pluralists, parties are supposed to perform a "brokerage" function...

States Congress we can see this tendency at work: senators and members of the House of Representatives vote in response to the pressures of the various lobbies rather than in accordance with the party line, and certain key interests have captured the parts of government that are supposed to be regulating them. What seems to keep the parties alive are institutional mechanisms such as the direct election of the president and the legislative framework of party registration, primaries, etc. For pluralists, parties are supposed to perform a "brokerage" function, mediating between the various interests and presenting policy packages which they hope will maximize their appeal to the voters by skilfully combining as many different group demands as possible. Nevertheless, the tendency of pluralist thought is to depreciate the role of parties and privilege that of interest groups.

Only if we accept the Marxist thesis that there are only two fundamental interests, that of the workers and that of the capitalists, can the politics of interests produce a system of stable, disciplined parties. Marxism, having no belief that a "common good" can be attained in a capitalist society, can embrace the idea of the political party and partisanship without reservations. For

Gramsci (1971, 227), parties are "the nomenclature for classes," and all Marxists believe that the working class has particular need of a strong party: "In its struggle for power the proletariat has no other weapon but organization" (Lenin, 1967, 440).

Marxism, however, is not part of the mainstream of liberal-democratic theory that has historically justified our contemporary democracy (although in Italy, for instance, it was one of the ideological influences on the Constitution). Nor, as Marxists would admit, do all parties in democracies represent distinct social classes in a clearcut fashion. Of all the other varieties of democratic theory, the only one that gives parties a key role is Schumpeter's "competitive elitist" theory—arguably one of the most impoverished from a normative point of view, though it claims for itself the virtue of a greater correspondence with empirical reality. For Schumpeter, the mass of the citizenry are uninformed and irrational, and elites must rule, but party competition within the elite is necessary to simplify the electorate's decision, to prevent tyranny, and to legitimate the system by giving the voters the illusion of consumer choice (Schumpeter, 1950, 269–83). Competitive elitism is a far from morally compelling form of democracy, and the role it reserves for parties, while necessary, is not particularly noble.

Given the lack of a strong justification for parties in liberal-democratic theory, what accounts for their ubiquity in modern democracies? Most simply, in any representative system association provides such a powerful advantage that parties inevitably form. The "justification" for parties, then, stems not from principle, or from the need to fashion compromises between interests, or from their utility as a barrier to tyranny, but rather from the more mundane functional characteristics of our political systems. Even where a popular assembly rather than a parliament ruled, as in ancient Rome, the election of magistrates led to the formation of parties; indeed, parties would have advantages even in a system with no election of representatives (e.g., a popular assembly with magistrates chosen by lot).

A party of some sort has been seen as a virtual necessity if one is to contest the U.S. presidency seriously, or aim at a majority in the House of Commons, and even at a purely local level it offers a considerable edge. Only a party can provide the money and the organization needed to win. In playing this key role of aggregating individuals into election-fighting coalitions, ideally parties also organize the alternatives offered to voters into a small number of well-publicized, coherent packages; they are valuable in reducing the voter's "information costs," especially since they tend to adhere to similar programs over time. Once an auto worker has identified the NDP, for instance, as the party most favourable to unionized workers, the worker may rationally vote for that party without troubling to find out its positions on each issue in each election. This simplifying role of parties is especially useful in allowing voters to assign responsibility for governmental policies and performance: where there is no party discipline, it is too easy for representatives to excuse themselves for failing to carry out their promises by citing the absence of majority support; individual voters have difficulty determining the truth of the matter.

At the same time, parties do from time to time perform the tasks indicated by liberal-democratic theory—advocating competing principles, representing and aggregating interests, and checking governmental high-handedness. They may also provide a useful way for citizens to participate in politics, thereby achieving another of the classical goals of democracy. From the point of view of competitive elitism, parties are also valuable because they recruit, select, and train leaders; the selection of the best leaders is a key function for Schumpeter and his followers.[2]

Historically, however, many political parties have been formed from the top down, so to speak, in a manner which reflects much more their functional utility or necessity for government than the opinions or interests of the people. In the British tradition this is expressed in the maxim, "The Queen's government must be carried on." This means that a majority must be found in the House of Commons to support the government, and some form of party organization is required to ensure this, particularly when members are elected by universal suffrage. In the 18th century, the cabinet, chosen in name and sometimes in fact by the king, was able to create a majority for itself using various forms of patronage and influence, giving rise to the court "party," and the raison d'être of opposition groups was often largely to gain a share of the spoils of office. The general election of 1832 was the first the cabinet "lost." Similarly, in many other countries party organization proceeded from government to Parliament to the country, giving rise to what Duverger has dubbed the "cadre party." Even in the postwar period, in countries such as Italy or Japan, the occupation of government has given long-time ruling parties considerable resources with which to maintain their electoral positions. More generally, institutional arrangements have either strongly encouraged the formation of parties (e.g., the election of the U.S. president) or directly enshrined them in law (e.g., U.S. laws regulating primaries, list systems of proportional repre-

sentation, or public funding of parties). In Canada, the cabinet system has stimulated party formation, while provisions for the assignment of broadcasting time and funding elections and political activity led in the 1970s to the institutionalization of parties, which had previously been only informal entities with no precise legal status (Courtney, 1978, 34, 36).

THE DECLINE OF PARTIES

◆ ◆ ◆

That parties lack a strong theoretical justification, owing their existence instead to more practical factors, simply reinforces other tendencies at work that seem to be dissolving parties as we know them. These tendencies interact, but one of the most powerful is a growing sense that parties do not matter, that whichever party wins the election, the actual range of choice open to government is small. This is more than the often-lamented narrowness of the range of choice offered by parties. Such a convergence has occurred in many countries, most notably the U.S., but by no means everywhere; elections are often fought with clear and distinct alternatives before the voters. However, other factors have intervened to make it difficult for the winning party to deflect policy in any significant way from the logic seemingly imposed by the situation. It is forced to abandon election promises and yield to the "necessary" solutions proposed by its officials. The governing party then becomes, as Poulantzas suggested (1980, 232–40), more a public-relations agency for the bureaucracy's policies than an independent source of ideas and initiatives.

Of course, there have always been limits to the ability of governments to effect fundamental change. The constraints of the capitalist economy often seem to impose certain kinds of solutions, or severely narrow the range of choice, unless the government is prepared and has sufficient popular backing to institute a virtual war economy. These constraints, however, have become much tighter and more evident in the past 20 years, since the end of the long postwar boom. Governments simply have less money with which to embark on new policies; they now also have less room to maneuver because of budget deficits. Also, the internationalization of the economy makes traditional Keynesian demand-stimulus measures less effective, as the Mitterrand government in France found in 1981–82. Balance-of-payments crises and runs on the currency await any government that overstimulates the economy or undermines the confidence of international investors. International agreements, such as the European Monetary System, and the end of capital and exchange controls have deprived governments of many policy instruments. They are therefore less able to deal with the root problems of slower economic growth and rising unemployment. These, rather than so-called "overload," provide the real explanation for the relative ineffectiveness of government action, but governing parties are the nearest and most obvious targets for disappointed voters.[3]

Another more tangible direction in which power has shifted from elected governments is toward independent bodies such as central banks and supranational institutions. Central banks, such as the Bank of Canada, have varying degrees of legal autonomy, but the real basis of their independence is the investment community, at home and abroad. It favours independent agencies rather than political control over currencies, which it considers less conducive to monetary stability and a positive climate for investment. Central banks' autonomy has been increasing in the past 20 years, with the adoption of monetarist policies in the late 1970s throughout the developed world and a massive shift in power to the holders of financial assets. The German Bundesbank is particularly powerful: the overriding goal of its policies has remained, controlling inflation at the expense, if necessary, of full employment and growth. The European Monetary System, dominated by the German mark, has forced Germany's partners to pursue similarly restrictive (or often more restrictive) policies in order to defend the parity of their currencies. The point is that the Bundesbank, and the other central banks to varying degrees, enjoy considerable autonomy and that their policies are not affected by changes in the make-up of the government. Even in the economically stronger countries, those which have not had International Monetary Fund teams impose conditions for loans, the maneuvering room of the government is limited.

In some countries, of course, the regular bureaucracy has traditionally been the major source of ideas and policies, and this naturally diminishes the role of the parties. France and Japan are perhaps the strongest cases. In Japan in particular, the interlocking network of bureaucrats, business leaders, and political bosses constitutes a power structure that prevents any one person from making fundamental changes; this is what van Wolferen (1989) means by the "enigma" of Japanese power. The system seems to be directed by an impersonal guiding hand, and the Liberal Democratic Party's function has been chiefly to provide democratic legitimacy for this power structure, making liberal use of the state's resources and the privileges of office in the

process. It is not clear that any radical changes will follow the Liberal Democrats' loss of their majority in 1993; after a brief period in opposition, they have returned to power in coalition with their erstwhile antagonists, the Socialists.

In Canada, as well, the bureaucracy is highly professional (in spite of a few politically motivated appointments at the top) and has generated many policy innovations, which have then been adopted by the party in power as its own. Though not part of the bureaucracy, royal commissions also have been a commonly source of nonpartisan policy advice and innovation.[4] But while a certain amount of interchange of personnel between the civil service, the ruling party, and business has occurred, especially in the last years of the long Liberal reign before 1957, there is not the same close and ongoing relationship in Canada as has evolved in Japan. Relations between elected politicians and bureaucrats may be close or strained, depending on the circumstances, though even in the latter case the power of the civil service in framing policy alternatives is considerable.

All these influences conspire to limit the room elected governments have to maneuver. There have been numerous examples of governments severely limited by economic circumstances that have reacted by reversing their original policies and long-standing commitments to their constituencies. A spectacular Canadian example was the Trudeau government's introduction of wage-and-price controls in the fall of 1975, after it had just won election the previous year by campaigning against the Conservatives' proposal of just such a plan (Meisel, 1979, 130). The Mitterrand government found it impossible to pursue "Keynesianism in one country" when other major economies were being squeezed by harsh monetarist measures. In 1976 the British Labour government was forced by International Monetary Fund (IMF) loan conditions to institute public-sector cuts that foreshadowed Thatcherism. In 1993, the Ontario NDP government, in response to a mounting deficit caused by the economic downturn, introduced a series of harsh cuts in public spending, including imposed cuts in public-sector pay. Even the Swedish Social Democrats in 1990 abandoned de facto the goal of full employment in their pursuit of monetary stability. In Canada, during the 1993 federal election campaign, few believed the Liberals were serious in their promise to refuse ratification of the North American Free Trade Agreement unless their conditions on matters such as labour and the environment were met; as it turned out, they did in fact ratify it, although they received few concessions.

There were alternatives in each of these cases, but the governments were genuinely under tremendous pressure to renege on their previous policy commitments. The "logic of the situation," as interpreted by policy advisors and powerful lobbies, seemed to point in a single direction. It would have taken considerable courage and commitment, and solid popular backing, to defy it. In some cases (e.g., the Mitterrand government), the only alternative might have been some measure of isolation from the international economy, with very serious consequences. Human agency has its limits. Nonetheless, it would perhaps be most accurate to say that these severe economic tests have revealed the latent weaknesses of many of these parties: their unresponsiveness to their members, their leaders' absorption into the existing networks of power, the degeneration of the parties from movements into simple electoral machines.

The result, of course, of government "U-turns" with respect to announced policies, or of the simple inability to fulfil promises to create jobs, to reduce the deficit, or to improve social services, is increased public disenchantment with the governing parties. These disappointments fuel cynicism about the democratic process itself, and often about parties as such. Party loyalties are strained—citizens become floating voters, and often angry protest voters, available for recruitment by new movements. These strains have affected parties of the left more seriously than those of the Right, but the latter have also failed to deliver economic prosperity and have suffered in their turn.

Another factor, in addition to the narrowing of policy alternatives and the growing role of the bureaucracy, that has contributed to the decline of parties is the increased importance of interest groups and social movements. In some political systems, parties themselves have been at the centre of subcultural networks of associations. Citizens are now more mobile and less likely to be part of tightly knit communities that reinforce party loyalties. In Europe, for instance, the destruction of traditional working-class neighbourhoods has undermined the socialist and labour parties, while the traditional religious subcultural networks are being weakened by secularization.

The fading of traditional cleavages and subcultures is viewed by social theorists such as Jürgen Habermas as resulting from an inevitable destructive process of rationalistic criticism of premodern values and patterns of behaviour. As these are subjected to public scrutiny, their weak intellectual foundations become apparent.[5] Many politically active citizens have broken with these "churches" and their world views and are bypassing the

parties to express their opinion. Grassroots social movements, such as environmentalism and feminism, have generally chosen to act outside established parties (though they have occasionally founded parties of their own, such as the Green Party in Germany). They have typically been unable to stomach the fact that established parties which have recognized their concerns have had to compromise them because of conflicting demands from other segments of their constituency. The party organizations have often appeared unwelcoming, already in the hands of other groups, and unable to offer the type of participatory politics the new social movements have sought. While the movements are also attempts to affirm new identities, the older parties have on the whole failed to provide either the symbols or the forum for such affirmations.

In Canada, this pattern has been evident as groups such as women's organizations (e.g., the National Action Committee on the Status of Women) or environmental groups (e.g., Greenpeace) have acted outside the parties. The parties too have been influenced by feminism and environmentalism, but have also seen major conflicts between these movements and other interests. The British Columbia NDP, which has been divided in recent

---

...the movements cannot fully identify with the parties...

---

years between supporters of logging, especially the forest unions, and conservationists, provides a textbook case of such conflict. As a result, the movements cannot fully identify with the parties, while some of their attempts to become parties themselves, such as the Canadian Green Party, are short-lived.

Of course, business interests have always exercised considerable power in all capitalist countries; sometimes this manifests itself as direct economic power (e.g., threats, open or implicit, to close factories, invest elsewhere, etc.), and in other situations it is wielded by interest groups. In Canada, the Business Council on National Issues (BCNI), founded in 1976, greatly enhanced the ability of business to engage in lobbying activity. It has been described as "the most powerful and effective interest group in Canada" (Langille, 1987, 70); its main objective has been to limit state intervention in the economy.

Other conventional interest groups, such as trade unions, have in some countries taken up issues like economic planning, social policy, or taxation that were previously the domain of the parties. In Sweden, for instance, the Landsorganisation (LO) union confederation is widely recognized as the source of innovative thinking for the Social Democratic Party, rather than the reverse. Liberal corporatist arrangements provide the greatest opportunity for this sort of expansion of union functions. Once again, the role of parties can be diminished.

Even in the absence of corporatist arrangements, interest groups have been able to exercise considerable influence in many Western democracies. For instance, the well-known phenomenon that Lowi (1967) dubbed "interest group liberalism" gives certain groups in the United States virtual control over the congressional committees and executive agencies which oversee their members' activities (the so-called "iron triangles"). This situation goes well beyond the interplay of different groups envisioned by pluralist theory. These entrenched interests make change very difficult, even if the "logic of the situation" dictates it (another demonstration that it is not truly ineluctable). Party allegiances are less relevant here than the strength of the interest group in the legislator's district, especially since the presidential system removes the incentives for tight party discipline.

The role of interest groups as opposed to parties is further enhanced by their importance as sources of campaign finance. American political action committees, furthermore, finance the campaigns of individual members of Congress: most funds are not channelled through the parties. Individual businesses, too, often exercise their own pull on politicians by contributing directly to their campaigns—in Japan and Italy, where recent scandals have revealed the extent of kickbacks and influence peddling, the bribes have generally gone to parliamentarians themselves or to factional leaders, not to the parties.

Moreover, the greater economic challenges facing governments during the past 20 years have created conditions favourable to powerful, charismatic leaders, who have often overshadowed their parties. Inflation, unemployment, deficits, and major industrial restructuring all have required stronger governments, able to take on vested interests in the name of their visions of the national good. The decline of parties has meant that they could not provide the fund of legitimacy and support governments needed for these actions. Instead, strong leaders, of whom Ronald Reagan in the U.S. and Margaret Thatcher in Great Britain were the prototypes, took over the function of gathering public support for new and wrenching policy shifts designed to respond to the radically changed climate of the late 1970s and

1980s. Both were able to garner votes beyond their parties' traditional constituencies on the basis of their own personal appeal and their own perception of the public mood. Both could be viewed as examples of "Bonapartism."

This term refers to the rule of leaders who are able to override even dominant interests in the name of their particular vision of the long-term national good. They generally come to power in times of acute conflict between dominant groups, or with the subordinate classes, or when the country is faced with extraordinary challenges; they typically have the charisma that allows them to appeal for support directly to the masses. They rise above parties, replacing them as sources of policy formation and political legitimacy. General de Gaulle, for example, made no secret of his contempt for partisan politics.

Reagan and Thatcher are less extreme cases of Bonapartism. Both, however, received mandates not only to attack the working class and the poor, though these were prime targets for both, but also to ignore the interests of many segments of business and industry. Thatcher came to power when Britain's economic decline had reached an acute stage, and when the working class appeared to be in need of a short, sharp lesson, having brought down the Heath government in 1974 and undone Callaghan's attempts to create an incomes policy. Her monetarism also imposed real hardship on many sectors of British manufacturing; the deindustrialization of Britain has hit some sectors of British business very hard. She dominated the Conservative party, as its constitution allowed her to do, and placed her own supporters in key positions of power. When she came into acute and open conflict with the dominant segment of business—the City of London—over European integration, however, she fell from power. Reagan, similarly, was deaf to the cries of many segments of the U.S. manufacturing industry for protection, pursuing instead a policy of trade liberalization, and ignored business opposition to his deficit spending.

Both leaders had forged a direct link to the electorate, based on an appeal to traditional values and racial insecurity. Reagan drew heavily on the support of the Christian Right, while Thatcher stressed the Protestant virtues of hard work and self-reliance; both combined these with strident patriotism, an aggressive posture in foreign policy, and support for strengthening the state against criminals and internal disorder.

In Canada as well, more and more leaders have come to overshadow their parties, not only in campaign appeals but also in policy formation (Carty, 1988,

24–28). John Diefenbaker may have initiated the trend, but Pierre Elliott Trudeau illustrated it more completely. Trudeau had had no connection with the Liberal party until his election to Parliament in 1965; yet three years later he was party leader and prime minister, winning an

---

...election campaigns are increasingly leader-centred.

---

election with a highly personalized campaign. In power, he showed little interest in party affairs or in Parliament, formulating policy with the aid of the civil service and a few trusted political advisors (Meisel, 1979, 129). It was after his return to office in 1980 that "Bonapartist" tendencies became most pronounced, as initiatives such as the National Energy Policy (NEP) alienated the most important sectors of Canadian business.

At the provincial level, too, leaders who are fresh recruits to the party and can put their stamp on it have been quite numerous in recent years (e.g., Ralph Klein in Alberta, Mike Harcourt in British Columbia). In addition, election campaigns are increasingly leader-centred. The electronic media, with their tendency to personalize the political struggle, seek out and focus on the leaders as symbols and spokespersons of their parties. Voters tend to pay greater attention to the leaders in making their electoral choices; this development has been reinforced by the importance of televised leaders' debates, which have played crucial roles in swinging the voters in at least two of the last three Canadian federal elections.

A well-known example of the predominance of leaders over parties is the candidacy of Ross Perot for the U.S. presidency in 1992. A billionaire, he was able to purchase the services of experienced political consultants, including the manager of Reagan's 1984 campaign, and large blocks of media time. In the end, in spite of his temporary absence from the race, he captured 19 percent of the popular vote. Most noteworthy is that he did this without the support of any existing political party, while his own organization, United We Stand America, was less a party than an ad hoc collection of personal supporters.

An even more extreme case of a leader creating a "party" around himself is the 1994 campaign of Italian media magnate Silvio Berlusconi, who in roughly three months organized a grouping known as Forza Italia ("Go Italy") that emerged from the election as the largest single party and catapulted him into the prime ministership. Berlusconi's personal motives for entering politics aside—his financial empire was in difficulty and threatened by antimonopoly legislation—his campaign carried Perot's methods to the nth degree. No fundraising was necessary, as his companies and his three television networks provided money and media time; Forza Italia is a network of supporters' clubs modelled on those of Berlusconi's soccer club, AC Milan; they were set up by employees detailed from his companies, especially his television-advertising sales network. "There are no policy committees, elected leaderships, or votes. Policy is decided from on high and fine-tuned through extensive market research" (Jacques, 1994, 4.1). While Berlusconi's success was made possible by the collapse of the Italian governing parties in the wake of massive corruption scandals, it is nonetheless symptomatic of trends in all advanced democracies, where disenchantment with parties and politicians has become widespread.

The trend toward stronger, more charismatic leaders, not all of the right, has been seen too in the already established parties: Craxi in Italy, Hawke in Australia, Nakasone in Japan, and Gonzalez in Spain, though in the event Craxi and Nakasone were unable to stave off the serious crises their parties were approaching. While technological developments and the personalizing effect of the mass media have contributed to the increased emphasis on party leaders, especially in the two-party systems, more important have been the new challenges and more difficult tasks that have faced governments over the past 15 years, which have created a need for reinforced support for state policies. One important channel through which this increased support has been generated is the selection of leaders with wide popular appeal.

All of these factors—the narrower room for maneuver available to governments and parties, the greater importance of interest groups, and more leader-centred politics—have combined to weaken parties' bases of support among the people. Whereas in the past, parties could rely on a large group of traditional supporters who had absorbed their politics with their mothers' milk, or at least from their families, today voters are much less firmly attached to one party and more likely to switch votes from one election to the next. In part this is because the issues and cleavages that gave rise to our party systems are now less relevant: for instance, few remember the events that made the Liberals in Canada the party of the great majority of Catholics and the Conservatives the party favoured by most Protestants. In part it is because of the erosion of traditional cleavages and subcultures. However, the rise of working-class subcultures over the past century-and-a-half demonstrates that, beside these processes of destruction, new traditions can also be created. Similarly, in our day the new social movements have given rise in some countries to new parties and world views (e.g., the German Green Party); anti-authoritarian, less materialist values have taken root in large segments of the population, particularly well-educated young people. These trends have been felt in Canada as well, but have lacked a clear national focus because of the regional fragmentation of the country and the persistence of ethnic and linguistic cleavages as major factors in politics. Since most parties remain wedded to their original subcultures, the new social movements, as mentioned above, have often chosen to operate outside of them. Some older cleavages

---

The upshot of these trends is a decline in stable partisan allegiance and increased electoral volatility.

---

inevitably lose their salience for voters, but parties, being complex organizations, often lag in adjusting to these changes. Their caution is understandable. Attempts by parties to "renew" themselves may succeed (e.g., the French Socialists in 1971, though the new party was more leader-centred than the old Section Française de l'Internationale Ouvrière [SFIO]), but there is always the risk of losing traditional supporters while failing to attract new followers (e.g., the Italian Communists' transformation into the Democratic Party of the Left in 1991 led to the splitting off of a sizable left wing).

As the bases of parties are being eroded, they are tempted to resort increasingly to the perquisites of office to maintain themselves in power. However, in a climate of growing cynicism and hostility toward parties, these expedients can be counterproductive, as the recent events in Italy and Japan demonstrate. Corruption discredits the entire party system and makes the electorate yet more volatile.

The upshot of these trends is a decline in stable partisan allegiance and increased electoral volatility. The 1993 Canadian federal election is a striking illustration of this volatility: the Conservatives fell from 43 to 16 percent of the popular vote and the NDP from 20 to 7 percent, while the new Bloc Québécois received 14 percent, and the Reform Party rose from barely 2 to 19 percent. But instability is also evident in other major democracies. Italy had seen the sudden rise of the

Northern League even before the appearance of Forza Italia on the scene, Sweden that of the New Democracy party, and Japan of a series of reforming parties. All of these new formations, and the Canadian Reform Party, have as part of their appeal a rejection of party politics as it has been conducted, and of party politicians as well. They are also markedly leader-centred. Beyond these immediately visible phenomena, the number of voters reporting that they have no party identification has been rising. Such increased electoral volatility might be interpreted as evidence of greater political knowledge and sophistication on the part of the citizenry, but in many cases it stems from a simple, often emotive reaction against the existing parties and their inability to solve the pressing problems besetting the country.

CONCLUSION

◆ ◆ ◆

The prospect is one of continued decline for political parties, as leaders take on increasing prominence. Yet this decline is not inevitable, and the disappearance of parties would impoverish our democracy. Without strong parties, democracies are subject to the seemingly ineluctable imperatives of the market economy and the soulless struggle for power of mighty interest groups.

Experiments with nonparty democracy have shown its weaknesses. At the turn of the century, American Progressives advocated "nonpartisan" city government in reaction to corrupt urban political machines. They saw local government in largely technocratic terms, and their attempt to depoliticize it served to mask underlying conflict of interests rather than to eliminate it. Well-organized interest groups were able to impose their agendas with relatively little competition or scrutiny. Depoliticization and nonparty councillors meant citizens had to work harder to inform themselves about the councillors' records, which resulted in lower voter turnout; elected officials became less, rather than more, responsible to the electorate. In most Canadian municipalities, the same defects can be seen to this day. The strongly technocratic flavour of Ross Perot's message is of a piece with this nonpartisan syndrome.

Parties are not only necessary to organize choice in a representative system; they can also play a positive role in enhancing democracy. They can provide the vehicle through which ordinary citizens can affect the course of policy; they can be agencies for political participation, leadership recruitment and selection, and political mobilization. Only parties can aggregate disparate interests around common purposes, forcing single-issue groups to take into account other viewpoints and considerations. They are not simply passive aggregators and brokers of existing interests; parties can also create new interests and world views, and shape existing ones. Only parties can, in this way, inject even a modicum of principle into public life. In the end, the new politics may have only its novelty to recommend it.

Notes

1. See Macpherson (1977, 112–14). Macpherson's work also contains many acute observations on liberal-democratic theory in general.
2. See King (1969) for a good summary of the functions parties are held to perform in liberal democracies.
3. I am indebted for these ideas to Clarke et al. (1984), chs. 1 and 2.
4. Royal commissions are formed to deal with particularly knotty policy issues, and when innovative solutions may be required. A notable example was the commission chaired by Justice Emmett Hall which laid the foundation for universal medicare in Canada (though it had been pioneered by the CCF in Saskatchewan). The Macdonald Royal Commission's 1985 report was arguably even more influential in opening the way for freer trade and a series of neo-conservative policy initiatives. The point is that royal commissions are generally nonpartisan, relying primarily on expert opinion, supplemented at times by submissions from interest groups.
5. See Habermas (1975), esp. Part II, ch. 7, and MacIntyre (1981).

References

Beer, S. 1969 (1965). *British Politics in the Collectivist Age*. New York: Vintage.

Burke, E. 1826. *The Works of the Right Honourable Edmund Burke*, Volume 2. London: C. & J. Rivington.

Carty, R.K. 1988. "Three Canadian Party Systems." In *Party Democracy in Canada*, edited by G. Perlin, 15–30. Scarborough: Prentice-Hall.

Clarke, H., J. Jenson, L. LeDuc, and J.H. Pammett. 1984. *Absent Mandate: The Politics of Discontent in Canada*. Toronto: Gage.

Courtney, J.C. 1978. "Recognition of Canadian Political Parties in Parliament and in Law." *Canadian Journal of Political Science* XI, 1: 34–60.

Gramsci, A. 1971. *Selections from the Prison Notebooks*, edited by Q. Hoare and G. Nowell Smith. London: Lawrence and Wishart.

Habermas, J. 1975 (1973). *Legitimation Crisis*. Boston: Beacon.

Jacques, Martin. 1994. "Big Brother." *The Sunday Times* (April 3): 4.1–4.2.

King, A. 1969. "Political Parties in Western Democracies." *Polity* II, 2: 111–41.

Langille, D. 1987. "The Business Council on National Issues and the Canadian State." *Studies in Political Economy* 24 (Autumn): 41–85.

Lenin, V.I. 1967 (1904). "One Step Forward, Two Steps Back." In *Selected Works*, Volume I. New York: International Publishers.

Lowi, T. 1967. "The Public Philosophy: Interest Group Liberalism." *American Political Science Review* 61, 1: 5–24.

MacIntyre, A. 1981. *After Virtue: A Study in Moral Theory.* Notre Dame, Ill.: University of Notre Dame Press.

Macpherson, C.B. 1977. *The Life and Times of Liberal Democracy.* Oxford: Oxford University Press.

Meisel, J. 1979. "The Decline of Party in Canada." In *Party Politics in Canada,* 4th ed., edited by H. Thorburn, 119–35. Scarborough: Prentice-Hall.

Poulantzas, N. 1980 (1978). *State, Power, Socialism.* London: Verso.

Schumpeter, J. 1950 (1942). *Capitalism, Socialism, and Democracy,* 3rd ed. New York and Evanston: Harper & Row.

Van Wolferen, K. 1989. *The Enigma of Japanese Power: People and Politics in a Stateless Nation.* New York: Knopf.

Terms & Concepts

Bonapartism
bureaucracy
cadre parties
competitive elitism
corporatist arrangements
Court "party"
depoliticization
direct democacy
disciplined parties

Edmund Burke
electoral volatility
Green Party
interest group liberalism
interest groups
iron triangles
parties' brokerage function
pluralism
policy innovations

political action committees
reforming parties
Ross Perot
Silvio Berlusconi
social movements
stable partisan allegiance
voter's information costs

Questions

1. What is a political party? What role do parties play in the operation of democratic government?

2. Amyot argues that the chief rationale for the existence of political parties in liberal democracies is a pragmatic one. Explain.

3. Are parties as constrained by their environments as Amyot says they are? Explain your answer.

4. What is the relationship between parties and nonparty organizations such as interest groups and social movements? What are the advantages and disadvantages of each for achieving political change?

5. How open should political parties be? Should just anyone be allowed to be a member of a political party?

6. Is Amyot too optimistic about the future of parties, given the evidence he has cited?

The Mass Media and Democracy

James W. Carey

Editors' Note

Carey tackles the thorny question of the relationships that exist between the kind of "public" we have and need in a democracy, and the media's role in creating this public. Currently such matters as the media's intrusiveness, people's right to "know," the obsession with personal detail, the focus on the sensational and/or the pictorial, the drive for profits, and the changing technologies we employ, are all matters of deep concern.

What is happening to the media and with what effects? There was a time when reporters would physically prevent photographers from taking pictures of Franklin Delano Roosevelt in a wheelchair. Nowadays, journalism is usually far more aggressive, and anything goes. Will the rest of the world adopt American-style political coverage, at least to some extent? Is jour-

nalism about "truth," or is it always a form of conversation in which we convey stories with a moral, social and mythic significance? Is it the recording or the formation of public opinion?

Canada is still, in some ways, quite different from the United States in its media coverage of politics and politicians, as David Taras and others have shown.[1] Canadians do not have an elevated First Amendment to bring out at every opportunity. (The First Amendment to the American Bill of Rights protects the freedoms of religion, speech, and peaceful assembly, as well as freedom of the press.) But we should not ignore the questions that Carey raises. What is happening to the audience and to our notions of a democratic public now? Carey's article is interesting in that after a great deal of gloom

and doom about the interplay between media and public, he ends on a very positive note. He sees great democratic opportunities as the media evolve.

Is Carey's conclusion compelling? In particular, does he come to terms with the power of television, and its effects on the public? Robert Hughes comments that "for most members of an audience, an audience far greater than print can claim, TV has taken over their image banks, their modes of social expression."[2] Network television has failed to provide a forum for the real discussion of American politics, says Hughes, and the prevailing wisdom is that television in America should be left to the "free market"—a market that is in fact an oligopoly. One does not have to read Chomsky to despair at what is—and is not—covered by the media.

1. David Taras, "A Question of Character: Political Reporting in Canada and the United States," in David Thomas, ed., *Canada and the United States: Differences* that Count (Peterborough: Broadview Press, 1993) 326–42.
2. Robert Hughes, "Why Watch It Anyway?" *New York Review of Books,* Feb. 16, 1995, 37–42.

John Chancellor was upset. Impeccably groomed and spoken, this visual icon of virtually the entire history of television journalism could hardly contain his distress. Beneath his characteristically genial manner, his anger showed, as he lectured at Columbia University's Du Pont Forum on what went wrong in the 1992 U.S. presidential election.[1] The catalog took more than 30 minutes: The election was the worst in history, worse even than the monumentally smarmy campaign of 1988; one no longer needed to belong to a political party to run for president; talk show hosts displaced journalists; the public filled the air with silly questions on ersatz television debates and call-in radio programs; faxes, "800-numbers," computer bulletin boards, private satellite hook-ups and electronic mail had conspired with talk-show hosts Arsenio Hall and Rush Limbaugh, and interviewers Larry King and Tabitha Soren to evacuate the role of journalism from presidential politics. In sum, Chancellor asserted that network journalism had declined, and the new news of endlessly chattering masses cluttered the electronic highway with trivia.

All good stories have a villain at the center, and this one was no exception: It had Ross Perot. Perot's electronic campaign circumvented party organization, presidential primaries and a national convention, as volunteers placed him on the ballot in state after state. Perot ignored local newspapers, radio and television and, in effect, told the national press that he could win without them—or by running against them. Perot demonstrated it was possible to run with one's own money and avoid restrictions on federal matching funds.[2] He laid down new rules for presidential politics: Avoid specifics; stay away from journalists; hold as few press conferences as possible; stay away from the serious interview programs; and cultivate electronic populism by exploiting call-in radio. Who, after all, needs Sam Donaldson? Worse yet, who needs John Chancellor?

Chancellor most of all mourned—and who can blame him—his own irrelevance and that of journalists like him. In his view, there was no one left to challenge the candidates, to hold their feet to the fire. The quality of campaigning was in decline because politicians had direct access to the public through media that offered neither threat nor intimidation. All this gave rise to the worst fear of the generation of journalists who had been affected by the Second World War: The new media had greased the highway of modern politics for demagogues and demagoguery. Chancellor had encountered the vampire of postmodern politics and found himself without a crucifix.

This episode serves to remind the reader that the following consideration of the mass media and democracy—which are always intertwined—occurs at a particularly opaque historical juncture. Something is afoot in modern societies that seems peculiarly tied to the decline of certain media that have defined the context of communications and democracy since at least the end of the Second World War. The media have changed decisively in the last 20 years, both as technologies and institutions. Yet democracy has changed also; the ends of political life have been reconceived in recent years. There is a widespread demand for less *pro forma* political representation, whether by the press or elected officials, and for more real participation.

Yet these changes only signal that the meanings of democracy and communication are historically variable. The meaning of democracy changes over time because forms of communication with which to conduct politics change. The meaning of communication also changes over time depending on the central impulses and aspirations of democratic politics. Neither communication nor democracy is a transcendent concept; they do not exist outside history. The meaning of these terms varies with available media and with whatever concrete notions of democracy happen to be popular at any particular time.

The journalistic side of the twentieth century can be defined as the struggle for democracy and an independent media against propaganda and subservience to the state. That struggle culminated during the first half of this century in the seizure of the means of communication by the demagogues of the 1930s and 1940s—Adolf Hitler and Josef Stalin—and their Cold War reincarnation of the 1950s, Joseph McCarthy—the ghost that still haunts U.S. journalism.[3]

While this struggle was imprinted upon the generation of the time, the fear of demagoguery seemed a curious hangover of a forgotten age for those in the post-McCarthy generations. Similarly, the quest for so-called objectivity seemed to a younger generation a curious absence of passion and commitment: a deliberate sitting out of history.

Published by permission of the *Journal of International Affairs* and the Trustees of Columbia University in the City of New York. *Journal of International Affairs* 47:1 (Summer 1993).

This historical, generational divide is what the hyperbolic phrase in the title "between the modern and the postmodern" is designed to catch. For John Chancellor was right—if only by implication—about one thing: A medium implies and constitutes a way of life. Whatever democracy as a way of life may be, it is constituted by particular media of communication and institutional arrangements through which politics is conducted, whether speech in the agora, the colonial newspaper and the pamphlet in the taverns of Philadelphia, the omnibus daily in the commercial city or the television network in an industrialized nation. Similarly, a medium of communication is defined by the democratic aspirations of those involved in politics: a conversation among equals, the organ of a political ideology, a watchdog on the state, an instrument of dialogue on public issues, a device for transmitting information or an arena for the struggle of interest groups. Modern journalism began around 1890 with the advent of a national system of communication and has had a pretty long run.[4] Its time now seems to be about up. Yet, there was democracy before modern journalism; and there will be democracy after it, despite difficult and dangerous transitions to be negotiated. The sections that follow contrast two historically specific forms of the relationship between journalism and democracy: journalism in a *public society* and journalism in a *national society*. The first form constitutes the original understanding of the press and the First Amendment in the United States.[5] The second form, in which the media acts more as a watchdog on the state, has been typical of the modern period that now seems to be coming to an end. These distinctions are important because it appears that the struggle today to recreate public life through new forms of communication such as cable television and talk radio are heavily inspired by images of democracy and public life from the colonial and early national periods. This article then discusses the potential for journalism and democracy in the years ahead.

This last discussion focuses primarily on U.S. experience. Nonetheless it can be instructive in a more international context for several reasons. New forms of communication rarely meet resistance in the United States: They are allowed to diffuse rapidly and penetrate deeply into the social fabric. Developments in the United States frequently foreshadow, though they never duplicate, changes that will occur in other countries. Second, the globalization of communication, and the creation of transnational audiences and markets—which are features of the contemporary period—have introduced similar problematic elements into the political life of all

democracies, not just the United States. The press may everywhere be part of the apparatus by which the accountability of the governors to the governed is achieved. Yet, just as the meaning of democracy and communication varies historically, it varies across nations as well. Thus, ultimately, the precise terms of accountability and the role of the press in each society must be examined on a country-by-country basis.

EVOLUTION OF THE PUBLIC

◆ ◆ ◆

The original understanding of journalism, politics and democracy in the United States emerged in the public houses and taverns of the colonial era. Pubs were presided over by publicans who were often publishers. Publicans picked up information from conversations in the pub and from travellers who often recorded what they had seen and heard on their journeys in log books stationed at the end of the bar. Publishers then recorded such conversation and gossip and printed it, in order that it might be preserved and circulated. They also

---

...journalism—reflected speech—was the ongoing flow of conversation, not in the halls of the legislatures, but in the public houses.

---

printed speeches, orations, sermons, offers of goods for sale and political opinions of those who gathered in public places, largely merchants and traders. Newspapers, which were circulated in public houses, animated conversation and discussion. Consequently, journalism—reflected speech—was the ongoing flow of conversation, not in the halls of the legislatures, but in the public houses.

This context provides the original understanding of the *public*: a group of merchants, traders, citizens and political activists—often strangers—who gathered to discuss the news. Describing Philadelphia on the eve of the Revolutionary War, Sam Bass Warner observed that

> gossip in the taverns provided Philadelphia's basic cells of community life....Every ward of the city had its inns and taverns and the London Coffee House served as central communication node of the entire

city....Out of the meetings at the neighborhood tavern came much of the commonplace community development...essential to the governance of the city...and made it possible...to form effective committees of correspondence.[6]

Today in the United States, the public is an abstraction and a philosophical term. "The public's right to know" is the worn slogan of modern journalism. The press justifies itself in the name of the public: The press exists to inform it, to serve as its extended eyes and ears and to represent and protect its interest. All privileges and prerogatives of the press, such as freedom of information laws or the right to keep news sources confidential, are rationalized in the name of the public.

The eighteenth-century public, which inspired democratic theory, is of a more humble origin. It was brought into existence by the conditions of the eighteenth-century city and the printing press. It was a concrete social group who gathered in public houses to talk, read the news together, dispute the meaning of events and relate political impulses to political actions. The public was elevated into a social form by the news and, in turn, the primary subject of the news was the public. The public formed because urban life was sufficiently developed so that strangers were regularly thrown into contact with one another. Technology allowed dissemination of newspapers and pamphlets, which provided a common focus for discussion and conversation. The public, then, was a society of conversationalists—or disputants. It was not, as it became during the modern period, a fiction or an abstraction. It was not a group of people sitting at home watching television or privately and invisibly reading newspapers. Nor was it the results of a public opinion poll.

The public space, in turn, depended on public habits, manners and talents, such as the ability to welcome strangers, to avoid intimacy, to wear a public mask and to shun the personal. As such, the public was taken to be both critical and rational. It was *critical* in the sense that nothing in public was taken for granted; everything was subject to argument and evidence. It was *rational* in the sense that the speaker was responsible for giving reasons for believing in any assertion; and there was no intrinsic appeal to authority. The public was, thus, more than a group of people or a mode of discourse: It was a seat of political power, located in the world between the state and the private sector. It was the only sphere in which power could wear the face of rationality, for it was the only sphere where private interest might be transcended.

The critical factor in the relationship between the public and journalism was that journalism was not an end in itself, but was justified in terms of its ability to serve and bring into existence an actual social arrangement, a particular form of democracy as discourse in a sphere of independent, rational, political influence. While freedom of the press was valued as an individual right, the importance of the press was predicated on the unspoken premise of the existence of the public, and not the reverse.

THE PUBLIC AND THE MEANING OF THE FIRST AMENDMENT

◆ ◆ ◆

Today, the First Amendment is often viewed as a loose collection of clauses on the freedoms of religion, assembly, speech and the press. Typically, U.S. citizens array the separate rights contained in each clause and the legal cases that fall under them. Today, the modern slogan "freedom of the press" belongs to those who own the presses or to journalists and the organizations for which they work. When read against the background of public life, however, the First Amendment is not a casual and loose collection of separate clauses or high-minded principles. It does not deed freedom of the press as a property right to journalists or any particular group. The First Amendment is simply a compact description of public life as it existed at the time the Founding Fathers developed the U.S. Constitution, and as they hoped it would continue to exist.

The First Amendment says that people are free to gather together, to have public spaces and to speak to one another free of the intrusion of the state or its representatives. They are further free to share what they have to say beyond the immediate place of utterance. Freedom of the press, in this case, means simply the right and ability to record and preserve, to enlarge and disseminate the conversation of the culture.

The public remains the implicit term of the First Amendment. It is the God term—the worshipped concept—of liberal society and the press. Without the public, neither the press nor democracy makes any sense. Today, however, this original conception of a public of discussion and disputation, independent of both the press and the state, has been abandoned. Public opinion, for example, no longer refers to opinions expressed in public and then recorded in the press. Public opinion is now formed by the press and modeled by the public opinion industry, polling and interest groups.[7] With the rise of the polling industry, the previous understanding of the public went into eclipse. The public has been replaced by the interest group as the object of analysis and key political actor, and the public has ceased to have a real existence. For much of the nineteenth century, political parties served as the principal means of influencing the distribution of economic resources and government privileges. But late in the century, interest and pressure groups developed as a new vehicle for pressuring governments. Thus, voting according to the party line in elections became less important, and interest groups operated in the private sector and behind the scenes to manipulate public opinion. As a result, the public faded into a statistical artifact or an audience whose opinions counted only insofar as individuals refracted the pressure of mass publicity. In short, while the word *public* continued in the English language as an ancient memory and pious hope, the public as a feature and factor of real politics disappeared.

Public life stands for a form of politics in which, in Jefferson's phrase, "We could all be participants in the government of our affairs."[8] Political equality, in its most primitive mode—to borrow and twist some lines from Bruce Smith—simply means the right to be seen and heard, or to have a public life.[9] When the life of a people is dominated by a few public figures or political celebrities, the rest of the population, denied the opportunity to be seen or heard, takes refuge and solace in private life and private pleasures. The passions for public life only grow and persist when people can speak and act as citizens, and have some guarantee that others see, hear and remember what they say. Therefore, the object of politics remains the desire to restore what Alexis de Tocqueville called the "little republics within the frame of the larger republic," and to create a palpable public to which each citizen can belong.[10]

BETWEEN TRADITIONAL PRESS AND MODERN JOURNALISM

◆ ◆ ◆

The transition from the original understanding of the press, the public and politics to journalism in the modern era was long and twisted. Throughout the nineteenth century, the public sphere divided into regional and class-based conflicting factions, organized around political parties and a partisan press. Journalism became an organ of such parties or ideologically aligned with political parties. Journalism began to express and reflect a bifurcated public sphere, as individuals joined politics through parties and the press.[11] Participation in the public sphere occurred more through parties, press, demonstrations and street parades, and less through public discourse. As the franchise was extended, legal participation rose to unprecedented and never-to-be repeated levels: Voter turnout averaged 77 percent in the last quarter of the nineteenth century. But popular politics, as Michael McGerr put it, "involved more than suffrage rights and record turnouts;"[12] that is, elections required visible support, mobilized through popular journalism and political parties. Thus, the transformation to a separation between politics and the public had begun.

THE MODERN ERA OF JOURNALISM

◆ ◆ ◆

The modern era of journalism stretched from the 1890s to the 1970s. It began with the birth of national magazines, the development of mass urban newspapers, the creation of primitive forms of electronic communication and the domination of news dissemination by the wire services.

Truly national media and a national audience in the United States were eventually supplemented by motion pictures, produced in Hollywood and distributed nationwide, and by radio in the 1920s. These media created a "great audience," a new collectivity in which peo-

These media created a "great audience," a new collectivity in which people were destined to live out a major part of their lives.

ple were destined to live out a major part of their lives. The media cut across the structural divisions in society, drawing their audience irrespective of race, ethnicity, occupation, region or social class. This was the first national and first mass audience—open to all. Modern communications media allowed individuals in nations as large as the United States to be linked, for the first time, directly to the "imaginary community of the nation," without the mediating influence of regional and other local affiliations.[13]

The modern period culminated in the network era of television, when the entire nation seemed to be assembled in front of the three commercial networks—CBS,

ABC and NBC—especially on the high holy days of politics, such as those surrounding the Kennedy assassination or the quadrennial political conventions.[14] The nation sat down to be counted as citizens of a 24-hour-a-day republic.

This rise of national media represented a centripetal force in social organization. Such media greatly enhanced the ability to control vast expanses of territory by reducing signal time and laying down direct lines of access among national centers—such as New York, Washington and Hollywood—and dispersed audiences.[15] This produced a remarkable potential for the centralization of power and authority.

The Progressive Movement and its Impact on Journalism

The period from the 1890s onward saw the creation of a variety of social and cultural movements that were reactions against and impulses toward the formation of a national society through a national system of communications. Movements and groups such as progressivism, populism, nativism, the know-nothings, women's suffrage, temperance, the Grange and ethnic or racial affiliations were all attempts to master, tame and direct the currents of social change. These movements expressed a restless search for new identities and developed new forms of social and cultural life, such as political parties, trade associations, professional groups and ethnic associations. They were organized by the new media, defined by the media, commented upon by the media and formed within the media. At a minimum, these movements were organized as a response to new conditions of social life brought about in part by the new media.

From the standpoint of journalism, the most important social movement was progressivism, which both redefined the past and projected a new democratic future. It contained economic, political and cultural elements which were closely connected. First, it was an attack on the plutocracy—concentrated economic power and the national social class that increasingly had a strangle hold over wealth and industry. The economic dimension of the progressive movement, however, also included the struggle by the middle-class professionals— such as doctors, lawyers, journalists and social workers—to become a national class and find a place in the national occupational structure and the national system of class influence and power. Thus, the professionals of the progressive movement were in many ways a less powerful imitation—a shadow movement—of the national class of plutocrats who ran and controlled industrial America.

Journalists were among these new progressive professionals. They formed national groups and lobbied to professionalize their standing through higher education. They sponsored histories of their profession and a new reading of the First Amendment in which the speech and press clauses became their possession. In effect, journalists became a new cultural elite with codes of ethical conduct justifying their new-found status in the nascent middle class professional world. They tried to figure out new ways of reporting on and commenting about this new world—a new professional ideology—which justified their place in the new order of things.

Second, progressivism was a movement of political reform at the national level and an attempt by the middle class and their intellectual allies to reclaim the cities from the political bosses and the urban machines. In many cases, the movement was an attempt to uproot the political influence of working-class groups who had seized city politics from local commercial and cultural elites during the great migrations before and after the Civil War. Progressivism was devoted to so-called good government by the middle class and created the chain of Better Government Associations that one still finds in major U.S. cities.

Journalists where usually allies of this movement for better government, in that they were committed to certain traditionally middle-class ideals of honesty and uprightness. Yet they also warred against the machines because city political bosses governed through the ward and patronage system and did not need the press to manage public opinion. Reform movements, in contrast, were dependent upon the publicity that only the press could give and thus assiduously courted and flattered the new journalists. Journalists were aligned with the progressive movement by both interests and ideology, although primarily through beliefs about modernity and the role of the press in the modernizing process.

Third, progressivism was a cultural movement that sought to define new styles of life, patterns of child rearing, modes of family life, taste in art and personal conduct. This cultural dimension was as important in the movement as the economic and political ones. Progressivism in culture became part of the outlook of the journalists who took up residence in the new national media, which formed the discourse of the nation.

The three wings of progressivism were joined to one common desire: to escape the merely local and contingent, to seek the distant and remote and to prefer the national over the provincial. The national media of communication—magazines, books and newspapers—were the arena where the progressive program was set out and the struggle for its legitimation occurred.

Muckraking

The initial impact of the progressive movement on journalism was the rise of muckraking in the first decade of the twentieth century. Initially, the muckraking journalists directed their attacks against the plutocracy and the business class in an attempt to expose corruption. Muckraking arose within magazines rather than newspapers, for the former had no affiliation with politics, let alone with a given political party. While they owed something to the crusading tactics of newspapers, muckraking magazines, like sensational newspapers, did not dwell long on any one topic, as Michael McGerr pointed out.[16] They were hit-and-run artists who exposed corruption or urged the passage of pro-consumer legislation, but they did not have the shape and persistence to constitute a tradition of journalism.[17] What muckraking

---

The press...became the independent voter writ large; its only loyalty was to an abstract truth and an abstract public interest.

---

did was promote a tradition of journalism that took as its task the unmasking of power. It strove to serve as watchdog, not only on the state, but also on interest groups.

Muckraking gave rise to propaganda analysis: the unmasking of attempts by both public and private interest groups to control and manipulate the press. It also demonstrated that democracy was no longer competition between political parties bearing explicit programs and ideologies. It had become a competition among interest and pressure groups that used the state, political parties and the press to control the distribution of economic rewards and social privileges. Moreover, the struggle among interest groups turned language into so-called public relations—an instrument in a struggle for advantage rather than a vehicle of the truth.

The Fourth Estate

In the twentieth century, new traditions of journalism and particular conceptions of the relationship between media and democracy formed themselves in mutual relief. The press, in effect, broke away from politics and

became the so-called Fourth Estate. It established itself, at least in principle, as independent of all institutions, including the state, political parties and interest groups. It became the independent voter writ large; its only loyalty was to an abstract truth and an abstract public interest.

This is the origin of the concept of *objectivity* in journalism, as Michael Schudson has shown.[18] Objectivity was a defensive measure, an attempt to secure by quasi-scientific means a method for recording the world, independent of the political and social forces that were shaping it. In this rendition, democratic media were representatives of the people because the people were no longer represented by political parties or the state. The media became the eyes and ears of a public that could not see and hear for itself—or indeed, talk to itself. Journalists went where public could not go, acquired information that the public could not amass on its own and tore away the veil of appearances that masked the play of power and privilege. The press seized the First Amendment and exercised it in the name of a public that could no longer exercise it on its own.

Paradoxically, this new role as representative of the public was contained within a sentiment that was increasingly antipopulist and antipublic. In a world ruled by interests and regulated by science, the public faded into a spectator. Journalism was diminished along with the public. In theory, at least, news was progressively separated from the truth. News was a blip on the social radar, an early-warning system that something was happening. The truth, however, became the exclusive domain of science. It was no longer a product of the conversation or debate of the public, or of investigations by journalists. Journalists merely translated the arcane language of experts—scientists in their labs, bureaucrats in their offices—into a publicly accessible language for the masses. By transmitting the judgments of experts, they ratified decisions made by that class—not those made by the public or public representatives.

Other than acting as transmitters, journalists performed one other vital function: publicity. News kept the experts honest, not by establishing the truth, but by turning on the hot light of scandal and publicity. As Walter Lippmann, who had more faith in publicity than in the news or an informed public, put it:

> The great healing effect of publicity is that by revealing man's nature, it civilizes him. If people have to declare, publicly, what they want and why they want it, they won't be able to be altogether ruthless. A special interest openly avowed is no terror to democracy; it is neutralized by publicity.[19]

Disengagement from Politics

While independent journalism legitimized democratic politics of publicity and experts, it also confirmed the psychological incompetence of most people to participate in it. A political system of "democracy without citizens" evolved.[20] A valuable role for the mass media was preserved, but the role of political parties and citizens diminished. First, independent print journalism weakened political parties, and then television decimated them. It reduced them to devices for fundraising for advertising and turned politics toward the cult of personality. Citizens, denied a public arena, became either consumers of or escapists from politics. Political journalism became, in Joan Didion's apt phrase, a game of "insider baseball."[21] The conversation of the culture moved outside the public realm and into private spaces. Increasingly, journalism became devoted to the sanctity of the fact and so-called objectivity, but invaded every domain of privacy with the hot light of publicity.

A journalism developed that was an early warning system, but one that kept the public in a constant state of agitation or boredom. It became a journalism that reported a continuing stream of expert opinion, but because there was no agreement among experts, it was more like talk-show gossip and petty manipulation than bearing witness to the truth. It was a journalism of fact without regard to understanding, through which the public was immobilized, demobilized and was merely a ratifier of judgments delivered from on high. It was, above all, a journalism that justified itself in the public's name, but in which the public played no role, except as an audience: a receptacle to be informed by experts and an excuse for the practice of publicity.

The media and democracy were increasingly reduced to a game and a dialectic of appearance and demystification, which tied the state, interest groups and

---

A political system of "democracy

without citizens" evolved.

---

the press together in a symbiotic relationship against the fragmented remains of the public. The game was played because each had something the other side needed. Interest groups and sources had newsworthy political information, the indispensable raw material needed to construct the news. Journalists could provide publicity slanted favorably or unfavorably. Elites sought to exchange a minimal amount of potentially damaging information for as much positively slanted coverage as

could be obtained. Journalists sought to extract information for stories that would bring acclaim or acceptance from editors and colleagues.

The public, however, watched this game as an increasingly alienated and cynical spectator: The public learned to distrust all appearances, whether mounted by elites or journalists, and to look at language as a mere instrument of interest and obfuscation. In this context, journalism could no longer link up political impulses with political action; it could produce publicity, scandal and drama, but it could not produce politics.

During the second half of the twentieth century, the average U.S. citizen was no longer interested in politics. Indeed, the title of E.J. Dionne, Jr.'s book, *Why Americans Hate Politics*, expresses a more active alienation from public life than is revealed by the low voter-turnouts that have marked the entire modern period.[22] The absence of participation is partially evidenced by active disengagement from political parties—and the rise of the independent voter, or more often, the independent non-voter.

The best evidence for the public's disengagement from politics was the beginning of a long-term decline in political participation, measured by voting, especially in presidential elections. Political participation continued to fall throughout the period of journalism in a national society with temporary blips and recoveries during certain periods, such as the Great Depression and Second World War. Yet the trend line was clear, and bureaucratic attempts to reverse it were ineffective, such as extending the franchise, easing voter-registration restrictions or democratizing the candidate-selection process through primaries. The overall decline of public involvement was even sharper than revealed by the conventional measures of voting in presidential elections, because it did not include the even more precipitous declines in primary, local and off-year congressional elections.[23]

Above all—as poll after poll showed—the public increasingly distrusted journalists and viewed them as a hindrance to, rather than an avenue toward, politics and reform.[24] The watchdog press—the adversary press—was exposed to even more skepticism during the period of its greatest success, namely during the Vietnam War and Watergate.[25] While the press dismissed the rising tide of criticism during these episodes as merely reactionary politics, the problem went deeper. In the public's eyes, the media had become the adversary of all institutions, including the public itself. As the press sought greater constitutional power, greater independence from the state and the removal of all restrictions on its activities and news-gathering rights, it pushed the legal case that it was a special institution with unique rights. These special rights were independent of the First-Amendment rights and different from—and often opposed to—the rights of ordinary people.

Ultimately, the public became an observer of the press rather than "participator[s] in the government of [its] affairs" and the dialogue of democracy.[26] The situation became one in which it was the media that needed to be protected, rather than the citizens' abilities to participate in politics. The individual was seen as remote and helpless compared to the two major protagonists—the government and the media.

Despite the criticisms of modern journalism, however, the U.S. press has also been a bulwark of liberty in our time, and so far there have been no examples of a better arrangement. Many notions of the press have served U.S. citizens well through some dark times in history: the press as watchdog; the independent press; a representative of the public; the unmasker of interest and privilege; the press that shines the hot glare of publicity into all dark corners of the republic; the seeker of expert knowledge among the welter of opinion; and the private citizens' informant. These notions are not perfect or without fault, but they have worked well and formed the understanding of a democratic press in the modern era. However, as the twentieth century progressed, the weaknesses of modern journalism became increasingly apparent and debilitating, especially when it began to be assaulted by technology.

MEDIA ENTERING THE POSTMODERN ERA

◆ ◆ ◆

This essay opened with the image of a dismayed television journalist lamenting the evaporation of the only journalism he had known, *modern journalism*. Actually, John Chancellor was feeling the force of something underway for close to two decades. Beginning in the early 1970s, the entire pattern of communication—the existing structure of the media and modern journalism—began to change.

Two technologies in particular were both the symptoms and symbols of the change: satellites and computers, the consequences of which reconfigured the map of communications and social relationships. Satellite broadcasting eliminated distance as a cost factor in communication. Computer technology not only altered all the parameters of numerical calculation, but through miniaturization widely diffused large-scale capacity for

information processing, storage and retrieval. The radiant arc of a communication satellite 22,300 miles above the earth synchronized time and transformed the globe into one homogeneous space. With perfection of this technology, the conquest of time and space—the dream of the nineteenth-century romantics—has now in a way been realized. Moreover, the aggressive transformation of publics into audiences—which in the late nineteenth century created the "imaginary community of the nation"—is now a global process.[27]

While cable and satellite have enlarged the scale and scope of communications, they also—paradoxically—have narrowed it. Cable television has radically expanded channel capacity, the variety of services available and the capacity to segment the audience; wedded to satellites, cable was able to penetrate 60 percent of U.S. homes by the 1990s. Multichannel systems, however, have fragmented the audience into narrow niches based on taste, hobbies, avocations, race and ethnicity.[28]

The combination of cable television and video cassette recorders, direct satellite broadcasting and interactive teletext splintered the "great audience" assembled by newspapers and television. Having reached their peaks of profitability and influence in the 1970s, newspapers and network television have receded as economic and political forces. Analysts continue to search for the meaning of these changes. They have attempted to express it through metaphors such as "the global village" and "spaceship earth."

CONCLUSION

◆ ◆ ◆

These complex and interrelated changes in the world of journalism and democracy erupted—to John Chancellor's dismay—in the new technology and politics of the 1992 election. What Chancellor missed, however, was the hopeful side of that election. Many of the phenomena that he found most troubling—call-in radio, public debates with public questioners, and spontaneous grass roots nominating movements—represented attempts by a fragmented and dispersed public, which had not completely lost and forgotten the image of a truly public life, to use the new technology and new media, designed purely for commercial purposes, to its own advantage.

The public is attempting to reform itself, outside the journalistic establishment, and to reassert both a public interest and public participation in the sphere of national politics. Rather than resisting these attempts or attempting to manage and orchestrate them, the press should assist the public's attempt to reassert a role in politics.

Today's public has inherited a journalism of the expert and the conduit, a journalism of information, fact, objectivity and publicity. This is a scientific conception of journalism: It assumes an audience to be informed and educated by the journalist and the expert. In their different ways, the methods of the journalist and the expert guarantee the truth and sanction the vocabulary of journalism as a record, a conversation and as an exercise in poetry and utopian politics.

...journalism ought to be conceived less on the model of information and more on the model of conversation.

The first thing to remember about journalism is that it derives its name from the French word *jour*, meaning day, and is, therefore, a daybook—a collective and public diary that records occurrences of the day. The importance of journalism is less that it disseminates news and information, and more that it is one of the primary instruments through which the culture is preserved and recorded and, therefore, available to be reconsulted. This notion supports Thomas Jefferson's basic justification for freedom of the press: The newspaper produced—compared to human memory or manuscript—a virtually indestructible record of the significant events in community life. The United States must return, in other words, to this journalism of record.

Second, journalism ought to be conceived less on the model of information and more on the model of conversation. Journalists are merely part of the conversation of U.S. culture; a partner with the rest of the public—no more and no less. This is a humble role for journalism, but in fact what we need is a humble journalism. Walter Lippmann was right: Journalism cannot tell the truth,

because no one can tell the truth. All journalism can do is preside over and within the public conversation: to stimulate and organize it, keep it moving and leave a record so that other conversations—history, art, science, religion—might have something off which to feed. The public will continue to reawaken when it is addressed as a conversational partner and encouraged to join the talk rather than sit passively as a spectator before a discussion conducted by journalists and experts.

Finally, journalism ought to be perceived not as an outgrowth of science, but more as an extension of poetry, the humanities and political utopianism. What would journalism look like if it were grounded in poetry, if that metaphor were realized, rather than the metaphor of objectivity and science? It would generate, in fact, a new moral vocabulary that might dissolve some current dilemmas.

In an earlier era, science could serve as the exemplification of our culture, and the scientist could be our hero. The sciences did enormous and important work in securing the foundations of liberal democracy. It is not surprising that journalism took science as its model and tried, in however degenerate a form, to imitate it. But that age is over.

Today the most important parts of U.S. culture are in the arts and humanities and in political utopianism. The public should not shrink from this new metaphor. Social life is after all the succession of great metaphors. The metaphor that has governed the understanding of journalism in this century has run into trouble. Neither journalism nor public life will move forward until the public actually rethinks and reinterprets what journalism is: not the science or information of culture, but its poetry and conversation. There will still be plenty of room left for investigations, for the Fourth Estate as a check upon tyrannical power. But there is good news for the First Amendment, journalists and the public. The re-creation of public life, as dangerous and difficult as it will be in an age of advanced technology, will bring the United States closer to the inspiring vision of journalism that has been the objective of democratic politics since the colonial era.

Notes

1. John Chancellor, "Seeing the Future," Keynote Speech, Alfred I. Du Pont-Columbia University Forum, 28 January 1993 (New York: Graduate School of Journalism, Columbia University, 1993).

2. Because Ross Perot did not take federal matching funds, he was exempt from the reporting and accounting requirements that bound other candidates.

3. See Edwin F. Bayley, *Joe McCarthy and the Press* (Madison, WI: University of Wisconsin Press, 1981).

4. In this article, *journalism* refers to both print and broadcast journalism.

5. The *press* refers to print and broadcast news media, both of which are covered, though in somewhat different ways, under the "freedom of press" clause of the First Amendment.

6. Sam Bass Warner, *Private City: Philadelphia in Three Stages of Its Growth* (Philadelphia: University of Pennsylvania Press, 1968) pp. 19–20; Alvin Gouldner, *The Dialectic of Ideology and Technology* (New York: Oxford University Press, 1976) pp. 95–6. Lest we be swept away by romanticism, it should be noted how tragically flawed the original idea of the public was, and it was this flaw that had something to do with the decline of the public sphere. It was a public, effectively restricted by race, class and gender; that is, the public consisted of middle-class men who had an interest and stake in public affairs, commerce, business or trade. Later, when public space began to fill with workers and artisans of another class, these merchants retreated into private spaces and the men's clubs that are still a feature of large cities. But these fatal imperfections do not diminish the historical importance of the public, as it was then defined, or the power of the concept to illuminate politics.

7. Benjamin Ginsburg, *The Captive Public: How Mass Opinion Promotes State Power* (New York: Basic Books, 1986).

8. Bruce Smith, *Politics and Remembrance* (Princeton, NJ: Princeton University Press, 1985) p. 252.

9. Ibid., p. 259.

10. Ibid., p. 269.

11. Participation was, strictly speaking, extralegal for the majority until the franchise was gradually extended to include all men, women and African-Americans.

12. Michael E. McGerr, *The Decline of Popular Politics* (New York: Oxford University Press, 1986) p. 5.

13. Benedict Anderson, *Imagined Communities* (London: Verso Books, 1983).

14. Daniel Dyan and Elihu Katz, *Media Events: The Live Broadcasting of History* (Cambridge: Harvard University Press, 1992).

15. Signal time refers to the gap time between the moment a message is sent and when it is received a function of distance.

16. McGerr, p. 134.

17. An example of pro-consumer legislation is the Pure Food and Drug Act. See Ibid., p. 134.

18. Michael Schudson, *Discovering the News* (New York: Basic Books, 1978) chapter 4. This argument has also benefited from the unpublished work of Patrick McGarry.

19. Clinton Rossiter and James Lane, eds., *The Essential Lippmann* (New York: Random House, 1963) pp. 226–7.

20. Robert Entman, *Democracy Without Citizens* (New York: Oxford University Press, 1989).

21. Joan Didion, *After Henry* (New York: Simon & Schuster, 1992) pp. 47–86.

22. E.J. Dionne, Jr., *Why Americans Hate Politics* (New York: Simon & Schuster, 1991).

23. *Congressional Quarterly*, "Presidential Elections Since 1789," 5th ed. (Washington, DC: Congressional Quarterly, 1991); Richard M. Scammon and Alice V. McGillivray, *American Voter* 18 (Washington, DC: Election Research Center, 1989).

24. D. Charles Whitney, "Americans' Experience with the News Media: A Fifty-Year Review," *The Media and the People* (New York: Freedom Forum Media Studies Center at Columbia University, 1985).

25. David Halberstam, *The Best and the Brightest* (New York: Penguin Books, 1983); Carl Bernstein and Bob Woodward, *All the President's Men* (New York: Warner Books, 1976).

26. Smith, p. 252.

27. Anderson, p. 49.

28. Cable systems with 150 channels are already in operation and systems of 500 channels are being tested.

Terms & Concepts

alienation	grassroots reform	postmodern politics
audience fragmentation	humble journalism	progressivism
bifurcated political sphere	imaginary community	public society
conversation	independent voter writ large	recreation of public life
demagoguery	insider baseball	renewed conversation
dialectic of appearance	journalism	symbiotic relationship
disengagement	muckraking	the great audience
first amendment	national society	watchdog
God term	news and truth	worshipped concept

Questions

1. How has "the public" changed, especially in the 20th century? How did the media change it? For example, do open-line shows allow people to express opinions that they would be ashamed to admit at a public meeting?

2. Did we really create "a democracy without citizens"?

3. Is there a chance that we can "reinvent" journalism and see it differently so that, once again, it helps to create a meaningful political life for citizens?

4. Is the United States a special case, or does Canada face very similar problems even if in somewhat muted form?

5. Should we see the media and what is conveyed as far closer to poetry entertainment and myth-making than to fact, reality, and truth?

Unit
Four   Discussion Questions

1. When we make institutional comparisons across political systems, what issues do we have to be particularly concerned about? Is the "transfer" of institutions easy?

2. Why are our institutions under stress? What likelihood is there of significant institutional change?

3. Political parties and the media are undergoing as much stress and pressure to change as are formal institutions (such as parliament). What impact do you think changes in these areas will have upon political life in general and upon electoral politics in particular?

Annotated
Bibliography

Achbar, Mark, ed. *Manufacturing Consent: Noam Chomsky and the Media*. Montreal: Black Rose Books, 1994. This is the companion volume to the video series of the same name.

Atkinson, Michael, ed. *Governing Canada: Institutions and Public Policy*. Toronto: Harcourt Brace Jovanovitch, 1993. Intended as a textbook, it contains excellent essays on a broad range of topics, all of current importance.

Bain, George. *Gotcha: How the Media Distorts the News*. Toronto: Key Porter Books, 1994. The media's role of political communication is by no means played impartially. Bain is a long-time journalist, who writes the "Media Watch" column in *MacLeans*.

Barry, John. *The Ambition and the Power*. New York: Viking Penguin, 1989. A lengthy and critical analysis of how Newt Gingrich rose to power at the expense of Jim Wright, the Speaker of the House.

Blais, Andre. "The Debate Over Electoral Systems." *International Political Science Review* 12:3 (1991), 239–60. A very useful summary and review of the empirical evidence regarding the merits of different electoral systems, especially ours.

Bogart, W.A. *Courts and Country: The Limits of Litigation and the Social and Political Life of Canada*. Toronto: Oxford Univerity Press, 1994. A good discussion of what can be expected from the courts, especially on the thorny issue of equality.

Burgess, Michael and Alain-G. Gagnon. *Comparative Federalism and Federation: Competing Traditions and Future Directions*. Toronto: University of Toronto Press, 1993. A comparative discussion of federalism, federation, and federal principles.

Cairns, Alan C. *Constitution, Government and Society in Canada*. Edited by Douglas Williams. Toronto: McClelland and Stewart Ltd., 1988. Beautifully crafted essays; mandatory reading for those who study Canada's constitution.

———. *Charter versus Federalism: The Dilemmas of Constitutional Reform*. Montreal and Kingston: McGill-Queen's University Press, 1992. Investigates, in vintage Cairnsian style, the deep divisions and difficulties encountered over the past 25 years.

Campbell, Robert M. and Leslie A. Pal. *The Real Worlds of Canadian Politics*, 3rd ed. Peterborough: Broadview Press, 1994. Five in-depth case studies, including the 1993 Federal Election and the defeat of the Charlottetown Accord.

Carty, R.K., ed. *Canadian Party Systems: A Reader*. Peterborough: Broadview Press, 1992. There are several excellent readers on the market; this one is particularly strong on historical developments as well as current issues.

Gagnon Alain-G and A. Brian Tanguay, eds. *Canadian Parties in Transition*, 2nd ed. Scarborough: Nelson Canada, 1995. A new edition of a comprehensive collection of essays by well known scholars. Clear and well organized.

Heard, Andrew. *Canadian Constitutional Conventions*. Toronto: Oxford University Press, 1991. A comprehensive review of what conventions are, and how they operate in Canada.

King, Anthony. "Overload: Problems of Governing in the 1970's." *Political Studies* 23:2–3 (1974), 284–96. This is a classic article outlining the "state overload" thesis. Still very useful.

Lijphart, Arend. "Democracies: Forms, Performance, and Constitutional Engineering." *European Journal of Political Research* 25:1 (January 1994), 1–17. The latest comparative work from the political scientist who first developed the idea of "consociational" democracies.

Mayer, Jane and Jill Abramson. *Strange Justice: The Selling of Clarence Thomas*. Boston: Houghton Mifflin, 1994. This is a highly critical account of the appointment of Clarence Thomas.

Morgan, Edmund S. *Inventing the People: The Rise of Popular Sovereignty in England and America*. New York: W.W. Norton, 1988. A classic dissection of the constitutional fictions we erect and defend — and upon which our system is based. Brilliantly argued.

Offe, Claus. *Contradictions of the Welfare State*. Edited by John Keane. Cambridge, MA: MIT Press, 1984. Capital cannot live with the welfare state and cannot live without it either. Important critical essays by a leading post-Marxist scholar.

Patterson, Thomas E. *Out of Order*. New York: Knopf, 1993. This is an attack on the cynicism of the press, and its recent manifestations. It argues for a more complex view of things.

Price, David E. *The Congressional Experience: A View From the Hill*. Boulder, CO: Westview, 1992. An insider's view of how Congress really works. An excellent example of "participant observation."

Sabato, Larry. *Feeding Frenzy*. New York: Free Press, 1991. Sabato's work focuses upon a discussion of journalistic scandals and sets the scene for our current preoccupation with "character," aggressivity and, of course, sales.

Smiley, Donald V. *The Federal Condition in Canada*. Toronto: McGraw-Hill Ryerson, 1987. Still one of the best analyses written on the subject.

Thomas, David M., ed. *Canada and the United States: Differences That Count*. Peterborough: Broadview Press, 1993. A collection of 19 essays on Canadian-American differences.

Tuohy, Carolyn J. *Policy and Politics in Canada: Institutionalized Ambivalence*. Philadelphia: Temple University Press, 1992. A sophisticated discussion of policy and institutions, with in-depth case studies.

Verney, Douglas. *Three Civilizations, Two Cultures, One State: Canada's Political Traditions*. Durham: Duke University Press, 1986. A sweeping historical analysis of Canada's traditions and contradictions.

Unit Five

Regimes and Change

• • •

Comparative politics is the field in which most students first study political regimes in detail. Introductory courses in this field, like those in international relations, have undergone frantic revisions during the first half of the nineties, and textbooks published as recently as three years ago have become anachronistic. Professors used to introduce students to liberal democracy, authoritarianism, and totalitarianism (of the latter, Communism was the only post-World War II variant). Alternatively, some textbooks chose to divide regimes into the First, Second, and Third Worlds. These categories were never watertight. For example, the term "First World" referred to political and economic criteria. The states included were economically developed liberal democracies. The concept of "Second World" referred to Communist states, but some classifications included only economically developed ones, whereas others included also developing Communist states. The "Third World" referred primarily to the stage of economic development. For example India, a constitutional democracy, and authoritarian Syria, were in the same category.

Today, such classification schemes seem to make little sense. Totalitarianism as we knew it has disappeared, and authoritarianism now covers too wide a range. The two most infamous variants of totalitarianism (Nazism and Stalinism) had more in common with each other than either had with other regimes. (Rubashov, the protagonist in Arthur Koestler's *Darkness at Noon*,[1] cannot tell the difference between a nightmare of his arrest by the Gestapo and the reality of his arrest by the GPU, the Stalinist secret police, because the *modus operandi* of both regimes is so similar.) On the other hand, the similarities between fundamentalist Islamic Iran, Saddam Hussein's Iraq, Fidel Castro's Cuba, and Lee Kuan Yew's Singapore are so few, and the differences so great, that merely calling the regimes totalitarian or authoritarian becomes misleading and confusing. So, of this older classification scheme totalitarianism as a category has no obvious examples, except perhaps, North Korea. Authoritarianism is, as noted, far too general to cover the diversity of regimes that might fit. Only one category (liberal democracy) seems to remain.

The three worlds do not fare much better. The Second World, which was comprised largely of East European or client states of the USSR, has virtually disappeared along with the collapse of the Soviet empire. Meanwhile, the Third World contains a range from New Industrialized Countries (NICs) like South Korea, a major exporter of manufactured goods, to countries like Malawi with a GNP (Gross National Product) per capita of less than $300. Here too, then, one category has disappeared, and another has become meaningless because of its enormous range. What should be put in their place?[2]

Before the collapse of the Soviet Union, the dynamics of the East-West conflict tended to support the status quo in the world. Communist countries stayed Communist, and the industrialized democratic states stayed democratic. In the Third World there were regime changes: some became Communist, some vacillated between short periods of democracy and authoritarianism, but most remained under some form of authoritarianism and were in many ways client states of either pole in a bipolar world. Whereas during the Cold War it was most interesting to study changes in economic development, since the end of the Cold War, regime change has become a hot topic.[3] Is it wishful thinking to expect that democracy can be created quickly from scratch in an ex-Communist state? Or is democracy, when it has come about with popular support, more resilient than we think? Are the demands for democracy in South Korea and Taiwan

and the building of a Statue of Liberty by Chinese students in Tiananmen Square evidence that economic development in *McWorld* leads to demands for democratic change? Or is a "new authoritarianism" evolving to cope with the pressures of development, allowing free rein to economic liberalism while holding off the "moral decay" of liberal democracy?

The collapse of the Soviet Union has been a catalyst for another major threat to existing states: nationalism. The Cold War tended to keep the forces of nationalism in check too, particularly in the Soviet sphere of influence; however, with the Cold War over, nationalities reasserted themselves and fragmented Eastern Europe into numerous new states in a process that is still unfolding. This breakup can be horrific as in Yugoslavia, dramatic as in the Baltic states, or peaceful as in the Czechoslovak Federation. The process of breaking-up has its own dynamics, something of particular interest to Canadians.

Change of an only slightly less dramatic nature has also been taking place within liberal democracies since the late 1970s. Neoconservatism has become the conventional wisdom. The welfare state is under assault because, we are told, it is too expensive and makes us too complacent in an interdependent world where competition can come from anywhere. But is the increase in the index of inequality (Gini coefficient) in most OECD countries[4] due to uncontrollable economic forces, or is it the desired outcome of a set of conscious policies by those who benefit most from this re-allocation of income? Be this as it may, the first target of neoconservatives have been the poor, the unemployed, and government bureaucrats. The results of these attempts at bureaucratic reform are discussed in this unit. The assault on social programs is still going on. The fallout is predictable: increasing economic polarization. But the most interesting question is whether this is really necessary. That question cannot be answered conclusively yet.

1. Arthur Koestler, *Darkness at Noon* (Harmondsworth, England: Penguin, 1947).

2. Samuel P. Huntington, *The Third Wave: Democratization in the Late Twentieth Century* (Norman: University of Oklahoma Press, 1991).

3. Francis Fukuyama, "Liberal Democracy as a Global Phenomenon," *PS: Political Science and Politics* 24, 4 (December 1991), 659–63.

4. *The Globe and Mail*, March 25, 1995, D4, citing statistics from "Income & Wealth," Joseph Rowntree Foundation.

Democracy in Europe

Nancy Bermeo

Editors' Note

Most of us are probably prepared to believe that the countries of Eastern Europe, now struggling to establish democracy, are likely to fail in their attempts to do so. Their communist past, their lack of strong civic cultures, their incredible economic dislocation, and their internal divisions all seem to presage political disaster. Nancy Bermeo asks us to reappraise such snap judgments, at least in the case of Poland, Hungary, the Czech Republic, and Slovakia. She suggests that we should compare their plight now with the situation that prevailed following the end of World War II in Europe, as well as with the failure of democracy in the interwar years between 1918 to 1939. She notes that the nations of Western Europe were able to survive the aftermath of World War II even though many of them, including France, came perilously close to civil war or breakdown. They not only survived and developed democratic systems of governance, but they became an essential world-stabilizing force.

Bermeo notes that prior to 1939, when democracies did crumble, notably in Germany, there were considerable differences between the situation then and the conditions in Eastern Europe now. She cautions against undue pessimism. Are there lessons to be learned? She suggests that there are, and one of them—perhaps the most important—is that we not give up too soon, or forget our responsibilities to the new democracies struggling to survive. She also makes the important point that a study of history can at least reveal to us the ways in which we often misuse historical analogies: democracies may be as difficult to destroy, once established, as they were to create. Bermeo's arguments give us hope even when they sound a note of warning, and her historical analysis is a useful scene-setter, for we are too inclined to forget the important details of earlier attempts at democratization and the differences between breakdown and crisis.

◆ ◆ ◆

THIS ESSAY PUTS OUR CURRENT social science thinking about Eastern Europe's new democracies into historical perspective and presents a case for cautious optimism. There is no "scientific" prediction here—if our work on regime change bears any resemblance to a science at all, it is to medicine and not to physics. Like physicians, we compare the case before us to other cases and we make an educated guess.

The agenda requires a comparative perspective but choosing a set of comparable cases is not easy. The dizzying pace of change in post-Cold War Europe has

"Democracy in Europe" reprinted by permission of *Dædalus*, Journal of the American Academy of Arts and Sciences, from the issue entitled, "Europe Through a Glass Darkly," Spring 1994. Volume 123, Number 2 (pp. 159–78).

forced us to grab on to all sorts of historical parallels to get our bearings. These range from Europe in 1066, to Muscovy in the 1600s, to the end of colonialism in Latin America. The choices are further complicated by the argument that these new European democracies are essentially incomparable. Martin Malia maintains that postcommunism (like communism itself) is "unique in human history."[1] There is much truth to this but it is still too early to know the extent to which these regimes will be defined by their communist antecedents.

I make the assumption that the East Central European regimes will be defined not solely by their communist past but by their European location. These regimes have already adopted the institutions of

---

This is, after all, the fourth wave of new European democracies since World War I...

European parliamentary democracies and the majority of their citizens aspire to be accepted as modern Europeans.[2] Though much of the recent history of this region *is* unprecedented, the aspiration to forge and maintain a "new" democracy on European soil is not. This is, after all, the *fourth* wave of new European democracies since World War I and there is much to be gained from viewing these new regimes in the context of their predecessors. The sets of democracies formed in the interwar years, in the years following World War II, and in the mid-1970s differ from the postcommunist regimes in important ways, but all of these new democracies faced problems of stability and consolidation. Their successes and their failures are relevant today not simply because they provide lessons from a common European home but because they have profoundly affected our thinking about democracies in general. Many of the remedies being prescribed for the troubles of Eastern Europe in the 1990s are forged through the analysis of these historical cases and many of our predictions about the future of new democracies today are based on what we believe about their earlier counterparts.

The argument for West European comparisons is strongest in the Central European states of Poland, Hungary, Slovakia, and the Czech Republic, and these are the contemporary focal points of this analysis. The Russian Federation is discussed as well but it remains in a separate analytic category because its status as a formal democracy is so recent.

THE MALADIES OF THE NEW DEMOCRACIES

◆ ◆ ◆

The tone of the literature on Europe's new democracies runs from triumphant to despairing. Jeanne Kirkpatrick opened a 1991 speech on postcommunism with the words "We won!"[3] but there is no shortage of pessimism in the social science community as a whole. On the contrary, the list of maladies allegedly affecting the new democracies in the East is long and troubling. The legacy of political history in these nations is said to be especially "unfriendly" to democracy and their current pools of leaders are said to lack the qualities required for the tasks of consolidation.[4] Communism is believed to have left behind a "distrustful," nondemocratic civil society[5] and a strong likelihood of serious performance failures.[6] Writers on both sides of the Atlantic warn of the drift toward populism and the ugliest forms of nationalism:[7] Leszek Kolakowski reminds the triumphant that the "victory of democracy" is far from assured and that there are "noncommunist forms of tyranny";[8] Adam Michnik writes that democracy's defense against "xenophobic authoritarianism" is weakening;[9] and Václav Havel writes that "demagogy is everywhere" and that citizens are becoming "more and more clearly disgusted" with their elected governments.[10]

The pessimistic forecasts for East Central Europe are easily matched by those for the former Soviet Union, where problems of leadership, political culture, and policy-making seem even worse. There, 126 different peoples live within the current federation and even the fundamental problem of national boundaries is unresolved.[11] The recent parliamentary elections, in which 23 percent of the vote went to Vladimir Zhirinovsky and his ultra-nationalist Liberal Democratic Party, simply confirmed the pessimism of many. The depth and breadth of the problems in the Russian Federation may mean that democracy is not a possibility and that the state is simply "too big to salvage."[12]

PREVIOUS DIAGNOSES

◆ ◆ ◆

We cannot know what these many maladies will lead to but we can learn something from putting our pessimism in historical perspective. Looking backward, we see the same degree of despair about Europe's new democracies in the years following World War II. As a 1955 article in the *American Political Science Review* observed: "the political communities" of the major continental countries "are fragmented into exclusive ideological movements...alienated from the West, politically apathetic or actively recruited to communism....The survival of parliamentary and democratic institutions" in Western Europe "is by no means to be taken for granted."[13]

Postwar analyses of German and Italian democracy were filled with foreboding. Studies of Germany's first several elections bemoaned the continued popularity of antidemocratic forces and concluded that the trend was "clearly against the center."[14] Analysts feared the weakness of the nation's political parties,[15] "the unparalleled apathy" of the population,[16] and even the political sympathies of the middle class.[17] Studies of Germany in the late 1950s revealed that only one-quarter of the adult population were "consistent supporters of democracy."[18]

The forecast for the new democratic regime in Italy was not much better. Studies of public opinion concluded that the "chances of democracy" there were "not good" and that parliamentary government was a "hypocritical fiction."[19] At least two serious analysts projected that Italy's future political system would be like Salazar's dictatorship in Portugal[20] and some even wrote of a threatening civil war.[21]

The pessimistic forecasts were not confined to the former Axis Powers. The French Fourth Republic was—justifiably—a source of great concern. As Gordon Craig reminds us, the "gloomier newspaper pundits" predicted a communist takeover in France by the end of 1947.[22] A 1949 article in *Foreign Affairs* described the public's "disgust" with parliament in a tone which presages the words of Václav Havel,[23] and a poll conducted in 1958 found that only 4 percent of the French public would actively oppose a military coup (four months later a military coup took place).[24] The Republic which had produced no fewer than twenty-five governments in twelve years was replaced by a new democratic system designed by Charles de Gaulle. Concern about the viability of French democracy continued, however, and Stanley Hoffmann has argued that it was not until the 1980s that the new democratic system was truly consolidated.

When another set of new democracies emerged in Southern Europe in the mid-1970s, scholars were again reluctant to be optimistic. An article by Juan Linz, which appeared in *Dædalus* in 1979, exemplified both the uncertainty and the pessimism of the period. The list of factors identified by Linz as "handicaps" to the Southern European regimes in the 1970s is remarkably similar to the list of maladies associated with the Central European states today. He cautioned that the new regimes in Greece, Spain, and Portugal were emerging at a time of simultaneous economic and ideological "crisis" which left "no clear models to follow or reject." Economic constraints meant that none of the states could "carry out the progressive policies" that would win them popular support. The uncertainty of national leaders, the "limited legitimacy of some of the participants," "the dangers of polarization, fragmentation or immobilism" inherent in their extreme multiparty systems, and "the serious threat of peripheral nationalisms" in Spain meant that each of the three new democracies was beset by "a crisis of legitimation."[25]

Objectively, concern for the crisis of Southern European democracy as a whole was neither intense nor long-lasting within the American scholarly community in general. The community paid little attention to Greece[26] and reservations about Spanish democracy soon gave way to laudatory discussions of Spain's peaceful and pacted transition.

Portuguese democracy *was* a source of special, if not enduring, concern due to its revolutionary beginnings and to the presence of a relatively popular pro-Soviet Communist Party. The image of Weimar Russia, used so frequently today, had an ironic parallel in the image of Bolshevik Portugal in the mid-1970s.[27] Henry Kissinger likened Mario Soares to the ill-fated Kerensky,[28] and even social scientists who were further removed from the front lines of the Cold War shared a profound pessimism regarding Portugal's future. A 1976 article in *Foreign Affairs* was representative of the contemporary mood:[29] it was profoundly pessimistic despite being written after democratic forces had already gained the ascendancy in the freely elected Constitutional Assembly, the provisional government, and the military. It argued that Portugal's democratic revolution was "doomed to face the worst of all possible worlds at the worst of all possible times," that "no group has the capability of easily or quickly destroying the other, but each has an incentive to seek to do so...," and that only "some miracle" would prevent a Spanish style "civil war."[30]

Thankfully, this bleak scenario was never played out. Conflicts were always resolved peacefully and within the realm of law. The parliamentary and presidential elections of 1976 proceeded without incident and gave overwhelming support to prodemocratic, mainstream parties—just as the elections to the Constitutional Assembly had done in the previous year.

There were many reasons to believe that the new democracies of Southern Europe would not prove viable. During the two centuries before these transitions, Southern Europe was a region of "unparalleled instability."[31] Scholars emphasized the "weak institutionalization" of interest groups,[32] the "fragile political attachments"[33] of the Southern European people, and their general lack of "civicness."[34] Yet, each of these regimes has held together for nearly twenty years and each is considered a fully consolidated democracy today.

This points toward two conclusions. The first concerns the actors who are most likely to challenge democratic rules and institutions. Despite grave problems, and unlike their predecessors in the interwar years, none of the postwar democratic regimes was successfully chal-

---

New democracies are indeed very difficult to create and maintain but successfully assaulting a democracy is very difficult as well.

---

lenged through parliament, through the executive, or through popular mobilization in the streets. The *only* regimes which *did* break down were targets of military revolts: The French crisis of 1958 led to a reconstructed democracy; the Greek military coup of 1967, which led to a vile dictatorship, was the *only* case of democratic breakdown in the entire postwar history of over twenty-one West European parliamentary regimes. These are very good odds.

The second conclusion is that we have despaired about new European democracies before and that things worked out better than expected. The social science community had sound reasons to doubt the viability of each of these new systems—in some ways they showed even less promise than those of East Central Europe today—but democracy in its many forms muddled through in all these states—and in the potentially difficult cases of Belgium, Finland, and Austria as well.

Why is it that the most despairing scenarios never came to pass in the West European cases? What can be learned from the erroneous predictions? The primary reason the likelihood of democratic breakdown was overstated was that no one considered the other half of the regime-change dilemma. New democracies are indeed very difficult to create and maintain but successfully *assaulting* a democracy is very difficult as well.[35]

THE PATHS BETWEEN CRISIS AND BREAKDOWN

◆ ◆ ◆

Democracies can be in crisis for a whole variety of reasons: they may have grave economic problems, unwieldy party systems, serious social cleavages, or all of these problems and more—but crisis and breakdown are two distinct phenomena. The paths between crisis and breakdown are not traveled as frequently as some of us imagine because these paths are treacherous in themselves. Antidemocratic groups who travel this terrain often fail and most do not attempt the journey at all.

The image of democratic "collapse" is misleading. Democratic political systems do not simply break down from exhaustion or from some set of structural maladies. They must be deliberately assaulted and disassembled. Some of the agents who contribute to this process may do so unwittingly, but ultimately democracies are disassembled by actors with power who think they have a better idea and organize to implement it.

Philippe Schmitter argues perceptively that democracy "has to be chosen" by "real live political actors" who "have plenty of room for making right or wrong" decisions.[36] The same can be said of those who seek to assault a democracy in crisis. If we are going to make any sense of the new democracies in Europe, we must think more systematically about who chooses dictatorship and about the paths they choose in the terrain between crisis and breakdown.

There are only a limited number of paths through which a democracy can be assaulted and destroyed. Military coups and foreign invasions constitute one set, but democracy can also be attacked through its own legitimate governmental structures.[37] These latter assault routes loom especially large in pessimistic forecasts for democracy in the East. This is a legacy of the failure of the new democracies of the interwar years, when antidemocratic forces triumphed over democratic groups through victories in national elections and nomination to executive office. Fascists played the democratic game and won—even though they played in gross violation of its basic rules. Whether this route will be traveled by antidemocratic forces in East Central Europe is a question for area specialists, but those who would hope to block these paths have much to learn from studying the historical cases in which they were traveled with success.

The cases of Italy and Germany are the most important because they have had such a profound effect on our thinking about democratic consolidation. The connections between political extremism and economic dislocation, between parliamentary immobilism and proportional representation, between authoritarianism and presidentialism, and between dictatorship and certain political cultures have all been graphically illustrated by these two tragic cases. Much of the pessimism about what may transpire in Europe's new democracies is based on observations that the frailties of these earlier democracies are being duplicated in another setting.

There are several similarities between today's new democracies and the democracies which gave way to fascism. Proportional representation has again proven to be a barrier to absolute majorities, and critics again accuse their newly democratic governments of immobilism.[38] Economic crises have contributed to the growth of nationalist-extremist parties and minorities are once again blamed for a whole range of economic and social ills.[39] In Poland and in the Russian Federation it is feared that presidential government may eventually deteriorate into some form of partially legitimated authoritarianism.

These sorts of parallels lead some analysts to conclude that antidemocratic forces in Central Europe will triumph just as their counterparts did in the interwar years. Both Mussolini and Hitler established political parties, competed in elections, won seats in the national legislature, and were then chosen to head governments by legitimate actors at the summit of their respective constitutional systems. Both these dictators took the governmental path to power and were assisted on the last leg of their journey by nominations to executive office from the King in Mussolini's case and the President in Hitler's case. But these facts should not be considered out of context.

Political scientists have given a great deal of attention to parliamentary institutions and elites in their analyses of the interwar breakdowns but what went on outside parliament and outside the rule of law was equally if not more important to the success of antidemocratic forces. Happily, these extraparliamentary factors have few parallels in the Central European cases, and the governmental path to power will not be so easy to negotiate.

Three critical qualities distinguish interwar Italy and Germany from the new democracies of Central Europe: armed extremism, bipolar extremism, and judicial dysfunctionality. The Italian and German democracies were greatly affected by the fact that World War I had left thousands of men on both ends of the political spectrum with arms, military experience, and little material security. For the communist Left, the success of the Bolshevik

Revolution provided a positive model for an armed assault on the state and on property in general. For the extreme Right, the violence perpetrated by the Left provided an excuse for counterviolence and a multitude of "preemptive" assaults. These assaults were the work of highly organized (if often decentralized) paramilitary organizations involving thousands of men. In both Italy and Germany, they targeted not only individual political actors but buildings, enterprises, and even the freely elected governments of large municipalities.[40]

In Italy, this meant that fascist squads dominated many rural areas and presented themselves as bastions against communist attack. They terrorized the populations of such cities as Ferrara, Ravenna, Cremona, Bologna, Parma, and Florence. From Naples they openly threatened the central government, deposed the freely elected socialist government of Milan, and brought thousands of armed men to riot in the capital *before* the infamous march on Rome.[41] Similarly, Hitler's S.A. (Storm Troopers) and S.S. marched throughout Germany by the thousands with weapons and uniforms long before Hitler formally came to power.[42] They regularly disrupted election campaigns, terrorized all who would "distract the minds" of the German people,[43] and even erected a cordon around Berlin during the presidential elections of 1932.

Amazingly, these and other flagrant violations of legality went unpunished. In Italy, fascist deputies brandished weapons in parliament, seized a communist deputy, and literally threw him out of the assembly yet they were never punished—despite the fact that their party commanded only 7 percent of the assembly seats. In both states, the judicial system usually failed to prosecute right-wing hooliganism, thereby lending legitimacy to the politics of coercion.

This dysfunctioning of the legal system existed in part because some magistrates were antidemocratic themselves but also because the decisions of those who were not antidemocratic were complicated by other factors. In both Germany and Italy, police and military forces often stood by as paramilitary organizations took massive coercive action on their own. Sometimes, as in Italy in 1921, elements of the army even lent fascist mobs trucks and weapons. Magistrates who sought to control right-wing violence often could not depend on the official coercive apparatus of the state to report crimes, arrest criminals, or even eschew criminal behavior themselves.

A second complicating factor derived from the effects of bipolar extremism on centrists. Centrists who might have been the foundation of the new democratic order were convinced that right-wing paramilitary organizations were needed as a bulwark against the sort of leftist revolution that had triumphed in Russia. This conviction enabled the far Right to play the center against the far Left, thereby ensuring the passivity of the judiciary.

Rather than charging fascist hooligans with crimes, centrists often relied on the fascists to assault their mutual enemies on the communist Left. The uneasy defensive alliances which at first ensured informal judicial immunity eventually became the voting alliances that endorsed the nominations of Mussolini and Hitler to executive power. The fact that Friedrich Ebert, a revered Social Democrat, called upon the *Freikorps* to

---

Fascism triumphed in the streets before it triumphed in governmental institutions.

---

crush the Red Army in the Ruhr in 1919 illustrates just how broad the effects of bipolar extremism were.[44]

Fascism triumphed in the streets before it triumphed in governmental institutions. Mussolini and Hitler took multiple paths to power. They assaulted their new democracies from several points. This must be emphasized if comparison between the interwar and East Central European democracies is to prove useful.

The bipolar extremism, bipolar violence, and judicial dysfunctionality that existed in interwar Germany and Italy from the very inception of their new democracies have no readily apparent parallels in the new East Central European democracies. Judicial dysfunctionality is not present because extremist violence is practically nonexistent. Even the breakup of Czechoslovakia was achieved without armed struggle or paramilitary activity. That a nation would actually disassemble itself through a "velvet divorce" seems a remarkable testament to what can be done *without* violence in this region.

The fact that all these democracies were established in the aftermath of a *cold* war rather than an open, armed conflict means that the structural foundations of paramilitarism are much weaker. In East Central Europe, there are no beleaguered veterans to form the bases of contemporary *Freikorps* or *arditi* and thus no ready foundation for extremist parties to engage in the politics of open coercion. Relatedly, there is no event

comparable to the Bolshevik Revolution which can serve as a positive example of armed struggle. On the contrary, both the citizenry and the elite of these new regimes seem to take special pride in the nonviolent nature of their revolutionary transformations. As the current president of Hungary reminds us, "not even a slap was heard" as these new democracies came into being.[45] Their interwar counterparts were radically different for they were rooted in both the violent revolutions that were the midwives of their birth and World War I.

Extremism certainly exists in the new democracies of Central Europe but it has not taken the same bipolar form that proved lethal for the interwar regimes. Whereas armed defenders of the ancien régime were active from the very inception of democracy in Italy and Germany, the old order poses little threat to democracy in Central Europe today—it had few defenders in 1989 and has even fewer now that so many apparatchiks have become "entrepreneurchiks."[46] Although the electoral appeal of former Communist Parties may be on the rise in some of these states, it has yet to approach the historic popularity of Communist Parties in the consolidated democracies of Western Europe.[47]

Another major difference between these new democracies and their ill-fated predecessors relates to political spectrums. The whole concept of a political spectrum running from Left to Right is problematic in the post-totalitarian systems. Forty years of communism have blunted the social and economic divisions which produced this spectrum in capitalist states,[48] and though the spectrum will likely emerge as marketization proceeds, the concept is of little use as a guide to understanding the ideologies of the current set of political parties. If we define the far Left as all those actors hostile to capitalism, we are forced to lump communists together with nationalists, who in terms of religiosity and other cultural values are extremely conservative. The far Right in this scenario would be hard to conceptualize and only some communists and some nationalists would fit this definition anyway. Alternatively, if we define the far Left as embracing all those actors who are hostile to "bourgeois democracy," we find ourselves in the same illogical position.

In any case, we are witnessing a dynamic that differs greatly from the polarities that led to the triumph of fascism. In interwar Germany and Italy, the antidemocratic Right seduced the center into an antidemocratic alliance by presenting itself as the defender of order and private property. Given the party landscape of the new democracies, this is an impossible scenario. No obvious postcommunist substitute for the left-right spectrum is available.

Identifying extremists in these systems is fairly easy but finding their polar opposites and arraying them on a spectrum with a center is extremely difficult. Where, for example, do we find the polar opposite of a nationalist party? Logically it would be an internationalist party. We might stretch a bit and argue that all those parties who are open to trade liberalization, foreign investment, and entrance to the European Community (EC) could be so defined—but can we call these parties extremist? Since access to the benefits of internationalism in Europe requires at least a facade of democracy today, this categorization makes no sense. In any case, the parties who have adopted these internationalist ideas define themselves as the democratic center and are seen as such by most outsiders.

The same problems emerge if we search for the polar opposite of populism. Populism is thought to be the major threat to these new democracies today and the troubling rise to power of Vladimir Mečiar in Slovakia shows us how powerful the appeals of populism can be. But who are the *anti*populists in these new regimes? They certainly exist but they do not subvert democracy and they are not extremists. They see themselves and are seen by others as centrists and as the very foundation of economic and political liberalism.

The bipolar spectrum that we have relied on in the past has to be modified to make sense of the East European democracies. The dynamic that produced centrifugal forces in interwar Italy and Germany is absent in these systems and thus the parliamentary paths to power will be harder to negotiate.

Extremism in Eastern Europe today has thus far resulted in centripetal movements, not the centrifugal movements that spelled the death of democracy in the past. Extremist forces exist, but nonextremists, despite their systems' many maladies, are still distancing themselves from the extremes. In Poland, Hanna Suchocka's seven party coalition came together in a deliberate alliance against the two alternative extremes of Olszewski's decommunization and the Polish Peasant Party's recommunization.[49] In Czechoslovakia, the reaction to Mečiar provides another example of centripetal distancing. As soon as Mečiar became an open advocate of nationalist populism, he was dismissed from the ruling centrist party. As soon as he succeeded in creating a large populist-separatist movement in Slovakia, his whole *state* was dismissed. Key Czech elites recognized the opportunity to rid their new regime of a potential liability and acceded to demands for separatism with surprising speed.

Many would characterize Mečiar as an antidemocrat, and he has certainly used the parliamentary paths to power with success, but it would be a mistake to see his victory as evidence that dictatorship is especially viable in these states. Mečiar's Slovakia is still, for all its shortcomings, a polyarchy and it does not, at present, seem to be a model that others would want to emulate. Now that Mečiar has achieved his main goal, his popularity has dropped dramatically. He is not reaping the benefits of association with the industrialized states of Europe and cannot make good on his populist promises. Philippe Schmitter and Terry Karl remind us that the austerity of the current world economy may have some "perverse advantages." Under current conditions, populism "cannot deliver the immediate rewards that have been its sus-

---

Inside the former Soviet Union the governmental path to dictatorship seems easier to negotiate.

---

tenance in the past" and neither the extreme Right nor the extreme Left has a plausible alternative system to offer.[50] The governmental path to dictatorship does not look very promising in the Central European states.

Inside the former Soviet Union the governmental path to dictatorship seems easier to negotiate. This is why references to Weimar Russia have multiplied since the parliamentary elections in December 1993. There are indeed some parallels here but there are dramatic differences too. To begin with, the chronologies of the two cases diverge in important ways. As our previous discussion illustrates, Hitler scored his electoral victories after many years of struggle in the streets. He built a vast (and armed) mass movement *before* playing the parliamentary game with much success. Zhirinovsky and his Liberal Democratic Party have done the opposite. They have scored an important electoral victory before developing a strong organizational movement. This means that they have substantially less to bargain with politically. Their voting base may be very fluid and since they are not a paramilitary organization, they pose no comparable physical threat to their adversaries or to public order more generally. Whether Zhirinovsky (or anyone like him) will succeed in creating the sort of organization a fascist movement requires remains to be seen but it will not be built in the same way or at the same pace as the Nazi movement. The mass unemployment that proved pivotal in the growth of armed extremism during

German fascism is not yet among Russia's many maladies, and bipolar extremism—with communists battling fascists in the streets—has not materialized either. In fact, it is the political *alliance* of these groups that troubles democrats most.

A second major distinction between these cases concerns the role of foreign democracies. The difference between a cold war and a real war matters greatly. There is no Versailles Treaty forcing massive and immediate troop reductions today.[51] Demobilization is a domestic affair and thus is not as easily manipulated by nationalists. There are also no debilitating reparations payments. Whereas the Allies' intransigence on reparations in the 1920s forced Weimar inflation to skyrocket,[52] Western advisers today are trying to control inflation instead. Rather than extracting reparations, they have provided billions in aid. They have also provided the possibility of eventual institutional links to the more advanced countries of Western Europe. These were of great importance to the consolidation of the new democracies of the 1970s. Though the time frame is obviously very different in this case, 'the acquisition of a European identity may be a powerful rationale for compromise and sacrifice' among important sectors of the Russian population. There was no European Community in the days of Weimar. The dynamics of exclusion and inclusion were dramatically different.

The most important difference between these cases may derive from their order of appearance. Those who defend Russian democracy today already know how the Weimar story ended and thus can learn from the errors of their predecessors—if they choose to do so. Three lessons seem particularly important. First, Hitler could not have traveled the governmental route to power without the assistance of *non*fascists. His nomination to the chancellorship in 1933 was not dictated by law or even electoral momentum. He had been defeated in his bid for the presidency by a substantial margin the year before and his party had actually lost two million votes since the previous parliamentary election.[53] Hitler was named to the chancellorship because nonfascists could not agree on an alternative candidate and because a small set of scheming politicians naively assumed they could control him in an almost exclusively non-Nazi cabinet. We now know that alliances with fascists are fraught with danger and that the argument for political distancing is stronger. We also know that fascism feeds on economic dislocation. This is a second lesson from the Weimar experience and presumably why Yegor Gaidar insists that Russia's chance to avoid fascism lies "in making the economy grow."[54] The sad irony is that the model of

economic growth which the West has exported to the East will *cause* rather than eliminate economic dislocation for some time to come. Policymakers who understand the history of fascism will realize that meaningful

---

Uncertainty is still the defining condition of these new regimes, and thus our efforts are best spent simply trying to understand them as they are today.

---

protection for those who are most threatened by marketization may be critical to the protection of democracy itself.[55]

The third lesson of Weimar is that nations take grave risks when they ignore extremist victories abroad. Here the contrast with the Russian case is especially dramatic. Whereas the nomination of Hitler to the chancellorship caused "no great sensation"[56] in the international press, Zhirinovsky's relatively minor victory in parliament has attracted attention across the world. The alarm bells have sounded, and, internationally, Zhirinovsky has immediately become a pariah, forbidden visas and publicly reviled by virtually all powerful heads of state. The international community of the 1930s treated Hitler very differently. The triumph of fascism in Germany (and Italy) has left a legacy of political learning that makes democrats more vigilant, if not wiser.

Whether vigilance will lead to a more successful defense of democracy in Russia (or elsewhere in Eastern Europe) is beyond the modest powers of social science to predict. As the opening section of this essay makes clear, our predictions about new democracies in Western Europe have been consistently mistaken and there is nothing to suggest that they will improve. The fact that these new regimes are struggling with the unprecedented task of creating market economies as well as democracies should make us particularly cautious. Uncertainty is still the defining condition of these new regimes, and thus our efforts are best spent simply trying to understand them as they are today.[57] Comparing the Central European democracies to other new democracies on the same continent helps us gain this understanding, but the comparison must be made with an eye toward differences as well as similarities. Pessimistic predictions based on partial parallels may lead us to give up on Europe's new democracies too soon.

Notes

1. Martin Malia, "Leninist Endgame," *Dædalus* 121 (2) (Spring 1992): 58.

2. Being accepted into the European Community is important for symbolic as well as economic reasons. Analysts from a variety of perspectives are united in emphasizing the multifaceted importance of joining Europe. See, for example, Jeffrey C. Goldfarb, *After the Fall* (New York: Basic Books, 1992), 9 and Adam Przeworski, "The East Becomes the South?: The Autumn of the People and the Future of Eastern Europe," *PS: Political Science and Politics* 24 (23) (March 1991): 23.

3. Jean Kirkpatrick, "After Communism, What?," *Problems of Communism* 41 (1–2) (January-April 1992): 7–10. The quotation is from the Editor's Introduction to the issue.

4. Grzegorz Ekiert, "Peculiarities of Post-Communist Politics: The Case of Poland," *Studies in Comparative Communism* XXV (4) (December 1992): 342–43. The one exception to this argument is Czechoslovakia which had a successful democracy from 1918 to 1938. Michael Bernhard, "Barriers to Further Political and Economic Change in Poland," *Studies in Comparative Communism* XXIII (3/4) (Autumn/Winter 1990): 320. Hannan Rose, "From Command to Free Politics," *The Political Quarterly* 64 (2) (April-June 1993): 160. Dankwart A. Rustow, "Democracy: A Global Revolution?," *Foreign Affairs* 69 (4) (Fall 1990): 86.

5. Ken Jowitt, *New World Disorder: The Leninist Extinction* (Berkeley, Calif.: University of California Press, 1992), 310. Benjamin Barber as quoted in Ekiert, "Peculiarities of Post-Communist Politics: The Case of Poland," 360–61. Sten Berglund and Jan Dellenbrant, "Prospects for the New Democracies in Eastern Europe," in Sten Berglund and Jan Dellenbrant, eds., *The New Democracies in Eastern Europe* (Brookfield, Ill.: Edward Elgar Publishing Company, 1991), 22.

6. Claus Offe, "Capitalism by Democratic Design? Democratic Theory Facing the Triple Transition in East Central Europe," *Social Research* 58 (4) (Winter 1991): 882. Sidney Tarrow, "Aiming at a Moving Target: Social Science and the Recent Rebellions in Eastern Europe," *PS: Political Science and Politics* 24 (1) (March 1991): 17.

7. See, for example, Giovanni Sartori, "Rethinking Democracy: Bad Policy and Bad Politics," *International Social Science Journal* XLIII (3) (August 1991): 447; Peter Gowan, "Western Economic Diplomacy and the New Eastern Europe," *New Left Review* 182 (July/August 1990): 77; Mary E. McIntosh and Martha MacIver, "Coping with Freedom and Uncertainty: Public Opinion in Hungary, Poland, and Czechoslovakia 1989–1992," *International Journal of Public Opinion Research* 4 (4) (Winter 1992): 388; and Michael Bernhard, "Barriers to Further Political and Economic Change in Poland," *Studies in Comparative Communism* XXIII (3/4) (Autumn/Winter 1990): 329.

8. Leszek Kolakowski, "Amidst Moving Ruins," *Dædalus* 121 (2) (Spring 1992): 55.

9. Adam Michnik, "The Church and the Martyr's Stake in Poland," *NPQ* 10 (3) (Summer 1993): 36.

10. Václav Havel, "Paradise Lost," *New York Review of Books,* 9 April 1992, 6.

11. Galina Starovoitova, "Weimar Russia?," *Journal of Democracy* 4 (3) (July 1993): 107.

12. Andrew C. Janos, "Social Science, Communism, and the Dynamics of Political Change," in Nancy Bermeo, ed., *Liberalization and Democratization* (Baltimore, Md.: Johns Hopkins University Press, 1992), 111.

13. Gabriel A. Almond, Taylor Cole, and Roy C. Macridis, "A Suggested Research Strategy in Western European Government and Politics," *American Political Science Review* XLIX (4) (December 1955): 1042–49.

14. Robert C. Schmid, "The German Election in Perspective," *American Perspective* III (4) (September 1949): 197.

15. Sigmund Neumann, "Germany's Unresolved Dilemmas," *Foreign Policy Bulletin* XXXII (2) (1 October 1952): 7.

16. J. Glenn Gray, "Denazification: An American Appraisal," *American Perspective* II (8) (January 1949): 421.

17. Harold O. Lewis, "German Parties and the Bundestag Elections," *American Perspective* III (4) (September 1949): 205.

18. K. W. Deutsch and L. J. Edinger, *Germany Rejoins the Powers* (Stanford, Calif.: Stanford University Press, 1959), 38. Serious scholars argued that "rigidity" and the inability to compromise were still the main features of political life and that only 20 percent of the new democracy's political elite had consistently opposed the Nazi regime. Sigmund Neumann, "The German Elections—Meaning and Impact," *Foreign Policy Bulletin* XXXII (23) (15 August 1953): 2; and Lewis J. Edinger, "Post-Totalitarian Leadership," *American Political Science Review* LIV (1) (March 1960): 75, 79.

19. Felix Oppenheim, "The Prospects of Italian Democracy," *The Public Opinion Quarterly* II (4) (Winter 1947–1948): 572–74. Oppenheim also said that the situation was not hopeless if the United States could help illustrate that democracy was compatible with bold social planning.

20. Vittorio Ivella, "Party Rule in the Democratic State," *Foreign Affairs* 28 (1) (October 1949): 75, and H. Stuart Hughes, "Italy under De Gasperi," *American Perspective* II (8) (January 1949): 419.

21. Hans Kohn, "Austria: Frontier Land of the West," *Foreign Policy Bulletin* XXXIII (8) (1 January 1954): 6. Many scholars wrote that democracy would be jeopardized without drastic redistributive reforms and that the communists and the Christian Democrats faced one another as "two distinct nations" unable even to communicate. See, for example, Clifford A. L. Rich, "Italy's Election Prospects," *Foreign Policy Bulletin* XXXII (12) (1 March 1953): 7, and Elizabeth Wiskemann, "Poverty and Population in the South," *Foreign Affairs* 28 (1) (October 1949): 88. Hughes, "Italy under De Gasperi," 414.

22. Gordon A. Craig, *Europe Since 1815* (New York: Holt, Reinhart and Winston, 1971), 714.

23. Jean-Marie Domenach, "Democratic Paralysis in France," *Foreign Affairs* 37 (1) (October 1958): 33.

24. Nicholas Wahl, *The Fifth Republic—France's New Political System* (New York: Random House, 1959), 20.

25. Juan Linz, "Europe's Southern Frontier: Evolving Trends Toward What?," *Dædalus* 108 (1) (Winter 1979): 204. Linz's point about a crisis of legitimation stands alongside his view that the majority of the citizens in these states seem desirous of a democratic system.

26. Virtually all the articles written in major social science journals on Greece were written by Greek or British scholars.

27. For examples of the Weimar parallel see Anders Åslund, "Russia's Road from Communism," *Dædalus* 121 (2) (Spring 1992): 8, and Starovoitova, "Weimar Russia?," 106–109.

28. Tad Szulc, "Lisbon and Washington: Behind the Portuguese Revolution," *Foreign Policy* 21 (Winter 1975–1976): 3. Henry Kissinger is said to have suggested the parallel to Mario Soares himself and warned the socialist leader that he was allowing excessive communist influence in government.

29. Tad Szulc, for example, wrote of the possibilities of a rightist coup or left-wing military regimes on the Peruvian or Algerian model. Ibid., 6.

30. Kenneth Maxwell, "The Thorns of the Portuguese Revolution," *Foreign Affairs* 54 (2) (January 1976): 258, 265, and 268. The order of these phrases is different in the original.

31. Richard Gunther, Hans-Jurgen Puhle, and P. Nikiforos Diamandouros, "Introduction: The Politics of Democratic Consolidation," in Social Science Research Council, *The New Southern Europe*, unpublished manuscript, 1993, 38.

32. Linz, "Europe's Southern Frontier: Evolving Trends Toward What?," 181.

33. P. Nikiforos Diamandouros and Richard Gunther, "Preface," in Social Science Research Council, *The New Southern Europe*, viii.

34. Philippe C. Schmitter, "An Introduction to Southern European Transitions from Authoritarian Rule: Italy, Greece, Portugal, Spain and Turkey," in Guillermo O'Donnell, Philippe Schmitter, and Laurence Whitehead, eds., *Transitions from Authoritarian Rule—Prospects for Democracy, Part I* (Baltimore, Md.: Johns Hopkins University Press, 1986), 7. Schmitter does not make this claim himself but states quite sensibly that these claims are often exaggerated.

35. The subject of how democracies are successfully brought down is under-theorized. Juan J. Linz, *Crisis, Breakdown, and Reequilibration* (Baltimore, Md.: Johns Hopkins University Press, 1978), 4–5, 13.

36. Philippe Schmitter, "Interest Systems and the Consolidation of Democracies," in Gary Marks and Larry Diamond, eds., *Reexamining Democracy* (London: Sage Publications, 1992), 158–59.

37. There are probably only five routes through which a democracy can be assaulted: military coups, foreign military invasions, executive coups, a triumph of an antidemocratic party at the polls, and nomination by legitimate actors within existing institutions. I discuss these routes at length in a forthcoming manuscript, *Democracy and the Legacies of Dictatorship*.

38. On Hungary see Jason McDonald, "Transition to Utopia: A Reinterpretation of Economics, Ideas, and Politics in Hungary, 1984–1990," *East European Politics and Societies* 7 (2) (Spring 1993): 239. See also Wojciech Maziarski, "The Powerlessness of the Powerful: Walesa Now," *EER* (January-February 1992).

39. George Schöpflin, "The Problem of Nationalism in the Post-Communist Order," in Peter Volten, ed., *Bound to Change: Consolidating Democracy*

in East Central Europe (New York: Institute for East West Studies, 1992), 34–35, 41; David Ost, "Labor and Societal Transition," *Problems of Communism* XLI (3) (May-June 1992): 49–50.

40. The enterprises here were typically left-wing publishing houses and newspapers.

41. For details on this see Adrian Lyttleton, *The Seizure of Power* (Princeton, N.J.: Princeton University Press, 1973) and Denis Mack Smith, *Mussolini* (New York: Vintage, 1982).

42. See, for example, Allan Bullock, *Hitler: A Study in Tyranny* (New York: Harper & Row, 1962) and Walter Struve, *Elites Against Democracy* (Princeton, N.J.: Princeton University Press, 1973).

43. Craig, *Europe Since 1815*, 568.

44. Ibid., 556–57.

45. Rudolf Tokes, "Democracy in Hungary: The First Hundred Days and a Mid-Term Assessment," in Volten, ed., *Bound to Change: Consolidating Democracy in East Central Europe*, 153.

46. Ellen Comisso, "Property Rights, Liberalism, and the Transition from 'Actually Existing' to Socialism," *East European Politics and Society* 5 (1) (Winter 1991): 187. Valerie Bunce and Maria Csanadi, "Uncertainty in the Transition: Post-Communism in Hungary," *East European Politics and Society* 7 (2) (1993); David Ost, "Labor and Societal Transition," *Problems of Communism* XLI (3) (May-June 1992): 49.

47. As of this writing in December 1993, the maximum percentage of the vote in a national election garnered by a reformed Communist Party in East Central Europe was 20.4 percent in Poland's 1993 election. This is well below the maximum percentage garnered by a Communist Party in the West: 34.4 percent by the Italian Communist Party in 1976.

48. On the problems with this spectrum see Editors, "Left, Right," *EER* 4 (2) (Spring-Summer 1990): 3. See also an article by X in the *British Journal of Political Science*. See Karol Modzelewski who argues that in Czechoslovakia, for example, the "views propagated by the traditionalist right with regard to the economy were in fact quite leftist." Karol Modzelewski, "A Temporary Truce?," *EER* (January-February 1992): 25.

49. Modzelewski, "A Temporary Truce?," 24.

50. Philippe Schmitter and Terry Karl, "The Types of Democracy Emerging in Southern and Eastern Europe and South and Central America," in Volten, ed., *Bound to Change: Consolidating Democracy in East Central Europe*, 64–65. Comisso makes the point that nationalism, too, can only thrive if it has something to offer politically. "If the international economy stays relatively open and major powers make it clear that nationalism has nowhere to go, its potential as a mobilizing ideology may prove much weaker than many believe." Comisso, "Property Rights, Liberalism, and the Transition from 'Actually Existing' to Socialism," 187.

51. The Treaty reduced the German army to 100,000 and the navy to 15,000. John Hiden, *Germany and Europe 1919–1939* (New York: Longman, 1993), 25.

52. Gordon Craig, *Germany: 1866–1945* (New York: Oxford University Press, 1978), 441.

53. Hitler lost the 1932 presidential election by six million votes. For a very careful study of the Nazi voting base, see Richard F. Hamilton, *Who Voted for Hitler?* (Princeton, N.J.: Princeton University Press, 1982).

54. *Moscow Segodnya*, 14 December 1993, as in *FBIS*, 14 December 1993, 27.

55. It is interesting to note that all three of the new democracies that emerged in the 1970s increased welfare spending substantially. The Spanish case is particularly instructive because it managed to consolidate democracy despite unemployment levels of 20 percent or more. A number of analysts attribute Spain's success to the quality of the social safety nets provided for Spanish workers. See Jose Maria Maravall, "Economic Reforms in New Democracies: The Southern European Experience," *East-South System Transformations*, Working Paper No. 3 (Chicago, Ill.: Department of Political Science, University of Chicago, October 1990), 25.

56. Craig, *Germany: 1866–1945*, 569.

57. Bunce and Csanadi, "Uncertainty in the Transition: Post-Communism in Hungary."

Terms & Concepts

apparatchiks
authoritarianism
Axis powers
bipolar extremism
Bolsheviks
civil society
demagogy
entrepreneurchiks

extraparliamentary factors
immobilism
judicial dysfunctionality
legitimation
marketization
paramilitary organizations
polyarchy
populism

proportional representation
reparations
Versailles
weak institutionalization
Weimar Russia
xenophobia

Questions

1. What are the key differences between the causes of the *breakdowns* that occurred in Europe prior to World War II and the *crises* we see today in Eastern Europe? Are there any similarities?

2. What do we learn when we put our current pessimism into historical perspective? Is there a developmental model to be found?

3. Is Bermeo's argument that we should take a longer-term, historical approach convincing? Why are the German and Italian cases so important?

4. What role does Bermeo's argument imply for Western countries?

5. A *usable* comparative perspective is not easy to find. Why is this so— and on what basis does she pick the countries she does choose to compare? Does she pick as her new democratic states only the very few that will fit the argument?

The "New Authoritarianism" in East Asia

Meredith Woo-Cumings

Editors' Note

East Asian states, in particular Japan and the "Four Tigers," (Singapore, Taiwan, Korea and Hong Kong) have become economic powerhouses. China is now also embarked on a program of economic revitalization. What route should it follow; what lessons can it learn from these other success stories; is the situation very different now than it was for say, Japan, and, perhaps above all, how is development linked to political culture?

These are the sorts of questions with which development theorists must grapple. If, for example, there really is a common East Asian political culture that lends itself to social and economic discipline and to commerce, China's future looks a lot brighter than if one assumes that the causes and conditions for an economic miracle were significantly different. Singapore seems to offer the Chinese a particularly attractive model of a kind of "New Authoritarianism"—an authoritarianism that is relatively soft compared to its predecessors, and which is outwardly focused in terms of the economy.

Singapore's successes also, however, had a great deal to do with the existence and creation of a public service that is efficient and not corrupt, with an educational system that can compete with any in the world, open to students on the basis of merit, and with the presence in power of a remarkable leader. Lee Kuan-Yew is the very model of a philosopher—king, or perhaps a benevolent and enlightened despot. He has presided over the creation of a carefully planned welfare state and a competitive economy. His is not the world of authoritarianism associated with a General Franco's Spain or South American dictatorships: the world of caudillo politics, family oligarchies and leaders on horseback.[1] This is a world of transnational actors, technocrats, stock markets and computers. It is an authoritarianism that nurtures entrepreneurs.

Meredith Woo-Cumings' argument sets the scene for the sweeping attack on liberal values that follows it in a speech by the Prime Minister of Singapore. He has no doubts as to what keeps the whole thing together. Woo-Cumings' explanations are far more subtle — and raise far more questions than they answer.

---

1. For a discussion of this older style of authoritarianism, see Juan J. Linz, "Authoritarianism," in Mark O. Dickerson, Thomas Flanagan and Neil Nevitte eds., *Introductory Readings in Government and Politics,* 4th ed. (Scarborough: Nelson Canada, 1995), 179–94.

In April I was in Tokyo for a conference on regional institutions. At a public forum afterward I gave a brief talk on the Asian Development Bank, but the audience seemed less interested in this low-profile bank based in Manila than they were in the scandal of the month—namely, the imminent caning of Michael Fay in Singapore. Most of the questions I fielded concerned the incident, and like most callers to American radio talk shows, the audience in Tokyo cheerfully supported the Singaporean resolve to cane the American teenager for his alleged vandalism. It seemed the world had suddenly discovered draconian politics in the Shining City in the Pacific, and liked it.

Political discipline and economic performance have always gone hand in hand in East Asia. For most of the past three decades Japan and the "Four Tigers" (South Korea, Taiwan, Hong Kong, and Singapore) experienced rapid economic growth under either one-man or one-party rule, with colonial Hong Kong not even permitted to exercise the right of self-determination.

In the last few years much has changed: the military has turned over the government to civilians in South Korea, and the dominant parties are allowing for greater electoral competition in Taiwan and Singapore—even the redoubtable Liberal Democratic Party in Japan briefly suffered the humiliation of being the opposition. Yet the East Asian nations remain profoundly conservative, distrustful of changes that purport to do away with the political formula that has served them well in the race to get rich. Moreover, the increasingly confident elites of the region do not appreciate hectoring by the United States about the shortcomings of their political system, not to mention chastisement of their venerable culture.

Hence the authorities in Singapore proceeded to give the American youth the promised whipping. Meanwhile the leadership in Beijing, with the connivance of the American business establishment, mocked the China policy of President Bill Clinton's administration, taking the steam out of Secretary of State Warren Christopher's human rights crusade this spring.

TAILORING THE AUTHORITARIANS' NEW CLOTHES
◆ ◆ ◆

In the heyday of Pax Americana, when American parochialism worked as well as universalism and the reigning social science idea was modernization theory, scholars and policymakers believed in the redemption and ultimate democratization of the heathens. Authoritarianism in East Asia was seen as an aberration, soon to be eclipsed by liberalism. Not so today. In the summer 1993 issue of *Foreign Affairs*, Harvard professor Samuel P. Huntington presented a stylized version of the global divide after the cold war that emphasized the remarkable persistence of cultural and civilizational boundaries. He singled out "Confucian civilization," along with Islamic civilization, as the most resistant to the Western perspective and hence a threat in the next phase of global politics. (He threw China and North Korea into the Confucian camp, but not Japan—an interesting departure that would not occur to any East Asian specialist.) Leaders in Beijing could not have been pleased that America's premier strategic thinker portrayed China as the next evil empire. But the argument on civilizational autonomy would be to their liking, if only to justify their human rights record.

The Chinese have not shrunk from proclaiming that Singapore-style authoritarianism as their formula for political and ideological stability while carrying out paramount leader Deng Xiaoping's economic reform program, since Communism would not serve the purpose. Their preferred term is "New Authoritarianism," connoting both continuity and change, the former occurring in the political and the latter in the economic realm—a political means of holding all other things "equal" while pursuing economic growth.

The new authoritarianism presupposes an older version. Latin Americanists equate the old authoritarianism with the caudillo or oligarchic politics characteristic of economies that relied on the export of primary commodities, or with the populist regimes that wanted to foster a self-reliant, indigenous industrial base—the Peronistas being the classic example. The new authoritarianism, according to the Argentine political scientist Guillermo O'Donnell, developed to provide stability in the transition from self-reliance to an export-led system, holding together the rapidly developing, outward-looking, capitalist economy, with transnational actors and technocrats as administrative linchpins.

Deng presumably had in mind a similar combination of continuity and change. Old authoritarianism in China would refer to the inward-looking, state-centric economic development Mao Zedong pursued. New authoritarianism, Chinese style, would correspond to the state-centrism of an outward-looking and coastal-oriented economy, with emphasis on light industrial exports, market reforms, and reliance on the private sector.

Tracing this political trajectory in the newly industrialized economies of East Asia is perhaps problematic, but if the Chinese emulated anything it was not the bureaucratic authoritarianism of the militarists in Latin America but the strong states of South Korea and Taiwan, and the industrial might of Japan. Openly emulating Japan is difficult for anyone to do in postwar Asia, however, which is why the Beijing leadership has made Singapore the shining example of "New Authoritarianism" and its presumed economic payoffs.

If the political economy of the People's Republic before 1978 was based on the predictability of political and economic outcomes (repression combined with state planning), and if Western liberal democracy rests on the

---

...the new authoritarianism seems to offer a way to have one's cake and eat it too.

---

predictability of procedures (rule of law, a formal constitution, regular elections, and so on) but not the outcomes of politics and markets, then the new authoritarianism seems to offer a way to have one's cake and eat it too. Political predictability reins in the anarchic behavior of both the market and the polity, through state intervention in the market and political behavior, but it does not become a Stalinist smothering of market and polity. This approach is said to be workable because it appears to have worked already in the "mirror of the future" for China: Japan, Taiwan, Singapore, and South Korea.

The attractiveness of the newly industrializing country model also comes from a sense that East Asian countries have essentially the same political culture. On this score, a whole phalanx of Western political scientists is available to help Deng out, pulling the concept of "culture" from the dustbin of history and informing the world that the success of East Asian capitalist economies is based on the region's traditional culture. But they introduce a new twist: instead of Weber's notion in *The Religion of China* that Confucian society squashed capitalist activity and possessed no "ethic" conducive to commerce, Confucius is suddenly active, promoting aggressive Confucianism, samurai Confucianism, post-Confucianism, and maybe one day even appearing in an Adam Smith tie.[1]

EXPLANATIONS FOR A MIRACLE

◆ ◆ ◆

So what is this East Asian political economy? For all the sound and fury about the East Asian miracle, there is no comprehensive thesis. At the more coherent end is Chalmers Johnson's 1982 work, *MITI and the Japanese Miracle*, which employs an institutional analysis, including a genealogy of prominent bureaucrats' careers, to unlock the secret of Japanese neomercantilism. Johnson vigorously eschews any cultural argument in this book, since a better one already exists in the political economy of "late" development. The developmental state that emerges from his study, however, is an ideal-type of Japan; the book does not provide a structural understanding of how things came to be the way they are.

Other writers merely assert that the East Asian state guides industrialization, or—in the neoclassical attempt to account for the state—that it pursues "hand-waving" and other such gesticulations to influence market mechanisms. Still less impressive are the cultural determinists mentioned earlier, who find causality emanating from residual categories labeled aggressive Confucianism, or historical evolution in a region assumed to have a common "tradition," or the diffuse concept of "emergence," which harks back to the modernization literature.

It is probably Johnson's ideal-type, however, that comes closest to Beijing's notion of an authoritarian valhalla at the end of the developmental path. *MITI and the Japanese Miracle* does not just explicitly include capitalist nations in East Asia other than Japan, but goes on to assert that what is unique about the East Asian political economy is its combination of "soft authoritarianism" and high-growth economies. This can be termed "plan-rational authoritarianism"—a deeply seductive notion for former Stalinists accustomed to plan-irrational outcomes (as Johnson puts it). In other words, Johnson takes us perilously close to the Dengist notion of new authoritarianism.

The developmental juggernaut in East Asia exhibits the following characteristics, according to analyses by Johnson and others, including my own work:

◆ autonomy of the state
◆ state-exercised financial control over the economy
◆ coordinated or corporatized labor relations (which are or had better be tranquil, even if this is achieved by terrorizing labor)
◆ bureaucratic autonomy (especially for key economic bureaucracies)
◆ "administrative guidance," which pushes some industries over others
◆ the existence of special private-sector organizations, especially general trading companies and industrial conglomerates favored by government (whether zaibatsu, keiretsu, chaebol, or caifa)
◆ a limited role for foreign capital[2]

This is an ideal-type of a statist utopia that would make Adam Smith turn over in his grave: the state wields power over society and the market at home, and holds foreign interests at bay by means of its formidable gatekeeping power. Whether this describes the reality of the East Asian industrial countries is another question entirely, but it is no wonder the Chinese leadership likes a formula that combines political stability, control of the gates against the imperialists, and rapid growth. It is a "Great Leap Forward" without the costs.

There is one problem with this picture, of course: it is a portrait of a capitalist developmental state. It does not matter whether the cat is black or white, Deng once said, so long as it catches mice. But as he himself must have learned during the 1989 Tiananmen revolt, the color of the cat does matter. The aforementioned characteristics of East Asian political economy may not be goods that can be chosen as if off a supermarket shelf. They are closely linked, and together form the gestalt of late capitalist development.

Development in East Asia is a temporal phenomenon, which makes it hard to emulate in different times and other countries. It took place in the context of a kind of benign neglect by a hegemonic power—the United States—which has tolerated neomercantilist practices so long as they occur in the interstices of the world market or when America dominates a broad range of industrial markets. Japan enjoyed such benign neglect from about the turn of the century to the 1930s,

and then again from the 1950s to about the mid-1980s. South Korea and Taiwan have had their chance from the 1960s to the 1990s, relying above all else on the vast American market. Seizing the opportunity created by United States sponsorship—in particular the decision to keep the American market open to East Asia's industrial commodities, in spite of increasing protectionist pressures—the capitalist states in East Asia built export powerhouses, while insulating their own markets and prevailing over their own societies. In the prophylactic realm they created, these states produced mechanisms that would serve as substitutes for—in economic historian Alexander Gerschenkron's formulation—"missing" prerequisites for an economic takeoff, the most important of these being entrepreneurial segments and domestic capital for industrialization.

THE CONSEQUENCES OF CAPITALISM

◆ ◆ ◆

The example of China immediately makes clear the hazards of pursuing this model in a different time and place. As several analysts have recently pointed out, if the textile sector were not so heavily protected—especially with the quotas and other barriers in the American market—China would quickly become the world's premier textile exporter. In the protectionist 1990s, as opposed to the open 1960s, textiles probably cannot be a "leading sector" for China as they were for South Korea and Taiwan. China cannot rely overwhelmingly on exports, as have other newly industrialized East Asian countries that have—Japan excepted—paltry domestic markets. China's huge domestic market must be able to absorb not only its own manufacturers but vast quantities of foreign imports as well, in part to assure continuing access to markets for its exports.

The 1960s and 1970s were also indulgent toward "soft authoritarianism," with much hortatory literature penned by political scientists touting the virtues of putting the military in the saddle of "political development." Paradoxically, China went from "hard" to "soft" authoritarianism just in time to get bashed for bashing Chinese students—a reprehensible and terrible action, but arguably not worse than what happened in South Korea in 1980 or Mexico City in 1968.

The East Asian newly industrialized countries, however, during the earlier periods erected a huge bureaucratic apparatus to incubate a nascent capitalist class. From this logic flowed a set of repressive policies that characterized prewar Japan and postwar South Korea and Taiwan: financial repression by the state, in the form of a non-market-determined, exceedingly low price for capital, so that large sums were transferred from savers to corporate borrowers; labor repression, so that a class could be broken and a new one created; discrimination against foreign commodities to protect domestic capital; and finally, repression of the popular sector, which is to say, democracy.

Thus in South Korea the historical task of the authoritarian state was the creation (not re-creation, as in more advanced capitalist countries) of a capitalist class. This was particularly urgent because Korea inherited a tiny capitalist class on liberation in 1945—Japanese colonialism having been less interested in incubation than infanticide when faced with independent Korean capitalist development.

If the authoritarian state in South Korea is thus viewed as an entity that has jump-started not just a stag-nant economy but an entire capitalist constellation—with the Korean conglomerates, the chaebol groups, the first major fruit—the implications of China's emulation of the South Korean political economy are highly interesting. They imply a transition from communism to capitalism, with the octogenarian Communists who cling to power in Beijing playing midwife to the birth not just of export-led growth but the capitalist classes their dictatorship of the proletariat was designed to quash.

What all this means is that authoritarianism in East Asia is an integral part of development strategy, useful not just for steadying societies in developmental flux but for creating the class that carried all before the modern world—the entrepreneurial class—and in the shifting of resources to that class. Authoritarian politics is not something genetically encoded in Confucian civilization, but a tried-and-true political arrangement in East Asia in its rush to industrialize.

Notes

1. See Kent Calder and Roy Hofheinz, Jr. *The Eastasia Edge* (New York: Basic Books, 1982); Lucian Pye, *Asian Power and Politics* (Cambridge: Harvard University Press, 1982); and Michio Morishima, *Why Has Japan Succeeded?* (New York: Cambridge University Press, 1982).
2. Chalmers Johnson, "Political Institutions and Economic Performance: The Government-Business Relationship in Japan, South Korea, and Taiwan," in Frederic Dexo, ed., *The Political Economy of the New Asian Industrialism* (Ithaca, N.Y.: Cornell University Press, 1987).

Terms & Concepts

caudillo politics
"Confucian civilization"
"Great Leap Forward"
hegemonic power
neomercantilist practices

"New Authoritarianism"
oligarchic politics
plan-rational authoritarianism
prophylactic realm
protectionism

Singapore-style authoritarianism
soft authoritarianism
statist utopia

Questions

1. What are the differences between the "old" authoritarianism of Mao's China, and the "new" authoritarianism China's leaders now wish to follow?

2. Why would Adam Smith supposedly "turn over in his grave" at the kind of economic regimes that have emerged in East Asia?

3. Can China expect to be able to practise a similar model of development to the one(s) others have been able to use so successfully?

4. What role does this kind of "soft" or "new" or "plan-rational" authoritarianism imply for a state's bureaucracy?

Social Values, Singapore Style

Goh Chok Tong

Editors' Note

In 1965, the young federation of Malaysia fell apart when Singapore was expelled in an extraordinarily rapid break-up. Upon leaving, Singapore faced enormous economic and social problems and "the situation seemed hopeless." Within five years Singapore was experiencing a boom; 30 years later it has become a world economic power. How was this accomplished?

Singapore is a society of amazing contradictions. It is a bastion of capitalism, yet government control is all pervasive and citizens are part of an all-encompassing welfare state. There is "virtually no poverty, no homelessness, and no begging."[1] Does the Singapore system have any larger, more global significance, or is it so small and unique, so driven by one remarkable man, Lee Kuan-Yew, that it is destined to be a transi-

tory and very local phenomenon? (It should be noted that a likely successor to Lee Kuan-Yew is his son, a trilingual graduate of Cambridge and Harvard known as BG Lee because he is also a former brigadier-general.)

Singapore offers a startling contrast to the liberal individualism of the West as well as to both the corrupt bureaucratic, incompetence of Eastern European Communism, and the frenzied, fanatical leader-worship in North Korea or Iran. In this speech, Singaporean Prime Minister Goh Chok Tong launches a sweeping attack on freedom, democracy, and liberalism, North American style. He does not apologize for what others have seen as Singapore's democratic shortcomings, including the preservation of a virtual one-party state. Instead he focuses upon the need for social equality and what

he terms "the rule of law." Note how all of this is then tied to family values and social discipline, and to a willingness to micromanage social and economic planning.

Does Singapore offer a model of "neo-authoritarianism" that might be followed by other countries, especially China? Is the price to be paid not only short-term constraints and a regime of coercion (the caning of foreigners being a notorious case of the latter) but also the long-term absence of a flourishing and sustainable democratic political culture? Or do we take our liberties as universal absolutes, and place far too high a value on some of them while ignoring communal and family needs? Tong makes it absolutely clear that there is a price to be paid for everything. He finds the price paid in the West far too high.

◆ ◆ ◆

1. See Stan Sesser, *The Lands of Charm and Cruelty* (New York: Alfred A. Knopf, 1993). Chapter one contains a readable discussion of what keeps Singapore Inc. so successful, and the price paid for that success.

Four years ago, I could not have predicted that we would do so well. Last year's growth of 9.9 percent was extraordinary. Its momentum has carried over to this year. We grew by 10.5 percent for the first half of this year. Even if the economy slows down in the second half, we should still end the year with more than 9 percent growth, which means civil servants will get a special bonus.

Our strong economic performance translated into higher wages and better schools, housing, and health care. Everyone has benefited, not just big businessmen, the graduates and professionals, but also small businessmen, workers, stall-owners, and taxi drivers.

Singaporeans living in Housing and Development Board [HDB] flats have seen big improvements in their standard of living. They own more luxury items like hi-fi sets, air conditioners, microwave ovens, and personal computers. Thirty-seven thousand HDB homes have maids, including 4,000 three-roomer households. Each year nearly half the HDB families have some members who go abroad for holidays.

Compare yourself with your counterparts in other countries and see how well you have done. If you are a technician or a teacher, compare yourself with techni-

---

Only with a set of political and social values grounded on sound moral principles can a country develop progressively...

---

cians or teachers elsewhere. If you are a taxi driver, compare yourself with taxi drivers in Thailand, Taiwan, London, or anywhere else in the world. How many of them own their homes? How many of them own shares? You are ahead of them.

How far ahead? Singaporeans now have one of the highest per capita incomes in the world. The World Bank ranks us eighteenth among 230 countries. We are ahead of Hong Kong and New Zealand, and just behind Australia.

It will not be easy to repeat the 8.1 percent annual growth of the last five years. But I am optimistic...The region is booming. We are seeing the greatest transformation in human history since the Industrial Revolution of the eighteenth century.

FAMILY AND MORAL VALUES

◆ ◆ ◆

I am reasonably confident that things will go well for the next five to ten years. At home, sound economic policies are in place. In the region things look calm but of course, one can never predict international relations. For success to continue, correct economic policies alone are not enough. Equally important are the noneconomic factors—a sense of community and nationhood, a disciplined and hard-working people, strong moral values, and family ties. The type of society we are determines how we perform. It is not simply materialism and pursuit of individual rewards which drive Singapore forward. More important, it is the sense of idealism and service, born out of a feeling of social solidarity and national identification. Without these crucial factors, we cannot be a happy or dynamic society.

These noneconomic factors translate into the political values the society has. Some of the political values we have are already ingrained and are good for our development. For example, society's rejection of corrupt practices and demand for a clean government and civil service. This is a basic expectation and it is a good political value. The more we enshrine this value, the more we ensure that crooked people do not assume responsible positions to make decisions affecting our lives. Only with a set of political and social values grounded on sound moral principles can a country develop progressively and win the respect of other nations.

Singaporeans have the right values to progress. Our Asian culture puts group interests above those of the individual. We have strong family and extended family ties. The generation of those over 40 has shared the hardships of the 1950s, 1960s, and 1970s caused by communists and communalists, and the uncertainties after separation from Malaysia when our survival was at stake. These experiences have tempered this older generation.

But societies change. They change with affluence, with technology, with politics. Sometimes changes are for the better, but sometimes changes make a society lose its vitality, its solidarity, make a people soft and [lead to] decline.

Singaporeans today enjoy full employment and high economic growth, and low divorce, illegitimacy, and crime rates. You may think decline is unimaginable. But societies can go wrong quickly. The United States and

---

From a transcript reproduced in *Current History* magazine, December 1994 (pp. 417–22).

British societies have changed profoundly in the last 30 years. Up to the early 1960s they were disciplined, conservative, with the family very much the pillar of their societies.

Since then, both the United States and Britain have seen a sharp rise in broken families, teenage mothers, illegitimate children, juvenile delinquency, vandalism, and violent crime. In Britain, one in three children is born to an unmarried mother. The same is true in the United States. A recent BBC program asked viewers to choose from a list of finalists the model British family. They chose a pretty divorcée, her boyfriend, and her five-year-old daughter by a previous marriage. The boyfriend did not even live with the divorcée. He came over only on weekends. This "family" won by an overwhelming majority. *The Times* of London, which reported this story, said that the BBC viewers chose them not just because they looked attractive but because they easily identified themselves with them.

This is a profound change in the British family structure. Many families have no man at the head of the household. The woman raises her children without him. The man is, as the *London Sunday Times* puts it, "a nonessential extra."

Some American and British thinkers are deeply concerned with this change in the moral fabric. *U.S. News and World Report* recently carried a series of articles entitled "America's New Crusade" on the loss of values in the United States. Twenty-five years ago the United States was swept by the hippie movement, the "flower power" people who smoked pot, promoted free love, believed in "doing their own thing," and opposed the Vietnam War. Today, one article says:

> Many Americans feel mired in a deep cultural recession and are struggling to escape by restoring old-fashioned values to a central place in their lives. It is Woodstock turned on its head 25 years later, a counterrevolution that esteems prayer over pot, self-discipline over self-indulgence, family love over free love.
>
> At the core of this pessimism is an increasingly frantic fear among Americans that the country is suffering a moral and spiritual decline.

It also quoted President Bill Clinton: "Our problems are beyond government's reach. They are rooted in the loss of values."

Singapore society is also changing. Singaporeans are more preoccupied with materialism and individual rewards. Divorce rates are rising slightly. There are some single parents, and some increases in drug addiction and juvenile delinquency.

Recently the *Straits Times* carried an advertisement showing a boy saying: "Come on, Dad. If you can play golf five times a week. I can have Sustagen once a day." I found the language, the way the boy speaks, most objectionable. Why put an American boy's way of speaking to a father into a Singaporean boy's mouth? Do your children really speak to you like that these days? These advertisements will encourage children to be insolent to their parents. Many American children call their fathers by their first names, and treat them with casual familiarity. We must not unthinkingly drift into attitudes and manners which undermine the traditional politeness and deference Asian children have for their parents and elders. It will destroy the way our children have grown up, respectful and polite to their elders.

Lesson 1: Do not indulge yourselves and your family, especially young children and teenagers.

As Singaporeans become more affluent, parents have increasingly indulged their children's whims and fancies. One small sign of this is the growing number of obese children in schools. Between 1980 and 1993, the obesity rate for primary school students went up three fold. I see this in kindergarten students in Marine Parade. There are more chubby children today than in the 1970s. Affluent parents who had poor childhoods want to spoil their children.

The schools are tackling the problem, but too many parents are not cooperating. They think chubby children are cute, because in the old days only wealthy people had chubby children. They do not know that doctors have found that fat cells in children make for a lifetime of problems.

In America, indulgent upbringing of children has brought sorry consequences. If you slap your child for unruly behavior, you risk going to jail. At a grocery store in the state of Georgia, a 9-year-old boy picked on his sister and was rude to the mother. The mother slapped him. A police officer saw red marks on the boy's face and asked if he had been slapped before. "I get smacked when I am bad," the boy said. The mother was handcuffed and hauled to jail for child abuse. She was released on S$33,000 bail. The charges were later dropped, not because the police felt they were wrong, but because they feared they could not prove to the court that the mother's slapping had caused excessive pain to her son.

British justice also seems to have gone liberal and soft. One teenager committed burglary and other offenses. To reform him, the judge sent him on an 80-day holiday to Africa: Egypt, Kenya, Tanzania, Malawi, Zambia, and Zimbabwe. I suppose this trip was meant to open his eyes to conditions in poorer countries. The safari cost British taxpayers £7,000 (US$16,000). Within a week of returning from this all-expenses-paid trip, the "Safari Boy," as he was dubbed by the press, went on a burglary spree. He was convicted. The sentence? A six-month stay in a young offenders institution, where the treatment is gentle.

The American and British peoples are fed up with rising crime rates, and want to get tough on crime. This is why Michael Fay's vandalism aroused such interest. Opinion polls showed that the American and British public supported the Singapore government's stand on the caning by large margins. But the liberal establishment, especially in the media, campaigned hysterically against the caning, not least because they felt that the ground in their own countries was shifting against them.

In Confucian society, a child who goes wrong knows he has brought shame upon the whole family.

Compare the attitudes of Michael Fay's parents and the parents of Shiu Chi Ho [a youth arrested along with Fay for vandalism]. Fay's parents were outraged instead of being ashamed. They went on radio, television, [and] talk shows, blaming everyone but themselves. Shiu's parents showed pain, avoided publicity, and considered leaving Singapore because of a sense of shame. On the other hand, Michael Fay, back in America, got drunk, and when his father protested, he tackled the father and wrestled him to the ground. I cannot imagine a Chinese son, or any other Asian son, physically tackling his father. But that may happen when sons call their fathers by their first names and treat them as equals. Familiarity can breed contempt.

In Confucian society, a child who goes wrong knows he has brought shame upon the whole family. In America, he may win instant stardom, like Tonya Harding, the ice skater who tried to fix her rival. The difference is stark between what traditional Asians demand of their children and what many Americans now allow theirs to become.

William Bennet, who was President [Ronald] Reagan's secretary of education, wrote an article in the *Asian Wall Street Journal* [March 16, 1993] titled "Quantifying America's Decline." From 1960 to 1990, the United States GDP grew by nearly 300 percent, welfare spending by 600 percent, and the education budget by 225 percent. During the same period, violent crime increased by 560 percent, illegitimate births and divorces by 400 percent. The only thing which went down was student performance: the [average] Scholastic Aptitude Test score dropped by 80 points.

What went wrong? People demand their rights, without balancing them with responsibilities and a sense of social obligation. As Mr. Bennet puts it: "American society now places less value than before on what it owes to others as a matter of moral obligation; less value on sacrifice as a moral good; less value on social conformity and respectability; and less value on correctness and restraint in matters of physical pleasure and sexuality."

This is the result of a me-first-and-society-last attitude to life.

Because we uphold tried and tested traditional values and inculcate them in our young, we are a different society. For instance, the *Straits Times* recently printed a letter from Naresh K. Sinha, a visiting professor at Nanyang Technological University from McMaster University in Ontario, Canada. It was an unsolicited compliment to standards of morality in Singapore. Two days before Mr. Sinha was due to leave Singapore, he went to a CPF [Central Provident Fund, a combination of Social Security, Medicare, and Individual Retirement Account for workers in Singapore] branch office to withdraw his Medisave contributions. To his horror, he discovered he had lost his passport. He panicked and made several phone calls. Meanwhile someone had found his passport and handed it to the police. The police called his office to ask him to go down to the police station and claim it. Mr. Sinha wrote:

> There are two amazing facts about this incident. The first is that someone took it immediately to the police station. The second is the efficiency with which the police were able to locate where I worked and inform me that they had my passport...This could be possible only because of the tough law enforcement in Singapore, coupled with the fact that the political leaders here have promulgated a strict code of ethics and morality.

Mr. Sinha lamented that during the last 33 years of his stay in North America, he had seen a steady decline in moral standards, followed by increasing crime and falling standards in education in both Canada and the United States.

I know Mr. Sinha's experience is just one example and there are others who lose their things and never get them back. But I cited Mr. Sinha's letter not to make us proud of ourselves or, worse still, smug. It is to highlight and hold up as examples the good deeds when they are done. In the same vein, I am pleased to see our newspapers, television, and police give prominence to Singaporeans who do honest deeds. Society must hold up these examples so that we can all emulate them and retain our strict code of ethics and morality.

Lesson 2: Compassion can be misguided.

We deal severely with criminals and antisocial elements. We have a reason: we have seen that in such cases, to be kind to the individual offender is to be cruel to the whole society and to him.

When Michael Fay was caned for vandalism, the United States media accused us of being barbaric. We know from experience that strict punishment deters criminals. In particular, it deters those who have been punished from repeating the offense. One United States television crew who was here covering the Michael Fay case interviewed a man who had been caned for participating in a gang rape. He told them that the caning was so painful that he would never commit the crime again. In other words, the punishment worked...

Welfare is the other area where misguided government compassion has led to disastrous results. The biggest welfare program in America is Aid to Families with Dependent Children [AFDC]. Under this program, women who are poor, unmarried, and have children receive welfare checks so long as they remain single and jobless. Result? The women don't get married and they don't get a job. For if they do, they will lose the benefits. So they produce more illegitimate babies.

Before 1960, one in twenty Americans was born out of wedlock. Now it is one in three. Among black Americans, two out of three births are illegitimate. Having babies without getting married is becoming the way of life for many Americans.

The AFDC program costs the United States taxpayers US$34 billion a year, enough to support our armed forces for 11 years!

Our compassion must never remove that spur that makes people work and pay for themselves. Nor should we undermine self-control, discipline, and responsibility.

Singapore is still a conservative society. Few children are born out of wedlock—one in a hundred...I was dismayed that Sumiko Tan, a *Straits Times* journalist whom I know to be a serious-minded young lady, could publicly reveal that she had once entertained the thought of having a child out of wedlock. Japan, despite its wealth, is still conservative, with only one child in a hundred born out of wedlock. Japanese women feel ashamed to have illegitimate children, and quite rightly so.

Lesson 3: Defend and strengthen family values.

One of our shared values is the family as the basic building block of society. Through the family we transmit values, nurture our young, build self-esteem, and provide mutual support. Schools can teach ethics, Confucian studies, or religious knowledge, but school teachers cannot replace parents or grandparents as the principal models for their children.

Many three-generation Singapore families live together. But this is giving way to single nuclear families. Even so, Singaporeans try to buy HDB flats near their parents so grandparents [can] help out with the grandchildren. Married children still have regular dinners or lunches with their parents.

But we have educated all our women and given them a difficult double role as homemaker and co-breadwinner. If the grandparents look after the children, the kids are not at risk. But they will be at risk if left entirely to the maids, or worse, grow up by themselves in front of televisions.

Furthermore, as we go regional, more families will have fathers who are frequently away, and mothers will have to bear the full burden of caring for the children and aged parents. We must help families to stay together, and encourage wives and young children to follow the fathers abroad, to China, Vietnam, India, or Indonesia.

Women's groups have pressed the government to change the Civil Service rule on medical benefits for family members of female officers. The cabinet has discussed this several times and is reluctant to do so. Changing the rule will alter the balance of responsibility between man and woman in the family. Asian society has always held the man responsible for the child he has fathered. He is the primary provider, not his wife. If a woman has a husband, the husband must be responsible for supporting his children, including meeting their medical costs. If she is an unmarried mother, her children will not be entitled to civil service medical benefits. But if she is widowed or her husband is incapacitated and she is the sole breadwinner, an exception is made and the government extends medical benefits to eligible children. If the boyfriend's child, or the woman's husband, can depend on the woman for medical benefits, [the] Singapore man will become a nonessential extra as in Britain.

I am not saying that woman is inferior to man and must play a subservient role. I believe women should have equal opportunities and men should help out at home, looking after babies, cleaning the house, and washing dishes. But we must hold the man responsible for the child he has fathered, otherwise we will change for the worse a very basic sanction of Asian society. We do not accept unmarried single-parent families.

See what has happened in the United States, the UK, and New Zealand in the last 20 years after their governments took the responsibility of looking after unmarried or divorced mothers and their fatherless children. The number of single-mother families skyrocketed out of control.

America, Britain, and several West European governments have taken over the economic and social functions of the family, and so make [the] family unnecessary and superfluous. Marriage to raise a family is now an extra, an optional extra, like optional extras when buying a car. As the pope observed, two lesbians, a dog, and a cat now form a family.

America's and Britain's social troubles, a growing underclass which is violence prone, uneducated, drug-taking, sexually promiscuous, is the direct result of their family units becoming redundant or nonfunctional. Some 20 to 25 percent of American and British children go to school not to study but to fight and make mischief. Teachers cannot control them. In America, many students carry guns to school and have shoot-outs.

The basic error was for governments to believe that they could stand in place of father and even mother. So they have an underclass which grows up unnurtured by mother or father, no family love and support, no role models, no moral instructions. It started with the best of intentions—compassion for the less fortunate. It ended in the dismantling of their family and the creation of troublesome, uncontrollable youngsters who in turn will become parents without forming proper families.

That is why our Small Families Improvement Scheme insists on the family staying intact. When the family breaks up, the payment stops. I know this is harsh, but it is right. We must never end up with our own version of Aid to Families with Dependent Children...

GOVERNMENT'S ROLE TO SUPPORT THE FAMILY

◆ ◆ ◆

We intend to reinforce the strength of the family. The government will channel rights, and benefits and privileges, through the head of the family so that he can enforce the obligations and responsibilities of family members. We will frame legislation and administrative

rules towards this objective. We already give tax rebates for support of parents and children. Children are allowed to top up their parents' CPF. Medisave can be used for parents, siblings, and the extended family. We encourage and will give support to such cross-generational transfers in the family and the extended family.

The government supports Walter Woon's Bill on the Maintenance of Parents. Parents who brought up their children should in turn be cared for by them. They should have legal recourse to seek financial support from their children as a last resort.

Edusave accounts are now in the name of students. We will amend the Edusave Act so that the accounts are jointly held by the students and parents, either the father or mother. The children are too young to have their apron strings cut. Joint accounts will underline and reinforce the family bond.

The government will introduce a new CPF housing grant scheme to help children buy HDB flats near their parents. We will remit a grant of $30,000 into the CPF account of households who purchase, as their first HDB flat, a resale flat in the New Town where their parents live. The $30,000 grant is to be used strictly as a capital payment to reduce the loan principal. The same conditions will apply as for first-time buyers of HDB flats—income eligibility, a five-year minimum period of occupation before resale or reapplication for another flat, and a premium or levy to be paid when they next buy a flat from HDB.

HDB currently allows unmarried mothers to buy HDB flats direct as well as on the resale market. One thousand unmarried mothers have done so. This rule implicitly accepts unmarried motherhood as a respectable part of our society. This is wrong. By removing the stigma, we may encourage more women to have children without getting married. After discovering this slip-up in our rules, we have decided no longer to allow unmarried mothers to buy HDB flats direct from the HDB. They have to buy them from the resale market.

LESSONS FROM TAIWAN

◆ ◆ ◆

Now, let me turn to a related subject. The Western media prescribe Western-style democracy and press freedom for all countries, regardless of their different histories, culture, traditions, and social evolution. They praise countries which follow their prescriptions: a free-wheeling democracy designed to produce alternating parties in government, and a press that treats the government party as an overlord to be gunned down and the opposition party as the underdog to root for. So the Western media praise Taiwan and South Korea but criticize Singapore because we do not heed their advice. We are the "authoritarian," "dictatorial" "PAP [People's Action Party] regime," "strait-laced" and "repressive."

The Economist in a recent report on Taiwan said: "The interests of Taiwan are more likely to be served...by the evolution of a system of pluralism which enables bad governments to be voted out and good governments to be voted in...Taiwan will then look just like any other independent democratic country, and have the same moral claims on the rest of the free world."

The Economist argued that Taiwan should become more "pluralistic" and "democratic," even though it acknowledged that Taiwan was "a society where votes are bought and free elections have proved to be very expensive." The *Asian Wall Street Journal* reported that the Taiwanese government is cracking down on election vote-buying, and in March indicted "436 politicians, including 341 of 858 councillors voted into office early in the year." In the Taoyuan county assembly, out of 60 councillors, 30 have been convicted of corruption and are appealing, 24 more are on trial, and 2 have been acquitted. That means only 4 out of 60 had no charges against them.

In the same issue of the *Asian Wall Street Journal*, an American academic, James Robinson, noted that in the forthcoming elections for mayor of Taipei, the Kuomintang candidate has "a budget of some US$20 million—in the league of a United States presidential campaign." Yet Robinson goes on to say: "The Taiwanese themselves marvel at how far their country has come in ten years, reforming itself and making its democratic processes durable. This polity has room to become more democratic, especially in privatization of television and radio and reform of campaign financing, but the democratic core is firm."

Now, let me quote the Taiwanese themselves. They have a serious magazine called *Commonwealth*. Ten years ago, [*Commonwealth*] sent a team here to produce a special edition on Singapore. Five years ago, it sent another team, and this year, a third team. Its editors and journalists have studied us closely over a period of 10 years.

The publisher and chief editor, Diane Ying, in her article "What Makes a Beautiful Dream Come True," says:

In ten years, Singapore has faced the reality coolly and soberly, sparing no effort in addressing its problems...

[On the other hand,] in ten years, loss of social discipline, confusion of values, rampant gangsterism and drug addiction, a crisis of national identity, poor leadership, and weakening of government power and public trust in Taiwan have left Taiwan further and further behind Singapore.

Taiwan has lost its goal and efficiency after lifting martial law: environmental pollution, backwardness of public construction, and worsening social order...

Most Taiwanese share the dream of having a clean environment, gracious living, a safe and stable society, and a clean and efficient government. What they want is social equality and rule of law, *not greater freedom and democracy*.

These are the words from Taiwan's leading intellectual magazine.

The Taiwanese have good reasons for going democratic, American style. Taiwan's leaders know too well that this is a very complex and delicate operation. But to survive they need the support of the United States media and Congress. Moreover, if Taiwan is democratic and China is totalitarian, then the West may support Taiwan if China uses force for reunification.

Western liberals, foreign media, and human rights groups also want Singapore to be like their societies, and some Singaporeans mindlessly dance to their tune. See what happened to President [Mikhail] Gorbachev because he was beguiled by their praise. Deng Xiaoping received their condemnation. But look at China today, and see what has happened to the Soviet Union. It's gone. Imploded! We must think for ourselves and decide what is good for Singapore, what will make Singapore stable and successful. Above all else, stay away from policies which have brought a plague of social and economic problems to the United States and Britain.

Let me end by quoting from a *U.S. News and World Report* editorial, "Where Have Our Values Gone?" which eloquently describes what it calls America's "moral and spiritual decline":

Social dysfunction haunts the land: crime and drug abuse, the breakup of the family, the slump in academic performances, the disfigurement of public places by druggies, thugs and exhibitionists.

We certainly seem to have lost the balance between societal rights and individual freedoms. There are daily confrontations with almost everyone in authority:...children against parents, mothers against matrimony, fathers against child support...

Gone are the habits America once admired: industriousness, thrift, self-discipline, commitment.

The combined effect of these sicknesses, rooted in phony doctrines of liberalism, has been to tax the nation's optimism and sap its confidence in the future.

America was not like this in 1966 when I was there as a student. In one generation, it has changed. Is it for the better or for the worse? That's for Americans to decide. But for me, a Singaporean, it is a change I would not want for my children and my grandchildren. Will Singapore, another generation from now, be like the United States today? This is not an idle question. Popular culture, television, rock music, the buy-now-pay-later advertisements, conspicuous consumption, the desire for more material goods, all combine to erode the traditional virtues of hard work, thrift, personal responsibility, and family togetherness.

Our institutions and basic policies are in place to sustain high economic growth. But if we lose our traditional values, our family strength and our social cohesion, we will lose our vibrancy and decline. This is the intangible factor in the success of East Asian economies, especially the NIEs [Newly Industrialized Economies] and Japan.

We have a built-in set of traditional values that have made our families strong. These values are tried and tested, have held us together, and propelled us forward. We must keep them as the bedrock values of our society for the next century. With no physical resources but with proper values, we have made the grade. To continue to succeed, we have to uphold these values which bond the family and unite our nation.

Terms & Concepts

authoritarianism
Edusave Act
Housing and Development Board
Maintenance of Parents Bill

People's Action Party
pluralism
pragmatic state capitalism
proactive economy

Small Families Improvement
    Scheme
traditional social values

Questions

1. Singapore is a country of amazing paradoxes. What appear to be the main ones?

2. What price is paid, in democratic terms, by Singapore's citizens? What aspects of Singaporean government control might Westerners accept? What impression do you get of the role played by women?

3. Singapore has been labelled "neo-authoritarian." Could this be a challenge to "democratic-capitalism" as a model for development? What are Singapore's biggest future political problems likely to be?

4. Would this model work anywhere else? What are the preconditions for its successful implementation?

5. Does this speech make highly selective use of examples to try and prove that North America's "moral and spiritual decline" is tied to liberalism?

Globalization and Governance

Donald J. Savoie

Editors' Note

A recurring theme in this reader is that the remarkable changes occurring in the world of politics now present a challenge to conventional political processes. Donald J. Savoie, one of Canada's leading writers on public policy, and most recently, author of *Thatcher, Reagan, Mulroney: In Search of a New Bureaucracy* (Toronto: University of Toronto Press, 1994), has focused on how well the government bureaucracy has adjusted, whether voluntarily or involuntarily, to this "strange new world," as Alvin Toffler refers to it.[1]

Some of the same forces identified in "Jihad Versus McWorld" (Unit One, Article 2) seem to be at work even inside Canada. At the same time as globalization and interdependence challenge the state from without, increasing regional differences challenge the state's capacity to manage the economy from within. How is the state to respond? One prescription attempted in Canada (and pursued with slightly more determination in the United States and certainly greater zeal in Great Britain) has been to liberate government from its bureaucratic integument by modelling bureaucratic decision-making on business management models. In all three countries this meant that policy decision-making was to be separated from administration of policy. It turns out, however, that business is not necessarily the ideal model for public service.

Margaret Thatcher's government privatized industries, contracted out some government services, and cut civil service employment back by 22%. What was left was fully reorganized along management models, including new hiring-criteria for civil servants. Ronald Reagan, not having as many government enterprises to privatize, cut back the civil service by over 7% within two years and brought in management reforms. Brian Mulroney's government initially cut the civil service by 5%, but by the end of his mandate, the civil service had swollen back to within less than two percent of its pre-1984 size. Here too, a cure was sought by bringing in new management practices.[2] More recently (and not covered

---

1. Alvin Toffler, *Powershift: Knowledge, Wealth and Violence at the Edge of the 21st Century* (New York: Bantam, 1990), 240–41.

2. Donald J. Savoie, *Thatcher, Reagan, Mulroney: In Search of a New Bureaucracy* (Toronto: University of Toronto Press, 1994), 247–74.

by Savoie), Ralph Klein's government in Alberta is cutting back the civil service drastically in personnel and functions, privatizing a wide range of government services, and bringing private sector style performance criteria to bear on what remains. But in all four cases the application of the private sector management model to the public sector seems to have left government bureaucracy hardly any more able to meet the new challenges than before. The article points to a lesson: simple solutions driven by an ideological agenda seem incapable of dealing adequately with the present challenges to the state. We need brand new ideas to deal with brand new problems.

◆ ◆ ◆

Globalization and the modern media are changing the art of governing. The post-war years provided reconstruction, strong economic growth, a firm belief in the ability of government to intervene in the economy, and a tremendous expansion of government spending. They were also quiet and stable years; countries were relatively free to shape domestic policy in isolation even of neighbouring countries. The media were not nearly so critical of government, especially in the pre-Watergate days. It might have been an environment ideally suited to the Sir Humphreys of the world, but this is no longer the case. The world depicted in George Orwell's novel *1984* has been turned upside down.[1] It is not a government élite that uses advanced technology to control the behaviour of citizens. Rather, it is politicians and, albeit to a lesser extent, government agencies, that are continually "watched, even hounded, as they attempt to go about their daily affairs."[2] To sum up, then, the world of relatively isolated national economies, linearity, discrete variables—and even common sense—inhabited by government officials is giving way to a new world. The new order is much more challenging and less deferential. It requires a strong capacity to adapt to change and to deal with more probing and better-informed media, policy communities or interest groups and the public.

I. THE RESPONSE

◆ ◆ ◆

How are national governments preparing their civil service to respond to the new world? There is little doubt that we have and are witnessing a worldwide frustration among political leaders with their civil services. Gerald E. Caiden, B. Guy Peters and Christopher Pollitt, among many others, have documented the numerous reform measures introduced during the 1980s.[3] Osborne and Gaebler insist that the reinvention of government is a "global revolution."[4] Scandinavian countries are busy "renewing" their national administration, France is attempting to decentralize its civil service, the Reagan administration implemented its Reform 88 initiative and *all* British Commonwealth countries have introduced a host of reform measures in search of a new "Public Management."[5]

This is not to suggest that all these reforms were designed to prepare the civil service to meet the challenges of the new world. They were certainly not part of a grand design to rethink the civil service as an institution.[6] Much of the political leadership that came to office in the 1980s neither arrived with a coherent plan to reform the civil service nor developed one subsequently.[7]

On the face of it, one could conclude that the reforms were incoherent, at times contradictory and even spiteful. One thing is certain—the political leadership of the 1980s, with few exceptions, became highly critical of the role of government in society. The new political rhetoric, if not the political agenda itself, took a decidedly conservative tack. The new agenda had many targets, including government as an economic manager, and the civil service was singled out for criticism. It would be wrong, however, to assume that only the political right had strong reservations about the civil service. In France, President Mitterrand has talked time and again about the need to overhaul the French civil service. Shirley Williams, a centrist politician who had worked well with public servants while in office, wrote after she left government that "My impression of the British Civil Service is that it is a beautifully designed and effective braking mechanism. It produces a hundred well argued answers against initiative and change."[8] John K. Galbraith, himself a leading proponent of the twentieth century for a greater role for government in society, recently observed that bureaucracy has given

---

Reprinted by permission of the author and the *Canadian Centre for Management Development,* Ottawa. The article is available in full on application to the Centre.

government a bad name.[9] Those few who still argued in the 1980s against tampering with the existing machinery of government and its "armies" of entrenched officials were dismissed by both the political left and right. Herbert Kaufman concluded that "antibureaucratic sentiment [had] taken hold like an epidemic."[10] The point here is that while the political leadership set out in the 1980s to overhaul the workings of their civil services without a well-thought plan in hand, there were precious few voices speaking on behalf of the status quo.

But what did the political leadership actually set out to accomplish? Though we know that it failed to step back to take a broader view of the problems before it began to introduce reform measures of one kind or another, it is clear that it set out to diminish the role of government in the economy, to reduce the influence of permanent officials on policy and the policy process, and to make government managers emulate the private sector. How did they go about accomplishing it? Rhetoric played a key role in the reforms. "Bureaucratic bashing" was often the order of the day and the rhetoric did not die down once the leadership took power. One still heard of the need to "deprivilege the civil service," to teach "bureaucrats a thing or two about political leadership," to cut an "overgrown and overweight" bureaucracy down to size, and to ensure that it would not let itself be "educated by bureaucrats."[11] The overall image of the civil service that emerged was that of a bloated and misdirected "behemoth staffed by incompetent zealots, hardly an image likely to encourage bureaucratic self-esteem."[12] Whether intended or not, the rhetoric served to undermine the confidence senior civil servants had in their institution. There is ample evidence that shows that morale in the civil service plummeted in the 1980s in most western countries.[13]

The political leadership also sought to check the influence of permanent officials on policy. The thinking was that officials were invariably wedded to the status quo, unwilling or unable to change direction, to be creative and to challenge conventional wisdom. The objective was to avoid the "Yes Minister" syndrome where public servants allegedly take hold of the agenda and direct the scope and pace of change—often giving the appearance of activity while, in fact, standing still.

How did the leadership seek to pursue this objective? The political leadership builds its strategy of containment around the notion that only politicians should define and move the political and policy agenda. It sought to redefine the role of bureaucracy so that senior civil servants would be managers rather than policy advisors or administrators. In brief, the 1980s saw an attempt to reapply the politics-administration dichotomy concept to government operations, with management replacing administration. The political leadership sought to recapture authority over policy by reforming the machinery and by appointing non-career public servants to key positions.

Efforts to reapply the politics-administration dichotomy were not in any way limited to Britain or the United States. They are also evident in Canada, New Zealand and Australia, among other countries. All in all, one can detect a declining faith in the neutral competence of public servants, with a good number of politicians and observers suspecting bureaucrats of "being biased rather than neutral in their policy perspectives and at times willing to sabotage policy proposals that political leaders want to put into effect."[14] The result is that expertise on public policy issues has begun to flourish outside of government offices in lobby firms, think tanks, public opinion surveys, ministerial offices, single issue groups and so on. In many ways, public policy expertise has been privatized.

But that tells only part of the story. Hand in hand with efforts to attenuate the influence on policy issues of permanent officials were—as we just noted—determined efforts to see senior public servants become managers rather than policy advisors or administrators. Indeed, the civil service, as an institution, was found particularly lacking not only on the policy front but also in managing government operations. The political leadership sent out not-so-subtle messages that they wanted "doers," or those with "a bias for action," rather than "tinkerers" and "can't do" types.[15] The thinking was that the glamour of government work over the years has been in policy, not in management. Indeed, senior officials have been happy to live with elaborate rules and regulations, as long as they were free to play a policy role. The view in some quarters is that the functional units were there to worry about rules dealing with personnel, administration and financial matters, whereas the senior officials' job was to concentrate on politicians and policy issues. Some go so far as to argue that in government, the managing of major departmental or agency programs traditionally has been a job for "junior personnel or *failed* administrative class people who are seen by the mandarins as not being able to make it to the top levels."[16]

The strategy to strengthen the management of government operations was built around two themes. The first was to send out messages that management abilities constituted the new road to the top rather than the policy skills of the "generalist."[17] The second was to look to the private sector for inspiration. The political leadership virtually everywhere in the western world, even in countries with left-of-centre parties in power, concluded that management practices in the private sector were superior to those in the public sector and that whenever possible, the public sector "should either emulate the private sector or simply privatize the function."[18] It set out to restructure government operations. The process was essentially designed to test a number of public sector activities by exposing them to competition. The measure entailed, among other things, the privatization of many crown or government corporations. Margaret Thatcher was the trail-blazer, but by the mid- and late 1980s privatization had become fashionable in much of the world. One observer reports that it began to spread "outward from Britain in the early 1980s affecting more than 100 countries through the world."[19]

The sale of government corporations or assets, however, was only a part of the privatization effort. Many governments began to contract out government operations and government jobs to the private sector. Contracting out is, of course, widely employed in the private sector where large firms decide what they should produce in-house and what ought to be produced by other firms under contract. It has become even more popular in recent years, with firms looking more and more at contracting out and divesting to the core in order to ensure a more concentrated focus on the "business of the business."[20] The political leadership of the 1980s felt strongly that government was producing too

---

...by the mid-1980s "public management" became the new fad in most western countries.

---

many of its services in-house, thus overlooking excellent opportunities to save public funds by contracting out services to the private sector; that large government had become unmanageable and should return to its core responsibilities, as defined by Milton Friedman and other neo-conservative thinkers. It was convinced that savings would be realized because contracting out would unleash competitive forces and expose the lack of efficiency and cost control found in government.[21] Contracting out held an added bonus for governments committed to reducing the size of their bureaucracies, since it transferred jobs from the public to the private sector.[22]

Still, no matter how broadly applied, privatization and contracting out could hardly affect all government operations. To be sure, the size of government could be reduced, but it was recognized that a wide range of activities would remain in the public sector and that large-scale government was here to stay. The political leadership decided to put in place new measures to see to it that these activities would in future be better managed. The importance of management in government was stressed time and again, and by the mid-1980s "public management" became the new fad in most western countries.

The new public management would concentrate as much on specific organizational units as it would on government-wide systems. It sought to transform public administrators into managers who would think, act and perform like private sector managers and run their government operations like private concerns.[23] The goal was to achieve greater efficiency, results, performance and value for money in individual government operations. Traditional approaches to public administration, the argument went, had overlooked these aspects, concentrating as they did on the policy advisory function, on the values of probity and on the maintenance of the process. In short, public administration had not kept pace with the increasing scale, scope and costs of modern government. The new managerialism would seek to break this pattern and to bring home the point that management in government involved a great deal more than controlling and supervising routine functions so that senior officials could be free to concentrate on policy issues.

The public management "fad" has had several themes—empowerment, improving service to clients and strengthening efficiency in government. There is no need to review the various measures in detail here since it has been done elsewhere.[24] Suffice it to stress once again that the new approach looked to better management practices as the key to strengthening efficiency in government operations, turned to the private sector for inspiration and deliberately downplayed the policy advisory function of public servants.

We also know that the 1980s saw the preparation of a host of "mission statements" everywhere in government operations, new efforts at "simplifying," "streamlining" and "deregulating" central agency policies and administrative requirements as well as attempts to "empower" line managers. Civil servants everywhere were told to "stay close to the customer." Empowerment and staying close to the customer would give rise to a new management culture which would be more open, responsive and place a stronger emphasis on management than the old "bureaucratic culture" it was replacing.

It is hardly possible to overstate the point that the purpose of empowering public servants at the point of delivery was not only to improve the delivery of government programs but also to open up the government bureaucracy. This would serve a number of objectives. It would force bureaucrats to deal directly with the complaints of the consumers, since they would no longer be able to hide behind centrally prescribed rules and controls. This would empower the public or the customer of government programs and force bureaucrats to deal with their views about what ought to be done. Invariably, this would serve to attenuate the influence of career officials on policy and programs.

II. LOOKING BACK

◆ ◆ ◆

What did the reforms seek to accomplish? To what extent did they get at the "deficiencies of governance" which, according to the *Club of Rome*, are at the root of the problem in the fast-changing global economy, and to what extent have the reforms prepared nation states and their civil service to deal with the new challenges?

The political leadership tried "this" and "that" in its attempts to reform the civil service. Lacking a grand design or a carefully crafted plan, the political leadership in various countries in the 1980s improvised from their first days in office. To be sure, the level of activity in reforming bureaucracy was intense and far-ranging. The 1980s left us with a series of new buzz words like empowerment, a new emphasis on service to clients, Rayner, Grace, Nielsen, privatization, contracting out, IMAA, Next Steps, reductions in the number of government departments (Australia), Special Operating Agencies, Total Quality Management, corporatization policy (New Zealand), PS 2000, pay-for-performance schemes, cuts in personnel, and the drive to separate policy advice from operational activities.

The reforms gave rise to several models of organization. Guy Peters reports on four. He points to the market model which calls for splitting up large departments into smaller entrepreneurial "agencies" or units. This model argues that public sector agencies are confronting the same managerial and service-delivery tasks as private sector firms. The participatory model, on the other hand, considers that hierarchical rule-based organizations inhibit effective management; it looks to the lower echelons of workers as well as clients for solutions and calls for flatter organizations. The temporary model enables government to respond more quickly to a crisis or rapidly increasing demands for services. By looking to temporary task forces or agencies, this model also deals with public perceptions of waste and empire building in government organization.[25] The fourth model, of course, is privatization, including contracting out, and new organization models to strengthen the hand of politicians over policy matters (e.g. chiefs of staff position and new policy units in ministerial offices, including the Prime Minister's Office in the case of Britain).

Though short of a grand design, we do know that the political leadership looked to the private sector for inspiration and to each other for guidance. Measures introduced in one country (e.g. Britain and executive agencies) were soon introduced in another (e.g. Canada and Special Operating Agencies). The same is true for virtually every other measure introduced in the 1980s to reform government operations. There are remarkable similarities in the approaches tried in various countries, despite different institutional structures and public service cultures. The degree of similarity is such that with respect to new approaches to management, it would seem that globalization is having as much impact on the public sector as it has on the private sector. Management techniques have moved from one country to another with great speed, as if there were no jurisdictional boundaries. Some of the more important similarities include "the assumption of public sector inefficiency, the recourse to the private sector expertise, the stubborn belief in the usefulness of merit pay, the tremendous emphasis on new accounting procedures" and sustained efforts to distinguish the policy formulation role from management.[26] On the policy side, however, the only thing that appeared to need fixing was the influence of permanent officials. Reducing their influence was relatively straightforward—import your own policy advisors, or look to partisan advice for help.

Ideology, fiscal pressure, and the self-fulfilling prophecies of bureaucratic bashing led the political leadership to focus reform efforts on management. Lack of rigorous management was seen as the culprit, rather than the policy advisory capacity of the civil service or the considerable discretion given to government departments in applying policies and delivering programs. In short, the focus was on the boiler-room aspects of governance. That is, efforts to strengthen the management capacity of government were directed at what James Q. Wilson and Henry Mintzberg have labelled "machine- or production-type organizations" rather than to departments with a high policy content.[27]

It is still too early to reach firm conclusions about improvements to government operations. In any event, a good number of observers question whether it is possible to measure qualitative performance in government operations. Still, a survey of reform measures in several countries reveals that the reforms had the greatest impact on machine- or production-like organizations, precisely those elements of government that already appeared to work best. These organizations produce a tangible product and the workload and level of productivity can often be measured. One wonders, however, how much more efficiency can be squeezed out of the Land Registry Office, Her Majesty's Stationery Office, Inland Revenue, the Passport Office, or the IRS. These agencies have not reduced staff; furthermore, they continually claim that they have insufficient financial resources to meet "client expectations."

The reforms, however, have had a negative impact on several fronts. As pointed out earlier, morale in the civil service has suffered greatly throughout the western world in the 1980s. There is plenty of evidence, including a number of surveys, to suggest that a mood of frustration gripped many civil servants, that it gave rise to a crisis in morale, and that the confidence civil servants have in their institution was badly shaken.[28] To career officials, the message from the political leadership was clear and hardly positive: a good part of the civil service had no intrinsic value since much of its work could be turned over to the private sector or to agencies employing people expected to behave as though they were in the private sector. When it came to policy matters, civil servants were felt to be of limited help. Best to turn to partisan policy advisors, to think tanks and to lobby firms for advice. All of this shook the values of public servants and their views of public service as well as what they considered to be the more noble side of their profession. One American official summed it up when he observed: "I might break and enter for my country but I would never do it for K-Mart or CitiCorp."[29]

It may well be that the civil service as an institution would have been challenged in the 1980s regardless of which political leadership was in office. The fact that both right-of-centre political parties (e.g. Britain, the United States, Canada) and left-of-centre ones (e.g. Australia, France and New Zealand) introduced similar reform measures speaks to this point. Indeed, the fact that a left-of-centre party, the Labour government in New Zealand, made the most radical use of the market-base model to reform the country's civil service suggests that fiscal problems, together with a widely shared sense that public bureaucracies were no longer appropriate for the challenges of the new world, were as important, if not more so, than political ideology.

III. LOOKING AHEAD

◆ ◆ ◆

Globalization, as noted earlier, requires above all a capacity to adjust rapidly to changes in the world economy.[30] It has become trite to write that the pace of change is breathtaking and that we are far more confident about what has gone before than about what lies ahead. We can no longer look to a world of more or less "stable regularities about which easy generalizations can readily be advanced."[31] Modern political theory and our traditions of governance have been built on a number of ideas, including—among others—a view of the nation state existing in relative isolation from other states except in war, diplomatic affairs and some trade issues; a mechanistic understanding of problem solving; and a relatively clear understanding of the roles, responsibilities and boundaries separating the rulers and citizens. These ideas no longer hold.

Where do nation states, in particular their civil services, fit in the new scheme of things? There is no denying that the role of nation states is being challenged from various directions—as we pointed out earlier—from above, from global corporations and from below. At the same time, we see the ability of nation states to implement new policy initiatives increasingly constrained because of international or regional trade agreements, and we see subnational regions growing restless and looking elsewhere for leadership. One such example is the Pacific Northwest Economic Region (PNWER). The enterprise is comprised of five American states (Washington, Oregon, Montana, Idaho and Alaska) and two Canadian provinces (British Columbia and Alberta) that have agreed to "collaborate" across national boundaries in six areas—expanding environmental products and services, creating markets for recycled materials, tourism, telecommunications, education and improving the region's labour force and expanding markets for selected products.[32] The two national governments remain thus far inconsequential actors in the initiative and in the process.

Alvin Toffler points to one of the most disturbing features of our "strange new world"—regional differences increasing economically, culturally, politically and technologically. He goes on to argue that as regional differences increase, it will be more and more difficult for national governments to manage economies with the traditional tools of a central bank, fiscal policy and national programs.[33] Therein lies the rub. Keynesian economics gave nation states the ability to manage national economies. It also, of course, fundamentally reshaped what governments do. Before Keynesian economics, the work of government was essentially of a routine nature, with government offices staffed largely with clerks processing application forms of one kind or another. By the end of the Second World War, however, governments everywhere expanded on all cylinders. Yet we did not initiate a fundamental rethink of the work-

---

There is a school of thought which suggests that Keynesian economics did not fail: the failure was in its application.

---

ings of government. New departments, new programs and new units, including new policy groups, were added to the existing machinery of government with the hierarchical nature of government remaining intact. In short, we established new agencies, hired new people, mostly young university graduates, and in the spirit of Keynesian economics we told them to be creative, to challenge the status quo and to come up with new solutions to old problems. Yet we did not attempt to remove the creative or policy shackles inhibiting government bureaucracies, to look to new ways of doing things or to jettison dated government programs and activities. In hindsight this may well have been a mistake, and in this sense a good number of our present-day problems with governance may well predate the globalization phenomenon. There is a school of thought which suggests that Keynesian economics did not fail: the failure was in its application. Politicians were unwilling to cut back government spending in good economic times and government bureaucracy became too rigid, unable to rid itself of redundant units, and too uncreative to chart a new course when it became necessary—hence John K. Galbraith's suggestion that "bureaucracy has given government a bad name."

The never-ending attempts to reform the civil service, beginning in the 1950s with the Hoover Commissions in the United States, carrying on in the 1960s with the Glassco Commission in Canada, Fulton in Britain, and the PPBS and PAR reforms in the 1970s, among others, speak to the inability of the machinery of government to accommodate the requirements of Keynesian economics. Calls for "letting the manager manage" and for putting in place objective evaluation criteria to assess the performance of programs ran up

against the reality of government operations where things can never be so simple and where things cannot always be measured. The requirements of partisan politics, officials fighting for turf, and accountability issues are just some of the forces that shape government decision making.

Neoclassical economic theory and globalization are now redefining the role of government, much as Keynesian economics did forty years ago. There are, of course, large differences between the two. Neoclassical theory tells us that a liberalized world economy is more efficient, more productive than a controlled or managed economy. The theory, however, tells us nothing about something that is key to its success, that is, how to get there, or how to make the transition from a managed economy to a liberalized one.

The reforms of the 1980s and early 1990s either overlooked these issues or sidestepped them. By and large, they sought to make government operations more efficient and to make them less rule-driven. They also sought to instil the notion of competition in public service thinking so that quality would get better and costs would come down. If these reforms in fact give rise to more efficient government operations, so much the better. But the reforms do not go far enough in preparing nation states to make the transition to a more liberalized world economy. The challenges for nation states are becoming clear—new cleavages are emerging, flowing out of a growing gap between the economically distressed and the economically secure, and between subnational regions as they integrate themselves differently in the global economy. The global economy, however liberalized, will require a strong capacity on the part of nation states to oversee its evolution. There is no global government ready to formulate and apply the necessary regulations; thus it is left to nation states to pick up the pieces as best they can and to provide the link between the global perspective and subnational regions, regions which are becoming increasingly frustrated over their inability to influence not only forces operating beyond their borders but even those shaping their own local economies.

In attempting to play a new role in the emerging scheme of things, nation states will have to look at the functioning of their democratic institutions and their requirements. If we have learned anything during the past thirty years, it is that attempts to reform the civil service as if political institutions do not matter invariably force reformers to work at the margin. Governance starts and ends with our democratic institutions to which a civil service is at least partially accountable. The wave of reforms we have seen either have begun with a deliberate decision not to ask fundamental questions about political institutions (e.g. Fulton) or have simply proceeded without asking how the reforms would be made workable in the political environment.

The time may well have come for public servants to say to Parliament, Congress, Cabinet and Cabinet committees "heal thyself" first before further civil service reforms can be attempted. Our political institutions were designed when things were simple and when nation states operated in relative isolation from one another. If the global economy now requires a well-honed capacity on the part of a national public service to innovate, to challenge the status quo, to take risks, to change course quickly, and to have the capacity to speak simultaneously to both the global perspective and to subnational regions, political leaders must attach some question marks to the workings of their own institutions, to what they do, and to how they do it.

There are still precious few rewards for calling a spade a spade or for risk taking in government bureaucracies, and plenty of career punishments for creating or mismanaging a political crisis or bureaucratic *faux pas*, particularly the ones reported in the media. Bureaucracy, as is well known, was designed to give priority to due process, to applying rules and regulations fairly, to responding to political direction from above, and to ensuring a full public accountability of its decisions and activities. In the hierarchical world of central bureaucracies, one looks up in order to serve political masters, the permanent secretary or other senior permanent officials as best one can. There is always a political crisis to manage, a "turf" war to be won and centrally prescribed rules and processes to observe. Talking about the need for greater emphasis on service to clients and establishing new executive or special agencies will only carry civil service reforms so far. Real reforms can take place only if political institutions are themselves reformed. In short, the search for less bureaucracy without less government may be possible if politicians look at the requirements of their own institutions.

The quality of governance in the new global order, however, extends beyond national political institutions and their civil service. New means of communication are making people stronger actors in the governance process. As we noted earlier, people are being empowered. This is not to suggest for a moment that they have the necessary knowledge to pressure politicians and their governments to pursue the "general public good." Robert A. Dahl's recent essay on the "problem of civil

competence" speaks eloquently to this issue.[34] If the objective in the global economy is to see people and regions reduce their reliance on government and to see the qualities of citizenship "restored,"[35] then public servants may well need to become teachers of public policy and governance. They may be called upon to act as "knowledge-based" advisors explaining the required trade-offs, and to assist in determining and explaining the parameters within which solutions must be found. This, in turn, will require redefining the relationship between politicians and career officials.

National civil services themselves must also look internally and strengthen their capacity to be creative, to challenge the status quo and to recommend and implement change. It is not too great an exaggeration to suggest that on the policy side, the quality of a civil service, "corresponds to the discretion available to be creative."[36] Again, recent reforms did not deal with this issue. The emphasis in the 1980s was on removing administrative—or better yet, management—shackles rather than policy shackles. If anything, the attempts to rediscover the politics-administration or management dichotomy served to undermine the policy role of civil servants. With the exception of cuts in the numbers and size of policy units, the policy machinery in government looks exactly as it did in the late 1970s.

Moreover, politicians sent out messages that they and their partisan policy advisors, their pollsters and their friends in lobby firms had the policy answers. There was declining faith in "neutral competence" on the policy front and "responsive competence" came in fashion.[37] Permanent officials with their well-honed capacity to read political signals understood the message clearly. There is evidence to suggest that there was a stronger tendency than there had been in the past for permanent officials to recommend safe policy options, what "politicians would wear," and an unwillingness to "say '*No Minister*' or at least '*Be Careful Minister*'."[38] In short, there was a reluctance to explain why things must be so, to provide objective or non-partisan advice to the powerful and to explain what kind of trade-offs are required if a certain decision is taken, and so on.

Perhaps the fear of strengthening the policy role of officials prevented the political leadership from reforming the policy formulation, coordination and evaluation machinery in government. Still, we know that the hierarchical nature of government departments, the dysfunctions of permanence and the "system" are inhibiting creative talents in government.

There is also, of course, the ongoing bureaucratic dilemma in which the urgent drives out the important, a dilemma which remains unresolved. Policy fire-fighting is the norm in policy units. Their criterion for success is how well senior officials and politicians are being served on the policy front. The problem here, of course, is that senior officials and politicians are rarely in a position to compare the work of their policy units with another across the street. Standards can change whenever there are changes in senior personnel or in politicians. In addition, in a collegial system, the expectations include securing the respect of other units in the department or other government departments. This is hardly conducive to developing a capacity to be creative or to challenge the status quo. Some officials in "policy shops" readily admit a reluctance to tackle "big" issues for fear of challenging the operational side of the department.[39] One official explained that his policy shop had "become irrelevant by attempting to be relevant and supportive of the operational side of the department."[40] Another reports that an inordinate amount of time was spent "keeping fingers in all areas to ensure that our side is protected in the interdepartmental game."[41] Again, we have seen precious few efforts thus far to deal with such problems.

At the risk of overstating the case, there was far more evidence in 1980 that the policy side of government and the ability of bureaucracy to be innovative and self-questioning needed more fixing than did the machine- or production-like agencies.[42] If nothing else, we needed a fundamental review of the merits of advising on policy from a sectoral or departmental perspective. The current machinery of government tends to compartmentalize thinking in government. It was no doubt appropriate at the turn of the century to establish vertical sectoral lines and deal with problems in agriculture, transportation and industry in relative isolation. Issues and challenges confronting nation states, however, now increasingly cross departmental lines. If key policy issues are more and more horizontal, then the bureaucratic policy formulation and advisory structures must become horizontal as well. Civil servants will have to bring a far broader and more informed perspective to bear on their work since issues are now much more complicated and interrelated.

The idea of looking at government operations from a framework that encourages the different assessment of different kinds of activities also holds promise. Such a framework could distinguish: (a) developmental agencies that design or create changes, or advise on them; (b) clerical delivery agencies, whose operating employees require relatively little training in providing certain services; (c) professional delivery agencies, which provide governmental services of a more skilled nature; and (d) control agencies, which act in some kind of control capacity vis-à-vis segments of the population (e.g., regulation), the population at large (army, police, etc.), or government itself (e.g., Treasury Board). In addition, new agencies should be distinguished in their "start-up" years from long established ones.

Each of these could use a different kind of structure to make them more effective. Developmental agencies seem to function best with "adhocracy" type structures, which must be highly flexible, decentralized, and provide relatively quick access to senior officials and to political authority. Professional delivery agencies, as well as many control agencies, tend to require a "professional bureaucracy" structure which could be decentralized. Neither of these structures, however, lends itself to performance measures. Clerical delivery agencies appropriately rely on the traditional structure of "machine bureaucracy," that is, centralized in power and formalized in procedure. They lend themselves to some form of performance measures.

All in all new approaches, particularly ones designed to strengthen the policy capacity of national civil services, are required for nation states to meet new challenges. Indeed, the challenges at hand have a great deal more to do with creativity, quick response to emerging problems and with a capacity to reconcile various interests both at home and even abroad then with squeezing more productivity out of the machine-like departments or administrative units. It only takes a moment's reflexion to appreciate some of the challenges ahead for nation states. Globalization and the legacies of the new "public management" are raising important issues of organizational complexity, including the problem of overlapping organizations dealing with overlapping issues, the need to strike a new balance between the public and private sectors, ensuring accountability in both the public and private sectors, and managing multi-organizational approaches to program delivery.[43]

It is also wrong to assume that the global economy, the rise of local or regional governments and the burgeoning international bureaucracy (e.g. United Nations) will leave in their wake little for national civil services to do. To be sure, the emerging world order or disorder is reshaping the international power structure and the impact on national civil services will be profound. The world is no longer divided along ideological lines, with two superpowers dominating the political landscape and military orientations. Yet many of the old problems remain, and new ones are constantly being added to the political agenda.

Although there is no denying that regional or local forces, often fuelled by ethnic, religious, cultural and economic differences, are running strong everywhere

---

...national governments will still be the ones asked to resolve old and new problems.

---

and are challenging nation states, it remains that national governments will still be the ones asked to resolve old and new problems. A recent incident off the coast of Newfoundland speaks to this issue.[44] The Canadian government imposed a two-year moratorium on groundfish, following the virtual disappearance of the northern cod off the coast of Newfoundland and Labrador. The moratorium extended to two hundred miles off the coast of Newfoundland and Labrador, or the area over which Canada holds jurisdiction. Spanish fishermen, however, have continued to fish on the "nose" of the Grand Banks which—at least as far as Newfoundland fishermen are concerned—is an important spawning ground for northern cod. The nose, however, is located just beyond the two hundred mile limit. A number of Newfoundland fishermen, with the full support of the Newfoundland provincial government, set out to sea in a large fishing trawler in the summer of 1992 to confront the Spanish fishing fleet. A television crew captured the confrontation which unfolded as follows: the Newfoundland ship came within fifty yards or so of a Spanish trawler and a spokesperson for the Newfoundlanders called the Spanish captain to express his displeasure and to ask him to leave the area. The Spanish captain replied that he was in international waters, that there were precious few fish left elsewhere, and that he and his crew had to make a living. The Newfoundlander replied that although the Spanish ship was beyond the two hundred mile limit, overfishing on the nose of the Grand Banks had serious implications for the local fishery and explained that he and his colleagues were also trying to make a living. At that point both sides agreed that they had a lot in common—they were fishermen, they wanted to continue to be fishermen, and they should make every effort to protect the fishery. They also agreed to a solution—they recognized that they could not resolve the problem themselves and concluded that both their "national" governments would have to meet to resolve the problem. The government of Newfoundland and Labrador sought to raise the issue at a U.N. sponsored conference "on high sea-fishing" but it was told that the problem was too "minor" to be dealt with at the United Nations.[45]

This story illustrates well the role nation states will have to play in future. The global economy can set the stage for national and local economies to compete and lay down the rules under which economies and firms must operate. It is hardly possible, however, to imagine a global economy taking shape without conflicts between firms, sectors, regions and nations or without far-reaching adjustments in some sectors and regions. The designers of the new order will have to be national politicians and national public services. They alone have the legitimacy. In short, national governments will have to take the lead in managing and resolving these conflicts, in paving the way for adjustments to take place and in integrating regional economies. To do so they will need "national" civil services with the capacity to be creative, to seek out compromises, to educate and to initiate and manage change. A well-honed capacity to manage programs, to squeeze more productivity out of machine-like organizations and to transfer activities to non-government bodies will not suffice.

Notes

1. Williams, *Problems of Governance, Political Participation and Administration of Justice in an Information Society*, p. 29.
2. Christopher Pollitt, *Managerialism and the Public Services* (Oxford: Basil Blackwell, 1988), p. 178.
3. See, among many others, Gerald E. Caiden, *Administrative Reform Comes of Age* (Berlin: Walter de Gruyter and Co., 1991) and B. Guy

Peters, *The Public Service, the Changing State, and Governance*, (Ottawa: Canadian Centre for Management Development, forthcoming.)

4. David Osborne and Ted Gaebler, *Reinventing Government: How the Entrepreneurial Spirit is Transforming the Public Sector* (Reading, MA: Addison-Wesley Publishing Co., 1992).

5. See, among others, Savoie, *Thatcher, Reagan and Mulroney*.

6. Ibid.

7. See, among many others, Geoffrey K. Fry, "The Development of the Thatcher Government's Grand Strategy for the Civil Service: A Public Policy Perspective," *Public Administration*, 62, 4 (Autumn 1984): 322–35.

8. Shirley Williams, "The Decision Makers," in *Policy and Practice: The Experience of Government* (London: Royal Institute of Public Administration, 1980), p. 67.

9. Quoted in *Dimension* (Winter 1986): 13.

10. Herbert Kaufman, "Fear of Bureaucracy: A Raging Pandemic," *Public Administration Review*, 59, 3 (1981): 1.

11. See, among others, Peter Hennessy, *Whitehall* (London: Fontana Press, 1989) and Savoie, *Thatcher, Reagan and Mulroney*.

12. Lester M. Solomon, and Michael S. Lund, "Governance in the Reagan Era: An Overview," in Lester M. Solomon and Michael S. Lund (eds.), *The Reagan Presidency and the Governing of America* (Washington: The Urban Institute Press, 1984), p. 14.

13. See, among others, Savoie, *Thatcher, Reagan and Mulroney*.

14. Francis E. Rourke, "Responsiveness and Neutral Competence in American Bureaucracy," *Public Administration Review*, 56, 6 (November/December 1992): 540.

15. Les Metcalfe and Sue Richards, *Improving Public Management* (London: Sage Publications, 1987); Pollitt, *Managerialism and the Public Services*; Savoie, *Thatcher, Reagan and Mulroney*.

16. See Williams, *Washington, Westminister and Whitehall*, p. 62.

17. Ibid.

18. Pollitt, *Managerialism and the Public Services*, p. vi.

19. See Madsen Pirie, *Privatization* (London: Wildwood House, 1988), p. 3.

20. See Rosabeth Moss Kanter, *When Giants Learn to Dance* (New York: Simon & Schuster, 1989), p. 96.

21. See M. Forsyth, *The Myths of Privatization* (London: Adam Smith Institute, 1983).

22. Metcalfe and Richards, *Improving Public Management*, chapter 8.

23. See, among others, John Greenwood and David Wilson, *Public Administration in Britain Today* (London: Unwin Hyman, 1984), p. 15.

24. See, among others, Savoie, *Thatcher, Reagan and Mulroney*.

25. See Peters, *The Public Service, the Changing State, and Governance*.

26. Pollitt, *Managerialism and the Public Services*, p. 181.

27. See James Q. Wilson, *Bureaucracy: What Governments Do and Why They Do It* (New York: Basic Books, 1989).

28. See, among many others, James D. Carroll et al., "Supply-Side Management in the Reagan Administration," *Public Administration Review*, 45, 6 (November/December 1985): 805–14.

29. Quoted in "Government," *Business Week* (Hightstown, N.J.: 14 October 1991): 100.

30. See Porter, *The Competitive Advantage of Nations.*

31. Williams, *Problems of Governance, Political Participation and Administration of Justice in an Information Society,* p. 10.

32. *Strategies for the Pacific Northwest Economic Region* (University of Washington: Northwest Policy Centre, 1991).

33. Alvin Toffler, *Powershift: Knowledge, Wealth and Violence at the Edge of the 21st Century* (New York: Bantam, 1990), p. 240–41.

34. Robert A. Dahl, "The Problem of Civil Competence," *Journal of Democracy,* 3, 4 (October 1992).

35. Marcel Massé, *Partners in the Management of Canada: The Changing Roles of Government and the Public Service,* The 1993 John L. Manion Lecture (Ottawa: Canadian Centre for Management Development, 1993).

36. See Joel D. Aberbach, and Bert A. Rockman, "Does Governance Matter—and If So, How? Process, Performance and Outcomes," *Governance,* 5, 2 (April 1992): 145.

37. See, among others, Francis E. Rourke, "Responsiveness and Neutral Competence in American Bureaucracy," *Public Administration Review,* 52, 6 (November/December 1992): 539–46.

38. See, among many others, Minutes of Evidence, Treasury and Civil Service Committee—Civil Servants and Ministers: Duties and Responsibilities (London: HMSO, 29 January 1986), p. 182.

39. Quoted in Savoie, *Thatcher, Reagan and Mulroney,* p. 214.

40. Ibid.

41. Ibid.

42. Rourke and Schulman, for example, argued that "bureaucratic think tank comes close to being an oxymoron." See Rourke and Schulman "Adhocracy in Policy Development," *The Social Science Journal,* 26, 2: 133.

43. Ali Farazmand, "The New World Order and Global Public Administration: A Critical Essay," in Jean-Claude Garcia-Zamor (ed.), *Public Administration in the Global Village* (Westport, CT: Greenwood Press, forthcoming), p. 29.

44. The fishermen's union captured the confrontation in a documentary film, *Troubled Waters,* a Burna-Olser Production, 29 April 1992, St. John's, the United Allied Food Workers, January 1993.

45. See "Fisheries crisis too small for U.N., E.C. official says," The *Ottawa Citizen,* 14 July 1993, p. A5.

Terms & Concepts

bureaucracy/civil service
contracting out
globalization
Keynesian economic theory
market-based government model

neoclassical economic theory
policy capacity
policy generalist
policy role
politics-administration dichotomy

private sector
privatization
public management
public sector
regionalization

Questions

1. What do neoconservative governments see wrong with government bureaucracy?

2. What are neoconservative prescriptions for modernizing government?

3. In what ways does public administration differ from business administration?

4. What are the dangers in reducing the policy function of bureaucrats?

5. How can the policy function of bureaucrats be increased without reducing accountability even further?

How Do Peaceful Secessions Happen*

Robert A. Young

Editors' Note

Robert Young's article tackles the question of national breakup from an unusual angle. He asks what we can learn about the process of secession in cases where it has been accomplished *peacefully*. There are not many such cases to choose from, but this does not make them unimportant—far from it. He notes the primacy of "high" state level politics in such cases, and he stresses that outcomes are "path dependent." This is the highest of high-stakes games, driven by history and nationalism—and by the personalities of ambitious leaders. (The attempted secession of Chechnya from the Russian Federation, and the resulting horrors, seems to be a graphic illustration of this latter point.)

Young provides a list of 13 generalizations about peaceful secessions. Many of them are counter-intuitive; we cannot rely upon our "common sense," for these are situations that are so uncommon as to leave us bereft of axioms based on experience. Political temperament, political culture and a willingness to compromise are all-important.

In Canada, in the past, open discussion of the prospect of Quebec's secession and its consequences has been avoided. It was a taboo subject, to be kept under wraps lest it gave credence to the very idea that it was a serious possibility. This has changed. Academic authors now routinely write of the kinds of problems we would face, the Bélanger-Campeau Commission held public hearings on the issues, followed in 1995 by the regional commissions established by the Parti Québécois. Some non-Francophone authors have, of late, gone so far as to suggest that the rest of Canada should actually encourage Quebec to leave.

Young's piece is a very useful corrective to both the view that secession is a subject best avoided as a topic of discussion, and to the "we're going to make it as difficult for you as possible" school of thought. He searches for patterns that might help us if things do fall apart. His 13 points are each of crucial importance, and his last observation is memorable: "There has never been a case of reunification after (peaceful) secession."

◆ ◆ ◆

*For comments on earlier versions of this paper, I thank Doug Brown, Ron Watts, Paul Boothe, Al O'Brien, Stéphane Dion, Philippe Faucher, Peter Neary, John McDougall, and participants in seminars at the University of Alberta, the University of Western Ontario, l'Université de Montréal, and the 1994 CPSA meetings. Research assistance was provided by Dwight Herperger, Allison Bramwell, and Cristine de Clercy. Funding from the Social Sciences and Humanities Research Council was essential to conduct the study, and the Institute of Intergovernmental Relations at Queen's University provided other forms of support.

I. INTRODUCTION

◆ ◆ ◆

The phenomenon of secession has recently attracted the attention of scholars working within a variety of theoretical perspectives. Spurred by events in the former U.S.S.R., specialists in comparative politics have returned to classic questions about nationalism and state viability.[1] Studies of the legal and moral issues around secession have begun to proliferate.[2] Political economists have engaged a process that lends itself well to calculation and strategic games.[3] And theories both deductive and inductive are emerging about the causes and process of secession.[4] Of course in particular countries, like Canada, where secession is a burning public issue, scholarly attention to all its causes, features and likely effects is intense.

In this context, the central purpose of this paper is modest and straightforward. It is to arrive at empirical generalizations about the politics of the process of secession. The objective is not to investigate the causes or consequences of secession; it is not to formulate theories about the relations between economic and social factors and political events; nor, finally, is it to predict when and

---

...political actors possess a high degree of autonomy in making decisions about secession and how to respond to it.

---

how particular secessionist movements may achieve their ends. The purpose is simply to explore how secessions have occurred in the past, and to search for general patterns in the political dynamics.

This is worth doing for several reasons. First, it seems important to study the politics of the transition from a single sovereign unit to two or more states, because the long term outcomes of secession may be highly path-dependent. That is, the nature of the "new" polities and the economic and political relations between them may depend critically on the process through which secession took place. Second, a primary focus on politics is justified to the extent that political actors pos-

sess a high degree of autonomy in making decisions about secession and how to respond to it. The societal constraints on decision-makers negotiating a new trade agreement, for example, may be far more binding than the constraints sensed by politicians who must decide how far to push secessionist demands, how to respond to them, or how to negotiate the unprecedented transition to separate sovereign entities. Finally, for analysts interested in particular cases, empirical generalizations about secession may assist in predicting how the process would unfold in other countries. Every country and every secessionist movement is unique, but this is precisely what renders predictions about each case unreliable (and contestable). Any evidence from comparative experience that suggests how the process might occur should be welcome to those who analyze particular systems. Inducing general patterns in the transition processes through which peaceful secessions have taken place is, in fact, possible: whether these generalizations illuminate other contemporary cases remains to be seen.

There is little point in summarizing the generalizations here. But the overall pattern is clear enough. After long and fundamental disputes, partisan realignments or external shocks cause one state to make an authoritative declaration of intent to end the union (or federation). This is accepted by the other government, in principle, a move that obviously distinguishes peaceful from contested secessions, since the only other alternative is to attempt violent repression.[5] Negotiations follow inevitably, and they are fast, limited to big issues, constrained by foreign powers, and conducted by small teams to which broad authority is delegated. Throughout this process, the two sides polarize, and there are substantial pressures to maintain national solidarity. Peaceful secessions occur constitutionally, and involve minimal changes to the existing constitutional order(s). But policies in the new states soon begin to diverge, and some friction continues, as is normal between interdependent, sovereign entities.

Before proceeding to elaborate the generalizations in more detail, this paper's limitations should be noted. The most serious is that there are few cases considered here. Most attention is devoted to only three—the secession of Singapore from Malaysia in 1965, of Hungary from Austria in 1867, and of Norway from Sweden in 1905. There is a handful of other cases to which some reference can be made, but these are mainly breakups of

Reprinted by permission of *The Canadian Journal of Political Science* and Robert Young. This article appeared in Volume 27:4, March 1994.

short-lived colonial federations, countries outfitted by the receding British Empire with generic (or "neo-classical") federal systems that did not long endure.[6] This small sample also ignores contemporary secessions from the former U.S.S.R., not because withdrawl from a communist empire is less relevant than some of the cases explored here—there undoubtedly is much to be learned from the C.I.S.—but because time and linguistic constraints have not allowed reliable information to be gathered. The breakup of the Czech and Slovak Federal Republic is of even greater interest, but I have treated it elsewhere in much more depth, using the same framework laid out here.[7] The empirical generalizations accommodate this case very well, and that they do fit a modern, industrial, Eastern European, and fully democratic country should increase confidence in their robustness and validity.

Second, the survey covers only cases of peaceful secession. Contested secessions are excluded. This is not because those cases are irrelevant; on the contrary, useful lessons and analogies have been drawn from them.[8] Moreover, contested secessions are far more numerous than peaceful ones. Bookman, for example, examines 37 secessionist movements, most of which emerged after WWII (the exceptions being Northern Ireland, Ukraine, and the Kurds), and only 12 of which were peaceful: these include six in the U.S.S.R. (where the central state was collapsing), three in Europe (Catalonia, Lombardy and Scotland), Tibet (where Chinese repression is enough to prevent any mass action, peaceful or not), and Peurto Rico and Quebec. The other movements were violent, or civil war resulted.[9] But contested secessions fall into a different class than that of interest here. For many purposes, it may be more fruitful to examine cases of "success", and to look for patterns in the transitions, than to focus on instances of civil war in the hope of discovering salutary lessons. So how has peaceful secession occurred in the past? What features have characterized the process?

i. Secession follows protracted constitutional and political disputes

While the event of secession is always abrupt, cases of peaceful secession have capped long periods of disagreement between the constituent units of a federation or empire. In a sense, secession results from an impasse about an important matter of principle, even though this may be only one of many irritants, or one which becomes important as the symbolic focus of autonomist yearnings.

In 1867, Hungary and Austria were separated through the Ausgleich (Compromise), which was finally sealed by its acceptance by the Austrian Reichstat on December 21.[10] This agreement provided a durable arrangement for the co-existence of territories that had been united but riven by fundamental conflict for almost two decades. As part of the 1848 revolutions that swept Europe, Hungary had achieved first a separate ministry responsible to the national Diet, and then had declared formal independence in April 1849. This revolt was crushed by the Russians who returned the errant state to the Austrian Emperor. After a period of authoritarian rule in the 1850s, a brief flirtation with a decentralized structure was followed in 1861 with a centralized, bicameral system. This the Hungarians boycotted for some years in a struggle for greater autonomy. Their local Diets generally refused to raise taxes or military recruits for the Imperial authorities. In April 1865, Francis Déak and other Hungarian moderates published a program for reform that envisaged a largely autonomous country, and the Emperor encouraged discussions to be held with Hungarian leaders because the central authorities were weakened by the boycott and by rapidly rising debt.[11] In early 1866 a new Hungarian Diet was called, and it worked out a program for negotiations. But these became serious only towards the end of the year, after Austria was defeated by the Prussians at Sadowa, and the Treaty of Prague dissolved the Germanic Confederation, essentially removing Austria from the Germanic system and making an internal re-ordering highly advisable.[12]

Norway, a Danish possession, was united with Sweden under King Karl XIII in 1814. While each country maintained separate citizenships, ministries, civil services, and courts, and while there was no joint legislature (formally), there were important joint and common functions. The King appointed each of the ministries, he could veto legislation, and, most critically, he conducted war and foreign policy.

Despite the fact that Sweden's main economic links were with Germany while Norway's were with England, there also was substantial economic integration. A common coinage was introduced in 1875, and joint tariff law prevailed after 1825. The tariffs covered a few items only, but were a cause of continuing dispute as Sweden sought to increase protection towards the end of the century; failing agreement, the joint laws lapsed in 1897.[13] But there were no serious economic disputes between the countries.

Deeper political integration was resisted, mainly by Norway. An 1850s plan for a confederal legislature failed, and Norway also blocked moves towards closer cooperation in 1871, causing much bitterness.[14] As under the Austro-Hungarian Ausgleich, it was the common royal prerogative that ensured some internal policy harmonization, through the veto power and the authority to select ministries. More important in an era of very limited government, the Crown's control over war and foreign policy enabled the countries to operate as a unit on the international stage, and although such an arrangement was not envisaged in the Riksakt (the Act of Union), the King was working through a Joint Council for diplomacy and foreign affairs by the late 19th century.[15] In the case of Sweden and Norway, however, growing nationalism and liberal demands for a fully responsible government led to the secession.

The immediate issue of contention was the Norwegian demand for a separate consular service. This led the countries near to war in 1895. Further negotiations over the issue opened in 1902. The stakes escalated in a bitter election campaign in Norway, won by the Conservatives who then had one last chance to find a negotiated solution.[16] In February 1905, however, the Norwegians refused the Swedish proposals; in March a coalition government was formed in Norway; then a consular bill was passed in the knowledge that the King would veto it and precipitate a crisis.

The secession of Singapore from Malaysia on August 9, 1965 was remarkable for the speed with which it was accomplished. But the final, very brief negotiations put the seal on a disengagement motivated by acrimony on several fronts. Discord had been growing almost since Malaysia was formed in September 1963. (Although this federation was very young, and in part was a contrivance of British Imperial withdrawl, it should be noted that the sovereign Federation of Malaya had been formed in August 1957, building upon the four-state Federated Malay States (1895) and the Federation of Malaya Agreement (1948). More important, under colonial rule, Singapore and the Malay states had been governed as an economic unit since the 19th century. The common Malayan dollar, for instance, had been issued by a Currency Board since 1906.[17] Interrupted by World War II, there had also been close (British-led) defence co-operation between the colonies since 1951.)

In this case there were disputes about central-bank arrangements that were protracted and tense and were unresolved at the time of secession.[18] As well, Singapore, which had supported the federation in part to gain fuller access to the Malayan market, was disappointed by the slow progress towards the goal of a full common mar-

ket, which was enshrined in Annex J of the 1963 constitution.[19] Other causes of friction included the distribution of tax revenues in the federation, economic favoritism towards the Borneo territories (Sabah and Sarawak), and Singaporean underrepresentation in Parliament and the Cabinet (a consequence of the asymmetrical powers that Singapore possessed under the constitution).[20] All these were aggravated by an undeclared war with Indonesia—the Confrontation—which put pressure on expenditures and led to the imposition of emergency-power rule.[21]

The major incompatability between the units, however, concerned race and the deep ideology that would underpin the federal political system. The accession of Singapore (80 percent Chinese) to the Federation posed a threat not only to the special privileges of the Malays (who became a minority overall), but also to the communitarian system through which the country traditionally had been governed. This was a system of elite accommodation between racial groups, largely achieved within the Alliance between the United Malay National Organization and the Malayan Chinese Association (UMNO-MCA). The Indian community, about 10 percent of the population, was also incorporated into this system. But communitarianism was challenged by Lee Kuan Yew of Singapore, through his People's Action Party (PAP), which advanced an ideology of progressivism, individualism, and pluralism, under the slogan of a "Malaysian Malaysia."[22] While the longstanding conflict was expressed through partisan competition, it went to the cultural and systemic foundations of the federation. PAP swept the 1963 elections in Singapore, then contested the 1964 elections on the mainland, albeit with little success. Undeterred, Lee Kuan Yew continued in 1965 to press for non-communal equality, and spearheaded the Malaysian Solidarity Convention to fight the Alliance, targeting the sensitive states of Sabah and Sarawak.[23] In the summer of 1965 there were serious race riots in Singapore, but even before this manifest unrest, it seems, the Tunku Abdul Rahman, prime minister of Malaysia, had concluded that Singapore's secession would be desirable for Malaysian stability.[24]

ii. The secessor state declares its intent to withdraw

This event is abrupt. In the West Indies case, the Jamaican referendum of September 1961 was immediately followed by a declaration that it would quit the Federation of the West Indies. In the case of Singapore, the situation was reversed: the Malaysian leader consulted his inner cabinet about Singapore's exit in July 1965, and declared his decision to the government of

Singapore upon his return to Kuala Lumpur on August 5. The announcement that Singapore would leave the federation was made in Parliament on August 9.

In the Austria-Hungary case, the Hungarian Diet drew up and approved a program for independence in early 1866. But war with Prussia was declared the following day. In July 1866, after the Empire's stunning defeats, Deák, the leader of the Hungarian moderates, met the Emperor, and in a famous interview was asked what Hungary wanted now that the realm was so weakened: he replied, "No more after Sadowa than before."[25]

In the Norwegian case, the declaration took two forms. The first was a Storting vote in favour of the principle of dissolving the union, passed under the new coalition government in March 1905. Then the consular bill was passed in May, and it was duly vetoed. The Norwegian ministry resigned. The final act came on June 7, when the Storting passed a resolution authorizing the ministry to continue as the government and to exercise the authority granted to the King under the constitution: it also dissolved the union.[26] This resolution passed unanimously.

iii. The predecessor state accepts the principle of secession: negotiations follow

This is a truism, *ex post facto*, but it reflects the most profound decision on the part of the leadership of the predecessor state—to accept that secession will occur. In the cases examined here, this is a bitter and very difficult decision. But it makes the fundamental difference between peaceful secessions and those that are violent.[27] This immense concession then sets in train all that follows, and the first item, obviously, is negotiations.

In the case of the breakups of colonial federations, it was the imperial power that generally had to accept that secession would occur. In late 1962, for instance, Britain recognized the right of Nyasaland (later Malawi) to secede from the Central African Federation: this led directly to a similar demand by Northern Rhodesia, and to the Victoria Falls Conference in June, 1963. Similarly, the British government accepted both the Jamaican referendum result and the decision of Trinidad to seek its own independence.[28] In Malaysia-Singapore, the normal situation was reversed. It was Lee Kuan Yew who had to swallow the bitter pill presented by Malaysia, and to negotiate as best as possible around the terms of secession which were presented to him and his colleagues.[29] The acceptance in Austria-Hungary was through the Emperor, who had come to the conclusion that the weakened realm could only be salvaged by placating the

Magyars through recognizing the principle of Hungarian independence. After his meeting with Deák, negotiations were opened.

Acceptance was most difficult in Sweden, where the populace as well as the government and the King was deeply shocked by the Storting's vote to sever the union. On the same day, however, despite some ministers' advocacy of war, the cabinet decided to proceed peacefully. This decision was confrmed by an extraordinary meeting of all party leaders the following day. Norwegian opinion was solid for sovereignty, war would be ruinous, and the Great Powers would isolate Sweden if it tried forceably to maintain the union. Negotiation represented the only viable course of action. Even Conservative newspapers declared that, after the Storting vote, the union had become "devoid of value for Sweden and, therefore, the use of force was unthinkable."[30]

iv. Secession is a momentous, galvanizing event

Despite contemporary slogans such as the "velvet divorce" or the "rupture tranquille," even peaceful secessions are times of much disruption and uncertainty. They mark profound changes in the relations between peoples and between states, and this is fully recognized at the time. Secession opens new possibilities and closes off options, and it does so in a compressed time period where the actors and arguments and choices are known to have big long-term consequences. Even peaceful separations are marked by considerable ferment.

There are always changes at the elite level. In the Hungarian case, for example, new leadership emerged in the moderate party during the early transition (in the person of Count Andrássy), and in Austria the minister-president resigned in some confusion after the major elements of the Ausgleich had been agreed. Coalitions formed and reformed in both Norway and Sweden. As discussed below, reflecting the turmoil of the transition, the internal politics and policies of the defederating units change a great deal.

There is also considerable mass unrest and excitement. In Singapore, racial tension and conflict continued after secession. In Austria, the Czechs and other minorities saw new opportunities for autonomy during the uncertainty of 1866–7, a prospect that led to external appeals to Russia and internal agitation by Prussia.[31] And in Norway-Sweden, secession was marked by huge public demonstrations in both countries, much chauvinism and tension, and the mobilization of defensive forces even as the negotiations about disengagement were taking place.[32]

v. The government is broadened and strengthened on each side, and there is a premium on solidarity

In order to undertake fundamental constitutional change, the governments of both the predecessor and successor state are strengthened. As discussed below,

---

...it is the leaders in place who assume responsibility for negotiating secession.

---

attention is focused on the immediate need to reach a settlement, rather than on other constitutional matters. Hence, it is the leaders in place who assume responsibility for negotiating secession. And in nonbipartite cases, it is the central government which negotiates. In the extreme case, Malaysia-Singapore, the state governments—including Sabah and Sarawak, which had entered the expanded federation with Singapore—were not even informed about the secession arrangements.[33]

But the national governments seek to augment their authority by broadening their bases of support. This occurs both in the period leading to the declaration of intent to secede and in the transitional period of negotiations. In Hungary, for example, the platform of demands that issued from the Diet in 1866 was forged by a special committee of 67 members, representing all factions, and by a strong executive committee of 15 members. In Singapore and Malaysia, PAP and the Alliance respectively had overwhelming majorities, so broadening was not necessary. But in Norway and Sweden, where the transition was particularly tense, this process was very evident.

In Norway there was a tremendous premium on solidarity in the spring of 1905 as the crisis developed. This is not to say that partisan considerations were entirely forgotten, for the radical Venstre party pressed a hard line on the consular issue. That matter decided, however, Norwegian politicians submerged their differences. A Special Committee of the Storting was established, and it took much initiative. Then a new coalition government was formed with broad representation, and until the June 7th vote and during the subsequent negotiations, this ministry relied heavily on the Committee.[34] In Sweden, after the vote, an Extraordinary Committee of the Riksdag was formed. It helped frame the national response to the Norwegian declaration, which consisted of a set of conditions to govern the secession. Then, in July, a coalition cabinet was assembled. This incorporated the opposition Liberals, and so it had a much broader composition than any preceding Swedish government.[35]

The crisis of secession, then, solidifies each side politically. And the sides polarize. These effects are undoubtedly less thoroughgoing than what occurs in contested secessions, when war entirely divides the states and forces internal unity. Nevertheless, those responsible for negotiations seek truly national support by submerging partisan and ideological differences for the duration of the crisis. And this effect is not confined to political elites. The plebiscite about secession forced upon the Norwegians by the Swedes as a pre-condition of negotiations carried by 367,149 to 184.[36] Such a margin could never have been achieved six months earlier. The process of secession, or the crisis of the transition, itself generates internal unity.[37]

vi. The negotiations involve few participants

Some cases examined here involve quasi-democracies characterized by a limited franchise and deference to regal or charismatic leaders. Nevertheless it still is striking that the negotiating teams have been very small in numbers, and this is the more remarkable when this feature is combined with the broadening of support discussed above. The paradox vanishes when one realizes that the teams incorporate the strongest leaders, of all factions, and that the same solidarity that arises from the national dimension of the crisis permits the delegation of substantial power to a very few representatives.

In Singapore-Malaysia, only the Prime Ministers were involved, aided by a few key members of their cabinets.[38] In East Africa, just as the Nairobi Declaration had been the product of the anti-colonial leaders from each state, so were the failed negotiations about federation conducted by them. In Austria-Hungary, the predecessor state was effectively represented by the minister of foreign affairs, Baron Ferdinand Beust, who was appointed in November 1866 and who alone conducted the serious negotiations which began in January 1867. In the case of Norway and Sweden, one immediate and critical issue to settle was whether Norway should invite a member of the Swedish Royal House (the Bernadottes) to take the throne: secret negotiations undertaken by one man had produced a solution—Prince Carl of Denmark—within a month (though confirmation was delayed until after the main negotiations were through, because the election of a King had implications for international recognition).[39] The main negotiations about secession and its terms, conducted at the Karlstad

Conference, involved Norwegian and Swedish delegations of only four members each.

vii. The settlement is made quickly

Negotiations about secession are not protracted. When a unit breaks up peacefully, the two sides disengage quickly, and the negotiations concern a relatively short list of items which are settled in principle. Singapore-Malaysia is the extreme case. The Tunku, Abdul Rahman, returned from London to Kuala Lumpur on August 5, 1965, and summoned Lee Kuan Yew in order to present him with the separation agreement, which was signed on August 7 and passed through parliament on August 9, effective immediately.[40] The Victoria Falls Conference that dissolved the federation of Rhodesia and Nyasaland took place in less than a week in June-July, 1963: the federation was terminated formally in December of that same year. The Jamaican referendum in favour of secession took place in mid-September 1961, and the Federation of the West Indies was wound up in May 1962. The Karlstad Conference opened on August 31, 1905 and negotiations were completed on September 22: then the Storting approved the arrangements on September 30, the Riksdag leggislated the abrogation of the Act of Union on October 16, the King abdicated, and the Storting unanimously elected Prince Carl of Denmark as Haakon VII on November 18.

The content of negotiations, of course, is primarily about the terms and conditions of disengagement. Even when it is not limited to this, but the framework for future relationships is also being established, events still move quickly. In the Austria-Hungary case, an extremely complex set of institutions was established under the Ausgleich. These were patterned on the Hungarian proposal of 1866. But serious negotiations began only in January 1867. By mid-February the Hungarian constitution was restored along with a responsible ministry, and Hungary approved the Ausgleich on May 29. In Austria, approval was delayed by an election and by the insistence that all financial arrangements be finalized; nevertheless, the Reichstat enacted the Compromise on December 21, 1867. The institutional structure of what Lloyd George called this "ramshackle realm" was settled within a year's time.

viii. The settlement involves a relatively short list of items

In cases of peaceful secession, negotiations centre on a few significant matters. This is not a sufficient condition for a quick resolution of the crisis, but it does appear to be a general feature of these secessions. The two parties settle the most pressing issues in framework agreements, leaving other matters and details to be worked out later.

The Singapore-Malaysia separation agreement, for instance, has only eight articles. It recognizes Singapore's sovereignty, commits the parties to a treaty on external defence and mutual assistance (spelling out four principles which mainly confer military rights upon Malaysia), establishes the principle of economic cooperation, repeals the economic-union provisions of the 1963 constitution, and releases Malaysia from its guarantees of Singapore's debt. In the case of Norway and Sweden, the Swedes imposed the prenegotiation condition of a plebiscite to sound Norwegian opinion. The actual negotiations concerned only:

1. Sweden's demand that Norwegian forts on the frontier be razed,
2. the establishment of a 10-kilometer neutral zone along the border,
3. guarantees for the unimpeded migration of the Lapps,
4. equal rights for transit and access to transfrontier watercourses (for railroads and water for log drives), and
5. an arbitration treaty to govern future disputes.[41]

Finally, in the Austria-Hungary case, the negotiations concerned not only the principles of disengagement—the restoration of the Hungarian constitution, a fully responsible ministry, and the coronation of Franz Joseph as King of Hungary—but also the mechanisms for future coordination. These were complex, involving a small number of common ministers, decennial agreements about each state's contributions to the common expenses and about the common tariff schedule, and a confederal system of "delegations" from each state to approve annual budgets. But much of this was left to be fleshed out in subsequent discussions and later practice. Hungary approved the arrangement even before the first fixing of tax contributions had been made.

ix. Foreign powers play an important role

This generalization holds in every case. The dissolution of the new Commonwealth federations was crucially dependent on Great Britain's approval of terms, and also on the probabilities of international recognition. In Malaysia-Singapore, the Confrontation with Indonesia made precipitous action more possible (and more necessary, from Malaysia's standpoint). But Indonesia also offered potential new markets to Singapore, which quickly assumed a friendlier stance towards it; in fact, after Singapore withdrew from the Combined Defence

Council in March 1966, Indonesia aimed to establish normal relations with the new state.[42] Despite Singapore's moves towards both non-alignment and a new relationship with the United States, its partners in the existing Anglo-Malayan Defence Agreement insisted that it continue to cooperate in defence with Malaysia.[43]

In Austria-Hungary, the threatened international position of the Empire was an underlying cause of disengagement. In the longer term it was also relations with Germany (through the 1879 Dual Alliance against Russia) that helped maintain the confederal system of the Ausgleich. This system mitigated the fear of absorption into Germany of the inhabitants of Cisleithania (especially the minorities) while diminishing the threat posed to the Magyars by the Southern Slavs.[44] More generally, the secession was peaceful and the new arrangement worked because outside powers—Germany, Turkey and Russia—each could pose as an ally of some internal minorities, and therefore presented threats to others.[45]

Norway-Sweden provides more examples. As the consular crisis mounted, the Norwegians immediately understood how important would be international

---

Peaceful secessions, without exception, are achieved through established legal processes.

---

recognition of their new state. This underlay both a vigorous public-relations campaign among the Great Powers and the decision to continue a monarchical system (with a Bernadotte as King, if necessary).[46] As well, fear of outside intervention in Scandinavia certainly helped lead both sides towards compromise when, even during the Karlstad Conference, each country contemplated war.[47]

x. The secession is accomplished constitutionally

Peaceful secessions, without exception, are achieved through established legal processes. Even such fundamental constitutional change occurs constitutionally. There is no legal rupture of the type associated with unilateral declarations of independence. Basically, this is a straightforward consequence of the predecessor state accepting the principle that secession will occur.

In Austria-Hungary, the restoration of the Hungarian constitution was effected through a royal let-

ter, and the Ausgleich was properly passed by the Diet. Similarly, the Austrian Diet amended the 1861 constitution to bring it into conformity with the new arrangement, and these changes to fundamental laws were duly sanctioned by the Emperor. In the Norway-Sweden case, established rules prevailed, as the Act of Union was abrogated by the two legislatures, the King abdicated from his Norwegian throne, and the new King was properly elected and crowned. In Singapore-Malaysia, although it took the Malaysian Parliament only three hours to do so, the constitutional amendment that eliminated Singapore from the federation was passed by the required two-thirds majority.[48] And the generalization holds for the new colonial federations that broke up: each failure was "marked by a constitutional act, like federation itself."[49] Even in the case of Iceland's separation from Denmark, in 1944 in the midst of war, when the Nazis controlled Denmark and the British were in Iceland, the matter was accomplished constitutionally. Iceland invoked a clause in the Act of Union that allowed for unilateral termination of the Act, and the decision was confirmed, as required, by a national plebiscite.[50]

xi. There are no other substantial constitutional changes in either the seceding or the predecessor state

This is a rather surprising fact, for one might anticipate that such a fundamental change as secession might either force or allow for other constitutional alterations. But this is not the case. The reasons appear to be twofold. The predecessor state and the seceding state especially seek stability, the first for damage-control and the other for international credibility. Second, for the significant policy changes which each state generally does undertake, constitutional amendment is not a prerequisite.

In any event there are some limited exceptions. In some short-lived colonial federations, the exit of one state—Jamaica and Nyasaland—led to the collapse of the rest of the federation. In Austria-Hungary, much of the drive for the new arrangements came from ethnic tension, not only between the two major ethnic groups but also between each and internal minorities. Hungary's Magyar majority was well served by their traditional constitution, and no post-secession change occurred there. In Austria, however, secession was accompanied by a vigorous debate about the degree of centralization that should obtain within the realm, with the non-Germanic minorities pressing the case for local autonomy. In the end, constitutional changes were enacted to confer the residual power upon the regional

Diets.[51] But provincial legislation still required the Emperor's approval, and the Crown also appointed the provincial governors and the presidents of the regional Diets; moreover, in 1873, direct elections to the central parliament replaced indirect election by those Diets, so further weakening their power.

There were policy changes, however. In Hungary, the separation allowed the continuance and heightening of social conservatism, including a firm policy of Magyar supremacy that was pursued in the linguistic and educational fields. In Austria, in contrast, the German-speaking Liberal Party introduced important social and economic reforms.[52]

In Malaysia, there were post-secession constitutional changes associated with ethnic issues, which had been made acute by Singapore's both joining and leaving the federation. In 1967, Malay became the sole official language, except in Sabah and Sarawak. But this had been due to happen in any event under the 1957 constitution.[53] Further, in response to sectarian violence, discussion of racial issues was outlawed between 1969 and 1971, under constitutionally invoked emergency powers. For its part, Singapore established a Constitutional Commission in March 1966. But there was no change until 1969, and this was minor: the Presidential Council was established to advise on legslation and to scrutinize it.

Again, while there was no constitutional change directly associated with secession, these was considerable policy change. Malaysia moved to diminish internal economic barriers. Singapore did much more. Under the slogan "Survival," the government moved towards *dirigisme*, towards the construction of a "tightly organized society," with National Service, new labour legislation attractive to investors, and a general stance favouring order and economic growth.[54]

In the Norway-Sweden case, policy changed in Sweden as the Liberals came to power in late 1905. But there was no constitutional change after secession. Norway provides a clear example of how secessionist states avoid unnecessary constitutional change, as its leaders decided to retain the monarchy so as not to offend the European powers (a choice ratified by plebiscite), and even extended an invitation to a son of the very monarch whose abdication would be occasioned by secession. There was no change in the form of government, in order to avoid a constitutional crisis simultaneous with secession, to placate Swedish rage, and to attain quicker international recognition. Subsequently Norway moved on several policy fronts to become one of the most liberal states in the world, but

apart from an extension of the franchise, this did not involve internal constitutional restructuring.

xii. Policies in the two states soon begin to diverge

In Austria-Hungary, secession produced two sovereign states. But, in contrast to the other cases, it was accompanied by new institutions for coordination. The keystone of the system was the monarch, Franz Joseph, who was Emperor of Austria and King of Hungary, and who chose separate ministries in each country, as well as special, common ministers for foreign relations, the military, and the joint finances to support these functions. This structure was successful in maintaining a common defence, monetary, and tariff structure until the Dual Monarchy collapsed during World War I. But there was tremendous friction between the two states, and this grew over time. The tariff negotiations broke down in 1897, only Austrian tolerance permitted agreement on the level of financial contributions, and the Hungarians sought more influence over the National Bank and the army. Moreover, domestic policies on minorities and religious matters began to diverge shortly after the Ausgleich was enacted; indeed, secession had come about in part to allow autonomy in these matters.

In Norway-Sweden, domestic policies did diverge along broad ideological lines. But there was also some coordination, within the Scandinavian framework. This was accomplished through informal mechanisms, like the Scandinavian Inter-Parliamentary Union, established in 1907, the Nordic Societies, established in 1919, and many voluntary associations.[55] In this, the common foreign policy of neutrality and isolation helped, as did the stabilizing presence of Denmark (and the later participation of Iceland and Finland). After the separation, the two (and three) countries sometimes passed parallel legislation, such as the Marriage Law of 1921–25, but this continued a tradition dating back to the monetary convention of the 1870s and the Bank Drafts Act of 1880.[56] Lindgren argues that the union of Norway and Sweden "itself formed a barrier", and that its dissolution "opened the way for an integration impossible under pre-1905 conditions."[57] But it would not do to overstate this case. The two countries never signed a mutual-defence treaty, Norway enjoyed a great-power guarantee of its borders, and the Kings did not meet until 1914. The development of genuinely integrative institutions awaited the formation of the Nordic Council in 1951.[58]

The countries of the colonial federations did not tend to harmonize policies upon dissolution. In Central Africa, economic integration had been deepened considerably in the federation era, and existing trade patterns did continue, even with the renegade state of Southern Rhodesia.[59] But this was a consequence of the abject dependence of Zambia on Rhodesian coal and hydro-electric power for its copper industry. Apart from this, integration eroded, notably when Malawi and Zambia issued their own currencies in 1963. In East Africa, similarly, there was an even longer history of cooperation among Tanganyika, Zanzibar, Kenya and Uganda, with a postal union dating from 1911, a customs union from 1917, and a common currency from 1920. These soon deteriorated after the projected federation failed. By 1965 Tanzania was imposing quotas on Kenyan goods, and the currency union was fractured in 1966. Generally, economic policies came to diverge sharply, and there were also military tensions between the former partners.[60]

Singapore-Malaysia provides a striking instance of policy divergence. Article VI of the separation agreement provided for cooperation in economic affairs and the establishment of joint committees and councils to promote it. But within a week of the secession, Singapore restricted imports of 187 manufactured goods from Malaysia. Malaysia retaliated. By October the govern-

> *There has never been a case of reunification after secession.*

ments had agreed to revert to the *status quo ante*; but when Malaysia announced it would work towards an internal common market within the federation, Singapore re-imposed tariffs. It then established a work-permit system for non-citizens, and Malaysia set up immigration controls.[61] Despite some later relaxation of these measures, Singapore's foreign-labour policy was dictated exclusively by its domestic interests.[62] In 1967, the currency union was ended. Singapore withdrew from the Combined Defence Council, and there was little cooperation in this area. There were no Prime Ministerial visits until the early 1970s.[63] Singapore was even thrown out of the Associated Chinese Chambers of Commerce in Malaysia.[64] As a consequence of nation-building policies on both sides, economic integration weakened. In 1964, Malay-peninsula imports from or via Singapore were 37 percent of the total, and exports were 28 percent: this dropped to 9 percent and 20 percent by 1975.[65] The federation itself was short-lived. But its breakup led to the erosion of an economy which had been integrating for decades.

xiii. Secession is irrevocable

There has never been a case of reunification after secession. Fundamentally this is because of two factors. First, the whole project of the seceding state is to acquire more autonomy. The exercise of these greater powers would be compromised by integrative arrangements. More important, though, are the effects of the transition itself. The process of secession marks both elites and masses. It affects them profoundly. Not only is there the psychic break, with the recognition that the community is fractured, but there also is the internal solidarity forged in the process of disengagement. Unity on each side develops through the crisis, and is built by a collective concentration on the Other. Hence each community is solidified through the transition process, and even where there is not great animosity between the two citizenries, the crisis forges separate identities and interests that cannot subsequently be subsumed in a new union. As Watts put it, delicately, "[w]henever secession has occurred, it has inevitably been accompanied by sharp political controversies which are not easily forgotten....the resentments aroused by the circumstances occurring at the time of separation have tended to persist and to discourage the subsequent creation of a looser form of association between the territories concerned."[66]

II. CONCLUSION
◆ ◆ ◆

There is little to add to this bare account of how peaceful secessions take place. Perhaps it is appropriate to emphasize, though, that these generalizations are quite robust. They hold true, more or less and mostly more, in circumstances separated by geography, culture, time, and degrees of democracy. It is also worth emphasizing that the process of the transition helps determine the long-term outcomes of the separation. In uncertain and unprecedented times, political leaders have considerable scope for taking decisions that have lasting consequences: the largest decision taken in the cases reviewed here was that the secession would not be contested. Moreover, choices are made about institutional arrangements, both domestically and between the two states, and institutions have enduring effects. Finally, it is tempting to speculate about how the standard pattern of peaceful secession might be fitted to the case of Canada and Quebec. But this is a larger task than can be accomplished here.[67] It is enough to have isolated the pattern.

Notes

1. Gertrude E. Schroeder, "On the Economic Viability of New Nation-States," *Journal of International Affairs* 45 (1992), 549–74; Amatai Etzioni, "The Evils of Self-Determination," *Foreign Policy*, 89 (1992–1993), 21–35.

2. Allen Buchanan, *Secession: The Morality of Political Divorce from Fort Sumter to Lithuania and Quebec* (Boulder: Westview Press, 1991); and Alexis Heraclides, "Secession, Self-Determination and Nonintervention: In Quest of a Normative Synthesis," *Journal of International Affairs*, 45 (Winter 1992), 399–420.

3. Donald Wittman, "Nations and States: Mergers and Acquisitions; Dissolutions and Divorce," *American Economic Review*, 81 (1991), 126–29; Pierre Simard, "Compétition Électoral et Partage des Pouvoirs dans un état fédéral," *Canadian Public Policy* (1991), 409–16; and Robert A. Young, "The Political Economy of Secession: the Case of Quebec," *Constitutional Political Economy*, 5 (1994), 221–45.

4. James M. Buchanan and Roger L. Faith, "Secession and the Limits of Taxation: Toward a Theory of Internal Exit," *American Economic Review*, 77 (1987), 1023–31; Stéphane Dion, "Why is Secession Rare? Lessons from Quebec," MS, December 1993; and Michael Hechter, "The Dynamics of Secession," *Acta Sociologica* 35 (1992), 267–83.

5. This article does not deal with a third class—the few instances like Western Australia in 1933–35 and Nova Scotia in 1868 where secessionist movements captured the support of popular majorities or elected representatives, but were simply ignored or "waited out."

6. These cases are discussed in Thomas M. Franck, ed., *Why Federations Fail* (New York: New York University Press, 1968): the "neo-classical" appellation is from his concluding essay, "Why Federations Fail," 167–99, 195. The other cases include the breakup of the West Indian Federation, the nonformation of the East African Federation, and the disintegration of Rhodesia and Nyasaland (the Central African Federation). As well, the secession of Iceland from Denmark (1944) is of some interest. See also Ronald L. Watts, *New Federations: Experiments in the Commonwealth* (Oxford: Clarendon Press, 1966); and Ursula K. Hicks, *Federalism: Failure and Success* (London: The Macmillan Press, 1978).

7. Robert A. Young, *The Breakup of Czechoslovakia* (Kingston: Queen's University, Institute of Intergovernmental Relations, 1994).

8. Ronald L. Watts, "The Survival or Disintegration of Federations," in R.M. Burns, ed., *One Country or Two?* (Montreal: McGill-Queen's University Press), 41–72. See also, for example, E. Wayne Nafziger and William L. Richter, "Biafra and Bangladesh: The Political Economy of Secessionist Conflict," *Journal of Peace Research* 13 (1976), 91–109; and Milicia Zarkovic Bookman, *The Economics of Secession*, (New York: St. Martin's Press, 1993).

9. Bookman, *The Economics of Secession*, Table 1.2, 31–34.

10. Leslie C. Tihany, "The Austro-Hungarian Compromise, 1867–1918: A Half Century of Diagnosis; Fifty Years of Post-Mortem," *Central European History* 2 (1969), 114–38: 115–16.

11. Arthur J. May, *The Hapsburg Monarchy 1867–1914* (Cambridge: Harvard University Press, 1951), 495–96 and note 22; and Thomas F. Huertas, *Economic Growth and Economic Policy in a Multinational Setting: The Hapsburg Monarchy, 1841–1865*, (New York: Arno Press, 1977), Table 8, 37–38.

12. May, *Hapsburg Monarchy*, 34–36.

13. Franz Wendt, *Cooperation in the Nordic Countries: Achievements and Obstacles* (Stockholm: Almqvist & Wiksell, 1981), 21.

14. Raymond E. Lindgren, *Norway-Sweden: Union, Disunion, and Scandinavian Integration* (Princeton: Princeton University Press, 1959), 49–51.

15. Ibid., 62–65.

16. Ibid., 95–111.

17. P.J. Drake, "Singapore and Malaysia: The Monetary Consequences," *Australian Oulook* 20 (1966), 28–35, esp. 28.

18. Chan Heng Chee, *Singapore: The Politics of Survival 1965–1967* (Singapore: Oxford University Press, 1971), 36–37.

19. Nancy McHenry Fletcher, *The Separation of Singapore from Malaysia*, Data Paper No. 73 (Ithaca: Cornell University Southeast Asia Program, 1969), 12–16.

20. See R.L. Watts, *New Federations: Experiments in the Commonwealth* (Oxford: Clarendon Press, 1966), 177, 257.

21. Ibid., 16–23; Nena Vreeland et al., *Area Handbook for Malaysia* (Washington: American University Foreign Area Studies, 1970), 74; James P. Ongkili, *Nation-building in Malaysia 1946–1974* (Singapore: Oxford University Press, 1985), 181; H.P. Lee, "Emergency Powers in Malaysia," in F.A. Trindale and H.P. Lee, eds., *The Constitution of Malaysia: Further Perspectives and Developments* (Petaling Jaya: Oxford University Press, 1986), 134–56.

22. Ongkili, *Nation-building in Malaysia*, 184–85.

23. Fletcher, *The Separation of Singapore*, 50–51, 56–66.

24. Lyon considers the possibility that the secession was a "contrived withdrawl" by Lee Kuan Yew; on balance, though, he agrees with most analysts that the event was an eviction: see Peter Lyon, "Separatism and Secession in the Malaysian Realm 1948–65," in W.H. Morris-Jones, ed., Institute of Commonwealth Studies, University of London, *Collected Seminar Papers on the Politics of Separatism*, No. 19, 1976, 69–78, esp. 74–76.

25. May, *The Hapsburg Monarchy*, 34.

26. Lindgren, *Norway-Sweden*, 130–31.

27. See John R. Wood, "Secession: A Comparative Analytical Framework," Journal 14 (1981), 107–34, esp. 125–27.

28. See Watts, *New Federations*, 311–12.

29. Ongkili, *Nation-building in Malaysia*, 186.

30. Lindgren, *Norway-Sweden*, 133–34.

31. May, *The Hapsburg Monarchy*, 50–51; and Victor-L. Tapié, *The Rise and Fall of the Hapsburg Monarchy*, (New York: Praeger, 1971), 304–05.

32. Lindgren, *Norway-Sweden*, 189–90.

33. Ongkili, *Nation-building in Malaysia*, 187–90.

34. Lindgren, *Norway-Sweden*, 128. The Committee refused to abide by the views of the ministry just before the decisive vote, but there was no min-

isterial crisis: "the times demanded that there be no constitutional or par-liamentary conflicts."

35. Ibid., 149–51.

36. Lindgren, *Norway-Sweden*, 167; and Nils Andrén, *Government and Politics in the Nordic Countries* (Stockholm: Almquist & Wicksell, 1964), 121.

37. In the Czech-Slovak case, the last three generalizations do not entirely hold. There was no clear, unequivocal declaration by either side of its intent to secede, nor was there a corresponding acceptance by the other of the principle that separation would occur; moreover, in neither state were broad coalitions formed to confront the national crisis. To some extent this was caused by the confusion and uncertainty that marked the re-emergence of democracy in Czechoslovakia, and by the massive challenges facing its governments. More fundamentally, though, there simply was not enough public support for secession in either republic. The whole separation took place through a gradual process of polarization, one that was spearheaded by partisan leaders who found it politically profitable to engage in mutual antagonism. In the June, 1992 elections, pluralities were won by these leaders—Vaclav Klaus of the Czech Republic and Vladimir Mečiar of Slovakia—and they could not agree to form an operational government at the federal level. Each then formed a tight coalition at the republic level, just sufficient to dominate the legislature, and polarization proceeded as they entered negotiations about ending the common state. As these took place, punctuated by provocative acts, threats, and feints towards sovereignty, public opinion shifted to the extent that pluralities in each republic favoured separation, and large majorities thought it inevitable. No referendum was ever held. Until the negotiations were well underway, a referendum would not have carried. But once they began, pressures to maintain national solidarity were evident. See Young, *Breakup of Czechoslovakia*, 11–18, 24–40. All the rest of the generalizations hold in this case.

38. Vreeland et al., *Area Handbook for Malaysia*, 75; Fletcher, *The Separation of Singapore*, 3.

39. Lindgren, *Norway-Sweden*, 155–66.

40. Gordon P. Means, *Malaysian Politics* (London: University of London Press, 1970), 294–95. The agreement is in Chan, *Singapore*, 58–59.

41. Lindgren, *Norway-Sweden*, 145–51.

42. Boyce, "Singapore as a Sovereign State," 24–25.

43. Vreeland et al., *Area Handbook for Malaysia*, 358–59; Chan, *Singapore*, 41–47; David Jenkins, "New Life in an Old Pact," *Far Eastern Economic Review*, November 7–13, 1980, 26–28.

44. John W. Mason, *The Dissolution of the Austro-Hungarian Empire, 1867–1918* (London: Longman, 1985).

45. Hence Deak's remark that "for us Austria's existence is just as necessary as our existence is for Austria" (Tihany, "The Austro-Hungarian Compromise," 118).

46. Lindgren, *Norway-Sweden*, 112–14, 127–31.

47. Ibid., 182–86.

48. In fact, it was passed unanimously, the PAP members having absented themselves by prior arrangement.

49. Franck, "Why Federations Fail," 170.

50. Andrén, *Government and Politics in the Nordic Countries*, 97–98.

51. May, *The Hapsburg Monarchy*, 37–38.

52. Mason, *Dissolution of the Austro-Hungarian Empire*, 16–18; and May, *The Hapsburg Monarchy*, 46–69.

53. Ongkili, *Nation-building in Malaysia*, 194–95; Vreeland et al., *Area Handbook for Malaysia*, 94; and Watts, *New Federations*, 234.

54. Chan, *Singapore*, 48–51, 22–5; and Stanley S. Bedlington, *Malaysia and Singapore: The Building of New States* (Ithaca, N.Y.: Cornell University Press, 1978), 210–43.

55. Lindgren, *Norway-Sweden*, 235, 245–46.

56. Gunnar Leistikow, "Co-operation between the Scandinavian Countries," in Henning Friis, ed., *Scandinavia—Between East and West* (Ithaca, N.Y.: Cornell University Press, 1950), 307–24: 311–18.

57. Lindgren, *Norway-Sweden*, 7.

58. Wendt, *Cooperation in the Nordic Countries*; and Erik Solen, *The Nordic Council and Scandinavian Integration* (New York: Praeger, 1977), esp. ch. 3.

59. Herbert J. Spiro, "The Federation of Rhodesia and Nyasaland," in Franck, ed., *Why Federations Fail*, 37–89, esp. 80.

60. Franck, "East African Federation," in Franck, ed., *Why Federations Fail*, 3–36, esp. 6–11, 17–8.

61. Chan, *Singapore*, 29–32.

62. Eng Fong Pang and Linda Lim, "Foreign Labour and Economic Development in Singapore," *International Migration Review* 16 (1982), 548–76.

63. Bedlington, *Malaysia and Singapore*, 247–48.

64. Chan, *Singapore*, 39.

65. Ibid., 33 note 48; and Vreeland et al., *Area Handbook for Malaysia*, 338.

66. Watts, "Survival or Disintegration," 69.

67. See Robert A. Young, *The Secession of Quebec and the Future of Canada*, forthcoming.

Terms & Concepts

asymmetrical powers	elite accommodation	quasi-democracies
autonomy	empirical generalizations	royal prerogative
bicameral systems	legality	secession
charismatic leaders	legitimacy	Storting
communitarianism	limited franchise	strategic games
Confederation	path dependent outcomes	unilateral declaration
deference	polarization	velvet divorce
diet	polities	
dirigisme	predecessor state	

Questions

1. Which of Young's generalizations seem particularly important for Canada? Is incremental break-up more likely than a dramatic rupture?

2. Are there any surprises to be found in his list of generalizations and general patterns? Explain why.

3. Are Young's cases too few, and too dissimilar, or are his generalizations "quite robust"?

4. What particular features of Canada's political system might make negotiations regarding secession extremely difficult? Who would negotiate for Canada? Who would negotiate for Aboriginal peoples?

5. Is splitting up a modern, developed, welfare state a far more difficult process than the examples provided by Young indicate, or do his generalizations reveal, even now, the essence of the problem?

Unit Five

Discussion Questions

1. Do these articles enable us to generalize about political change or is each case unique and of very limited applicability?

2. Which of the major ideas discussed elsewhere in this reader seem of particular relevance when discussing the problem of "regime change"?

3. How is the complex relationship between democracy and capitalism linked to the current debate about regime change?

4. In what ways do these selections reveal the crucial importance of political leadership and need for an honest, efficient, meritocratic state bureaucracy?

Annotated
Bibliography

Ash, Timothy Garton. *In Europe's Name: Germany and the Divided Continent*. New York: Random House, 1993. Even when a former communist state is fully and voluntarily absorbed by the strongest economy in Europe, adjustment to the changes is problematic.

Chaliand, Gerard and Jean-Pierre Rageau. *The Penguin Atlas of Diasporas*. New York: Viking Press, 1995. If one wants to know who moved where, and when, this is a fascinating study.

Cohen, Lenard J. *Broken Bonds: Yugoslavia's Disintegration and Balkan Politics in Transition*, 2nd ed. Boulder, CO: Westview Press, forthcoming 1995. Provides essential, detailed information on the crisis leading up to the war—and what went wrong.

Cook, Curtis, ed. *Constitutional Predicament: Canada After the Referendum of 1992*. Montreal: McGill-Queen's University Press, 1994. A collection of very thoughtful essays by prominent Canadian political scientists.

Glenny, Misha. "Yugoslavia: The Great Fall." *New York Review of Books* March 23, 1995. An expert's review and commentary on recent books about the Yugoslavian nightmare.

Goldman, F.M. *Russia, The Eurasian Republics and Central/Eastern Europe*. Guilford, Conn: Dushkin, 1994. An annual edition of news and analysis from the region.

Heilbroner, Robert. *Twenty-First Century Capitalism*. Don Mills, Ont.: Anansi Press, 1992. The futurist-economist considers capitalism after the year 2000.

Huntington, Samuel P. *The Third Wave: Democratization in the Late Twentieth Century*. Norman: University of Oklahoma Press, 1991. An account of the processes and explanations for democratization around the world.

Inglehart, Ronald. "The Renaissance of Political Culture." *American Political Science Review* 82:4 (December 1988), 1203–29. The author of several important studies of "new social values" examines the changing academic debate regarding the role of "political culture."

Lemco, Jonathan. *Turmoil in the Peaceable Kingdom*. Toronto: University of Toronto Press, 1994. Lemco deals with the implications of Quebec sovereignty for Canada and the United States.

Savoie, Donald. *The Politics of Public Spending in Canada*. University of Toronto Press, 1990. Savoie shows how extremely difficult it is to bring about major bureaucratic change.

Sesser, Stan. *The Lands of Charm and Cruelty*. New York: Alfred A. Knopf, 1993. A readable discussion of developments in East Asia, especially the New Authoritarians. Chapter one deals at some length with Singapore, and how change has been dealt with.

Smith, Hedrick. *The Russians*. New York: Ballantine, 1984. An acclaimed perspective on the Soviet Union by a western correspondent who lived in Moscow for more than 20 years. After reading it, the implosion of the USSR is no longer such a surprise.

———. *The New Russians*. New York: Avon, 1991. A post-Gorbachev update of *The Russians* (1976, 1984).

Weaver, Mary Anne. "Report from Cyprus." *The New Yorker*, August 6, 1990. Shows how even seemingly totally interdependent island communities cannot co-exist peacefully.

Young, Robert A. *The Secession of Quebec and the Future of Canada*. Montreal: McGill-Queen's University Press, 1995. The author applies some of the observations gained from his comparative work on secessions ("Breakup") to the possibility of Quebec secession.

———. *The Breakup of Czechoslovakia*. Kingston: Institute of Intergovernmental Relations, 1994. Further evidence of the conditions necessary for a peaceful breakup.

Unit Six

The Nature of Politics

...

A Final Footnote to Rally Those Who Grudge the Price

Bernard Crick

Editors' Note

Bernard Crick is one of the United Kingdom's best known political theorists. He is the author of an acclaimed biography of George Orwell[1] and a prolific essayist in the Orwellian tradition. Probably his best known work is a book entitled *In Defence of Politics,* written in 1962, "largely to share with a German friend grounds for hoping that her people could exorcise the past and establish a political or republican tradition of active citizenship."

Crick defends "mere politics" against both its obvious enemies (such as those who wish to stamp out politics by coercion or some enforced orthodoxy, or by a belief in technocratic rule) and against more subtle "enemies," namely those who claim to be its friends. Such friends, be they liberals, socialists, conservatives, or academics, may well participate in the political process, but they harbour deep doubts and corrosive suspicions about whether or not we really do need open, divisive, conflict and genuine power sharing.

Over the years, Crick has added what he calls "Footnotes" to each new edition. These are, in fact, not footnotes but essays intended to bring the reader up to date or to make a particularly relevant point in further defence of politics. The Footnote reproduced here is his latest one, added to the fourth edition in 1992. He now wants to consider how best to view and defend politics in the light of the enormous changes that have taken place since the mid-1980s. As he wrote this most recent addition, the Berlin Wall fell, Communism was in full flight, and he had to consider anew what advice to give to his German friend about how we should live our political lives as *citizens*, not as mere consumers.

He notes that democracy itself, if defined solely as majority rule, is a problem. So too is intransigence and the cry of "no surrender" that comes from cultural communities under threat. Even asking the question as to "who is right" is, he says, to start from the wrong place. Perhaps, above all, there is the complexity of things, which are made so much more difficult to resolve when what Crick considers to be "normal" politics has broken down—or has never been allowed to exist.

"A Final Footnote to Rally Those Who Grudge the Price" is a fitting piece with which to end this volume of essays which explores our new political world and our old political concepts. Crick writes of the attitudes and values—and the courage—we need if we are to maintain a viable, healthy polity. What Crick is saying, after a lifetime of political study and involvement, has applicability in constitutional democracies old and new, and may have special meaning for Canadians as we struggle to come to terms with our political future, with our identities, and with our tendency to ask "who is in the right?"—even when there isn't an answer.

---

1. Bernard Crick, *George Orwell: A Life* (London: Secker and Warburg, 1980).

There was an old man who supposed
That the street door was partially closed,
    But some very large rats
    ate his coat and his hats
While that futile old gentleman dozed.

EDWARD LEAR

'The charge of elitism never fails to amaze me because the same people who make it will also criticise you for not prescribing their brand of revolution to the masses. A writer wants to ask questions. These damn fellows want him to give answers. Now tell me, can anything be more elitist...? As a writer I aspire only to widen the scope of self-examination. I don't want to foreclose it with a catchy, half-baked orthodoxy...Writers don't give prescriptions,' shouted Ikem. 'They give headaches.'

Uproarious laughter.

'Well, on that note we say thank you to Dr. Osodi for a most entertaining evening.'

CHINUA ACHEBE, ANTHILLS OF THE SAVANNAH

The price of free politics, indeed of peace, can be high. Thirty years ago I began by saying that I simply wanted to make some old 'platitudes' pregnant: that politics is the conciliation of naturally different interests, whether these interests are seen as material or moral, usually both. The activity is to be honoured as the key to freedom, whatever the behaviour of actual politicians.

The thought is perennial, but circumstances have changed and the strategy of this book might be different today. Two sets of circumstances have changed, both greatly for the better; but not without a price. Firstly, the inefficiency of Communist central command economies has been empirically and dramatically demonstrated (just as eighteenth-century and early nineteenth-century reformers had demonstrated the inefficiency of old autocracy in terms of political and economic theory). Secondly, everywhere autocracies now seem less stable than parliamentary regimes, whereas thirty years ago the right-wing dictatorships of Spain and Portugal seemed, for example while not unshakeable, yet realistically to be accepted as part of the most probable order of things in the immediate future. And during this period military government came and went in Greece. These countries that seemed worrying exceptions to the European tradition of civic politics and parliamentary government, suddenly proved comforting examples of the long-term strength of these traditions and their appropriateness to modern conditions. And now demands for multi-party systems, parliamentary liberties and judicial protection of human rights gain ground throughout South America, even in many African countries. These demands will, of course, meet with varying fortunes: as old Machiavelli argued, more shrewdly than either Marx or modern social scientists (be they free-market economists or sociologists), there is <i>Fortuna</i> as well as <i>Necessità</i> in all forms of political life. However, these tendencies were afoot even before the astounding and heartwarming events of 1989 in Eastern Europe and the equally astounding but tragic events in China.

These events were, of course, a consequence of the reforms of the Gorbachev era, themselves a product of the failure of the Communist Party's vision of total and transformatory control. But there were no other straws for him to snatch at than moving towards (but always a relative term) a free-market economy and free political institutions. Almost everywhere this now seems the only real alternative to either autocracy or totalitarianism, although the forms and modulations political regimes can take are infinite. Political cultures always have a particular and peculiar cultural setting, and are difficult to attain where there has been no prior experience of either entrepreneurial or civic spirit, only a theoretical appreciation of observed and idealized examples elsewhere. But the events in the USSR were only a necessary condition, not a sufficient one, for the revolutions in Eastern Europe. The Communist one-party regimes in Hungary and Poland had already been visibly undermined, over a period of time and amid complex events and steady pressures. But what was so totally unexpected, heartening, indeed heroic (no sane prophets or pundits emerged to say, 'told you so'), was that crowds in Czechoslovakia, East Germany and Romania took to the streets so suddenly, risking their lives for freedom. Neither in Prague and Brno nor in Berlin and Dresden was it clear at the time that the army and the police would not fire—in Romania they did, and in China with terrible effect; no one could be sure that the servants of the oppression would suddenly perceive enemies of the state as fellow human beings, fellow countrymen, fellow citizens even.

Excerpted from <i>In Defense of Politics</i>, 4th ed., by Bernard Crick (pp. 242–72). Reprinted with permission by George Weidenfeld & Nicolson Limited.

Perhaps few governments, even of free societies, can be entirely happy in an uncomplicated way at the spectacle of the masses suddenly becoming a people and tearing down their government, however iniquitous. Should it not have been a time for public political joy? And even if not joy for the freedom of others, at least joy that the long fear of an annihilatory world war was over? Yet there was failure in the West of moral imagination. There was a lack of immediate response, even by great words (which are important), certainly from President Bush and Prime Minister Thatcher, those two self-perceived leaders of 'the Free World' who seldom lacked for instant rhetoric. Margaret Thatcher was not alone in seeming shamefully obsessed by fears of *what it would all cost the taxpayer*, and by ungenerous antique fears of German unity. Perhaps only private people could rise to the heights of those revolutionary events. The day the Berlin Wall was breached I played Beethoven's Ninth Symphony three times between radio and television bulletins; and when eventually I got through on the phone to Berlin to the German friend for whom I first wrote this book, to try to give grounds for hope in troubled times, I discovered that she had done the same. Whether through poor German or good politics I had *always* misheard the key word '*Freude*' of the final chorus as '*Freiheit*'. But for that heroic moment, both freedom and joy. Only later the bathos, the price to be paid. Mrs Thatcher was sometimes not entirely wrong.

So in this final Footnote I want to reflect on the high price of freedom, peace and politics. And I want to do this not by discussing in detail the new problems created or revealed by the break-up of the old Soviet Empire and

---

So I...look at some great and continuing problems and dilemmas, not to solve them but to be realistic about the price worth paying for free politics.

---

the end of the Cold War, but by speculating more generally on the nature of what can appear to be insoluble political problems. Perhaps the examples I took in the book were too glib, or writing during the Cold War it was too easy to make a rhetorical contrast between political rule and totalitarian rule; for anyone free to choose, the choice was obvious. So I now am my own

critic and look at some great and continuing problems and dilemmas, not to solve them but to be realistic about the price worth paying for free politics.

I have argued all too easily that all advanced societies contain a variety of values and interests, and that conflicts between them are best settled politically. Politics, it is still important to labour the old Aristotelian point, is both historically and logically prior to democracy. There are some situations in which any simple application of democratic majority rule can make political resolutions more difficult, even stimulate more violent conflict. In Israel and Palestine, in South Africa and—a smaller example, but in some ways more incorrigible—Northern Ireland, the democratic argument has been part of the problem. 'We have the majority and we'll do what we will with it.' My chapter 'A Defence of Politics Against Democracy' was not an argument against 'democracy', only against seeing it as the answer to everything, a single universal and overriding value (Tocqueville and J.S. Mill had long ago said everything that needs to be said on this). Political rule, I said, existed before democratic government, and some dictatorships have rested on popular support and been the stronger for it.

Normal politics breaks down or is impossible to create when rival groups pursue policies which they say admit of no compromise and which are believed to be totally exclusive and contradictory, at least as formulated by the protagonists. Consider Israel and Palestine, Northern Ireland and South Africa. In each of these areas, and elsewhere too, there are normal people who believe that the very survival of their communities as cultural identities, which is so much part of their own self-identity, is threatened by any political compromises whatever of the kind advocated in this tract. 'The slippery slope', 'the thin end of the wedge', 'give an inch, they'll take a yard', 'our land for ever' or 'no surrender!', they say.

Our response to such challenges is often to take the moral high ground and to raise like a flag the question of justice. Who is in the right? 'Oh, I know the history is complicated, but who *basically* is in the right?'

WHAT IS THE QUESTION?

◆ ◆ ◆

Is this always the right question? An English country story has an almost Hassidic wisdom about it. 'How do I get to Biddicombe?' 'I wouldn't start from here if I were you.' So I want to start with a mild humanistic protest against the prevalence of restating the arguments of the protagonists as if these are possible solutions. Intellectuals and concerned journalists should not 'join in' and 'take sides', as if they were lawyers in an advocacy system seeking to win a case, rather than arbitrators in a tribunal seeking to establish the facts and considering how to obtain the best possible *settlement*, to settle for a peace of conciliation acceptable to the rival parties—not for an ideal solution, nor possibly even a permanent solution. Much good reporting and commentary is also marred not only by clear partisanship, but by presenting problems only in terms of the day-to-day reporting of recurrent injustices, especially the violent injustices, commited by one side or the other. This creates a danger of responding passionately to symptoms and not thoughtfully to causes; the public in Western democracies outside our three troubled areas must sometimes wonder what the underlying conflicts are really about, why are they doing this? 'The atrocities of the terrorists' and the 'excesses of the security forces' are events which are themselves part of the propaganda battle, and often manufactured or provoked for that purpose. And all factual 'balance sheets' of incidents and atrocities are highly subjective in their assumptions. While it is important to ask activists what they want, and to listen empathetically to nuances in their replies, it is just as important, sometimes more so, to stand back from the struggle and to ask other observers close to the ground (such as old-fashioned reporters, churchmen, teachers and small businessmen) what they think is *possible*. One should try to establish a way of looking at extreme problems that can do justice to the claims of rival groups when they each or all may have a quite plausible and, to the individuals involved, even a fully just case.

Politics is a conciliating activity or process, not a set of substantive rules needing agreement or consensus (as unthinking politicians say when trying to be thoughtful) about 'fundamental values' or even 'the rule of law'. Politics can change laws peacefully and find paths of compromise amid differing values so long as there is a broad consensus about procedures. There is more agreement in societies like the USA and the member states of the European Community about *how* to conduct disputes than about the *ends* of policy. Such a distinction is both sensible and civilized. Writing about political education I invoked the concept of 'procedural values': a minimal respect by political activists for freedom, toleration, respect for truth, as well as empathy and willingness to resolve disputes by discussion.

But what happens when these prior conditions for politics do not exist, when 'procedural values' themselves are hotly contested? The three cases I mention, Northern Ireland, Israel/Palestine and South Africa, are at least intellectually interesting to the political thinker, even if there were not moral and practical reasons for all our interests as compelling as in the ethnic complexities, rivalries and hatreds of Eastern Europe, the Balkans, the Russian confederation and many African states and Indian provinces. Political leaders in these situations can appear either not to perceive the complexity of the interests to be satisfied (as if their perceptions are affected by the intensity of the conflicts), or believe that the very safety of the state or the survival of their people, as the case may be, is threatened by any political articulation from rival interests. They then conceive it as their moral duty not to compromise but to oppress, eradicate or simply stolidly and often bloodily endure. They see their opponents as beyond political persuasion. They see them as threatening not merely their basic interests and beliefs but all that they are, their very being, their precise human, cultural identity: thus as literally beyond reason, like another order of beings. They confuse the old order with all possible types of order, even though its autocratic incompetence may have been a cause of disorder. *All* political opposition becomes seen as inherently subversive. Such terrible fears can arise from religious, ethnic, national or class prejudice: the others are not like us as a people and never can be, and nor have we anything to learn from them. And this is often a reciprocal relationship, a self-fulfilling prophecy. 'Treat people like rats,' said Arthur Koestler, 'and they will learn to bite your fingers off.'

When large numbers of people are treated as enemies of the state and its rulers, then they may come to attribute to themselves a complete and artificial unity. To amend Browning, 'Oppression makes [even] the wise man mad.' This unity may be false culturally and hard to sustain politically ('Blacks' and 'Whites', 'Arabs' and 'Jews', 'Irish' and 'Brits'; 'they are and we are all the same') hard to sustain, that, is, without repression within one's own ranks—'act like a *true* Black!', or a true White, Serb, Uzbeki, whatever. Nationalism for the time of struggle is so unifying and intoxicating that it often tempts leaders elsewhere to continue 'the struggle' even after victory, or victory enough. And there are cases when some of the disenfranchised and dispossessed are as prejudiced, violent and irreconcilable as the rulers. Orwell once said with great honesty that after becoming anti-imperialist it took him twenty years more to realize that 'the oppressed are not always right'. He did not mean they were wrong in not wanting to be oppressed; but they were not right, nor necessarily specially admirable, in everything else. Western friends of the oppressed have often been embarrassing idealizers; I prefer Mark Twain's humanism, 'God damn the Jews; they are as bad as the rest of us.' (As a young man I demonstrated against the British attack on Suez and chanted praises of Colonel Nasser. A distinction could have been made.) Orwell's remark is salutary. However, the commonsense moral view must remain that rulers normally have more opportunity for reform, therefore carry a greater moral responsibility for failure to act effectively against endemic disorder, poverty, injustice and (the most telling monitor of all) widely different death-rates between different classes or ethnic groups. Mortality tables are a good rough indicator of political justice or injustice. More revolutions take place because governments break down through the ineptitude of conservatives than through the prophecies, schemes, courage, guns and luck of revolutionaries.

In other words, what happens when normal politics breaks down or remains minimal and locked in a dominant community which is either not accepted by a clear majority of the inhabitants (as in South Africa) or by minorities who consider themselves rightfully a majority but frustrated by boundaries unjustly and arbitrarily drawn (as in Ireland and Palestine)? One odd feature of the actual regimes in these three cases is that none of them are pure autocracies; each has some kind of working parliamentary system, indeed a vigorous and by no means superficial political life within the dominant community. Nonetheless the existing institutions did not furnish a mutually acceptable framework for the resolution of conflicts; rather the discontented see them as part of the problem. The disenfranchised do not merely want, like most American Blacks, to be treated as ordinary Americans; they want fundamental institutional changes as well as in the balance of powers between the communities. Both sides may then refuse to negotiate at all, or in the absence of acceptable common institutions, can negotiate only slowly and suspiciously about how to negotiate—while events can take their bloody course.

One could call such problems 'insoluble' for two formal reasons: (i) that no internal solution likely to guarantee peace can possibly satisfy the announced principles of the main disputants; and (ii) and that any externally imposed solution or enforced adjudication is likely to strengthen the desperation and self-righteousness of the threatened group (I first heard the phrase 'laager mentality' in Ulster, long before I heard it in South Africa; and Israel knows 'settler mentality' and 'uncompromising defence of the settlements' too). No one can win in terms of their expressed objectives, 'victory' would be 'defeat', pyrrhic at least. Indeed almost any gain for one side is immediately pictured as a potentially fatal loss for the other. Therefore there typically emerges an ideology and personal ethic of defiant heroism: 'sacrifice for the cause', 'to die for one's people', 'the blood sacrifice', 'better to die fighting than live in subjection', etc. The style of thinking of Zionist settler and PLO, IRA and UDF, and AWB (*Afrikaner Weerstandsbeweeging*), Inkatha's warriors and the ANC's *Umkhonto we Sizwe*, all these have had real similarities with each other as well as famous differences (indeed each, to some extent, 'inspired' the other). And governing communities in such situations commonly claim a unique religious identity, even destiny, as well as an ethnic peculiarity. They are especially prone to irrational fears and to hunting down 'the enemy within the gates' as well as 'the enemy without'.

EQUAL JUSTICE?

❖ ❖ ❖

In all three cases one can become deeply impressed, almost obsessed, with the equal justice of the broad case put by *both* regime and rebels—if one knows something of their history and grants their basic premises of argument. Anyone who cannot see the plausibility of the other side's case in each of these three instances cannot think, let alone act, politically.[1] Empathy is painful but may be a better starting point for any possible conciliation than trying to decide '*who is right?*' whether by historical argument (who got where first); by a balance sheet of rights and wrongs (like a judicial arbitration); or by utilitarian argument (who makes or could make the best use of 'the land' or 'our land'). Empathy can be painful and fraught with misunderstandings because supporters of tough and beleaguered regimes are so unused to empathetic understanding, especially from foreign observers, that they can mistake it for moral support. And their opponents may similarly regard any scepticism about their means or ends as hostility, or signs of support for the enemy. Overseas supporters who have generously adopted them as 'a cause' are often especially virulent: 'So you actually went *there*! [Spain, Greece, Israel, South Africa—at different periods]. You don't believe in a *total* boycott?'

Albert Camus once raged against his fellow intellectuals in France who thought it their duty to take sides in the Algerian War and to provide justifications for 'the right to slaughter and mutilate', each basing their arguments mostly 'on the other's crime':

The role of the intellectuals cannot be...to excuse from a distance one of the violences and condemn the other. This has the double result of enraging the violent group that is condemned and of encouraging to greater violence the violent group that is exonerated. If they do not join the combatants themselves, their role (less spectacular, to be sure!) must be merely to strive for pacification so that reason can have a chance.

Some may follow my 'obsession' or painful empathy into Israel-in-Palestine and Ulster-in-Ireland but find it perverse when applied to South Africa. Certainly there are clear arguments why racial prejudice is morally more unjust than religious bigotry or the conceits and constraints of class; and the numbers excluded from the franchise in South Africa are impressive by any standard, especially in a state that claimed to be parliamentary and democratic even in part. But in each of these cases, South Africa not least, a large part of the basic problem is the desperation of historic communities to preserve their identity (originally Afrikaners against the British, quite as much as both the indigenous and migrant peoples against the oppression of both; and sometimes Black against Black).

To have abolished legal Apartheid and sought to remove institutions that can violate basic individual human rights is a necessary but not a sufficient condition for stability and justice in South Africa. Quite apart from the problem of lives stunted by poverty, many—surely most?—individuals in South Africa find a large part of their human identity in being a member of a specific community. And each of these communities can appear, at least, to threaten the others, hence threatening each individual's basic sense of identity, not simply their economic interests or acquired beliefs in democratic (or other) political institutions. To say, as the ANC for instance have often appeared to say (more often their supporters outside Southern Africa), that 'one person one vote' constitutes a solution, is only to point to part of the problem. And this is the same in Northern Ireland and in Israel where the use that the majority made of their power has been both crucial and partial.

In such situations neither side can gain a victory except at a price too great for normal men and women to contemplate or endure ('Where they make a desert they call it peace', cried Tacitus of Rome's razing of Carthage). And in such situations nor can any established juridical or democratic criteria be applied to reach a mutually acceptable result peaceably. The breakdown of normal politics creates the need for a kind of politics that can find guarantees for continuing communal identities as well as common citizenship. Few politicians, few thinkers even, have even begun to consider the implications of a truly pluralistic democracy. What constitutes a community within a state with different legal rights, whether religious, ethnic or territorial? And if to some degree or other such communities may enforce their own rules, how far should the state go in not merely monitoring those rules but in insisting that individuals (especially women and adolescents) are not imprisoned in their communities? Legal Apartheid is an abomination but in most countries intermarriage between people of different communities (where community involves a strong ethnic or religious loyalty) is still not easy; and in most countries tensions between community values and individual rights hit women particularly hard.

Suppose leaders talked a language of generally *acceptable* compromises rather than democratically *agreeable* solutions? The price for any such accommodations would be painfully high in each of the three cases, in terms of previously announced 'unnegotiable positions' and what communities and their existing leaders conceive to be their rights, both rights against others and rights to manage their own internal affairs without interference. In each case it would involve talking seriously and respectfully to people who may have done 'unforgivable things'. But paying a high price has to be faced at some stage if the alternative in each case would be (as is so often threatened when trying to bring the unruly to the negotiating table) chaos, anarchy or the breakdown of the social order—as actually occurred in Yugoslavia in 1992; or even more likely, a sad continuation of present levels of instability, violence, poverty, tension and injustice—as has been the fate of Northern Ireland since 1968 (to give only a small and local example).

Any objective study of the basic problems of instability and violence in these three areas would show their complexity and might stress the *differences* within what only their opponents and foreign supporters see as a united and monolithic Catholic, Protestant, Arab, Jewish, Black or White camp. Activists on the ground, when one talks to them, are commonly more frank and realistic than their leaders about divisions in their own camp, and talk more about them, almost to a fault, than about the nature and iniquities of their enemies. Nonetheless, in each case the fate of 'moderates' who have attempted to use these differences within their communities to build a political base for compromise is not encouraging. A community when it fears that its very existence is threatened rallies to leaders who can be sure to defend it utterly and by all means, even if those leaders' beliefs and methods (as with the Revd Dr Paisley) are not normally acceptable. Such leaders are in many respects unrepresentative except as militant defenders. But advocates of moderation are so often outflanked on both wings.

When anyone cries 'I've a solution', one knows one is dealing with a fanatic, an innocent or crank.

A scholarly study also might find few direct comparisons between the circumstances of the three areas and offer no easy answers. Almost certainly, there are none. Each area is historically and sociologically unique. The common factors are found not in the empirical facts but in *how we perceive* these problems and in how we try to resolve them. Perhaps the very complexity of them or perhaps a natural impatience at their bloodiness and violence tempts us into specious comparisons and general 'solutions'. These solutions are usually a list of 'self-evident' abstract principles so presented as to lead deductively to a card castle of detailed institutional proposals, favouring one side. When anyone cries 'I've a solution', one knows one is dealing with a fanatic, an innocent or crank. 'Patience and time', said Tolstoy's General Kutusov to his young officers eager for an immediate all-or-nothing battle with Napoleon.

Strictly speaking, and there is need to speak strictly, only *puzzles* have clear solutions. *Problems* (especially political problems) can either be said to have many possible solutions, or no solutions, only resolutions, settlements, compromises or even ameliorations; none perfect, but several, perhaps many, ranging from the more-or-less positively agreeable to the more-or-less tolerably acceptable. Real differences of interest may continue but they can, with will, skill, resources and good fortune, sometimes be made or become less intense, more peaceful. When idealists aim to eradicate 'the causes of prejudice', as is often said amid multi-ethnic tensions, they can put the cart before the horse: it is a far more ambitious and long-term goal than containing the consequences of prejudice by law enforcement, reasonable settlements and good behaviour. Indeed, eradication of prejudice would need a prior settlement before it could be sensibly attempted. If we can understand what our differences really are and even tacitly agree to differ, then we can share the same house without any great affection but with reasonable civility—if only because we may both have nowhere else to go.

Such settlements will neither be perfect nor what anyone deeply involved would have rationally agreed to in advance of events and negotiations. Some would say that this is because of the inherent imperfection of human nature (what Reinhold Niebuhr called 'Christian realism'), but I think it a sufficient explanation to point to the simple logical truth that free actions are unpredictable. So we need a way of thinking about such conflicts that neither offers too much nor too little. Reckless impatience in remedying injustice is the mirror of feckless delay by states in tackling conditions that create and sustain suspicion and hostility among communities who live in the same territory and who each claim it as their own.

THE PRICE TO BE PAID

◆ ◆ ◆

My moral is not 'peace at any price' but the terribly high price of 'victory' if it come to winner-take-all. The price of any negotiated peace in such situations is high enough and painful enough, in terms of disappointing the aroused expectations of activists, but it must be paid if ever the main actors come to want peace more than the triumph or the glory of the continual sacred struggle. A desire for peace can come through exhaustion and weariness (as in Ireland in 1919 and 1920) or through moral conviction amid a diminished fear of losing communal identity. When these conditions begin to appear then, and only then, outside aid and pressure can be of much help, indeed sometimes crucial; until then, each of

---

The highest price of peace is to give up hopes of total victory, to realize the limits of power, and to tell one's followers so.

---

the three situations suggests that external interventions can actually increase fears and prove counter-productive. And inevitably the form of such interventions owes far more to the nature of the domestic politics of the 'donors' than to any objective appraisal of the needs of the 'receivers'.

The highest price of peace is to give up hopes of total victory, to realize the limits of power, and to tell one's followers so. Israel must not, indeed cannot, be displaced but equally it cannot for ever govern areas which are predominantly Arab; nor can it deny to Arabs in these areas the right to be governed how they choose and by whom they choose. Northern Ireland cannot be governed peaceably from either Dublin or London alone. The province (and it is a province not a state, nor even a normal part of a state, both in relation to Ireland and to Great Britain) *inherently faces both ways*. Few people in the North act as if their identity was exclusively Irish or exclusively British: but leaders do not come to terms with this in their policies, being trapped in a mind-set of conventional nationalism. And populist leaders of ethnic or religiously identified communities are necessarily more responsive to their peoples. The Anglo-Irish Agreement of 1985 pointed a broad way forward towards institutions of joint responsibility, dual citizenship and bi-communal equality; but its effectiveness was hampered by the exclusion of one community in its formulation. In South Africa any lasting compromises must be between communities, openly or covertly, in the text or between the lines. The ending of Apartheid and the freeing of labour in a more rational capitalist market are steps forward which both sides support, though expecting different consequences; but the non-Whites are so disadvantaged that deliberate economic and social reforms by the state are needed, even if by careful stages through time.

As argued in the previous 'Footnote to Rally Fellow Socialists', the nature of time in society must be considered. What kind of changes (whether of income, education, health, the structure of the economy or basic attitudes) take what kind of 'investment lead-time'? 'Rome was not built in a day' or, as William Blake said, 'eternity loves the products of time'. A real conviction can grow that 'things must change' or at least 'cannot go on as they are'. But opposition leaders must realize that real changes in attitudes among ruling class and real changes in skills and educational attainment among the dispossessed are the work of decades, sometimes generations, not of a parliamentary session, a 'night of long knives' or any mythical 'first hundred days'. Lasting revolutions are long processes, not quick events. The distinction between revolution and evolution is not absolute. The reforming politician with a sense of time (like Lincoln) is a statesman indeed; the conservationist politician who uses time as an excuse for delay is, indeed, a timeserver. No modern state can now turn back, only attempt to make realistic, the rising tide of expectations among its dispossessed, nor frustrate the free movement of people and the free expression of ideas: for these are externally triggered, not so often by deliberate pressure but simply by communications and involuntary example. Both man and monkey are mimetic. Example is a most potent force in politics.

I have stated two general reasons why at least two of these problems might be insoluble. A third contingent one emerges in looking at the three areas separately: the virtual impossibility of successful armed rebellion against each of the governments concerned. But also not to forget that there can be severe political, moral and international limitations on the force that each government can use against internal subversion: hence the relative ease of spasmodic violence and terrorism. The real hope of many terrorists in Israel and Palestine and in South Africa was not to bring down a regime and to take over the state, but to force a government to the negotiating table. (The IRA has been divided on this issue.) In each case terrorism by itself is unlikely to force negotiation. It can stiffen resolve, heighten fears in the regime and provoke counter-terror. But terror when used tactically in combination with demonstrations, strikes, riots and propaganda, can sometimes succeed—and, seen in that light, can *in principle*, under extreme oppression, have some justification. At least it makes it absurd to demand that the oppressed forswear all violence as a condition of negotiations. In such circumstances, negotiations offered by the government are unlikely to be genuine unless constrained; both parties in any real negotiations must believe that the consequences of them breaking down would be worse violence and instability than ever before.

An important difference emerges between terrorists who have political aims—or more precisely those who however vague, idealistic or impractical are their stated aims, yet are capable of acting politically—and those whose behaviour is stridently anti-political, those to whom *the Struggle* and heroic defiance have become a way of life, ends in themselves. The PLO, the IRA and the ANC all seem to have had, at various periods, real divisions between politicals and militants, as well as tactical disagreements. The politicals can be seen as extremists having some genuine claim to be representative of, as well leaders of, a mass popular *movement*, but the militants while claiming to represent *their* people, in fact act like a *sect*. A sect is internally motivated. Any sect is difficult enough to deal or bargain with, and many sects, mutual rivals for leadership of a movement, are almost impossible to deal with. (The growth of Islamic fundamentalism proves to be a common problem to Israel, Algeria, Egypt, Syria and the PLO.) The PLO and the ANC were not divided into clearly institutionalized political and military wings: each exhibited shifting and tactical moves back and forth from one to the other.

From a stalemate of subversive terror versus state terror, neither able to win but neither able to escape the other, can sometimes emerge a qualified general ground for hope: out of the very eye of the storm can come war-weariness and the meeting face to face of key or leaders on both sides.

THREE MAXIMS

◆ ◆ ◆

Three general perspectives or maxims of political thought seem relevant to intransigent situations. The first maxim concerns the nature of state power. Despite all the abuses of coercion in so many familiar instances, *the limitations of state power should never be forgotten.* There is the inability of governments, when the modern technology of radio is added to time-honoured rumour, to silence both internal criticism and news from else-where; and there is the proven inefficiency of over-regu-lation and over-centralization. There is a vital difference between power as unchallengeability (no one else can do it, even if I can't) and power as the ability to carry out a premeditated intention (getting things done). Some gov-ernments can't be overthrown but they can neither by force prevent unrest nor carry their own people into eco-nomic reforms or new ways of working. The state's power to get things done, to reform a decayed economy, depends both on an ability to mobilize and convince the beneficiaries of reform, but also on an ability to delegate or devolve authority to agents or elected bodies far from the centre. This balance of central control and local ini-tiative is difficult to find; but not impossible, just diffi-cult. Good political judgement is difficult.

'Power' to be powerful needs redefining as legiti-mate authority. Authority is the respect that we give to someone for their skill in performing a function that we think is needed. To get such authority, it is not foolish or empty to say, governments actually have to act legiti-mately. Their skills have to last and they have to learn to adapt and never to forget that, in the last analysis (as the saying used to be), both power and authority rest on consent. In uncharted transitional situations it is indeed difficult for governments, even when they have accepted the need to negotiate, to treat yesterday's gunmen as the responsible opposition leaders or even as coalition col-leagues next month, and to face the possibility of losing power in free elections next year. But the price of refus-ing to negotiate—perpetual uncertainty, debilitating insecurity, economic decline and foreign ostracism—can

come to seem even higher. The price is so high, however, that regimes often come to the edge but then go back or sit on their hands. This is why the common well-meant demand that in such situations oppositions should totally renounce the tactics of civil disobedience or of violence can be both unrealistic and unwise. For the price the regime has to pay is so unwelcome and begrudged that pressure has to be kept up or else the government may lapse back or simply play for time hopefully or hopelessly, simply putting off harsh com-promises and facing the fact that the other side can gain office.

The second maxim is that *there can never be peace in the world while we believe that for every nation there must be a state and that the state or national parliament, even, must be fully sovereign.* The need for entrenched guarantees to communities is at the heart of so many problems, whether such guarantees are protected by courts or international treaties. In both Israel and Palestine and in Ireland and Northern Ireland even repartition with better demographic boundaries would still leave many on the wrong side of the line and in each one a formidable territorial problem: the Catholic areas of Belfast and Arab Jerusalem. Questions of minority rights leap across state boundaries: consider the Armenians and the Kurds. Many areas of the world do not fit expectations based on the European experience since the seventeenth century of national state formation and the almost universal emulation or imposition of it elsewhere: consider South America and Africa. Political power is not indivisible, it can perfectly well be divided and limited. The Treaty of Rome is a clear enough exam-ple. Elements of federalism and federal thinking are almost inevitable in any lasting settlements, or frame-works for peaceable evolution by consent in divided areas. But some new federal constitutions may have to be communal as much as territorial. The state needs binding constitutionally against harming its own minori-ties, and sometimes to prevent it favouring them dispro-portionately; and individuals need protecting by Bills of Right against both state and community.

'Pluralism' was once a philosophy of the state criti-cal of the theory of sovereignty. Some groups, it was argued, do have a relative autonomy that is beyond the power of the state. 'All power is federal', said the young Harold Laski. That is doubtful. We have to think case by case, and function by function within those cases. But some power to be effective can only be federal. Sovereignty thinking, like simple-majoritarian-democra-tic thinking, can again be more part of the problem than the dominant necessity in any 'solution' or resolution. The claim of 'sovereignty' often precludes any genuine constitutional restraints, hence makes any negotiation still depend on the goodwill (which may be wholly lacking) of the majority or the powerful minority in government. But two or more nations can inhabit one state and preserve their identities. We in the United Kingdom should sometimes look under our noses, as well as to Canada and Belgium, etc. The United Kingdom is a multi-national state not a single nation state, albeit and arguably with inadequate or inappropriate political institutions. Most Scots and Welsh want a parliament both as positive symbol and as a democratic protector of their nationhood, but not a separate state.[2]

Again, only puzzles have unique solutions; problems can be resolved to tolerable levels, if never wholly removed, in different ways.

The third maxim is that *the basic philosophical concept of a free action as an unpredictable action* (one not logically entailed or determined by an necessary circumstances) *must be related to the nature of political negotiation*. Only in efficient autocracies are the outcomes of 'negotiations' predictable, and efficient autocracies are getting hard to find. Certainly what the leaders of rival groups in the three particular areas say they each want as their unnegotiable objectives are relatively unlikely to occur. They confuse political negotiation with a negotiated military surrender. So if the real object of the struggle is not 'revolution' or 'victory' but is 'to bring to the table' the reluctant parties, then it is wise, while never going into negotiations without preparation, yet to be open-minded about what will emerge. No one will convert the other but in the nature of the problems and of negotiation, no one will get all they want or even quite what they expect. Precise outcomes in difficult situations are unpredictable. Again, only puzzles have unique solutions; problems can be resolved to tolerable levels, if never wholly removed, in different ways. Safeguards, privileges, rewards, opportunities and legal and social rights can all take many forms, and are all negotiable.

By the mid-1980s, for instance, both British and Irish governments began to perceive Northern Ireland as a common problem, so that to some degree they have tried to act jointly, 'in collusion' even (as the rival irreconcilables and invincibles see it). They were uncertain what framework to advocate, both what might work and what might prove acceptable to their very different constituencies. Neither side brought a draft of the 'Anglo-Irish Agreement 1985' with them to the table. It emerged from negotiation, or some might say (but with hindsight) from the logic of the situation. The Intergovernmental Council that emerged was not an instrument of government but rather a reasonably stable forum for consultation and continuing negotiation. But very probably it points, as some fear and others hope, towards some kind of evolving joint authority, joint citizenship and some working doctrine of communal equality.[3] But to some on both sides, any negotiation was selling the pass. So sectarians commonly refuse to negotiate or try to wreck negotiations, until their own followers either grow weary of them and rebel, or too often, alas, drop out of politics entirely leaving the fanatics and the 'incorruptibles' unrestrained and pretending to speak for them.

'Oppression makes a wise man mad', and not all begin by being equally wise. But happily this is not always true: oppression can bring out the best in human beings. I found hope not just in new ideas about constitutional arrangements but in what one found when talking to Black South African political leaders recently released from long years in brutal prisons; one found qualities not always associated with normal politics in comfortable, consumer-driven societies: courage, dignity, irony not anger, tactical skill, empathetic understanding of their oppressors rather than a hunger for revenge, and an ability to state the essence of their case cogently—that is, briefly and with absolute relevance as if genuinely to persuade other reasonable people. But if the other side were not so good at persuading, and often, like elsewhere, seemed trapped in their own history, while it made it more difficult to understand their true case and what are their minimal demands, yet it made it more urgent to do so and to take them fully seriously.

So this penultimate defence of politics is a plea for outsiders and observers not to give unqualified and uncritical support to one side or another in the most difficult political problems—Serbs or Croats, say—nor to offer glib solutions. Some causes are more worthy of qualified support than others, but all conflicts need understanding historically and empathetically and all causes benefit from critical support ('A writer', said Orwell, 'can never be a loyal member of a political party'—he was member of a party when he wrote that.)

Such difficult problems must, indeed, be tackled not evaded, for moral as well as prudential reasons. Decent people should scorn arguments that our government (and all others) should only be concerned with Croatia and Serbia, say, if our material interests are concerned;

...but the greatest good we can do in extreme situations is to keep a clear head and offer independent, critical intelligence, not to add to the passion of the commitments that kill and maim.

---

or should only have helped President Gorbachev or President Yeltsin for the immediate sake of British trade. Common humanity is sufficient reason for the concern, even involvement, of all thinking people; but the greatest good we can do in extreme situations is to keep a clear head and offer independent, critical intelligence, not to add to the passion of the commitments that kill and maim. There is a danger that outsiders can indulge their own passions, as if the tragedies of the world were a street theatre, with either no effect on the problems or bad ones. There is a need for both influence and critical judgement (in Kant's sense) from outsiders, and for insiders to force themselves mentally to act like dispassionate outsiders. Spectators *do* see more of the game than the players.[4] Informed spectators can influence, not a particular game perhaps, but the general way in which it is played. Such influence is at best indirect: the observer should neither volunteer for the Front nor make high-brow propaganda for the better cause. He or she should try to suggest the preconditions for negotiations between the actual parties involved and stand ready to help, if asked, in assisting or implementing any transitional arrangements. Because such situations involve real and terrible dilemmas and are not perverse tests or puzzles made for our solving, outcomes can vary and will always disappoint, somewhat; there are no perfect or unique solutions. Concerned persons should be less concerned to predict and support most-favoured outcomes and be more willing to imagine and to accept many possible and often quite unexpected outcomes which will give peace and reduce both violent death and death by neglect of state action.

ON SECOND THOUGHTS

◆ ◆ ◆

These considerations lead to two substantial afterthoughts, perhaps second thoughts. I am unrepentant in my argument about the primacy of political thinking over both economic and legal thinking; but in reacting against the exaggerated claims of Marxist economicism and Conservative legalism, I may have underestimated their relative importance. To be told that to observe 'the rule of law' is the overriding maxim for social justice and peace is a dangerous half-truth: those who say so forget that laws can be iniquitous and judges hostile to liberty and to reform. Socrates broke the law, to begin the whole tradition of free political speculation; so did Brutus; and citizens in Eastern Europe did so spectacularly in 1989, and on a humble scale (foreign readers must forgive parochial triviality) an unjust tax in Britain, the Poll Tax, was destroyed by public disobedience and protest at about the same time. And certainly uncontrolled free markets can no more create the conditions for social justice than can state control: neither the writing of Adam Smith nor Karl Marx are self-sufficient guides to policy (leaving aside that what they both said is somewhat different from what has been made of them by enthusiastic followers and by enthusiastic enemies).

The new struggles for liberty, however, have involved a far greater revival of constitutional law and speculation than seemed relevant or likely thirty years ago. Abrupt attempts to move overnight from an ideology of state control to an ideology of 'a free market in everything' (as old Hungarian friends now say) may, indeed, be a running from one total and rigid ideology to another, both lacking in historical and sociological insight, and may prove dangerous rejections of political thinking about intermediate positions and transitional means. Yet it is now clear that some form of free market, in some context of public law, is a necessary condition for liberty and the institutions of political rule. (I could have said this more clearly in the section on 'Equality' in the 'Footnote to Rally Fellow Socialists'.) Gorbachev realized that in order to get some *perestroika*, some *glasnost* had to be tolerated, but *glasnost* was not containable and this produced the need for more *perestroika* than he had bargained for and prepared for.

So a word, finally, on each of these reservations. If the main precondition for peace and justice in the post-Cold War modern world is a change from centralist sovereignty thinking to pluralistic thinking, then negotiation in extreme situations must take a more legalistic form than has been common of late in European political thought and practice, scarcely at all in the new nations. Negotiations themselves will be about constitutional devices and the only possible outcome will be a just, or acceptable, and better (not perfect) set of constitutional arrangements. Working through these arrangements, substantive issues of social policy would, in the near or middle future, be settled; but not in the constitution itself. Constitutions cannot settle economic policy, neither prescribe redistribution nor embalm or protect specified and precise property rights for ever. The most that can and should be hoped for from negotiation is to reach a consensus on procedures: agreement on rules by which substantive problems can, within a framework of government, be resolved; and also agreement on more difficult processes by which constitutions themselves can be changed.

Put it this way. Remember that the thirteen colonies in British North America that revolted against the homeland found a common bond in a constitution that they created themselves. Constitutionalism was itself a founding and a bonding belief which long preceded any sense of an American nation. A clear and firm sense of American nationhood emerged only during a long and bloody civil war to defend what even then and now was called, not 'the State', but 'the Union'. The first stages of the French Revolution were constitutional, heavily influenced by the American example and by the writings of the Anglo-American republicans and constitutionalists. Only when foreign invasion occured and internal violence became endemic did nationalism stir, and was stirred, and 'sovereignty of the people' became a sufficient constitutive principle to the Jacobin leadership who used and abused it in the name of 'the people'. The predominant reformist and emancipatory idea everywhere in Europe and the Americas in the early and mid-nineteenth century was to gain or be given 'a just constitution'. There was the American anti-monarchical slogan, 'a government of laws and not of men'; and there was the idea of the German parliaments of 1848 to create a 'Rechtstadt', a state bound by enforceable laws. The belief in general legal rules rather than paternal particularism, 'each case on its merits', was in part a response to particular difficulties of conflicting community, group and ethnic loyalties within states. Britain was and is the exception (to my mind now, the unfortunate exception).

Throughout the latter part of the nineteenth century and into the decade of colonial emancipation in the middle of this century, nationalism seemed to hold sway nearly everywhere, often at the expense of constitutional beliefs that governments should be restrained in some agreed areas by enforceable laws which can only be changed by special procedures. The nation, on the contrary, should have no restraints put upon it, or rather on its devoted leaders: popular sovereignty should be absolute. But there are many areas of the world where different peoples are inextricably bound together by geography or by economic dependence on each other. The collapse of Soviet power released suppressed nationalist passions for ideas of complete independence or of 'ethnic cleansing', which even if possible, prove economically disastrous and morally intolerable. Leaders of the emancipated East European states, of the Baltic Republics, and of the Ukraine and Georgia, etc., have had to consider the practical compromises of 'sovereignty' that states in Western Europe had already taken for their own betterment.

In these areas some of the reasons why constitutional government first arose may be recreating themselves, with the added complexity that relations between 'sovereign states' themselves (as in the EC) can need binding by litigable and enforceable law. National states are not the only possible form of human government, nor necessarily the best. And the idea that the mere assertion of sovereignty can create power sufficient for economic, political and even cultural independence, is a sadly absurd illusion.

FINAL THOUGHTS
◆ ◆ ◆

The revolutionary events of 1989 in Eastern Europe have changed the history of the world. But they arose basically from a simple but profound perception by Gorbachev that the economic problems of his country cold only be solved politically, not by central command. Nothing has changed the truth of that perception. Economic reform needs political reform, and in the precise sense of trying to create a political system and civic culture, which is not an easy task (as my discussion of the formal conditions for the stability of political systems would indicate). And there were, of course, repercussions far beyond Europe; as in a terse remark by Gorbachev in July 1988 that 'there must be a political solution to the Southern African question'. That meant that there would be no more training of guerrillas or money for arms, whether in Africa, the Middle East, South and Central America, or anywhere else.

All this was so unexpected. No political scientists can claim to have predicted these events. The image of

---

The image of the study of politics as aspiring to science rather than to good judgement (say again, political judgement) took a humbling knock.

---

the study of politics as aspiring to science rather than to good judgement (say again, political judgement) took a humbling knock (even though such great events leave many scholars undisturbed, still grazing happily in their own narrow fields).[5] Economists had for long proved in theory the inevitable inefficiency of production and distribution of goods and resources in command economies without a price mechanism, and that price mechanisms depend on a free market. But few of them expected that in practice the greatest of these systems would actually break down. Most observers simply thought that it did not work well and could still work worse. Their theories seemed like the rhetoric of Burke who tried to prove that the French Revolution was impossible in the same breath as he berated the iniquities of its success.

Travelling and lecturing in Czechoslovakia shortly after the November risings of 1989, I was startled to provoke puzzled and angry objections by referring (for once without thinking) to 'the November *revolution*'. That very word, like 'socialism' (even with its Western democratic handle firmly nailed to the new broom), was almost untouchable because of its abuse and over-use by the Communist Party. So before we could establish a normal vocabulary to discuss quite what had happened and why that November, I had to go backwards in time to talk about why it is sensible to call the American War of Independence a revolution (certainly in terms of its international consequences) and I had to distinguish patiently between stages of the French Revolution.

The November events were revolutions in certain obvious senses. They were revolts that aimed at far more than a change of government, rather to create a new regime, to transform many basic social institutions and also basic values; and they arose suddenly and almost spontaneously, triggered (to recycle an old concept) by inherent contradictions in the ideology of the ruling class (an ideology of production that could not produce, an ideology of labour that even alienated the working class). But also, like most previous revolutions, the very drama of the events, the very awfulness of the old oppression, combined to create exaggerated expectations of what freedom could immediately bring. And, of course, the revolution swept away one system of distribution, which worked after a fashion, even if so badly, without there being another ready to put in its place.

In fact, of course, no revolution has ever made or could make a complete break from the past; nor are social systems like machine-tools that can be simply bolted into the floor and substituted for outmoded ones. People have traditions, memories and habits. Rome wasn't built in a day and when we rebuild we have to use a lot of old materials, and on the same old site using most of the same people—people perhaps radically changed, but not transfigured; and among those radical changes, the unreal expectations, certainly unreal in the short term.

Small wonder that new regimes come under threat when they have to call for continued economic hardships, perhaps even more than before, to rebuild from the mistakes of the past. The workers have heard all that before. Disillusionment can come quickly, as happened in the former Soviet Union itself, especially when the greatest price of transition to a free economy is something as fundamental and hitherto unexperienced as unemployment coupled to the rising price of necessities. Apart from the risk of violent death, there is no human circumstance that can so discredit a regime and cause many of its inhabitants to drop out from, despise and turn against civil society, as continued mass unemployment.

There are great dangers in trying to leap from one extreme to another too precipitously: as if one can move from a total central command economy to an unregulated free market as easily as spinning a coin. If we seek to cross from one side of a mountain torrent to another we look for stepping-stones. The great mistakes of command economies are uneconomic subsidy of so-called basic industries, more often symbolically important (like coal and steel in Communist ideology) than economically effective. But not all subsidies are of that kind. I heard Hungarian friends say that *all* subsidies must be removed, even from public transport, from hospitals and from nursery education. When I said weak British things like, 'isn't that going too far?' or 'isn't that wrong?' or simply 'why?', they recited paragraphs to me from the writings of Professor Hayek. What I most tried hard to say was, 'isn't all this politically imprudent?' 'shouldn't you move cautiously and selectively?' They then read me more passages from Hayek.

There can be a fundamental misunderstanding of the nature of Western capitalism. Its early origins were, in some sense, spontaneous, perhaps arguably even a natural tendency. But its institutional development depended not merely on sweeping away a lot of old mercantilist laws, but on the state bringing in new kinds of regulation, notably Company Acts, commercial law in general, regulation of stock markets, and on a great deal of state subsidy of education and the infrastructure for transport and sanitary cities. Borrowing arguments from Neal Ascherson, I bored my Hungarian friends with an account of how much more regulation of this kind there was in the Federal Republic of Germany, far more than was thought good in Thatcher's Britain. That was a better argument; they listened with puzzled patience to my amateur account of the reasons for the success of the post-war West Germany economy, whereas they reacted impatiently to a brave woman colleague of theirs who went on and on about Swedish social-democracy proving the possibility of mixed economies.

Such middle ways are possible (as I argued in the Footnote on socialism), but perhaps her audience simply didn't want a middle way. But the theoretical point is that just as there was no such thing as a totally totalitarian regime (the desire for total power was real enough, but attempts to exercise it were ramshackle and destructive), so there has never been such a thing as a totally free economy. All economies are mixed economies, and some are more mixed than others. However, it as well to accept that truism: to make deregulation an end in itself can actually threaten a transitional political order. Real leaders must be prudent, must exercise political judgement, must encourage but not surrender completely to the competitive imperatives of the free market.

These conversations caused me to worry that the old regime, Communism I mean, had discredited not only even the mildest elements of democratic socialism and social democracy; it had discredited any respect for politics itself. My basic argument seemed very important to some of them (more so than here), but puzzled others who were in such a mood of reaction against the immediate past that they wanted to take the politics out of everything, even the politics of a freely elected parliament. They imagined that they would thus create a more efficient market economy more quickly; in fact, I argued, they could end up being governed by bureaucrats, lawyers and accountants. Someone has to regulate markets; the real question is whether they are accountable or not to the governed. Totalitarianism indeed was less a relapse into barbarism, as some have argued, than a false

modernism: an attempt to remake humanity scientifically and bureaucratically into something more predictable, mechanical and controllable, quite other than human.

To warn against exaggerated expectations is not to belittle the progress that there was. That there are great problems in Eastern Europe in the 1990s, partly the legacies of the past and partly the inadequacy of foreign aid, is no argument for putting the clock back. If we can regret the separation of the Czechs and the Slovaks, we can count it as a blessing that the breakup was peaceful—unlike the bloodshed and anarchy as Yugoslavia tore itself apart. The past was bad enough elsewhere in Eastern Europe, even if not always in immediate material terms to all sections of society, because there was no hope of peaceful change.

Orwell once remarked, in an essay on Koestler, that the 'essence of being human is that one does not seek perfection':

Perhaps, however, whether desirable or not, it [the Earthly Paradise] isn't possible. Perhaps some degree of suffering is ineradicable from human life, perhaps the main choice before man is always a choice of evils, perhaps even the aim of Socialism is not to make the world perfect but to make it better. All revolutions are failures, but they are not all the same failure.[6]

Betterment has resulted, and free politics is part of that betterment because it is both means and end. It is right that all mankind should live in free political systems and that free political systems have their own means of adjustment, advance, self-renewal and betterment.

Times of transition always entail a high price. Mankind cannot live for long in anarchy or chronic instability, without hope and reasonably clear expectations; but cannot be human or free either if expectations are fixed and rigid. The price of change has been heavy in the Eastern block but is worth paying. How easy to say to others! How shameful and lacking in civic spirit that people in the free countries of the West have been so grudging and stinting, found so many rationalizations, so petty-minded and selective, against helping the liberated to restructure their economies on the scale plainly and urgently needed. 'Are people really so lacking in humanity and vision, or do all our politicians misread us,' have no confidence that they can persuade us to look beyond our noses, and thus fail to lead us?

Have they narrowed politics to questions of marginal rates of taxation at the expense of the greater public values of our whole civilization? Men and women are citizens as well as consumers. The price of liberty is more than eternal vigilance (especially when the objects of our vigilance now appear comfortably on screen); it is eternal commitment to political activity. What has been most proved in the last decade has been the weakness of autocracy, iron regimes have proved fragile; but, alas, the altruism and public spirit of the free, while strong and noble on occasion, is dangerously spasmodic. We are all too apt to watch rather than to act, are too fearful of losing immediate comforts to defend intelligently our own long-term interests by helping others.

Notes

1. Some of us stipulated *empathy* for political viewpoints other than one's own as a formal criterion for 'political literacy' in drawing up guidelines for political education in schools. See Bernard Crick and Alex Porter (eds.), *Political Education and Political Literacy* (Longman and Hansard Society, London: 1978).

2. See 'Devolution, Decentralism and the Constitution' in my *Political Thoughts and Polemics* (Edinburgh University Press, 1990), and 'The Sovereignty of Parliament and the Scottish Question' in Normal Lewis (ed.), *Happy and Glorious: The Constitution in Transition* (Open University Press, Milton Keynes: 1990).

3. See 'Northern Ireland and the Theory of Consent' in my *Political Thoughts and Polemics*, ibid.

4. See Ronald Beiner, *Political Judgment* (Methuen, London: 1983).

5. When, for instance, the British Political Studies Association held their annual conference at Easter 1990 they were not willing or able to change their programme to include any discussion of the momentous events of the Autumn before.

6. Quoted in 'Orwell and English Socialism' in my *Essays on Politics and Literature* (Edinburgh University Press, 1989).

Terms & Concepts

altruism
autocracy
command economies
Conservative legalism
empathy
Fortuna
glasnost
Gorbachev era

laager mentality
legitimate authority
Machiavelli
Marxist economicism
mixed economies
Necessità
perestroika
pluralism

political thinking
politics
procedural values
simple-majoritarian-democratic
   thinking
Treaty of Rome

Questions

1. What does this article reveal about Crick's view of politics? What is the essence of politics for him, and how is the need for "politics" illustrated by the three examples he has chosen?

2. What are Crick's three "maxims"? How are they linked to his view that political problems don't really have "solutions," and that empathy is as important as asking "who is right"?

3. Why does Crick remain an optimist in the face of such evidence of hatred, implacable hostility and escalating violence? What makes him think that even crises that have lasted for decades can be resolved? Is there recent evidence to support him?

4. Does Crick have unreasonable expectations about the price people should be prepared to pay, and what politics can accomplish? What is the alternative?

5. Crick says that he is "unrepentant in my argument about the primacy of political thinking over both economic and legal thinking." What does he mean by this, and does he say that he has modified his views at all since *In Defence of Politics* first appeared?

Conclusion

According to one Central Intelligence Agency employee, "(now) we rely on history books to identify which communities are located where... we have done more historical maps in the last two years than we have in the past 50. We're always back in the library now, pulling out old sources and historical atlases."[1] The CIA's cartography department is hard at work because, in the "old" days of the Cold War, maps were created based upon satellite data that revealed military sites and installations, whereas now the need is for demographic maps that provide details on ethnic, religious, and national makeup, as well as on the environmental situation.

As Cold War maps become obsolete, so do the economic, political, and ideological frameworks that were generally taken for granted. The Golden Age of the welfare state did not last for very long. The Reform liberalism of the Hobhouse, Green, Keynes, Roosevelt, King, and Pearson eras has developed profound inner contradictions—and may be in a state of crisis.

Challenges to the hegemony of "liberal" ideas are not new. But to the critical perspectives provided by feminists, neo-Marxists, environmentalists, nationalists, and populists, several important factors must be added. Our faith in liberal democracy has been fuelled by 50 years of Cold War and the presence of an illiberal enemy. We thought that we could afford the welfare state, and we believed that western economies would continue to dominate globally. But paradoxically, as global economic forces come to dominate national economies Canadians may retreat into ever more parochial identities, stressing local autonomy and control. Why should Albertans care any more about Newfoundlanders than about starving orphans in Bosnia? Why should we allow a remote national government to spend our tax dollars? Thus, under the stress of deficit and debt cutting, some very angry and intolerant sentiments may emerge.

There is no doubt that the citizens of the wealthy industrial states will continue to face agonizing ethical dilemmas. Who is to be taken aboard the "lifeboat"? What kind of aid—and how much—will be given to the Third World? To what horrors and injustice will the citizens of the "developed" world have to (or choose to) close their eyes? Legally, the democracies of Europe and North America can pride themselves on having abolished slavery and emancipated women. But in many parts of the world men, women, and children often toil in appalling conditions to produce the very products we consume so conspicuously, or are even bought and sold as sexual chattels. To some degree we close our eyes because we do not know what to do; we accept the vagaries of chance and assume that the existence of the unfortunate is unavoidable or even necessary. In these respects, are we not far closer to the Greeks and their attitudes to slavery as a social and economic necessity than we realize? This is an argument developed by Bernard Williams. He concludes that, "In important ways, we are, in our ethical situation, more like human beings in antiquity than any Western people have been in the meantime."[2]

Charles Taylor, a noted Canadian political philosopher, has argued that what we are experiencing is a sense of impending breakdown, to which the name "hypertrophy" is sometimes given. He defines this as the fear that we are "becoming too much what we have been...the fear that the very things that define our break with earlier 'traditional' societies—our affirmation of freedom, equality, radical new beginnings, control over nature, democratic self-rule, will somehow be carried beyond feasible limits and will undo us."[3] Our hubris could get us! Our new world may thus be the very opposite of what was intended; it may see an increasing retreat into guarded, walled enclaves of privilege. City life could become increasingly dangerous, as police battle for control over areas that gangs consider their turf, as the wealthy drive their luxury cars over pot-holed streets and do not dare to stop until the safety of an underground parking lot is reached.[4] Large groups of recent immigrants may also be forced into increasingly violent action to assert their rights. The landscape can therefore be made to look positively medieval—tiny city-states, armed gangs, hired mercenaries (as protection), the threat of plague-like pandemics—coupled with high technology entertainment and information.

How are we to cope with our new world? Is it really turning into a cross between Huxley's dystopian vision (but a world on prozac, not soma) and a Hieronymus Bosch painting of the apocalypse, as victims are torn apart? To answer this we are drawn back to politics, for such questions raise the not inconsequential matter of what kind of polity we want to create, and thus return us to our current dilemmas. On the right, are divisions between those who are staunch free marketeers wanting the state out of most if not all forms of regulation, and those who are deeply concerned about the erosion of "traditional" values and see the market as responsible for an unacceptable level of corrosive social change. On the left is disarray. The old intellectual left, rooted in the alliance with labour, committed to protectionism and to the preservation of an industrial assembly-line economy (sometimes referred to as "Fordism"), has a difficult time meshing with the new left of feminists, environmentalists, and other rights-bearing groups. Communitarians of various kinds plead for a renewal of community, but what, in practice this really means is not clear. The whole left/right debate crumbles on a number of fronts, from the ideological to the pragmatic.

As we approach the end of the 20th century, the international system looks, in some respects, more like the 19th century, at least in the sense that it is a multi-polar world. But the situation is different in that the great powers are not all European, weapons and warfare are radically different, and there is now only one military superpower, although it may be in a state of serious economic decline. Nineteenth century rivalries were played out over territory in remote parts of the globe. The British and French Empires confronted each other at the forlorn outpost of Fashoda in the Sudan. Nowadays mere territorial control is not as important to major powers, even though, on the ground, the struggles over who controls a hill or a village are just as important as they always were. Nonstate actors are extremely powerful. Civilizations may be redefining their boundaries, and cultures are challenging each other in ways not experienced since the industrial revolution. Islam confronts the secular world of the Enlightenment. John le Carré estimates that, in Europe alone, there are 35 ethnic or national entities demanding autonomy or sovereignty. He takes issue with "our careless modern assumption that as trade borders fall and systems of communication change, the countries of the world will be brought closer together. Nothing could be further from the truth."5

We also still face enormous problems of post-Cold War cleanup, with costs expected to be in the hundreds of billions as we realize the legacy of 40 years of nuclear weapons production. Another trend to note is the attack on our elites, often led by people who want to see *themselves* as the new leaders and thinkers. There is nothing

necessarily wrong with being fed up with experts; there can be a healthy, democratic, side to anti-elitism, but such a sentiment "will come to nothing if it simply turns into fodder for demagogues"6—and if it manifests itself as shallow anti-intellectualism.

Thus, as we look around our political world, there are numerous reasons for despair and pessimism, and many of the articles in this reader raise excruciatingly difficult questions. What can we do about renewable resource extinction and its attendant political consequences? Are we facing the prospect of a quarter-century of ongoing moral and spiritual crises, sapping our political will? How will the forces of Jihad and McWorld collide and evolve? What will happen to democracy in the process? Can we reinvent the economic marketplace, and how is the public domain to co-exist with the new world of transnational capitalism and privatization? Are political institutions impotent? Is our civic culture disintegrating? Does the populist response inevitably go hand-in-hand with nativism and territorial nationalism? What can be done to tackle the problems of representation, and can we re-establish meaningful forms of public discourse and conversation?

Involvement in public political activity seems one obvious answer, at least for North Americans. But the price to be paid for so doing if you are, for example, a Saudi woman, or an Algerian journalist, or a Burmese democrat, or an Italian magistrate, or even a British author, can be very high indeed. You may pay with your life, and the lives of family and friends. Even where political participation is allowed, we seem to have run out of answers, or perhaps cannot even pose the right questions. Some would in fact argue that our problems are due to too much participation and too excessive demands on the state. At a time when problems appear to be intractable and many citizens are retreating into a privatized world of entertainment, we expect our leaders to have the remedies for what ails us, and we still make Enlightenment-rooted assumptions about our abilities to identify and solve all our problems.

Yet in spite of such an abundance of gloom and possible doom, we hope that the articles chosen also convey glimmers of hope and some grounds for cautious optimism. At a time when we often seem to be providing 18th and 19th century responses to late 20th century problems (note the current flood of references to Adam Smith, social Darwinism, race, population control, biology, and the undeserving poor), many of the authors encourage us to see our challenges and difficulties as having both old and new components. It is not *simply* a postmodern world where the confident, sweeping, assumptions of yesteryear—about science, history, economics, the state, progress and democracy—have given way to incoherence and flux. (One might perhaps argue that hypermodernism is stacked on top of traditionalism.)

The contributors urge us to examine history anew and with greater care; they reveal how we must guard against easy generalizations and undue pessimism; they attempt to see things in context; they do not underestimate the resiliency of democracy, or its capacity for reinvention. Democracies may be facing what is, at bottom, a moral crisis, and it is important to see this crisis in historical perspective. We have experienced many of these problems before, and have usually proffered similar cures. The trick is to sort out what is different, for history does not simply repeat itself, and the "lessons" to be learned must be treated with the greatest of care. What historians *are* able to do is prevent the overt misuse of historical examples, but the profession itself has become hazardous, and even as eminent a historian as Eric Hobsbawm now admits that "I used to think that the profession of history, unlike that of, say, nuclear physics, could do no harm. Now I know that it can." Telling people that a 1000-year old shrine is, in fact, of fairly recent vintage, or that others have a legitimate claim to it, is not something that remains academic![7]

As the list of key terms for each piece was assembled, it became even more apparent that certain ideas and concerns are now widespread. There is the stress upon the importance of civil society. There is frequent mention of forms of federalism, or confederalism, as possible avenues of institutional renewal. Populism is discussed in numerous places. There is an attempt to defend "politics" and political institutions against the assumed efficiencies of the "marketplace." It is not that the pervasiveness of such ideas is novel or unexpected; what stands out are the ways in which the themes pop up in so many different contexts. What is also noteworthy is the repeated stress on the importance of a reasoned and thoughtful historical perspective.

Finally, it is important to remember that actions do not always speak louder; we are not dealing in "mere words." Words have great power: they can bring about agreement and compromise and increased tolerance. They can give us hope and confidence. Politics and politicians—disparaged, reviled, vilified—remain our hope, as long as, by politics, we have in mind the kind of activities and attitudes that Bernard Crick (Unit 6, Article 25) so ably defends.

We hope that both teachers and students will find articles in this volume that go beyond what can be provided in an introductory text. The intent is to provide greater depth, more opportunity for debate, and a challenge to the unthinking acceptance of authoritative definitions, which texts, by their very nature, usually provide. Our political concepts are more nuanced, especially these days, than students are sometimes led to believe—but not so nuanced that we cannot examine and unravel them carefully and see their importance for us as citizens as we struggle to brave our protean, turbulent, new world.

Notes

1. Thomas L. Friedman, "Cold War Without End," *New York Times Magazine* (Aug. 22, 1993), 28–30.
2. See Bernard Williams, *Shame and Necessity* (Berkeley: University of California Press, 1993).
3. Charles Taylor, "Alternative Futures: Legitimacy, Identity and Alienation in Late-Twentieth-Century-Canada," in *Reconciling the Solitudes* (Montreal: McGill-Queen's University Press, 1993), 60.
4. Thomas Homer-Dixon uses this limousine metaphor to describe the air-conditioned existence of the post-industrial regions, surrounded by the rest of humankind. See Robert Kaplan, "The Coming Anarchy," *Atlantic Monthly* (January, 1994).
5. John Le Carré, "After the Cold War: The Shame of the West," *Globe and Mail*, December 15, 1994, A27.
6. Louis Menaud, "The Trashing of Professionalism," *New York Times Magazine* (March 5, 1995), 41–43.
7. Eric Hobsbawm, "The New Threat to History," *The New York Review of Books* (December 16, 1993), 62–64.